THE BLOOMSBURY
HANDBOOK OF
21ST-CENTURY FEMINIST THEORY

Available from Bloomsbury

The Bloomsbury Handbook to Octavia E. Butler
Edited by Gregory Hampton and Kendra R. Parker

The Bloomsbury Handbook to Katherine Mansfield
Edited by Todd Martin

The Bloomsbury Handbook to Edwidge Danticat
Edited by Jana Evans Braziel and Nadège T. Clitandre

The Bloomsbury Handbook of Posthumanism
Edited by Mads Rosendahl and Jacob Wamberg

Forthcoming from Bloomsbury

The Bloomsbury Handbook to Sylvia Plath
Edited by Anita Helle, Amanda Golden, and Maeve O'Brien

The Bloomsbury Handbook to Edith Wharton
Edited by Emily J. Orlando

The Bloomsbury Handbook to J. M. Coetzee
Edited by Andrew Van der Vlies and Lucy Graham

The Bloomsbury Handbook of the Digital Humanities
Edited by James O'Sullivan

The Bloomsbury Handbook to New Approaches
in Cultural And Memory Studies
Edited by Brett Ashley Kaplan

The Bloomsbury Handbook to Agatha Christie
Edited by J.C. Bernthal and Mary Anna Evans

The Bloomsbury Handbook to Cold War Literary Cultures
Edited by Greg Barnhisel

The Bloomsbury Handbook to Contemporary American Poetry
Edited by Craig Svonkin and Steven Gould

The Bloomsbury Handbook to the Medical-Environmental
Humanities
Edited by Scott Slovic, Swarnalatha Rangarajan, and Vidya Sarveswaran

The Bloomsbury Handbook to D.H. Lawrence
Edited by Annalise Grice

The Bloomsbury Handbook to Ageing in Contemporary
Literature and Film
Edited by Sarah Falcus, Raquel Medina, and Heike Hartung

THE BLOOMSBURY HANDBOOK OF

21ST-CENTURY FEMINIST THEORY

Edited by Robin Truth Goodman

BLOOMSBURY ACADEMIC
LONDON • NEW YORK • OXFORD • NEW DELHI • SYDNEY

BLOOMSBURY ACADEMIC
Bloomsbury Publishing Plc
50 Bedford Square, London, WC1B 3DP, UK
1385 Broadway, New York, NY 10018, USA
29 Earlsfort Terrace, Dublin 2, Ireland

BLOOMSBURY, BLOOMSBURY ACADEMIC and the Diana logo
are trademarks of Bloomsbury Publishing Plc

First published in Great Britain 2019
Paperback edition published 2022

Cover design: Eleanor Rose
Cover image © Ociacia / iStock

A catalogue record for this book is available from the British Library.

A catalog record for this book is available from the Library of Congress.

ISBN: HB: 978-1-3500-3238-5
PB: 978-1-3502-6840-1
ePDF: 978-1-3500-3240-8
eBook: 978-1-3500-3239-2

Series: Bloomsbury Handbooks

Typeset by Newgen KnowledgeWorks Pvt. Ltd., Chennai, India
Printed and bound in Great Britain

To find out more about our authors and books visit
www.bloomsbury.com and sign up for our newsletters.

CONTENTS

FIGURES

ACKNOWLEDGMENTS

Immense thanks are due to the writers of this volume. All of them have invested time, energy, and intellectual insights toward making this volume cutting-edge, original, and smart.

Thanks are also due to feminists who came before us and laid out the concepts that we are still using. Some of the work for this volume was done in Kate Millett's East Village apartment immediately before her death. Kate Millet was an inspiration for feminism, and I mourn her loss.

I'd also like to thank Jeffrey Di Leo. His invitation for me to contribute to his own *Bloomsbury Handbook of Critical Theory* sparked the idea for this project. David Avital and Clara Herberg at Bloomsbury have been fantastic to work with and supportive of the project throughout. I'm happy to see their continued interest in feminism and critical theory.

Additionally, a number of people have been very helpful in suggesting writers, reviewing drafts, advising, and talking through ideas. I express gratitude to Elisabeth R. Anker, Emily Apter, Anne Coldiron, Barry J. Faulk, Mary A. Favret, Paul Fyfe, Timothy Parrish, and Rebekah Sheldon.

And finally, I'd like to thank Kenneth J. Saltman, my intellectual soulmate.

CONTRIBUTORS

Sarah Afzal currently teaches undergraduate composition and literature courses in the English department at Florida State University. She studies literature with an emphasis on Postcolonial Literature and Feminism, Gender, and Sexuality Studies. She is particularly interested in exploring marginalized and socially and politically repressed voices and identities in postcolonial societies. She is also interested in personal narratives that explore the partition of the Indian subcontinent.

Emanuela Bianchi is Associate Professor of Comparative Literature and affiliated with the Department of Classics and the Program in Gender and Sexuality Studies at New York University. She is the author of *The Feminine Symptom: Aleatory Matter in the Aristotelian Cosmos* (2014) and is currently writing a book on nature, hegemony, and kinship in ancient Greece.

Avtar Brah is Professor Emerita at Birkbeck College, University of London. She is a pioneer in the field of Diaspora Studies. Her book *Cartographies of Diaspora* generated key debates in this field. Her publications include the books *Cartographies of Diaspora: Contesting Identities; Hybridity and Its Discontents: Politics, Science, Culture* (coedited with Annie Coombes); *Thinking Identities: Racism, Ethnicity Culture*; and *Global Futures: Migration, Environment, and Globalization* (coedited with Mary Hickman and Mairtin Mac an Ghaill). She is a member of the Academy of Social Sciences, UK. In 2001 she was awarded the MBE for services to Race and Gender. She is a member of the Editorial Collective of the journal *Feminist Review* and the International Editorial Board of the journal *Identities: Global Studies in Culture and Power*.

Anne Cong-Huyen is the Associate Librarian of Digital Pedagogy at the University of Michigan Library. She was formerly the Digital Scholar at Whittier College, coordinator of the Digital Liberal Arts center, Mellon Postdoctoral Fellow in the Humanities, and Visiting Assistant Professor of Asian American Studies at the University of California, Los Angeles. Her research interests include digital pedagogy, literature and media of migration and labor, and women of color feminisms. Her work has appeared in the *Journal of e-Media Studies* (2013), *Debates in the Digital Humanities 2016* (2016), *Between Humanities and the Digital* (2015), and the open-access publication *Digital Pedagogy in the Humanities*. She holds leadership positions in HASTAC, FemTechNet, and the Digital Humanities Caucus of the American Studies Association and is a founding member of the #transformDH collective. Anne can be reached on Twitter @anitaconchita. You may find out more about her work at anitaconchita.org.

Marios Constantinou received his PhD from the New School for Social Research. He is the editor of *Badiou and the Political Condition*, as well as of special issues on *Space and Event* (*Environment & Planning D: Society and Space*) and *Imperial Affect* (*Parallax*). He is currently translating Jodi Dean's *Publicity's Secret* into Greek. His writings and essays appeared in *Third Text, Parrhesia, The Year's Work in Critical and Cultural Theory, Angelaki,*

Parallax, Thesis Eleven, Postcolonial Studies, and elsewhere. They all attempt from different angles to retrieve the counter-imperialist truth of the political from different angles.

Bridget Crone is Lecturer in Visual Cultures at Goldsmiths, the University of London. Her work as a curator and writer weaves together forms of speculation and enquiry across fields of practice to propose new forms of encounter between body, time, and the image. Recent exhibitions include *Propositions for a Stage: 24 Frames of a Beautiful Heaven* (2017) and *Spectral Ecologies* (2017). Her published works include *The Sensible Stage: Staging and the Moving Image* (2017, edited collection, second edition Intellect); "Flicker-Time and Fabulation: From Flickering Images to Crazy Wipes" (in *Fictions and Futures*, 2017); "Opera as Method in the Work of Grace Schwindt" (2016); "Liquid States and the Image" (in *Technologism*, 2015); and "Curating, Dramatization and the Diagram" (in *The Curatorial: Philosophy as Curating*, 2013).

Susan Ferguson is Associate Professor in both the Digital Media and Journalism, and the Youth and Children's Studies programs at Wilfrid Laurier University in Ontario, Canada. Her publications engage variously with feminist political economy, childhood and children's culture, and public discourse and democracy. Her articles on Social Reproduction Feminism appear in *Critical Sociology, New Politics, Socialist Register, Studies in Political Economy* and *Race, Gender and Class*. Her most recent journal article in this area addresses debates within Intersectionality Feminism and appears in a special issue of *Historical Materialism* which she has coedited. She is currently working on a book about the social reproduction of capitalist childhoods.

Luise von Flotow has been teaching Translation Studies at the University of Ottawa since 1996. Her main research interests include feminism, gender and translation, cultural diplomacy and translation, and audiovisual translation. She is also a literary translator, most recently publishing *They Divided the Sky* (2013), a translation of Christa Wolf's *Der geteilte Himmel*, and *The Stalinist's Wife*, a translation of France Théoret's *La femme du stalinien* (2013). Her most recent scholarly publications are *Translating Women: Different Voices and New Horizons*, edited with Farzaneh Farhazad (2016); *Translation Effects: The Making of Contemporary Canadian Culture*, edited with Kathy Mezei and Sherry Simon (2014); and *Translating Women* (2011).

Robin Truth Goodman is Professor of English at Florida State University. Her published works include *Gender for the Warfare State: Literature of Women in Combat* (2016); *Literature and the Development of Feminist Theory* (edited collection, 2015); *Gender Work: Feminism after Neoliberalism* (2013); *Feminist Theory in Pursuit of the Public: Women and the "Re-Privatization" of Labor* (2010); *Policing Narratives and the State of Terror* (2009); *World, Class, Women: Global Literature, Education, and Feminism* (2004); *Strange Love: Or How We Learn to Stop Worrying and Love the Market* (cowritten with Kenneth J. Saltman, 2002); and *Infertilities: Exploring Fictions of Barren Bodies* (2001). She is currently completing a monograph entitled *Promissory Notes: On the Literary Conditions of Debt* and editing another volume for Bloomsbury called *Understanding Adorno, Understanding Modernism*.

Henriette Gunkel is Lecturer in the Department of Visual Cultures at Goldsmiths, University of London. She is the author of *The Cultural Politics of Female Sexuality in South Africa* (2010) and coeditor of *Undutiful Daughters: New Directions in Feminist Thought and Practice* (2012), *What Can a Body Do?* (2010), and *Frieda Grafe. 30 Filme*

(2013). She currently works on a monograph on Africanist Science Fictional interventions and on three coedited volumes: *Futures & Fictions* (Repeater, forthcoming), *Visual Cultures as Time Travel* (forthcoming), and *We Travel the Space Ways: Black Imagination, Fragments and Diffractions* (Duke University Press, forthcoming).

Susan Hekman is Professor Emeritus of political science at the University of Texas at Arlington. She has published widely in feminist theory. Her recent books are *Private Selves/Public Identities*, *The Material of Knowledge*, and, with Stacy Alaimo, *Material Feminisms*. Her most recent book, *The Feminine Subject*, was published in the fall of 2014 by Polity Press.

Margaret R. Higonnet, Professor of English and Comparative Literature at the University of Connecticut, has worked on a range of topics including the literature of the First World War, feminist theory, comparative literature, Thomas Hardy, and children's literature. Her work on women in the First World War has had three focuses: elegiac poetry, nurses' and soldiers' memoirs, and texts that inculcate a war culture for children. Her comparative studies of women address issues of realism, cultural definitions of gender, and women's narrative voices. Her current work on female realism connects with her study of women's photographically documented memoirs as well as women's focus in the nineteenth century on labor. She is also coeditor of a two-volume comparative study of realism in the nineteenth and twentieth centuries.

Laura Hughes is Visiting Assistant Professor in the Department of French Literature, Thought and Culture at New York University. She works on critical archiving in French literature and thought, focusing on how the process of creating and preserving writing is imprinted by the body, sexuality, and matter. Her current book project is a study of Hélène Cixous's and Jacques Derrida's archived friendship.

Aída Hurtado is Luis Leal Endowed Chair and Professor in the Department of Chicana and Chicano Studies, University of California, Santa Barbara. Dr. Hurtado is a social psychologist whose research focuses on intersectional feminisms and Latinas/os' gender socialization. Her most recent work is a feminist analysis of racialized masculinities, which is the focus of her new book *Beyond Machismo: Intersectional Latino Masculinities* (coauthored with Mrinal Sinha, 2016). Dr. Hurtado is the recipient of the Women of Color Psychologies Award (from the Association of Women in Psychology), the SAGE Award for Distinguished Contributions to Gender Equity in Education Research (from the American Educational Research Association), and the Outstanding Latino/a Faculty in Higher Education Award (from the American Association of Hispanics in Higher Education).

Joy James is the F.C. Oakley 3rd Century Professor at Williams College. She is the editor of a number of texts on radical abolitionism and the author of *Seeking the Beloved Community*.

Mina Karavanta is Associate Professor of Literary Theory and Cultural Studies in the Faculty of English Studies of the School of Philosophy of the National and Kapodistrian University of Athens. She has published on postcolonial studies, gender studies, literary theory, and comparative literature in international journals and collections and has coedited special issues on cultural studies and literary theory. She has also coedited two collections of articles, Edward Said and Jacques Derrida: Reconstellating Humanism and the Global Hybrid (2008), and Interculturality and Gender (2009). She is one of the editors of *Synthesis*, a peer-reviewed Anglophone journal of comparative literary studies (http://synthesis.enl.uoa.gr/) that boasts an international academic board. She is currently working on her monograph, *The Postnational Novel: Literary Configurations of Community in the Anglophone Novel of the Twentieth-First Century.*

Kyoo Lee, Professor of Philosophy, Women & Gender Studies at John Jay College and the Graduate Center, CUNY; author of *Writing Entanglish: Come in Englysshing with Gertrude Stein, Zhuangzi …* (2015) and *Reading Descartes Otherwise: Blind, Mad, Dreamy, and Bad* (2012); coeditor of journal issues on "Derrida in China Today" (*Derrida Today*), "Safe" (*Women's Studies Quarterly*), and "Xenophobia & Racism" (*Critical Philosophy of Race*), is a theorist and writer who works widely in the interwoven fields of the Arts and the Humanities. A coeditor of philoSOPHIA: *A Journal of transContinental Feminism*, she also serves on the boards of *Belladonna**, *Derrida Today, Simone de Beauvoir Studies,* and *Women's Studies Quarterly.*

Kathleen Long is Professor of French in the Department of Romance Studies at Cornell University. She is the author of two books, *Another Reality: Metamorphosis* and the *Imagination in the Poetry of Ovid, Petrarch, and Ronsard and Hermaphrodites in Renaissance Europe*, and editor of volumes on *High Anxiety: Masculinity in Crisis in Early Modern France, Religious Differences in France,* and *Gender and Scientific Discourse in Early Modern Europe.* She has written numerous articles on the work of Théodore Agrippa d'Aubigné on gender in early modern Europe and on monsters. She is preparing a translation into English of *The Island of Hermaphrodites* (*L'isle des hermaphrodites*), a book-length study of the works of Agrippa d'Aubigné, and another on the relationship between early modern discourses of monstrosity and modern discourses of disability.

Shannon Davies Mancus is the Hennebach Visiting Assistant Professor of Environmental Humanities at the Colorado School of Mines. Her work can be found in *Performing Ethos* and *The Cambridge History of Science Fiction*, and her manuscript project focuses on the ways in which genre functions as a performative framework for environmentalist narratives. She is one of the current heads of the ecomedia working group for the Association of the Study of Literature and the Environment, as well as the Digital Humanities Liaison for the Environment and Culture Caucus of the American Studies Association. Her work focuses on the political performativity of environmentalist media in visual and popular culture.

Maria Margaroni is Associate Professor in Literary Theory and Feminist Thought at the University of Cyprus. She has held Visiting Fellowships at the Institute for Advanced Studies in the Humanities (University of Edinburgh) and the Centre for Cultural Analysis, Theory and History (University of Leeds). Her publications include *Julia Kristeva: Live Theory* (with John Lechte, 2004), *Metaphoricity and the Politics of Mobility* (with Effie Yiannopoulou, 2006), *Intimate Transfers* (with Effie Yiannopoulou, special issue of the *European Journal of English Studies*, 2005), *Violence and the Sacred* (special issue of *Philosophy Today*, 2012), and *Textual Layering: Contact, Historicity, Critique* (with Apostolos Lampropoulos and Christos Hadjichristou, 2017). She is currently finishing her monograph focusing on the thought of Julia Kristeva.

Rita Mookerjee is a PhD candidate studying literature at Florida State University. She specializes in Caribbean women's writing and food studies. Her work has been featured in the *Routledge Companion to Literature and Food*, the *Bloomsbury Handbook to Literary and Cultural Theory*, and *Palaver Journal*.

Caitlin Newcomer is Assistant Professor of English at College of the Canyons. Her work focuses on twentieth- and twenty-first-century American poetry and feminist poetics, with a special interest in women's experiments in long-form poetry, lyric subjectivity, and representations of motherhood.

Anca Parvulescu is Professor of English at Washington University in St Louis. She is the author of *Laughter: Notes on a Passion* (2010) and *The Traffic in Women's Work: East European Migration and the Making of Europe* (2014). She works in modernist literature, feminist theory, and Eastern Europe.

Alison Phipps is Professor of Gender Studies at the University of Sussex. She is a political sociologist focusing on how neoliberalism shapes feminism, especially within institutions and on media and social media platforms. Her 2014 monograph *The Politics of the Body* explored how the dominant macropolitical coalition of neoliberalism and neoconservatism framed and circumscribed feminist rationalities and politics. She is now working on her next monograph, entitled *Personal Business: Neoliberalism and the Politics of Sexual Violence*. Alison is also currently leading research focused on the interactions between neoliberal higher education cultures and issues of equality and diversity, through the Changing University Cultures (CHUCL) project.

Masood Raja is Associate Professor of English at the University of North Texas. He is the author of *The Religious Right and the Talibanization of America* (2016) and *Constructing Pakistan: Foundational Texts and the Rise of Muslim National Identity, 1857–1947* (2010).

Nicole Simek is Associate Professor of French and Interdisciplinary Studies at Whitman College. She specializes in French Caribbean literature, with research interests in the intersection of literature and politics, trauma theory, postcolonial critique, and sociological approaches to literature. Her publications include *Hunger and Irony in the French Caribbean: Literature, Theory, and Public Life* (2016) and *Eating Well, Reading Well: Maryse Condé and the Ethics of Interpretation* (2008), as well as the coedited volumes *Feasting on Words: Maryse Condé, Cannibalism, and the Caribbean Text* (2006) and an issue of *Dalhousie French Studies on Representations of Trauma in French and Francophone literature* (2007).

Fanny Söderbäck is Assistant Professor of Philosophy at DePaul University. She holds a PhD in Philosophy from the New School for Social Research and taught philosophy for several years at Siena College. Fanny has edited *Feminist Readings of Antigone* (2010) and is a coeditor of the volume *Undutiful Daughters: New Directions in Feminist Thought and Practice* (2012). She is also the editor of a special issue of *philoSOPHIA: A Journal of Continental Feminism* on the topic of birth. Her work has appeared in scholarly journals such as *Signs: Journal of Women in Culture and Society*, *Journal of Speculative Philosophy*, and *Journal of French and Francophone Philosophy*. She is working on a book manuscript titled *Revolutionary Time*, which treats the role of time as it appears in the work of French feminist thinkers Julia Kristeva and Luce Irigaray. She is the codirector of the Kristeva Circle.

Alison Sperling is currently a postdoctoral fellow at the ICI Berlin Institute for Cultural Inquiry. Her research examines twentieth- and twenty-first-century literature and culture with specific attention to nonhuman modes of embodiment and temporality through queer and feminist theory, science studies, disability studies, and eco-criticism. Her essays appear in *Rhizomes*, *Girlhood Studies*, and *Paradoxa*, with forthcoming work on plant studies and speculative fiction.

Hortense J. Spillers is the Gertrude Conaway Vanderbilt Chair in English at Vanderbilt University. Her collection of essays, *Black, White and in Color: Essays on American Literature and Culture*, juxtaposes inquiries in feminist studies, minority discourse, and psychoanalytic theory, as well as American and African American literatures. Her essays have appeared in a number of journals, most recently in *Small Axe* and *boundary 2*. She is at work on two big projects—*The Idea of Black Culture* and *The Life and Status of Women under Revolutionary Conditions in Emergent Haiti, the Modern French State, and the Early United States*.

Mihoko Suzuki is Professor of English, Cooper Fellow in the Humanities, and founding director of the Center for the Humanities at the University of Miami. During fall 2016 she was Ruth and Clarence Kennedy Professor in Renaissance Studies at Smith College. She is the author of *Metamorphoses of Helen: Authority, Difference and the Epic* (1989) and *Subordinate Subjects: Gender, the Political Nation, and Literary Form, 1588–1688* (2003); and the editor of volume 3 of Palgrave's *History of British Women's Writing, 1610–1690* (2011). She has coedited *Debating Gender in Early Modern England 1500–1700* (2002); *Women's Political Writings, 1610–1725* (4 vols., 2007); *The Rule of Women in Early Modern Europe* (2009); and *Early Modern Women: An Interdisciplinary Journal* (2011–18). She is completing *Antigone's Example*, on women's political writing in various genres during times of Civil War.

Rashmi Varma teaches English and Comparative Literary Studies at the University of Warwick. She is the author of *The Postcolonial City and Its Subjects: London, Nairobi and Bombay*, and has recently coedited a special issue of *Critical Sociology* on Marxism and Postcolonial Theory: What is Left of the Debate? She is the founder-member of the journal *Feminist Dissent*.

Aimee Armande Wilson is Assistant Professor of Humanities at the University of Kansas, where she specializes in modernist literature and reproductive justice. Her work has appeared in *Modern Fiction Studies*, *symploké*, and *Genre*. She is the author of *Conceived in Modernism: The Aesthetics and Politics of Birth Control* (2016).

Michelle M. Wright is the Augustus Baldwin Longstreet Professor of English at Emory University in Atlanta, Georgia, where she teaches courses on the African diaspora, black Europe, and black feminist and queer theory. She is the author of two monographs, *Becoming Black: Creating Identity in the African Diaspora* (2004) and *Physics of Blackness: Beyond the Middle Passage Epistemology* (2015), and coeditor of three volumes: *Domain Errors! A Cyberfeminist Handbook*, with Faith Wilding and Maria Fernandez (2003), *Reading the Black German Experience, A Special Issue of Callaloo*, with Tina M. Campt (2003), and *Blackness and Sexualities*, with Antje Schuhmann (2007). She is also coeditor with Jodi Byrd of the book series Critical Insurgencies in conjunction with the Critical Ethnic Studies Association (CESA) and Northwestern University Press.

Effie Yiannopoulou is Assistant Professor of English and Cultural Theory at the School of English, Aristotle University, Greece. She has researched and published work in the fields of twentieth-century women's writings, Black British and British Asian literature, and postcolonial and cultural theory. She is especially interested in theories of mobility and community building and their impact on cultural, racial, and gender identities. She has coedited *Metaphoricity and the Politics of Mobility* (2006), *The Flesh Made Text Made Flesh: Cultural and Theoretical Returns to the Body* (2007), and *The Future of Flesh* (2009).

Ewa Plonowska Ziarek is Julian Park Professor of Comparative Literature at the University of Buffalo, a senior research fellow at the College of Fellows at Western Sydney University, and a visiting faculty in the Institute for Doctoral Studies in the Visual Arts, University of Maine. Most recently, she coauthored *Natality and Biopolitics: Towards Democratic Plurality and Reproductive Justice* with Rosalyn Diprose Arendt (2019). Her other books include *Feminist Aesthetics and the Politics of Modernism* (2012); *An Ethics of Dissensus: Feminism, Postmodernity, and the Politics of Radical Democracy* (2001); and *The Rhetoric of Failure: Deconstruction of Skepticism, Reinvention of Modernism* (1995); and coedited volumes, such as *Intermedialities: Philosophy, Art, Politics* (2010); *Time for the Humanities* (2008); and *Revolt, Affect, Collectivity: The Unstable Boundaries of Kristeva's Polis* (2005). Her interdisciplinary research interests include feminist political theory, modernism, feminist philosophy and psychoanalysis, and critical race theory.

Introduction

ROBIN TRUTH GOODMAN

KEYWORD: FEMINIST THEORY

This book comes at a time of major transition and radical change in the way gender is publicly recognized and organized, from debates worldwide over transsexuality and gay marriage as well as regressions in abortion and birth control policy, to austerity measures, sweatshop labor, war, environmental policies, and migration policies that cause misery disproportionately to women, and new arrangements of labor that substitute robotics for bodies and service for manufacturing. In light of these transformations, it is impossible to consider feminism as having produced a settled body of theory. Especially in the language it uses to describe itself, feminism must be presented in active development.

When we initially started to work on this volume, feminism was a word becoming rarefied in popular culture and sometimes in academia, vilified, and often rejected by our students even as they may have accepted its major premises. In the early aughts, Governor Jeb Bush of Florida could proudly proclaim to marchers and activists that the Equal Rights Amendment (ERA) was outdated like bell-bottoms. In the past year, however, young women and men have been wearing T-shirts extolling feminism, putting pro-feminist bumper stickers on their cars to answer to feminism's call, some choosing their courses for their feminist content, and, despite Jeb's prophecies, the ERA is back on the table. Even the *New York Times* has marked International Women's Day in 2018 with recognizing that women die too and their deaths should be commemorated in *New York Times* obituaries. Much of popular culture and its political landscapes have come to an open embrace, even a celebration of a certain form of street feminism. This includes not only millennial TV programs like *Girls* that show young women negotiating independent financial lives and a multiplicity of sexual arrangements, and commemorations of women superheroes like *Wonder Woman* as she is given her first feature-length blockbuster, but also a near-victory of a female presidential candidate in the United States, record numbers of female candidates running for office in the 2018 midterm elections, protesters against the US president wearing "pussy hats," celebrities and politicians speaking out against sexual harassment, and media-savvy movements on college campuses against sexual assault, with women carrying their mattresses on their backs to class to expose university inaction on harassment allegations. On International Women's Day in 2018, 5.3 million Spanish women stopped working, causing an economic slowdown, while laws were loosened in Saudi Arabia and women went jogging as well as started to drive cars (even though women's rights activists remain incarcerated). In Ireland, voters approved a referendum that legalized abortion. There have been marches of thousands of women in Brazil, large movements against sexual violence in India, and crowds of women turning up in protest to argue against their government's repressions of reproductive freedoms in Poland, and the "Ni Una Menos" (Not One Less) movement in Argentina (against femicides and domestic abuse) has succeeded in bringing abortion legalization bills to the legislative floor. Women protestors at the US Supreme Court were right to hold up red signs saying "Feminists Are the Majority."

In 1997, Wendy Brown could begin an article in the feminist journal *differences* by stating, "There is today enough retrospective analysis and harangue concerning the field of women's studies to raise the question of whether dusk on its epoch has arrived, even if nothing approaching Minerva's wisdom has yet emerged" (79), and in the early aughts, Toril Moi could agree that "Today, ... the future of feminism is in doubt. Since the mid-1990s, I have noticed that most of my students no longer make feminism their central political and personal project" (1735). Yet, twelve years later, the resurgence of popular interest in feminism defies Moi's tragic prognostication and warning: "If feminism is to have a future, feminist theory—feminist thought, feminist writing—must be able to show that feminism has wise and useful things to say to women who struggle to cope with everyday problems" (1739). Obviously, women who struggle to cope have decided that feminism was and still is the place to turn.

The question that confronts us is no longer if feminism has a future but rather whether the sort of feminism that has arisen in the political emergency of our present is adequate to that emergency. As Susan Watkins observes, "Of all the opposition movements to have erupted since 2008, the rebirth of a militant feminism is perhaps the most surprising" (5). Yet, she goes on to say, what is most surprising about this "return" to feminism is that feminism had never really gone away but had been absorbed as "a mantra of the global establishment" (5), becoming a rallying cry for the expansion of global power and losing some of its critical edge. In this context, for instance, Women's Studies programs reached—as Biddy Martin assessed it—"a point of stasis" (102) (where the stultification of the terms of the debates led to loss of "critical and intellectual vigor" as well as a depoliticization) and generally turned to "gender studies," which often focuses curriculum on description and empirical studies over theory and is less overtly concerned with concepts and critical tools than with affirming present gender manifestations as the truth of gender. Lee Edelman might call this turn from theory "a certain positivization" where the "signifier of presence, of identity, is increasingly *made* present, resulting in a reification of difference, in a quest for its actualization" as the first move toward "violent assurances," the denial of identity as a question, and "an avowal of authority" (151).

Alongside this disciplining, rigidifying, and administrative turn of much Women's Studies, feminism's revival has been met with a mainstreaming of extreme right-wing positions against women and feminism, often calling for attacks on women, following a series of incidents like "Gamergate" where women journalists and bloggers were sent hundreds of threatening Twitter messages because they expressed aversion to the "neomasculinist" content of online subcultures. As Angela Nagle has documented, in the face of "a revived feminist movement [that] was trying to change the culture" (24), "Gamergate brought gamers, rightist chan culture, anti-feminism and the online far right closer to mainstream discussion and it also politicized a broad group of young people, mostly boys, who organized tactics around the idea of fighting back against the culture war being waged by the cultural left" (24). Even as we must seriously combat this renewed acceptability of violence against women, we are still compelled to ask what it means to have the media/political spectacle direct and absorb both the feminist and the anti-feminist impulse in the same gesture? That is, we should be questioning whether the irresistibility of feminism in the media and popular culture also limits the types of interventions feminism can make in the name of justice, if it highlights women's individualized grievances and spectacularizing victimizations in order not to take feminism's global demands seriously, if it is so invested in entertainment, glamor, and fashion as "empowerment" that it cannot recognize the banality, neglect, and dispossession that frames many ordinary lives, and if it answers to individual needs rather than to the global crises induced by enduring wars, growing numbers of refugees, environmental risk, cuts to social safety nets, austerity policy, increasing debt, intensifying economic polarization at the expense of working people, and a growing sense of labor's obsolescence worldwide.

Up until now, feminism has responded to this global emergency in a variety of ways. One way has been "[t]he revalorization of all girlie things in popular culture," as Jane Spencer notes: women's affirmation through emphatic feminine display. Another way has been the promotion of entrepreneurial feminism as a dominant transformation in the work/consumption promise, where traditionally "female" traits are held up as the benevolent welcoming arm of the increasingly polarized economy and the new corporatisms. Identity-talk certainly has its pitfalls. It tends to allow both empiricism and calculation to take control of what counts as legitimate articulations. In the face of massive global transformations (often called "neoliberalism"), the time may at long last be now to find alternatives to the forms of identity that are always looking to settle the concrete and the quantifiable, and yet this type of identity keeps popping up, as though everyone knows its political limitations but needs to hold on to it nevertheless. With this type of identity, social conventions get lodged in bodies as though the bodies make them real, creating certainty, and the bodies rather than the arguments are what is at stake, as though the bodies *are* the arguments. This can make thinking about what "ought to" or "might" be trapped in what "is," as though the "is" were inevitable. Though Civil Rights and anti-imperialist struggles have and should have a great influence on the development of feminist theory, neither movement insists on considering the body as the limit to thought nor on posing the body as evidence of righteous outcomes, good intentions, insight, or reason. Additionally, as Wendy Brown has astutely pointed out, identity-talk seems "to breed a politics of recrimination and rancor, of culturally dispersed paralysis and suffering, a tendency to reproach power rather than aspire to it" (*States of Injury* 55); it tends to posit the body as the site of injury and politics as a cry of pain and woundedness for the state to remedy, rather than as a positive struggle for a vision of a better world or a plan to take over and hold power.

The politics of cultural affirmation may take us in unsavory directions. As the former Trump Administration strategist Steve Bannon told Robert Kuttner of the *American Prospect* after the 2017 white nationalist rally in Charlottesville, Virginia, where one protestor was killed, "The Democrats …, the longer they talk about identity politics, I got 'em. I want them to talk about racism every day. If the left is focused on race and identity, and we go with economic nationalism, we can crush the Democrats." The point here is not to worry about Democrats and Republicans, or liberals and conservatives, but rather to understand identity-talk as creating blockages. Though it is difficult at best to take Bannon's version of reality seriously, his cynical response does characterize liberalism at a standstill in ways that are familiar. Identity focuses public participation largely around calls for rights and equality while reducing suffering predominantly to what can be made visible and counted. It also might be seen as creating communities with seemingly hardened and uncrossable boundaries, while suggesting that the body essentially is inscribed with specified ideas, consciousness, and political program. Feminism should, rather, be a politics of disidentification with what appears as the "is," an articulation, as Jacques Rancière says about politics, of what we could have in common against those who want to divide us into these countable parts.

Talk about identity often assumes a transparent but false connection between the biological body and a body of knowledge or experience. Identity assumes that what people can know, think, feel, and experience can be seen on the surface of their bodies, and what they can do and say in order to be understood is reduced to a meaning and a course of action that appear, in public, on that surface. It binds people to others not because they find there sympathetic ideas. Rather, identity constrains populations behind shields of abstracted, idealized stereotypes while reducing politics to interest and thought to instrumentalism. It confines feminist questions to social concerns that, as Linda Zerilli argues, are "framed ... in the language of social utility" (7), depoliticized, and instrumentalized within the framework of a specific problem that can be fixed (most likely through inclusion): that, for example, rights and recognition ought to be expanded to currently disenfranchised groups. This type of rights discourse assumes certain needs as "self-evident and beyond dispute," as Nancy Fraser has pointed out, not taking into account that "the interpretation of needs is itself a political stake, indeed sometimes *the* political stake" (145) and, as such, is never self-evident. Miring us in our statistics and empiricism, identity-talk, in other words, promotes a type of politics that bureaucratizes inequality within an unwinnable game of "catch up." Rather, as feminists, we have an imperative to reimagine the terms in which we live together and make judgments about the world we want to live in.

Another feminist tactic is identity critique, that is, questioning the possibility of a subject that speaks as "woman." Such a move has put feminism in a bind, as it says simultaneously that women should demand rights as women and then also that "women" and "men" are falsely hegemonic categories, based on exclusions, that limit experience and truth for the purposes of social ordering (sometimes a division of labor). As Linda Zerilli defines the problem, "posited as a unified category given in advance of politics, 'women' generates exclusions; posited as 'a site of permanent openness and resignifiability,' 'women' precludes the possibility of speaking collectively" (170). The conflict between these two positions has trapped feminist thinking in an echo chamber. Much ink has been spilt nuancing, say, the category of women so that it does not presume its own universal representation, so that the category of women does not speak in the name of white privilege by erasing racial, ethnic, sexual, national, ability, age, and class differences. On the other hand, feminists have also exhibited resolve in reviving an idea of feminist agency even without being able to construct a women's subjectivity-in-common. Meanwhile, feminist thinkers influenced by Judith Butler, for example, have demonstrated that "woman" is an appropriable category, constantly being remade and reconstructed, whose meaning is never finalized.

Rather than extending the present indefinitely, as burrowing inside an identity tends to do, the critique of identity puts identity into circulation, allowing sexual difference to take shape and become coherent as it congeals inside a historical stage that it, at the same time, participates in formulating and dismantling. In other words, we have not always lived and will not always live in the regime of sexual difference that we currently inhabit. *The Bloomsbury Handbook of 21st-Century Feminist Theory* is about uncongealing— it understands that the terminology that constitutes feminist politics is constantly overturning and reorganizing what counts as a feminist subject. Instead of answering the call of the Symbolic to decide once and for all what a woman is or what "woman" does or what the contents of feminism should be, the *Handbook* focuses on the politics of saying and acting, tracing concepts through time by foregrounding a set of thought processes and terminologies that have gone into treating the "woman question" for feminism and teasing out what ideas have been unleashed. In order to do politics differently, we need to think differently about how we think and about what words we use to think it, about organizing how we live together and with whom we share the world, and we need to think differently, too, about how thinking is already in the world that we experience, sometimes sedimented in conventions but oftentimes crashing against the walls.

Another major theme that has captured feminist thinking is agency and power. In the face of dominant structures, institutional forces, oppressive ideologies, and historical atrocities, much feminism must seek out possibilities of change, of taking control, mechanisms for disrupting powerful symbols and mythological systems and drawing out oppositional potentialities. Most famously, perhaps, Judith Butler introduced the question of agency as a problem when the gendered body "cannot be isolated from the dynamics of power from which it is wrought" (xxv), when "one cannot disavow power as the condition of its own possibility" (xxv). Sometimes, this formulation can mean that oppositional power comes from the same place as oppressive power and is at home inside of it. In response, some feminists have turned to media images as sources of empowerment. In the introduction to their field-setting volume *Third Wave Agenda*, Leslie Heywood and Jennifer Drake, for example, look to pop stars to find prototypes "of female ambition" for they often combine "individualism, combativeness, and star power" (4). As Claire Hemming corrects some of the misreadings of agency in feminist thought post-Butler, "Judith Butler's conclusion to *Gender Trouble* ... argues for a view of agency ... on the basis that its overassociation with individual capacity ignores both the vagaries of power and the ways in which power acts to make individuals *feel agented* as part of how it operates" (206). Though Butler definitely promotes a view of agency that is socially dependent and vulnerable, another type of agency has often subsequently been advanced in response as enacting identifications with shiny corporate products, fashion mavens, and popular celebrity.

This type of agency, however, since it acquires power in its repetitions of hegemonic representations, does not necessarily pass oppositional muster, often reinvesting the hierarchies and exploitative relations that their corporate managers imbue in their image. One outcome of this spin on agency, for example, has been a wielding of feminism within the temporal logic of imperialism: if (such views say) Western feminists have achieved a high level of visibility in culture, if femininity is seen as a pleasure-loving prize rather than a desultory liability, if women have at last achieved some level of "equality" in the workplace, then the places where women are disparaged and repressed must fall outside the borders of the West, maybe even in a different, regressive time. Such a racist and supremacist premise justifies military interventions for the purpose of "white men saving brown women from brown men" (296), as Gayatri Spivak has notoriously elaborated.

Contingently, feminist agency that borrows its forms from the existing power structure often reiterates commercialized messages that counter feminism's commitment to freedom. Rosalind Gill, for example, has countered this feminist obsession with locating agency: "One of the problems with this focus on autonomous choices is that it remains complicit with, rather than critical of, postfeminist and neoliberal discourses that see individuals as entrepreneurial actors who are rational, calculating and self-regulating. The neoliberal subject is required to bear full responsibility for their life biography no matter how severe the constraints upon their action" (436). Angela McRobbie agrees: "gender retrenchment is secured, paradoxically, through the wide dissemination of discourses of female freedom and (putative) equality" (720). This, for McRobbie, means "that there is no longer any place for feminism in contemporary political culture" (720). Such

market-oriented forms of agency taken up in contemporary feminism tend to individu-
alize responsibility, commercialize empowerment, and equate freedom with product
choice. As Butler intended "agency" to be a practice of creating new norms by disrupting
the Symbolic, a redefining of "agency" in conformity with social norms tends to dull
feminism's capacities toward reenvisioning the political in any other way besides getting
more shine from what is already established, or feeling a glow from binding ourselves
to the call of the dominant. The transfer of feminism's agency into the socially normal
and the Symbolic—in its most egregious forms, into a stylization of naturalized forms
of the body, extracting images of our future from media screens—aligns some feminism
with neoliberal power. The obsession with locating agency within poststructuralism is
dispiriting and often requires an array of qualifiers and conditions that limit the area
of possibilities in which either individual or collective agents can exercise control. This
insistence on an agency that is gradually surrendered dovetails with a political effort
to depoliticize citizens and knowledge, injecting a sense of helplessness, victimization,
and powerlessness within democratic cultures by raising the question of whether democratic institutions can institute democratic agency. *The Bloomsbury Handbook* seeks to
comb feminism for ideas to rethink political subjectivity and rebuild political, cultural,
and social life nationally and globally. Instead of locating agency in care of the self, the
Handbook takes seriously the agency of grabbing at hegemony through intellectual life
and rethinking where we fit in language. As feminists, we must seize control of the means
of identification by unsettling the present form of the Symbolic.

Additionally, *The Bloomsbury Handbook of 21st-Century Feminist Theory* produces
a story of feminism's long history that veers off from the dominant direction of contemporary feminist historical sequencing. The standard historicization of the movement
presumes that feminism's early connection to socialism fractured because of its tendencies
to universalize the experience of "women's oppression" and gave way to a "difference
feminism," hyphenization model, or an "identity politics" that sought a broader inclusion
of race, class, ethnicity, nationality, age, ability, and sexual orientation. It finally moved
into a "postmodern feminism" that questioned the very possibility of reference and
representation altogether in its broad philosophy of difference and its espousal of "the
end of master narratives." "Postmodern feminism" then itself came under attack because
its aversion to representation limited the possibility of representational politics under the
name of feminism, and so feminism turned back to a post-feminist, materialist orientation, or a "Third Wave." This deconstruction of the monolithic subject for which new
feminists have criticized the previous generation is characterized, Shelly Budgeon writes,
by "diversity, fragmentation, and a series of internal contestations" (1), where feminism is
said to have achieved many of its aims and now has turned to "widening the parameters
of a feminist agenda" (3) by challenging the categories of gender and affirming difference.

Such a view of stages or waves relegates feminist history to a false coherence following
a course of transformation through radical breaks of self-awareness. It does not take into
account what Joan Scott has remarked as the feminist "invention of tradition," where the
"subject of feminism" emerges variously at different moments in response to political and
social needs, at once reproducing and masking "conflict, antagonism, or contradiction"
(49) by rewriting its traditions. The third wave of contemporary feminism, instead of
treating language as productive, similarly to the poststructuralist models that the third
wave often says are its origin points, still treats language as repressive as it "relies upon
representing second wave feminism as ethnocentric and overly concerned with imposing
similarity upon women's difference" (Budgeon 5). Though one might expect that the next

sentence would display an example of such an egregious act on the part of the second wave, this does not occur, and the author instead throws down with the word "sisterhood" as the underlying indicator that dominates, defines, saturates, and maligns the feminism of the past as exemplary of the ethnocentric bias and the repression of difference.

One might be able to locate instances of the kind of condensed "sisterhood" narrative that Bludgeon dislikes in the feminist archive, but one will also, certainly, come upon even more counter examples—like Simone de Beauvoir, who many consider a "foremother" of the second wave for influencing a preponderance of its writings (more on this below). Leslie Heywood and Jennifer Drake define their "Third Wave" project as being "hard at work on a feminism that strategically combines elements of these feminisms [equity feminism, gender feminism, and poststructuralism], along with black feminism, women-of-color feminism, working-class feminism, pro-sex feminism, and so on" (3). There is no work cited to show what is "new"—how the "Third Wave" has broached something never before tried that bridges insurmountable gaps and developed techniques where the previously excluded can now, newly, play a part. Rather, the idea projected here is that "these feminisms" did not acknowledge the existence of the politics of race and pro-sex and, indeed, could not acknowledge this existence because of the essentialism embedded in what they defined as feminist goals and in the universalist subject (like "sisterhood") they claimed for feminism. The present feminism is, therefore, doing something different in kind. This staging of feminist history gives the "Third Wave" the power to characterize the "First and Second Waves" retrospectively as malignant, monstrous, out of synch, and out of touch in order to differentiate the past from the triumphal self-congratulations of a feminism having learned its lessons that its mothers could not learn (though what those lessons were remain obscure). What is more, such rhetoric essentializes feminism, reducing complex and varied philosophical debates in order to reject them all as, at best, unworthy and uses this as the reason for not engaging with them seriously.

Within this model, the historical breaks are meant to assert a radically new awareness that is vaguely situated with references like "then in the eighties or nineties," temporally locating a grand, momentous event and a climatic realization inside an expansive, ill-defined temporal span with fuzzy borders. Authors and ideas can thus be split between these contexts, taking on different meanings depending on which context is staking the claim. Sometimes, for example, poststructuralist thinkers are the good guys for celebrating difference, while other times they are the evil villain for their idealisms, ethnocentricities, class privileges, or lack of engagement with "reality" or history. This model of feminism's history advances by setting off its present moment from its naïve and unfortunate past and expanding this present indefinitely, often severely lashing out at its past in order to do so. One may even wonder how the framing of feminist history through a sequential (or sometimes nonsequential) series of waves rules out utterances and acts that do not adhere to that paradigm or cannot be captured in these time categories.

One can surely find examples where earlier feminists were anti-racist and anti-imperialist, or when feminist principles and ideas have been used to further anti-racist and anti-imperialist causes. For example, the Combahee River Collective of black feminists was formed "most obviously," they write in their foundational statement, "in connection with the second wave of the American women's movement beginning in the late 1960s" (177). Why are feminists the primary target of the feminist critique of racism, homophobia, and transphobia when racism, homophobia, and transphobia on the political plane have become so toxic and identifiable? Why not focus this vituperative political energy on the racists? Is every subject that gets posed as speaking for feminism assuming that every woman has the same experience, or that feminism would need to speak for all women's experiences in order to speak as feminist? Is an angry allegation of racism against one's philosophical and ideological forbearers the same thing as critique? What is lost and what is gained in this turn of feminism against feminism for universalizing the subject? Does the second wave really have nothing to offer except for a repetition of racisms of its past? Cannot some of the projects it developed—for example, freedom or multiplicity—also be appropriated toward freedoms and multiplicities that answer to our current moment? By acknowledging its concepts as necessarily in flux between contexts, as useful because they can effect understanding across temporal schema, this *Handbook* focuses on feminist theory's major concepts in order to explore how these concepts are more than what they have been or what they seem; how they cannot be restricted to particular historical stages, their contexts, and meanings; and how they could—really, must—redirect the field and its inquiries toward unpredictable futures.

These stories that feminism tells of itself have come under fierce scrutiny in the last ten years or so. The generational framing of the feminist project has recently been criticized by feminist critics like Elizabeth Grosz and Clare Hemmings for limiting and homogenizing what gets included in the discussion and for being insensitive to potential lines of possibly radical politics and research that get smothered by the dominant narrative. "[I]n times of social upheaval and political and economic crisis such as our own," Elizabeth Grosz counsels, "it is more crucial than ever that we access resources—intellectual or conceptual resources as much as political and fiscal ones—that enable us to understand the logic at work in culture, social relations, or individual psychology, its points of vulnerability and its capacity for change" (96). She goes on: "[T]he task of philosophy is to create concepts and, especially, to create new concepts, even if these concepts resonate and recall other concepts, concepts inherited or given, but always made over again, always revived and created again if the concept is to do the work of thought" (96). Clare Hemmings, meanwhile, advises about the importance of not trapping the history of the treatment of women in a closed historical past because such a placement gives a false sense of security in the overcoming of sexism's worst past practices. "We . . . need," she writes, "to examine the ways in which Western feminist stories about the recent past coincide unnervingly with those that place Western feminism firmly in the past in order to 'neutralize' gender equality in its global circuits" (11). The model of different historical levels of feminism tends to homogenize both past and present and so often also tends to shift the burden of the past onto cultures that have "not yet achieved" the feminist momentum of the contemporary West. According to these perspectives, she argues, "a shared global feminist future requires the fantasy of a shared oppressive past, already moved beyond in the West, but culturally present for the South and the East" (149). *The Bloomsbury Handbook* challenges this dominant temporal structure by extracting concepts—concepts that are still necessary—from their confinement in historical periodizations or disciplinarity and addressing them toward the future.

The negativity of these emergent feminist temporal themes toward their antecedents does not brake at the academy's doors but floods into feminism's popular appearances. In the list of 2017 US Academy Award nominees, four films focused on maternal abuse of daughters: Greta Gerwig's *Lady Bird*, Allison Janney's *I, Tonya*, Martin McDonagh's *Three Billboards Outside Ebbing, Missouri*, and Sean Baker's *The Florida Project*. These films were nominated partly on the basis that they were apparently by and/or about women, in the midst of a crisis of abuse against women in Hollywood. Following the revelations that the mogul film producer Harvey Weinstein had engaged in decades of

sexual harassment and assault on a slew of industry women, other performers and celebrities were systematically accused of an array of acts, ranging from unwanted advances,
unsavory comments, bad jokes, uninvited flirtations, and sex acts outside the norm to
domestic abuse and serial pedophilia (followed by similar accusations in other spheres).
Coined "#MeToo" or "Time's Up" on multiple social media platforms, this campaign
of outing resulted in a barrage of negative publicity that was frequently the cause of the
career downfall of the alleged perpetrators: sometimes talented artists and comedians
and sometimes politicians, doctors, restaurateurs, and sports managers. Nevertheless,
the resulting celebration of films that blamed mothers for atrocities committed against
daughters is a disturbing reflection on these events as well as on feminism in our times.

Much was said about these "#MeToo" events, and it is not my intention here to replay
the repertoire of themes and issues that framed the public discussion. Nor is it my intention to downplay the horror of the revelations of rape and abuse of power that surround
Harvey Weinstein and others like him. I am concerned for the most part, rather, with the
way "#MeToo" expands the category of "misconduct" in a way that mixes up assault,
for example, with forms of sexual discomfort due to unfamiliar or undesired encounters.
Such a rhetorical gesture succeeds in portraying all sex as coercion, even if its victims only
realize it many years later. This follows, in the United States, on the overextension of Title
IX regulations, the federal Civil Rights Office, and Equal Opportunities offices on college
campuses in the United States that, during the Obama years, together issued a vendetta
on all college sex as dangerous—and often traumatizing. During these years, university
Title IX officers, human resource personnel, and administrators encouraged reporting
and investigations on any act a student found disturbing or uncomfortable, including
classroom content, and even made faculty members responsible for reporting on any
(private or public) student disclosure, no matter the student's will. Sexual paranoia on
campus, Laura Kipnis has detailed, is "fundamentally altering the intellectual climate in
higher education as a whole, to the point where ideas are construed as threats" (5). It "is
a formula for intellectual rigidity," she goes on, "and its inroads on campus are so effectively dumbing down the place that the traditional ideal of the university—as a refuge for
complexity, a setting for the free exchange of ideas—is getting buried under an avalanche
of platitudes and fear" (5). Though certainly victims of rape and sexual abuse deserve
redress, the discursive climate on campuses—putting rape in the same basket as the discomfort experienced in learning about the politics of rape in the classroom—put intellectual life at risk and chilled relations between faculty and students. Faculty members were
threatened with disciplinary action for saying something unpopular or not informing
authorities of sensitive and private disclosures students might make in office hours for the
purpose of seeking adult guidance.[1] It may be worthwhile to ask if there is a connection
between the capture of feminism by a politics of trauma and our current neoliberal political environment where agency to influence the circumstances of social life has been
diminished along with the democratic institutions that supported it.

Restricting the vast multiplicity of sexual behavior or making sex—especially sex acts
outside of the dominant or the normalized—guilt-ridden have historically been strategies that backfired for feminism, and the "#MeToo" spectacle—even as it exposed some
monstrous acts and some villainous criminals—on a more general level also posed some
challenges and pointed toward a number of possibly alarming setbacks for feminism at
this moment of its rekindled popularity. For example, the feminist subject was unified
and redesigned as a subject of injury, acted upon rather than acting and defined through
inescapable suffering and trauma, whose speech was confined to lament.[2] Politics was

privatized through psychological pain, and the idea of justice reduced to a declaration or multiple declarations: justice took place as a collective media vilification—like a mob action—that more or less labeled sexual acts across the spectrum as one type of horrible criminal affliction on women. Part of how this was accomplished was by conflating sexual assault, sexual harassment, sexual misconduct (a term not defined either by general usage or by law across locations), and discomfort or annoyance, thereby blurring the line between consent and coercion.[3] Another consequence was a severe denial of the ambiguities that are an inherent part of all communication (as feminist theory has taught us for the last three decades or more) but of sexual expression in particular and, contingently, the production of an ideological assumption that all sex is damaging. As Laura Kipnis points out, "If the prevailing story is that sex is dangerous, sex is going to feel threatening more of the time, and anything associated with sex, no matter how innocuous (a risqué remark, a dumb joke) will feel threatening" (9). Another particularly disturbing outcome was an impassioned debate between those who thought perpetrators who are racial minorities should themselves be understood as victims of violence as they suffer from the residues of colonial repression (Beliso de Jesús et al.; Alcoff), and those who believe that protecting communities of color by silencing victims is perpetuating the abuse (Collective). Either way, certain bodies are attributed guilt essentially, agency is assumed as exclusively tied to victimhood and pain, and responsibility for criminal acts is removed from the individual committing the act and put onto world geopolitical history, group identity, or racial background as the body becomes a type of passive objectivity devoid of subjectivity. The issue sets up a hierarchy of suffering between disenfranchised groups that much feminist scholarship has tried very hard to overcome.

Even considering the feminist pride of those who spoke out, sexual repression has never been a good tactic for feminism, especially sexual repression legislated juridically, and, in fact, it catapults us back into the essentialized, singular subject that unifies "women" by defining them as symbols through pain, vulnerability, and disempowerment—like children under the protective management of the state. As Beatriz Preciado succinctly summarizes, "when abolitionist feminists ask the state to regulate the representation of sexuality, they are granting too much power to a patriarchal institution whose historical goal has always been the subjugation of the female body and the reinforcement of the masculine gaze and enjoyment" (338–9). As well, as noted in a letter from a French feminist collective to *Le monde* that was cited in the US press as "Catherine Deneuve's anti-feminist letter" (even though the collective explicitly called itself feminist, and Catherine Deneuve was only one of the 100 participants, who were mostly writers, artists, actresses, and activists of some renown), "Such a fever to send the pigs to slaughter [also called a limitless 'wave of purification' and compared to censorship], far from helping women to be autonomous, in reality serves the interests of the enemies of sexual liberation, religious extremists, the worst reactionaries, and those who believe, in the name of a substantial conception of well-being and of the Victorian moralism that goes with it, that women are special types of beings, children with adults' faces demanding to be protected" (my translation). My intention here is not to demote, belittle, or denigrate the traumatic personal pain that results from sexual aggression. Certainly, the number of reports of intense degradation and humiliation testify to a systematic abuse of women that has been systematically covered up or non-reported. Rather, I am criticizing the broadening of the categories of sexual criminalization over an array of sexual acts in terms that make sexual crime unrecognizable as such and all sex acts—particularly non-normative or unexpected ones—terrifying. As well, I am calling attention to the problem the public declaration of victimhood poses for politics, in that it does not account for how private pain can be translated into public action and channeled for institutional change rather than retribution alone.

Other critics of "#MeToo" have noted how it participates in a broader neoliberal clamping down on racial minorities and workers. JoAnn Wypijewski of the *Nation* worries about "the crippling of due process and the ratcheting up of criminalization" (15)[4] and a politics of punishment and fear that reignited a history of "sexual panic," where allegations of misconduct are also part of a culture of incarceration, racism, and an excuse for "the expansion of state violence" (15). "The War on Sex," she remarks, "now drives the fastest-growing imprisoned population" (15), whose ideology can be traced back to the lynchings of the post-Reconstruction era that Ida B. Wells documented. Although expressing no love for the likes of Bill Cosby, Harvey Weinstein, Larry Nassar, and others of their ilk, Wypijewski faults an education (in which the "#Me Too" campaign plays a part) that teaches women to be powerless and afraid as well as an economic system that uses humiliations of all sorts—not only sexual abuse but also physical endangerment, routinization, de-unionization, job displacement, low pay, precarity—to control the workforce.[5]

Hollywood's response to the exposure of sexual abuse was to acclaim women artists and applaud women-centered themes in many of their Academy Award–nominated films (though the awards for "Best Picture" and "Best Director" were still given to a male-directed film with a corny if not childish and hardly feminist romantic plot, *The Shape of Water*). It can be argued that such films were not necessarily friendly to feminism despite the public pride in the public exposures of sexual harassment and assault against women in Hollywood as a type of courageous feminist speech. Rather, all these films made sexual assault into a private family matter and, in particular, the mother's fault. The trend I am addressing of the maternal ogre, however, is a misplaced allegory that blames the past generation of women for abusing its children and also forms the identity of the female protagonist—the maturing autonomous subject, or the body of liberation, or the break into free self-expression—against injury-inflicting, abusive feminist predecessors. The films in fact displace the causes of pain caused by poverty, social alienation, austerity policies, domestic violence, and political neglect onto the mothers who, for the most part under-recognized in the films themselves, were striving to build courageous autonomous lives in the midst of social challenges and hardships. Leaving poverty, mediocrity, or boredom behind can only be achieved, in the logic of all these films, through hating the mother.[6] In the context of "#MeToo," the films could be seen as blaming the past generation for not assuming the necessary autonomous subjectivity that this new generation was willing, daringly, to assume in stepping forward to make public denouncements. By not being feminist in the right way, the prior generation could be seen as guilty for not protecting their daughters and permitting the continuation of the sexist culture that led to their sexual assault.

The trend in feminism to separate from a prior feminist generation, to represent that generation as inadequate and compromised—as "ethnocentric," racist, universalizing, heterosexualizing, deterministic, and essentializing, indelibly white and blind to otherness, against a "new" poststructuralist-informed, enlightened acclaim of fragmentation and multiplicity, of difference and inclusivity, and of justice—leads similarly to a depoliticizing of the feminist past and a charge of past failures as the criminal naïveté (or worse, e.g., racism, heterosexism, and imperialist formation) of feminism's second-wave pioneers. Not only does such a perspective blame feminists for the political, social, and discursive limits imposed on them by the historical moment, but it also flattens their critique within a singularized, uncomplicated, bare-bones parameter and upholds a new feminist identity as escaping from those limits onto a new plateau of sophistication and personal pride, purity of vision, fashionable self-awareness, and limitless cultural sensitivity.

Ironically, perhaps, such a move of separation from the past does not separate these contemporary feminist outlooks from the standpoints of the past against which they pose themselves. In fact, perhaps, the debasing of the mother is a site that continually appears in feminist theory even while it constantly is revised into different forms and meanings. Actually, feminist rhetoric has been built upon mother hatred as early as Freud's patient Dora and the feminist appropriation of her for her hysterical defiance and schizoid speech. Freud's conclusion that Dora hated her mother out of jealousy for the father, though preposterous, allowed him to attribute her despair to psychic imbalances, thermodynamic currents, and personal failings rather than, as the case implies, to social alienation and socially sanctioned domestic and sexual abuse. Yet, feminist theory—like Cixous, for example[7]—wanted to appropriate her as a hero for breaking free from the repressive social structure and language that defeated her mother.

Simone de Beauvoir, as well, is well known and well criticized for her scorn of motherhood. For Beauvoir in *The Second Sex*, mothers reduce women to the hated particularity by seeking "eagerly to sacrifice their liberty of action to the functioning of their flesh: it seems to them that their existence is tranquilly justified in the passive fecundity of their bodies" (495). After all, Beauvoir ruminates disdainfully, "It is in maternity that woman fulfills her physiological destiny; it is her natural 'calling,' since her whole organic structure is adapted for the perpetuation of the species" (484). As mothers are trapped in the immanence of the body, prototypes of women's situation, Beauvoir also derided her own mother on her deathbed: "Only this body, suddenly reduced by her capitulation to being a body and nothing more, hardly differed at all from a corpse—a poor defenseless carcass turned and manipulated by professional hands, one in which life seemed to carry on only because of its own stupid momentum" (*A Very Easy Death* 20).

While cancer reduced her mother to pure physicality, though, Beauvoir's memoirs are much more conflicted about her mother than her negativity about motherhood in *The Second Sex* or about her mother's body in the memoir would imply: as Beauvoir despises the bourgeois conformism that consumed her family life, represented by her mother's frustrations, she definitely sees her mother as the point of resistance, the line that lures her from the unintellectual confinement of her conservative provincial childhood toward the freedom that she seeks in philosophical practice. "The principal function of . . . Mama was to feed me" (*Memoirs* 6), she remembers, because "[t]he world became more intimately a part of me when it entered through my mouth than through my eyes and my sense of touch" (6). Her mother's feeding reduces Simone to her situation of biological need but also provides an opening, giving her access to another knowing beyond the pure inertness of physicality. Identification with the mother's body became both a hated regression into the atrophied, nonautonomous identity of her past *and* the uncontrolled transcendence, the break into the future in another sensible, material, and intellectual form. This repeats at her mother's death: "my own mouth was not obeying me any more: I had put Maman's mouth on my own face and in spite of myself, I copied its movements. Her whole person, her whole being, was concentrated there, and compassion wrung my heart" (*A Very Easy Death* 31). Feminism here is not singularized or universalizing but rather split with difference. Beauvoir asks us what would it mean, as a feminist, to speak through the mother's mouth, or outside one's own mouth, or to feel the mouth of the past or of another, and why would such speaking cause fear? Beauvoir is aware that her mother represents a world of social alienation that she wants to leave behind. Even so, she does not bury her mother inside the immanence of identity which seems to reach down from her mouth even into the malignancy of her cell structure. "[A]t the same time," she reflects at the moment of her mother's death, admiring her grasp at every bit of remaining life, "in every cell of my body I joined in her refusal, her rebellion" (*A Very Easy Death* 105). Beauvoir's engagement with the memory of her mother is multifaceted and irrepressible inside her own reach toward a future philosophical language for feminism.

The Bloomsbury Handbook approaches history differently than the transcription of the waves. It takes on an alternative approach by situating discussions around a term that is constantly being revised in its feminist encounters, speaking through our mothers' mouths. Alternatives exist that neither get bogged down and trapped in the past nor repress it wholeheartedly, and perhaps will surprise us with new beginnings. Instead of enslaving our speech to already existing narratives that have been washed out and wrapped up in over-small packages, and instead of expanding the present as the transcendent moment of truth, *The Bloomsbury Handbook* traces feminist history's time through its constitutive vocabulary. Rather than echoing the rhythms of fashion, where ephemeral image constellations and shiny surfaces pop up as "new and improved" attractions and then pop out with the regulated and unmemorable cycles of the clock, the backstory of feminist discursive engagements animate the deep structures of feminist thought and politics in future time. *The Bloomsbury Handbook* shows feminism's past as operative in and essential to its current needs, offering a rich set of concepts, images, and ideas for feminism to stake in its claims to the future even while questioning the pasts in which they play a part. Thinking about current feminist theory in relation to what feminism's next step will be, this *Handbook* considers feminism as a theory that is vital and living.

* * *

The keywords in *The Bloomsbury Handbook of 21st-Century Feminist Theory* are organized in three major sections: Subject, Text, and World. Together, the three areas touch on a range of ideas and questions. Broadly speaking, the words together bring out vital interconnections in feminist thinking, where the individual, the social/political context, and writing are all insufficient in themselves to account for women's place and the shape of feminist thought, where—as one of the contributors, Susan Hekman, has written—"we are both separate and collective beings" (7) and, similarly, we are combinations of material and symbolic stuff. These keywords were chosen by the contributors as vital points of interest in their own research in feminist theory.

Feminist theory has long been involved with investigating subjectivity, often turning back to Freud and psychoanalysis to search for alternatives to its disembodied traditions in philosophy. In keeping, the subject of feminism was never isolated. In her inaugural work on this topic, Juliet Mitchell argued that the subject was how ideology entered and inflected social life, reproducing conservative and out-of-date identifications: "the world breaks in on us violently," she reiterates in her "Introduction" to the 1999 edition of her classic work *Psychoanalysis and Feminism*, "and its impingement is registered as a 'trace'" (xxii). The sense of the subject being *in* and *of* the body as well as being larger than the body, engaged in material practices where the body's limits overlap with a broader sociality and relatedness, sometimes makes the feminist subject undo its attachment to the human and humanism even as it, as well, plays a part in those narratives. The critique of the feminist subject as inheriting the autonomous, imperialist subject born in reason, centered, and self-knowing has been rejected in favor of a subject whose vulnerability always links it to all sorts of others, including not only those dispossessed by geopolitical and technological alignments but also those who set awry the very category of the human.

Yet, the contemporary practice of rejecting past feminists as insufficiently aware of differences—the practice of drawing a line in the sand between "then" and "now" in the name of some new form of materialism or post-ness—seems to define feminist subject-ivity anew in the old philosophical form of independent heroism that underlies thinking after Kant. In these versions, feminist consciousness breaks from its past, sheds off the world that brought it into being. The insights of second-wave feminism, however, place the subject firmly in a situation, as Hekman shows, that is, in the situation of the social, language, and embodiment. This subject-in-the-world, or what Kristeva calls this *sujet-en-procès*, demands the deconstruction of the romanticized, individuated subject-abstraction of moral reason or existentialism that can—on its own, through an act of will—burst out of its "is" toward idealist, transcendent freedom.

The feminist subject, then, exists only inasmuch as it is in, of, for, and as the world. Feminism has always been a worldly endeavor. The term "world" has also received quite a bit of attention in literary studies in recent years, partly because of rising interest in teaching literatures in translation. As a result, some warnings have been put out. David Damrosch, for example, has warned that "world" could easily merge into the term "NATO"—and then really only half of those countries—leaving the rest—the less powerful—outside of its purview, or that the term "world" could make literature "ideologically complicit with the worst tendencies of global capitalism" (456). But this would be only the world as space, what Pheng Cheah has called a "vulgarization" of the world: "a world," says Cheah, "is precisely what cannot be represented on a map" (8), an "opening that puts all beings into relation" (9). Indeed, the "world" for Emily Apter is a relation that transpires across bad translations; the "world" exists through the open intersections of concepts that do not quite meet. Gender plays a part because "[g]ender trouble gradually merges with translational difference as such, discernible in words that defy translation" (168), meaning that gender makes worlds. This has become increas-ingly clear in cultures of migration, where, as Aihwa Ong, for example, articulates it, states have the capacity to make "female migrants available for employment overseas, where they are exposed to conditions of violence and neo-slavery" (163). Here the glo-balization of high tech calls out to women workers from across borders who can assume needed emotional, nurturing, and domestic labor functions in other national settings, so that gender becomes a key translatable good, an ideological relation gathering meanings in its translations and mistranslations. The term "world" is thus imbued with a mish-mash of discrepant, even clashing subjectivities, sensibilities, sensitivities, languages, genders, systems, and historical processes, all of which throw "woman" into turmoil and up for grabs.

Introduced in translation, the subject/world interconnectivities and crossings that form as gender in feminist theory thus also rely on new vocabularies, reconsidering lost pos-sibilities in old vocabularies and remobilizing language. The very idea of a language for feminism is caught up in sets of vital questions that now pervade critical theory, like whether the epistemological claims of the feminist focus on language as underlying sub-jectivity have gone too far in erasing ontology, or in what sense feminism, feminist theory, and feminist politics benefit or do not benefit from a theoretical positing of the body as the inert matter on which language operates.

Within cultural theory following Raymond Williams, keywords have been a way to present to generations of readers a selection of issues that have guided profes-sional practitioners. The words are screens for a variety of meanings and a range of discussions: past, present, and future. As such, these words house unsettled political momentum and yet-to-be-realized conflicts, potentials, and interrogations. Taking into account intersections and nonintersections between diverse applications, organizing without fixing meanings, keywords like these that follow are always in open historical movement.

NOTES

1 These campus Title IX policies are being dismantled by the US Department of Education under the directorship of the Secretary of Education for the Trump administration, Betsy De Vos. Unfortunately, De Vos is at the same time dismantling support for rape victims because, she says, perpetrators have been unfairly treated. This will surely lead to increased crimes against women, especially violent crimes. The prior implementation of Title IX protections by equally labeling anything uncomfortable, unwanted, unexpected, misunderstood, badly expressed, suggestive, spoken, acted, or violently coerced as "misconduct"—rather than defining criminal sex acts differently from sex acts and sexual knowledge in general—may have, at least in part, paved the way for De Vos to claim that all sexual aggressors have been unfairly treated. In other words, policies that were meant to extend the category of sexual violation by including a broad range of acts inside it may have ended up supporting the argument that punishments for any sort of sex act, including criminal ones, were being administered arbitrarily.

2 As Bonnie Honig has argued, a politics of lament does not interrupt power, and it is not a political model for seizing power. It often works to invoke and reestablish the hierarchies that cause the injury. Often, lament puts the issue beyond politics, in a space of sentimental moralism. Honig invites us to "consider the limits of tragedy for politics" (70).

3 "We are today sufficiently informed to admit that the sexual impulse is by nature offensive and wild, but we are also sufficiently aware to not confuse a clumsy flirtation with sexual aggression" (Millet et al., my translation).

4 Rafia Zakaria, also in the *Nation*, has elaborated on this problem of due process to which sexual harassment policy gives rise in the post–Civil Rights era. In the US Supreme Court decision in *Burlington Industries v. Ellerth* (1998), Zakaria argues, the Court decided that employees could sue their employers for creating a "hostile environment." This meant that employers could "evade liability for the actions of their harassing employees" as long as the employer could "show first that they took reasonable care to prevent" the behavior by following preventive and corrective bureaucratic rules. Because of the need of the accuser to prove that the employer's rules and enforcement were inadequate rather than proving that a particular criminal act was committed by an individual, the costs of filing and pursuing a case are prohibitively high and the standard of evidence of the employer's inaction contingently unreachable for many victims, who risk losing their employment just for pursuing a claim and who need to get confirmation of their allegations from substantial numbers of other employee witnesses. Without recourse to the courts to bring perpetrators to justice, it stands to reason that victims would turn to other possible means of exposure and retribution. In the absence of any workable enforcement mechanism in the current law, it is not surprising that "#MeToo" victims would have turned to the airwaves to look for justice, or that students at universities would turn to internalized "kangaroo court"–like setups for hearings, thereby privatizing the means of adjudicating criminal acts. Zakaria concludes that the law could transform the way victims respond to harassment by forcing employers to hold the perpetrators responsible and making it costly to keep the perpetrators employed.

5 As Bryce Covert points out in another article in the *Nation*, the "#MeToo" campaign did not extend into the food and hotel industries where sexual harassment runs rampant.

6 Such films contrast sharply with Taylor Sheridan's *Wind River*, another 2017 film that got no mention in the Oscars. This film similarly shows the sexual abuse and murder of young girls but blames it on the racism of US First Nation reservation and development policy rather than on mothers. These 2017 nominated films also contrast with feminist filmmaker Chantal Akerman's 2015 film *No Home Movie* about her mother's death. In that film, the mother is often filmed off to the side, in low angle, outside of the frame or in partial frame, or from the back, and finally disappears from the frame altogether as the living room is filmed too low and off to the side but empty, as though the emptiness was always there and waiting. The mother is never situated inside a narrative of causation in relation to the daughter—as, for example, the *cause* of the daughter's pain and rejection, as she is in the Hollywood films discussed here.

7 "You, Dora, you, the indomitable, the poetic body, you are the true 'mistress' of the Signifier. Before long your efficacy will be seen at work when your speech is no longer suppressed, its point turned in against your breast, but written out over against the other" (343).

WORKS CITED

Alcoff, Linda Martín. "This Is Not Just About Junot Díaz." *New York Times*, May 16, 2018. https://www.nytimes.com/2018/05/16/opinion/junot-diaz-metoo.htmlo. Accessed May 26, 2018.

Apter, Emily. *Against World Literature: On the Politics of Untranslatability*. London: Verso Books, 2013.

Beauvoir, Simone de. *Memoirs of a Dutiful Daughter*. Trans. James Kirkup. New York: HarperCollins, 1959.

Beauvoir, Simone de. *The Second Sex*. Trans. H. M. Parshley. New York: Vintage Books of Random House, 1989.

Beauvoir, Simone de. *A Very Easy Death*. Trans. Patrick O'Brian. New York: Pantheon Books, 1965.

Beliso de Jesús, Aisha et al. "Open Letter against Media Treatment of Junot Díaz." *Chronicle of Higher Education*, May 14, 2018. https://www.chronicle.com/blogs/letters/open-letter-against-media-treatment-of-junot-diaz/. Accessed May 26, 2018.

Brown, Wendy. "The Impossibility of Women's Studies." *differences: A Journal of Feminist Cultural Studies* 9.3 (1997): 79–101.

Brown, Wendy. *States of Injury: Power and Freedom in Late Modernity*. Princeton, NJ: Princeton UP, 1995.

Budgeon, Shelley. *Third Wave Feminism and the Politics of Gender in Late Modernity*. New York: Palgrave, 2011.

Butler, Judith. *Gender Trouble: Feminism and the Subversion of Identity*. New York: Routledge, 1990, 1999, 2006.

Cheah, Pheng. *What Is a World? On Postcolonial Literature as World Literature*. Durham, NC: Duke UP, 2016.

Cixous, Hélène. "The Laugh of the Medusa." In Feminisms: An Anthology of Literary Theory and Criticism. Ed. Robyn R. Warhol and Diane Price Herndle. New Brunswick, NY: Rutgers UP, 1993, pp. 334–49.

Collective. "In Scholarly Debates on #MeToo Survivor Support Should Take Precedence." *Medium*, May 23, 2018. https://medium.com/@nsscollectiveeditorial/collective-editorial-survivor-support-should-take-precedence-71a2f6230157. Accessed May 26, 2018.

Combahee River Collective. "Combahee River Collective Statement." *Feminism in Our Times: The Essential Writings, World War II to the Present*. Ed. Miriam Schneir. New York: Vintage Books, 1994.

Covert, Bryce. "When Harassment Is the Price of a Job." *The Nation* 306.6 (March 5, 2018): 12–20.

Damrosch, David with Gayatri Chakravorty Spivak. "Comparative Literature/World Literature: A Discussion with Gayatri Chakravorty Spivak and David Damrosch." *Comparative Literature Studies* 48.4 (2011): 455–85.

Edelman, Lee. "I'm Not There: The Absence of Theory." *differences: A Journal of Feminist Cultural Studies* 21.1 (2010): 149–60.

Fraser, Nancy. *Unruly Practices: Power, Discourse and Gender in Contemporary Social Theory.* Minneapolis: U of Minnesota P, 1989.

Gill, Rosalind. "Culture and Subjectivity in Neoliberal and Postfeminist Times." *Subjectivity* 25 (2008): 432–46.

Grosz, Elizabeth. "The Practice of Feminist Theory." *differences: A Journal of Feminist Cultural Studies* 21.1 (2010): 94–108.

Hekman, Susan. *The Feminine Subject.* Cambridge: Polity Press, 2014.

Hemmings, Clare. *Why Stories Matter: The Political Grammar of Feminist Theory.* Durham, NC: Duke UP, 2011.

Heywood, Leslie, and Drake, Jennifer. "Introduction." *Third Wave Agenda: Being Feminist, Doing Feminism.* Ed. Leslie Heywood and Jennifer Drake. Minneapolis: U of Minnesota P, 1997, pp. 1–20.

Honig, Bonnie. *Antigone, Interrupted.* Cambridge: Cambridge UP, 2013.

Kipnis, Laura. *Unwanted Advances: Sexual Paranoia Comes to Campus.* New York: HarperCollins, 2017.

Kuttner, Robert. "Steve Bannon, Unrepentant." *American Prospect*, August 16, 2017. http://prospect.org/article/steve-bannon-unrepentant. Accessed March 5, 2018.

Martin, Biddy. "Success and Its Failures." *differences: A Journal of Feminist Cultural Studies* 9.3 (Fall 1997): 102+.

McRobbie, Angela. "Top Girls?" *Cultural Studies* 21.2–5 (2007): 718–37.

Millet, Catherine, et al. "Nous défendons une liberté d'importuner indispensable à la liberté sexuelle." *Le Monde*, January 13, 2018. http://www.lemonde.fr/idees/article/2018/01/09/nous-defendons-une-liberte-d-importuner-indispensable-a-la-liberte-sexuelle_5239134_3232.html#JbS8DXEe8uJIJrzu.99. Accessed January 13, 2018.

Mitchell, Juliet. *Psychoanalysis and Feminism: A Radical Reassessment of Freudian Psychoanalysis.* New York: Basic Books, 1974, 2000.

Moi, Toril. "'I am Not a Feminist, but …': How Feminism Became the F-Word." *PMLA* 121.5 (2006): 1735–41.

Nagle, Angela. *Kill All Normies: The Online Culture Wars from Tumblr and 4chan to the Alt-Right and Trump.* Winchester: Zero Books, 2017.

Ong, Aihwa. "A Bio-Cartography: Maids, Neo-Slavery, and NGOs." *Migrations and Mobilities: Citizenship, Borders, and Gender.* Ed. Seyla Benhabib and Judith Resnick. New York: New York UP, 2009, pp. 157–84.

Preciado, Beatriz. *Testo Junkie: Sex, Drugs, and Biopolitics in the Pharmacopornographic Era.* Trans. Bruce Benderson. New York: Feminist Press, 2013.

Rancière, Jacques. *Dissensus: On Politics and Aesthetics.* Ed. and trans. Steven Corocran. London: Continuum Books, 2010.

Scott, Joan. *The Fantasy of Feminist History.* Durham, NC: Duke UP, 2011.

Spencer, Jane. "Introduction: Genealogies." *Third Wave Feminism: A Critical Exploration.* Ed. Stacy Gillis, Gillian Howie, and Rebecca Munford. New York: Palgrave, 2004, pp. 9–12.

Spivak, Gayatri Chakravorty. "Can the Subaltern Speak?" *Marxism and the Interpretation of Culture*. Ed. Cary Nelson and Larry Grossberg. Champaign: U of Illinois P, 1988, pp. 271–313.

Watkins, Susan. "Which Feminisms?" *New Left Review* 109 (January and February 2018): 5–76.

Wypijewski, JoAnn. "#Me Too: What We Don't Talk about When We Talk about …" *The Nation* (March 19/26, 2018): 12–18.

Zakaria, Rafia. "The Legal System Needs to Catch Up With the #MeToo Movement." *The Nation* (April 18, 2018). https://www.thenation.com/article/the-legal-system-needs-to-catch-up-with-the-metoo-movement/. Accessed April 18, 2018.

Zerilli, Linda M. G. *Feminism and the Abyss of Freedom*. Chicago, IL: U of Chicago P, 2005.

PART ONE

The Subject

CHAPTER ONE

Subject

SUSAN HEKMAN

The question of the feminine subject has, of necessity, been at the forefront of feminist theory. Who is "woman"? How does she relate to "man"? To "human"? As feminists have grappled with these questions, they have come to realize the enormity of the issues involved. It does not suffice to define woman as man's opposite yet his equal. Nor is it sufficient to declare the humanity of woman. It became clear to feminists early on that "human" is defined in masculine terms. Once feminists began to examine these questions, it seemed that we were embarking on a quest that had no obvious method or answer.

In 1949 in *The Second Sex* (*TSS*), Simone de Beauvoir plunged into this morass by asking, "What is a woman?"[1] On one level, it might seem too simplistic to begin with Beauvoir. She is not the only feminist or even the first to ask this question. The value of Beauvoir's work, however, is the profundity of her analysis. More so than any previous theorist or many who succeeded her, Beauvoir understands that to attempt to define the feminine subject entails calling into question the entire tradition of Western philosophy and theology. It also necessitates redefining the "human." Although Beauvoir does not state this as clearly as we might like, a careful reading of *TSS* leads to these conclusions. Beauvoir does not have an answer to the questions she raises, but she defines the radical path that feminist theory must follow in the search for the subject.

The question of the human is from the outset central to Beauvoir's exploration of "woman." She first approaches the issue of what it means to be human in *The Ethics of Ambiguity* (*EA*).[2] Employing male pronouns throughout her discussion, Beauvoir asserts that being human is ambiguous in that we are both separate and collective beings. At the core of her theory is the assertion that all human beings are on a moral plane as seekers of freedom. But as she begins to develop this assertion, complexities arise. Women in Western countries, she asserts, lack an apprenticeship in freedom and even consent in their servitude.[3] In *EA*, Beauvoir does not pursue this issue, but in *TSS* it becomes her principal focus. The One/Other relationship that defines the human, she claims, is primordial, and the One is gendered masculine. It follows that women, who are the Other rather than the One, are denied full subjectivity.

This premise is the impetus behind *TSS*. Beauvoir declares that the purpose of her book is to assess the condition of women. This she does in great detail, looking at women from the perspectives of biology, religion, philosophy, and social condition. Her analysis probes both the causes and consequences of women's inferior status in society. It is easy to interpret *TSS* as doing only this, and many of her interpreters have done so. But there is more going on here than an empirical analysis. What if we read Beauvoir's analysis not only as a brutally accurate description of the roots of women's inferiority in society but, rather, also as a definition of the challenge that women must meet and transcend? What if Beauvoir is saying, in effect, that the One/Other dichotomy gives women no way out and it is incumbent on us to develop a new approach—a feminist approach—to find that way? And, finally, what if Beauvoir is saying that our tradition and culture fail to provide a way out and introducing women entails deconstructing the whole edifice?

This more radical interpretation of Beauvoir fits the tenor of *TSS* more accurately than the conventional interpretation. Interpreting Beauvoir this way clarifies the claim that Beauvoir begins the feminist search for the subject. She makes it clear what is at stake here—the entire Western tradition—and that our search for a subject will entail reinventing the human. It is unfortunate that Beauvoir does not state this as clearly as she might have. It is also unfortunate that she provides us with only a sketch of what that subject might look like. But the overall message is clear: we need to start from scratch, and we need to define our own terms.

What is important about Beauvoir, then, is that she throws down the gauntlet for subsequent feminist explorations of the subject. She outlines the path that these explorations must follow without herself providing us with specifics. Although feminist theorists after Beauvoir have approached the question of the subject from a variety of perspectives, they have all implicitly acknowledged Beauvoir's thesis—that our task constitutes a radical challenge to the tradition that has defined "woman."

As feminists moved into this unchartered territory, a particular pattern emerged. First, these thinkers agree with Beauvoir that what is required is, quite literally, a new form of life. They concur that masculinist theorists will be of no help in defining this new form.[4] Second, each of the major approaches to the subject adds a theoretical element absent from previous theories. If we think of these theorists as building a new edifice, each major theory adds a brick to that edifice as it is constructed. The third element of the pattern, however, is less positive. There is a tendency among feminist theorists to characterize their theories as correcting the errors of previous theories. Instead of defining their contribution as adding to the cumulative enterprise of constructing a radically new subject, most theorists have tended to characterize their predecessors as wrong and their position as correcting these errors. This tendency is unfortunate. Feminist theory would be better served by theorists acknowledging their participation in a common enterprise than by criticizing their predecessors.

The so-called French feminists, principally Julia Kristeva, Luce Irigaray, and Helene Cixious, were the first to answer Beauvoir's call to redefine the subject. They exemplify the pattern described above nearly perfectly. They concur that we need a radically new approach to the subject. In characterizing their approach, Alice Jardine asserts that they are "diving into the wreck of western culture."[5] Second, the theoretical elements that these theorists add to the task of defining the subject are psychoanalysis and language. Beauvoir's disdain for psychoanalysis is well known. Against this, the French feminists embrace psychoanalysis as an analytic tool. Furthermore, they are clear that at the center of the status of woman as "Other" is language. Our language defines women as inherently inferior; no alternatives are available. What is required, Irigaray insists, is to "jam the theoretical machinery."[6]

Unfortunately, however, these theorists fit the third element of the pattern as well. They claim that Beauvoir had not sufficiently broken away from the tradition she critiqued but was still bound to humanist assumptions. As a consequence, they define the characterization of the subject they propose as a necessary corrective to Beauvoir's errors. These theorists begin a regrettable tradition in feminist theory that finds it necessary to reject a predecessor in order to advance one's own theory. Instead of criticizing Beauvoir's "errors," it would be much more fruitful—and accurate—to define the emphasis on psychoanalysis and language as compatible additions to the understanding of the subject that they are jointly constructing.

The next major contribution to this edifice is the feminist exploration of the relational subject. It is beyond question that this is a major step forward for the understanding of the feminine subject. At the center of the Western tradition stands the Cartesian subject: autonomous, individual, and separate. This subject not only defines full subjectivity for humans but also defines the opposite of this subject, the relational, connected subject, as inferior. The Cartesian subject embodies the essence of the fully human that only men can achieve. Women's relational self prevents her from achieving this full subjectivity.

The effort by feminists to define, rather than dismiss, the relational self is a watershed event in the evolution of the feminine subject. The tradition paid scant attention to this subject because it was defined as inherently inferior and hence not worthy of attention. By focusing on the relational subject, feminists in a sense brought her out of the shadows. But more importantly, by claiming equality for the relational subject, feminists in effect challenged the hegemony of the Cartesian subject; the Cartesian subject's exclusive definition of subjectivity was called into question.

Perhaps the most influential proponent of the relational subject is Carol Gilligan. Although Gilligan does not have the philosophical sophistication of some other relational theorists, what she accomplishes in *A Different Voice* is nothing short of revolutionary.[7] What appears on one level to be merely an empirical analysis of how women's moral reasoning differs from that of men, what Gilligan is actually accomplishing is a challenge to the entire Western tradition. Her argument is directed against one aspect of that tradition: the understanding of moral reasoning as necessarily involving abstraction, removal from circumstances, and the appeal to universal principles. The belief that this style of moral reasoning, and it alone, will produce singular and absolute moral truth was constitutive of Western thought.

Gilligan's counter is deceptively simple. Through a careful analysis she concludes, first, that women's moral reasoning is different from that of men and, second, that it is equally valid. Her first conclusion would receive little resistance. The second, however, embodies the radical element of her argument. It calls into question the definition of moral truth extant in the tradition. In that tradition, there can be only one moral truth and that truth is arrived at through the abstract principled reasoning defined by the Cartesian subject. There is no room for a second equally valid truth.

The parallel here between Gilligan and Beauvoir is striking. Both effect a radical displacement of the tradition, but neither offers a philosophical satisfying account of this displacement. We wish both had done so. But the net effect remains: both challenged the sacred cows of Western thought and suggested a radical alternative. Gilligan's work resonated strongly with a cross-section of women because she reaffirmed what they already knew—that their moral reasoning was different but equally valid from that of the accepted version. But in so doing she brought down the long tradition that established the sole validity of Cartesian morality.[8]

There is another parallel between Gilligan and Beauvoir as well. From a Beauvoirian perspective, Gilligan fails to challenge the One/Other dichotomy at the center of Western thought. Her strategy, instead, is to attempt to elevate the status of the Other to equality with the One. Subsequent work will reveal this to be a futile strategy. We need to displace this dichotomy, not try to redefine it. But this does not diminish the importance of the relational subject in feminist thought.

The theorists discussed thus far have followed Beauvoir's lead by attempting to redefine "woman" apart from masculinist theories. But there are two exceptions to this pattern: liberal feminism and Marxist/socialist feminism. In both of these cases, feminists attempted to base their theories of the subject in masculine theories. The failure of these attempts reinforces Audre Lorde's famous statement that the master's tools cannot dismantle the master's house.

The connections between liberalism and feminism go back well before Beauvoir to the liberal tradition of Wollstonecraft, Mill, and Elizabeth Cady Stanton. But, as Zillah Eisenstein argues in *The Radical Future of Liberal Feminism*, the contradictions between liberalism and feminism doomed this association from the beginning.[9] The sexually egalitarian and collectivist roots of feminism are fundamentally incompatible with liberalism's patriarchal individualism. Despite this, many attempts have been made to link the two. We live in a society founded on liberalism, a society in which women are overcoming many aspects of patriarchy. It seems to follow that feminists should embrace liberalism because it fosters equality and freedom, two key feminist values. But the argument for liberal feminism always founders on the contradictions that Eisenstein describes. Theorists such as Susan Moller Okin and Martha Nussbaum make impressive arguments for liberal feminism.[10] But they cannot overcome the impossibility of fitting feminism into the individualism of liberalism and the Cartesian subject on which it is founded. The defenders of liberal feminism inevitably produce theories that are neither feminist nor liberal.

The relationship between Marxism and feminism is equally complex. As with liberalism, the connection between the two seemed initially obvious. Both are libertory theories that hold out hope for freedom from the oppression of capitalism and patriarchy, respectively. But it soon became clear that the connection between Marxism and feminism was indeed an "unhappy marriage." Marxist feminism did not fit into either feminism or Marxism. This became particularly obvious with the advent of the most significant element of Marxist feminism: feminist standpoint theory. Central to Marxist standpoint theory is the claim that the proletariat standpoint discovers the true reality of capitalism. This creates two problems for feminism: first, we must resolve which is truer—the feminist standpoint or the proletariat standpoint; second, we must decide which feminist standpoint is the truest given the diversity among women.[11] Neither problem can be solved within the framework of Marxism. Once more we are driven to the conclusion that the two approaches are incompatible and prove Beauvoir right: it is impossible to fit the feminine subject into a masculinist theory.

In 1988, Elizabeth Spelman's book *Inessential Woman* advanced a thesis that, ten years earlier, would have been heresy in feminist theory: that we should abandon the unitary definition of "woman."[12] Spelman's book was not unique. It was an expression of a profound change that swept feminist theory in the late 1980s and 1990s: the turn from difference to differences. Instead of exploring the difference between men and women, feminist attention shifted to detailing the differences between women. This shift fundamentally affected the effort to define the feminine subject. Instead of trying to define the "true" feminine subject, the effort shifted to defining the range and diversity of feminine subjects.

This effort took several different forms. One aspect was the turn to postmodernism. In the 1990s, postmodernism overwhelmed the feminist movement. Its a radical challenge to the Western tradition and particularly to the centerpiece of that tradition—"man"—seemed custom-made for feminism. If the subject is a fiction and there are no essences or absolute truth, then the problem with "woman" that Beauvoir describes quite literally disappears. The One/Other dichotomy that, for Beauvoir, traps women in inferiority disappears as well. The postmoderns agree with Beauvoir that our language traps women in inferiority but they go on to claim that we must deconstruct this language as a way out.

Postmodernism moved the search for the feminine subject into entirely new territory. If "woman" is wholly constituted by discourse, then our task must be to change the discourse of "woman." But from a postmodern perspective, this is no easy task. Since "woman" does not have an essence, we cannot remove her inferiority by proposing an alternative essence. Instead, we must initiate a radical inquiry into the political constitution and regulation of identity.[13] What we must do, claims Judith Butler in *Gender Trouble*, is to open up new possibilities in the definition of gender.[14] Redefining "woman," she claims, cannot provide emancipation because it is discursively constituted by the political system from which it seeks emancipation.

Postmodernism offers a rich resource for feminist theory of the subject. Theorists such as Butler opened up understanding of the linguistic constitution of "woman" that was unique and insightful. But it is not clear that the search for the feminine subject is advanced by postmodernism. Postmoderns assert that redefining woman is not a productive strategy and, indeed, that it is counterproductive. This position creates problems for the definition of a feminist politics that we might employ to achieve the political transformation that feminists seek. What Butler and other postmodern feminists argue is that we must open up the category of gender by exploring gender identity that does not conform to cultural norms. For many feminists, this is not a sufficient blueprint for feminist politics or the feminine subject. They argued that feminist politics requires a concrete strategy and a definition of woman that can ground that strategy.

Another significant challenge to the universal feminine subject came from the turn to race and ethnicity. In the 1980s, a spate of books and articles emerged that challenged the hegemony of white feminist thought. The concerns raised in these books broadened and deepened the search for the feminine subject begun by Beauvoir. Increasingly, feminists came to realize that the oppression of women that feminist had categorized took many forms and that feminism did not necessarily emerge from the women most victimized by sexist oppression. bell hooks, for example, argued that the one-dimensional perspective of the feminist movement must be corrected with a counter-hegemony.

From a Beauvoirian perspective, the turn to race and ethnicity complicates the search for the feminine subject. For Beauvoir and subsequent theorists, the oppression women face was constituted solely by gender. Now it was becoming clear that other factors come into play as well. It also became clear that it is not possible to neatly separate the influences of gender, race, sexuality, and the other factors that cause oppression. This realization led to the rise of an issue that dominates feminist discussions of difference today: intersectionality. Intersectional analysis focuses on the multiple sources of oppression, emphasizing that oppression cannot be reduced to one type and that oppressions work together to create injustice.[15]

Criticisms of postmodernism's exclusive focus on linguistic construction lead to another approach to the feminine subject, a turn to the material. While claiming to deconstruct dichotomies, in particular the dichotomy between the discursive and the material, in practice postmodernism privileges the linguistic and effaces the material. What is needed, it seemed clear, was a new approach that would accomplish what the postmoderns failed to do without returning to the essentialism of the "old materialism." Feminists need an approach that can talk about the materiality of women's bodies and women's pain without ignoring the linguistic or lapsing into essentialism.

What emerged is a perspective commonly labeled the "new materialism." The approach is wide-ranging, encompassing philosophy of science, cultural studies, body studies, and the posthuman. Rooted in the path-breaking work of Karen Barad and Nancy Tuana, the new materialists have "brought the material back in." There is a sense in which the new materialists' approach encompasses all the aspects of the feminine subject that previous theorists have emphasized. They agree that women have been oppressed through linguistic constructions that extend for millennia, but they also assert that women have bodies that experience pain and are distinct from masculine bodies. Bodies are the point of intersection between patriarchal structures and women's lives. We need to be able to talk about the linguistic construction of patriarchy as well as the real experience of women's lives.

As exciting as it is, the new materialism is not the culmination of the search for the feminine subject. It is, rather, the latest iteration of that search. If we look back on the trajectory of the search for the subject since Beauvoir, three things are clear. First, the post-Beauvoirian efforts to define the subject are cumulative in nature. Each builds on rather than repudiates previous attempts. Second, we have not found the "true" feminine subject, nor should we be looking for her. Our searching is ongoing; we should not be looking for the truth, a decidedly masculine quest, but, rather, continuing the conversation begun by Beauvoir. Third, the root of the problem we are facing, as Beauvoir realized, is that the human is defined in masculine terms. It follows that what we must face is not just relieving the stigma of the "Other" from women but also redefining the human itself, transcending the One/Other dichotomy.

The contemporary theorist who takes on this challenge most directly is Judith Butler. This may seem counterintuitive given Butler's position as the foremother of feminist postmodernism. But in her recent work, Butler turns away from a strict linguistic constructionism and develops what amounts to an ontological position on the subject. In a series of books published in the early 2000s, she explores questions around norms and identity that lead to a redefinition of the human.

Butler begins with the relationship between norms and resistance. She argues that the norms that define gender allow some possibility for resistance; they do not wholly determine us. This argument speaks to Beauvoir's assertion that we become "woman" through socialization. What Butler is arguing here, however, is more complicated. She asserts that the subject is not merely the passive recipient of power but is also the site of agency and resistance. That this resistance is not simple is clear from all of her previous work. But it is possible. She concludes, "Power attaches a subject to its own identity. Subjects appear to require this self-attachment, this process by which one becomes attached to one's subjecthood."[16]

What this means in the context of our discussion is that it is unavoidable that we are socialized by the norms of our society; they give us our identity, which, she claims, is a necessity for a "livable life." My identity as a woman, furthermore, also gives me agency and the possibility of resistance. I can push against the norms and fashion a new identity. In a sense this is what feminism is all about. But then Butler raises a problem: what if the identities available in my society fail to offer me a way of being? She asserts, "A normative conception of gender can undo one's personhood, undermining the capacity to persevere in a livable life."[17] The consequence is that I am denied an ontology, a being, and because

I must have an identity to lead a livable life, I am denied that as well. It follows that "for those who are still looking to become possible, possibility is a necessity."[18]

What this comes down to is that norms allow us to "be," but for some subjects being is not a possibility. If certain persons are not classified as human in relation to existing norms, they are denied an ontology; they have no possibility of being. For most of us, resistance is possible within the normative framework constituting gender. But what if the norms make it impossible to "be" at all, precluding an identity for certain kinds of subjects? The only option for these subjects is to challenge the norms that confer recognition, that grant being to some subjects but not to others. What is required, Butler declares, is nothing less than to challenge what it means to be human.

Before detailing how Butler proposes to challenge the definition of the human, it is worth noting that her argument circles back to Beauvoir. For Beauvoir, the One/Other distinction that defines the human is primordial. Women are caught in this definition; they have no escape. Beauvoir hints that our only option is to challenge this primordial distinction that locks women into inferiority but she does not say so explicitly. Butler is picking up this hint and filling in the missing pieces.

How, Butler asks, can we change our conception of the human? How do we alter the category of the human to include the excluded? Butler's answer to this question in her recent work revolves around the question of kinship. In most societies, and ours is no exception, kinship is intimately tied to state legitimization; the state decides who legitimately belongs to whom. In our society, the contemporary legitimization of gay marriage has extended the realm of acceptable personhood by making same-sex marriage legitimate. Historically, marriage is inseparable from kinship, from the definition of legitimate relationships. Every culture has kinship rules that are fundamental to the norms that define it. By legitimating gay marriage, our society has altered these rules. Thus, by challenging the kinship rules rooted in marriage, we have challenged the basic structure of society.

Butler turns to "postkinship" studies in anthropology in order to pursue these claims. Her thesis is that new kinship and sexual relationships can compel a rethinking of culture itself. A more radical social transformation than that made possible by the legitimization of gay marriage is to refuse to allow kinship to be reduced to family or sexuality to marriage.[19] Calling into question traditional forms of kinship displaces the central place of biological and sexual relations. Furthermore, sexuality outside the field of monogamy may open us to a different sense of community.[20] New kinship and sexual arrangements break the homology between nature and culture, redefining the fundamentals of society. Challenging kinship thus challenges the norms that define not only sexual relations but also the realm of the human itself. Butler concludes by asserting that we must call into question the framework that silences certain subjects by denying them humanity.[21] Addressing the exclusion of some subjects from the realm of being, Butler concludes, must become our foremost political priority. Our politics must be oriented around broadening the norms that define human life.

Thus the argument about the feminine subject once more comes back to Beauvoir. The problem is not the definition of women in our culture but, rather, the exclusion of women from full humanity, full subjectivity. In order to address this problem, we must redefine the human, not just "woman." This emphasis on the human broadens feminists' search for the feminine subject. It also reveals the deeply radical nature of that search. Who is human and who is not, as Butler makes so clear, challenges the foundational norms of our society.

In *TSS*, Beauvoir defines Christianity as one of the principal forces in effecting women's subordination. This claim has been echoed in subsequent feminist analyses of Christianity, both by feminist theorists and feminist theologians. These works have revealed another aspect to the redefinition of "woman," which is the goal of feminism: redefining "woman" entails redefining "God." The conception of God in Christian thought is closely tied to the definition of the human. For Christians, both God and human are masculine. As Mary Daly put it so succinctly, "If God is male, then male is God." It follows that feminist theologians' attempt to redefine God and hence the human parallels and enriches feminist theorists' attempt to redefine the feminine subject.

Tracing the parallel between these two traditions begins with Mary Daly's *The Church and the Second Sex*, an analysis of Beauvoir's book from a Christian perspective.[22] Originally published in 1968, Daly republished the book with what she labeled a "new feminist postchristian introduction" in 1975 in which she repudiated most of her arguments in the original book. In the body of the book, she initially agrees with Beauvoir that in the fight for sexual equality the Catholic Church is the enemy. Following Beauvoir, she details the oppression that women have suffered over the centuries and links many of these to the church. These oppressions, furthermore, are still evident in the contemporary church. Although women have made progress in the present, she argues that the church has refused to adapt to the situation of modern women.

But Daly's agreement with Beauvoir is tempered by another perspective. She advances a series of arguments that have become themes of contemporary feminist theology: religious doctrines are not static; they can change as society changes. Today, she asserts, there are promising elements in Christian thought that can improve sexual relations. Christian documents on women, furthermore, reveal ambiguity if not contradiction.[23] She concludes, "The equal dignity of all human beings as persons is the essence of the Christian message."[24] She thus counters Beauvoir's argument of despair with hope:

> Simone de Beauvoir rejects Christianity as burdensome baggage inherited from the past. The life-affirming alternative to this is response to that liberating Power which calls us to transcend the archaic heritage and move forward toward a future whose seeds are already within us.[25]

In Daly's "new feminist postchristian introduction" to the 1975 book, however, she totally repudiates this optimism. Criticizing her own work in the third person, she argues that "Daly" was unable to see that sexism is inherent in Christianity. She castigates "Daly" for attempting to save Christianity in the face of her own evidence that this is impossible.[26] These arguments form the core of Daly's subsequent work that is characterized by a radical rejection of not only Christianity but also the structure of patriarchy as a whole.

Despite this departure from Beauvoir, however, Daly's work exhibits a significant parallel with that of *TSS* in her concern with the human. Like Beauvoir, Daly realizes that the key issue here is not the feminine subject but transforming our conception of the human. Particularly in *Beyond God the Father*, Daly attempts to find a religious language that will foster human becoming: "To exist humanly is to name the self, the world, and God. The 'method' of the evolving spiritual consciousness of women is nothing less than this beginning to speak humanly—a reclaiming of the right to name."[27] And "in beginning to come to grips with the problem of our own self-naming in the world in which women are nameless, feminism is implicitly working out a naming toward God."[28]

Daly's radical rejection of the Christian tradition is not echoed in the work of contemporary feminist theologians. The extensive and complex literature that constitutes feminist theology attempts to redeem elements of the tradition that are not incompatible with feminism. Feminist theologians challenge the androcentric interpretation of the Bible. They point to pervasive feminine imagery in scripture, claiming that it saturates the text. They reinterpret the history of the early church to emphasize the leadership roles that women assumed.

Many of these themes come together in what is the most feminist-oriented contemporary theology: process theology. Even Mary Daly in her post-Christian phase asserts that process theology comes closest to anticipating the dawn of rising woman consciousness.[29] Process theology embodies several themes that are distinctly feminist. Process theologians emphasize a relational self far removed from the Cartesian self. Their definition of God rejects the androcentric, all-powerful, removed, and controlling God of the tradition. Their God is in-the-world, involved in human experiences and sympathetic to our lives. Furthermore, process theologians posit a human connection to the nonhuman world that breaks down the human/nonhuman dichotomy. Their theology is one of becoming, not being, where nothing is fixed.

Janet Soskice in her introduction to *Feminism and Theology* tries to answer the question of why feminist theology should matter to feminist theorists. She points out that Christianity is still very much a part of our culture, that many women are deeply involved in religious institutions, and that many women come to religion without dropping their feminism. She concludes, "Feminists must surely be willing to concern themselves with the curious interaction of women, theology, and God."[30]

There is, however, a deeper reason why feminist theorists and feminist theologians should listen to each other. I have argued that our underlying concern as feminists must be the redefinition of the human. In our culture, the definitions of human and God have been inextricably intertwined. It is no coincidence that both God and human have been defined in androcentric terms. It follows that in order to be successful in redefining the human, we must also redefine God. Several feminist theologians are aware of this. Rosemary Radford Reuther asserts that "the central principle of feminist theology is the promotion of the full humanity of women" and that "whatever diminishes or denies the full humanity of women must be presumed not to reflect the divine" (18–19). Fiorenza echoes this in her comment that Christ's work was not being a male but being a new human (15).

My argument, then, is that the work of feminist theologians can deepen and broaden the concerns of feminist theorists. Rejecting feminist theology as an oxymoron stands in the way of our common goal: redefining the human. And the benefits of working together are significant. As the process theologians have emphasized, a conception of God as in-the-world displaces the androcentrism of the tradition. A God who is present in every moment of experience and sympathetic to our humanity changes everything for women and men and offers us a new way of being human.[31]

NOTES

1 Simone de Beauvoir, *The Second Sex*, trans. Constance Borde and Sheila Mallovany-Chevallier (New York: Knopf, 2010).

2 Simone de Beauvoir, *The Ethics of Ambiguity* (New York: Philosophical Library, 1948).

3 Ibid., pp. 37–8.

4 Two notable exceptions to this pattern are liberal feminism and Marxist feminism. Below I will argue that the failure of these perspectives reveals the validity of the other approaches.

5 Alice Jardine, *Gynesis: Configurations of Women and Modernity* (Ithaca, NY: Cornell University Press, 1985), p. 153.

6 Luce Irigaray, *This Sex Which Is Not One*, trans. Catherine Porter (Ithaca, NY: Cornell University Press, 1985), p. 78.

7 Carol Gilligan, *In a Different Voice* (Cambridge, MA: Harvard University Press, 1982).

8 This is, of course, only one way of reading Gilligan. Her many critics have called her analysis into question on empirical, philosophical, and sociological grounds. For a defense of my interpretation here, see Susan Hekman, *Moral Voices/Moral Selves* (University Park: Penn State Press, 1995).

9 Zillah Eisenstein, *The Radical Future of Liberal Feminism* (New York: Longman, 1981).

10 Susan MollerOkin, "Humanist Liberalism," in *Liberalism and the Moral Life*, ed. Nancy Rosenblum (Cambridge, MA: Harvard University Press, 1988), pp. 39–53; Martha Nussbaum, *Sex and Social Justice* (New York: Oxford University Press, 1999).

11 Susan Hekman, "Truth and Method: Feminist Standpoint Theory Revisited," *Signs* 22, no. 2 (1997): 341–65.

12 Elizabeth Spelman, *Inessential Woman* (Boston, MA: Beacon Press, 1988).

13 Judith Butler, *Gender Trouble*, 2nd edn. (New York: Routledge, 1999), pp. xxi–xxii.

14 Judith Butler, *Gender Trouble* (New York: Routledge, 1990).

15 Patricia Hill Collins, *Black Feminist Thought: Knowledge, Consciousness, and the Politics of Empowerment* (New York: Routledge, 2004), p. 2.

16 Judith Butler, "Bodies and Power Revisited," in *Feminism and the Final Foucault*, ed. Dianna Taylor and Karen Vintges (Urbana: University of Illinois Press, 2004), p. 190.

17 Judith Butler, *Undoing Gender* (New York: Routledge, 2004), p. 1.

18 Ibid., p. 31.

19 Judith Butler, "Is Kinship Always Already Heterosexual?" in *Left Legalism/Left Critique*, ed. Wendy Brown and Janet Hailey (Durham, NC: Duke University Press, 2002), pp. 254–5.

20 Judith Butler, "Global Violence, Sexual Politics," in *Queer Ideas*, ed. CUNY Center for Lesbian and Gay Studies (New York: The Feminist Press, 2003), p. 206.

21 Judith Butler, *Frames of War* (New York: Verso, 2009), p. 168.

22 Mary Daly, *The Church and the Second Sex* (New York: Harper and Row, 1975).

23 Ibid., pp. 73–4.

24 Ibid., p. 83.

25 Ibid., p. 222.

26 Ibid., pp. 17–18.

27 Mary Daly, *Beyond God the Father* (Boston, MA: Beacon Press, 1973), p. 8.

28 Ibid., p. 37.

29 Ibid., p. 188.

30 Janice Soskice and Diana Lipton, *Feminism and Theology* (Oxford: Oxford University Press, 2003).

31 My discussion here is limited to the Christian tradition. I would take the discussion too far afield to explore the human in other religious traditions.

WORKS CITED

Beauvoir, Simone de, *The Ethics of Ambiguity*. New York: Philosophical Library, 1948.

Beauvoir, Simone de, *The Second Sex*. Trans. Constance Borde and Sheila Mallovany-Chevallier. New York: Knopf, 2010.

Butler, Judith, "Bodies and Power Revisited." *Feminism and the Final Foucault*. Ed. Diana Taylor and Karen Vintges. Urbana: U of Illinois P, 2004.

Butler, Judith, *Frames of War*. New York: Verso, 2009.

Butler, Judith, *Gender Trouble*. New York: Routledge, 1990.

Butler, Judith, *Gender Trouble*, 2nd edn. New York: Routledge, 1999.

Butler, Judith, "Global Violence, Sexual Politics." In *Queer Ideas*. Ed. CUNY Center for Lesbian and Gay Studies. New York: The Feminist P, 2003.

Butler, Judith, "Is Kinship Always Already Heterosexual?" *Left Legalism/Left Critique*. Ed. Wendy Brown and Janet Hailey. Durham, NC: Duke UP, 2002.

Butler, Judith, *Undoing Gender*. New York: Routledge, 2004.

Collins, Patricia Hill, *Black Feminist Thought: Knowledge, Consciousness, and the Politics of Empowerment*. New York: Routledge, 2004.

Daly, Mary, *Beyond God the Father*. Boston, MA: Beacon P, 1973.

Daly, Mary, *The Church and the Second Sex*. New York: Harper and Row, 1975.

Eisenstein, Zillah, *The Radical Future of Liberal Feminism*. New York: Longman, 1981.

Gilligan, Carol, *In a Different Voice*. Cambridge, MA: Harvard UP, 1982.

Hekman, Susan, *Moral Voices/Moral Selves*. University Park: Penn State P, 1995.

Hekman, Susan, "Truth and Method: Feminist Standpoint Theory Revisited." *Signs* 22.2 (1997): 341–65.

Irigaray, Luce, *This Sex Which Is Not One*. Trans. Catherine Porter. Ithaca: Cornell UP, 1985.

Jardine, Alice, *Gynesis: Configurations of Women and Modernity*. Ithaca: Cornell UP, 1985.

Nussbaum, Martha, *Sex and Social Justice*. New York: Oxford UP, 1999.

Okin, Susan Moller, "Humanist Liberalism," *Liberalism and the Moral Life*. Ed. Nancy Rosenblum. Cambridge, MA: Harvard UP, 1988.

Reuther, Rosemary Radford, *Sexism and God-Talk: Toward a Feminist Theology*. Boston: Beacon Press, 1983.

Soskice, Janice, and Diana Lipton, *Feminism and Theology*. Oxford: Oxford UP, 2003.

Spelman, Elizabeth, *Inessential Woman*. Boston, MA: Beacon P, 1988.

CHAPTER TWO

Identity

MICHELLE M. WRIGHT

As one might imagine, any discussion on the future of black feminist politics of identity must engage with both the past and the present moment. Unsurprisingly, this triple temporal lens is both enlightening and confusing. On the one hand, the number of conferences, anthologies, special issues of journals, symposia, and scholars who self-identify as working on black feminism has increased in the past fifteen years. On the other hand, as Marlon Bailey has pointed out, of the fourteen PhD-granting Black Studies programs in the United States, only four have full-time faculty who work in gender and/or sexuality.

Even further, while the reasons and the interpretations would differ, most scholars who work on issues of identity, specifically black gender and sexuality, would agree in this moment that black feminist studies[1] today look quite different from what appeared to be their congealing moment in the 1980s with the appearance of *This Bridge Called My Back*, *All the Women Are White, All the Blacks Are Men, But Some of Us Are Brave*, *Home Girls: A Black Feminist Anthology*, and *Zami: Towards a New Spelling of My Name*.

Perhaps most strikingly, the cross-racial and ethnic alliances that gave us the volumes on black feminist identity above do not appear to be as strong or as frequent—at the very least, we do not yet have a twenty-first-century equivalent to *This Bridge*, *Home Girls*, or *All the Women Are White*. Equally important, however, is the way in which contemporary black feminist politics has also edged away from the rather exciting possibilities of a dialogic agency opened up by Mae Gwendolyn Henderson in her essay "Speaking in Tongues: Dialogics, Dialectics and the Black Woman Writer's Literary Tradition" and, more recently, Kimberlé Crenshaw's concept of intersectionality.

Crenshaw's development and application of intersectionality was clearly set within the context of the US legal-juridical system and used to demonstrate that those bodies deemed to possess more than one vulnerable identity (race, gender, sexuality, class) were accordingly punished for it with harsher sentences and penalties. Yet, as scholars such as Jennifer Nash[2] have noted, the term has since been unmoored from its context. Its application seems to align more closely with perhaps the most influential text informing contemporary black feminist politics: Hortense Spillers's classic "Mama's Baby, Papa's Maybe, an American Grammar Book." This canonical piece, still a staple in Women, Gender, and Sexuality Studies and black and African American studies departments, squarely turns its ire toward the white US heteropatriarchy, not the least for attempting (and often succeeding) to pervert gender and sexual relation between black individuals (most especially the heterosexual black female) as well as between black and white communities.

In determining the future of black feminist politics on identity, we could in fact propose a fulcrum of sorts, one in which Henderson's notion of a multivalent black female identity weights one end and Spillers's construction of a deeply damaged black female identity the other, with Crenshaw's intersectionality as the fulcrum. Henderson explicitly theorizes the multiple identities of the US black female as a multivocal power that ostensibly allows her to connect more easily and more frequently (i.e., dialogically) with other social identities. Spillers sees this black female as clearly more marginalized by her racial and gendered identities, unavoidably twisted this way by centuries of slavery and Jim Crow practices. I would argue that Crenshaw can be seen hanging in the balance because, on the one hand, Crenshaw's intersectionality can be read as a "double yoke" (oppressed by two burdens: race and gender), as Nigerian British feminist writer Buchi Emecheta[3] once described it. On the other hand, however, Crenshaw's observations could be taken to argue that black feminism's fluency with the complex conflations that sexism and racism formulate is well-suited to understanding itself as an axis that connects to a much broader range of issues when it comes to the ways in which oppression, bigotry, and prejudice operate at both the institutional and individual level.

For the moment, it seems, more attention is being paid to the devastating cost of being black and female in predominantly white Western nations than to the rather rich confluences, intersections, and moments in which black feminists and their allies prevail in the face of daunting odds. Make no mistake, we do need, have needed, and will always need scholarship, art, and activism that locate, detail, analyze, and protest the numbing ways in which black female bodies are sacrificed: sacrificed to the amour propre of the heteropatriarchal state; sacrificed to maintaining the wealth of the ultrarich; sacrificed to the egos, drives, and desires of heterosexual white men and women—and, it must be said, sacrificed to the ego, drives, and amour propre of black heteropatriarchy and black heterosexual men (although this last category is still woefully neglected by all but a few bold and insightful activists, artists, and academics). At the same time, we do need to continue to understand, analyze, and describe how, in spite of the barrage of violence and cruelty thrown our way, so many black women both remain and become stronger, more compassionate, more courageous, and a site of inspiration for both themselves and others.

As a bourgeois black woman academic, I have always leaned more toward the Henderson side of this intersection: I know so little and want to know so much more about the ways black feminist studies boasts our ability not only to accurately represent black women but also to provide considerably more accurate and inclusive ways for understanding the human condition itself in all of its variety. While I do not believe that black women exist as some sort of Rosetta stone for the rest of the human race/all living things, I do believe that it is one of the better disciplines to lay bare the deeply uneven terrain that theorists ignorant of black feminism leave in their wake: terrain that they believe has been leveled but in fact is still lumpy with unacknowledged sacrificial bodies.

More specifically, this "lumpy terrain" reflects the ways in which too many discourses on racial justice ignore the specifically masculinist logics they apply to their critiques. For example, the wanton killing of black denizens in white Western nations by police often restricts itself to those murders committed in the public sphere: on sidewalks, public parks, streets, highways, and other venues where, consciously planned or not, other citizens must witness the power of the state to liquidate black bodies at will. Of course, these executions need to be publicly criticized frequently and ferociously, but by routinely ignoring a more private sphere—jail cells, the backs of police cars and vans, and within the home—these discourses sweep the lynched and bullet-riddled bodies of black women and girls, also victims of murderous police, under the carpet. They are the lumps, the bodies sacrificed to a scholarly imagination that reduces the complexity of racial oppression to a masculine contest in which the only agents are black men and white men, the rest of collateral damage.

In this essay, I want to try to lay bare the fundamental ways in which black feminism—or, more specifically, black queer feminism—calls attention to and seeks to solve these "lumpy terrains" in ways that are broadly applicable by taking three broad theoretical concepts—time, space, and knowledge—and showing how a black feminist politics on identity provides a sophisticated and inclusive schema for all bodies. Many others before me have pointed out (and I will cite a few of them along this way) that gender and sexuality studies have, like race studies, often been mistaken as a set of practices that are scenario-specific, falsely contrasting them against white Western male heterosexual cultural and intellectual productions that are supposedly "universal." Sylvia Wynter has cannily argued that this is possible only because the latter has determinedly and doggedly shaped the concept of what is human into its own image. Here I will try to show (perhaps not as cannily as Wynter) that black queer feminist politics on identity endures and at times flourishes because it captures, analyzes, defines, and theorizes so well, so accurately, those performances, assumptions, machinations, and designations that mark, mold, and define all individuals and collectives who must from time to time or in a plethora of moments negotiate and interpellate themselves through these overdetermined social identities.[4]

TIME

Writing about time alone is both impossible and unavoidable. It is impossible because, as Kathryn Yusoff at Queen Mary University of London put it to me in an e-mail, one ends up either "spatializing time or temporising space." It is unavoidable because it doesn't seem yet possible to write about time and space equally: one term must always end up qualifying the other, as in Yusoff's description.

With that caveat in mind, I nonetheless want to try and focus first on the nature of temporality because our familiarity with it shapes our understandings not only of space but also our concept of knowledge. More so, I think, than space or knowledge, time is most often our most immediate template for understanding abstract ideas.

While most philosophers and scientists freely admit that time remains elusive, may or may not exist, and may take many more forms than we realize, Western discourses on knowledge and identity almost always deploy a particular imagining of time with a certainty that belies our explicit confusion over the exact nature of temporality. Time is almost always depicted as a time line, usually fleshed out as a linear progress narrative, in which time is a force that moves "forward," driven by the natural dynamic of progress (or, in the case of pessimistic concepts of progress, malevolent human and state agencies inhibit this drive that is nonetheless still imagined as a natural physical force from which all human beings are meant to profit by birthright).

Progress is typically understood as eradication and accumulation. Old, anti-progressive practices and methods, such as human slavery and less efficient technologies, are eradicated, replaced by progressive practices and methodologies that we know to be progressive because they are accumulative: free of slavery, a population's birthrate now increases, as does our lifespan. Older, less efficient machines produced less, while newer, more efficient machines produce more product (with quality taking a backseat to quantity when necessary).

When it comes to gender identity, our concept of progress is more easily attached to the male body as we tend to imagine the female body as first and foremost a site for reproduction, even as the "product" of that reproduction—human babies—is typically given its earliest social identity through a present or absent male (the last name or family name). The extension of that social identity—of social belonging and ancestry, also known as the family tree—is also ordered in that they are extended but also pruned according to patrilineal logic: men beget men through the neutral vessels of women.

Almost all racial and ethnic collectives tend to define their larger collective as comprised of pyramidal heteropatriarchal family structures (i.e., households headed by men, or female-run households, but the presence of the latter is understood as an absence: a black man should be where the woman is but cannot because of racist oppression). This means that the linear logic used to define the history (past), contemporary moment (present), and future prospects of that collective upends traditional biology: men, whether white or of color, beget other men. Surnames and often even first names are replicated, from man to man, and the more the better, as same-named offspring are numbered—and accumulation meant to bespeak some form of racial progress on a smaller scale.

The censure that molds the African American family tree highlights the precarity of this device of self-cloning men because the antebellum reproduction of the slave woman was almost wholly controlled by white men, an overwhelming number of whom raped their slave women. The capitalist logic that legally allowed white men to procreate black slaves creates a fair number of question marks on those eighteenth- and early- to mid-nineteenth-century roots and branches of black US family trees. In some of these family trees, black women appear as the earliest progenitors, a symbolic parthenogenesis that within one to two generations gives way to the patrilineal again. At the same time, the desire in most racial and ethnic collectives to adhere strictly to the myth of discrete racial boundaries so that race itself can be passed down as masculine birthright produces two quandaries: first, the fact that interracial liaisons continue today, so we are not rid of nonblack fathers, and they will continue to roil our attempts at racially pure family trees so long as we honor the myth of self-cloning men. Second, black women will not only continue to be ignored as procreators but will also remain that "weak link" because we still look to fathers, rather than mothers, to understand or at least negotiate the racial identity of children. In other words, rather than simply deprive black women, patrilineal logic and its attendant myths highlight both black male vulnerability and the unreliability of racial essentialisms as a viable analytic, especially when it comes to origins.

A black feminist "family time" rids us of these problems—we need not look anxiously and continuously at/for our origins and ancestors for racial confirmation and belonging, especially as those origins and ancestors fade ever further into the background, shrouded more and more distortedly by our present wishes, needs, and desires. In the black feminist anthologies mentioned above, and in many other black feminist works besides, genealogies are not summoned to authenticate identity: identity and belonging are achieved through an affirmation in the now. One need not know one's great-great-grandfather or grandmother in order to be sure who one is and, even further, one can relinquish the complicated process of inversion by which one attempts to synchronize with one's past by in fact forcing the past to suit the political beliefs of the present. Blackness, after all, has gone by many names, as have black men and women, and many of our antecedents used names and deployed logics that we find distasteful today—names that we now determine to be degrading and logics that praise and honor people and events we now decry as almost beneath mention.

Home Girls: A Black Feminist Anthology, edited by Barbara Smith, begins with Beverly Smith's expression of frustration from its famous sister anthology, *This Bridge Called My Back*: "because I feel people don't understand where we came from ... Sometimes I do wish people could just see us in the context we grew up in, who our people *are*" (vii, emphasis my own).[5] That this quote is in fact a requote frames the frustration as a perpetual one and by introducing the quote before its author conveys a sense of it being less a quote than an echo, an echo that does not come *through* the ages but *in* the ages because the readers of *Home Girls*, the readers of *This Bridge*, and the readers of this essay are all creating that past by imagining that echo. An echo, after all, is heard in the moment; it does not bundle itself up for a long journey from the past into the present to be heard. In like kind, the quote itself moves between present (I feel/people don't understand), past (where we came from), and back to the present (who people are) tenses. Both of these strategies of presentation upend the assumption that time is a neat tripartite system of clearly delineated past, present, and future. In marking this desire to be understood and located as a desire of comingled tenses, a desire of the *now* that speaks for all ages imagined and thus summoned, Smith neatly dispenses the need for an ancestral line: one need not seek the benediction of the ancestors for this volume even as one nonetheless longs for an established sense of belonging. While linear time as the progress narrative-cum-history is an obsessively annotated and abridged myth, revealing its mythological status does not eradicate that very human longing to nonetheless seek it out as a source for identity formation: if we did not desire it, why else would it exist as such a cherished and enduring fabrication?

In fact, far from expelling the desirability of myth from black feminist identity, many black feminist scholars, writers, and activists of Smith's generation elaborate on and call attention to it. Audre Lorde does not write a biography, a genre that typically promises a linear progress narrative of the self, beginning with one's ancestors. She instead dubs her genre a "biomythography"—a mythological writing of the self—and dubs that self "Zami," a regraphing that does not attempt to erase its antecedent but in fact highlights, in the title, that this is "a *new* spelling of my name." Lorde, in other words, suggests that rather than a genealogy of self, she is best served by a palimpsest, in which earlier traces, or older spellings, are also part of the now of her identity.

To upend (but not dismiss, only relinquish as a truth and perhaps maintain as a desire) the linear progress narrative, that linear arrangement of accumulation and progress, then, can overlap with a more spatial understanding of time because the now becomes less of a moment and more of a space in which we summon and acknowledge the presence of "other times" in our present, specifically other pasts and other futures, all sharing the space with us.

SPACE

While time produces the black male as object and the white male as subject, with gender and sexual minorities generally left unrepresented (or represented in absentia by a default heterosexual masculinity and therefore not represented at all), space bifurcates, however unevenly, between the masculine public and feminine private, with the latter designated a devolution of the former, a hierarchy within a hierarchy. Within this schema, many public spaces enjoy peer relationships to one another—the court house, the legislature, the office, the social club—reflecting the luxuriously privileged overlapping networks of the homosocial and the state. This conflation of spaces translates into a conflation between the male body and state power because the male body retains those powers supposedly confined to official spaces (the courthouse, the legislature, the office, etc.) and extends them to the social club, the gym, the golf course, the limousine, and so forth.

Because black bodies were brought into the United States as property, there is an ugly twist here rarely shared with other minorities who immigrated (this distinction does not, however, establish any clear or fixed hierarchy of oppression between different racial or ethnic minority collectives). Like most slave states, male and female slaves are both understood as operating within the wholly private sphere, whether at work in the fields or in the house, meaning the black space is a devolution of the white private sphere.

Perhaps what is most empowering and enriching about the spaces enjoyed by the dominant white male collective (n.b.: not all white men, by any stretch) is their series of lateral relationships: the privileged member may flow freely from one to the other and thus enjoy a range of access (to other bodies, superiors and peers for work and romance, disempowered bodies for service). What is clearly most disempowering for those black spaces is their lack of accesses, the fact that they are not so much space as enclosures—and that this is an established norm, informing past, present, and most likely futures.

As Katherine McKittrick sums up in *Demonic Grounds: Black Women and the Cartographies of Struggle,*

> Dominant geographic patterns can often undermine complex interhuman geographies by normalizing spatial hierarchies and enacting strict spatial rules and regulations. More than this, "normal" places and spaces—of comfort, wealth, peace, safety—are hopefully seductive: they allude to the idea that finding and living the "normal" within existing spatial hierarchies is a geographic achievement. (146)[6]

In the quote above, McKittrick reflects on the ways in which the past is very much present in our space, taking the form of "dominant geographic patterns" that come, almost inevitably, with hierarchies, hierarchies that distort one's sense of self and agency to the degree that one may simply aspire to live "normally," an aspiration for a norm that, McKittrick warns, is nonetheless replete with levels of oppression, no matter how seductive it appears.

Demonic Grounds analyzes a form of black spatial female agency that successfully negotiates temporality, specifically the past and the present, whether it be the garret where escaped slave and acclaimed author Linda Brent/Harriet Jacobs hid for seven years or the empty contemporary auction block at a US southern plantation that is now a tourist site. For McKittrick, black women's spatial agency is entwined with a polytemporal performance and state of mind, the ability to live beyond the single temporality (the past, present, or future alone) and thus cross temporal boundaries even when completely still.

This is similar to the "shared" space I allude to at the end of the section on time and which here can be understood as a polytemporal space. While McKittrick focuses on negotiation, here I want to focus on the very different type of agency that the polytemporal space provides, one significantly different from the agency imagined by white and black men who have theorized Western subjectivity—Emmanuel Kant, Thomas Jefferson, G. W. F Hegel, Jacques Lacan, Martin Delany, Alexander Crummel, W. E. B. Du Bois, and Frantz Fanon.

In the Enlightenment-inflected subjectivities imagined by the figures above, agency is both the means and proof of total self-actualization: to think is to do. And yet all of these theorists conceive of subjectivity along dialectical lines, meaning that there must be an Other against which the subject achieves *his* definition of being self-conscious and rational. In other words, all of these forms of subjectivity, our most famous, are predicated on a hierarchical structure, a fact that Western political science and economic theory has never been able to bypass: in order for some people to enjoy forms of freedom, others must be deprived of those forms (most often control over one's body and one's labor).

A black feminist agency borne in the polytemporal space rejects this hierarchization, beginning with the rejection of the unified subject because to acknowledge the polytemporal space is to acknowledge one's body as an unstable conflation of temporalities, of other selves over which we cannot exert total control because they are not often neatly aligned with one another. Rather than being transcendental—outside of all space-times—the polytemporal space is a complicated conflation containing more than we can ever acknowledge or observe. Our agency and our ability to choose is necessarily hampered from the confusing polytemporality that bears it because there is no unified thought, action, or choice that could ever speak to all of those selves in the moment.

To inhabit the polytemporal space is to *choose* and *know*, but choose and know without omniscience or omnipotence; the one is the many, but the many are not one.

KNOWLEDGE

In white-majority Western nations, we are taught our alphabet, our numbers, our histories, and our scientific discoveries within a linear form. We are taught our social identities, whether in history, anthropology, political science, or around the kitchen table, within a linear form. The linear form implies that information achieves the important level of knowledge when it is put into a causal line in which one piece of information begets the next. In such an arrangement, as one can imagine, it is the first piece of information that always retains pride of place because it is the originator, the starter of the sequence, and the little god of this epistemology.

When it comes to knowledge, origins tend to possess human agents, and those agents are most often assumed to be white and male even when other knowledge sources contradict that claim.[7] We are taught that science is the discovery and then application of universal physical principles, and therefore intrinsic, transcendent, and that their birthplace is in Europe under the aegis of white men. However, this runs afoul of simple logics because we now have a paradox in which scientific practices were formalized in Europe beginning in the fifteenth century, and yet the chemistry, biology, and physics that begat metallurgy, medicinal practices, and gun powder (to name just a few technological innovations) radically predate the so-called invention of these sciences in Europe.

There is an important lesson here in this contradiction: that a line comprised of causal information is entitled to a title, such as a formal discipline, with a host of distinguished midwives. Information that exists outside of the white Western purview and defies the dates and names needed for a genealogy simply becomes a humanless practice performed by humans. In other words, physics gets the imprimatur of ancient Greece and Thales as its creator, but metallurgy does not get a history and all of its appurtenances until it can be located within a European time line.

Disciplinary and ideological genealogies, then, offer little in the way of black feminist agency—much less black male agency, tied as they are to a linear history in which the primary malefactor is represented by those white European and then US enterprises that purchased the bulk of their human cargo from the "slave coast" of West Africa. The

African American progress narrative-cum-history—and for that matter, any history of a besieged diasporic collective—will represent that minority collective as its colonized/dispersed/enslaved object rather than its agent.

This is a far less elegant equation than that famously offered by Sylvia Wynter and her determination that the colonial system did far more than rob the colonized of their rights—according to Wynter, the colonizer also permanently shunted the colonized from consideration as human altogether. Like Saidiya Hartman's *Scenes of Subjection*, Wynter, most famously in "On How We Mistook the Map for the Territory," argues that the white Western world has successfully deprived the black collective of that most cherished status for white Western democracies: human.

Yet Wynter's concept of history is strictly linear and understands that linear progress narrative not as an attempted representation of space-time but of space-time itself. Equally striking, Wynter primarily relies on white and black male thinkers to represent this confrontation and its devastating aftermath, returning us to a representation of the world where men beget men and white men can ensure black men never appear on this time line as humans.

In 2012, the playwright Jackie Sibblies Drury completed "We Are Proud to Present a Presentation about the Herero of Namibia, Formerly Known as Southwest Africa, from the German Sudwestafrika, between the Years 1884–1915," a darkly comedic meta-play about a group of well-meaning thespians attempting to represent and perform the demise of the Herero, a historical collective from East Africa who were colonized by the German state in the late nineteenth century and then subjected to genocide. Drury's play tackles two metaphysical questions about knowledge and representation well-known in literary studies but also a key component to performance art. The first question is a version of postcolonial critic Gayatri Spivak's question if the subaltern can speak.[8] That is, if the colonized can only communicate with the colonizer in the language of the latter, can they ever really accurately communicate all the blatant and nuanced ramifications of their condition?

Not coincidentally, "On How We Mistook the Map for the Territory" draws heavily on Frantz Fanon's exploration of this question in *Black Skin, White Masks* (and which he answers with an unqualified negative). Drury's play agrees, as its middle-class, relatively privileged performers scratch their well-groomed heads and exhaust their pampered bodies in trying to find ways to understand the ultimately deprivileged: those who have been eliminated from the earth and almost but not quite from historical memory.

The second question pursued by "We Are Proud to Present" is closely related: how does one do justice to a group who leave behind no trace, no clues as to how they were, what they thought, what they created, and what they believed? The second answer is as bleak as the first: one cannot; one, at best, can only signify the failure of signification—which, of course, is Drury's play in a nutshell.

Drury, like Wynter, deploys the linear form of time; space and thus knowledge are purely affairs of the linear progress narrative, where one is either "off" or "on" the line (and, if one is a minority, most likely off). Black queer feminist space-time steps back from the transcendental, universal claims that the linear progress narrative seeks to make. Drury's exploration, like Wynter's, uses linear genealogies assumed to be complete because to be in the present moment means one is "ahead of" the past, forward, in front of it—and therefore empowered to evaluate the present status of past knowledge or—in the case of Drury—evaluate the history of the Herero as effectively lost. As such Wynter, like Fanon, observes the ugly and distorted white Western linear progress narrative and determines that black (male) identity is located quite explicitly off that time line in a state of alienation.

One cannot argue with this conclusion: both Wynter and Fanon offer deeply knowledgeable, logically elegant, and compelling eloquent arguments that do indeed show the sad degree to which white Western epistemologies not only offer no space for the black subject but also insist on that black (male) "no-space" in order to bring themselves into being. After all, a progress narrative is a relative thing; it requires an object fixed in space-time against which to measure one's own forward velocity, one's progress.

Yet black queer feminist politics need not argue with either Fanon or Wynter (at least in this case): it can easily agree that yes, linear formations of knowledge are forbidding, fundamentally inaccurate in nearly all assumptions, and of course hostile to both diversity and nuance. The two-dimensional world is often a world of absolutes, even when deployed by one as clever as Fanon to measure the possibility of black female agency in *Black Skin, White Masks*. We see him weighing the complexity of female identity through the rather reductive lens of heterosexual relationships:

> Every woman in the Antilles, whether in a casual flirtation or in a serious affair, is determined to select the least black of men.... . I know a great number of girls from Martinique, students in France, who admitted to me with complete candor—completely white candor—that they would find it impossible to marry black men.... . All of these frantic women of color in quest of white men are waiting.... . what they must have is whiteness at any price. (47–48)[9]

The linear logic of this questionable argument about black female (heterosexual) identity allows a few to stand in for the total collective, and for one individual's recollection (Fanon's) to operate as a transcendent and transparent communicator for universal truths. Indeed, any argument in which the text claims to be able to speak for an entire collective most likely asserts its truths through this two-dimensional format.

Yet, we can stand here in this moment and bring in the complexity of Fanon—an anti-colonial intellectual who studied under white scholars, writing in French while condemning it as the language of the colonizer (and thus incapable of conveying the true sentiments of meaning of the colonizer) — and we can see, rather than the two-dimensional logic organizing the page, considerably more complex competing truths, all of which call attention to the conflict with the meta-narrative and thus fold in on themselves and as a whole, accordion-like. For Fanon to study under and work in a white colonial regime and use the colonizer's language offers two entwined possibilities, similar to the alogical statement "you can't trust me: I always lie." Either Fanon is, as his argument claims, under the distorting influence of the colonizer, thus rendering his arguments equally false and distorted, or he is successfully communicating a cogent, insightful, and far-seeing anti-colonial critique, in which case his premise that the language of the colonizer cannot be used to express the ideas of the colonized is false. No matter which conclusion one comes to, Fanon's meta-narrative is a time bomb for two-dimensional logic. This truth calls attention to itself quite memorably in his screeds against black women: armed with the treacherous language of the colonizer, he can only produce an analysis of black Caribbean womanhood that reflects what he imagines to be the ugly assumptions of the white colonizer about his desirability for black women, and his own more ambivalent lust.

We can ask if this is deliberate or not, but the answer in this polyvalent moment of past, present, and future is yes and no and who knows and there is nothing to know because who knows if the question even has, much less deserves, an answer: it depends on what information one is looking at, what angle one is taking—and the knowledge that, whatever the conclusion, it is only a partial conclusion shrouded by the limitless and yet largely unknowable present moment. The bleak truths found on a time line are not false but will collapse in on themselves when presented with the polyvalent present moment, a space for many more dimensions of knowledge and consideration.

Similarly, black feminist politics of identity can also respond to Drury because the history of the Herero is not in fact lost. Like much if not possibly most of our past, we don't know what we don't know because the past is not laid out behind us, clearly marking what we do know and what is lost. Rather than only mourn what is lost according to our two-dimensional time line, we might also interpellate ourselves into the present moment and ask ourselves how what we think is lost might remain. We can begin with the sobering fact that, despite the best attempts of murderous regimes, a whole people can never be entirely eliminated because collectives are not two-dimensional dots traveling on time lines: people wander, people escape, and they often leave traces. This fact is not celebratory: to be nearly decimated is, in many moments, to be decimated. Yet with the Herero we do have those who escaped, those who bore witness, and their testimony is available in both printed form and online sites (some in fact spurred by Drury's play).

This answer does not entirely solve the more pressing question in Drury: how can one accurately represent the subaltern? The answer here is that no one moment can ever accurately represent any individual because we construct and reconstruct our polyvalent identities in various forms in different moments. While this is hardly a superpower, some sort of omnipotent shape-shifting—it is far more often immediate reactions to often negative stimuli—it also means the black queer feminist politics on identity itself cannot be reduced to a single two-dimensional trajectory with some sort of clear (if porous) origin, a string of related events to flesh out the meaning of the time line, or even a clear goal.

The future of black queer feminist politics of identity, in this moment, offers a broad variety of trajectories. With this moment here as our only contingent origin, we can see how moving beyond linear time, space, and knowledge opens up a multitude of possibilities, from the garret to the classroom, from Wynter to the Herero, and always, always in this moment, with our polyvalent (un)knowing selves in the center.

NOTES

1 For the purposes of this essay, "black feminist studies" will also include sexuality as one of its analytical lenses. I will elaborate on sexuality in any instances where this would be unclear.

2 Jennifer Nash, "Re-Thinking Intersectionality," *Feminist Review* 89 (2008): 1–15. Online.

3 Buchi Emecheta, *Double Yoke* (New York: Braziller Press, 1983).

4 See *Physics of Blackness: Beyond the Middle Passage Epistemology* for my explanation as to how interpellation is ultimately an act of the self in epiphenomenal time.

5 Barbara Smith, ed., *Home Girls: A Black Feminist Anthology* (New Brunswick: Rutgers UP, [1983] 2000).

6 Katherine McKittrick, *Demonic Grounds: Black Women and the Cartographies of Struggle* (Minneapolis: University of Minnesota Press, 2006).

7 The desire to imagine all creators as male crosses racial lines as well. A recent blogspot at MIT (http://www.mit.edu/~thistle/v9/9.01/6blackf.html) asserts that black feminism itself is born out of "Black Liberation movements" (i.e., the Black Panthers) when in fact black feminism, unsurprisingly, was created by black feminists over a century earlier (see Paula Giddings's *When and Where I Enter*).

8 Gayatri Spivak, "Can the Subaltern Speak?" in *Marxism and the Interpretation of Culture*, ed. C. Nelson and L. Grossberg (Basingstoke: Macmillan Education, 1988), pp. 271–313.

9 Frantz Fanon, *Black Skin, White Masks*, trans. Charles Lam Markmann (New York: Grove Press, 1967).

WORKS CITED

Emecheta, Buchi. *Double Yoke*. New York: Braziller P, 1983.

Fanon, Frantz. *Black Skin, White Masks*. Trans. Charles Lam Markmann. New York: Grove P, 1967.

McKittrick, Katherine. *Demonic Grounds: Black Women and the Cartographies of Struggle*. Minneapolis: U of Minnesota P, 2006.

Nash, Jennifer. "Re-Thinking Intersectionality." *Feminist Review* 89 (2008): 1–15. Online.

Smith, Barbara, ed. *Home Girls: A Black Feminist Anthology*. New Brunswick: Rutgers UP, [1983] 2000.

Spivak, Gayatri. "Can the Subaltern Speak?" *Marxism and the Interpretation of Culture*. Ed. C. Nelson and L. Grossberg. Basingstoke: Macmillan Education, 1988: 271–313.

CHAPTER THREE

Difference

HORTENSE J. SPILLERS

GETTING STARTED

One forgets what the world was like before "difference" carried an echo—before this apparently ordinary word, which used to bear the full uncomplicated weight of universal sexual arrangements, came crashing down at our feet in a new order of conceptual difficulty. It is fair to say that some of the blame might be posted at the threshold of the 1960s when radical transformation was the watchword of the day—at least an inquiry into the matter might start there with what has been called in feminist circles "second-wave" feminism, or women's movement that blossoms anew in the metropolitan centers of the globe in the aftermath of the Second World War, and while we do not customarily posit an alignment of motives between wars and women's response to their own status, it is a matter of interest to this observer that women's renewed call to domestic arms unfolds in view of a spatiotemporal horizon that overlooks radical change along a broad waterfront of stress points in social, political, cultural, and historical relations: in race, gender, ethnicity, concepts of the nation-state and nationalisms, and the impulsion to a new global synthesis of geopolitical persuasions with the United States commanding a position of leadership. Precisely because war's aftermath had engendered the fall of a myriad of idols, the belief in spirit drooping down in the midst of things, where differences between the sexes, for example, were thought to be immutable, became as vulnerable to doubt and suspicion as the supposed inferiority of the "darker races." The emergence, then, of a more complex sense of difference as one of the solid achievements of second-wave feminism occurs, according to Nancy Fraser, within the wider context of agitation from an "anti-imperialist New Left, as a radical challenge to the pervasive androcentrism of state-led capitalist societies in the post-war era."[1] Fraser's elegant summary renders succinct a massive entanglement of elements, some strands of which we will attempt to decipher here.

DEFINING DIFFERENCE

As familiar as the new difference is by now, it is quite remarkable to my mind that one cannot say in a word exactly what it is—if it is an idea or a concept, then what does it mean? We are, therefore, reduced, or relegated, to describing its *effects* rather than tracing its movement across a predicate, as we might in a definition—"difference is ...." In any case, difference is already assigned a history, if the decennial mark is to be credited. In the introduction to another volume of keywords related to gender, Catharine Stimpson notes that during the 1960s and 1970s, "women's studies explored the question of difference between women and men in three ways, to all of which feminism provided intellectual energy and insights and a moral and political framework."[2] In one of the first volumes of writing to explore difference as a critical tool of feminist inquiry, Hester Eisenstein observes that difference is a "theme" that is "integral to modern feminist thought from at least the time of the publication of Simone de Beauvoir's *The Second Sex*, and in particular since the rebirth of the women's movement in the late 1960s."[3] In both Stimpson's and Eisenstein's readings, difference becomes a kind of torque that makes things happen, that sends them into rotation through a variety of transformations: in Stimpson's outline, the first of the differences between women and men were exposed early on in the career of second-wave feminism as the "consequence of men's dominance over women, of hierarchical patriarchal structures, and of phallocentrism" (12). In the second instance, women's achievements, despite drawbacks in their assertion of historical agency, were highlighted in the attempt to revise and correct the record. Stimpson here notes the important contributions of Carol Gilligan's *In a Different Voice* to the effort to retrieve a notion of women's particular strengths of care and compassion, poised as a counterweight to the phallocentric boast,[4] and in the third instance of the play of difference, we observe what might well be a shot across the bow, insofar as "woman" itself, by the early 1980s, fractures across the fault lines of race, class, historico-cultural circumstance, "age, religion, sexuality, nationality, status as citizens." In short, this "third approach" inaugurates a thematics of diversity (13). In doing so, certain practitioners of the 1980s, among them, Barbara Smith and Akasha Gloria Hull,[5] bring to stand black women's studies and studies of women of color, exemplified, for example, in *This Bridge Called My Back*,[6] which led more or less directly to (1) intersectional theory that undergirds critical race theory of which Kimberle Crenshaw is a pioneer[7] and (2) gender studies that not so ironically encompass analyses of male sexuality. Gayle Rubin's "sex/gender system," examined in "The Traffic in Women,"[8] provided a nuance in the study of difference that not only instantiated a theoretical differentiation between *sex* and *gender* as a gain in argumentative and conceptual subtlety but perhaps also laid the groundwork for the American reception of French feminist theory and a deepening grasp of the entire repertoire of human sexuality/sexualities across the register of identity and performance.

Once gender breaks away from *sex* as its own discrete, but not unrelated, calculus of motives, *feminine* and *masculine* and *male* and *female* then lay hold of differentiated theoretical terrain that perhaps echoes the nature/culture split: Stimpson points out that "*gender* does not mean sex but the social and sexual relationships between the sexes and the place assigned to members of each sex within these relationships" (6). For example, "control" over women, she contends, signals the operations of gender, as does the permissibility of the rape of women by men. Biological and anatomical differences between *male* and *female* (which time-honored closure will open onto new curricular objects and subjects at century's end and beyond) have often enough stood in for, or disguised, the operations of gender; as Stimpson puts it, studies of biological femaleness and maleness, frequently flawed and erroneous, are nonetheless pressed into service at times as justification for maintaining "normative gender arrangements."

A striking example of this elision is offered by Joan Scott in a reading of the infamous Sears case. In this particular instance, not only were gender and sex analyses confounded, which redounded to the distinct disadvantage of the women workers represented in the case,[9] but also the bugaboo of fraudulent choice between "equality" and "difference" was paraded with a vengeance.

In 1984, the Equal Employment Opportunity Commission (EEOC), pursuant to Title VII of the 1964 Civil Rights Act,[10] filed suit against Sears for sex discrimination when historians Alice Kessler-Harris and Rosalind Rosenberg testified on opposite sides of the case. A writer for the *New York Times* called the Sears–EEOC fracas "the last of a series of landmark sex-bias cases brought by the Government against major corporations."[11] The EEOC, we are told, spent eleven years and a whopping $22.5 million in legal fees preparing for combat with the "retailing giant" and lost, but more than that, the outcome apparently set askew relations between Rosenberg and Kessler-Harris, as it also engendered recriminations and hostility among feminist colleagues and associates, more broadly speaking. In any event, Scott advances a reading of it as a prime instance of what she considered an unfortunate, but avoidable, feminist bind. In short, the debacle dramatized two position-takings: on the one hand, "those who argue that sexual difference ought to be an irrelevant consideration in schools, employment, the courts, and the legislature" belong to what Scott calls the "equality category" (391). The "difference category," on the other, is comprised of those "who insist that appeals on behalf of women ought to be made in terms of the needs, interests, and characteristics common to women as a group" (391). Asserting in the latter instance the "positivity" and "specificity" of group difference by race, sexual orientation, cultural signature, and degrees of ability/disability, the "difference" contingent, according to Iris Marion Young, redefines "the meaning of difference so that it no longer means exclusive opposition and deviation from a norm, and reveal[s] that the liberal humanist ideal of universal standards according to which everyone should be measured tends to perpetuate disadvantage and silence the specific culture and experience of some groups."[12] Scott contends that the "clashes over the superiority of one or another of these strategies" have generated not only a useless bifurcation of motives but also "new classificatory labels," as in "cultural feminism, liberal feminism, feminist separatism, and so on" (391). In order to steer around what Martha Minow named "the difference dilemma"—focusing on difference or ignoring it altogether—Scott suggests that feminists "need to ask how the dichotomous pairing of equality and difference itself works" (391). In other words, what is required here, she argues, is a sustained examination of the terms of the "existing political discourse," which would evince the necessity to understand *context*. In the Sears case, "equality-versus-difference" did not "accurately depict the opposing sides."

As Scott describes it, Rosalind Rosenberg's testimony on the defendant's behalf and the arguments by Sears's legal team pursued the "difference" strategy. Apparently, the Sears defense claimed that women's sexual difference, rather than discrimination, would explain hiring practices and differential promotional outcomes at the retailer's. Several factors of the judicial and evidentiary staging of the case strike an observer as peculiar: for one thing, the EEOC "had no individuals to testify that they had experienced discrimination." Instead, the commission lawyers grounded their case on "biased job applicant questionnaires and statements by personnel officers" (392). Against primarily statistical-based evidence, the testimony offered by the historians "could only be inferential, at best," and as we might imagine, what would count as an "interpretive premise" in scholarship was treated as "matters of fact" in the courtroom (392). Above all, Kessler-Harris's "carefully nuanced explanation of women's work history was forced into a reductive assertion by the Sears lawyers' insistence" that she "answer questions only by saying yes and no" (392). Juxtaposing Kessler-Harris's earlier published work on differences between male and female laborers with her testimony in the Sears case, Rosalind Rosenberg attempted to show that her colleague "had misled the court" (392).

As Scott explains it, difference, treated as an unalterable finality by the court, might have been better understood in relationship to women's work history, if Kessler-Harris could have shown that the term "worker" was predicated on "male reference," which "could not account for all aspects of women's job experiences" (392). But in connection with employers who sought to rationalize discrimination on the basis of sexual difference, it would have been tactically astute to "deny the totalizing effects of difference by stressing instead the diversity and complexity of women's behavior and motivation" (392–3). Rosenberg's holding to a strict argument that "unproblematically linked socialization to individual choice" apparently complemented the binary style of response preferred by the court, and moreover, the world beyond scholarship and publishing more broadly speaking, which revels in "prevailing normative views" (393). Allowed little margin for nuance, Kessler-Harris was not able to lay hold of a "simple model that would at once acknowledge difference *and* refuse it as an acceptable explanation for employment patterns at Sears" (393). The subtler arguments advanced by Kessler-Harris were ultimately rejected "as contradictory or inapplicable" (393). The presiding judge, finding in the retailer's favor, upheld the chief arguments of the defense "that an assumption of equal interest was 'unfounded' because of differences between women and men" (393). The outcome here, as disappointing as it might be, is all too predictable: not only did the EEOC suffer massive loss "but the hiring policies of Sears were implicitly endorsed" because cultural and historical difference, "redefined as simply the recognition of 'natural' difference," was embraced as "real and fundamental" (393).

If the Sears case is analyzed as a crucial instance of movement across a discursive field, which Scott rightly identifies as a "political field," then feminists would be called upon to confront, on the one hand, "the unmasking of the power relationship constructed by posing equality as the antithesis of difference" and, on the other, "the refusal of its consequent dichotomous construction of political choices" (394). Scott contends that feminists should not abandon difference, as "it has been our most creative analytic tool" (394), but at the same time, feminism cannot allow its arguments to be forced "into preexisting categories and its political disputes to be characterized by a dichotomy that (it) did not invent" (394).

On this point, it is useful to recall that equality, as Michael Walzer put it, carries a negative valence (394). Related to egalitarianism, with its echoes in eighteenth-century revolutionary France, equality, in the context of the US Republic, traces back to abolitionist politics of the nineteenth century in which case it was aimed "at eliminating not all differences, but a particular set of differences" and, generally speaking, "a different set in different times and places" (394). In the American instance, abolitionist equality referred quite specifically to race in the remapping of its social and political meaning at slavery's end in accordance with the putative aims of democratic citizenship and belonging. Equality, then, "presumes a social agreement to consider obviously different people as equivalent (not identical) for a stated purpose" (394). As we see here, "the political notion of equality" does not eschew difference at all but "includes, indeed depends on, an acknowledgment of the existence of difference," or said another way, "if individuals or groups were identical or the same there would be no need to ask for equality," which, Scott suggests, might be defined "as deliberate indifference to specified differences" (394). This discursive and historical analysis leads Scott to the conclusion that the actual enemy in the Sears case and in "equality-vs-difference" in general is "categorical thinking," in this instance, "about gender" (395). Sameness or identity between men and women is not a sociopolitical goal but, rather, "a more complicated historically variable diversity than is permitted by the opposition male/female, a diversity that is also differently expressed for different purposes in different contexts" (395). Practically speaking, though, feminists inhabit a world that operates by binary choice in its most pressing decisions. Under such circumstance, how, then, to pursue a truer social value, the refusal "to oppose equality to difference and insist continually on differences—differences as the condition of individual and collective identities, differences as the constant challenge to the fixing of those identities, history as the repeated illustration of the play of differences, differences as the very meaning of equality itself" (395)? Since 1988, when Scott's words were penned, differences have not only thrived but indeed proliferated in a vertiginous gigue of virtually unique porous individual identities on a shared stage of sociality. Today, presumed common ground, if the academic state of things in cultural criticism yields some clue, appears to have become an undesirable, even a defunct, idea. But perhaps this is a story for another day, although it inscribes the "future of difference" that we could not have guessed from the vantage of the 1980s.

COMPARATIVE AND CONTRASTIVE READINGS

One of the single points of agreement among the contingents and proponents of difference was identified nearly a decade before Scott's writing by Alice Jardine, who noted, after Nancy Miller, that "Western culture has proven to be incapable of thinking not-the-same-as without assigning one of the terms a positive value and the other, a negative."[13] But the intercalation of French feminisms, perhaps already prepared by the American reception of *The Second Sex*, as early as H. M. Parshley's English translation of 1953, shifted the focus of the debate, and even if difference did not by any means retire from the field, it appears to have been absorbed in the rerouting of a feminist topography: "this sex that is not one," for instance, not only embraced difference but also renamed it as the principal heuristic of a superior practice and understanding that we would come to recognize as a *feminine écriture*. In the introduction to *New French Feminisms: An Anthology*, the editors note that the writers represented in the volume "are engaged separately, and in some cases collectively, in an attempt to formulate a theory that would account for women's specificity" (Marks and Courtivron xii). A perusal of Elaine Marks's and Isabelle Courtivron's table of contents reveals right away the identity of French women intellectuals whose projects would indeed come to enhance the Anglo-American feminist library as a significant chapter in the history of Western thought in the post–Second World War period, Hélène Cixous, Julia Kristeva, Margaret Duras, Monique Wittig, and Luce Irigaray prominent among them. Luce Irigaray's *This Sex Which Is Not One*, for instance, not only accounts for "women's specificity" but also boldly pronounces on such difference by way of what Judith Butler would declare a little over a decade later as a "return to biology" (30). Perhaps one of the most brazen paronomasic (punning) gestures that a reader might imagine, *Ce Sexe qui n'en est pas un*, originally published by Editions de Minuit in 1977, manages a sustained investigation, in relatively short order, of the West's "dominant phallic economy" on the basis of the "architecture," we might say, of the human female genitalia; this stunning display of the convergence of poetic imagination, theoretical *savoir faire*, and the ineluctable conformity effected between a numerical figure and an abiding conceptual notion is both light-hearted (at least in its title) and as serious as a heart attack in what it insistently summons its reader to grasp: The "woman," here the embodied female figure in all its magisterial difference from the male, is "within herself ... already two—but not divisible into one(s)—that caress each other" (Irigaray 24). This symmetrical "twoness," predicated on the anatomy of the vulva, instantiates in woman an entirely different register and economy of desire—unlike the male and its organ that wants a sheath or depression in which to situate itself. It follows, then, that woman's desire, subjected to the rule of the phallus, or the logic of phallogocentrism, is "submerged" by the latter "that has dominated the West since the time of the Greeks" (25). The logic of phallogocentrism in Irigaray's argument is grounded in the "predominance of the visual," as woman "takes pleasure more from touching than from looking" (25, 26). Woman's inauguration into this "dominant scopic economy" has been costly, and that is to say, "her consignment to passivity" (26). The extended train of abjection that attaches to the "look" courses right through our own contemporaneity from the "beauty pageant" to the twitter mouth-feed of the president of the United States.

The numerical figures of *one* and *two* yield work in this essay always on at least a couple of registers—the literal and the figurative, the tenor and the vehicle—in a consistency of motives that drives what seems to point to an unalterable opposition between male and female anatomy that is winkingly intimated in the old, unreflected difference of the pre-1960s "Vive la difference," but in this case, the outcome is riddled with cultural implications that are fatal for women, especially within the context of heterosexual eroticism and political representation in its discursive regimes: "The *one* of form, of the individual, of the (male) sexual organ, of the proper name, of the proper meaning ... supplants, while separating and dividing, that contact of *at least two* (lips) which keeps woman in touch with herself, but without any possibility of distinguishing what is touching from what is touched" (26; emphasis Irigaray). This movement of inflection that commences from the apparent singlicity of the penis and proceeds to the proper name and the ownership of property, with its roots in juridical personality and the law, is analogously configured in what follows from the female "lips" in inevitable contact—for one thing, the rupture of women's pleasure as the male organ "divides" and "separates," and with this disturbance, the woman's sex is not only *not* counted as "one," or a sex, but because it is not, it is, therefore, considered as *none*. In Irigaray's version of phallic economy, the woman is not a "second sex," as Beauvoir would have it, but, rather, no sex at all, not even the male's "other." As the "reverse of the only visible and morphologically designatable organ ... the penis," the woman is left with maternity that serves to fill "the gaps in a repressed sexuality" (26, 27). But this otherwise genial sexuality in Irigaray's hands is capable of performing the double duty of both reproductive work and the work of pleasure, insofar as it is "always at least double." What is more, "it is plural ... sex organs more or less everywhere" (28). For this reason, "the geography of her pleasure is far more diversified, more multiple in its differences, more complex, more subtle, than is commonly imagined" (28). The ramifications of woman's sexual multiplicity engender notations along several impression points from the morphological to the ontological, axiological, conceptual, and material. This multiplicity that "really involves a different economy more than anything else" eschews "the linearity of a project, undermines the goal-object of a desire, diffuses the polarization toward a single pleasure, disconcerts fidelity to a single discourse," as Irigaray supplements this repertoire of gifts with the woman's refusal of the fixity of meaning in the play and orchestration of language (29–30).

Self-nearness in this scheme appears to evade the alienation inherent in property-owning with its tilt toward male *exteriority* and the latter's representability—in other words, a significant portion of the male body is located "outside" itself, so to speak, as the male would attempt to "show" this outside to himself and the world in acts of displacement onto things that "represent" him—in short, his thing(s), his properties. To the contrary, the woman, with her multiple *interiority*, constituted by a sexual architecture of involuted folds, enters into the "ceaseless exchange of herself with the other," Irigaray contends, "without any possibility of identifying either" (31). Might it be said, then, that on the basis of female sexuality, with its plural dimensions, the woman is already her own other? But in the traditional social order, how the woman *expresses* her *interiority*, inasmuch as property is not it, is precisely a problem for thought and political movement. Irigaray, capitalizing on the notion of *exchange*, remarks, "For woman is traditionally a use-value for man, an exchange value among men; in other words, a commodity" (31).

These Marxist inflections in Irigaray's writing demark one of the pathways that feminist thought has taken over the decades in varied combinations with disciplinary practices and investments spread across the precincts of the human sciences; to my mind, this fertile cross-pollination of creative and intellectual energies has done more to expand the region of literary study and the "English Department" (where I sit) than any single factor of radical change in the academy that we can imagine, which, as a result, has not only enabled the growth of interdisciplinary regimes but also undergirded the development of a recalibrated regimen of learning and higher education. In other words, any degree program in the contemporary era must confront, sooner or later, in one way, or another, and to whatever extent, the massive production of feminist scholarship and minority discourses and their related visionary transformations that have redirected the conceptual/symbolic traffic around questions of race, gender, and sexuality. Not that the global scene, especially in its North American and transatlantic iterations, had not been ready for it—from roughly 1912 and the outburst of new impulses in seven fields of the arts—writing (poetry, the novel, drama), music, painting, dance, photography, architecture, and film—creative possibilities were awakened that would match the tectonic shifts in technological advancement and innovations in material culture, including the automobile and the assembly line. From that angle, the movements in critical race studies and women's studies appear to have been inevitable. Moreover, the "rise of theory," as the afterlife of philosophy and its reterritorializations onto unwonted ground, collides with the Left political movement from the 1960s forward to give rise to the world of ideas as we know it now.

The theoretical efflorescence in women's studies might be considered one of the most perdurable contributions of second-wave feminism, ironically, in gestures of critical inquiry that displace "the subject of feminism" and its "object." Two examples of such displacement emerge between the mid-1980s and the turn of the century in the researches of Teresa de Lauretis on the cinematic apparatus and that of Judith Butler in rhetoric and philosophy. If "women" and "woman" were once presumed to be more or less unproblematical locutions—one knew what the latter meant by way of broad sympathetic identification—then the ease of reference would be cancelled by feminist theory itself: in *Alice Doesn't*, which examines the semiosis (or play of signs) in the cinematic imagery of a handful of films, Lauretis notes early on the difference between these twin terms: "By 'woman' I mean a fictional construct, a distillate from diverse but congruent discourses dominant in Western cultures (critical and scientific, literary or juridical discourses), which works as both their vanishing point and their specific condition of existence" (5). The difficulty here is Lauretis's "vanishing point," which I take to mean that punctuality at which the object of the fiction disappears in/into the accomplishment of a goal, while the object itself doubles as the condition by which the fiction exists in the first place. If this reading is correct, then "woman"—"nature and mother, site of sexuality and masculine desire, sign and object of men's social exchange" (5)— never operates as a subject/subjectivity but, rather, "finds itself" trapped in objecthood as both the closure and enablement of certain cultural processes; contrarily, "women" means "the real historical beings who cannot as yet be defined outside of those discursive formations, but whose material existence is nonetheless certain, and the very condition of this book" (5)—just as if "women" were the point of theorization all along! There's more: "The relation between women as historical subjects and the notion of woman as it is produced by hegemonic discourses is *neither a direct relation of identity*, a one-to-one correspondence, *nor a relation of simple implication*" (5; emphasis mine). If that is so, then "what is finally at stake," with its Marxist/Althusserian overtones, "is not so much how 'to make visible the invisible' as how to produce the conditions of visibility for a different social subject" (8–9). If differences among women had become thematically and theoretically available to discourses about women by women, then it became central procedure to what could be thought as "the subject of feminism" in driving a cleavage between a subject and what the latter had divined as its "own" thing—seemingly, we were light years away from "Ce Sexe qui n'en est pas un."

Shortly after *Alice Doesn't*, Lauretis advances the arguments posed in that text by inquiring "how to theorize gender beyond the limits of 'sexual difference' and the constraints that such a notion has come to impose on feminist critical thought" (ix). Reading with and beyond Foucault, Lauretis in *Technologies of Gender* wants to propose, with respect to representation and self-representation, that gender is also "the product of various social technologies, such as cinema, as well as institutional discourses, epistemologies, and critical practices" (ix). Having had the veil of mystery ripped off "woman" in its difference to "women," one had been alerted by such assertions to a heady and an unexpected eventuality—*all* the ontological assumptions about a self that "she," by mimetic will, had maintained throughout a lifetime seemed suddenly thrown into crisis—"she" was nothing more, or less, than a "fiction" and the moment of convergence of a myriad of discursive formations so that, quite possibly, there was no there there. It is difficult now to recall exactly what such revelations felt like in the moment of their utterance, but for sure Lauretis's putative disposition in these essays closely aligns with portions of cultural and discursive content that sharpens the line of critical demarcation between the world *before* women's studies and the world *after*; another way to put the matter would bookend Gayatri Spivak's crucial translation of Jacques Derrida's *De la Grammatologie* (1974) and the close of the century during which time span the theoretical scaffolding that had secured the humanistic project gives way. We could also drive the front end of this time line back to the publication of Richard Macksey's and Eugenio Donato's *Structuralist Controversy* (1966), which introduces a US audience to many of the figures (heavily French nationals), whose thought would assume dominance over the next half century, and opens the way to the creation of the School of Criticism and Theory that will commence at the University of California, Irvine, in 1974. The events cursorily outlined here provide the staging and backdrop for shifts in the curriculum, as they lend a clue to nodal points along the trajectory of feminist theorizations.

In Lauretis, "the female subject of feminism" does not demark a redundancy because "gender," "sexuality," and "woman/women" have been unmoored from their customary milieu precisely by way of the torque of "difference." A multiple subject, the "female subject of feminism" is "constructed across a multiplicity of discourses, positions, and meanings which are often in conflict with one another and inherently (historically) contradictory" (x). Lauretis takes this formulation one more turn of the screw: "By the phrase 'the subject of feminism' I mean a conception or an understanding of the female subject as not only distinct from Woman with the capital letter, the *representation* of an essence inherent in all women ... but also distinct from women, the real, historical beings and social subjects who are defined by the technology of gender and actually engendered in social relations" (8–9; emphasis Lauretis). But here comes the rub: "the subject of feminism" that Lauretis means "is one *not* so defined" (10). The sentence continues on the other side of a comma in apposition to this unanticipated veto—"one whose definition or conception is in progress, in this and other feminist critical texts" (10).

Could we assume that this seeming elision is inadvertently erroneous and that what is meant is something like: "but, rather, one whose definition or conception is in progress?" In any case, we might be justified in concluding that Lauretis's "subject of feminism," in its infinitely dynamic character, cannot be captured between a capital letter and a period but instead runs on beyond the confines of the signifying chain, in excess of it. Lauretis does not make such claims, but it seems to me that her "subject of feminism" brushes the threshold of an undecidable, or perhaps tips over into it. Precisely so, it is the case, then, that the "very subject of women," in Judith Butler's estimation, "is no longer understood in stable or abiding terms" (1).

In the opening chapter of *Gender Trouble*, Butler lays out her protocol on the basis of two "controversial terms"—*representation* on the one hand, "which serves as the operative term within a political process that seeks to extend visibility and legitimacy to women as political subjects," and on the other, *politics* that constructs the subject "with certain legitimating and exclusionary aims, and these political operations are effectively concealed and naturalized by a political analysis that takes juridical structures as their foundation" (1, 2).

The trick of juridical power is that it "inevitably 'produces' what it claims merely to represent" (2). This stealthy operation accounts for the dual character of the political, insofar as it is both juridical *and* productive. The opening gambit against what Butler rehearses as the "metaphysics of substance" rolls out here in her challenge to law's temporal sleight-of-hand: the subject of feminism may not be a subject that stands "before" the law, both in the sense, as I understand it, of "before" as a standing *in* the law (as in equality) and "before" as an index of duration, as "before" the time that the subject arrives *at* the law. The subject and the "befores" are "constituted by the law as the fictive foundation of its own claim to legitimacy" (3). In short, the subject of feminism is "always already" "produced," according to certain exclusionary aims, by the "normative function of language which is said either to reveal or to distort what is assumed to be true about the category of women" (1). We have had occasion to observe a particularly pellucid instance of the "normative function of language" at work in the courts of America in our brief notes on the Sears case earlier in this writing. The latter would not be the first time and, unfortunately, not the last either when an interpretive premise such as Butler offers demonstrates "the rubber meet(ing) the road."

As an antidote to fixities of the normative order, Butler proposes a "radical rethinking of the ontological structures of identity," inclusive of the sex/gender system (5–7) and a view of gender, a "complexity whose totality is permanently deferred, never fully what it is at any given juncture in time" (16). Running parallel to the notion that gender inscribes a kind of closure is the fiction, or misprision, of the "internal coherence of the subject ... the self-identical status of the person," in short, the narrative of identity that is not secured by the "logical or analytical features of personhood" but, rather, by "socially instituted and maintained norms of intelligibility" (16–17). Butler's "domain of intelligibility" is produced and driven ahead by the "heterosexual contract," or as Adrienne Rich put it, "compulsory heterosexuality"; both concepts match up with Butler's "heterosexualization of desire" with its attendant "asymmetrical oppositions between 'feminine' and 'masculine,'" grasped, in turn, "as expressive attributes of 'male' and 'female'" (17). The conclusion that Butler reaches through this analysis of the "metaphysics of substance" is that "gender is not a noun," that is to say, "constituting the identity it is purported to be" (24–25). Rather, it is "always a doing, though not a doing by a subject who may be said to preexist the deed" (25). Reading Nietzsche's "the deed is everything" against the grain, Butler promulgates a corollary that the philosopher, she offers, "would not have anticipated or condoned," and that is this: "There is no gender identity behind the expressions of gender; that identity is *performatively constituted* by the very 'expressions' that are said to be its results" (25; emphasis mine).

By turns, feminist theory arrives at a virtually undecidable "subject of feminism," of an infinite variety of loci and dispositions, in the social and institutional staging of a performativity; what the thematics of "difference" has yielded from this vantage is a wide open horizon of uncertainty, which inaugurates a scene of possibilities. Among the latter is the firm instauration, by the 1990s, into the new century, of feminist studies/gender studies/theory as a *curricular object* that interpolates, or intrudes, itself in the midst of the human sciences as a worthy contender for institutional and capital regard. What began in "maxims and surprise," to quote poet Gwendolyn Brooks, has eventuated in the smooth purring of a medium-sized jet engine or, to shift registers, an evacuation of a street-felt intensity.

STRIDES TOWARD DIVERSITY

But some feminisms took another turn or, more precisely, brought other discursive and experiential persuasions to bear alongside the theoretical; if one reads in isolation either the contributions of Anglo-American feminists or the work produced by black and women of color feminists, the appearance of separate aims would be unmistakable. Even with the occasional acknowledgment among feminists of a shared terrain of values, the plain truth is that the respective historical and political orientation of these communities of scholars and writers conduced to asymptotic lines of investigation. I have often wondered why this apparent outcome is the case, as any attempt at systematic explanation disappears into fog. My hunch, however, is that one of these enfilades of critical inquiry regards "postmodernism" and what it valorizes with a highly skeptical, or an ironical, eye, while the other more readily accepts its tenets and procedures—the decline of the "grand narrative" of history, the deconstruction of "presence," and the "death" of the subject, prominent among them. Any extended look at this query, which we cannot engage here, would then go on to ask why these disparate positions prevail, and the answer seems to be the intervention of "race" and the introduction of the "racialized" subject to the gender/power calculus. Some commentators, however, would argue that "race" is neither an "intervention" nor an "introduction" of any sort to any of the topics related to the sex/gender system, but that it is always already there as the founding prototype of difference in modernity. Even if we agree that "race" is among the West's most perdurable and precious mysticisms, we would also have to admit its unfailing power to effect actual material reality, assume the "looks" of the era in which it appears, and disseminate social value in a way that determines winners and losers. One would be right to answer back that the protocols of the sex/gender system do enough of the same thing most of the time that the pairing of "women" and "minorities" justly resonates with a great deal of force in the world, but as far as I can tell, without wishing to engage the old and unhelpful game of "ranking oppressions," the stigmata of race throw the racialized subject into the threat zone of mortal danger, however tempered or suspended, and *this* makes the difference.

When the editors of *All the Women Are White, All the Blacks Are Men, But Some of Us Are Brave* named their volume, we can well imagine laughter in the room, but not for long and not without the reflex of irony that makes the comedic ever aware of its twin. As the editors explain in the introduction, the text "fulfills a long-term need for a reference text and pedagogical tool" in relationship to black women's studies, which the book was instrumental in bringing into existence at that moment (Hull, Scott, and Smith xxviii). Growing out of a project initiated by Barbara Smith, during her tenure as a member of the Commission on the Status of Women in the Profession (established by the Modern Language Association of America [MLA]), the book was accepted for publication during the winter of 1977–8 by the founding editor of the Feminist Press, Florence Howe; a distinguished feminist scholar and activist in her own right, Howe became the third woman president of the MLA in 1973. The sense of urgency that accompanies *All the Women Are White* is palpable, as the text is called upon to do double duty as both a miscellany and political manifesto. What the title aptly captures is the interstitial situatedness of black women, caught precisely at Lauretis's "vanishing point" in the legislative sweepstakes of civil rights law: as the courts understood "women," they were white people; as the system understood "blacks," they were male people; but as the editors make clear, in case anyone entertained doubt, some "women" were not white, and even "blacks" engendered "women." Such common-sense comprehension turned out to be far less common in places where it mattered, for example, sites of employment, courts of law, among them, than we might have suspected.

A genial solution to this dilemma was posed from the theoretical field a little over a decade later, as we mentioned earlier in this writing, in Kimberle Crenshaw's paradigm of *intersectionality*. A law professor, Crenshaw proposes that the "monocausal" focus on gender "tends to downplay the intersection of gender subordination with race and class" (111). The interplay of converging social and political themes in the lives of black women is defined by Crenshaw as a "structural intersectionality." Material, ideological, and political factors play at once on this conceptual stage, which also evinces in this case an extra good, and that is to say, its figural ease. Perhaps what an American audience takes for granted gains pointed emphasis in another. Black British feminist and writer Reni Eddo-Lodge makes this observation: "America, with its grid-like road system, neatly packed full of perfect rectangles and squares, was the right place for the birth of this metaphor" (159). Although US urban topography is a bit less schematic than Eddo-Lodge asserts here—the notorious traffic circularities of the nation's capital, for example—the intersecting American road of perpendicular angles offers a very useful analogy on the conceptual serviceability of the notion of convergence. The dynamism inherent in intersectional theory approaches the multiplicity of subject positions at stake in Lauretis's "technologies of gender," or Butler's gender as a repertoire of performative practices, but the delineation of features of identity contextualizes race and gender *in relation* to other factors.

This dialogical paradigm appears to have licensed and enabled the archival and historiographical emphases that would come to characterize black feminist criticism and theory as an interdisciplinary project. In short, the weight of history as it is expressed in systematic gestures of anti-black violence cannot be overstated as the central underpinning of black theorization from the earliest years of Black Studies movement on predominantly white campuses across the United States to current iterations of cultural studies. If we could isolate a single anxiety of influence that has decisively configured the nexus between the gender problematic and black feminist thought, we might call it the slavery-carceral complex. At the intersection itself of theories of democratic governance and varied formulations of public policy, the slavery-carceral complex, though we could certainly plot its time line, consists in a repertory of motifs that not only riddle US democracy with contradiction but also throw into crisis the very concept of subject formation in its racialized reference. In any case, the turn to the historiographical register brought the historian and the literary critic onto common ground, as the latter asked questions of the historical in new ways. For example, Deborah McDowell's and Arnold Rampersad's *Slavery and the Literary Imagination* (1989), proposing to examine slavery's discursive and rhetorical regimes, propels the narrative of the former enslaved to the foreground of literary analysis; as the narratives had crucially served the historian as primary source material toward an understanding of the conduct of slavery's protocols, the editors' wish "to have the community of scholars pay closer attention to the body of writing known as slave narratives" advanced the important work of the Institute of Afro-American Culture, convened by the late Darwin Turner over the course of the 1970s, at the flagship campus of the University of Iowa. The institute would become an early training ground for young black postdocs who had taken PhDs in traditional fields of humanistic study but were now responding to their own summons as historical actors to bring to fruition black studies as an elaboration of the human sciences. One of the first fellows of the Afro-American Institute was Frances Smith Foster, whose *Witnessing Slavery* (1979) brings the study of the narratives into conversation with post-1960s contexts and imperatives.

If we decide that slavery, though long past, nonetheless maintains an afterlife, then we are called upon to account for its systematic reincarnations in the contemporary world; it was precisely this vexatious problematic and its ramifications that defined a "subject of feminism" that the second-wave movement could not accommodate within its customary analytical parameters—in brief, the "racial contract," if we might call it such, assigned affiliation and belonging on the basis of material interests and above all, the mandates of history, which dictated a different conceptual path for black feminists: the researches of Angela Davis, bell hooks, Claudia Tate, Ann du Cille, Hortense Spillers, and, more recently, Saidiya Hartman and Daphne Brooks, among others, emerge within this fraught context of contestation between the 1980s and the present; situated quite differently as regards the sex/gender system, because of the effects of slavery, black women as "subjects of feminism" were thought to inscribe processes of "ungendering" (Spillers). But the entire point of movement was to rupture the silence brought on by historical disaster. One of the key anthologies of the period marks precisely the import of language in overcoming silence in its very title—Cheryl A. Walls's *Changing Our Own Words: Essays on Criticism, Theory, and Writing by Black Women*. Illuminating some of the stakes entailed in differences among women as a crucially irreducible feature of feminist interrogation, *Changing Our Own Words* not only provided a platform for prominent black feminist figures of the day but also reinforced the notion that a critical aspect of feminist work unfolded as a collaborative gesture. One of the most fruitful of such engagements has yielded the work of Chandra Talpade Mohanty and M. Jacqui Alexander in the field of Third World/postcolonial feminisms.

In their introduction to *Feminist Geneaologies, Colonial Legacies, Democratic Futures*, Mohanty and Alexander succinctly sum up those differences that we have attempted to define against the grain as the mark of alternative feminist theories and praxes. As they explain the work of their anthology, *Feminist Geneaologies* "aims to provide a comparative, relational, and historically-based conception of feminism, one that differs markedly from the liberal-pluralist understanding of feminism, an inheritance of the predominantly liberal roots of American feminist praxis" (xvi). Perhaps we could say that the entire feminist project in its elaboration over time has been working toward an *expansion* of the concept of the human, if not a reformulation of it altogether; the doing so will certainly necessitate going beyond geophysical and nationalist limitations toward the global imagination as well as exceeding the liberal subject in its myopic gaze. In short, in the irretrievable play of difference along its various lines of stress, feminist movement continues to call us to our better angels.

NOTES

1 Nancy Fraser, "Feminism, Capitalism and the Cunning of History," in *Feminist Theory: A Reader*, eds. Wendy K. Kolmar and Frances Bartkowski, 4th edn. (New York: McGraw Hill, 2013). Part VII. 1995–2012, pp. 555–60; quotation at p. 556.

2 Catharine R. Stimpson and Gilbert Herdt, eds. *Critical Terms for the Study of Gender* (Chicago, IL: University of Chicago Press, 2014); p. 12.

3 Hester Eisenstein and Alice Jardine, eds. *The Future of Difference* (Boston, MA: G.K. Hall, 1980); xv.

4 *In A Different Voice: Psychological Theory and Women's Development* (Cambridge, MA: Harvard University Press, 1982).

5 *All the Blacks Are Men, All the Women Are White, but Some of Us Are Brave*, eds. Gloria Hull, Patricia Bell Scott, and Barbara Smith (New York: Feminist Press, 1982).

6 Cherrie Morago and Gloria Anzaldua, eds. *This Bridge Called My Back: Writings by Radical Women of Color* (Watertown, MA: Persephone Press, 1981).

7 Mari J. Matsuda, Charles R. Lawrence, III, Richard Delgado, and Kimberle Williams Crenshaw, eds. *Words That Wound: Critical Race Theory, Assaultive Speech, and the First Amendment* (Boulder, CO: Westview Press, 1993).

8 "The Traffic in Women: On the 'Political Economy' of Sex," in Toward an Anthropology of Women, ed. Rayna R. Reiter (New York: Monthly Review Press, 1975).

9 Joan W. Scott, "Deconstructing Equality-versus-Difference: Or, the Uses of Post-Structuralist Theory for Feminism," in *Feminist Studies Reader*, eds. Wendy K. Kolmar and Frances Bartkowski. 3rd edn. (New York: McGraw-Hill, 2010; Part VI: 1985–95, pp. 388–97).

10 The 1964 Civil Rights Act, which legislation effectively mooted the "separate but equal" practices, enacted in the United States as an outcome of *Plessy v. Ferguson* (1896), reenforced the concept of the equal protection of the law, already championed in the Fourteenth Amendment of the US Constitution, and by way of Title VII of the Act, prohibited "employers from discriminating against employees on the basis of sex, race, color, national origin, and religion. It generally applies to employers with fifteen or more employees, including federal, state, and local governments." https://www.eeoc.gov

11 Samuel G. Freedman, "Of History and Politics: Bitter Feminist Debate," *New York Times*, Archives 1986.

12 Iris Marion Young, "Difference and Social Policy: Reflections in the Context of Social Movements," in *The Feminist Philosophy Reader*, eds. Alison Bailey and Chris Cuomo (New York: McGraw-Hill, 2008); Chap. 8: Feminist Political Philosophies, pp. 638–48; quotation at pp. 638–39.

13 Alice Jardine, "Prelude: The Future of Difference," in *The Future of Difference*, xxv.

WORKS CITED

Beauvoir, Simone de, *The Second Sex*. Trans. H. M. Parshley. New York: Vintage Books, 1974.

Butler, Judith. *Gender Trouble: Feminism and the Subversion of Identity*. New York: Routledge, 1990.

Eddo-Lodge, Reni. *Why I'm No Longer Talking to White People about Race*. London: Bloomsbury Circus, 2017.

Eisenstein, Hester, and Alice Jardine, eds. *The Future of Difference*. Boston, MA: G. K. Hall, 1980.

Fraser, Nancy. "Feminism, Capitalism, and the Cunning of History." *Feminist Theory: A Reader*. Eds. Wendy K. Kolmar and Frances Bartkowski, 4th edn. New York: McGraw Hill, 2013.

Freedman, Samuel G. "Of History and Politics: Bitter Feminist Debate." *New York Times*, Archives 1986. Mobile.nytimes.com.

Gilligan, Carolyn. *In a Different Voice: Psychological Theory and Women's Development*. Cambridge, MA: Harvard UP, 1982.

Hull, (Akasha) Gloria, Patricia Bell Scott, and Barbara Smith, eds. *All the Women Are White, All the Blacks Are Men, but Some of Us Are Brave*. Old Westbury: The Feminist P, 1982.

Irigaray, Luce. "This Sex Which Is Not One." Trans. Catherine Porter with Carolyn Burke. Ithaca: Cornell UP, 1985.

Lauretis, Teresa de. *Alice Doesn't: Feminism, Semiotics, Cinema*. Bloomington: Indiana UP, 1984.

Lauretis, Teresa de. *Technologies of Gender: Essays on Theory, Film, and Fiction*. Bloomington: Indiana UP, 1987.

Marks, Elaine, and Isabelle de Courtivron, eds. *New French Feminisms: An Anthology*. New York: Schocken Books, 1981; ix–xiii.

Matsuda, Mari J., Charles R. Lawrence, III, Richard Delgado, and Kimberle Williams Crenshaw, eds. *Words That Wound: Critical Race Theory, Assaultive Speech, and the First Amendment*. Boulder, CO: Westview Press, 1993.

McDowell, Deborah E., and Arnold Rampersad, eds. *Slavery and the Literary Imagination*. Selected Papers from the English Institute, 1987. Baltimore, MD: Johns Hopkins UP, 1989.

Mohanty, Chandra Talpade, and M. Jacqui Alexander, eds. *Feminist Geneaologies, Colonial Legacies, Democratic Futures*. New York: Routledge, 1997.

Rubin, Gayle. "The Traffic in Women: On the 'Political Economy of Sex.'" *Toward An Anthropology of Women*. Ed. Rayna R. Reiter. New York: Monthly Review P, 1975.

Scott, Joan W. "Deconstructing Equality-versus-Difference: Or, the Uses of Post-Structuralist Theory for Feminism." *Feminist Theory: A Reader*. Eds. Wendy K. Kolmar and Frances Bartkowski, 3rd edn. New York: McGraw Hill, 2010; Part VI: 1985–95; 388–97.

Spillers, Hortense J. "Mama's Baby, Papa's Maybe: An American Grammar Book." *Black, White, and in Color: Essays on American Literature and Culture*. Chicago, IL: U of Chicago P, 2003.

Stimpson, Catharine R., and Gilbert Herdt, eds. *Critical Terms for the Study of Gender*. Chicago, IL: U of Chicago P, 2014; 12.

Wall, Cheryl A., ed. *Changing Our Own Words: Essays on Criticism, Theory, and Writing By Black Women*. New Brunswick, NJ: Rutgers UP, 1989.

Young, Iris Marion. "Difference and Social Policy: Reflections in the Context of Social Movements." *The Feminist Philosophy Reader*. Eds. Alison Bailey and Chris Cuomo. New York: McGraw Hill, 2008.

CHAPTER FOUR

Birth

FANNY SÖDERBÄCK

INTRODUCTION: FEMINISM AND BIRTH

Since Simone de Beauvoir's early analysis and critique of patriarchy as a system that, among other things, reduces women to mothers and confines them to the realm of reproduction, feminists have been wrestling with the question of whether birth and motherhood pose a threat to or promote women's liberation. In an early assessment of the relationship between feminism and birth, Mary O'Brien suggests that feminist theory in fact starts "within the process of human reproduction" (8). Almost three decades later, Imogen Tyler notes that birth "remains a pressing political question for feminism" (2). To be sure, many of the topics so pertinent to feminist theory—from emancipatory issues such as reproductive rights, the right to work and equal pay, and women's health, to more conceptual concerns such as time, embodiment, desire, and sexual difference—force us to return to questions of birth and reproduction.

This chapter looks at the role birth has played in feminist discourse across disciplines—as a philosophical concept, as a lived experience, and as a battleground for women's rights—and maps the terrain of a set of highly contested and ideologically embedded questions about our shared beginnings in the event of birth and the role that women have played, play, are expected to play, or refuse to play in the realm of reproduction. In what follows, I grapple with the philosophical privileging of death over birth, the paradoxical ways in which women have been systematically robbed of their active role in procreation while at the same time being locked in the reproductive sphere, and, finally, the role reproductive technologies have played in feminist discourse about birth, and the importance of intersectional analysis to avoid the all-too-common bias toward white and Western, cisgendered, straight, middle-class, able-bodied experiences and discourses about birth.

THE HUMAN CONDITION OF BEING BORN

In the Western philosophical canon, the human condition has been framed first and foremost in terms of mortality. As Robin May Schott puts it, "Fewer philosophers have looked to the concept of birth in order to find a horizon of meaning or an inspiration for philosophical reflection, as Heidegger and innumerable other philosophers have done with the topic of death" (1). When broaching the question of our finitude as one concerned with death alone, we obscure and overlook equally important questions: What does it mean to be born? What does it mean to think the human condition as marked not only by death (and a meaningful relation to our death-to-come) but also by birth (and the capacity to reflect on our having-been-born)?[1] And what would it mean to think human finitude in terms of the lived embodied experience of inhabiting a time span *between* birth and death? These are questions that are curiously absent from traditional philosophical accounts but that appear with increasing frequency in feminist philosophical work.[2]

Much feminist attention to the human condition of birth draws from Hannah Arendt's insistence, in *The Human Condition*, that the fundamental category of political thought should be natality rather than mortality (9). Adriana Cavarero has argued that the central position of natality within Arendt's work "brings about a subversive shift in perspective with respect to the patriarchal tradition that has always thrived on the category of death" (*In Spite of Plato* 6–7). Indeed, in a 1971 lecture at The New School for Social Research, Arendt declared that if "the Greeks defined man as the 'mortal', men are now defined by their natality, as the 'natals'" (quoted in Bowen-Moore 22). What this means, for Arendt, is that humans first and foremost get identified as having a supreme capacity for beginning—the fact of birth conditions us to break out of predictable patterns, to institute change, to take initiative, and to bring about novelty.

Arendt, however, makes a point of distinguishing our first appearance in the world through the event of birth from our capacity to appear again, through action and speech, on the shared scene of political life. With action, she suggests, "we insert ourselves into the human world, and this insertion is like a second birth, in which we confirm and take upon ourselves the naked fact of our original physical appearance" (Arendt 176–7). This "second birth"—our ability precisely to begin anew through action—ultimately takes center stage in the Arendtian corpus. The capacity for beginning is announced by the birth of a child, but it is only actualized as freedom once we put it to work in a shared space of equals. If Arendt is the supreme thinker of (political) natality, she is thus not really a thinker of (embodied) birth, and this has led feminists to critically examine her work.[3] Lisa Guenther eloquently voices one such criticism: "the opposition between a laborious, private, and feminine labor of reproduction and an active, public, political, and apparently sexually undifferentiated 'second birth' conspires to reduce the maternal body to a biological or animal condition for a human existence from which she herself is excluded" (*Gift of the Other* 40). In short, Arendt's discussion of natality offers an important corrective to the philosophical tradition's one-sided focus on death and mortality, but she nevertheless perpetuates that same tradition's erasure of birthed embodiment and maternal agency, by insisting on a version of natality that remains curiously abstract-disembodied and detached from the gendered horizon of birth.[4] As such, Arendt's account is limited, but it has propelled a body of feminist work that seeks to challenge, in more profound ways, the philosophical paradigm of death, offering instead both ontological and ethical accounts grounded in the fact of birth.

It is interesting to note that much of such feminist work comes out of a British academic context.[5] Christine Battersby's "fleshy metaphysics" has been formative in this regard. In *The Phenomenal Woman*, natality (here understood as fundamentally embodied and rooted in sexual difference, contra Arendt) is the first of a series of concepts put to work to challenge patriarchal metaphysics and ontologies that take for granted Enlightenment ideals of equality and autonomy. From the vantage point of natality—and a critical examination of women's role as birth- and caregivers—Battersby proposes that we articulate a metaphysical framework grounded in ontologies of dependence, relationality, and a constitutively ambiguous relationship between "self" and "other" (8–9). What attention to birth can do, in other words, is to upend false (masculine) fantasies about sovereign subjectivity and offer instead a more complex ontology of selfhood that acknowledges our leaky, relational, interdependent, and precarious nature—the fact that we are con-stitutively exposed and given over to others, never simply "thrown" into the world but indeed delivered there by another, most paradigmatically (although not necessarily) our mother. And if traditional accounts of human mortality have tended to emphasize death as distinctly our own, feminist work on birth also forces us to rethink death in relational terms, as exemplified by the work of Alison Stone ("Natality").[6]

Stone, also a British feminist philosopher, seeks to overcome philosophy's neglect of the human condition of birth. Her forthcoming *Being Born: Birth and Philosophy* offers perhaps the most systematic philosophical analysis of birth to date. In the introduction, she lists several issues that come into focus when we take natality to be a defining fea-ture of human life, namely dependency, relationality, situatedness, embeddedness in webs of social power, vulnerability, radical contingency, various forms of natal anxiety (the awareness that we are not masters in our own house), as well as a temporal structuring of human life and experience that does not always privilege the future (as Heidegger, because of his focus on death, would have it) but that sees the past as no less fundamental a temporal mode of human experience.

If Arendt's account of natality was wholly embedded in a discourse about new beginnings, radical futurity, and our capacity for novelty, it is indeed the past that is at stake for many feminist thinkers who urge us to grapple with the human condition of birth. Attending to birth means shifting the emphasis in the stories we tell about our past. From where do we come? From whom do we originate? If philosophical, theological, and political concerns with origins and foundations have been deeply patriarchal-paternal in nature—the male appropriation of birth ranges from the Socratic midwife, to genesis myths that attribute exclusive procreative powers to male gods, to the founding fathers of modern nation-states—feminist thinkers have sought to reclaim maternal origins and women's active role in birthing (and having birthed) not only babies but also works of art, philosophical ideas, and political ideals.

At the foundation of much feminist thought about birth lies the claim that our culture is marked by matricide (Jacobs). Paradigmatic in this regard are the by now major bodies of work by French feminist Luce Irigaray and Italian feminist Adriana Cavarero. From her early *Speculum of the Other Woman* to her more recent *In the Beginning, She Was* and *To Be Born*, Irigaray has perhaps offered the most systematic account of the erasure of our maternal-material beginnings and the matricide that founds patriarchal culture.[7] Her famous reading of Plato's cave—one that takes the cave to be a perverted mirror image of a womb, or *hystera*, establishing the now common view that the founding moment of metaphysics (our journey out of the cave into a Platonic heaven of abstract-universal forms) is premised by the erasure and silencing of our maternal-material beginnings—has been both tone-setting and disputed in the feminist literature (Irigaray 243–364).[8] Speaking more recently of the matricide that founds our culture, Irigaray asks why man has "likened the woman's part in generation to a simple nourishing environment, keeping for himself providing for the germ of individuation" and wonders how it is possible that "this error has remained ignored for so long" (*In the Beginning* 81).

Cavarero similarly returns to Plato in an attempt to trace the trajectory by which women, and mothers, have been written out of the story about human origins.[9] Her early *In Spite of Plato* is exemplary among texts that try to subvert the patriarchal-paternal philosophical paradigm of death and reclaim (as in steal back, give voice to) repressed feminine-maternal experiences and figures, such as Penelope, Demeter, and Diotima, all of whom have a rich and complex relationship to the human condition of birth. But while the male appropriation of birth might begin in ancient Greek mythology and philosophy, it certainly doesn't end there. It is indeed symptomatic, Cavarero notes, that Arendt's example of the original scene of birth as a locus for plurality is the creation of Adam and Eve—two individuals who, notoriously, were not really *born* at all, but rather *created* by a paternal-disembodied God (Arendt 8; Cavarero, "'A Child'" 20). As Cavarero puts it, "Arendt does not highlight the concept of birth as coming from a mother's womb, but accepts the Greek [and, we might add, biblical] meaning of birth as coming from nothing" (*In Spite of Plato* 6). Again, we are reminded that Western patriarchal culture is founded on a matricidal logic, one that depends on repression, erasure, and a denial of our maternal-material roots: "Man, with a masculine—universal—neutral valence, is a term from a language that has turned its gaze away from the place of birth, measuring existence on an end point that bears no memory of its beginning" (69).

THE FEMALE CONDITION OF GIVING BIRTH

If women have been deprived of their active role in procreation, having been allotted instead a docile role as mere receptacles, or erased altogether as birthing agents (what I have described above as the matricide that founds our culture), they have arguably, as Beauvoir maintained, at the same time been equated with the function of motherhood and the reproductive realm. This paradox is the result of a double repression of sorts: the forgetting of woman *as* mother and, at the same time, the forgetting of woman as anything *other* than mother. Along these lines, Nancy Tuana has convincingly argued that women, paradoxically, have been *robbed* of their role in procreation while simultaneously being *reduced* to the role of mothers, and that upholding them to such double standard has served to maintain women's perceived inferiority (111). From ancient Babylonian and Greek creation myths, via the biblical Genesis, to modern science, the female power to give birth has been both *underemphasized* (as a way of denying such female power and appropriating it onto an all-powerful masculine divinity or medical-scientific establishment) and *overemphasized* (as a way of establishing women's inferiority to men by way of tethering them to the embodied realm of biological labor and the survival of the species).

This paradoxical double repression has given rise to debate in the feminist literature, where scholars of birth and motherhood are navigating the challenging task of reclaiming women's power to give birth while at the same time liberating women from the social demand that they be mothers. Navigating this minefield typically entails tackling fraught issues such as essentialism, embodiment, and sexuality,[10] and demands that we engage in critical examination of the oftentimes heteronormative, ableist, classist, racist, and cisnormative features of traditional as well as feminist attempts to grapple with issues of birth and reproduction (as I will do in the final section of this chapter).

Beauvoir's analysis of women's lived experience, which is clearly guided by an awareness that women have played and continue to play an all-too important role in reproduction and child-rearing, has been formative, especially for early feminist debates about birth and motherhood.[11] For Beauvoir, one of the foremost reasons for the oppression and othering of women is their role in procreation, which has locked them in a state of immanence and prevented them from embracing their human capacity for transcendence and freedom. She "cautions women against assuming the role of mother and getting caught in the trap of reproducing the species at the expense of other projects" (Oliver, "Motherhood" 762). Beauvoir's own commitment to a feminist-existential emancipatory project that seeks to liberate women from such a state of facticity is thus tied to a critique of the institution of motherhood as we know it. It is telling that her chapter on motherhood opens with a twelve-page discussion of abortion and offers only two pages on the experience of giving birth (Beauvoir 524–35, 547–9; see also Stone, "Beauvoir" 123). While Beauvoir's rejection of motherhood has been overstated, and interesting analysis has emerged that paints more complex and ambivalent a picture of her views on motherhood,[12] it is clear that for Beauvoir reproductive labor as we know it represents an obstacle on the path toward women's liberation. Questions about birth are thus intimately tied up with women's capacity to choose *not* to give birth—by making contraceptives and family planning more widely accessible and by making abortion legal, accessible, and affordable.

To be sure, the social expectation that women reproduce is far-reaching and powerful. As Battersby puts it, "Whether or not a woman is lesbian, infertile, post-menopausal or childless, in modern western cultures she will be assigned a subject-position linked to a body that has perceived potentialities for birth" (16). Judith Butler speaks of a "compulsory obligation on women's bodies to reproduce" (*Gender Trouble* 115). And such compulsory obligation is, of course, intimately tied to social and economic inequalities between women and men such that women's liberation ultimately rests on their capacity to reproduce without being swallowed up by the demands of maternal labor; their right to embody motherhood in ways that challenge traditional norms and expectations; or their ability to reject motherhood altogether. Women's "troubling talent for making other bodies" (Haraway 253 n8) continues to haunt those who are now or are about to become mothers, those who choose not to be mothers, those who struggle to become mothers, or those who have given birth but don't identify as mothers.[13]

As much as some feminist and queer-theoretical work from the last few decades has sought to reject the centrality of motherhood as a feminist issue and question the very value of reproduction (oftentimes because of worries about the biological essentialism and heteronormativity that pervade much work on motherhood and reproduction),[14] a body of feminist thought has also emerged that seeks to challenge specifically *patriarchal* accounts of reproduction, birth, and motherhood, offering more complex analysis instead that depicts women as birthing agents rather than victims laboring under the weight of species life. Under this rubric, we might include the following: (1) historically situated work that seeks to challenge the patriarchal-scientific rendering of women as passive receptacles, as well as the profound medicalization of pregnancy, labor, and delivery; (2) psychoanalytical work that attempts to correct and move beyond traditional Oedipal accounts that reduce mothers to objects of incestuous desire and representatives of mute embodiment; and (3) phenomenological work that grapples with the multifaceted lived experience of gestation and childbirth. I want to examine each of these in some detail, in an effort to explain the stakes in these bodies of work and to show how they have contributed to a more nuanced portrayal of women's role in procreation.

First, historically, traditional scientific accounts of reproduction have tended to reduce women to a role of passivity. As Kelly Oliver puts it, "The history of medical and biological accounts of conception and gestation construct the maternal body as a passive container that exists for the sake of the 'unborn child'" (*Family Values* 13). Feminist assessments of reproductive biology and science tend to bring attention to, and challenge, the all-too-common view that mothers are passive, inferior, and helpless, which arguably has served to justify women's lack of citizenship and rights. In her chapter on biology in *The Second Sex*, Beauvoir offers a historical analysis of how the role of women in procreation has been reduced to passive receptivity, from Aristotle via Hippocrates to modern science (21–48). The ancients established the long-lasting view that woman is a mere passive receiver while man is the sole creative agent in procreation.[15] Tuana's analysis of the primacy of the male begetter in embryological theory from ancient to modern science confirms this view: "He was the master artist of human generation; she merely supplied the raw materials for his work" (130).[16]

But the most comprehensive account of the medicalization of birth and the scientific rendering of women as passive objects can be found in Adrienne Rich's seminal *Of Woman Born*. Here, Rich argues for the need to "distinguish between two meanings of motherhood," namely "the *potential relationship* of any woman to her powers of reproduction and to children," on the one hand, and "the *institution*, which aims at ensuring that that potential—and all women—shall remain under male control," on the other (13). In a chapter treating the history of obstetrics, Rich is careful to point out that questions about how women have given birth, who has helped them, how, and why, are not neutral-scientific but rather political in nature (128). She traces the development from a time when birth tended to be in the hands of female midwives to one dominated by the male province of modern obstetrics,[17] foreshadowing a present (at least in the United States) where birthing rarely happens without intense medical interventions, such as induced labor through the use of the synthetic hormone Pitocin or the rupturing of membranes; pain relief such as epidural anesthesia; and assisted delivery through the use of forceps, vacuums, episiotomy (surgical cuts to the perineum), or cesarean sections.[18] The shift from midwifery to obstetrics, and the concomitant relocation of labor and delivery from homes to hospitals, depended on an ideological turn that involved a two-century epidemic, starting in the seventeenth century, of "puerperal fever" (a misnomer for a deadly kind of blood poisoning) that killed not only Mary Wollstonecraft but also thousands of other women who had been forced to give birth in hospitals. At a time when "antisepsis, asepsis, contagion, and bacterial infection were still unheard-of," physicians, surgeons, and midwives alike were potential carriers of bacteria, but "the hands of the physician or of the surgeon, unlike those of the midwife, often came directly from cases of disease to cases of childbirth," which led to an increased risk for infection (Rich 151). Even entirely uncomplicated births meant almost certain death for laboring women.[19]

While the problem of contagion has been mostly eliminated in US hospitals with access to clean water and disinfectants, the *alienation* of medicalized labor remains a reality for many women today: "The loneliness, the sense of abandonment, of being imprisoned, powerless, and depersonalized is a chief collective memory of women who have given birth in American hospitals," Rich asserts (176). Iris Marion Young confirms this view, maintaining that "woman's experience in pregnancy and birthing is often alienated because her condition tends to be defined as a disorder, because medical instruments objectify internal processes in such a way that they devalue a woman's experience of those processes, and because the social relations and instrumentation of the medical setting reduce her control over her experience" (56). American birthing narratives often do give voice to this sense of alienation. Naomi Wolf, for example, speaks of the "loneliness and strangeness" that characterized her own birthing experience, one marked by a "seemingly inevitable high-tech intervention" that left her feeling like a passive adjunct in the delivery room, someone lacking an active role in the process, disempowered by social shame, fear, and unwanted (as well as unexplained) medical interventions (135–8).

In light of the intense medicalization of birth—and the resulting alienation women attest to feeling in the delivery room—we witness a renewed call for so-called "natural" birth, a resurgence in home birthing, and increased demand for doulas and midwives as an alternative to the "male province" of obstetric care. These movements are extremely important as a step for women to reclaim birth as their own domain. But it is worth noting that such developments and trends by and large remain limited to the Global North. As Candace Johnson has pointed out, "For some women, medical intervention in pregnancy and childbirth is inherently oppressive, whereas for other women such intervention is a marker of privilege" ("Negotiating" 65). In her own work, Johnson draws from in-depth interviews she conducted with pregnant women and recent mothers in Canada, the United States, Cuba, and Honduras (Johnson, *Maternal Transition*). It is worth noting, in light of her research, that every day approximately 830 women die from preventable causes related to pregnancy and childbirth (roughly 303,000 per year), usually due to limited access to quality antenatal and maternal care. Ninety-nine percent of these deaths occur in the Global South (WHO). In the United States, "a black woman is 22 percent more likely to die from heart disease than a white woman, 71 percent more likely to perish from cervical cancer, but 243 percent more likely to die from pregnancy- or childbirth-related causes," and "black infants are twice as likely as white babies to die before their first birthday" (N. Martin). Birth is still very much a matter of life and death for birthing women in large parts of the world, including in the United States, especially if they are black, and the call for "natural" birth must be understood in relation to power dynamics, privilege, and access to quality maternal care.[20]

Second, feminists have been compelled to correct deeply entrenched views about birth and motherhood embedded in the psychoanalytic tradition and to challenge an Oedipal logic premised by a "silent mother and threatening father" (Oliver, *Family Values* 56). According to the traditional Oedipal model formulated by Sigmund Freud and developed by Jacques Lacan, if the child is to be able to enter into the sociolinguistic sphere, separation from the mother is required. As Oliver puts it, "Because she is associated with nature, the mother must be left behind, killed off, in order for the child to be social" (*Family Values* 54). Psychoanalytic theory thus follows the matricidal logic examined by Irigaray and others, and it is precisely in the works of Freud, and by extension Lacan, that Irigaray locates the erasure of birth, the compulsory rupture with the mother, and the concomitant assumption that subjectivity and agency are inherently paternal-masculine (*Speculum* 13–129).

There is a rich and interesting body of work that feminists tend to draw from as they seek to challenge the primacy of the father and turn attention back to the mother and to the possibility of maternal agency. From Melanie Klein's focus on a pre-Oedipal stage of development, and the role of the maternal breast (good or bad) for early psychic development (Klein), via D. W. Winnicott's emphasis on the mother–infant dyad and the good enough mother (Winnicott), to Jessica Benjamin's insistence that mothers are active agents in the process of infantile socialization, which is to say that no paternal law is needed to tear children away from their mothers (Benjamin), psychoanalysts have contested the Freudian-Lacanian assumption that an unbridgeable gap, or abyss, separates maternal nature and paternal culture (*Family Values* 53–61).

The most important—as well as contested—thinker of the role of the maternal in psychosexual development is, arguably, Julia Kristeva.[21] On the one hand, Kristeva "retains a version of the traditional Freudian-Lacanian view that the paternal figure is necessary as the 'third term' to break up the mother-child pair and thereby introduce the child into language and social life" (Stone 62). As such, Kristeva upholds the inevitability of matricide: "For man and for woman the loss of the mother is a biological and psychic necessity, the first step on the way to becoming autonomous. Matricide is our vital necessity, the sine-qua-non of our individuation" (Kristeva, *Black Sun* 27–8). On the other hand, as Stone has pointed out, Kristeva "qualifies and transforms the idea of the paternal third term, and re-appraises early maternal relations, in ways that point in anti-matricidal directions" (Stone, *Feminism* 62).

While those of us who have a mother, in different ways, try to separate from her in order to become differentiated individuals and speaking beings, we also remain entangled with her as we experienced her in the earliest stages of our life[22]—the organizing force of our most archaic affective and bodily environment, what Kristeva names the *semiotic chora* (*Revolution* 25–30). Throughout the course of life, we maintain a complex bond to this archaic relationship, and it erupts in works of art, poetry, and other sublimated forms of expression. And as the process of separation begins, early on in life, it is far from clear-cut or absolute. Instead, it is marked by an ambivalent process of continual redrawing of boundaries—what Kristeva names *abjection*. Since the infant feels like it is "one" with its mother, the very process of separating from her inevitably involves a sort of self-separation, or splitting. The process can be violent, painful, and messy: "During that course in which 'I' become," Kristeva writes, "I give birth to myself amid the violence of sobs, of vomit" (*Powers of Horror* 3).

In "Stabat Mater"—arguably her most important essay on motherhood—the very structure of the essay incorporates two polar aspects of the maternal figure: on the one hand, the most idealized and phantasmatic of them all—the figure of the Virgin Mary— and on the other hand, what Kristeva herself refers to as "the real experience that fantasy overshadows"—a poetic account of pregnancy and childbirth grounded in her own personal-singular experience thereof ("Stabat Mater" 234). As Kristeva has noted elsewhere, woman as mother tends to be either altogether *absent* or overly *idealized* (*This Incredible Need* 47). She is either depicted as a *hole* (at the root of the Hebrew word for woman, *nekeva*) or as a divine or royal *whole* (in the form of the Virgin Mother). Kristeva's work is an attempt to overcome this false and damaging dichotomy, and to develop an account of maternity that is more complex, more ambiguous, more messy. Marked by desire and disgust both at once, the maternal cannot be done away with or silenced, nor can it be pinned down in an idealized or frozen image. We must reckon with the mother, wrestle with the experience of motherhood and our relationship to our mothers, or else we are missing something about who we are, who we can be, and how we might be otherwise.

Third, then, there is a body of feminist phenomenological work that seeks to account for this lived experience not only of motherhood but also of pregnancy and childbirth. Indeed, phenomenological work on pregnancy specifically has become so common (although mostly very recently, and notably with a bias toward distinctly Western experiences and contexts) that an anthology gathering a host of current contributions is now available (Bornemark and Smith). Like Kristeva, feminist phenomenologists writing on these issues tend to challenge and complicate both the reduction of women to passive vessels of gestation and the idealized image of motherhood. They insist on narratives that acknowledge and give voice to the complex-ambiguous-messy nature of motherhood and maternal subjectivity. We find an early example of this already in Beauvoir, who describes gestation as a thoroughly ambiguous and contradictive phenomenon. The expectant woman, she notes, can experience pregnancy "both as an enrichment and a mutilation; the fetus is part of her body, and it is a parasite exploiting her; she possesses it, and is possessed by it; it encapsulates the whole future, and in carrying it, she feels as vast as the world; but this very richness annihilates her, she has the impression of not being anything else" (Beauvoir 538). Maurice Merleau-Ponty—whose work on embodied perception has been deeply influential for feminist phenomenologists—paints a similarly ambivalent picture of pregnant embodiment, identifying the source of such extreme ambivalence to the perceived loss of unified selfhood (101).[23]

 Indeed, what many feminist phenomenological accounts of pregnancy, childbirth, and mothering have in common is their insistence that these experiences force us to revise basic Western assumptions about personhood, such as the perceived unity of the subject, the boundedness of our bodies, the autonomy and integrity of the self, or the "mineness" that we tend to attribute to the ego.[24] Even intersubjectivity is troubled by pregnancy, since it involves one subject (gestating mother) and one subject-to-be (fetus), and is therefore perhaps better described in terms of *intercorporeality*.[25] It has been argued that pregnancy, childbirth, and mothering have their own temporality and challenge basic Western philosophical presuppositions about time and temporal experience.[26] And it is evident that they put to test Western dualistic distinctions such as self/other, own/alien, same/different, active/passive, inside/outside, subject/object, reason/affect, and mind/body.[27] If traditional philosophers have managed to mostly ignore the phenomenon of pregnancy— "for philosophy, it is as if pregnancy has never happened" (Smith 15)—feminist philosophies of pregnancy, childbirth, and mothering set out to transform, scrutinize, and decenter the very nature of philosophy as we know it, and its most fundamental conceptual presuppositions.[28]

 The characterization of the pregnant body as fundamentally "split"—which serves to undermine basic distinctions between subject and object—originates in Kristeva's discussion of the manner in which "cells fuse, split, and proliferate; volumes grow, tissues stretch, and body fluids change rhythm, speeding up or slowing down," within the "simultaneously dual and alien space" of gestation ("Motherhood" 237). In her now classic "Pregnant Embodiment: Subjectivity and Alienation," Young draws from Kristeva as well as Merleau-Ponty as she considers "some of the experiences of pregnancy from the pregnant subject's viewpoint" and describes pregnant bodily existence as "decentered, split, or doubled in several ways" such that the pregnant woman "experiences her body as herself and not herself" (46).[29] As Oliver has pointed out in her reading of Young, pregnancy "opens the body to otherness in ways that make the experience porous physically and mentally. This porosity … can be a model for more open relationships with others and a more porous notion of subjectivity than philosophers typically provide" ("Motherhood" 772–3).

 This view of pregnancy as an experience that complicates the boundaries of self and other as well as self and world, and the birthing process as "the most extreme suspension of the bodily distinction between inner and outer" (Young 50), runs through much work on pregnancy and childbirth (Lupton 52–5). Gail Weiss uses similar language to describe her own pregnancy and highlights again the potential of birth to challenge traditionally held Western views about subjectivity: "Fluidity and expansiveness, rather than the myths of wholeness and closure (which I don't believe any of us, male or female, ever truly experience) were the tangible signs of this newly discovered bodily integrity" (53). And beyond pregnancy and birth, even the first weeks of motherhood "can provide fecund insights into this blurring of subject and object, of transcendence and immanence" in what Sally Fisher has described as "a continuous, lived dance of self and other" (197).

 Young is careful to remind her readers that the analysis she offers is limited to "the specific experience of women in technologically sophisticated Western societies" (47).

Indeed, much has been written on how technological equipment such as ultrasound imaging plays a central role in shaping the kind of experiences we have examined here.[30] But it is also worth noting that the Western bias in much phenomenological work on pregnancy in no way is limited to the role of technology or even medicalization. Insofar as this body of work by and large seeks to challenge Western notions of selfhood, time, or dualist thinking, they are for the most part implicitly assuming that pregnant embodiment itself is a Western phenomenon. As Deborah Lupton points out, Western individuality "differs radically from the relational model of personhood and embodiment common in non-western cultures, which depends on creating and maintaining social ties with other persons/bodies and which views bodies as communal rather than as individuated from each other" (53). There is not much work on the lived experience of pregnant embodiment in non-Western cultural contexts where autonomous selfhood, linear time, or dualist constructions of reality are not the norm, and where the experience of pregnancy would not represent an anomaly. A welcome exception is Tsipy Ivry's *Embodying Culture*, an ethnographic study comparing two contexts, Israel and Japan, that both rely heavily on medicalization and sophisticated technology, but where differences in cultural conceptions of embodiment and personhood inevitably shape the lived experience of pregnancy as such (Ivry 123–228).

Young also notes that her analysis is limited to chosen pregnancies (47). Caroline Lundquist has taken it upon herself to expand Young's account to include experiences of unwanted pregnancies so as to offer a more inclusive phenomenological analysis that can account for "rejected" pregnancies (unwanted pregnancies that nevertheless must be carried to term) and "denied" pregnancies (in which the gestating parent is unaware of their pregnancy until the very end of the gestational process). In the case of rejected pregnancies, experienced for example by victims of rape who are forced to carry the fetus to term, "the fetus is *radically* other, even hostile," and the splitting that Kristeva and Young spoke of becomes a "radical internal division between 'the flesh which engenders flesh' and the desiring or willing subject who cannot control that incarnate teleological process" (Lundquist 143). It is not rare that this experience of being torn from within culminates in infanticide, or at the very least abuse or neglect of the newborn child—all topics rarely discussed in the literature on pregnancy and birth.

Talia Welsh has stressed that feminist phenomenological accounts of pregnancy, childbirth, and mothering importantly have not only philosophical but also practical import: they "are both descriptive and prescriptive; they point out lacunae in universal theories of the subject as well as the political dangers of consciously or unconsciously ignoring our experiences of birth and dependence" (283). A case in point would be Fisher's account of her own postpartum experience, one that inspired her not only to reconceive theories of embodiment and subjectivity but also to make her own philosophical analysis a conceptual basis for a "practical, political critique of workplace policies in the U.S. [such as maternity and family-leave laws] that are inherited from our liberal political tradition," and that presuppose that "once the baby is born the woman returns to being a distinct, unified, and separate individual again, according to our Western notion of personhood" (194–5).

To be sure, the legal terrain of pregnancy and childbirth extends far beyond maternity and family-leave laws, and current debates on reproductive technologies, queer and trans parenting, or intersex births—to mention but a few of the most thorny issues—shed sharp light on how this "Western notion of personhood" is indeed a thing of the past, one that feminist scholarship on birth has troubled so deeply that it is rendered obsolete.

THE FUTURE OF BIRTH

The rapid development of reproductive technologies, as well as radical transformations of kinship structures, troubles not only the Western notion of personhood in general but also assumptions—including feminist ones—about pregnant embodiment, birth, and motherhood. Mapping these issues has become increasingly complicated as one is bound to navigate the constant redrawing of the legal and scientific landscape in real time. As I am writing this chapter, the birth of the first baby in the United States gestated in a transplanted uterus is announced (Grady),[31] and this event certainly raises questions about the future of birth and motherhood. We live in a world in which one must not be born with a womb in order to gestate and birth a child.[32] The recent explosion in the global surrogacy industry is far from the only phenomenon "expanding or disturbing the prevalent construction of parentage" (Lewis 97). From Aldous Huxley's *Brave New World* to P. D. James's *Children of Men*, science fiction authors have a long-standing interest in the dystopias of human reproduction, but reality is catching up, and scholarly work is desperately trying to keep up with current developments.

It is beyond the scope of this chapter to account for the many developments in reproductive technologies that have emerged since the birth of Louise Brown, the world's first baby to be conceived by IVF, in July of 1978 in Manchester, UK. These forty years of reproductive innovations have sparked a range of feminist responses, from optimistic jubilance to suspicious ambivalence to downright hostility. On the optimistic end of the spectrum, Shulamith Firestone's *The Dialectic of Sex* celebrates reproductive technologies as the key to women's liberation and freedom (Firestone). More ambivalent views regarding the potential of reproductive technologies are expressed in Rita Arditti, Renate Duelli Klein, and Shelley Minden's anthology *Test-Tube Women*: "Each time a new technological development is hailed the same question arises: is this liberation, or oppression in a new guise?" (2). And on the truly hostile end of the spectrum are collections like *Man-Made Women*, edited by members of the group FINRRAGE (Feminist International Network on New Reproductive Technologies and Genetic Engineering), as well as a report put together by that same group, declaring that "the female body, with its unique capacity for creating human life is being expropriated and dissected as raw material for the technological production of human beings" (FINRRAGE 233). The debates that have unfolded since then cover a host of more or less controversial issues, including, but not limited to, contraception, sterilization and abortion, egg and sperm donation, in vitro fertilization and assisted reproductive technologies, embryo freezing and stem cell research, prenatal screening, intersex births and sex selection, surrogacy and artificial wombs, as well as cloning, gene selection, and eugenics.

In this context, it seems essential to take note of the fact that not only traditional but also feminist discussions of reproduction, pregnancy, and childbirth have perpetuated normative assumptions about birth-givers as Western, female, straight, white, middle-class, and able-bodied. As Kaila Adia Story has noted, "The dominant portrayal of what is, and what it means to be a 'mother' ... remains locked within a reductive and imaginary prism of white supremacy, heteronormativity, and sexism" (1). To be sure, we must challenge the all-too-common assumption that birth is an altogether "natural" event, and that nature somehow privileges some births and birth-givers over others in hierarchical fashion. It is no coincidence that trans-exclusive radical feminists (TERFs) such as Janice Raymond combined deeply held transphobic views with intense suspicion of assisted reproductive technologies—both couched in the name of "real" and "natural" women, allegedly under attack by medically created "artificial" women. As Sophie Lewis has pointed out in an important article mapping the shared roots of transphobia and feminist critiques of surrogacy, for scholars like Raymond, "transition surgeries and contract pregnancies were two facets of a seemingly omnipotent 'male' war on or invasion of the 'female'" (Lewis 103).

With a growing body of work in trans studies, and with increased visibility of nonbinary and trans identities, the age-long association of women with gestation and birth, and the concomitant assumption that all birth parents are mothers, is coming to an end. Future work on reproduction and birth will inevitably have to pay more attention to experiences that trouble and disrupt such associations, descriptively and normatively. Indeed, the autobiography of Thomas Beatie—one of the first transmen to go public about his pregnancy and birthing experience—fundamentally challenged ingrained social expectations about who gives birth, and how (Beatie).[33] And while there is not much work in this area as of yet, some is emerging that seeks to grapple with the lived experience of trans pregnancy and birth, oftentimes with the aim to improve medical practice and policies (see, e.g., Light et al.).[34]

There is an overwhelming tendency in feminist work on birth and reproduction to discuss these issues as if they were racially neutral, which is to say that they mostly have been treated from an implicitly white standpoint. As Dorothy Roberts points out in her seminal *Killing the Black Body*, "The feminist focus on gender and identification of male domination as the source of reproductive repression often overlooks the importance of racism in shaping our understanding of reproductive liberty and the degree of 'choice' that women really have" (5). Indeed, "books on racial justice tend to neglect the subject of reproductive rights; and books on reproductive freedom tend to neglect the influence of race" (4).

Since Roberts set out to correct this imbalance, and to account for the manifold ways in which black women's reproductive lives have been subjected to insidious forms of white supremacist violence and injustice—ranging from the ideology of Mammy and white slave owners' widespread use of rape for the purpose of impregnating black women, to forced sterilization and scientific experiments devoted to proving the biological inferiority of black folk, to the contemporary stereotyping of black mothers as immoral, neglectful, and domineering welfare queens, media stories about hopelessly defective crack babies, and massive racial discrepancies in maternal health care and infertility treatment—a body of work has emerged that speaks specifically to racial dimensions of reproduction and racist tendencies in the literature on birth and reproduction. This includes work that considers cultural differences in birthing practices (Ivry; Johnson), work that examines global perspectives on reproductive technologies (Browner and Sargent; Ragoné and Twine), work that shares birthing stories from people of socioeconomically and racially diverse backgrounds (Apfel), and work that speaks specifically to the lived experience of black motherhood (Collins; Craddock; and Story).

To be sure, much work lies ahead in terms of addressing racial inequalities in maternal health and reproductive rights. Black women in the United States are three to four times more likely to die from pregnancy or childbirth-related causes than white women are. The imbalance has persisted for decades, and in some places, like New York City, the gap is widening.[35] It is also worth noting that "black women are nearly twice as likely to have infertility problems as whites, and when they undergo treatment, there's much less likelihood that the treatments will succeed" (N. Martin). Most researchers agree that the problem isn't race but racism. Twenty years ago, Roberts found herself "in the midst of an explosion of rhetoric and policies that degrade Black women's reproductive decisions" (4). The observation remains acutely applicable to our own present. And while we hear less these days about forced sterilizations and mandatory insertions of Norplant (a risky hormonal birth control implant), we have a long way to go to undo racial reproductive inequities and overcome the racial bias that marks much feminist work on birth and reproduction.

Of equal importance is the need to make more widely available and visible counternarratives that depict the lived experience of black motherhood in all of its richness and uniqueness, not just in terms of inequity and oppression. Echoing Kristeva's call for complex and ambivalent accounts of motherhood that refuse both the idealized image of the Virgin Mother and the degrading image of mothers as passive vessels, Patricia Hill Collins calls for accounts of black motherhood that reject the "mother glorification" that she attributes to "Black men who routinely praise Black mothers, especially their own," as well as the social stigma of the "bad" black mother, such that black motherhood can be described in more complex and multifaceted terms, as the "fundamentally contradictory institution" it in fact is (188, 211). For Collins, as much as motherhood for many black women comes at the expense of their own freedom, she is careful to point out that for many, it remains "a symbol of hope" and an "empowering experience," and it can "foster a creativity, a mothering of the mind and soul, for all involved" (214–5).

Collins notes that "othermothers—women who assist bloodmothers by sharing mothering responsibilities—traditionally have been central to the institution of Black motherhood," and that "these women-centered networks of community-based child care have extended beyond the boundaries of biologically related individuals to include 'fictive kin'" (192–3). Such mothering networks, firmly rooted in African American culture, seem particularly salient as a reproductive model for our own times, marked across racial, social, and sexual strata by the deterioration of social security programs and public education, the widespread displacement of refugees, epidemic infertility combined with increased pressure that women carry unwanted pregnancies to term, and other reconfigurations that demand that we rethink reproduction and motherhood as lived social realities.

So, the future of birth, what is it? The beginning of new forms of birth or the end of birth as we know it? Perhaps more now than ever, birth is indeed a pressing political question, and feminists are in no way in agreement about how it should be treated. As much as this chapter has been an attempt to delineate some central themes and topics, I hope more than anything that it has served as a reminder of how diverse and complex the experience of birth, and feminist thought on birth, is, and ultimately must remain.

NOTES

1 For an analysis of what it would mean to take on the Socratic imperative to learn how to die precisely *as* a mother, where the exercise of learning how to die is born out of the very experience of mothering and childbirth, see Schueneman.

2 See, for example, Battersby, Cavarero (*In Spite of Plato*, *Inclinations*), Guenther, Irigaray (*To Be Born*), O'Byrne, Stone ("Natality," *Being Born*), and Söderbäck ("In Search," "Natality or Birth?").

3 See, for example, Cavarero ("'A Child,'" *Inclinations*), Dietz, Guenther (*The Gift of the Other*), and Söderbäck ("Natality or Birth?").

4 Peg Birmingham objects that Arendt in fact *does* develop an account not only of the second birth of action but also of the first birth that she claims is required for action to take place.

She locates such an account in Arendt's engagement with Heidegger's discussion of natality in *Being and Time* (Birmingham).

5　Indeed, British academic work on birth has been influential in recent years. This might in part be attributed to the events and publications coming out of MaMSIE: Mapping Maternal Subjectivities, Identities and Ethics, an interdisciplinary network based in the Department of Psychosocial Studies at Birbeck University. Since 2009, MaMSIE has been publishing the online journal *Studies in the Maternal*, edited by Lisa Baraitser and Sigal Spigel, and this has been a central forum for recent reflections and debates on reproduction, pregnancy, birth, motherhood, parenting, and childcare across disciplinary and practice boundaries.

6　For an extended discussion of the need to think birth and death—natality and mortality— *together* (rather than as two distinct issues), see also Schott.

7　Irigaray notes, "Our society and our culture operate on the basis of an original matricide" (*Sexes* 11), and adds that Western man "did not work out his maternal beginning but put it into the unthought background of his story and history" (*Key Writings* ix). For a more extended analysis of this dimension of Irigaray's work, see Söderbäck ("In Search").

8　For a lucid analysis of this passage, one that focuses on the matricidal logic that it uncovers, see Jones. For a more critical reading, see Butler (*Bodies* 3–27).

9　For an overview of the Platonic appropriation of birth and birth-giving powers, see DuBois and Sandford.

10　See, for example, the special issues of *Hypatia* on motherhood and sexuality (Ferguson) and French feminist philosophy (Fraser and Bartky).

11　See Lázaro (87) and Oliver (761).

12　See, for example, LaChance Adams and Stone ("Beauvoir"). In an interview from 1982, Beauvoir herself clarifies that "motherhood in itself is not something negative or something inhuman," but rather that it is motherhood as a patriarchal reality, what she calls "enslaved motherhood," that is a problem (Beauvoir, Simons, and Todd 18).

13　The latter might apply to surrogates, birth mothers who give their child(ren) up for adoption, or gestating and birthing transmen who identify as fathers.

14　The seminal radical feminist rejection of motherhood is arguably Firestone. For a queer challenge to the very logic and idealization of reproduction, see Edelman.

15　"The woman you call the mother of your child is not the parent, just a nurse to the seed, the new-sown seed that grows and swells inside her. The *man* is the source of life—the one who mounts" (Aeschylus 260–1).

16　For a discussion of how social gender roles are projected onto reproductive biology, such that biology textbook discussions of conception reflect common societal views of male activity and female passivity by producing myths about agile-aggressive sperms and passively awaiting eggs, see E. Martin. For an updated account that looks at how Martin's argument holds true into the twenty-first century, see Campo-Engelstein and Johnson. Oliver has examined how medical discourse has rendered mothers not only passive but also invisible (*Family Values* 14–34).

17　Rich dates "the beginning of the transformation of obstetrics into a male province" to 1663, with "the attendance of a court physician named Boucher on Louise de la Vallière, the favorite mistress of Louis XIV" (139).

18　One in three children in the United States is delivered by cesarean section (CDC), which is more than double the rate recommended by the WHO.

19　"In the French province of Lombardy in one year no single woman survived childbirth" (Rich 151).

20 It is also important to note, as Johnson does, that Western "trends toward midwifery care and breastfeeding, which reclaim the 'natural', woman-centered models of birthing and caring, have created pressure for women to move in this direction despite possible inclinations to the contrary" ("Negotiating" 71). Such trends might risk reinforcing the patriarchal tendency to associate women with the natural realm, thus maintaining male control over the cultural-technological realm. They can also have unfortunate effects on women who want to feel empowered, rather than guilt-ridden, in their decision-making processes as they prepare for labor, delivery, and motherhood. I can personally attest to the sense of failure I felt when, after sixty-six hours of attempting a "natural" birth, I ended up having a cesarean section.

21 For a more careful treatment of Kristeva's work on motherhood, as well as a critical engagement with Butler's influential reading of it, see Söderbäck ("Motherhood").

22 These accounts of course do not tell us much of those who grow up outside of traditional Oedipal configurations, such as orphans, or children of same-sex or single parents.

23 Talia Welsh has pointed out that, while feminist phenomenologists have criticized Merleau-Ponty for failing to account for gendered experiences in general and pregnant embodiment in particular in his *Phenomenology of Perception*, he did in fact address the phenomenon of pregnancy in his lectures on child psychology and pedagogy that he gave at the Sorbonne from 1949 to 1952, just after the publication in French of *The Second Sex* (287–8). It is perhaps worth noting that "the father of phenomenology," Edmund Husserl, in fact also discussed issues of motherhood and pregnancy. For discussions of this, see Oksala, and Smith (29–40). For an analysis of pregnancy and birth that draws from the work of Heidegger, see Staehler.

24 Scientific research supports the notion that pregnancy and childbirth undo these basic models of selfhood. For example, a study in 2012 concluded that, because cells can migrate through the placenta between the mother and the fetus, fetal cells can be found not only in the mother's lung, thyroid, muscle, liver, heart, kidney, and skin, as was previously known, but also in her brain. In the study, male cells were embedded in the brains of women and had been living there, in some cases, for several decades (a condition called chimerism). Robert Martone, who describes the phenomenon as a "reminder of our interconnectedness," comments on the findings: "We are accustomed to thinking of ourselves as singular autonomous individuals, and these foreign cells seem to belie that notion, and suggest that most people carry remnants of other individuals."

25 Sara Heinämaa has argued, to the contrary, that we ought to view the intrauterine relationship between gestating mother and fetus as properly intersubjective. Pregnant embodiment, she asserts, establishes "a relationship of proto-communication between two subjects that are not equal in their powers, capacities, or positions but despite their asymmetry form a couple of mutually dependent subjects" such that "the analysis of pregnancy is relevant to the philosophical discussion of the foundations of intersubjectivity and *Mitsein* or coexistence" (33).

26 For more extended discussions of temporal dimensions of pregnancy, childbirth, and mothering, see Baraitser (66–89), Kristeva ("Women's Time"), and Söderbäck ("Motherhood").

27 For an influential analysis that seeks to trouble any and all clear-cut distinctions between self and other, see Irigaray's conversation with the biologist Hélène Rouch on the mediating function of the placenta ("On the Maternal Order"). See also Bracha Ettinger's work on what she has coined the "matrixial borderspace"—a concept that is meant to describe intrauterine presubjectivity (*Matrixial Borderspace*). For an analysis that challenges the distinction

between activity and passivity during pregnancy, see Jonna Bornemark's discussion of gestational "pactivity" (270).

28 Johanna Oksala has stressed the need to articulate a phenomenology of birth that is concerned not with "marginal or regional subthemes in phenomenology," nor with simply "adding gender-specific analyses of experience" or "vivid descriptions of labor pains," but rather as one articulating "a critical current going through the whole body of phenomenological thinking reaching all the way down to its most fundamental tenets," which is to say that it would "radically rethink such fundamental phenomenological questions as the possibility of a purely eidetic phenomenology and the limits of egological sense-constitution" (88–9). Bornemark and Nicholas Smith confirm this view, asserting that "pregnancy is clearly not just one experience among many. The experience of pregnancy activates the most basic problems of transcendental phenomenology: the structure of the self, its relation to otherness, and the genesis of intentional life as such" (8).

29 What is at stake, for Young, is the way in which pregnancy "reveals a paradigm of bodily experience in which the transparent unity of self dissolves" (47).

30 See, for example, Lupton and Mills.

31 Since 2014, eight other babies have been born to women who had uterus transplants, but all were in Sweden. The recent birth at Baylor University Medical Center in Dallas was a result of the first successful attempt in the United States and confirmation that the procedure can be replicated beyond the Sahlgrenska University Hospital in Gothenburg.

32 While extrauterine gestation is still very much in an experimental stage, in 2017 researchers were able to gestate a premature lamb in an external womb (a so-called Biobag) for four weeks (Flake et al.). Alan Flake, the lead author of the study, is careful to point out that, to the extent that similar experiments could be used for gestating humans (a reality that he claims is about four years away), it would be a matter of developing a support system for premature infants, not artificial wombs for growing babies from scratch: "It's complete science fiction to think that you can take an embryo and get it through the early developmental process and put it on our machine without the mother being the critical element there" (Becker).

33 Not all gender-queer folk saw the publication of Beatie's autobiography as a step forward, however. Jack Halberstam, for example, wonders "what price was paid, and by whom," in "this riot of visibility," wherein the image of Beatie's pregnant belly sensationalized trans parenthood: "He was far from being, in his own words, the 'first pregnant transman,' he was simply the first posttransition transgender male to go public with his decision to keep his female reproductive organs and then to use them" (77). Halberstam further worries that "rather than promoting a queer narrative about difference and gender shifts, his story ultimately came to rest upon an all too familiar narrative of humanity and universality—it is universal to want a child, it is only human to want to give birth" (78).

34 While there is not much work on trans parenting available, there is certainly a rich body of literature on queer parenting in general and lesbian mothering in particular. For two salient examples, see Moraga and Park. There is also some work that seeks to challenge established norms regarding sex assignment at birth. For an influential analysis that focuses on the medical response to the birth of intersex infants, see Fausto-Sterling (45–77).

35 In 2001–5, the risk of death was seven times higher for black mothers in New York City. Today, black mothers there are twelve times more likely than white ones to die from childbirth (N. Martin).

WORK CITED

Aeschylus. *The Oresteia*. Trans. Robert Fagles. New York: Viking P, 1979.

Apfel, Alana. *Birth Work as Care Work: Stories from Activist Birth Communities*. Oakland: PM P, 2016.

Arditti, Rita, Renate Duelli Klein, and Shelley Minden, eds. *Test-Tube Women: What Future for Motherhood?* London: Pandora P, [1984] 1989.

Arendt, Hannah. *The Human Condition*. Chicago, IL: U of Chicago P, [1958] 1998.

Baraitser, Lisa. *Maternal Encounters: The Ethics of Interruption*. Milton Park: Routledge, 2009.

Battersby, Christine. *The Phenomenal Woman: Feminist Metaphysics and the Patterns of Identity*. New York: Routledge, 1998.

Beatie, Thomas. *Labor of Love: The Story of One Man's Extraordinary Pregnancy*. Berkeley, CA: Seal P, 2009.

Beauvoir, Simone de. *The Second Sex*. Trans. Constance Borde and Sheila Malovany-Chevallier. New York: Alfred A. Knopf, [1949] 2010.

Beauvoir, Simone de, Margaret A. Simons, and Jane Marie Todd. "Two Interviews with Simone de Beauvoir." *Hyptia: A Journal of Feminist Philosophy* 3.3 (1989): 11–27.

Becker, Rachel. "An Artificial Womb Successfully Grew Baby Sheep—and Humans Could Be Next." *The Verge* (26 April 2017). Accessed at https://www.theverge.com/2017/4/25/15421734/ artificial-womb-fetus-biobag-uterus-lamb-sheep-birth-premie-preterm-infant, December 12, 2017.

Benjamin, Jessica. *The Bonds of Love: Psychoanalysis, Feminism, and the Problem of Domination*. New York: Pantheon Books, 1988.

Birmingham, Peg. "Heidegger and Arendt: The Birth of Political Action and Speech." *Heidegger and Practical Philosophy*. Ed. François Raffoul and David Pettigrew. Albany: State U of New York P, 2002.

Bornemark, Jonna. "Life beyond Individuality: A-subjective Experience in Pregnancy." *Phenomenology of Pregnancy*. Ed. Jonna Bornemark and Nicholas Smith. Södertörn Philosophical Studies 18. Stockholm: Södertörn U, 2016.

Bornemark, Jonna, and Nicholas Smith, eds. *Phenomenology of Pregnancy*. Södertörn Philosophical Studies 18. Stockholm: Södertörn U, 2016.

Bowen-Moore, Patricia. *Hannah Arendt's Philosophy of Natality*. London: Macmillan P, 1989.

Browner, Carole H., and Carolyn F. Sargent, eds. *Reproduction, Globalization, and the State: New Theoretical and Ethnographic Perspectives*. Durham, NC: Duke UP, 2011.

Butler, Judith. *Bodies That Matter: On the Discursive Limits of "Sex."* New York: Routledge, [1993] 2011.

Butler, Judith. *Gender Trouble: Feminism and the Subversion of Identity*. New York: Routledge, [1990] 1999.

Campo-Engelstein, Lisa, and Nadia L. Johnson. "Revisiting 'The Fertilization Fairytale': An Analysis of Gendered Language Used to Describe Fertilization in Science Textbooks from Middle School to Medical School." *Cultural Studies of Science Education* 9 (2014): 201–20.

Cavarero, Adriana. "'A Child Has Been Born unto Us': Arendt on Birth." Trans. Sylvia Guslandi and Cosette Bruhns. *philoSOPHIA: A Journal of Continental Feminism* 4.1 (2014): 12–30.

Cavarero, Adriana. *Inclinations: A Critique of Rectitude*. Trans. Amanda Minervini and Adam Sitze. Stanford: Stanford UP, [2014] 2016.

Cavarero, Adriana. *In Spite of Plato: Feminist Rewriting of Ancient Philosophy*. Trans. Serena Anderlini-D'Onofrio and Áine O'Healy. Cambridge, UK: Polity P, [1990] 1995.

Centers for Disease Control and Prevention (CDC). *National Center for Health Statistics: Births— Method of Delivery*, 2017. Accessed at https://www.cdc.gov/nchs/fastats/delivery.htm, December 5, 2017.

Collins, Patricia Hill. *Black Feminist Thought: Knowledge, Consciousness, and the Politics of Empowerment*. New York: Routledge, [1990] 2009.

Corea, Gena, et al., eds. *Man-Made Women: How New Reproductive Technologies Affect Women*. Bloomington: Indiana UP, 1987.

Craddock, Karen T., ed. *Black Motherhood(s): Contexts, Contours and Considerations*. Ontario, CA: Demeter P, 2015.

Dietz, Mary G. "Feminist Receptions of Hannah Arendt." *Feminist Interpretations of Hannah Arendt*. Ed. Bonnie Honig. University Park: Pennsylvania State UP, 1995.

DuBois, Page. "The Platonic Appropriation of Reproduction." *Feminist Interpretations of Plato*. Ed. Nancy Tuana. University Park: Pennsylvania State UP, 1994.

Edelman, Lee. *No Future: Queer Theory and the Death Drive*. Durham, NC: Duke UP, 2004.

Ettinger, Bracha L. *The Matrixial Borderspace*. Minneapolis: U of Minnesota P, 2006.

Fausto-Sterling, Anne. *Sexing the Body: Gender Politics and the Construction of Sexuality*. New York: Basic Books, 2000.

Feminist International Network on New Reproductive Technologies and Genetic Engineering (FINRRAGE). "International Conference Lund—Sweden." 1985. Accessed at http://www.finrrage.org/wp-content/uploads/2016/03/Finrrage_Conference_Lund_Sweden_1985.pdf, December 13, 2017.

Ferguson, Anne, ed. "Special Issue: Motherhood and Sexuality." *Hypatia: A Journal of Feminist Philosophy* 1.2 (1986).

Firestone, Shulamith. *The Dialectic of Sex: The Case for Feminist Revolution*. New York: Farrar, Straus and Giroux, [1970] 2003.

Fisher, Sally. "Becoming Bovine: A Phenomenology of Early Motherhood and Its Practical, Political Consequences." *Philosophical Inquiries into Pregnancy, Childbirth, and Mothering: Maternal Subjects*. Ed. Sheila Lintott and Maureen Sander-Staudt. New York: Routledge, 2012.

Flake, Alan W., et al. "An Extra-Uterine System to Physiologically Support the Extreme Premature Lamb." *Nature Communications* 8, 2017. Accessed at https://www.nature.com/articles/ncomms15112, December 12, 2017.

Fraser, Nancy, and Sandra Bartky, eds. "Special Issue: French Feminist Philosophy." *Hypatia: A Journal of Feminist Philosophy* 3.3 (1989).

Grady, Denise. "Woman with Transplanted Uterus Gives Birth, the First in the U.S." *New York Times* (December 2, 2017). Accessed at https://www.nytimes.com/2017/12/02/health/uterus-transplant-baby.html, December 12, 2017.

Guenther, Lisa. "Being-from-Others: Reading Heidegger after Cavarero." *Hypatia: A Journal of Feminist Philosophy* 23.1 (2008): 99–118.

Guenther, Lisa. *The Gift of the Other: Levinas and the Politics of Reproduction*. Albany: State U of New York P, 2006.

Halberstam, Judith. "The Pregnant Man." *The Velvet Trap Light* 65 (2010): 77–8.

Haraway, Donna J. *Simians, Cyborgs, and Women: The Reinvention of Nature*. New York: Routledge, 1991.

Heinämaa, Sara. " 'An Equivocal Couple Overwhelmed by Life': A Phenomenological Analysis of Pregnancy." *philoSOPHIA: A Journal of Continental Feminism* 4.1 (2014): 31–49.

Huxley, Aldous. *Brave New World*. New York: Harper, 1932.

Irigaray, Luce. *In the Beginning, She Was*. London: Bloomsbury, 2013.

Irigaray, Luce. *Key Writings*. London: Continuum, 2004.

Irigaray, Luce. "On the Maternal Order." *Je, Tu, Nous: Toward a Culture of Difference*. Trans. Alison Martin. New York: Routledge, [1990] 1993.

Irigaray, Luce. *Sexes and Genealogies*. Trans. Gillian C. Gill. New York: Columbia UP, [1987] 1993.

Irigaray, Luce. *Speculum of the Other Woman*. Trans. Gillian C. Gill. Ithaca, NY: Cornell UP, [1974] 1985.

Irigaray, Luce. *To Be Born*. London: Palgrave Macmillan, 2017.

Ivry, Tsipy. *Embodying Culture: Pregnancy in Japan and Israel*. New Brunswick, NJ: Rutgers UP, 2010.

Jacobs, Amber. *On Matricide: Myth, Psychoanalysis, and the Law of the Mother*. New York: Columbia UP, 2007.

James, P. D. *Children of Men*. London: Faber and Faber, 1992.

Johnson, Candace. *Maternal Transition: A North-South Politics of Pregnancy and Childbirth*. New York: Routledge, 2014.

Johnson, Candace. "Negotiating Maternal Identity: Adrienne Rich's Legacy for Inquiry into the Political-Philosophical Dimensions of Pregnancy and Childbirth." *philoSOPHIA: A Journal of Continental Feminism* 4.1 (2014): 65–87.

Jones, Rachel. *Irigaray: Towards a Sexuate Philosophy*. Cambridge, UK: Polity P, 2011.

Klein, Melanie. "Notes on Some Schizoid Mechanisms." *The Selected Melanie Klein*. Harmondsworth, UK: Penguin Books, [1946] 1986.

Kristeva, Julia. *Black Sun: Depression and Melancholia*. Trans. Leon S. Roudiez. New York: Columbia UP, [1987] 1989.

Kristeva, Julia. "Motherhood According to Giovanni Bellini." *Desire in Language: A Semiotic Approach to Literature and Art*. Ed. Leon S. Roudiez. Trans. Thomas Gora, Alice Jardine, and Leon S. Roudiez. New York: Columbia UP, [1977] 1980.

Kristeva, Julia. *Powers of Horror: An Essay on Abjection*. Trans. Leon S. Roudiez. New York: Columbia UP, [1980] 1982.

Kristeva, Julia. *Revolution in Poetic Language*. Trans. Margaret Waller. New York: Columbia UP, [1974] 1984.

Kristeva, Julia. "Stabat Mater." *Tales of Love*. Trans. Leon S. Roudiez. New York: Columbia UP, [1983] 1987.

Kristeva, Julia. *This Incredible Need to Believe*. Trans. Beverley Bie Brahic. New York: Columbia UP, [2006] 2009.

Kristeva, Julia. "Women's Time." *New Maladies of the Soul*. Trans. Ross Guberman. New York: Columbia UP, [1979] 1995.

LaChance Adams, Sarah. *Mad Mothers, Bad Mothers, and What a "Good" Mother Would Do: The Ethics of Ambivalence*. New York: Columbia UP, 2014.

Lázaro, Reyes. "Feminism and Motherhood: O'Brien vs Beauvoir." *Hypatia: A Journal of Feminist Philosophy* 1.2 (1986): 87–102.

Lewis, Sophie. "Defending Intimacy against What? Limits of Antisurrogacy Feminisms." *Signs: Journal of Women in Culture and Society* 43.1 (2017): 97–125.

Light, Alexis D., Juno Obedin-Maliver, Jae M. Sevelius, and Jennifer M. Kerns. "Transgender Men Who Experienced Pregnancy after Female-to-Male Gender Transitioning." *Obstetrics & Gynecology* 124.6 (2014): 1120–7.

Lundquist, Caroline. "Being Torn: Toward a Phenomenology of Unwanted Pregnancy." *Hypatia: A Journal of Feminist Philosophy* 23.3 (2008): 136–55.

Lupton, Deborah. *The Social Worlds of the Unborn*. Basingstoke: Palgrave Macmillan, 2013.

Martin, Emily. "The Egg and the Sperm: How Science Has Constructed a Romance Based on Stereotypical Male-Female Roles." *Signs: Journal of Women in Culture and Society* 16.3 (1991): 485–501.

Martin, Nina. "Black Mothers Keep Dying After Giving Birth: Shalon Irving's Story Explains Why." NPR All Things Considered (December 7, 2017). Accessed at https://www.npr.org/2017/12/07/568948782/black-mothers-keep-dying-after-giving-birth-shalon-irvings-story-explains-why, December 8, 2017.

Martone, Robert. "Scientists Discover Children's Cells Living in Mothers' Brains." *Scientific American* (December 4, 2012). Accessed at https://www.scientificamerican.com/article/scientists-discover-childrens-cells-living-in-mothers-brain/, December 12, 2017.

Merleau-Ponty, Maurice. *Child Psychology and Pedagogy: The Sorbonne Lectures 1949–1952.* Trans. Talia Welsh. Evanston, IL: Northwestern UP, 2010.

Mills, Catherine. "Making Fetal Persons: Fetal Homicide, Ultrasound, and the Normative Significance of Birth." *philoSOPHIA: A Journal of Continental Feminism* 4.1 (2014): 88–107.

Moraga, Cherríe. *Waiting in the Wings: Portrait of a Queer Motherhood.* Ann Arbor, MI: Firebrand Books, 1997.

O'Brien, Mary. *The Politics of Reproduction.* Boston, MA: Routledge & Kegan Paul, 1981.

O'Byrne, Anne. *Natality and Finitude.* Bloomington: Indiana UP, 2010.

Oksala, Johanna. "A Phenomenology of Birth." *Feminist Experiences: Foucauldian and Phenomenological Investigations.* Evanston, IL: Northwestern UP, 2016.

Oliver, Kelly. *Family Values: Subjects Between Nature and Culture.* New York: Routledge, 1997.

Oliver, Kelly. "Motherhood, Sexuality, and Pregnant Embodiment: Twenty-Five Years of Gestation." *Hypatia: A Journal of Feminist Philosophy* 25.4 (2010): 760–77.

Park, Shelley M. *Mothering Queerly, Queering Motherhood: Resisting Monomaternalism in Adoptive, Lesbian, Blended, and Polygamous Families.* Albany: State U of New York P, 2013.

Ragoné, Heléna, and France Winddance Twine, eds. *Ideologies and Technologies of Motherhood: Race, Class, Sexuality, Nationalism.* New York: Routledge, 2000.

Rich, Adrienne. *Of Woman Born: Motherhood as Experience and Institution.* New York: W. W. Norton, [1976] 1995.

Roberts, Dorothy. *Killing the Black Body: Race, Reproduction, and the Meaning of Liberty.* New York: Vintage Books, [1997] 1999.

Sandford, Stella. *Plato and Sex.* Cambridge, UK: Polity P, 2010.

Schott, Robin May, ed. *Birth, Death, and Femininity: Philosophies of Embodiment.* Bloomington: Indiana UP, 2010.

Schueneman, Brooke. "Creating Life, Giving Birth, and Learning to Die." *Philosophical Inquiries into Pregnancy, Childbirth, and Mothering: Maternal Subjects.* Ed. Sheila Lintott and Maureen Sander-Staudt. New York: Routledge, 2012.

Smith, Nicholas. "Phenomenology of Pregnancy: A Cure for Philosophy?" *Phenomenology of Pregnancy.* Ed. Jonna Bornemark and Nicholas Smith. Södertörn Philosophical Studies 18. Stockholm: Södertörn U, 2016.

Söderbäck, Fanny. "Motherhood According to Kristeva: On Time and Matter in Plato and Kristeva." *philoSOPHIA: A Journal of Continental Feminism* 1.1 (2011): 65–87.

Söderbäck, Fanny. "Natality or Birth? On the Human Condition of Being Born." *Hypatia: A Journal of Feminist Philosophy* 33.2 (2018): 273–88.

Söderbäck, Fanny. "In Search for the Mother through the Looking Glass: On Time, Origins, and Beginnings in Plato and Irigaray." *Engaging the World: Thinking After Irigaray.* Ed. Mary C. Rawlingson. Albany: State U of New York P, 2016.

Staehler, Tanja. "Who's Afraid of Birth? Exploring Mundane and Existential Affects with Heidegger." *Janus Head* 16.1 (2017): 139–72.

Stone, Alison. "Beauvoir and the Ambiguities of Motherhood." *A Companion to Simone de Beauvoir*. Ed. Laura Hengehold and Nancy Bauer. Hoboken: Wiley-Blackwell, 2017.

Stone, Alison. *Being Born: Birth and Philosophy* (forthcoming). Accessed at https://www.academia.edu/34019302/Draft_Introduction_to_Being_Born and https://www.academia.edu/34472130/Chapter_Two_Questions_about_Natality_DRAFT_, November 30, 2017.

Stone, Alison. *Feminism, Psychoanalysis, and Maternal Subjectivity*. New York: Routledge, 2012.

Stone, Alison. "Natality and Mortality: Rethinking Death with Cavarero." *Continental Philosophy Review* 43 (2010): 353–72.

Story, Kaila Adia, ed. *Patricia Hill Collins: Reconceiving Motherhood*. Ontario, CA: Demeter P, 2014.

Tuana, Nancy. *The Less Noble Sex: Scientific, Religious, and Philosophical Conceptions of Woman's Nature*. Bloomington: Indiana UP, 1993.

Tyler, Imogen. "Introduction: Birth." *Feminist Review* 93 (2009): 1–7.

Weiss, Gail. *Body Images: Embodiment as Intercorporeality*. New York: Routledge, 1999.

Welsh, Talia. "The Order of Life: How Phenomenologies of Pregnancy Revise and Reject Theories of the Subject." *Coming to Life: Philosophies of Pregnancy, Childbirth, and Mothering*. Ed. Sarah LaChance Adams and Caroline R. Lundquist. New York: Fordham UP, 2013.

Winnicott, D. W. "The Theory of the Parent-Infant Relationship." *Maturational Processes and the Facilitating Environment: Studies in the Theory of Emotional Development*. New York: International Universities P, 1965.

Wolf, Naomi. *Misconceptions: Truth, Lies, and the Unexpected on the Journey to Motherhood*. New York: Anchor Books, 2003.

World Health Organization (WHO) fact sheet on maternal mortality. 2016. Accessed at http://www.who.int/mediacentre/factsheets/fs348/en/, December 1, 2016.

Young, Iris Marion. "Pregnant Embodiment: Subjectivity and Alienation." *On Female Body Experience: "Throwing Like a Girl" and Other Essays*. Oxford: Oxford UP, [1984] 2005.

CHAPTER FIVE

Body

MARIA MARGARONI

INTRODUCTION: AFTER THE "CORPOREAL TURN"

The body as a powerful attractor of desires, affects, imaginaries, and a site of theoretical reflection was actually foregrounded in feminist studies in the 1980s–1990s, in the context of the wider "corporeal turn" in social and cultural theory. As a number of theorists insist, however, "the body" (*this* body in its situatedness) has consistently remained a major concern throughout feminism's long history—from Mary Wollstonecraft's astute analysis of eighteenth-century bourgeois ideals of feminine beauty to first-wave feminists' critical appropriation of Enlightenment discourse in their attempt to refute biological determinism, Simone de Beauvoir's phenomenological rethinking of "a woman" as an embodied process of becoming, the 1960s radical and black feminists' reclamation of the sexed, gendered, racialized body no longer as the passive ground of women's oppression but as a site of struggle and a source of power, to the more contemporary multiple engagements with corporeality in light of postmodern, queer, or transgender theorizations of subjectivity and the new challenges we are facing at this advanced stage of a biopolitical technocapitalism.

This chapter takes the form of a dictionary-in-mutation—a corpus in transition, in other words, which comes to *be* (much like Frankenstein's creature) out of the remains of what Claire Colebrook aptly calls feminism's "bodily questions," its body tropes, "body-image[s]," "body-thing[s]," "body-effect[s]" (126). In structuring my analysis around key cluster concepts that have been enthusiastically invested in, obsessively refuted, or meticulously theorized in feminist scholars' engagement with the problem that the naturally or the socially marked body has constituted for an emancipation-oriented feminism, my aim is to attempt a historically informed mapping of (existing or emerging) feminist ontologies, semiologies, and epistemologies of the body. As I shall demonstrate, such new or newly invested corporeal vocabularies open up fresh perspectives on twenty-first-century enfleshed existence and are developing in the context of some of the most heated debates currently defining the field of feminist theory after the "corporeal turn": (a) the debate originating from the publication of Judith Butler's *Gender Trouble* (1990); (b) the open question of sexual difference, as taken up by psychoanalytic, postmodern, and new materialist feminists; (c) the ambivalent responses to versions of posthuman and cyber feminism, which seem to reproduce Western *somatophobia*; and finally, (d) the debates centering on new directions in corporeal feminist thought, such as Catherine Malabou's retheorization of embodiment in terms of plasticity, Deleuzean-inspired post-anthropocentric approaches to the body, or Elizabeth Grosz's experimentation with an evolutionary materialism of life and time.

PART A: GRAVITY FIELDS

Mud

In *The Book of Genesis*, one of the seminal origin texts in Western thought, the material weight of the human body, its taking on life out of "the silt of the earth,"[1] is consistently gendered and associated with humanity's inevitable destiny, its proneness to fall from paradise into a miserable, death-bound existence. Returning to this origin story in her analysis of the myths that have produced "woman" as a being relative to the "absolute human type," namely Man, Simone de Beauvoir demonstrates how the gesture feminizing the "material envelope" of Man is paradigmatic of a wider *somatophobia* in Western patriarchal tradition, an attitude that conceptualizes life in dualistic terms (*Second Sex* 5, 167). In "man's eyes," Beauvoir writes, life "is consciousness, will, transcendence, it is intellect; and it is matter, passivity, immanence, it is flesh" (167). Unable to carry the weight of his materiality, a "curse" that ties him to what William Blake calls the "matron Clay" and destines him to death, man rebels "against his carnal condition" (*Second Sex* 168–70). More importantly, Beauvoir argues, he comes to experience disgust for his "limited body" and for "woman who imprisons him in the mud of the earth" (*Second Sex* 169).

It is this dualistic metaphysical tradition, developing as an alliance between misogynism and what Elizabeth V. Spelman terms "psychophilic somatophobia" (40), that can account for the "unbearable weight" of the "withness" of the female body, as Susan Bordo traces it in her compelling reading of contemporary cultural phenomena such as the spread of anorexia nervosa and other eating disorders (2). Indeed, it is not difficult to see how the spirit of feminism as a revolutionary movement has been weighed down by an internalized discomfort with bodily matters, which first-wave feminists were all too keen to relegate to the brute state of nature and condemn as the source of women's oppression: "I discern not a trace of the image of God in either sensation or matter," writes Wollstonecraft. "Refined seventy times seven, they are still material" (134). The feminist's aim, then, according to her, was to help women enlarge their nature through cultivation and, thus, "mount" along with man, "the arduous steeps of knowledge" (137).

An important strand of second-wave feminism focused precisely on those philosophical, scientific, or theological concepts of "matter" that forced early feminists to define women's right to freedom in terms of a necessary ascension to the realms of disembodied reason. Following up on Beauvoir's own attempt to theorize embodiment outside the framework of biological determinism, thus making it possible for women to claim the possibility of transcendence from within their enfleshed situation, French feminists such as Julia Kristeva and Luce Irigaray committed themselves to developing less hylomorphic epistemologies of matter. Through their reconceptualization of our material/maternal origins and their theorization of new body-invested terms (e.g., "the semiotic *chora*," "signifiance," "semanalysis," "flesh," "the sensible transcendental"), these theorists have thrown light on material processes of self-ordering and their significance in refiguring a materialist feminist politics. Notably, in *Ethics of Sexual Difference*, Irigaray returns to the paradigm of a feminized earth as the material envelope of Man and turns the tables on patriarchal thought by tracing a resistance-in-the-feminine in the very qualities of mud that, according to Beauvoir, made it distasteful to man: namely, its layered oozy nature, its density, stickiness, viscosity, mucosity.

Despite the significance of this materialist legacy taken up by other scholars such as Bracha Ettinger, Elizabeth Grosz, Rosi Braidotti, and Catherine Malabou, among others, the heaviness of earthly materiality continues to be felt in post-1990s feminist theory. In her introduction to *The Beauty Myth*, Naomi Wolf insists that we have not yet freed ourselves "from the dead weight that has once again been made out of femaleness" (19). In her debut novel titled *Dietland*, Sarai Walker exposes the dark consequences of women's desire to shrink and inhabit a gravity-free wonderland. In *The Rejected Body*, Susan Wendell critically engages with similar gravity-free imaginaries of the body, celebrated in versions of poststructuralist and cyber feminism. Quoting Carol Bigwood, she argues, "'The poststructuralist body ... is so fluid it can take on almost limitless embodiments. It has no real terrestrial weight.' A body experienced has both limitations and weight" (168). The experienced body weighed down to earth by illness, disability, weakness, and dying is what she calls the "rejected body" that, she argues, remains an embarrassment to feminism (93). In *The Rhetorics of Feminism*, Lynne Pearce notes the proliferation of body *metaphors* in poststructuralist accounts of the subject, a rhetorical "shift that," she goes on to add, "will be undertaken with some impunity by all those who still regard women's bodies as the site of their most material oppression and violation" (126–7). Indeed, in her portrayal of the cyborg, one of the wildest and catchiest body metaphors in contemporary feminism, Donna Haraway predictably embraces the ironic complicities of techno-myth at the expense of what comes forth as a passé mélange of earth and patriarchal ideals of a maternally connoted nature. In one of her apophatic moments, she writes, "The cyborg would not recognize the Garden of Eden; it is not made of mud and cannot dream of returning to dust" (151).

Interestingly, in a recent discussion with Malabou on the master and slave paradigm in Hegel's *Phenomenology of Spirit*, Butler returns to the gesture of corporeal dispossession Beauvoir describes in *The Second Sex*, by means of which, as we have seen, man disavows his body by shifting the burden of weighty materiality onto woman. Reading the Hegelian episode through her earlier analysis of Beauvoir[2] and her more recent concern with neo-imperial politics and forced migration, Butler helps us reread the recurring narrative that binds bodily materiality to the "silt of the earth." For if the body (in its material substance) *is* earth, it too can be owned and possessed, conquered and usurped, commodified and exploited. The gesture, then, that Beauvoir identifies and Butler reiterates (both in their reading of Hegel) connotes, not simply man's fear to *be* a body but also his desire to *have*, his need to affirm his autonomy through possessing the bodies of others. In this light, "You be my body for me," as Butler succinctly puts it (Malabou and Butler 632), functions as an alternative origin story that, like Engels's own account,[3] brings together the emergence of the patriarchal family and the institution of an economy of slavery, one which, as Bibi Bakare-Yusuf argues, involves the violent deconstruction of the enslaved body. In other words, if the male Western subject disavows "the" body as the silt of the earth, this is not merely because it condemns him to mortality but, as Butler suggests, because it exposes him to the threat of being *bound* to life qua materiality and, hence, to another. "You be my body for me," then, appears to be at the origins of patriarchy as much as of the Western colonial project. As a distinct form of *somatophobia*, it is the product of Western man's desire to remain "unbound," master of all who are destined to carry his burden of materiality for him, be they women or enslaved "savages." This is precisely what Catherine Kellogg spells out in her analysis of the Butler/Malabou exchange, which, she rightly insists, needs to be seen in terms of "the history of regarding both the body and the land as property" (83). She writes, "The link ... is between the takability (indeed rapability) of certain kinds of juridically described bodies, and the plundering of land, territory and livelihood" (93).

In the face of a neocolonial global situation where to be *bound* is synonymous with to *be* a body (i.e., of the "silt of the earth" but with no claim to earth), it is no wonder that bodily materiality has come to constitute a form of *terra nullius* repeatedly placed under erasure in neoimperial practices as much as in popular cultural representations. In this light, the dialogue initiated by Butler's reflections above could not have been more topical.

Mark

In the previous section, my aim was to focus on the weight of earthly materiality, especially as this has been experienced and continues to be experienced not merely by female subjects (the privileged carriers of bodily weight in patriarchal Western thought) but also by all the dispossessed who find themselves trapped in the gravity field of neocolonial politics. In this section, I would like to turn to another metaphor that has dominated discussions of embodiment in feminist theory, especially post-1960s: namely, the metaphor of the *marked* or the culturally inscribed body. In this context, the body is not reduced to the viscous muddiness of its matter. Instead, it is perceived as an inert, receptive surface, the layered site of all sorts of social, cultural, discursive markings that produce a useful, disciplined, normalized subject. "Let's face it," Hortense Spillers writes. "I am a marked woman ... In order for me to speak a truer word concerning myself, I must strip down through layers of attenuated meanings, made an excess in time, over time, assigned by a particular historical order, and there await whatever marvels of my own inventiveness" (656).

As a conceptual model, the body qua passive surface of inscription constitutes the point of convergence of multiple lines of thought and philosophical frameworks: that is, Friedrich Nietzsche's metaphorics of corporeal branding through what he calls *mnemotechnics* (61), Michel Foucault's analyses of the body as "totally imprinted by history" (148), structuralist anthropological accounts of "primitive" and "civilized" forms of body inscription, the poststructuralist textualization of the body as much as the psychoanalytic production of psychic cartographies of the body, erotic bodily zones, and body parts. In all of these frameworks, metaphors of the body as the product of various writing systems, a clean slate, a blank page, a palimpsest, a coded network, an informational pattern, a text, a script, and a web of equally fictional narratives proliferate. As Grosz notes, the body is approached as "a purely surface phenomenon, a complex, multifaceted surface folded back on itself, exhibiting a certain torsion but nevertheless a flat plane whose incision or inscription produces the (illusion or effects of) depth and interiority" (*Volatile Bodies* 116).

Intended as a response to theories of biological essentialism grounded in a natural(ized) body, this paradigm has been very useful in feminist and gender theorists' attempts to understand the multiple cultural mechanisms that are responsible for the production of sexually, racially, legally, medically marked bodies, bodies that are *more* or *less* valued and, hence, are not equally livable. Yet, the asymmetrical emphasis on the ideological and the culturally constructed body along with a deterministic understanding of what we might call the inscribing work of culture has rendered this model of embodiment both conceptually problematic and politically disabling. In her introduction to *Bodies That Matter*, Butler acknowledges that the "relation between culture and nature presupposed" by theories of cultural construction "implies a culture or an agency of the social which acts upon a nature, which is itself presupposed as a passive surface" (4). As a result, the "natural" is systematically degraded "as that which is 'before' intelligibility, in need of the mark, if not the mar, of the social to signify, to be known, to acquire value" (*Bodies That Matter* 4–5). Butler's early theorization of gender performativity aims precisely at debunking dualistic concepts of "nature," thus reconceptualizing the process of construction in ways that permit her to restore some form of agency "within a network of deeply entrenched cultural norms" ("Sex and Gender" 37). To this end, she shifts attention away from matter as such, foregrounding "a process of materialization that stabilizes over time" (*Bodies That Matter* 9). Construction, then, is for Butler a "temporal process" rather than a single, effect-bound act. It involves not merely the subject's internalization of inscribed norms but also his or her gestures of dis-identification, his or her repeated failures and resistances, his or her conscious or unconscious opening up of norms to the Derridean strategy of (re)iteration and hence to "a potentially productive crisis" (*Bodies That Matter* 10).

It would be hard to deny the powerful impact of Butler's refiguration of the surface politics of the body on the imaginaries of gender theorists and gender activists alike. To begin, Butler has helped us appreciate the phantasmatic production of bodily morphology. She has restored the dynamism of Beauvorean becoming in processes of gender construction. She has reclaimed a politics of *acts*, as opposed to a politics grounded in the struggle for recognition among preexisting identities. More importantly, perhaps, she has alerted us to the punitive mechanisms at work in the unsuccessful or unconvincing performances of gender. Butler's intervention in the debate between biological essentialists and cultural constructionists has been decisive in that she reconceptualizes the culturally marked body as a dynamic *field of interpretive possibilities* ("Sex and Gender" 45), thus opening up a space for what Spillers calls "the marvels of my own invention." Adrienne Rich's call to "writing as re-vision" becomes in Butler a call for new styles of corporeal writing, for ironic and subversive reinscriptions of oppressive cultural histories that have left their traces on our bodies (33). From Cindy Sherman's "Untitled" series to Orlan's reincarnations through the use of cosmetic surgery, countercultural practices such as body piercing and tattooing, public or private drag performances, and the multiple "fictions of gender" that continue to materialize through elective body alterations are only few examples of the multiple interpretive possibilities still open to the human project of corporeal becoming (Halberstam 13).

Paradoxically, as Pearce notes, Butler's theory of body performativity is "the most striking and familiar instance of disembodied thinking in 1990s feminist and cultural theorizing" (144) because, for all its merits, it remains grounded in a poststructuralist view of language where the referent can only be experienced "as a kind of absence or loss" (*Bodies That Matter* 67). As a result, it has become the privileged target of theorists who feel wary of modes of thinking that reduce the body to a discursive field and acknowledge the gravity of only one kind of materiality, namely, the materiality of the signifier. In *What Is a Woman? And Other Essays*, Toril Moi does not hesitate to argue: "Ultimately, Butler loses sight of the body that her work tries to account for: the concrete, historical body that loves, suffers, and dies" (49). Moi does, indeed, have a point. In *Bodies That Matter*, the body seems to be deprived of any form of dynamism or agency. It is "that which" persists *passively* as "*a demand in and for language*, a 'that which' which … calls to be explained, described, diagnosed, altered or within the cultural fabric of lived experience, fed, exercised, mobilized, put to sleep" (67). As Pheng Cheah in his turn also suggests, "The dynamism she attributes to bodily materiality remains a function of sociohistorical form, where form is the anthropologistic process of signification *sans* subject" (118). What is lost, then, in Butler is "the possibility that matter could have a dynamism" in itself (119). This is what Cheah calls "mattering" (123) and Grosz attributes to the differences of multiple corporeal forces. In her own critical engagement with models of bodily inscription, Grosz insists on raising questions that lead us to take seriously the "stuff" of the page on which culture leaves its marks (*Volatile Bodies* 119). She argues, "If the writing or inscription metaphor is to be of any use for feminism … the specific modes of materiality of the 'page'/body must be taken into account" (*Volatile Bodies* 156).

All of the above make it clear that it is equally important, as Wendell emphasizes, to understand the body as *a cause*, not merely as a series of surface effects (175). It is also important, Moi would add, to rethink *our* body in Beauvoirean terms, that is, not as a thing that carries its meaning on its surface but as a situation (65). She explains, "To consider the body as a situation, … is to consider both the fact of having a specific kind of body and the meaning that concrete body has for the situated individual" (81). This is precisely, in my view, the kind of thinking Jay Prosser invites us to engage in in his *Second Skins*. Taking as his starting point "the elision of the experience of embodiment (of how bodies actually feel) in contemporary theories of transsexual and other bodies," Prosser sets out to produce theory out of the distinct situation of living in a transsexual body—hence his reliance on autobiographical narrative (92). Our theories, he writes, "are not simply costumes for our experience of our bodies," for they are "formed by and reformative of them" (96). It is, then, imperative to "reinsert into theory the experience of embodiment" and locate the points where "our experiences of our bodies resist or fragment our theoretical generalizations" (96).

Meat

In Pat Cadigan's cyberpunk novel *Synners*, one of the protagonists, aptly named Visual Mark, has a brain implant and dreams of leaving behind the "outside meat-inhabited world" (416) through what he perceives as an enlargement of himself, his gradual integration into the wider context of the web: "He lost all awareness of the meat that had been his prison for close to fifty years, and the relief he felt at having laid his burden down was as great as himself. His *self*. And his *self* was getting greater all the time, both ways, greater as in more wonderful and greater as in bigger" (251). As Deborah Lupton notes, this depiction of the body as "the meat" constitutes a common *topos* in much cyberwriting, from William Gibson's *Neuromancer* (1984) to the present (100). Indeed, in contemporary techno-capitalism, the fate of the biological human seems to be rather uncertain, given the increasing availability of multiple technological interventions that modify and hybridize the human body, giving rise to what for Lupton is a "utopian discourse" (100) that promises the cybertraveler a clean escape from "the meat-problem" (Cadigan 325). The dream of "coding the body," Nick Land in his own turn argues, points to the cybertraveler's desire to "escape from the clumsily underdesigned, theopolitically mutilated, techno-industrially pressure-cooked and data-baked, retrovirally diseased, tortured, shredded zombie meat" (192–3).

Though appropriated cautiously and translated in more ironic terms, this utopian dream of stepping out of "the germo-somatic 'meat circuit'" (Land 193) has turned out to be most attractive to a number of feminist and gender theorists. Drawing on Haraway's cyborg manifesto, such theorists have developed a kind of cyber-veganism in the context of which, Prosser rightly suggests, the sexed; racialized; age-, surgery-, or illness-marked meat is treated as a form of "virus" one needs to defend against (90). "Now the material flesh ... has become the marker of retrogressive identities," he writes (90–1).

But what is it about material flesh or meat that unnerves the advocates of "transgenic" or "virus free gender" (Prosser 90)? Land gives the following definition of "meat": "disinherited animal tissue simultaneous with fate, spontaneous, orphan and mutable matter" (193). What seems to be at stake, then, in this renewed denial of the body is not matter qua earth or *res extensa* but *animate* matter in its mindless abandonment, *life* in its organic mutability and vulnerability, or what Braidotti calls *zoe*, drawing on Gilles Deleuze and Giorgio Agamben: this "scandal, this wonder, this *zoe* ... this aching meat called my 'self,'" expressing "the abject/divine potency of a Life that consciousness lives in fear of" (252). On my reading, the meat phobia that characterizes versions of post or transhumanism (including versions of posthuman feminism) is the index of a desire to disavow *not* the human but the *inhuman* that precedes, coexists with, and surpasses the human. Indeed, despite popular representations of posthumanism and transhumanism, these intellectual movements have taken a historical form that can be seen as the return of classical humanism and an epitomization of the human as a systematic figuration of species arrogance. Theorists as diverse as Mike Featherstone, Roger Burrows, Lupton, Anne Balsamo, Vivian Sobchack, Kathleen Woodward, Braidotti, and even Haraway herself in a 1991 interview[4] caution against the uncritical appropriation of meat-phobic discourses that seem to have fallen into the lure of the "God trick" (Sobchack 209). Downloading the "self" into dataspace may, after all, be yet another reenactment of the mind over body dualism, while the dream of artificial intelligence as our common language may turn out to be a renewed version of the old: that is, in Featherstone and Burrow's words, "the dream of reason, with its quest for total control, order and pure unsullied communication" (16).

In this light, twenty-first-century feminism may do well to resist a utopianism of technological prosthetics and a "discourse of transgenics," which, as Prosser astutely claims, "ends up resembling that of nineteenth-century *eugenics*" (91), though it may embrace the enabling possibilities technology offers for what Max More calls "morphological freedom" (Ferrando 222). It may opt to mobilize "the infidel heteroglossia" of a cyborg politics, though it needs to remain aware of the complicity of cyborg discourses to C³I or, in Haraway's terms, "command-control-communication-intelligence" (150, 181). What is more, twenty-first-century feminism cannot afford to forget, as Cheah insists, that in the current "situation of global neocolonialism" oppression works as much on the disavowed meat as on subjects' consciousnesses, leaving its tracings in (for example) "the digestive tract" of the superexploited "by inequalities in food production and consumption" (120–1). Given that the utopian gesture of denying the hunger-driven, defecating, desiring meat can only be performed from a position of privilege, feminism may do well to reinvest in *a politics of the meat* or a politics of the inhuman, as Deleuzean-inspired feminists such as Braidotti, Grosz, and Cheah understand the term. The inhuman, Grosz explains, refers to "the animal, plant, and material forces that surround and overtake the human" (*Becoming Undone* 11). These forces, she adds, are "a necessary reminder of the limits of the human, its historical and ontological contingency; of the precariousness of the human as a state of being, a condition of sovereignty, or an ideal of self-regulation" (12). Taking my cue from this understanding of the inhuman, I would now like to turn to some emerging or newly invested body concepts that, in my view, invite us to rethink feminism's commitment to the body and its inhumanizing, life-affirming lessons.

PART B: MOBILITY VECTORS

Force

Grosz turns to the Nietzschean concept of force in an attempt to respond to Irigaray's call to think the "unthought of human becoming" (quoted in *Time Travels* 171). In her 2005 *Time Travels*, Grosz insists on the need for feminism to reevaluate its concepts and key questions. It "is time to move beyond the very language of identity and gender, to look at other issues left untouched, questions unasked, assumptions unelaborated" (171). Grosz is critical of the thoroughgoing absorption of feminist concerns with the body in identity politics—a politics, in other words, that centers on affirmations of who one *is* rather than on exploring the potential to overflow one's being in response to a changing environment. She argues that we need to return to some of the questions that have been "deemed the most offensive and disputed within the last decades: *not* the body ... but messy biology, ... *not* ideology, ... but force, energy, affect ... and *not* gender, ... but sexual difference" (171).

I find this direction that lays the groundwork for a corporeal feminist philosophy most promising. Ahead of her time, Angela Carter writing at the height of identity politics in the UK and the United States has already alerted us to the inadequacy of questions foregrounding the desire for recognition. Her female characters, though caught in a number of gender traps, grow through an ambiguous embracing of natural, subindividual forces. Her Red-Riding Hood, wolf-Alice, tiger-bride come to *be* at the crossroads of meta-morphic events and unpredictable encounters. In her novels and stories what is at stake is not identity or gender but the different enfleshed becomings of subjects brought and held together through desire, loathing, pain, and pleasure. It is precisely these embodied ontologies of becoming that Grosz associates with force, a term she uses to reconceptualize freedom, no longer as an activity of the mind but as "the struggle of bodies to become more than they are" (*Becoming Undone* 72). The aim of feminism as a revolutionary movement, according to her, should not be the liberation of a preexisting subject (e.g., women) but "the struggle to render more mobile, fluid, and transformable the means by which the female subject is produced and represented" (*Time Travels* 193). As feminists, then, we may find it enabling to shift the focus of our politics away from issues relating to subjectivity, choice, consciousness, or will to questions centering on forces, affects, actions, encounters, and events. Grosz argues in favor of a "politics of *imperceptibility*" that strives to account for "the pre-personal forces at work in the activities of sexed bodies, institutions, and social practices" (*Time Travels* 194–5). As Cheah notes, this direction in feminist thought that he retraces in the work of Foucault may allow us to appreciate "a dynamism that obeys an inhuman temporality ... incalculable for human political reason" (128). Indeed, I would argue that one of the reasons why Toni Morrison's *Beloved* remains one of the strongest political responses to white supremacy is its ability to mobilize the force of this inhuman temporality that connects the flow of milk within Sethe's body (a flow cut off by the slave owners) with the rash of blood from her infant daughter's wound. It is this force that constitutes the substance of Sethe's inhuman resistance, an apotropaic corporeal event that stops the slave owner in his tracks.

It is significant, I believe, that Grosz's elaboration of the concept of force enables her to rethink one of the central problems in feminist and gender studies, namely, the problem raised by the across-species event of sexual difference. The thinker par excellence of sexual difference is indisputably Luce Irigaray, the first theorist who has insisted on approaching this difference as an ontological and philosophical, rather than a biological, issue. Due to her consistent claims that the difference between man and woman has a foundational significance, serving as the prototype of all other differences, Irigaray has repeatedly been accused of essentialism and found guilty of heteronormativity. Though (as a linguist) she does tend to lapse into moments of the crudest essentialism, at her best Irigaray has succeeded in conceptualizing sexual difference as the interval necessary in the context of any relation, that is, not only in the relation between man and woman but also in those established between human and human, the human and the divine, or the human and the world. Grosz agrees with Irigaray that sexual difference "is the issue in our time" (*Ethics* 7). According to her, "Sexual difference is universal, an ontological condition of life on earth rather than a performatively produced artifact as Butler's work claims" (*Becoming Undone* 107). A force rather than a stable fact, it demonstrates that embodied beings are always sexed *and* sexually differentiated. It is also the proof that "force itself" is always "divided, differentiated, sexualized" (*Time Travels* 172). In contrast to Irigaray who tends to define sexual difference as the interval between two, Grosz theorizes it as the relational mode of "at least two" (*Time Travels* 176). As such, it "does not yet exist," for it does not mark the difference between preexisting entities (176). Sexual difference, she writes, "is entirely of the order of the surprise, the encounter with the new" (176), the generative force of the future. This is why, in her view, sexual difference, reconceptualized as the force of our inhuman materiality, is *not* an obstacle but the conceptual crucible within which we need to continue raising some of the most pressing questions for feminist theorists today: that is, "how to move beyond the sexes as we know them, and beyond sexuality as it is usually practiced? But also, how to understand this dynamism as always bifurcated and bifurcating, driven primarily by difference?" (*Time Travels* 180).

Form

Sexual difference constitutes the focus of Malabou's own attempt to open up new materialist directions in twenty-first-century feminist philosophy. In *Changing Difference*, she expressly sets out to move beyond "a feminism without women" (6). Her aim is to change the terms of the essentialism versus anti-essentialism debate and to reclaim "empirical femininity" as an essence that is empty but resistant to its deconstruction (v, 36). "I seek recognition for a certain feminine space that seems impossible, yet is also very dangerous to try to deny," she writes (2). Bringing together Irigaray's thinking of sexual difference as primarily ontological and her own rereading of Heidegger's philosophical account of the difference between Being and beings, Malabou is able to show the connection between the "pluralizing of gender differences" we are currently witnessing and "the pluralizing of ontological difference undertaken in France" by post-Heideggerean philosophers such as Emmanuel Levinas and Jacques Derrida (6). "Can we say," she asks, "that there are ontological differences as one says that there are genders and that in both instances ... difference is more than duality?" (7).

Malabou invites us to rethink the relation between sex and gender (i.e., one's sexed specificity and his or her gendered forms) in terms of the relational mode that characterizes Being and being. If Being and being are different but can "exchange modes of being" (36), then "[t]ransvestism comes with difference" (37). Rather than the *chorismos/bar* that keeps preexisting entities separate, sexual difference needs to be conceptualized, instead, as the mobile space of (ex)change and "reciprocal metamorphosis" (37). It is the space of play and substitutability, the principle of ontological passing that makes possible "the passing inscribed at the heart of gender" (40).

Through showing that essence (and "woman" as essence) can "go in drag," that is, that it can arrive in the flesh of different forms, Malabou insists on refusing the double bind we are currently facing in feminist theory: Would it be "more feminist," she asks, to "avoid the mark of sex" in order to rethink and reinvent gender? Or, would it indeed be more feminist to "claim that empirical femininity cannot be erased and is resistant to any neutralizing roller?" (*Changing Difference* 9, 36, 39). From her perspective, essence is not a fixed property but the always-present potential of change. Malabou challenges the metaphysical opposition between being and appearing, essence and form, *ousia* and *morphe*. Form, she argues, cannot "be left hanging like a garment in the chair of being or essence" (*Ontology of the Accident* 17). Following up on Irigaray's own rethinking of form beyond its metaphysical understanding and her insistence that birth is "the entrance into a morphology, … into the morphology of the female or male sex" (Mulder 177), Malabou ventures to reconceptualize form as inextricable from what she calls the plasticity of materiality. "Plasticity" is a concept Malabou first introduces in *The Future of Hegel*. As she defines it, plasticity refers to the receiving and giving of form. It is, at the same time, the (creative or destructive) change of form—*trans*formation as much as absolute *de*formation. Drawing on recent neurobiological research, Malabou mobilizes the concept of plasticity in an attempt to reexamine the interplay between history and biology, nature and culture, determinism and freedom (Bhandar and Goldberg-Hiller 4). Following her line of thinking, if our arrival in sexed form cannot be denied, neither can it be denied that this form remains open to invention. "To construct one's identity," she explains, "is a process that can only be a development of an original biological malleability, a first transformability. If sex were not plastic, there would be no gender" (*Changing Difference* 138).

Surprisingly, then, Malabou succeeds in occupying an impossible position between affirming and negating sexual difference. On the one hand, she insists on enfleshed morphological specificity that points to the existence of some form of essence or material resistance. On the other hand, she foregrounds the plasticity of this essence, its openness to unexpected inventions of form, and new histories of embodiment. Given the novelty of her work, it is still early to predict the futures of a plasticized understanding of sexed difference. In his *Plastic Bodies* (2014), Tom Sparrow sets out to investigate one such possible future. Critically appropriating Malabou's materialism, his aim is to rethink not only the freedom of embodiment but also freedom as necessarily embodied, indeed, intercorporeal. As he argues, the project of a theory of corporeal plasticity is to activate anew Foucault's commitment to the aesthetic potential of embodiment beyond and in spite of constraining technologies of the body. "The body is an aesthetic phenomenon," he claims (230). As such, it is an assemblage of sensations, affects, supple surfaces, and intensities—all singular enough to produce "*this* body at *this* location" yet sufficiently plastic to allow a multiplicity of unimaginable connections and metamorphoses (226).

Flesh

The term "flesh" has often been used as a synonym for raw animate matter, what I have discussed as "meat" in this chapter. In my final section I intend, instead, to take as my starting point the phenomenological understanding of "flesh." As Emmanuel Falque points out, the distinction between "flesh" and the "body" is central in the wider phenomenological tradition, from Edmund Husserl and Maurice Merleau-Ponty to Michel

Henry. Whereas the term "body" refers to weighty, spatialized, objectified materiality, "flesh" stands for the "organic, or better [the] living body," that which undergoes the experience of its own embodiment (Falque 139). Rather than a thing in the world, it is the intentional connectedness of consciousness and the world. For Merleau-Ponty, in particular, "flesh" is the interrelatedness (indeed, the reversibility) of being and the world, subject and object, inside and outside. To draw on Grosz's account, "flesh" in Merleau-Ponty's thought is "the condition of both seeing and being seen, of touching and being touched"; it is "being's most elementary level" (*Volatile Bodies* 95, 100).

The phenomenological conceptualization of "flesh" in opposition to the "body" has been most useful in feminists' attempts to reclaim the female subject's corporeal existence beyond the systematic objectification and commodification of women's bodies. Feminist philosophers from de Beauvoir and Irigaray to Butler, Moi, Grosz, and Iris Marion Young, among others, have returned to this phenomenological tradition, sometimes reading it against the grain, in order to do justice to the complexity of embodied human existence while, at the same time, correcting this tradition's sex blindness. For example, both Irigaray and Young have taken Merleau-Ponty to task for grounding his analysis in a concept of "flesh" that remains neutral and is, as a result, incapable of accounting for the distinctness of women's corporeal experience. Demonstrating Merleau-Ponty's forgetting of the feminine/maternal in his invocation of an anonymous, not-yet sexually differentiated flesh, Irigaray succeeds in retheorizing "flesh" in ways that enable her to move beyond what for Falque is a serious *aporia* in the phenomenological tradition. In other words, she succeeds in thinking incorporation and incarnation side by side. Indeed, Irigaray is concerned neither with "body" nor with "flesh" in isolation but with the "body of flesh," as Falque puts it in his analysis of Henry (163). There "is never a 'lived experience of the body' independent from a 'materiality,' or even an 'organicity' that carries it," he insists (163). Similarly, "flesh" in Irigaray is a sensible transcendental. Though, as Mulder notes, it refers to "sensible, tangible, libidinal, maternal matter," it functions, simultaneously, as "a productive source and resource of relating and speaking, of being and becoming" (174).

It is interesting, I believe, that in her seminal essay "Mama's Baby, Papa's Maybe" Spillers comes to reiterate the phenomenological distinction between "body" and "flesh," remobilizing it in the interests of producing an ontology of freedom rooted paradoxically in the enslaved black body as its "zero degree" (659). According to Spillers, "flesh" is "a primary narrative" of human personhood that remains legible from generation to generation despite the "hieroglyphics" of torture that remark it, concealing it "under the brush of [colonial] discourse, or the reflexes of [sexist and racist] iconography" (659). Flesh, Spillers writes, is "the concentration of 'ethnicity,'" the vulnerable site where "biological, sexual, social, cultural, linguistic, ritualistic, and psychological fortunes" converge (658, 659). It is flesh that gets expropriated through the European "theft" of black bodies, that which is disciplined and reduced to exchangeable property in the economy of slavery (658).

Significantly, in her recontextualization of the concept of "flesh," Spillers invokes both the intentionality traditionally associated with it and a kind of pathos that contemporary phenomenologist Michel Henry insists is originary and nonintentional. As Falque explains, the pathos Henry attributes to this other, nonintentional flesh relates to its "carnal auto-affection," that is, the capacity of flesh to experience joy, pain, hunger, anxiety *under* the skin (146, 147). It is, then, flesh as *sensible*, beyond the phenomenological distinction between the sens*ing* and the sens*ed*. In her analysis of a form of "human and social irreparability" that she connects with the European violation of black flesh, Spillers foregrounds the "seared, divided, ripped-apartness" of flesh (659). In a similar vein to

Henry, she perceives the flesh as "the site of my greatest passivity, and thus of my noblest receptivity (of my own life and of the absolute Life in me)" (Falque 147). For both thinkers, this originary flesh can be violated and yet persists. What is more, it is inextricable from the singularity of the human person, his or her "profound intimacy" that, according to Spillers, was disrupted through the captivation of the black body (Spillers 658). As Falque points out, Henry's auto-impressional flesh "is always only *mine*—neither 'yours', nor 'someone's', nor even 'ours'" (147).

Reading Spillers's employment of a concept of "flesh" in light of Henry's own rethinking of this concept may turn out to be useful, I think, especially for a critical feminist theory that cannot afford to forget the "materialized scene[s] of unprotected female flesh," enacted again and again in the context of persistent economies of slavery (Spillers 660). It is precisely in such scenes where a "laboratory prose of festering flesh" operates that Bakare-Yusuf locates the perseverance of a counter-memory of freedom (314). Drawing on Spillers, she insists that there is always a memory of the "flesh" in the enslaved body. In her view, this memory can return, reviving the body's capacity for resistance, transformation, and healing: The body, she writes, "was and still is capable of being something quite beautiful, quite sensuous, quite joyous" (321). Indeed, it is this return of "flesh" in the newly liberated bodies of ex-slaves that Baby Suggs in Morrison's *Beloved* orchestrates at the Clearing: In "this here place," Baby Suggs tells friends and strangers, "we flesh, flesh that weeps, laughs; flesh that dances on bare feet in grass" (88). And it is this return of "flesh" that Beloved herself seeks when she asks Paul D. to touch her "inside part" and call her name (117).

In a discussion with Cheah and Grosz, Butler cautions against an uncritical employment of the concept of "flesh": "'Flesh,'" she argues, is "a wonderful rhetorical word that makes everyone think that they have arrived finally at the true end of embodiment and materiality" (Cheah and Grosz 33). On the other hand, Spillers posits her counter-hegemonic history of "crimes against the *flesh*" as the possible source of "a praxis and a theory, a text for living and for dying and a method of reading" (559, 660). Caught in what feels like a double-bind, twenty-first-century feminists may, like Lewis Carroll's Alice, discover that the wonder of sexed metamorphic embodiment relies as much on the theorist's suspicion (and smiling suspension) of enfleshed materiality as on the victim's committed resistance to any sovereign's vicious disparagement of it.

NOTES

1 This is the translation of the relevant *Genesis* passage (*Genesis* 2:7), which Emmanuel Falque uses in "Is There a Flesh Without Body?" (164).

2 See Butler, "Sex and Gender."

3 See Engels, "The Origin of the Oppression of Women."

4 See Penley and Ross, 1991.

WORKS CITED

Bakare-Yusuf, Bibi. "The Economy of Violence: Black Bodies and the Unspeakable Horror." *Feminist Theory and the Body: A Reader.* Ed. Janet Price and Margrit Shildrick. Edinburgh: Edinburgh UP, 1999, pp. 311–23.

Bhandar, Brenna, and Jonathan Goldberg-Hiller, eds. *Plastic Materialities: Politics, Legality, and Metamorphosis in the Work of Catherine Malabou.* Durham, NC: Duke UP, 2015.

Bordo, Susan. *Unbearable Weight, Feminism, Western Culture, and the Body*. Berkeley: U of California P, 1993.

Braidotti, Rosi. "Meta(l)flesh." *The Future of Flesh: A Cultural Survey of the Body*. Ed. Zoe Detsi-Diamanti, Katerina Kitsi-Mitakou, and Effie Yiannopoulou. New York: Palgrave Macmillan, 2009, pp. 241–61.

Butler, Judith. *Bodies That Matter: On the Discursive Limits of "Sex."* New York: Routledge, 1993.

Butler, Judith. "Sex and Gender in Simone de Beauvoir's *Second Sex*." *Yale French Studies* 72 (1995): 35–49.

Cadigan, Pat. *Synners*. London: Gollancz, 2012.

Cheah, Pheng. "Mattering." *Diacritics* 26.1 (1996): 108–39.

Cheah, Pheng, and Elizabeth Grosz, "The Future of Sexual Difference: An Interview with Judith Butler and Drucilla Cornell." *Diacritics* 28.1 (Spring 1998): 19–42.

Colebrook, Claire. "Is Sexual Difference a Problem?" *Deleuze and Feminist Theory*. Ed. Ian Buchanan and Claire Colebrook. Edinburgh: Edinburgh UP, 2000, pp. 110–27.

De Beauvoir, Simone. *The Second Sex*. Trans. Constance Borde and Sheila Malovany-Chevallier. New York: Vintage Books, 2011.

Engels, Friedrich. "The Origin of the Oppression of Women." *History of Ideas on Woman*. Ed. Rosemary Agonito. New York: Perigee Trade, 1978, pp. 273–88.

Falque, Emmanuel. "Is There a Flesh Without Body? A Debate with Michel Henry." *Journal of French and Francophone Philosophy* XXIV.1 (2016): 139–66.

Featherstone, Mike, and Roger Burrows. "Cultures of Technological Embodiment: An Introduction." *Cyberspace/Cyberbodies/Cyberpunk: Cultures of Technological Embodiment*. Ed. Mike Featherstone and Roger Burrows. London: Sage, 2000, pp. 1–19.

Ferrando, Francesca. "The Body." *Post- and Transhumanism: An Introduction*. Ed. Robert Ranisch and Stefan Lorenz Sorgner. Bern: Peter Lang, 2014, pp. 213–26.

Foucault, Michel. "Nietzsche, Genealogy, History." *Language, Counter-Memory, Practice: Selected Essays and Interviews*. Ed. Donald Bouchard. Ithaca, NY: Cornell UP, 1977.

Grosz, Elizabeth. *Becoming Undone: Darwinian Reflections on Life, Politics, and Art*. Durham, NC: Duke UP, 2011.

Grosz, Elizabeth. *Time Travels: Feminism, Nature, Power*. Durham, NC: Duke UP, 2005.

Grosz, Elizabeth. *Volatile Bodies: Toward a Corporeal Feminism*. Bloomington: Indiana UP, 1994.

Halberstam, Judith. "F2M: The Making of Female Masculinity." *Feminist Theory and the Body: A Reader*. Ed. Janet Price and Margrit Shildrick. Edinburgh: Edinburgh UP, 1999, pp. 125–33.

Haraway, Donna J. "A Cyborg Manifesto: Science, Technology, and Socialist-Feminism in the Late Twentieth Century." *Simians, Cyborgs, and Women: The Reinvention of Nature*. New York: Routledge, 1991, pp. 149–81.

Irigaray, Luce. *An Ethics of Sexual Difference*. Trans. Carolyn Burke and Gillian C. Gill. New York: Continuum, 2004.

Kellogg, Catherine. "'You Be My Body for Me': Dispossession in Two Valences." *Philosophy and Social Criticism* 43.1 (2017): 83–95.

Land, Nick. "Meat (or How to Kill Oedipus in Cyberspace)." *Cyberspace, Cyberbodies, Cyberpunk: Cultures of Technological Embodiment*. Ed. Mike Featherstone and Roger Burrows. London: Sage, 2000, pp. 191–204.

Lupton, Deborah. "The Embodied Computer/User." *Cyberspace, Cyberbodies, Cyberpunk: Cultures of Technological Embodiment*. Ed. Mike Featherstone and Roger Burrows. London: Sage, 2000, pp. 99–112.

Malabou,Catherine. *Changing Difference: The Feminine and the Question of Philosophy*. Trans. Carolyn Shread. Cambridge, UK: Polity P, 2011.

Malabou,Catherine. *Ontology of the Accident: An Essay on Destructive Plasticity*. Trans. Carolyn Shread. Cambridge, UK: Polity P, 2012.

Malabou, Catherine, and Judith Butler. "You Be My Body for Me: Body, Shape, and Plasticity in Hegel's *Phenomenology of Spirit*." *A Companion to Hegel*. Ed. Stephen Houlgate and Michael Baur. Oxford: Blackwell, 2011, pp. 611–40.

Moi, Toril. *What Is a Woman? And Other Essays*. Oxford: Oxford UP, 1999.

Morrison, Toni. *Beloved*. New York: Vintage Books, 1997.

Mulder, Anne-Claire. "Incarnation: The Flesh Becomes Word." *Dialogues*. Ed. Luce Irigaray, *Paragraph* 25.3 (November 2002): 173–86.

Nietzsche, Friedrich. *On the Genealogy of Morals/Ecce Homo*. Trans. Walter Kaufmann. New York: Vintage Books, 1969.

Pearce, Lynne. *The Rhetorics of Feminism: Readings in Contemporary Cultural Theory and the Popular Press*. New York: Routledge, 2004.

Penley, Constance, and Andrew Ross. "Cyborgs at Large: Interview with Donna Haraway." *Social Text* 25.26 (1991): 8–23.

Prosser, Jay. *Second Skins: The Body Narratives of Transsexuality*. New York: Columbia UP, 1998.

Rich, Adrienne. "When We Dead Awaken: Writing as Re-Vision." *On Lies, Secrets and Silence: Selected Prose 1966–1978*, London: Virago, 1986, pp. 33–49.

Sobchack, Vivian. "Beating the Meat/Surviving the Text, or How to Get Out of this Century Alive." *Cyberspace, Cyberbodies, Cyberpunk: Cultures of Technological Embodiment*. Ed. Mike Featherstone and Roger Burrows, London: Sage, 2000, pp. 205–14.

Sparrow, Tom. *Plastic Bodies: Rebuilding Sensation after Phenomenology*. London: Open Humanities P, 2014.

Spelman, Elizabeth V. "Woman as Body: Ancient and Contemporary Views." *Feminist Theory and the Body: A Reader*. Ed. Janet Price and Margrit Shildrick. Edinburgh: Edinburgh UP, 1999, pp. 32–41.

Spillers, Hortense. "Mama's Baby, Papa's Maybe: An American Grammar Book." *Literary Theory: An Anthology*. Ed. Julie Rivkin and Michael Ryan. Oxford: Blackwell, 1998, pp. 656–72.

Walker, Sarai. *Dietland*. London: Atlantic Books, 2015.

Wendell, Susan. *The Rejected Body: Feminist Philosophical Reflections on Disability*. New York: Routledge, 1996.

Wolf, Naomi. *The Beauty Myth: How Images of Beauty Are Used against Women*. New York: HarperCollins, 2002.

Wollstonecraft, Mary. "A Vindication of the Rights of Woman." *The Norton Anthology of English Literature*, vol. 2. Ed. M. H. Abrams et al. New York: W. W. Norton, 1979, pp. 112–37.

CHAPTER SIX

Affect

ANCA PARVULESCU

How and when does one become a feminist? This is the question animating Sara Ahmed's recent *Living a Feminist Life* (2017). The narrative it provides as an answer begins with a feeling that something is amiss in one's world. One feels it on one's skin; alienation is a sensation. In time, as a function of repetition and the irritation that comes with it (repetition is also something one feels on one's skin), one begins to reflect on both the feeling and its eloquent repetition. Knowledge, feminist knowledge, slowly develops as the outcome of dwelling on a feeling. As Ahmed's narrative advances, one begins to read feminist books, feminist classics, and one realizes one is not alone: others have had similar feelings and similar thoughts in response to those feelings. Feminist consciousness breaks through, one day, for some, as the by-product of such a realization, which functions as a constitutive affective event. Feminist theory is necessarily a form of affect theory because the feminist subject is constituted affectively.

Attachment to the affective event that births the feminist subject shapes the feminist life, which in Ahmed's account blurs the distinction between theory and practice and between practice and politics. A theory of the good feminist life is a practice of the good feminist life. Ahmed renames this loyal subject: the feminist killjoy. *Living a Feminist Life* ends with a manifesto titled "The Killjoy Manifesto," which belongs to a long series of attempts to rewrite and reclaim the anti-feminist figure of the feminist killjoy.[1] What the feminist killjoy kills is crucially not joy but the ideology of happiness women are socialized to desire as a life. The feminist killjoy is committed to stirring things up in search of an alternative to happiness and a more just world, where she and other feminists can feel somewhat at home. Importantly, the feminist killjoy is not humorless; she both produces humor and laughs in certain circumstances: "we laugh often in recognition of the shared absurdity of this world; or just in recognition of this world" (Ahmed, *Living* 245). Principle 4 of the Killjoy Manifesto, nonetheless, reads, "I am not willing to laugh at jokes designed to cause offense" (261). Affect theory promises to offer a framework in which to understand and possibly to intervene in some of the thorniest debates in contemporary life.

In 2017, Ahmed is not alone either in retracing feminist theory as affect theory or in her return to the figure of the feminist killjoy and its counterpart, the humorless feminist. For Lauren Berlant, affect theory is a subset of ideology critique, offering a more attuned and more descriptive style of critique at a time when critique seems to be in need of redefinition.[2] Affect studies address questions ranging from the scale of the intimate to that of the world, from the subjective to the economic, from the ineffable to the structural. It promises to account for what are often contradictory, messy affective clusters, both personal and collective. "People leak or spray affectively all over the place" ("Humorlessness" 312), Berlant writes. Cruel optimism constitutes such a cluster, naming the desire for a life that promises a narrative of happiness but often delivers cruelty, to which the subject nonetheless remains attached. Berlant offers a revised concept of the Spinosist *conatus*: we sometimes persevere in the bad in order to survive.

Berlant too is invested in retheorizing the humorless subject, including implicitly the feminist humorless subject. In Berlant's account, the humorless subject is overly focused on the micro-adjustments that put together an appearance of sovereignty—an appearance of being in control and of knowing what to do next. In this context, Berlant is skeptical of both "the humorlessness of commitment" and "the commitment of humorlessness" ("Humorlessness" 310). Privilege attaches to humorlessness, Berlant argues, which is unequally distributed across the social field. Not everyone can afford to, in Berlant's words, "withhold the cushion of generosity, wit, or mutually hashed-out terms of relation" (310). Not everyone can afford to, as Ahmed advises, go on a smiling strike. Some subjects, often women, are expected to conciliate social situations in order to make or sustain a living.

Ahmed and Berlant offer examples of contemporary theories of affect—one focused on the urgency of what it understands as the political; the other committed to a non-judgmental, at points even tender, tracing of affective attachments that might well be needed for contemporary psychic survival. Albeit in different keys, Ahmed and Berlant are invested in the work of affective description and redescription of the normative. They both participate in the "affective turn," the wave of scholarship on affect in the first two decades of the twenty-first century, paralleled in intensity only by the concentration of early modern writing on the passions and the eighteenth-century constellation of writing on feeling.[3] They are also separate from it in that they both, unlike many contemporary theorists of affect, invoke and rely on a feminist genealogy of theorizing emotion and affect in the 1980s. They work with a receptive genealogy of feminist theory's engagement with emotion and affect—indeed, with an awareness that work on emotion in the 1980s was often work on affect.

FEMINIST GENEALOGIES

Genealogies of feminism are highly passionate affairs. They constitute sites of affective density, saturated with a range of feelings. Scholars tend to be deeply invested in some narratives of feminism's trajectories—and oppose others with equal passion. Beginnings are especially contested sites: starting a genealogy with Juana Inés de la Cruz, Harriet Jacobs, Simone de Beauvoir, or Gayle Rubin yields different narratives about different feminist projects, with different feminist personae, and in different critical styles. It remains important to trace multiple feminist genealogies, revolving not only around multiple figures but also multiple conceptual configurations. One such conceptual genealogical configuration traces the feminist literature on emotion and affect, which sometimes risks being erased within the broader "affective turn."[4] Genealogical work placates the temptation of claiming a fresh start for the affective turn, which rhetorically produces its necessity by clearing the critical field either into a quasi *tabula rasa* or a selective and limited, interested genealogy.

Feminist theory's engagement with affect and emotion has taken myriad forms. It has detailed a Bildung in proper femininity, retracing the historical socialization of women into gendered feeling norms. It has described various forms of emotional attachment to objects, situations, and structures. It has dramatized consciousness raising as a form of emotion work, whereby one transitions from a feeling of loneliness to one of community. Among the rhetorical forms that consciousness-raising draws has been the use of the personal voice, arguably one of the ways of accessing emotions. Calls for change often involve a feminist theory of the event reliant on a subject's porous affective receptivity. Accounts of feminist solidarity have had to account for both the benefits and risks of thinking through empathy. Feminist encounters with psychoanalysis have often focused on the latter's theorization of affect. Theories of racialization have sometimes described race as an effect of a consequential, emotion-filled encounter. The workings of power have been revealed to be anchored in feeling, including various forms of attachment to oppression.

In the following, I identify three clusters of feminist scholarship on affect and emotion in the 1980s. The first cluster is concerned with a political economy of emotional and affective labor as seen through Arlie Russell Hochschild's *The Managed Heart: Commercialization of Human Feeling* (1983). The second cluster revolves around feminist epistemology and its turn to emotion, as seen through Alison M. Jaggar's essay, "Love and Knowledge: Emotion in Feminist Epistemology" (1989). The third cluster centers around Audre Lorde's essay "The Uses of Anger" (1981) and the theorization of emotion in black feminist thought. Genealogically, the texts around which I group these tendencies concentrate the stakes of three influential, interrelated feminist debates in the 1980s. Gayle Rubin's retrospective words on her influential essay, "The Traffic in Women: Notes on the 'Political Economy' of Sex" (1975), are eloquent in these three cases as well; they are pieces of "amber that preserve those heady conversations and that moment in time" (12).

The Managed Heart revisits several tenets of feminist materialism in order to identify emotion as a resource that contemporary forms of capitalism, the service industry and the care industry in particular, enlist.[5] In this line of work, workers mine their emotional reservoir and sell it as labor. Hochschild defines emotion as an orientation: "a way of knowing about the world" (29). As a perspective on the world, emotion "warns us of where we stand vis-à-vis outer or inner events" (Hochschild 28), thus constituting a form of "pre-action" (56). Anticipating Ahmed, Hochschild rejects the model of a subjective "inside" of emotion (17) and proposes an understanding of emotion as relational and interactional, a function of social exchange. Using a word Berlant picks up, Hochschild argues that emotion is a "lubricant" (167) in social exchange. The fact that women more than men are traditionally called upon to lubricate exchange reflects power arrangements and inequality in expectations for emotional production and management. Expectations are part of the habitus, translating into "feeling rules," taught by both family and school. In time, they yield gendered specializations in emotion (Hochschild 170) and thus gendered emotional roles and jobs. They become body through the sedimentation of requirements for physical appearance that include heels, weigh-ins, makeup, smiles, and so forth, which, in time, sculpt surface into a body.

At times, Hochschild describes flight attendants' attempts to "preserve a sense of self by circumventing the feeling rules of work" (xviii). The agency Hochschild claims for flight attendants (locating female agency was an imperative in 1980s feminist theory) is anchored in the preservation of this "real" self, as is the possibility of placating emotional burnout (197). In particular, since smiling materializes into their signature emotional labor, Hoschschild imagines flight attendants reclaiming their smile (127). At other times in *The Managed Heart*, however, Hochschild seems well aware that this "true" self, which one would cultivate in the private sphere, is itself estranged. Anticipating her collaboration with Barbara Ehrenreich in *Global Woman: Nannies, Maids and Sex Workers in the New Economy* (2002), she acknowledges that many contemporary emotional labor jobs are located in the private household. What Hochschild calls emotional transmutation is not strictly a transfer of emotion from the private realm to the public sphere; it is, rather, multidirectional. The analogy between cabin and living room, which Hochschild struggles to dismantle, is not in fact a mere analogy not only because flight attendants are recruited on account of specialized emotional skills developed in the family but also because the emotional skills developed on the job prepare flight attendants for future careers in the family. On the one hand, women who come from large families are thought to be better equipped for situations in which, as one flight attendant recalls, they "tuck people into bed" (Hochschild 122) as proto-mothers (176). On the other, the family "quietly imposes emotional obligations of its own" (69). There is an ongoing looping effect between the family household and the cabin: "The atmosphere of the private living room, which a young flight attendant is asked to recall as she works in the airplane cabin, has *already borrowed* some of the elements of that cabin" (161). *The Managed Heart* is a second-wave feminist learning text, revealing how the private/public analytical divide (itself carrier of the true/false self divide) collapses, in the course of research on emotion: "Schooled in emotion management at home, women have entered in disproportionate numbers those jobs that call for emotional labor outside the home" (181).

If Hochschild's book can be seen as a node of second-wave feminist work on emotional labor and economy, Alison M. Jaggar's essay "Love and Knowledge: Emotion in Feminist Epistemology" (1989) constitutes a node for feminist epistemology's engagement with emotion.[6] Like Hochschild, Jaggar turns to emotion because of its historical association with woman. Jaggar starts her argument with a familiar two-column set of keywords, a signature rhetorical strategy in second-wave feminist theory: "Not only has reason been contrasted with emotion, but it has also been associated with the mental, the cultural, the universal, the public, and the male, whereas emotion has been associated with the irrational, the physical, the natural, the particular, the private, and, of course, the female" (145).[7] In this framework, Jaggar sets out to dispel stereotypes of "cool men and emotional women" (158).

Arguing against an understanding of positivist epistemology as limiting emotion to the choice of object, followed by "dispassionate inquiry" (155), Jaggar proposes alternative modes of knowing through emotion. For Jaggar, emotions and the "physical disturbances" coterminous with them are socially constructed. We are socialized into emotion and the language of emotion; the work of ideological reproduction is often done through "recalcitrant" emotion (164). Our "first impressions" or "gut reactions" are nothing but habitual emotional responses. Emotions are historically specific, an insight that has led to a large literature on the history of emotion over the last two decades. And emotions are culturally specific; indeed, in dialogue with Catherine Lutz, Jaggar argues that the very reason/emotion dualism is Eurocentric; words for emotions are often untranslatable across languages. The work of tracing the impact of the word "emotion" as it travels into non-Western linguistic contexts and is translated through various translingual practices remains to be done.[8]

For Jaggar, like for Hochschild, emotions and expressions are mutually constitutive engagements with the world, shaping the purportedly objective exercises of observation and description: "emotion directs, shapes and even partially defines observation ... What it is selected and how it is interpreted are influenced by emotional attitudes" (154). Indeed, they have shaped modern Western science and its purportedly objective findings. Most importantly, what emotions do is selectively focus our habits of attention (Jaggar 154). At the same time, they help "motivate new investigations" (161), a Cartesian argument that Ahmed traces as well (*Cultural*). Anticipating contemporary debates concerning the affect of various critical schools, Jaggar calls for an awareness that "efforts to reeducate our emotions are necessary to our theoretical investigation" (164) and are instrumental to the creation of a plurality of affective theoretical styles.[9] One such emotional style would circle around Jaggar's titular love; if Hochschild sees a circuit of emotion circulating between the family household and the service sector, Jaggar traces a parallel line between the family household and the philosophy department.

Like Hochschild, Jaggar emphasizes the appropriateness of feeling in a given situation and the possibility of affective misfit, which she calls "outlaw emotion" (160). Here is Jaggar's example: a woman of color feels anger in response to a room's laughter at a racist joke (160). Because "the hegemony that our society exercises over people's emotional constitution is not total" (160), emotions can function as incipient analyses of power and inequality, leading to potential critique. Subcultures, including feminist subcultures, are formed around outlaw emotions. In a move Berlant develops, Jaggar acknowledges a potential mismatch between emotion and politics: "we may still continue to experience emotions inconsistent with our conscious politics" (163); and she foregrounds the possibility of "emotional deception and even self-deception" (165).

Jaggar's essay is representative of a strand in the feminist theory of the 1980s that oscillates productively between epistemology and a certain kind of ontology: "interaction between how we understand the world and who we are as people" (164).[10] In this conversation, ontology acquires a forceful affective dimension. Audre Lorde's "The Uses of Anger" both belongs to and challenges this body of literature. If Jaggar turns to the exemplarity of love, Lorde argues for the recognition of anger as black women's ontology and calls for its deployment as a mode of feminist affective relation. "The Uses of Anger" was given as a talk at the National Women's Studies Association in 1981 and subsequently published in *Sister Outsider: Essays and Speeches* (1984).[11] It predates both Hochschild's book and Jaggar's essay and can be read as a background to both. The poet-theorist warns that "I do not want this to become a theoretical discussion" (Lorde 278), thus marking the emergence of a very particular kind of feminist theory, with its signature emotional style. Throughout, Lorde deploys the word "use" ("the uses of anger") creatively as a gesture against a certain mode of theorizing that risks remaining abstract and academic. Since "anger is loaded with information and energy" (280), feminists can tap it as a resource—a resource not for the labor market or philosophical argumentation but for politics.

Lorde's essay is both precise and creative in its affective use of pronouns—an embodied "I," a plural "you," a hospitable "we." It is written and delivered under the sign of urgency. It uses anecdote as condensed, embodied historical knowledge. Lorde deploys the sentence "My response to racism is anger" as a performative refrain (278, 283). Nonparadoxically, the cool, matter-of-fact statement forcefully amplifies the message that anger is an appropriate response to racism, as appropriate as the fear of the bear in William James's famous philosophical example.[12] Lorde cautions that there are different kinds of anger—*angers*—and calls for acuity in distinguishing between them: "the anger of exclusion, of unquestioned privilege, of racial distortions, of silence, ill-use, stereotyping, defensiveness, misnaming, betrayal, and coopting" (278). While some of these angers might be punctual, responding to specific situations, for Lorde anger is a mood, functioning in an ontological *longue durée*. Crucially, anger can become a relation: "Anger is the grief of distortions between peers" (Lorde 282). Unlike guilt or fear or rage, anger can be used as a relation of equality; Lorde could have subtitled her essay "How to Do Things with Anger." Anger travels on a horizontal plane of relation—like friendship or partnership.[13]

A notable operative keyword for Lorde is *clarity*: anger brings clarity. She rewrites the meaning of the word in modern European philosophy, where claims to knowledge have often relied on tropes of clarity, as in Descartes' search for "clear and distinct" scientific claims (*Meditations*). Lorde suggests that anger is an "act of clarification" (280); it constitutes a usable "spotlight" (278). If Jaggar traces the afterlives of "dispassionate observation," Lorde proposes that, for some, it is anger that clears the field of observation: "I have suckled the wolf's lip of anger and have used it for illumination" (285). It is not only that the reason/emotion dichotomy never held but also that in some situations emotion might be more conducive to illumination than a *cogito* fantasized as independent of the passions.

One of the most eloquent images in Lorde's essay calls out the white feminist who "cannot see her heelprint upon another woman's face" (284). The foot on someone's face is a symbol of colonialism and the racial regime of domination it inaugurated. Robinson Crusoe is often visually depicted with his foot on Friday's face. In Lorde's image, Crusoe is a modern white woman in heels. Her heels might be a sign of her oppression (Hochschild's flight attendant is forced to wear heels), but they should not blind her to other women's oppression, in which the well-heeled woman participates. Anger is here a way of framing the sedimentation of inequality *among* women.

Lorde goes on to acknowledge that she might be guilty of blindness herself, failing to recognize other women of color as "other faces of myself" (284). Face becomes *form* in Lorde's writing. Racism is a face. Oppression is a face. So is fear. Anger is a face. So is solidarity. Face is nonetheless also a verb; Lorde calls upon her audience to "face each other's angers" (282). Her last sentence: "We welcome all women who can meet us face to face, beyond objectification and beyond guilt" (285). This is not Levinas's face-to-face without a face; it is, precisely, a call to read the microexpressions of the face, the face as expression.

These three, nonexhaustive clusters of feminist theory (Hochschild, Jaggar, Lorde), and the complex relation between them, bear witness to a period in the 1980s when emotion and affect were objects of intense feminist interrogation. Importantly, as we have seen with Lorde, the insights developed within this body of work consequentially turned to an investigation of feminism's own affective histories, especially histories of racialization and affective complicity. Subsequently, they turned to an interrogation of feminism's affective investments in a transnational frame. In the 1990s, a body of feminist work sketched the figure of the sentimental feminist benefactor who imagines herself saving brown women from brown men.[14] Feminist affect theory became a tool to rethink and newly pluralize the feminist project itself.

EXPRESSION AFTER THE EXPRESSIVE SUBJECT

How do we think expression *after* the affective turn? Does expression die with the expressive subject? Once we sever the link between the subject's interiority and expression, what is left of expression? If, as Ahmed revising Judith Butler argues, bodies come to matter through emotional encounters, is the ensuing "surface" expressive? Is expression inevitably linked to emotion or are there ways to think affective expressivity? One way of foregrounding the importance of genealogical work is to acknowledge the fact that it yields a set of old/new questions.

The focus on the physicality of emotion in the three clusters above is a symptom of feminist theory's central preoccupation with the body. Indeed, it could be argued that feminist theory's affective genealogies constitute a subset of feminist theories of the body. One of Hochschild's most enduring contributions remains her detailed description of the choreography of a smile. Jaggar goes to great length to emphasize that emotions and their "physical disturbances" are co-constitutive; we cannot think one without the other. Lorde develops a complex theory of the face in order to draw out difference *within* anger.

In the meantime, thinking about expression has fallen out of favor in contemporary affect theory.[15] Rei Terada writes *Feeling in Theory: Emotion after the "Death of the Subject"* (2001) against what she calls "the expressive hypothesis" (11). Expression, in this account, is guilty of advertising and verifying modern subjectivity—in particular subjective interiority and depth. In a similar vein, Ranjana Khanna follows Fredric Jameson in his diagnosis of postmodern culture's post-expression predicament: "This waning of affect is a result of the fact that there is no subject remaining, and no expression. It is, in fact, a deconstruction of the subject as expressive being" (214). The purportedly disappearing subject is "an original subject with depth, a centre and feeling" (214); since expression is thought to be a function of the subject's depth, it disappears alongside this subject. In a familiar move, Khanna follows Derrida, himself following Levinas, to "seek out risk in relation to an alterity without a face" (230).

It would seem that we move away from expression if we work with a too-sharp distinction between emotion and affect. This distinction is often attributed to Brian Massumi and his followers, for whom formed, namable emotions capture the open potentiality of unformed, ineffable affect. Indeed, for Massumi, "Emotion is the intensest (most contracted) expression of that capture" (96).[16] Since the possibility of the new is tied to affect, the *expression* of emotion closes off affect's creative possibilities. As affect and emotion become polarized in this fashion, expression largely falls off the conceptual map. The genealogy of feminist theory proposed here, however, tells the story of a shrinking distance between the concepts of emotion and affect. This story becomes legible if we read this genealogy generously, in a hospitable key that historicizes its signature moves: its over-preoccupation with agency and thus a certain subjectivity, its lists of operative dichotomies, and its emotional styles. It is the argument of this essay that the feminist theory of the 1980s applied itself to a conceptual conglomerate I have been referring to as "emotion *and* affect," with an emphasis on the conjunction.[17]

Let us return to Hochschild once again. She emphasizes that flight attendants successfully sever the relation of emotion to a cause (113), with emotion thus becoming largely autonomous, independent of both subject and object, as Massumi would argue is the case with affect. Workers are estranged from their smiles; they are "*on* them but not *of* them" (Hochschild 8); they are "an extension of the make-up" (8). Flight attendants experience "separations of 'me' from my face" (37). The emotions Hochschild focuses on are not only friendliness, love, gratitude, fear, sincerity, and niceness but also clusters of feelings, often without a name, "intangibles" (101).

Hochschild's central concepts, emotion and emotional labor, are anchored in the realities of flight attendants' gendered lives, which have changed considerably since the 1980s. Nonetheless, her insights offer an arc of comparison to conceptualizations of what today we call affect and affective labor.[18] What the worker sells is her personality, conducive to successful teamwork (Hochschild 115). Not coincidentally, "self-sellers" are often encouraged to imagine themselves as self-employed (109). They can work any-where, indeed, often at home. Today, one recognizes here precedents for the contem-porary debates on affective labor and the creative class. Given the widespread demand for emotional labor, Hochschild announces that "we are all partly flight attendants" (11). On account of our emotional deep acting, "We are all students of Stanislavski" (194). Given Hochschild's focus on emotion *and* gender, however, unlike for other theorists of affect, the fact that "we are all flight attendants" asks us to pay attention to the workings of gender.[19] If we are to speak, with Gilles Deleuze and Félix Guattari, alongside Massumi, of "affective athleticism" (Deleuze and Guattari 172), we might want to remember that if anybody is an affective athlete, it is the female flight attendant.

Hochschild draws on Constantin Stanislavski's distinction between surface and deep acting. When a flight attendant feigns a smile, she is surface acting. Since this effort can be exhausting, she soon realizes it is easier to actually be nice. Stanislavski suggests that one can make this transition by imagining that one is not serving a rude stranger but a relative or a friend. This is deep acting, generator of affective authenticity on the job. The dis-tinction is crucial to Hochschild because it allows her to account for situations in which flight attendants retreat from deep acting to surface acting. Hochschild locates agency in surface acting: if I display a fake smile, I am in control of my smile, therefore I have agency. The politics of *The Managed Heart* is anchored in this possibility. Hochschild, however, knows that the distinction between authenticity and phoniness does not hold; the "true self" is irretrievable lost, because it has always been lost already in the family, which enforces its own emotional labor. And so is the distinction between surface and deep acting. The flight attendant does not have to recall a narrative situation in which she helped a family member; all she has to do is, in the blink of an eye, activate a smile. She has no need for narrative memory or, for that matter, any interiority; the smile is already a form of memory, lodged in the muscles of the face.

Feminist theory in the tradition of *The Managed Heart* attends to microexpressions—not necessarily as manifestations of a subject's emotional activities but as floating sub-jective and nonsubjective traces. The smile of the flight attendant is not *her* expression; it is not the property of a subject, and yet it remains expressive. Hochschild details the work of transmutation, the travel of emotion and expression between family and workplace, before acknowledging that transmutation fails. What we are left with is not so much emo-tional labor as expression labor (Hochschild 136). Methodologically, what this means is that sometimes we need to start with the face, start from expression—a smile, a tear, a blush—in order to understand the workings of affect.[20]

In her recentering of expression, Hochschild is invoking a long and diverse tradition that goes beyond feminist theory. Descartes, despite having his name associated with caricatures of the "Cartesian subject," emphasizes in *The Passions of the Soul* that passion and expression reinforce each other, albeit not in a straightforward way; the face more often than not deceives or simply does its own bidding as a function of habituation. William James, for his part, concerns himself only with affective states that have a bodily counterpart. Suffice it to say that Darwin's book on emotion is titled *The Expression of Emotion in Man and Animal*. Walter Benjamin develops a theory of modernist physi-ognomy concerned with "the face of things." Perhaps most surprisingly, although Deleuze and Guattari are considered to belong to the affect side of the emotion/affect distinction à la Massumi, they are deeply invested in a theory of expression: "all the material becomes expressive" (Deleuze and Guattari 90).[21]

Among other things, the genealogy of feminist theory's engagement with emotion and affect in the 1980s takes the form of an invitation to rethink expression—in and beyond feminist theory. Within the sphere of what Hochschild calls expression work, we can focus on micro-expressions (131)—the micro-expressions differentiating the various angers in Lorde's account, for example. Or we can focus on posture—the face-to-face in the same account. We can draw on James's investment in the legibility of a range of expressions— changes on the skin, patterns of breathing or sweating or crying, contractions of the muscles, positions of the spine, and a range of gestures. Attending to this level of bodily detail, affect theory as expression theory becomes an analysis not of what is hidden below the surface but precisely of the surface.

As a conclusion, a brief encounter with a passage in Virgina Woolf's novel *Orlando* might offer an example of the inescapability of expression after the turn to affect. Published in 1928, the novel is arguably itself a combination of feminist theory and affect theory; it could be included in an extended version of the feminist genealogical map proposed above. The passage that concerns us appears at the beginning of the novel, as young Orlando is introduced to the Queen:

> Such was his shyness that he saw no more of her than her ringed hands in water; but it was enough. It was a memorable hand; a thin hand with long fingers always curling as if round orb or sceptre; a nervous, crabbed, sickly hand; a commanding hand too; a hand that had only to raise itself for a head to fall; a hand, he guessed, attached to an old body that smelt like a cupboard in which furs are kept in camphor; which body was yet caparisoned in all sorts of brocades and gems; and held itself very upright though perhaps in pain from sciatica; and never flinched though strung together by a thousand fears; and the Queen's eyes were light yellow. All this he felt as the great rings flashed in the water and then something pressed his hair—which, perhaps, accounts for his seeing nothing more likely to be of use to a historian. And in truth, his mind was such a welter of opposites—of the night and the blazing candles, of the shabby poet and the great Queen, of silent fields and the clatter of serving men—that he could see nothing; or only a hand.

Orlando reads a hand; the reader reads Orlando's reading of a hand. The hand is an expressive surface; formally, the hand becomes face. This is the Queen's hand, but if the hand expresses something it is not her interiority, which remains opaque. Woolf's narrator makes sure the reader does not have access to the Queen's soul. The hand—its shape, texture, pose, movement—expresses a relation. Woolf is ironic of the reading the hand might have been given historically, in classic physiognomy and chirology (the science of the hand), where the Queen's hand might have come across as unambiguously commanding, a function of her power. Instead, in Orlando's reading, the hand is both upright and vulnerable—commanding, but also fearful. A visual object, the hand unproblematically carries information about the Queen's bodily smell and her health. Woolf's scene foregrounds the fact that the expression of the hand is a function of Orlando's guessing—his "gut reaction." It is filtered through modernist affect attached to Orlando's point of view, not the Queen's. Orlando's affective makeup in the scene is messy and ambiguous (he "sprays affectively all over the place," Berlant might say). Shyness and excitement, desire and disgust, freely intermix. What the hand expresses, what it is memorable for, is the fact that there is expression, both historical and punctual, circulating, free-floating, object- and subject-free, but nonetheless participating in the creation of meaning in any given chronotope. The possibility of reading Woolf's scene, partially and nondefinitively, is a function of expression as a complex mode of affective legibility.

*I would like to thank the students in the Fall 2017 Research Lab at Washington University in St. Louis for stimulating discussions on emotion and affect and for sharing with me the writing process of this essay.

NOTES

1 Since the feminist killjoy has often been described through her inability to laugh, responses to this stereotype within second-wave feminism have often focused on laughing women. See, in particular, Cixous and Morris. For recent accounts, see Parvulescu (*Laughter*) and Felski (*Literature*).

2 On the need to rethink critique, see Anker and Felski.

3 It would have to be asked why we are witnessing a period of renewed interest in the emotions in the first decades of the new millennium. The answer to this question would have to reassess, among other things, the place of emotion in contemporary capitalism, developments in neuroscience, as well as the theorizing of emotion along structuralist/poststructuralist lines. For two arguments in this direction, see Hemmings ("Turn") and Leys.

4 On genealogies of feminist studies of emotion and affect, see Stephens, Pedwell and Whitehead, and Lutz ("What").

5 The materialist feminist literature of this period, which often focused on the mobility of affective labor between the family household and the job market, has been collected in a number of anthologies. See Edmond and Fleming, Malos, and Hennessy and Ingraham.

6 Jaggar is in conversation with other theorists who worked on emotion in the 1980s; see especially Spelman and Lutz.

7 In 1986, Lutz offered a comprehensive and influential review of assumptions made about emotions in Western cultures ("Emotion").

8 On translingual practice, see Liu.

9 While contemporary affect theorists often take feminist critics to be embodiments of paranoia or other forms of hermeneutics of suspicion, Felski reminds us that "feminism also cranked up the level of positive affect and literary enthusiasm. Reclaiming the work of women writers, attending to overlooked genres, forms, and themes, triggering waves of excitement, recognition, and curiosity, it inspired to take the study of literature to heart" (*Limits* 29).

10 On this oscillation, see Hemmings ("Affective").

11 On the broader moment in 1980s black feminist theory, see Christian, Collins, and hooks.

12 William James theorized emotion, in his case fear, starting from an anecdote of an encounter with a bear.

13 In the 1980s, Scheman (1980) and Spelman (1989) theorized anger as a moral imperative (one *ought* to be angry in certain situations). In "Anger and Insubordination," one of the essays of the 1980s to have foregrounded anger as a feminist emotion (Jaggar cites a version of the essay delivered as a talk in 1982), Spelman engaged with Lorde's essay on silence in *Sister Outsider* (1984), but, eloquently, not with "The Uses of Anger." The silence surrounding the missed encounter between Spelman and Lorde over the question of anger is itself thick with affect. Spelman subsequently opened *Inessential Woman* (1988), one of the texts of second-wave feminism that took on the question of race *in* feminism, with a motto from Lorde: "There is a pretense to a homogeneity of experience covered by the word *sisterhood* that does not in fact exist" (1).

14 See Spivak.

15 Expression has, of course, been of continued and ambivalent interest in art history and remains one of the foundations of American Sign Language.

16 Given Massumi's distinction between emotion and affect, expression appears to belong to the realm of qualifiable emotion. And yet, in arguing that something is lost if we study emotion strictly at the semiotic level, Massumi argues that what is lost is "the expression event": "the expression-event is the system of the inexplicable" (87). It could be argued that the use of the word "expression" on both sides of the emotion/affect distinction is a result of our deficient critical vocabulary. But could it be that expression in fact belongs on both sides?

17 Drawing on James, Ngai focuses on the transition between emotion and affect, which allows us to decipher affective traces *in* emotions.

18 See Atkins and Weeks.

19 For an exemplary account in this line, see Ditmore.

20 On the choice of a methodological starting point for work on emotion and expression, see Elias.

21 Massumi writes in his introduction to *A Shock to Thought*: "For many years, across many schools, 'expression' has been anathema. The underlying assumption has been that any expressionism is an uncritical subjectivism ... Communication, Deleuze and Guattari agree, is a questionable concept. Yet they hold to expression. '*What takes the place of communication is a kind of expressionism*'" (xiii). It should be possible to attend to Deleuze and Guattari's thoughts on expression without fully subscribing to their understanding of communication.

WORKS CITED

Ahmed, Sara. *The Cultural Politics of Emotion*. New York: Routledge, 2014.

Ahmed, Sara. *Living a Feminist Life*. Durham, NC: Duke UP, 2017.

Anker, Elizabeth. S., and Rita Felski, eds. *Critique and Postcritique*. Durham, NC: Duke UP, 2017.

Atkins, Lisa. "Feminism after Measure," *Feminist Theory* 10.3 (2009): 323–9.

Benjamin, Walter. *The Arcades Project*. Cambridge, MA: Belknap, 2002.

Berlant, Lauren. *Cruel Optimism*. Durham, NC: Duke UP, 2011.

Berlant, Lauren. "Humorlessness (Three Monologues and a Hairpiece)." *Critical Inquiry* 43. 2 (Winter 2017): 305–40.

Butler, Judith. *Bodies that Matter: On the Discursive Limits of "Sex"*. New York: Routledge, 2011.

Christian, Barbara. *Black Feminist Criticism: Perspectives on Black Women Writers*. New York: Teachers College P, 1985.

Cixous, Hélène. "The Laugh of the Medusa." Trans. Keith Cohen and Paula Cohen. *Signs* 1.4 (Summer 1976): 875–93.

Collins, Patricia Hill. "Learning from the Outsider Within: The Sociological Significance of Black Feminist Thought." *Social Problems* 33.6 (1986): S14–S32.

Darwin, Charles. *The Expression of Emotion in Man and Animal*. London: Penguin, 2009.

Deleuze, Gilles, and Félix Guattari. *What Is Philosophy?* Trans. Hugh Tomlinson and Graham Burchell. New York: Columbia UP, 1994.

Descartes, René. *Meditations on First Philosophy*. Trans. John Cottingham. Cambridge: Cambridge UP, 1986.

Descartes, René. *The Passions of the Soul*. Trans. Stephen H. Voss. Indianapolis: Hackett, 1989.

Ditmore, Melissa. "In Calcutta, Sex Workers Organize." *The Affective Turn*. Ed. Patricia Ticineto Clough and Jean Halley. Durham, NC: Duke UP, 2007.

Edmond, Wendy, and Suzie Fleming, eds. *All Work and No Pay: Women, Housework, and the Wages Due*. Bristol: Falling Wall P, 1975.

Ehrenreich, Barbara, and Arlie Russel Hochschild. eds. *Global Woman: Nannies, Maids and Sex Workers in the New Economy*. New York: Holt, 2002.

Elias, Norbert. "Essay on Laughter." Ed. Anca Parvulescu. *Critical Inquiry* 43.2 (Winter 2017): 281–304.

Felski, Rita. *Limits of Critique*. Chicago, IL: U of Chicago P, 2015.

Felski, Rita. *Literature after Feminism*. Chicago, IL: U of Chicago P, 2003.

Hemmings, Clare. "Affective Solidarity: Feminist Reflexivity and Political Transformation." *Feminist Theory* 13.2 (2012): 147–61.

Hemmings, Clare. "Invoking Affect: Cultural Theory and the Ontological Turn." *Cultural Studies* 19.5 (2005): 548–67.

Hennessy, Rosemary, and Chrys Ingraham, eds. *Materialist Feminism: A Reader in Class, Difference and Women's Lives*. New York: Routledge, 1997.

Hochschild, Arlie Russell. *The Managed Heart: Commercialization of Human Feeling* [1983]. Berkeley: U of California P, 2012.

hooks, bell. *Feminist Theory: From Margin to Center*. Boston, MA: South End P, 1984.

Jaggar, Alison M. "Love and Knowledge: Emotion in Feminist Epistemology." *Gender/Body/ Knowledge: Reconstructions of Being and Knowing*. Ed. Alison M. Jaggar and Susan R. Bordo. New Brunswick: Routledge, 1989, pp. 145–71.

James, William. "What Is an Emotion?" *Mind* 9.34 (April 1884): 188–205.

Khanna, Ranjana. "Touching, Unbelonging, and the Absence of Affect." *Feminist Theory* 13.2 (2012): 213–32.

Levinas, Emmanuel. *Totality and Infinity: An Essay on Exteriority*. Trans. Alphonso Lingis. Pittsburgh, PA: Duquesne UP, 1969.

Leys, Ruth. "The Turn to Affect." *Critical Inquiry* 37.3 (Spring 2011): 434–72.

Liu, Lydia. *Translingual Practice: Literature, National Culture and Translated Modernity*. Stanford, CA: Stanford UP, 1995.

Lorde, Audre. "The Uses of Anger." *Women's Studies Quarterly*, 25.1/2 (1997): 278–85.

Lutz, Catherine. "Emotion, Thought and Estrangement: Emotion as a Cultural Category." *Cultural Anthropology* 1.3 (1986): 287–309.

Lutz, Catherine. "What Matters." *Cultural Anthropology* 32.2 (2017): 181–91.

Malos, Ellen, ed. *The Politics of Housework*. Cheltenham: New Clarion P, 1980.

Massumi, Brian. "The Autonomy of Affect." *Cultural Critique* 31 (Autumn 1995): 83–109.

Massumi, Brian, ed. *A Shock to Thought: Expression after Deleuze and Guattari*. New York: Routledge, 2002.

Morris, Meaghan. "in any event ..." *Men in Feminism*. Ed. Alice Jardine and Paul Smith. New York: Methuen, 1987, pp. 173–181.

Ngai, Sianne. *Ugly Feelings*. Cambridge, MA: Harvard UP, 2007.

Parvulescu, Anca. "Laughter and Literature." *Oxford Research Encyclopedia of Literature*, 2017. doi: 10.1093/acrefore/9780190201098.013.43.

Parvulescu, Anca. *Laughter: Notes on a Passion*. Cambridge, MA: MIT Press, 2010.

Pedwell, Carolyn and Anne Whitehead, "Affecting Feminism: Questions of Feeling in Feminist Theory." *Feminist Theory* 13.2 (2012): 115–129.

Rubin, Gayle S. *Deviations: A Gayle Rubin Reader*. Durham, NC: Duke UP, 2011.

Scheman, Naomi. "Anger and the Politics of Naming." *Women and Language in Literature and Society*. Ed. Sally McConnell-Ginet, Ruth Borker and Nelly Furman. New York: Praeger, 1980, pp. 174–87.

Spelman, Elizabeth V. "Anger and Insubordination." *Women, Knowledge, and Reality*. Ed. Ann Garry and Marilyn Pearsall. Winchester, MA: Unwin Hyman, 1989, pp. 263–73.

Spelman, Elizabeth V. *Inessential Woman: Problems of Exclusion in Feminist Thought*. Boston, MA: Beacon P, 1988.

Spivak, Gayatri Chakravorty. *A Critique of Postcolonial Reason: Toward a History of the Vanishing Present*. Cambridge, MA: Harvard UP, 1999.

Stanislavski, Constantin. *An Actor Prepares*. Trans. Elizabeth Reynolds Hapgood. New York: Theater Arts, 1958.

Stephens, Elizabeth. "Bad Feelings: An Affective Genealogy of Feminism." *Australian Feminist Studies* 30.85 (2015): 273–82.

Terada, Rei. *Feeling in Theory: Emotion after the "Death of the Subject."* Cambridge, MA: Harvard UP, 2001.

Weeks, Kathi. *The Problem with Work: Feminism, Marxism, Antiwork Politics, and Postwork Imaginaries*. Durham, NC: Duke UP, 2011.

Woolf, Virginia. *Orlando: A Biography*. Oxford: Oxford UP, 2008.

CHAPTER SEVEN

Sex

RITA MOOKERJEE

There are few subjects that strike anxiety in Western minds the way that sex does. This anxiety has historically stunted sex discourse and postponed crucial discussions of sex, gender, and orientation. In her iconic "Thinking Sex" essay, Gayle Rubin writes,

> This culture always treats sex with suspicion. It construes and judges almost any sexual practice in terms of its worst possible expression. Sex is presumed guilty until proven innocent. Virtually all erotic behaviour is considered bad unless a specific reason to exempt it has been established. The most acceptable excuses are marriage, reproduction, and love. Sometimes scientific curiosity, aesthetic experience, or a long-term intimate relationship may serve. But the exercise of erotic capacity, intelligence, curiosity, or creativity all require pretexts that are unnecessary for other pleasures, such as the enjoyment of food, fiction, or astronomy. (Rubin 150)

As such, feminist thinkers are now tasked with dismantling models that conceive of sex and gender in shameful and binary terms that subjugate sexual minorities and advance the heterocentric values of late capitalism. This chapter will frame an emergent sexual politics of inclusivity as well as sex positivist ideologies while tracing the phenomenology of sexual identity, thereby illustrating how feminist theory has transformed in the late twentieth and twenty-first centuries with specific regard to sex practices, presumed deviance, and fluidity. The importance of destigmatizing sex work will also be discussed. Ultimately, this chapter signals the inextricability of queer theory from feminist studies and calls for more attention to be paid to gender-nonconforming and trans subjects.

FUNDAMENTALS OF TWENTY-FIRST-CENTURY SEX DISCOURSE

Before inspecting contemporary feminist perspectives of sex and sex practices, it is helpful to clarify and define a number of terms that often get used interchangeably. While many texts make use of the word "sex" to mean the biological determinants of male and female bodily difference, "sexuality" emerged as a term in the nineteenth-century West to refer to an individual's orientation and desire as well as the sum of physical acts that constitute the practice of sex. These definitions of sex and sexuality relied heavily on the gender binary, which has since been proven to be an inadequate litmus test. Definitions of sex and sexuality prior to the twenty-first century account for these concepts without carefully evaluating them within the contexts of power and orientation. Feminists have worked to dismantle the presupposition that gender and sex are interchangeable terms, dismissing any notions of biological determinism between gender, sex, and sexuality. In the following sections, the words "woman" and "women" will refer to both bodies that are biologically female as well as individuals who self-identify as female, regardless of the identity they were assigned at birth. Keeping this criterion in mind, this chapter will present the myriad ways in which sexuality has evolved and taken on new, hybridized forms with gender nonconformity and queerness in mind.

In the 1970s, a new class of artists and thinkers emerged in the United States with the goal of crafting paradigms that would later serve as the basis for gender and sexuality studies. Queer women, trans women, and gender nonconforming people face entirely different standards of value, desirability, respectability, and power than women who identify with the gender identity they were assigned at birth, also known as cisgender. Ideas of queerness have impacted contemporary feminist writing, ensuring that nonnormative identities are neither erased nor homogenized. As Lee Edelman posits in *No Future: Queer Theory and the Death Drive*, "queerness can never define an identity, it can only ever disturb one" (Edelman 17). In keeping with Eve Kosofsky Sedgwick's original definition in *Tendencies*, the word "queer" will be used to refer to lesbian and bisexual women, female-identifying people, as well as "the open mesh of possibilities, gaps, overlaps, dissonances and resonances, lapses and excesses of meaning when the constituent elements of anyone's gender [and sexuality] aren't made (or *can't be* made) to signify monolithically" (Sedgwick 7). The second half of this definition is offered for posterity so that the ideas presented in this chapter may be adapted to describe future notions of gender, sex, and feminism.

SEX, LAWS, AND POWER

It is almost inevitable that theoretical discussions of sex and sex practices will call forth Sigmund Freud and Michel Foucault. Freud's hypothesis that children exist as inherently sexual beings suggests that sexuality is an innate human trait. While Freud's studies allowed for thinkers to situate sex as a naturalized discourse of power, scholars of modern gender studies agree that his psychoanalytic findings are reductive and reinforce the increasingly flimsy gender binary. In the introduction to *The History of Sexuality*, Michel Foucault unfolds the term "sex" to explain how it signifies "not only biological functions and anatomical traits but sexual activities as well as a kind of psychic core that gives clues to an essential, or final meaning to, identity" (Butler, "Sexual" 60). Foucault locates the production of sex as a category within the eighteenth century, wherein Europe saw a decline in starvation and disease (142). Without the constant threat of death, Europeans turned their attentions to sustaining and preserving their families. Herein lies a defining moment in human history where heterosexual, reproductive sex was not only normalized but valorized. But a new set of political demands emerged from this period of ostensible stability: "The 'right' to life, to one's body, to health, to happiness, to the satisfaction of needs, and beyond all the oppressions or 'alienations,' the 'right' to rediscover what one is and all that one can be" (Foucault 145). In Foucault's terms, this is how we can see sex as both a political and juridical force. Sex is produced by power.

Yet as Lauren Berlant and Michael Warner explain in "Sex in Public,"

Heterosexuality is not a thing. We speak of heterosexual culture rather than heterosexuality because that culture never has more than a provisional unity. It is neither a single Symbolic nor a single ideology nor a unified set of shared beliefs. The conflicts between these strands are seldom more than dimly perceived in practice, where the givenness of male-female sexual relations is part of the ordinary rightness of the world, its fragility masked in shows of solemn rectitude. Such conflicts have also gone unrecognized in theory, partly because of the metacultural work of the very category of heterosexuality, which consolidates as a sexuality widely differing practices, norms, and institutions; and partly because the sciences of social knowledge are themselves so deeply anchored in the process of normalization to which Foucault attributes so much of modern sexuality. Thus when we say that the contemporary United States is saturated by the project of constructing national heterosexuality, we do not mean that national heterosexuality is anything like a simple monoculture. Hegemonies are nothing if not elastic alliances, involving dispersed and contradictory strategies for self-maintenance and reproduction.

Thus heterosexuality becomes a paradoxical prescriptive embedded in public and private apparatuses and value systems. As Judith Butler clarifies in *Feminist Interpretations of Michel Foucault*, "the law constructs sex, producing it as that which calls to be monitored and *is* inherently regulatable" ("Sexual" 64). The regulation process occurs in discourse such that "any social displays of nonidentity, discontinuity, or sexual incoherence will be punished, controlled, ostracized, reformed" (65). Butler points to Luce Irigaray to outline one deficiency of Foucault's argument—the subtext that the regulating discourse of sex really only constitutes masculinity, thereby positioning the feminine as erased or abject (68). With Irigaray's assertion in mind, Butler posits that "both masculine and feminine reduce to the masculine, and the feminine, left outside of this male autoerotic economy, is not even designatable within its terms or is, rather, designatable as a radically disfigured masculine projection, which is yet a different kind of erasure" (68). Consequently, in order to understand how sex as a discourse produces identity, we must also recognize how sex has the capacity to erase and oppress.

Butler's central critique of Foucault is his demarcation of "an era of epidemics" which, in 1976, he believed had ended (71). The AIDS epidemic of the twentieth century posed threats to sex as a broad political category and to all queer bodies that were already pathologized and reviled within a heteronormative worldview. Returning to the regulatory nature of sex discourse, since queerness is thought to be "pathological from the start, then any disease that homosexuals may sometimes contract will be easily conflated with the disease that they already are" (70). All of this filters into the Freudian notion of the death drive, which Edelman discusses in *No Future*. Edelman combats the amalgamation of queer identity and the death drive since "the death drive dissolves those congealments of identity that permit us to know and survive as ourselves" while "the queer [insists] on disturbing, on queering social organization" thereby giving queer subjects a means of self-reification and survival (Edelman 17). While the AIDS epidemic has historically been associated with queer men, queerness in women was believed to result in a number of devastating bodily ailments. In *Desire in Language*, Julia Kristeva asserts that female homosexuality can only lead to a splintering of social taboos resulting in permanent psychosis.

Technological advancement once appeared to be the key to both the annihilation of madness and disease (including HIV/AIDS) and the prolonging of human life. However, Butler reminds us that it is progressive technology itself that is systemically withheld[1] from oppressed communities as a means of governance and regulation; technology is a lens that magnifies sexual nonconformity. Within medicojuridical discourse, homosexuality is situated as a fixed conduit of death (Butler, "Sexual" 71). The concealment of queerness does not put an end to societal persecution and neither does the explicit revealing of queerness. For Foucault, what is important is finding a way to perform "resistance[2] to the diagnostic category … that does not reduplicate the very mechanism of that subjection" (69).

In locating and identifying normative sex, Foucault notes a grand irony: "To deal with sex, power employs nothing more than a law of prohibition. Its objective: that sex renounce itself. Its instrument: the threat of a punishment that is nothing more than the suppression of sex … Your existence will be maintained only at the cost of your nullification" (Foucault 84). The regulatory mechanisms of power over sex require sex to be hidden in the first place, and so any sort of sexuality or sex practice that deviates from the normative male/female pairing is doubly taboo. For Foucault, bodies that are already "sexed" are therefore invisibly governed by regulatory laws that dictate gender conformity and desires and also serve as hermeneutic tools for identity formation (Butler, *Gender* 130).

BODIES BEYOND

Of course, not all subjects can be understood within regulatory sex discourse or the rigid laws of heteronormativity. In *Gender Trouble*, Butler discusses Foucault's work with the published journals of Herculine Barbin, an intersex person assigned female gender identity at birth (henceforth abbreviated as AFAB) who lived in the nineteenth century. Both Foucault and Butler use the term "hermaphrodite" to describe Herculine Barbin. Contemporary gender studies scholars and medical experts have agreed[3] that this term is not only derogatory, but also reductive and stigmatizing. It arose from what can now be deemed arbitrary medical evaluations of genital structures and gonadal tissue and has since been replaced with the nineteenth-century word "intersex," which refers to a "variation in genital anatomy" including but not limited to "ambiguous genitalia," differing internal and external genitals, and various congenital conditions (Reis xi). Butler explains that Foucault's publication of Herculine Barbin's journals gives us a place to evaluate and "expose the constitutive contradiction of [an] anti-emancipatory call for sexual freedom" today (Butler, *Gender* 130). There is value in studying the journals that Foucault edited but not in the sense that he envisioned.

Butler reminds us that while Foucault correctly separates the somatic body (and its functions) from social behaviors, he incorrectly anticipates that the case of Herculine results "in a happy dispersal of these various functions, meanings, organs, somatic and psychological processes" and an escape from heterocentric desire. It remains difficult to see where Foucault detected this opportunity for dispersal since Herculine chronicles their[4] life as tragic and unsatisfactory, and once their anatomical secret[5] is revealed, the authorities force them to live life as a man. Herculine eventually commits suicide. In Foucault's interpretation, Herculine's time in the convent before they are identified as intersex represents a "utopian play of pleasures" "effectively free of the juridical and regulatory pressures of the category of 'sex'" (133). Herculine is sexually attracted to women and is able to enjoy that desire until they are discovered within the hyperfeminized space of the convent.

Though Herculine's intersex subjecthood does not in itself unlock freedom, Butler reveals a key concept from Foucault's study: "that homosexuality is instrumental to the overthrow of the category of sex" (136). In *Undoing Gender*, Butler posits that "sexual difference is the site where a question concerning the relation of the biological to the cultural is posed and reposed, where it must and can be posed, but where it cannot, strictly speaking, be answered" (Butler *Undoing* 186). It seems that a large part of this type of questioning revolves around legitimization. Can a sexual identity have legibility/ visibility without legitimacy? Prior to the recent legalization of same-sex marriage in the United States, "improvisation [was] always necessary for the speech act of pledging, or the narrative practice of dating, or for such apparently noneconomic economies as joint checking" (Berlant and Warner 562). Yet Butler, writing in the millennium and the Third Wave, anticipates subjects who do not consider legality to be the measure of their sexual actualization, especially if "sexuality is already thought of in terms of marriage and marriage is already thought of as the purchase on legitimacy" (106). While there are concrete advantages to having that sort of legitimacy, and same-sex marriage in the United States is now relatively attainable, there are many other conflicts dealing with ideas of sexuality and sex practices. It seems as though we have entered what Butler terms "the field outside the disjunction of the illegitimate and the legitimate" wherein "nomination itself falls into a crisis" (105, 108). This movement outside of the legitimacy binary shows the inherent plurality of sex and sexual identity. Sex surpasses the boundaries of the law and the somatic body. This is how we are able to arrive at notions of the trans.

TRANS IDENTITY AND TERF BATTLES

With the birth of queer studies, foundational scholars like Sedgwick and Lee Edelman developed trans-inclusive language, but some feminist works continue to perpetuate a cis-centric worldview. While some intellectuals implicitly present a limited idea of what a woman is or can be, others explicitly define the category of woman through heteronormative language, thereby stratifying various groups and fueling a radical feminist politics of exclusion. In *Gyn/Ecology: The Metaethtics of Radical Feminism* and *Websters' First New Intergalactic Wickedary of the English Language*, Mary Daly uses supernatural/fantasy language in a literary tradition that parallels revolutionary feminist works like Donna Haraway's "Cyborg Manifesto." Throughout the beginning of *Gyn/Ecology*, there are moments where it seems that Daly is gesturing toward the trans. She writes of "multiply mobile" subjects and departs from classical images of woman as Mother Nature or Supreme Goddess (Daly xlvii). Her invocation of the supernatural via ghosts, hags, and witches also suggests a pivot toward the nonnormative, but ultimately Daly's assertions about sex and gender remain myopic and derogatory.

In one chapter of *Gyn/Ecology*, Daly asserts the following:

> Today the Frankenstein phenomenon is omnipresent not only in religious myth, but in its offspring, phallocratic technology. The insane desire for power, the madness of boundary violation, is the mark of necrophiliacs who sense the lack of soul/spirit/ life-loving principle with themselves and therefore try to invade and kill off all spirit, substituting conglomerates of corpses. This necrophilic invasion/elimination takes a variety of forms. Transsexualism is an example of male surgical siring which invades the female world with substitutes. Male-mothered genetic engineering is an attempt to "create" without women. (Daly 70–1)

Here, Daly makes an error commonly found in early feminist writing: conflating motherhood with womanhood, consequently condemning not only trans women but any female subjects who are uninterested in or incapable of producing children. She restricts female identity to the body, thereby reinforcing notions of sex that had been dismantled by scholars in decades prior. Moreover, she dismisses trans bodies altogether by likening the gender reassignment process to the practice of white people in blackface or males playing dress-up in female bodies (67). Arguably, the most extreme example of Daly's trans-exclusionary radical feminist (hereby referred to as TERF) sentiments consists of her depiction of the "transsexual world of christian [*sic*] myth" wherein the holy ghost is the female portion of the trinity and God "manages not only to impregnate Mary physic-ally, producing the 'Incarnate Word', but also to fecundate the souls/minds of the faithful, engendering 'supernatural life' " (229). By casting trans subjects as actors in the staging of Christianity and Frankenstein's monsters, Daly couches their identity in a fantasy world, or at least divorces trans identity from political life. Though this analogy is perplexing on its own, Daly fails to imagine intersex bodies within the equation altogether despite her explicitly intersex breakdown of the Holy Trinity.

Similar concepts continue to crop up in women's writing, and they all seem to indicate a deep anxiety about what to "do with" and "say about" trans and gender nonconforming people. In "Feminist Solidarity After Queer Theory: The Case of the Transgender," Cressida Heyes explains that even in good faith, feminist thinkers who write[6] on trans topics are "held captive by a picture within which the history of fetishizing trans people combines with a lack of critical attention to the privilege of being stably gendered to erase the possibility of a feminist politics" but "this picture needs to be made visible *as a* picture before it can be dispelled" (1100). Without locating the specific issues, needs, and concerns of the trans community, feminist writers sustain a connection to an essen-tialist definition of trans identity. In reinscribing these reductive ideas, TERF intellectuals inhibit the discourse on normative and nonnormative sexual identities and practices.

REDEFINING SEX FROM THE MARGINS

While the problems with cishet-centric language are apparent to contemporary feminist scholars, cishet notions of femininity, womanhood, and lesbianism continually creep into theoretical discourse. To use Gayle Rubin's words, "Popular sexual ideology is a noxious stew made up of ideas of sexual sin, concepts of psychological inferiority, anti-communism, mob hysteria, accusations of witchcraft, and xenophobia" (152). A present goal of feminist theory is to create room for all subjects within discussions of gender and sexuality. With the growth of queer theory within the field of gender studies, new conversations have emerged about the practices of sex. In *Sister Outsider*, Audre Lorde guides readers beyond cishet binaries and into broader ideas about the erotic. Lorde explains that eroticism has historically been stigmatized and "devalued" in discussions of sex: "On the one hand, the superficially erotic has been encouraged as a sign of female inferiority; on the other hand, women have been made to suffer and to feel both con-temptible and suspect by virtue of its existence" (53). In the colloquial sense, eroticism has been reduced to an excess and conflated with the obscene and the pornographic, which Lorde argues against since "pornography emphasizes sensation without feeling" while the erotic encompasses both. Second-wave feminists drew a line between pornog-raphy and erotica, arguing that both the production and rhetoric of porn is fundamentally misogynistic. Today, women and queer people have forged new subgenres within the porn industry in order to offer pro-women/pro-queer sexual material. With these concepts in mind, it proves easier to envision desire on a spectrum, mirroring the larger categories of LGBTQIAA, which are pliable and fluid.

A concept that emerges from recognizing the erotic as a core component of feminist ideology is sex positivity[7] or pro-sexuality. The groundwork for these movements was laid by many members of the second wave. For example, Gayle Rubin explicitly uses the term "pro-sex" in her writing. While sex positivism and pro-sex ideas are not interchangeable, they will be used in tandem in this chapter. Both concepts view sex and/ or freedom[8] from oppressive sex categories as a fundamental tenet of current feminist discourse and also work to inspect the economies and politics that emerge from sex practices. Sex positivists examine what kinds of sex qualify as feminist and/or progressive. Elisa Glick explains that pro-sex feminist ideology contains "the interlocking of public and private spheres" and has the potential to illustrate "individual and/or collective identity not only as a basis for political organization but also as a site of political activism itself" (20). Drawing from Butler, Glick discusses the place of sexual agency in that it "is not located in a pre- or extradiscursive space, but rather within the gaps of dominant sex/gender ideology: gaps that may be exploited for the project of social transformation" (32). Berlant and Warner note that eroticism is also fraught when conceptualized outside of monogamous couple sex:

> Affective life slops over onto work and political life; people have key self-constitutive relations with strangers and acquaintances; and they have eroticism, if not sex, outside of the couple form. These border intimacies give people tremendous pleasure. But when that pleasure is called sexuality, the spillage of eroticism into everyday social life seems transgressive in a way that provokes normal aversion, a hygienic recoil even as contemporary consumer and media cultures increasingly trope toiletward, splattering the matter of intimate life at the highest levels of national culture. (Berlant and Warner 560)

These conversations about nonnormative sex practices and feminism emerged in the 1980s, largely on the subject of BDSM. Sex-positive feminism works in the opposite way of censorship and state-sanctioned sexual condemnation promoted by second-wave scholars like Andrea Dworkin, Catherine MacKinnon, and Robin Morgan along with groups like Women Against Pornography. Rather than denouncing all sexual material and sex acts as reinscriptions of patriarchal norms, sex positivists and pro-sex thinkers advocate for sex to be enacted and embraced as self-exploration. Though these ideologies seek to empower sexual minorities and women, Glick maintains that pro-sex movements are too individualistic and libertarian. She also argues that lauding subversive sex culture creates a hierarchy of legitimacy, but sex positivists actually envision sex practices within broad categories. Of course, having sex does not stand in for revolution; as Pat Califa states in *Macho Sluts*, it is not possible for queer people or women to "fuck our way to freedom." Pro-sex feminist thinking does, however, create opportunities for people's emancipation from sexual systems that are rooted in patriarchal oppression. If pro-sex feminism allows the individual to become sexually emancipated, then that individual is still part of a collective feminist movement against cishet patriarchal models of sex.

In actuality, the trouble is not that pro-sexuality/sex positivism "revalues disparaged sexual identities and styles, but that it stops there" (Glick 26). In other words, sexual representation becomes the goal, thereby stunting the potential for pro-sexuality/sex positivity to actually enact social change. While visibility improves, oppressive structures remain unchallenged. Though scholars have praised pro-sex ideology and written about it since the 1980s, the quotidian labor of the pro-sex movement emerges first from "communities that organize politically around identity categories" in the same way that the Stonewall rioters performed the labor of queer resistance before queer studies was constructed as a field (30).

Since the "valorization of radical sexual practices as politically subversive often depends upon collapsing the distinction between fantasy and reality," the question of enactment comes into play (40). How can different kinds of sex be made visible without becoming spectacles? How can sex-positive practices be enacted and validated in *both* the public and the private? How can these ideologies function outside of physical sexual exchange? Can sex positivism transcend the personal? In order to answer these questions, sex positivism and pro-sexuality must first become integrated within general value systems. For example, sex education, sex shops, and pro-queer/pro-women pornographers all need to (and can) overlap in some articulation of sex positivity. Though this seems idealistic, emergent works of sex-positive theory coupled with political action have already helped to integrate pro-sex ideology into the lexicon. The denunciation of "slut-shaming" is evidence of this; feminists actively work to reclaim the word "slut[9]" and force others to interrogate their perceptions of women and sexuality. This can be understood as a sex-positive effort since the word itself now bears an outmoded connotation in addition to a derogatory one. Presently, scholars and activists "struggle to clarify [feminist] values so that women's sexual[ity] [and the sexual identities of queer people] are not co-opted and commodified" (Nguyen 158).

SEX WORK

Glick's strongest critique of pro-sex feminism is its "refus[al] to conceptualize sexual relations ... in terms of social regulation" (22). Her contention draws attention to sexual economies and how some—those forced to operate outside of normative legal and social confines—have not been given sufficient attention in feminist theory. Returning to the ideas of sexual regulation that Foucault observed, queer and feminist sexual economies have had to exist in the underworld; images of escorts, black market midwives, and back alley plastic surgeons come to mind. As such, an inclusive feminist ideology must recognize the history of exploitation within these economies and combat the sociocultural stigma that situates sex work[10] as immoral. As Gayle Rubin chronicles in "Thinking Sex," the late nineteenth century was a popular time[11] for campaigns against prostitution (143). The 1950s saw major shifts in sexual rhetoric, namely a nascent anxiety about "sex offenders," which was often just an oblique way of saying homosexual (145). Stigmas around prostitution resurged[12] in the late 1970s, and the efforts to inhibit sex work have remained consistent; "states and municipalities have been passing new and tighter regulations on commercial sex. Restrictive ordinances have been passed, zoning laws altered, licensing and safety codes amended, sentences increased, and evidentiary requirements relaxed" (146). In 2017, the US House of Representatives introduced Bill 2480, the "Empowering Law Enforcement to Fight Sex Trafficking Demand Act," which grants federal funding from the Edward Byrne Memorial Justice Assistance Grant (Byrne JAG) in the interest of increasing police involvement with sex work cases ("United States").

This attitude toward the disenfranchised doubly relegates female/queer sex workers to the margins. In *Profit and Pleasure*, Rosemary Hennessy notes that "racialized and gendered divisions of labor [suggest] that there are more lesbians than gay men living in poverty and proportionately more of them are people of color" (140). With commodi-fied images of gay identity as glamorous, the media "blot[s] from view lesbians, gays, and queers who are manual workers, sex workers, unemployed, and imprisoned" (140–1). Pro-sex feminism can work to address subjects outside of the "class-specific 'bourgeois (homosexual/queer) imaginary' " (141).

CONCLUSION

In *Undoing Gender*, Butler clarifies that there is no need to destroy sexual difference as a categorical signifier but maintains that it "registers ontologically in a way that is permanently difficult to define" (Butler, *Undoing* 186). In order to refine feminist discourse about and around sex and sexuality, scholars must push the boundaries of existing paradigms so that multifaceted subjects can become legible and pursue legitimacy on their own terms. As Lorde states, "it is not difference which immobilizes us, but silence. And there are so many silences to be broken" (Lorde 44). Feminism is inextricable from queer studies. In the best interests of both fields, feminist theory must recognize the limitless potential for new modes of sex.

NOTES

1 In 2017, President Donald Trump has sought to cut a fifth of the multibillion dollar budget dedicated to purchasing antiretroviral drugs for about twelve million people around the world (Harris).

2 In Butler's words, this is "why Foucault will not confess or 'come out' in *The History of Sexuality* as a homosexual or privilege homosexuality as a site of heightened regulation" (69).

3 There is still some debate about the use of "intersex" as a category. Some feel that this term is isolating. Disorders of sex development (DSD), a term used by the medical community, is criticized for pathologizing an identity that does not necessarily require medical attention (Reis xv). Scholars like Elizabeth Reis work to create language that accurately describes sexual difference without stigmatizing it, and it is safe to assume that this language will continue to evolve.

4 While Butler uses "s/he" as Herculine's pronoun, "they/them" pronouns do not rely upon the gender binary and therefore serve as more adequate set of identifiers.

5 Herculine does not describe or define their genitalia in the journals. Foucault includes a dossier with medical examination notes describing Herculine as "feminine in the upper part, with a fine skin" with a "*cul de sac*" instead of a vagina and a "well-defined *membrum virile*, capable of erection" (198).

6 Heyes spends most of her argument taking the works of Janice Raymond and Bernice Hausman to task for dismissing transgenderism as simply a technological intervention or the equivalent of a black person wanting to become white.

7 Yet not all pro-sex/sex positive advocates are feminists, and therefore sex positivity is not feminist by default. Its use as a feminist principle in this chapter is contingent upon subjects who align themselves with these terms in the interest of advocating for queer and women's rights.

8 This includes abstaining from sex entirely or identifying as an asexual subject.

9 The SlutWalk is a movement that began in Toronto in response to a police officer's remark that "women should avoid dressing like sluts in order to not be victimized" (Nguyen 159). The SlutWalk attempts to dismantle a twofold misconception: "one, that it is socially permissible to judge, objectify, and morally categorize women based on their appearances

and, two, that women, rather than the rapists, attackers, assailants, bullies, and aggressors, are responsible for sexual violence committed against them" (159). Heather Jarvis and Sonya Barnett organized a march for people united "under the banner of 'slut'" who dressed in revealing outfits or walked partially nude (159). The march was then replicated by people all over the world. There is some debate as to whether or not the SlutWalk is an effective means of protest since "slut" has not been fully reclaimed in the manner of a term like "queer."

10 Midwifery is not included in this category, but it is a historically underregulated profession in the United States. NPR Illinois aired a story in 2016 titled "The Black Market For Midwives" chronicling the appeal and dangers of at-home births. Midwifery is peripherally related to sex work in that it is an intimate service performed by women that is depreciated in the United States due to the capitalist patriarchy's insistence that hospital births are technologically advanced and therefore safer.

11 Anti-masturbation rhetoric was also rampant during this period, both in the United States and in England.

12 Interestingly, this is also the time wherein conservatives protesting sex education in schools and abortion move "from the extreme fringes to the political centre stage" (147).

WORKS CITED

Butler, Judith. *Gender Trouble*. New York: Routledge, 1990.

Butler, Judith. "Sexual Inversions." *Feminist Interpretations of Michel Foucault*. Ed. Susan J. Hekman. University Park: Pennsylvania State UP, 1996, pp. 59–76.

Butler, Judith. *Undoing Gender*. New York: Routledge, 2004.

Berlant, Lauren, and Michael Warner. "Sex in Public." *Critical Inquiry* 24.2 (1998): pp. 547–66. www.jstor.org/stable/1344178.

Daly, Mary. *Gyn/Ecology: The Metaethics of Radical Feminism*. Boston, MA: Beacon P, 1990.

Edelman, Lee. *Queer Theory and the Death Drive*. Durham, NC: Duke UP, 2004.

Foucault, Michel. *Herculine Barbin*. New York: Pantheon Books, 1980.

Foucault, Michel. *The History of Sexuality, Volume 1: An Introduction*. New York: Vintage Books, 1990.

Freud, Sigmund. *Three Contributions to the Sexual Theory*. Trans. A. A. Brill. New York: Journal of Nervous and Mental Disease, 1910.

Glick, Elisa. "Sex Positive: Feminism, Queer Theory, and the Politics of Transgression." *Feminist Review* 64.1 (2000) 19–45. www.jstor.org/stable/1395699.

Harris, Gardiner. "Cuts to AIDS Treatment Programs Could Cost a Million Lives." *New York Times*, https://nyti.ms/2rRFhAJ. Accessed August 1, 2017.

Hennessy, Rosemary. *Profit and Pleasure: Sexual Identities in Late Capitalism*. New York: Routledge, 2000.

Heyes, Cressida J. "Feminist Solidarity after Queer Theory: The Case of Transgender." *Signs* 28.4 (2003): 1093–120. www.jstor.org/stable/10.1086/343132.

Irigaray, Luce. *This Sex Which Is Not One*. Trans. Catherine Porter with Carolyn Burke. Ithaca: Cornell UP, 1985.

Kristeva, Julia. *Desire in Language: A Semiotic Approach to Literature and Art*. New York: Columbia UP, 1941.

Lorde, Audre. *Sister Outsider*. Berkeley, CA: Crossing P, 1984.

Nguyen, Tram. "From SlutWalks to SuicideGirls: Feminist Resistance in the Third Wave and Postfeminist Era." *Women's Studies Quarterly* 41.3/4 (2013): 157–72. www.jstor.org/stable/23611512.

Reis, Elizabeth. *Bodies in Doubt: An American History of Intersex*. Baltimore, MD: Johns Hopkins UP, 2012.

Rubin, Gayle. "Thinking Sex." *Culture, Desire, and Sexuality: A Reader*. Ed. Richard Parker and Peter Aggleton. eBook. New York: Routledge, 2007, pp. 143–78.

Sedgwick, Eve Kosofsky. *Tendencies*. Durham, NC: Duke UP, 1993.

United States House of Representatives. H.R.2480—Empowering Law Enforcement to Fight Sex Trafficking Demand Act. Congress.gov. https://www.congress.gov/bill/115th-congress/house-bill/2480/text. Accessed July 13, 2017.

CHAPTER EIGHT

Intersex/Transgender

KATHLEEN LONG

Is it possible to imagine a post-gender world? Our social interactions and our lives are so thoroughly governed by bigenderism that we cannot move, speak, dress, work, gesture, look, express emotions, or think without either conveying or violating an assigned or assumed gender role (Gilbert 94). If we are "read" to be male or female, and do something or appear in some way transgressive of that role, we will elicit confusion, upset, shaming or ridicule, or even anger and violence. We are supposed to practice our roles and refine our gender presentation. So, what we do in our daily lives is enforce these gender roles upon ourselves by means of minute-by-minute performances of gender: how we walk, talk, greet others, react to danger or affection or cold or heat. In the wake of Judith Butler's groundbreaking *Gender Trouble*, feminist and queer critics are aware of the performative nature of gender and how it can be used to enforce or subvert gender roles. But much of feminist criticism remains in the thrall of bigenderism. Miqqi Alicia Gilbert defines " 'bigenderism' as the view that accepts the rules of gender and does not permit or allow for variations, exceptions, and/or deviations from the norm" (95). These rules "establish that there are two and only two genders, and that everyone must be one or the other," which "means that trans folk cannot exist" (95). It should be noted that these rules mean that intersex individuals cannot exist, either. Even in discussions critical of bigenderism, bodies that do not conform to its rules are often effaced.

Thus, it should not be surprising that while recent feminist and queer criticism has embraced transgender as a means of calling bigenderism into question, intersex has yet to be fully considered in this context, although David Rubin's recent study, *Intersex Matters*, is a significant step in this direction. Butler, for example, sees queer theory as being "opposed to the unwanted legislation of identity" (*Undoing Gender* 7). But the categories of male and female persist in this account of gender: "Gender likewise figures as a precondition for the production and maintenance of legible humanity" (11). Gender is seen as a subject position that may or may not be related to the body; in this context, intersex further complicates queer theory by presenting bodies that are only legible within the system of bigenderism by means of extensive mediating intervention, whether surgical, legal, or conceptual. That is to say, intersex always already confounds bigenderism. Intersex individuals who prefer not to be designated as male or female thus choose a subject position that is illegible even in the domain of gender theory. Frequently, until quite recently, intersex infants underwent sex assignment surgery; as Butler says, "Here the ideality of gendered morphology is quite literally incised in the flesh" (*Undoing Gender* 53). But even in Butler's account, the complex materiality of that body upon which the surgery is performed is subordinated to the felt sense or performance of one gender or the other; in this way, gender theory remains normative. This is where the intersection of disability studies and gender studies can be useful in acknowledging that the materiality of bodies does have a role in our interactions with the world around us, and in how we become legible to that world, something Rosemarie Garland Thomson has underscored in connecting the two fields (6–7). Acknowledging corporeal differences, without categorizing them in ways that are as value-laden as gender inevitably is, opens up the possibility of transforming social institutions, cultural assumptions, and physical structures to meet the demands of the body, rather than shaping the body to meet the demands of these constructions.

The difference between this surgery and reassignment surgery, hormone therapy, or other interventions for transgender individuals is one of consent: bigenderism is so crucial to our social interactions that it has been seen as necessary to enforce it medically on intersex infants even before any possibility of consent or choice. As Iain Morland makes clear,

> Here is another key reason why the medicalization of intersex is a fundamentally erroneous project: it mistakes social norms and their transgressions for properties of bodies, which can be modified or disambiguated through clinical interventions. But ambiguity is an interpretation, not a trait; and one cannot do surgery on a norm. ("Intersex" 113)

In the case of intersex individuals, as well as of anyone else not conforming to gender norms, the gap between these norms and the variations present in human bodies underscores the limited and limiting nature of bigenderism relative to human experience.

A "third gender," which exists conceptually somewhere between male and female, does not solve the problems posed by bigenderism, for several reasons. The first reason is perhaps clearest in relation to intersex individuals; even from medieval times, a range of gender variations was noted by anatomists, theologians, surgeons, and jurists. These variations exceed the simple notion of male, female, and a third sex. The second is that the notion of a third gender also essentially keeps bigenderism intact: there is male, female, and the other who is neither male nor female. Rather than limiting human possibilities to these two or three genders, perhaps we could turn to the notion of human variation, of all humans being different from each other, as the norm. This concept of the norm, which turns the usual understanding of the term on its head, elaborated by Georges Canguilhem in the mid-twentieth century and already suggested by Michel de Montaigne in the late sixteenth century, is a valuable critical reaction to the marginalization of those who do not fit neatly into the categories created in order to interpret and understand humanity.

Then how many genders are there? Since the time of Aristotle, some have believed that there was only one, with women being simply a defective or monstrous version of men (Laqueur 63–113). Others believed that there were two: male and female (Daston and Park, "Hermaphrodites in Renaissance"). Still others believed three, or even six, as Medieval Kabbalistic thought proposed (Boyarin 117–36). Some believed in a spectrum of gender, from manly man to womanly woman, with no defined limit on the possible variations (Long, *Hermaphrodites* 51). Accompanying these theories of gender from ancient times to the present day were questions about whether gender was a fixed or mobile state of being: could women become men and men become women (Paré 31–3)?

Twenty-first-century feminism has returned to these questions, considering not only the number of genders, but the nature of gender. In 1993, Anne Fausto-Sterling suggested five sexes. Throughout the 1990s, Suzanne Kessler, Cheryl Chase, and Alice Dreger all

focused these discussions on intersex individuals, calling into question the ethics of surgi-
cally reassigning male or female identities to intersex infants. These discussions found a
wider audience in the context of broader feminist engagement with gender (Butler, *Gender
Trouble* and *Undoing Gender*), suggesting that feminist thought could benefit from a more
sustained engagement with the concept of intersex. The recent work of Rubin; Morland;
Downing, Morland, and Sullivan; and Gayle Salamon (2010) has indeed suggested that
intersex and transgender individuals can offer new and much-needed critical perspectives
on our understanding of gender.

In fact, gender has been one of the crucial categories used as a means of rendering
bodies legible to human understanding for millennia; questions concerning the viability
of these categories have existed for just as long (Cadden 201–27). Well into the nineteenth century, medical treatises suggest that if one's gender cannot be readily established
as male or female, one might not be fully human. This normative understanding of gender
may be one explanation for why discussions of intersex and transgender are most frequently found, even well into the modern era, in treatises on monsters or monstrosities.
Yet our methods for selecting the signs used to interpret bodies within the system of
gender are revealed to be factitious in the face of gender ambiguity: we decide that certain
bodily signs are male or female in nature, then use those signs to impose a gender identity. But what if those signs contradict each other, or remain unclear? The insistence on
the part of early modern and modern teratologists, as well as the sexologist, John Money,
on developing yet more elaborate models of interpretation suggests an obsession with
imposing gender regularity within the parameters of clearly delineated binary gender. In
turn, these models demonstrate the problematic logic of binary gender and undermine
the regularity they seek to establish. Salamon aptly questions our ability to understand the
complexities of the body:

> I seek to challenge the notion that the materiality of the body is something to which
> we have immediate access, something of which we can have epistemological certainty,
> and contend that such epistemological uncertainty can have great use, both ethically
> and politically, in the lives of the non-normatively gendered. (1)

The insistent need for this impossible epistemological certainty has driven the medical
and legal responses to intersex individuals since medieval times (DeVun 17–37).

In this context, it should be easy to see that the present and future of feminism will
be enriched by the interventions of "critical intersex studies as both an ally to and a critical interlocutor for feminist, queer, and trans studies alike," in Rubin's words, because
"feminist scholarship still has much to learn from the various 'sexed others' against which
and in relation to hegemonic systems of bodily categorization take shape." For Rubin,
"Learning from the history of intersex is a process of unlearning received accounts of
gender's history" (69). I propose to extend that history a little further, in the hopes
of providing new insights into gender. The critical parameters of this history will be
slightly different from those of most recent work on gender, because of the historical
link between discussions of intersex and transgender individuals and those of humans
represented as "monsters." One of the best-known early modern works associating
intersex and transgender with "monsters" is Ambroise Paré's *On Monsters and Marvels*
(1573), first published alongside his treatise on surgery. One of the best-known modern
works that repeats this link is Isidore Geoffroy Saint-Hilaire's pioneering treatise on
teratology, *A General and Particular History of Anomalies of Organization in Man and
Animals* (1832–7),[1] which situates intersex individuals between relatively functional

anomalies and the more gravely impaired "monstrosities." Both authors were crucially influential in their own time and well after, but they both also met with critical responses. Montaigne questioned the association of corporeal difference with monstrosity reflected in Paré's work, and Canguilhem questions the categories of normal and pathological first suggested in Geoffroy Saint-Hilaire's work. Both philosophers arrive at the conclusion that individual experience in a given environment cannot be mapped onto some universal truth about the body and its functioning, and that therefore bodies cannot simply be deemed "normal," "monstrous," or "pathological." For Montaigne and Canguilhem, the desire for a knowledge that masters or controls the body is itself monstrous, closing off both an awareness of the limitations of human knowledge and the possibility of new understandings of ourselves and of the world around us. In the context of these critical approaches to concepts of the normal or the natural, bodies that cause us to call the binary concept of gender into question reveal the failures of that system of organizing the human.

Intersex and transgender thus have a longer history than is generally recognized, and at moments that history confounds any teleological narrative of increasingly complex understandings of gender over time. Early modern France was a time and place where discussions of gender, and of the gender status of intersex humans (called "hermaphrodites" in that period and up to and well into the twentieth century), became heated, underscoring divisions between the surgeons, who worked directly with their patients, and doctors, who taught medicine and anatomy but had less contact with patients and more of a theoretical understanding of gender based largely on the works of Aristotle. Theorists of gender in early modern Europe, particularly in France, remarked on the tension between the social and juridical demands that all bodies be sorted into either male or female, and their own observations that not all bodies were so easily sorted (Long, *Hermaphrodites* 29–47). The regularly recurring interest in intersex underscores both the persistence and the precariousness of the male/female binary. Until the late twentieth century, discussions of intersex also place it in a larger context of anatomical diversity, associating it first with the monstrous and then with the pathological. More recent discussions separate intersex from this context, with the result that intersex becomes a "problem" of gender and sexuality, rather than a normal or natural aspect of human variation. The link between gender and sexuality is particularly troubling in the work of John Money, as the projection of predicted sexuality onto infant's bodies was used to justify surgical procedures to assign gender to intersex infants. The problematic ethical dimensions of these procedures have been explored in depth (Dreger, *Intersex*; Rubin; Morland; Downing, Morland, and Sullivan).

Foucault's presentation of intersex in the person of Herculine Barbin as "a subject position both produced and ultimately foreclosed by the cultural logic of sexual dimorphism," as Rubin so cogently puts it (63), reduces intersex once more to the parameters of binary gender. Butler, in her assessment of Foucault's account, uses Barbin's gender ambiguity as evidence of the performative nature of gender, inevitably linked to sexuality and its regulation (127–37). These critical articulations of intersex enter into the logic of what Rubin calls "intersex exceptionalism":

Intersex exceptionalism is the view that intersex bodies are historically extraordinary, isometric objects of study—objects like no others—that reveal spectacular truths. Intersex exceptionalism is problematic because it presumes that "minus a few exceptions the system works just fine." That is to say, intersex exceptionalism hypostatizes ideas about the nature of atypical sex and gender nonconformity and, on the other hand, renaturalizes—rather than calls into question—the embodiments of people with non-intersex anatomies and cisgender or gender-conforming presentations, as well as the gendered operations of medical, legal, and social systems more broadly. (64–5)

There are multiple issues inherent to this exceptionalism. Intersex individuals are not seen as such—individual subjects of their own lives—but rather as "objects of study" that provide an abjected and indistinct "other" to ground concepts of gender normativity. These approaches also ignore differences among intersex bodies themselves, which prevent a uniform and depersonalizing mapping of characteristics and experiences. The word intersex stands in for a range of bodies and experiences that cannot be reduced to a uniform other, or even a range of categories or types.

The term "intersex" was introduced in the 1940s and came into general use in 1993, when the Intersex Society of North America was founded by Cheryl Chase. Intersex people prefer this term to "hermaphrodite," a term that from ancient times until at least the 1940s was used in association with the concept of the monsters. Monsters were all creatures, human and animal, that did not fit into the categories devised by humans to understand the world around them.

But the term "intersex" suggests that there is a sex that hovers somewhere between male and female, again reflecting misleading notions of the bodies we designate with this term. Since 2005, when pediatric endocrinologists agreed upon this term, "disorders of sex development" has dominated medical discussions of bodies that we deem not to be clearly male or female. The term "disorders" also resonates disturbingly with the history of teratology, thus relegating these bodies once more to the realm of the monstrous. Elizabeth Reis has proposed a less problematic phrase, "divergence of sex development" (535–43), which seems better, but still suggests that these bodies are diverging from something normative. All of this terminology still suggests that people with bodies we do not deem normal according to our cultural standards of gender are a problem to be solved, rather than just being an integral part of humanity and nature.

Since not all people fit into one or the other gender, these categories are not entirely accurate in their representation of humanity. When one considers dimorphic gender in the broader sense, in terms of characteristics other than gonads or genitals that we stereotypically associate with male or female, even fewer people fit into these neat categories. Perhaps it should be argued that this sort of categorization is itself monstrous, marginalizing people who are different from the norms we have devised. Yet, as the discussion of terminology above suggests, we have yet to find a way to talk about gender that does not remain within the parameters of male and female; we are not yet ready to be a post-gender world.

THE NORMAL AND THE PATHOLOGICAL: ORGANIZING GENDER

Current critical discussions of "normative" sexuality and gender owe their origins to Canguilhem's more general discussion of the normal (and to Foucault's brief summary of his work in *Abnormal*, 49–50). In responding to natural and medical philosophers such as Isidore Geoffroy Saint-Hilaire (1805–1861), who focused intensely on the project of classifying all anomalies in humans and animals, and most particularly on classifying what he called "hermaphrodites," Canguilhem proposes a model of understanding anatomical and physiological differences that is relevant both to the field of disability studies and to that of gender studies, presenting bodies as active and ever-changing participants in dynamic systems.[2] While the current separation of intersex bodies from those we might now consider "disabled" might be an understandable reaction to the stigma associated with disability, it also precludes the consideration of both early modern and modern discourses of the body that presented anatomical difference in a more positive light. A return to these discourses, via Canguilhem, might provide useful avenues for understanding intersex.

Early modern medical and philosophical thinkers did not separate sex and gender, and they were keenly aware that the social conventions for seeing human bodies in terms of gender dimorphism were not necessarily a reflection of the bodies that they observed around them. This contradiction creates a tension in many of these works, as authors insist on finding an organizational system that could justify assignment of intersex individuals to the male or female gender but fail repeatedly to create coherent models. We still feel such a deep-rooted need to put bodies "in order" that we have considerable trouble questioning that need and that order, and fall back instead on the association of gender nonconformity with the abnormal. While the way in which we read bodies as gendered is obviously intertwined with our understandings of sexuality, thinking about gender through a different lens, one suggested by a critique of early modern and modern teratological works, demonstrates how we use our constructions of gender to normalize or marginalize a range of different bodies. This in turn explains the twentieth-century insistence on shaping intersex bodies through surgery and other forms of medical manipulation in order to fit into gender identities as we imagine them to be.

As Daston and Park have pointed out, the discussion of gender ambiguity became particularly intense in early modern France ("Hermaphrodites in Renaissance," "The Hermaphrodite").[3] The fact that binary gender is deeply ingrained in the language and culture of France may help to explain the intensity of these debates. French is a grammatical gender language, meaning that all nouns, even those designating concepts or inanimate objects, have a gender. Unlike Latin, from which it evolved, French does not have the options of nouns with neuter gender or common (both male and female) gender, so all nouns are either masculine or feminine. As modern linguistic research suggests and some early modern texts recognize, this insistent division of the world and everything in it into masculine or feminine precludes the capacity to conceive of ambiguous or uncertain gender and tends to support stereotypical understandings of dimorphic gender (Prewitt-Freilino 268–81).

The tension between the complexity of observed gender differences and the cultural/linguistic imperative to designate humans as male or female is already apparent in Paré's treatise *On Monsters and Marvels*. In his chapter "On Hermaphrodites or Androgynes, That Is to Say, Which Have Two Sets of Sex Organs in One Body," Paré suggests the existence of six sexes: male and female, and four categories of hermaphrodites (his term), male, female, indeterminate ("neither one nor the other"), and "male and female hermaphrodites." Those in this last category of hermaphrodites, "with both sets of sexual organs well-formed," must be designated as male or female, even if their bodies do not present a clear gender:

> [B]oth the ancient and the modern laws have obliged and still oblige these latter to choose which sex organs they wish to use, and they are forbidden on pain of death to use any but those they will have chosen, on account of the misfortunes that could result from such. For some of them have abused their situation, with the result that,

through mutual and reciprocal use, they take their pleasure first with one set of sex
organs and then with the other: first with those of a man, then with those of a woman.
(Paré 27)

Recent research suggests that the legal imperative that all individuals should be either
male or female took precedence over a sense that not everyone could be designated as one
or the other gender (Laflamme). For Paré, most people presenting as ambiguously gendered can still be designated male or female on medical grounds, but the "double" hermaphrodite, male and female, poses a particular set of problems, having no clear legal status
and being able to play either the masculine or feminine role. There is a tension between
the reality of bodies that are not clearly legible as male or female, and the legal imperative
that everyone fit into this rigid norm. The neuter hermaphrodite, the individual whose
observable characteristics cannot be read as either stereotypically masculine or feminine,
disappears from the discussion altogether, suggesting the cultural necessity of gender,
and the difficulty of thinking outside of its parameters. Although Paré lists four types of
hermaphrodites, thus implying the existence of six genders, all of these types are then
regrouped into male or female, or vanish from the text. As anatomists and surgeons continue to write about more and more cases of intersex, the potential number of variations
increases, and thus Caspar Bauhin, a professor of anatomy at the University of Basel,
proposes a spectrum of gender, from manly man to womanly woman, with a range of possible types between these two poles (Long, *Hermaphrodites* 51; Bauhin A2v–A3). Still, all
humans must remain within the parameters of male and female; there is no possibility of
thinking outside of this system in the medical domain, even if not all bodies map onto it.

This insistent call to categorize bodies according to gender is linked to wider questions
of how we constitute the human and, in this context, connects early modern theories to
modern ones, as Elizabeth Bearden's recent essay on the resemblances and distinctions
between concepts of the natural and the normal makes clear. This is quite evident in
the work of Isidore Geoffroy Saint-Hilaire, considered to be the father of modern teratology (the science of abnormal development) because of his influential treatise on
the subject, *General and Particular History Anomalies of Organization in Man and the
Animals*, cited above. Whereas, as Dreger points out, Geoffroy Saint-Hilaire proposes
to naturalize bodies he sees as anomalous (*Hermaphrodites* 35), he still designates many
of these bodies, including conjoined twins, as monstrous and even designates what he
calls hermaphrodites as more monstrous than merely anomalous (Geoffroy Saint-Hilaire
2: 2).[4] While Fausto-Sterling has asserted that his system of classification makes "intersexuality virtually invisible" (37), his chart of "hermaphrodisms" actually underscores the
complexity as well as the factitious quality of gender designations.

In his work, Geoffroy Saint-Hilaire divides bodies into the categories of anomalies,
hermaphrodites, and monstrosities; none of these bodies is presented as normal, but
each category has a different "gravity" or severity of what he presents as abnormality.
Anomalies are bodily differences that do not significantly impair functioning; monstrosities are bodily differences that do impair functioning and often threaten the possibility of
life. He insists that his work is modern, dividing the history of the "science of monstrosities" into three periods: that of fables, or imaginary accounts; the "positive period," when
knowledge of monstrous bodies was gained through direct observation, but no theories of
bodily difference were developed; and the "scientific period," when rational explanations
were elaborated in order to account for anomalies and monstrosities (1: 4–9). He focuses
intently on how to include nonnormative bodies (which he called monsters in all of his

work) in the natural order of things, how to integrate them into a system of thought, rather than leaving them on the margins as singularities, the mode of thinking about nonnormative bodies that dominated the medieval and early modern periods (Daston and Park, *Wonders* 116). The solution he proposes is his "theory of arrested or retarded (slowed) development" ("théorie de l'arrêt et du retardement de développement"), a solution borrowed from the work of his father and of other anatomists:

> Up until this point, all that has been seen in phenomena of monstrosity are irregular arrangements, bizarre and disorderly bodily forms ... For the idea of strange and irregular beings, this theory substitutes the more true and philosophical one, of beings delayed in their development .... Monstrosity is no longer a blind disorder, but another order equally regular, equally subject to laws.[5] (Geoffroy Saint-Hilaire 1: 18)

This emphasis on order and law echoes Paré's insistence that the "double" hermaphrodite be assigned a gender in order to conform with the law. The laws invoked by Geoffroy Saint-Hilaire impose a hierarchy; anomalous bodies, whether "disabled" or indeterminately gendered, are presented as a lower form of life on the evolutionary scale that places the human on the top. Their development has been stopped or slowed, and therefore they have not achieved perfect humanity. This concept of bodily difference, based on a work of comparative anatomy of human and nonhuman animals, itself dependent on the assumption of human superiority, is underscored by the insistent use of the term "monstrosity" in Geoffroy Saint-Hilaire's work, a term he uses to convey the nonviability of an organism. Thus, his theory is both based on and confirms a hierarchy of anatomical superiority (the normal) and inferiority (the anomalous), and he places what he calls "hermaphrodisms" beneath the realm of the normal but not quite in the realm of the monstrous. This near association of intersex with the monstrous connects Geoffroy Saint-Hilaire's work with early modern treatises on monstrosity.

Geoffroy Saint-Hilaire has particular difficulty coaxing "hermaphrodisms" into an orderly system; already, he has not determined whether they are anomalies or monstrosities, arguing that they are the former until puberty and more like the latter after that (2: 33). Although he condemns Paré as not scientific enough (1: 72), he reuses his categories of hermaphrodites listed in *On Monsters* in his "General and Methodical Table of Hermaphrodisms" (2: facing 36): masculine, feminine, mixed, and indeterminate. He augments this list with three additional categories: the complex masculine hermaphrodite, the complex feminine hermaphrodite, and the "bisexual" hermaphrodite, for seven genders in all. This last category seems to blur into the "mixed" category above it, but Geoffroy Saint-Hilaire insists that humans with perfect organs of both sexes do not exist, thus inserting a fiction into his "scientific" system of organization, which as a result seems somewhat tenuous.

The *Atlas* of illustrations to this treatise offers an additional, somewhat more complex, system of organization, one placed on a grid rather than a chart (Figure 8.1). This grid is quite striking, because among twenty images of diverse bodies, it is the only one that replaces the bodies in question with rectangles representing body parts. This reduction of intersex bodies to geometric forms underscores the symbolic use of those bodies, as the system of organization overrides a more naturalistic form of representation. The grid format implies a comprehensive and closed system, one that contains all possibilities, thus mirroring Geoffroy Saint-Hilaire's goal of including all of nature, even that which is deemed singular or monstrous. As promised in the introduction to this treatise, it imposes order on those bodies, and this order in turn imposes a hierarchy. There are

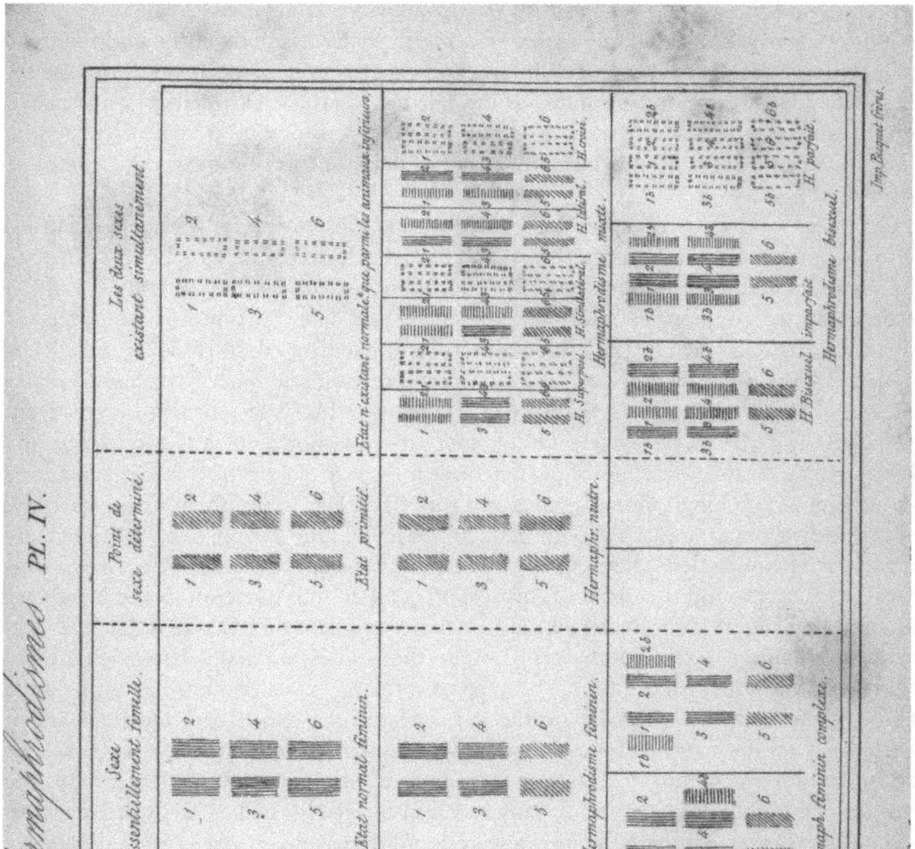

FIGURE 8.1 Isidore Geoffroy Saint-Hilaire, *Histoire générale et particulière des anomalies de l'organisation chez l'homme et les animaux* (*A General and Particular History of Anomalies of Organization in Man and the Animals*), *Atlas*, Plate 4, "Hermaphrodismes" ("Hermaphrodisms"). Courtesy of the Division of Rare and Manuscript Collections, Cornell University Library.

four columns and three rows: the first row designates normal states of "sexual apparatus" ("appareil sexuel"); the second, abnormal states without excess body parts; and the third row, abnormal states with excess parts. In other words, the grid moves from normal states at the top to the most abnormal states at the bottom. In the top row, the "essentially" male individual is presented first, and on the left, the "essentially" female. The simple states of indeterminate sex and the two sexes simultaneous in one individual complete the top row.

In Geoffroy Saint-Hilaire's system, six body parts determine what he calls sex. In his guide to the grid, he explains his method: each part is designated by a number, 1 through 6. The numbers 1 and 2 represent the two internal parts (the ovaries or testes), 3 and 4 represent the medial parts (the uterus or prostate), and 5 and 6 represent the external parts (the clitoris and vulva or the penis and scrotum). Geoffroy Saint-Hilaire adds: "The even numbers represent the left side, the odd numbers the right" (Geoffroy Saint-Hilaire 4: 5; see also Dreger, *Hermaphrodites* 141). Numbers 1 bis, 2 bis, and so on represent additional body parts as necessary. The gender of these body parts is represented by hatching on the rectangles: horizontal hatching indicates male parts, vertical hatching female, diagonal hatching indeterminate, and tiny hatching, in the form of dots around the edges, indicates parts that are both male and female. Our author explains that these latter parts can be imagined "theoretically, but do not yet exist in reality" (Geoffroy Saint-Hilaire 4: 5). Once again, the order of this system is called into question by the imaginary bodies used to make it seem balanced. In a further complication of this system, the dots are made up of either horizontal or vertical lines, thus indicating male or female parts. In the "normal" (but nonexistent) double hermaphrodite, the "male" double parts are on the right side of the body, the "female" on the left, a placement consistent in ancient, medieval, and early modern views that associated the feminine with the left or sinister side of the body. The level of detail in this grid suggests an effort to create an all-encompassing system, one that takes every variation into account, but it also makes this system impossible to interpret. I have lingered on my description of it, to underscore both the obsessive nature of this need to order bodies that resist such categorization and the futility of this effort.

Even at first glance, the chart itself seems problematic; while it is a chart of "hermaphrodisms," it includes the "normal masculine state" ("état normal masculin") and the "normal feminine state" ("état normal féminin"). Does this mean that these states are also potentially hermaphrodisms? What happens at this point in the chart is a blurring of the lines between normative gender, male and female, and "hermaphrodisms," which calls bigenderism into question as much as it normalizes intersex. In the second row of this chart, the "essentially male hermaphrodite" is characterized by internal and medial organs that are masculine, and external parts that are indeterminate; the "essentially female hermaphrodite" has feminine internal and medial organs and indeterminate external organs. But in his narration of particular cases, Geoffroy Saint-Hilaire recognizes that each part could potentially be one of three types (remember, the fourth type, the "perfect" hermaphrodite, exists only theoretically) so the number of possible variations increases (and these variations are imagined throughout the chapters on "hermaphrodisms," 2: 61–173). The rectangles representing the "neuter" or indeterminate hermaphrodite are identical to those in the first row, which indicate the "primitive state," perhaps that of the undifferentiated fetus. The fourth column in this second row then reveals a further proliferation of gender types, in its representation of "mixed hermaphrodisms." There is "superimposed hermaphrodism," in which internal parts are identified as belonging to one gender (in this grid, masculine), medial to another (here, feminine), and external a third (here, indeterminate); "semilateral hermaphrodism", in which one medial part is masculine, the other feminine, and internal parts are masculine, external indeterminate; lateral hermaphrodism (male on one side, female on the other); and "crossed hermaphrodism," with dotted parts representing male-ish internal parts on one side, female on the other, with the reverse for medial parts. In these first two rows, this grid has shown us fourteen gender possibilities.

The third row, that of abnormal states with excess parts, presents seven more genders: two types of complex masculine hermaphrodism, two types of complex feminine hermaphrodism, and three types of "bisexual" hermaphrodism. These types include between eight and twelve body parts that indicate gender. If the types represented are indicative of all of the possibilities, then Geoffroy Saint-Hilaire has offered us twenty-one possible gender types; if it is suggestive of other possible combinations (with male, female, indeterminate, or double parts substituting for the parts that are represented), then the possible number of variations increases dramatically. Thus, in the attempt to "naturalize" anatomical differences within the confines of binary gender, Geoffroy Saint-Hilaire creates a system that causes genders to proliferate in a vast number of different forms. Depending on how the chart is interpreted, there could be as many genders as there are humans on earth, or perhaps even more.

Furthermore, the column for the indeterminate hermaphrodite with excess parts remains blank, while the nonexistent "perfect" hermaphrodite finishes out the grid. In the right-hand columns of the second and fourth rows, the categories are further divided into subcategories, creating a proliferation of possibilities that threatens the order of the grid. Thus, the system devised for putting these bodies in order seems to represent instead the unruly diversity of genders. This attempt to reduce human beings to a system, the depersonalizing of individual bodies to rectangles representing "types," reveals the violence of attempts to theorize bodily diversity in systematic ways, as well as the conceptual insufficiency of these systems. As Rubin states, "it is the obsession with gender and sex *normativity* that transforms intersex into a medical problem" (81). Geoffroy Saint-Hilaire's grids show the lengths to which this obsession might go.

The problematic nature of this grid, which imposes a conceptual order on living bodies whose capacities exceed or exist outside of the realm of this order, reflects Canguilhem's more general criticism of Geoffroy Saint-Hilaire's work. As he considers the teratologist's classification of anomalies with more severe impairment as monstrosities, he questions the judgment concerning the *importance* of this impairment: "For the naturalist importance is an objective idea, but it is essentially a subjective one in the sense that it includes a reference to the life of a living being, considered fit to qualify this same life according to what helps or hinders it." Canguilhem also points out that Geoffroy Saint-Hilaire himself recognized the subjective nature of impairment in his considerations of functionality and of harm or disturbance to the individual (134), and then rejects the ascription of pathology to physical differences that do not have a pronounced effect on functioning:

> As long as the anomaly has no functional repercussions experienced consciously by the individual ... the anomaly is either ignored ... or constitutes an indifferent *variety*, a variation on a specific theme; it is an irregularity like the negligible irregularities found in objects cast in the same mold. It might form the subject of a special chapter in natural history, but not in pathology. (135–6)

In Canguilhem's view, the experience the individuals have of their own lives is the crucial determinant. This view is supported by the narrative in Geoffroy Saint-Hilaire's treatise, as he offers examples such as that of Adélaïde Préville who lived happily as a woman all of her life, but was discovered to have predominantly masculine genitalia during her autopsy; in this and other cases, he suggests that the personal preferences of the individual, which he calls "penchans," should serve as some indication of gender (2: 72). As Canguilhem suggests, the quality of life as perceived by the individual determines whether medical intervention is warranted: "But diversity is not disease; the *anomalous* is not the pathological. Pathological implies *pathos*, the direct and concrete feeling of suffering and impotence, the feeling of life gone wrong" (137). Further on, he rejects systematic "scientific" assessments of bodily functions: "*The living being's functional norms* as examined in the laboratory are meaningful only within the framework of *the scientist's operative norms*" (145). The way in which we assess individuals in a scientific or laboratory environment tells us something about what they are like in that environment and nothing about what they are like in their daily lives. Similarly, a system of categorizing bodies tells us a great deal about the system itself, its creator, and the cultural environment in which it was created, and very little about the bodies it claims to "put in order." The reduction of intersex individuals to a series of rectangles in a grid tells us nothing of value about those individuals; it tells us a great deal about the problematic nature of the desire to create an epistemology that puts bodies "in order."

What Canguilhem's theories of the normal and the pathological seek to explore is the subjective nature of illness and impairment, as well as of good health and normality. In the context of this approach to diversity, the individuals concerned are the ones who determine how to live their lives, whether to seek medical intervention, and whether they feel impaired by physical difference or by the environment which does not accommodate that difference, or which makes it a "problem." Writing in the context of the French Resistance to the Nazi Occupation, Canguilhem is pushing back against the notion of physical difference as a problem, as well as resisting the scientific regimentation of bodies as more or less normal or pathological, with the goal of designating some for destruction. As Foucault has demonstrated in his account of quarantines in plague-infested towns, the grid is a method of extreme control over bodies, one that organizes society into a system of surveillance and self-surveillance (44–52): "It is not a question of driving out individuals but rather of establishing and fixing them, of giving them their own place, of assigning places and of defining presences and subdivided presences" (46). Canguilhem's emphasis on the subjective experience of the individual, also suggested in Geoffroy Saint-Hilaire's narratives in distinction to his charts and grids, provides a useful alternative to theories and paradigms of gender that reify intersex as a form of exceptionalism (in Rubin's terms) that reduces individuals to a homogenous category of the unintelligible other (66). The normative/nonnormative binary that informs this reification is simply refused by Canguilhem. For him, diversity and variation *are* normativity.

In this regard, Canguilhem echoes the ideas of Michel de Montaigne, who chooses an Augustinian approach to anatomical diversity over the Aristotelian notions of departure from an ideal type or excess or lack of parts, all of which condemn nonnormative (and all female) bodies to the domain of the monstrous (Long, "Montaigne" 309–10). After describing a child with a conjoined headless parasitic twin, and performing a refusal of interpretation of this child that serves as a critique of the political uses of monstrosity, he describes an individual with indeterminate gender: "I have just seen a shepherd in Médoc, thirty years old or thereabouts, who has no sign of genital parts. He has three holes by which he continually makes water. He is bearded, has desire, and likes to touch women" (Montaigne 539). While the beard and the sexual activity might be indicators of gender, these were problematic signs in the early modern period; bearded women were known to exist (Fisher 112–17), and the original French for "likes to touch women," "recherche l'attouchement des femmes" ("he seeks the touch of women," Montaigne 713) hovers between activity, considered a male attribute, and passivity, associated with females. His conclusion concerning these two individuals is Augustinian: "What we call monsters are not so to God, who sees in the immensity of his work the infinity of forms he has comprised in it" (539). This view of difference is a recurrent theme in Montaigne's work, appearing most prominently in the final essay of his third book, "Of experience": "Nature has committed herself to make nothing separate that was not different" (815). Canguilhem offers a similar view of anatomical difference as a universal attribute of humankind: "An anomaly is a fact of individual variation which prevents two beings from being able to take the place of each other completely" (137). In the face of this diversity, Montaigne sees the pursuit of systematic knowledge in the form of organization of bodies and behavior into absolute immutable categories as a futile gesture:

> Who has seen children trying to divide a mass of quicksilver into a certain number of parts? The more they press it and knead it and try to constrain it to their will, the more they provoke the independence of this spirited metal; it escapes their skill and keeps dividing and scattering in little particles beyond all reckoning. This is the same; for by subdividing these subtleties they teach men to increase their doubts; they start us extending and diversifying the difficulties, they lengthen them, they scatter them. (816)

For Montaigne, individual experience of one's own health and illness overrides the imperatives of orderly categories of medicine: "Experience is really on its own dunghill in the subject of medicine, where reason yields it the whole field" (826). He derides the presumption that man can understand his own body, and those of others, in any systematic or universalizing way.

Canguilhem's refusal of the dichotomy normal/abnormal or normal/pathological in favor of a more universal diversity also offers an alternative to Foucault's formulation of sex as an effect of sexuality (Butler, *Undoing Gender* 129), which echoes Money's approach to sex reassignment surgery on intersex infants. Money attributed sexuality to nonverbal infants, reading anatomy that was not fully developed as potentially sexually active within the heterosexual matrix, and thus inscribed the sexuality onto their bodies by means of surgery. Money also tried to elaborate systems to predict sex (gender), including his "seven variables of sex": " 'chromosomal sex; gonadal sex; hormonal sex; external genital morphology; accessory internal genital morphology; assigned sex and rearing; and gender role' " (Morland 110). As Morland demonstrates in his analysis of this system, the "discreteness of the seven sexual variables ... led Money to two contradictory positions," as these variables could " 'vary independently of one another' " (111) thus creating inconsistencies within an individual, not unlike the different body parts that could develop independently of each other, some becoming male and some female, in Geoffroy Saint-Hilaire's system. Morland points out that Money wanted "classificatory criteria" that were unambiguous, so that he might sort the individuals into the categories of male and female, and underscores the tautological nature of this pursuit (116). What is problematic here, and what informs many of the medical and critical responses to intersex, is the expressed need for certainty and order, something both Montaigne and Canguilhem knew was impossible in the realm of the corporeal.

Bodies themselves are always already sites of resistance to rationalizing forms of knowledge; they constantly escape the control of systems of thought that they are used to validate. They are measured, sorted, and categorized, but they come up short, or tall, or simply different from what is expected of them. We respond by creating new systems for them, or by shaping bodies to fit the old ones, but in the end, the body's possibilities will always exceed our capacity to know and to control them. In the context of this reality, gender cannot function as a fixed system; this is something theorists of gender already knew in the early modern era.

INTERSEX/TRANSGENDER: THE CASE OF MARIN LE MARCIS

One well-known early modern case unites a discussion of transformation of gender identity with that of intersex and suggests that gender variation and gender fluidity are related, but not identical. It presents gender variation as a preexisting state that is not legible in terms of bigenderism, while fluidity calls into question the static or fixed nature of gender. The story of Marin le Marcis as told by Jacques Duval in his treatise on hermaphrodites (and childbirth) is well known through Foucault's and Greenblatt's accounts of it, but it offers a richer view of gender indeterminacy and gender mobility than these versions have conveyed and allows a brief view of the complexity of early modern understandings of gender. In Paré's accounts of gender transformation in *On Monsters* (31–3), which follows his chapter on "hermaphrodites," the newly born men are given clothing that establishes their new-found gender, along with a new name, both apparently granted by religious authorities. Thus, bodily transformation is authorized by established social institutions. The situation is somewhat different for Marin le Marcis, the young man who had been born and baptized a female, who took on men's clothing and married a widow in adulthood, and who was thus accused of violating gender norms and sentenced to death in Rouen in 1601.[6] It is clear in Jacques Duval's account of this case, published in 1612, that the law does not permit individuals to determine their own gender identity and confirm it by means of clothing.

The rhetoric of Duval's account expresses gender ambiguity in the context of a culture dependent on the strict gendering of everything into masculine and feminine. This is perhaps why Marin's case has been read as that of a hermaphrodite, when it could so easily fall into the category of Paré's transgender males. The opening lines of this account, in the chapter sixty-two of his treatise, *Des Hermaphrodits*, evoke the complexity of Marin's gender:

> In this category we will also place Marin le Marcis, who having been baptized, named, dressed, raised & educated as a girl, up until the age of twenty years, after which he felt the signs of his virility, changed his clothing, and had himself called Marin instead of Marie. (Duval, 383–4)[7]

Duval insistently uses the masculine form of the past participle even as he is describing Marin's childhood as a girl, thus underscoring the dissonance between the official view of his gender and the identity that Marin wants to establish for himself and that Duval seeks to confirm in order to save Marin's life.

Marin works as a chambermaid until he is twenty-one, when he meets Jeanne le Febvre, and reveals his "virile member" to her. They fall in love, and he introduces her to his parents, whose only objection to the proposed marriage is the young widow's poverty and two dependent children. They apply to abjure their Protestant faith and marry within the Catholic Church, openly sharing the story of Marin's newly revealed identity (Duval 386–9). Much of this portion of the narrative is Duval's summary of Marin's own testimony, and thus at least to some degree his own version of his story.

When Marin is arrested and examined, the two surgeons involved find no sign of masculine traits in him,[8] so another examination is undertaken, with the same results. While his wife says that Marin's physiology is much like that of her dead husband's, all of his former employers state that he only showed signs of being a girl. Marin is told that "he had offended God and Justice, to have called himself a man, when no one had found any signs of that, but rather all the signs of a girl."[9] Marin is convicted of taking the clothing of a man and usurping a man's name, thus engaging in impersonation. He is also convicted of sodomy, but as Duval's marginal note points out, this crime would require having a penis, a fact which would invalidate the conviction. According to the court documents, "Marie" le Marcis is condemned to be burned alive, Jeanne, to be publicly beaten (Duval 393–4).[10]

Marin's appeal of this sentence leads to him being examined once more. The signs that his body presents seem to offer contradictory versions of gender. He is solidly built,[11] with short hair, but this hair is neither wiry nor soft.[12] He has a moustache,[13] but his voice is high and feminine,[14] and he has a large chest with breasts.[15] He has a large stomach, large buttocks and thighs, and is very hairy all over, much more so than a woman would be. He has a small clitoris, and where the vulva should be, the examining surgeons find something that resembles a small penis (Duval 400–1). Marin's body offers a wealth of contradictory signs, and so eludes clear interpretation.

Nonetheless, since Marin's life is at stake, Duval seeks to establish masculinity by means of the erection of the penis and ejaculation, and performs an invasive clinical examination of Marin's body to find the proof. This examination saves Marin from execution (Duval 402–5). Duval criticizes his colleagues for reading only the external signs, and not considering what nature had hidden: "I began to blame to myself the negligence of those, who wanted to judge by inspection of the exterior, that which nature had kept and hidden in a more secret room" (Duval 405).[16] The external signs are no longer reliable as markers of gender; for Duval, sight does not indicate an underlying truth. In this, he is the heir of Montaigne. He stays within the realm of empirical inquiry, however, in suggesting here that touch or feeling is a better indicator of gender than visual cues; the body cannot be read, but felt, by Duval and by Jeanne, who testifies to her experience of Marin's masculinity, as well as by Marin himself. In the end, the contradictory signs on and in Marin's body cause Duval to call him a "Gunanthrope" or womanly man (Duval 407); the name implies that both gender identities are present in one person.

Duval's insistence that the signs of gender vary according to the situation of the person being observed suggests that he sees gender as a contingent, and not fixed, quality of the body. As a "gunanthrope" with both masculine and feminine characteristics, Marin can become more feminine or masculine depending on his context. When he slept in a comfortable bed, ate well, had plenty of exercise and fresh air, adequate sleep, and frequent sex with his wife, he looked and acted more like a man. In prison, sleeping on a straw mat, eating bread and water, engaging in little activity, getting no fresh air, no sunshine, little sleep, and no sex, he takes on the appearance of a woman. Thus, gender is again read through stereotypical characteristics imposed on men and women by social norms; men are active, women passive. These characteristics also speak to the deprivation and subordination that shape gender in this period, creating a sort of circular enforcement of gender roles: women are deemed weaker, so they are afforded less food and freedom to move, thus making them weaker. The fear engendered by the criminal trial, the constant surveillance of an unpleasant prison guard, and the lack of freedom all contribute as well to his feminization by changing his dominant humors from sanguine to phlegmatic or melancholic. Since he is forced to wear women's clothing throughout the trial and even afterward for a number of years, his appearance is further feminized. These external influences have helped to further shape Marin's body (Duval 416–18; Long, *Hermaphrodites* 84). This account presents an intersex individual whose body changes in response to different contexts and elicits opposing interpretations, bringing the tales of intersex and transgender individuals together in one person.

The sentence of the court mirrors this complexity, as Marin is required to live as a woman until he is twenty-five years old, without sexual contact with other people of one or the other gender. Ten years later, Duval describes him as bearded and living as a man, in "an even better manly state,"[17] working as a man's tailor. He "undertakes, performs, and completes all duties pertaining to a man, he has a beard on his chin, and has that which is necessary to content a woman, and to beget children by her" (Duval A7).[18] These basic signs of masculinity confirm Marin's chosen gender. But throughout his detailed account, Duval conveys both the complexity and mobility of gender in this case, suggesting that one's reading of the gendered body is driven by the context in which it is found. Thus, Duval's treatise also underscores the intersections between transgender and intersex identities, the signs that are used to designate individuals with these identities as male or female, and the inconstant and indecipherable nature of those signs.

CONCLUSION

What is extraordinary about Marin's story is both his desire to be accepted by social institutions of Church and State as male and his persistent quest for self-determination (even when faced with a death sentence). He manages to use the judicial system to confirm the gender he has chosen, in the face of strong opposition on the part of the medical establishment (none of the professors of medicine from the Sorbonne would even touch his body to perform an examination). This confirmation allows him, eventually, to live the life he has chosen, with the person he loves, exercising a profession by means of which he prospers. In spite of a physiology that does not conform to stereotypical notions of binary gender, he is living what Canguilhem would call a normative life; he has adapted to his surroundings, and is thriving. The judicial system, unable to determine his gender definitively, bent to his will, albeit reluctantly, and did not break.

This tale, placed alongside Geoffroy Saint-Hilaire's rigid and yet dysfunctional system for organizing gender variations, suggests that gender functions best as an improvisational category, one that bends to the circumstances and desires of those who choose to participate in it, rather than as a system of organization that "fixes" bodies according to rigid yet arbitrary stereotypes that do not reflect the range of possibilities in humanity. Such allowance for variation and improvisation creates the possibility for everyone to thrive, regardless of gender, and to move beyond the limitations that bigenderism imposes on all of us. Marin offers us what Susan Stryker and Talia M. Bettcher call "transgender agency—that is, of trans people making conscious, informed choices about the best way to live their own embodied lives" (7). Intersex individuals have been demanding this agency as well; the ability to determine their own embodiment and how best to live it.

While self-determination is crucial, it remains constrained by a system that reduces bodies to two genders, rather than recognizing the potential infinite variation of differences. Sandy Stone sees this potential in trans bodies:

> The disruptions of the old patterns of desire that the multiple dissonances of the trans-sexual body imply produce not an irreducible alterity but a myriad of alterities, whose unanticipated juxtapositions hold what Donna Haraway has called the promises of monsters—physicalities of constantly shifting figure and ground that exceed the frame of any possible representation. (232)

But Stone sees this variation as occurring in expression or representation, thus effacing the possibility that this variation might already be present in bodies themselves, meaning that variation exceeds the norms.[19] This is what intersex thought can contribute to our understanding of gender; this is what Montaigne and Canguilhem already knew.

Many of the possibilities raised by the case of Marin le Marcis and by twenty-first-century feminists—a myriad of alterities, the mobility of gender and the possibility of personal agency in determining one's gender, the performance of gender, and the idea that we do not have unmediated access to the materiality of the body—resonate throughout early modern culture, in satirical novels like *The Island of Hermaphrodites*, in plays, poetry, alchemical works, and medical treatises.[20] Yet, these ideas seem to vanish by the end of the early modern era, along with an understanding of the inherently nonnormative nature of material bodies, giving way to more normative concepts of gender. The recursive nature of the work we are undertaking once again underscores the persistence of bigenderism even in the face of examples of its limitations and its failures. The work of twenty-first-century feminism will be to flip this script on its head and explore the possibility that it is the norms themselves that are not normal.[21]

NOTES

1 The full French title gives an idea of the scope of this work: *Histoire générale et particulière des anomalies de l'organisation chez l'homme et les animaux, ouvrage comprenant des recherches sur les caractères, la classification, l'influence physiologique, les rapports généraux, les lois et les causes des monstruosités, des variétés et vices de conformation, ou traité de tératologie* (*A General and Particular History of Anomalies of Organization in Man and Animals, a work including research on the nature, classification, physiological influence, general relations, laws and causes of monstrosities, variations and defects in form, or treatise on teratology*).

2 See, in particular, his chapter on "A Critical Examination of Certain Concepts: The Normal, Anomaly and Disease; The Normal and the Experimental," 125–49.

3 See also Jones and Stallybrass, and Epstein, who connect nonnormative gender with other forms of corporeal difference.

4 "The second group [hermaphrodisms, mentioned earlier in the text] is, on the contrary, closer to the monstrosities" ("Le second est, au contraire, plus voisin des monstruosités"). Geoffroy Saint-Hilaire repeats this sentiment later in the text, claiming that "after puberty, he becomes almost a monstrosity" ("après la puberté, il devient presque une monstruosité," 33); this is in contrast to Julia Epstein's claim that he only designates severe anomalies as monstrous: "He

reserved 'monstrosity' only for severe anomalies such as anencephalous (headless) births" (100). All translations of Geoffroy Saint-Hilaire's text are my own.

5 "Jusqu'ici on n'avait vu dans les phénomènes de la monstruosité que des arrangemens irréguliers, des conformations bizarres et désordonnées... . À l'idée d'êtres bizarres, irréguliers, elle substitue celle, plus vraie et plus philosophique, d'êtres entravés dans leurs développemens... . La monstruosité n'est plus un désordre aveugle, mais un autre ordre également régulier, également soumis à des lois."

6 The best-known assessment of this case is undoubtedly that of Greenblatt, in his chapter, "Fiction and Friction," *Shakespearean Negotiations*, pp. 73–86. Unfortunately, Greenblatt sees Marin as "grotesque," thus condemning his nonnormative gender presentation to the realm of monstrosity. An interesting but somewhat inaccurate account of the case is presented by Foucault in his lecture from "22 January 1975," from *The Abnormal*, 68–70 (see note 10, below).

7 "Sous ceste espece nous mettrons aussi Marin le Marcis, qui ayant esté baptisé, nommé, vestu, nourri & entretenu pour fille, iusques à l'aage de vingt ans: apres qu'il eut senti indices de sa virilité, changea d'"habit, & se faisant appeller Marin, au lieu de Marie." See also Ferguson, particularly the discussions of the story of Mary from Michel de Montaigne's Journal de Voyage and of Marin le Marcis (146–8).

8 "ne trouver en luy aucun signe de verilité."

9 "il avoit offencé Dieu & la justice, de s'estre dit homme, veu qu'on n'en avoit trouvé aucuns indices, mais au contraire tous signes de fille."

10 It should be noted that Duval only uses the name "Marie" when he is quoting court documents or others' accounts of the young man's life. Foucault, although acknowledging that Marin took on a masculine name (which he mistakenly gives as "Martin"), uses "Marie" consistently throughout his brief summary of the case (68–9). Foucault also does not seem to understand that Marin was being tried for sodomy, a somewhat inventive charge because of the lack of legal guidelines for trying women in same-sex relationships; thus, Marin is being tried for his actions, not his intersex status. Foucault is also mistaken about the outcome of the case; once he reached the age of majority, Marin resumed his masculine identity, lived with Jeanne, and, according to Duval, had sexual relations with her. I have chosen to return in some detail to Duval's original account of this case in order to offer a more accurate reading of it.

11 "Il avoit le corps trappe, fourni, bien ramassé."

12 "la chevelure courte, de qualité entre dure et molle."

13 "La levre superieure noircissante, par le poil copieux & noir."

14 "la voix claire & fort semblable à la feminine."

15 "poitrine large, ornee de tetins gros & glanduleux en forme de mamelles."

16 "Je commençay blasmer à part moy la negligence de ceux, qui vouloient par l'inspection de l'exterieur, juger et decider de ce que nature avoit retenu, & reconcé en un plus secret cabinet."

17 "meilleure habitude virile."

18 "entreprend, faict, execute tous exercices à homme appartenans, porte barbe au menton, & à dequoy contenter une femme, pour engendrer en elle."

19 "This is a treacherous area, and were the silenced groups to achieve voice we might well find, as feminist theorists have claimed, that the identities of individual, embodied subjects were far less implicated in physical norms, and far more diversely spread across a rich and complex structuration of identity and desire, than it is now possible to express" (Stone 232).

20 *L'Isle des Hermaphrodites*, first published in 1605. See also Benserade, *Iphis et Iante*, first performed in 1632, and Long, "Gender and Power in the Alchemical Works of Clovis Hesteau de

Nuysement" (137–62) and "Lyric Hermaphrodites" (163–87), in *Hermaphrodites in Renaissance Europe* for alchemical and poetic representations of intersex and transgender individuals.

21 See Dreger (*One of Us*) and Davis for considerations of the future of the concept of "normal."

WORKS CITED

Barbin, Herculine. *Herculine Barbin. Being the Recently Discovered Memoirs of a Nineteenth-Century French Hermaphrodite*. Trans. Richard McDougall. New York: Pantheon Books, 1980.

Bauhin, Caspar. *De hermaphroditorum monstrosorumque partuum natura ex Theologorum, Jureconsultorumque, Medicorum, Philosophorum, et Rabbinorum sententia libri duo.* Oppenheim: Galleri, De Bry, 1614.

Bearden, Elizabeth B. "Before Normal, There Was Natural: John Bulwer, Disability, and Natural Signing in Early Modern England and Beyond." *PMLA* 131 (2017): 33–50.

Benserade, Isaac de. *Iphis et Iante*. Ed. Anne Verdier. Vijon: Lampsaque, 2000.

Bettcher, Talia Mae. "Intersexuality, Transgender, and Transsexuality." *The Oxford Handbook of Feminist Theory*. Ed. Lisa Disch and Mary Hawkesworth. New York: Oxford UP, 2016, pp. 407–27.

Boyarin, Daniel. "Gender." *Critical Terms for Religious Studies*. Ed. Mark C. Taylor. Chicago: U of Chicago P, 1998, pp. 117–36.

Butler, Judith. *Gender Trouble*. New York: Routledge, 1990.

Butler, Judith. *Undoing Gender*. New York: Routledge, 2004.

Cadden, Joan. *Meanings of Sex Difference in the Middle Ages: Medicine, Science, and Culture*. Cambridge: Cambridge UP, 1993.

Canguilhem, Georges. *The Normal and the Pathological*. Trans. Carolyn R. Fawcett. New York: Zone Books, 1991.

Downing, Lisa, Iain Morland, and Nikki Sullivan. *Fuckology: Critical Essays on John Money's Diagnostic Concepts*. Chicago: U of Chicago P, 2015.

Daston, Lorraine, and Katharine Park. "The Hermaphrodite and the Orders of Nature." *GLQ* 1 (1995): 419–38.

Daston, Lorraine, and Katharine Park. "Hermaphrodites in Renaissance France." *Critical Matrix* 1 (1985): 1–19.

Daston, Lorraine, and Katharine Park. *Wonders and the Order of Nature, 1150–1750*. New York: Zone Books, 1998.

Davis, Lennard. *The End of Normal: Identity in a Biocultural Era*. Ann Arbor: U of Michigan P, 2014.

DeVun, Leah. "The Jesus Hermaphrodite: Science and Sex Difference in Premodern Europe." *Journal of the History of Ideas* 69 (2008): 193–218.

Dreger, Alice. *Hermaphrodites and the Medical Invention of Sex*. Cambridge, MA: Harvard UP, 1998.

Dreger, Alice, ed. *Intersex in the Age of Ethics*. Hagerstown, MD: University Publishing Group, 1999.

Dreger, Alice. *One of Us: Conjoined Twins and the Future of Normal*. Cambridge, MA: Harvard UP, 2005.

Duval, Jacques. *Des hermaphrodits, accouchemens de femmes, et traitement qui est requis pour les relever en santé*. Rouen: David Geuffroy, 1612.

Epstein, Julia. *Altered Conditions: Disease, Medicine, and Storytelling*. New York: Routledge, 1995.

Epstein, Julia. "Either/Or—Neither/Both: Sexual Ambiguity and the Ideology of Gender." *Genders* 7 (1990): 99–142.

Fausto-Sterling, Anne. *Sexing the Body: Gender Politics and the Construction of Sexuality*. New York: Basic Books, 2000.

Ferguson, Gary. "Early Modern Transitions: From Montaigne to Choisy." *L'Esprit Créateur, Transgender France*. Ed. Todd Reeser. 53.1 (2013): 145–57.

Fisher, Will. *Materializing Gender in Early Modern English Literature and Culture*. Cambridge: Cambridge UP, 2006.

Foucault, Michel. *Abnormal: Lectures at the Collège de France, 1974–1975*. Ed. Valerio Marchetti and Antonella Salomoni, trans. Graham Burchell. London: Picador, 2003.

Geoffroy Saint-Hilaire, Isidore. *Histoire générale et particulière des anomalies de l'organisation chez l'homme et les animaux, ouvrage comprenant des recherches sur les caractères, la classification, l'influence physiologique, les rapports généraux, les lois et les causes des monstruosités, des variétés et vices de conformation, ou traité de tératologie* (*General and Particular History of Anomalies of Organization in Man and the Animals, Work Including Research on the Nature, Classification, Physiological Influence, General Connections, Laws and Causes of Monstrosities, Varieties, and Vices of Formation, or Treatise on Teratology*), 4 vols. Paris: Baillière, 1832–7.

Gilbert, Miqqi Alicia. "Defeating Bigenderism: Changing Gender Assumptions in the Twenty-First Century." *Hypatia*, special issue on *Transgender Studies and Feminism: Theory, Politics, and Gendered Realities*, 24 (2009): 93–112.

Gilbert, Ruth. *Early Modern Hermaphrodites: Sex and Other Stories*. Basingstoke, UK: Palgrave, 2002.

Jones, Ann Rosalind, and Peter Stallybrass. "Fetishizing Gender: Constructing the Hermaphrodite in Renaissance Europe." *Body Guards: The Cultural Politics of Gender Ambiguity*. Ed. Julia Epstein and Kristina Straub. New York: Routledge, 1991, pp. 80–111.

Karkazis, Katrina. *Fixing Sex: Intersex, Medical Authority, and Lived Experience*. Durham, NC: Duke UP, 2008.

Kessler, Suzanne. *Lessons from the Intersexed*. New Brunswick, NJ: Rutgers UP, 1998.

Laflamme, Mathieu. "Is It a He or a She? Trials of Hermaphrodites and the Construction of Legal Gender Definitions by the Judicial System of Old Regime France." Paper submitted for the workshop, *Extraordinary Bodies in Early Modern Nature and Culture*, Uppsala, Sweden, October 26–7, 2017.

Laqueur, Thomas. *Making Sex: Body and Gender from the Greeks to Freud*. Cambridge, MA: Harvard UP, 1992.

Lane, Riki. "Trans as Bodily Becoming: Rethinking the Biological as Diversity, Not Dichotomy." *Hypatia*, special issue on *Transgender Studies and Feminism: Theory, Politics, and Gendered Realities*, 24 (2009): 136–57.

Long, Kathleen P. *Hermaphrodites in Renaissance Europe*. Farnham, UK: Ashgate, 2006.

Long, Kathleen P. "Montaigne, Monsters, and Modernity." *Itineraries in French Renaissance Literature: Essays for Mary B. McKinley*. Leiden: Brill, 2017, pp. 305–29.

Montaigne, Michel de. *The Complete Essays of Montaigne*. Trans. Donald M. Frame. Palo Alto, CA: Stanford UP, 1965.

Morland, Iain. "Intersex." *Postposttranssexual: Key Concepts for a Twenty-First-Century Transgender Studies*, special issue of *Transgender Studies Quarterly*. Ed. Paisley Currah and Susan Stryker 1.1 (2014): 111–15.

Morland, Iain, ed. *Intersex and After*, special issue of *GLQ* 15.2 (2009).

Paré, Ambroise. *On Monsters and Marvels*. Trans. Janis L. Pallister. Chicago, IL: U of Chicago P, 1982.

Prewitt-Freilino, Jennifer L., T. A. Caswell, and E. K. Laakso. "The Gendering of Language: A Comparison of Gender Equality in Countries with Gendered, Natural Gender, and Genderless Languages." *Sex Roles* 66 (2012): 268–81.

Reis, Elizabeth. *Bodies in Doubt: An American History of Intersex.* Baltimore, MD: Johns Hopkins UP, 2012.

Rubin, David A. *Intersex Matters: Biomedical Embodiment, Gender Regulation, and Transnational Activism.* Albany: SUNY, 2017.

Salamon, Gayle. *Assuming a Body: Transgender and Rhetorics of Materiality.* New York: Columbia UP, 2010.

Stone, Sandy. "The *Empire* Strikes Back: A Posttransexual Manifesto." *The Transgender Studies Reader.* Ed. Susan Stryker and Stephen Whittle. New York: Routledge, 2006.

Thomson, Rosemarie Garland. "Integrating Disability, Transforming Feminist Theory." *NWSA Journal*, special issue on *Feminist Disability Studies* 14.3 (2002): 1–32.

Stryker, Susan, and Talia M. Bettcher. "Introduction: Trans/Feminisms." *Transgender Studies Quarterly*, special issue on *Trans/Feminisms* 3 (2016): 5–14.

Wolff, Étienne. *La Science des monstres.* Paris: Gallimard, 1948.

CHAPTER NINE

Experience

ALISON PHIPPS

INTRODUCTION

This chapter rethinks the role of experience in contemporary feminist politics, set in the context of the neoliberal commodification of first-person narratives. Building on existing analyses of what experience *is* in relation to the epistemological and political, it asks questions about what experience *does*. Through the examination of two key case studies, I argue that the appropriation of "survivor stories" and rhetorical use of distressing experiences by the powerful and privileged, often in collaboration with conservative agendas, turns them into a kind of "investment capital" in what Sara Ahmed terms "affective economies" (45), by mobilizing them to generate feeling and create political gain. In the process, structural dynamics are masked; the privileged are able to capitalize on the personal and deflect critique by marginalized groups whose realities are invisibilized or dismissed, even as they are spoken for. This also has a polarizing effect, which inhibits connections across differing experiences: indeed, we often participate in *selective empathies* where we discredit the realities of those who articulate opposing politics.

This chapter does not intend to play into what Ahmed identifies as contemporary dismissals of feminism as being primarily a politics of emotion (based on the already pathologized and assumed emotionality of femininity), which juxtapose this against mainstream politics presumed to be grounded in reason (170). Nor do I wish to rehearse the tendency she identifies in some strands of feminist thought and politics to see the emotional and experiential as a problem (171). However, in keeping with the constructive tradition of contextualizing feminisms within particular conditions of knowledge production (Hesford and Diedrich; Lamm), I wish to highlight and problematize some ways in which experience has become commodified in the contemporary feminist political field. I end with a plea to resist this commodification and the selective empathies it generates, while situating our first-person politics through structural analysis.

EXPERIENCE IN FEMINIST THEORY

"The personal is political," argued Carole Hanisch in 1969. It was a revolutionary phrase that illuminated the Women's Liberation Movement of the 1970s and after, coined in response to claims that consciousness-raising was navel-gazing with no coherent program for social change. The sentiment was not, of course, original: an early, and iconic, example of testimonial activism is Sojurner Truth's 1851 speech to the Akron Women's Rights Convention, which infused sociopolitical critique with rawness and immediacy through her experiences of pain and violence (see Brah and Phoenix). As Danielle McGuire documents, the US civil rights movement was rooted in a powerful (and now largely obscured) sexual violence politics articulated through personal narrative. Famous activists such as Ida B. Wells, whose speeches situated the rape of black women by white men within an analysis of racist oppression (McGuire xviii), and Rosa Parks, who was "an antirape activist long before she became the patron saint of the bus boycott" (xvii), were at the forefront of a dynamic congregation of women who "deploy[ed] their voices as weapons" (xix) by testifying about their assaults.

The fact that we associate the politicization of experience with second-wave radical feminism speaks to the structural racism of the feminist movement; a key focus for this chapter is the continued dynamics between privilege and marginality in feminist politics. While (largely white) radical feminists used the personal as a basis for activism, (largely white and middle-class) feminist academics codified this through epistemological theorizing. This posed a direct challenge to the established belief that "personal problems" should not be a basis for knowledge or be brought into the public arena. A research base was built, focusing on gendered experiences, which fed these theoretical confrontations with the generic (white, masculine) "knower" (Code) and operationalized the principle of "theory in the flesh" (Calderón et al. 521). The construction of feminist knowledge-making as a language of speakers and hearers (Code) also brought to light the impossibility of objective analysis (Haraway; Code) and generated pedagogies based on the sharing and discussion of narratives (Huber et al.; Belenky et al.).

This institutionalization of the politics of the personal prompted challenges from those relegated to the margins, particularly the black feminists to whom so much was owed. The concept of intersectionality developed by Crenshaw and others, and explorations of how Western feminisms had been co-opted by colonial discourses and projects (Mohanty, *Under Western Eyes*), exposed the false universalism of "women's experience" and the construction of the feminist "knower" in the image of privilege (Baldwin). In response, it was argued that those on the perimeters of feminism had access to special forms of insight: Hill Collins's exploration of the structural and discursive spaces occupied by black women/scholars as "outsiders within" ("Learning") uncovered hidden forms of creativity and distinctive and important standpoints on self, family, and society. Ideas of epistemic injustice (Code) and questions about who can know and speak (Spivak) continue to be central to feminist theory and activism and are also central to the analysis in this chapter.

As the second wave of feminism turned into the third, the status of experience was secured. Conversations between feminist epistemologies and postmodern theory, and a "turn to narrative" in social science research (Huber et al. 217), generated beautiful, nuanced auto-ethnographic work. Structures such as colonialism and their relationships to identity, gender, and sexuality were illuminated in new ways (see, e.g., Jiménez), and first-person narratives from the sex industry gave complex insights into gendered objectification (see, e.g., Egan, Frank, and Johnson). Munro and others argue that we are now witnessing a fourth wave of feminism in which the internet plays a key role: in online spaces, intersectional feminists use storytelling as an antidote to the invisibility and silencing that characterize oppressions based on race, class, and gender (see also Steele; Wilkins). This has generated a veritable treasure trove of grassroots blogs, photoblogs, and social media archives. Within this, women of color, sex workers, and trans people tell of societal oppressions and personal traumas, around which social movements have coalesced. For instance, the Tumblr of American trans girl Leelah Alcorn, who took her own life in 2014 after leaving a detailed account of the cruelty of so-called conversion therapy, inspired a petition against the practice with more than 300,000 signatories (Pilkington).

Across its third and fourth waves, feminism has also been central to the theorization of emotion and the so-called affective turn in social, political, and cultural theory (see Pedwell and Whitehead). These have been attempts to write embodied experience back into analysis, often grounded in the conviction that postmodernism has written it out: although, as Clare Hemmings argues, this ignores the prior contributions of postcolonial and feminist thinkers ("Invoking Affect"). A central concern within studies of emotion and affect is how these phenomena shape/are shaped by the political sphere. For instance, Ann Cvetkovich's work explores publics formed in and by trauma, such as lesbian cultures around incest, or HIV and AIDS activism. Ahmed uncovers how the politics of emotion creates social and cultural Others through the generation of affect and constitution of subjectivities. Sianne Ngai analyzes the political work done by negative emotions such as envy, anxiety, and paranoia in a variety of cultural artifacts. There has also been attention to the relationship between feminism and pain, building on Wendy Brown's insights into the limitations of "wounded identities" (*States of Injury* 52–76), although not necessarily subscribing to her conclusions about letting them go (see Ahmed).[1] Experience, then, remains foundational to feminist theorizing but continues to be contested in a number of ways.

EXPERIENCE IN FEMINIST POLITICS

The discussion in this chapter draws from the perspectives above, alongside contestations around epistemic privilege and marginality and critical theorizations of experience itself. Experience must be differentiated from emotion and affect, which themselves have often been used interchangeably (Gorton 334).[2] Joan Scott defines experience as a "linguistic event" (793)—I argue that this is also embodied, and often suffused with emotion/affect, but not reducible to either. In similar ways to the theorists of affect mentioned above, my interest is in how experience enters the political. I find Ahmed's concept of "affective economies" (45) useful; this describes emotions as a form of capital, generated by the circulation of objects (such as bodies) and signs (such as the burning cross). I start from the premise that these objects and signs are often situated within experiential narratives. Experience can therefore be described as a kind of "investment capital," a currency of objects and signs that generates further capital in the form of feeling. My analysis focuses on how experiences are "invested" into feminist politics, often as part of battles for epistemic privilege or political gain. As part of this process, some "personals" become more important politically than others.

I also draw on the work of Scott and Linda Alcoff, who have both theorized how experience operates as epistemology and politics. Scott examines the "turn to experience" in historical analysis, arguing that although this made a diversity of stories and oppressions visible, it tended to reify personal narrative as the origin of explanation, in the process dehistoricizing it and essentializing identities. If experience is our starting point, she contends, we lose a focus on the historical conditions that shape and produce it and risk shoring up rather than contesting ideological systems. Alcoff charts critiques of "speaking for others": those emerging from the development of situated epistemologies in which we cannot fully know another's truth and those based on awareness of the relationships of privilege and power, from local to geopolitical, in which testimonial forms exist. My analysis builds on and develops this work, grounded in the idea of the epistemological authority of experience (Scott 783), but moving from epistemology to politics: examining what experience *does* as it enters the feminist field. It explores the acts of speaking for others and speaking for oneself, as a means of gaining political purchase in adversarial debates. It reflects on how personal narrative can *actively* be used as a tool of silencing that works to reinforce the power of the dominant through capitalizing upon emotional responses and invisibilizing structural dynamics.

This chapter is situated in the "discursive publics" (Rentschler and Thrift 239) of contemporary Western feminism, which encompass academic, activist, and public/media discussions. Although this field is broad, Rentschler and Thrift argue that contemporary feminisms in the West are increasingly defined by what registers across media platforms. Furthermore, due to the permeation of media and social media into scholarship, often set within agendas around research impact, more academics (including myself) are visible and active in these spaces. This certainly does not constitute the whole of contemporary feminism: these "discursive publics" are dominated by voices from the UK and North America. Nevertheless, this has been identified as a field where high-profile debates are being constructed (Rentschler and Thrift). Like all discursive contexts (Alcoff 15), this is a highly politicized arena. Through the phenomena of what Park and Leonard call "Twitter feminism" or what Loza terms "hashtag feminism," and the increasingly influential feminist blogosphere (Keller), activists from diverse and often marginalized communities are speaking for themselves and with each other and entering into dialogues with more privileged academics and journalists who are being held accountable for their ideas. Experience and affect are key to these publics, partly due to the testimonial conventions of mainstream and social media, and also reflecting the influence of standpoint theory upon contemporary intersectional feminisms.

My analysis is also situated within the logics and practices of neoliberalism. This is a much-contested, much-discussed (and some might say overused) term; nevertheless, it refers to a socioeconomic-political framework that, although not the root of all contemporary evils, is an important shaping structure. This "market-political" rationality (Brown, "American Nightmare" 691) has cascaded economic principles into the social realm as part of the assumption that societies function best with a minimum of state intervention (Harvey). Political and social problems are converted into market terms, becoming individual issues with consumption-based solutions (Brown, "American Nightmare" 704). As Brown contends, this privatization and commodification of social life has structured subjectivities ("American Nightmare" 693). The rationalities of neoliberalism atomize, interiorize, and neutralize: the neoliberal self is an individualized one (Beck and Beck-Gernsheim), constructed around the principles of agency and self-governance. Neoliberal reflexive projects of the self are characterized by introspection and narratives of self-actualization (Giddens), often with economic metaphors (see, e.g., Johnson; Rousmaniere). As part of this, experience and emotion have accrued value as forms of intelligence that can serve life and career goals for those in advantaged social positions (Hochschild; Ahmed).

Within this framework the personal has simultaneously grown and shrunk as difference has flattened out into "diversity" alongside a "tabloidization" (Glynn) and "testimonialism" (Ahmed and Stacey) in which, perhaps in place of politics, popular culture and debate have been saturated with feeling. The phrase "disaster porn" has been coined by Molotch to describe the contemporary fascination with the troubles of others, which provides a repository for guilt or schadenfreude. In this narcissistic and therapeutic neoliberal moment, as Ahmed argues, personal pain can be depoliticized or co-opted as it accumulates and stagnates in what Brown calls "wounded identities" (*States of Injury* 52–76), which both legitimate and depend upon state power.[3] For example, Carolyn Pedwell has highlighted how personal tragedies can be appropriated and mobilized by politicians and privileged "experts" who use empathy as a technology of access to disadvantaged lives. In a marketplace of experience, the privileged inevitably have more platforms from which to narrate (see also Ahmed 33), and the marginalized are often spoken for within agendas that are not their own. I will show in this chapter that these characteristics of the neoliberal context are also evident within feminist politics.

EXPERIENCE AS CAPITAL: TWO CASE STUDIES

The neoliberal commodification of distress is particularly germane to feminism, due to the enduring co-constitution of femininity and pain (Baker) and the centrality of experience to feminist epistemologies and politics. The contemporary movement is also situated in a dynamic with neoconservative frameworks, in which the strategic use of women's victimization narratives by neo-imperialist and carceral projects, often in collaboration with liberal or radical feminist groups, can produce a defensive rejection of these narratives by third-wave and intersectional strands (Phipps). This architecture surrounds the interactions that constitute feminist discursive publics; these are characterized by contention and debate in which personal experience often becomes capital. I present two key examples below: the mobilization of "survivor stories" by sex industry abolitionists and the use of the rape experience in trans-exclusionary feminist politics. In both, experience is deployed by privileged feminists (frequently in association with conservative agendas) who wield particular narratives to generate emotion and make political gains.

"Survivor Stories" in Sex Industry Politics

The sex industry "survivor" is an abiding and central figure in feminist politics. Famous second-wave abolitionists Andrea Dworkin (herself an ex-sex worker) and Catharine MacKinnon made the voices of women exploited in pornography central to their legislative lobbying. Since then, such "survivor stories" have acquired corporate gloss and wider exposure, as a key rhetorical tool for what Agustín has termed the "feminist rescue industry" constituted by policymakers, NGOs, women's groups, and international organizations focused on using the criminal law to "save" women from commercial sex. The relationship between this "industry"[4] and neoconservative social and political projects has been captured by Elizabeth Bernstein with the term "carceral feminism." This encapsulates how feminist opposition to the sex industry has bolstered and colluded with agendas around strengthening migration controls and the punitive power of the state (see Bumiller for an exploration of this dynamic in relation to sexual violence). The "survivor stories" of this carceral feminism tap particular forms of Western empathy (see Pedwell) and are frequently deployed as capital in debates around legal regulation of the sex industry and sex workers' rights.

For example, in 2013, following two UN reports which advised that commercial sex should be decriminalized in order to help reduce HIV and AIDS and promote the human rights of sex workers (Global Commission on HIV and the Law, United Nations Development Programme), international organization Equality Now launched a campaign entitled "Listen to Survivors." This used experiential narratives to urge the UN to instead promote measures criminalizing the demand for sexual services. In a rhetorical sleight of hand, all these narratives concerned trafficking and commercial sexual exploitation, even though both UN reports had opposed these practices and distinguished them from the consensual sale of sex. The phrase "trafficking and prostitution" was common among the stories: an example of the metonymy Ahmed identifies in which words (such as "Islam" and "terrorist") are stuck together to evoke particular responses (76), and a tactic often used by sex industry opponents to discredit sex workers' demands for rights (Massey, Congdon). Many of the narratives also recounted childhood sexual abuse and domestic violence, and some contained references to HIV and AIDS, in opposition to the UN reports that had linked sex industry decriminalization with a reduction in these conditions. The narratives also contained graphic descriptions of rape and physical violence.

Similar "survivor stories" have been used by sex industry abolitionist initiatives in countries such as the UK, Ireland, the United States, Canada, and France (see, e.g., Turn Off the Red Light; End Demand; New York State Anti-Trafficking Coalition; Congdon). Common to all are harrowing accounts of victimization and suffering, including experiences of physical and sexual violence and abuse, problematic substance use, unwanted pregnancy, and sexually transmitted infections. These stories are deployed in support of a particular legislative agenda, usually that of "ending demand" for commercial sex through criminalizing clients and third parties. However, such maneuvers rarely incorporate analyses that tie specific experiences to distinct parts of law or working practices: instead, the fact of suffering is used to bolster a sweeping moral case against the sex industry as a whole. This is usually done without reference to evidence that client criminalization creates additional risks for sex workers and does not necessarily reduce prostitution (see, e.g., Jessen; Levy, *Criminalising*). There are links here with campaigns against female genital cutting, which center "native informants" with harrowing personal accounts of trauma (Carle; United Nations; ITV News; Rudulph), but which often feed a politics defining all Muslim communities as inherently and uniquely misogynist, or all African countries as ignorant and "backward," with little regard to the historical and cultural specificities that frame particular practices (Njambi).

Of course, the distress caused by experiences of forced prostitution and genital cutting should not be denied; however, this should not foreclose an analysis of what such "survivor stories" do. Often, in relation to the sex industry, they are used to gain political advantage over grassroots groups who argue for decriminalization. The capital provided by experience, bolstered by the "moral authority of suffering" (Lorde 294), is deployed to dismiss sex workers' demands for labor rights as proceeding from atypical and inauthentic positive experiences of the industry.[5] This dynamic was recently apparent in debates around Amnesty International's draft decriminalization policy, when the diverse global coalition of sex workers united behind it were depicted as an unrepresentative minority in the international press, compared to the "survivors" spoken for by its opponents (see, e.g., Lewis; Moran). The power relations at work in "survivor stories" draw on the long tradition of white feminist empathy which, according to Hemmings ("Affective Solidarity" 154), is a way of cannibalizing the Other (see also Ahmed; Pedwell). In this case, however, there is a double-oppression at work: the sex industry survivor is cannibalized by the abolitionist agenda, and her story is also used as political capital to deflect opposition coming from another Other (the sex worker advocating for labor rights). The problematic practice of speaking for others (see Alcoff) becomes extra-pernicious in this example, wielded as a weapon against Others who are speaking for themselves.

Rape in Trans-Exclusionary Feminism

The investment of experience as a form of capital in sex industry debates is to do with ownership of the "authentic" narrative of selling sex. "Survivor stories" are used to defeat opponents, principally performing exclusions of sex workers deemed "not representative" because they are engaged in opposing forms of politics. Another key example of the use of experience to perform exclusions is the politics around trans women's inclusion in women-only space. Here, the rape experience in particular becomes capital, mobilized by trans-exclusionary feminists alongside a construction of trans women as predatory, dangerous, and essentially male. This politics is part hatred and part fear, both of which concern border anxieties and the construction of boundaries between selves and others (Ahmed 51, 76). Furthermore, as Ahmed argues, hate is used as a defense against injury (42–3): in this case, an imagined threat of injury from the trans woman is warded off by the mobilization of another injury, the experience of being raped by a cisgender man.

In her book *Excluded*, Julia Serano describes being interviewed by a graduate student visiting Camp Trans, the yearly demonstration and event by trans women and allies protesting the Michigan Womyn's Music Festival's policy of "womyn-only space." It was only a matter of time, Serano writes, before the line of questioning arrived at the "penis issue" (30). At this point, she recalls, the student's partner "burst out with questions of her own":

> While there were several of us being interviewed, she turned directly to me, and in a terse and condescending tone of voice, said: "How dare you! You have no idea what many of these women have been through. Don't you understand that many of them are abuse survivors who could be triggered by you? Can't you see why some women might not feel safe having you and your penis around?" (31)

This outburst encapsulates perfectly how trans-exclusionary feminism deploys the experience of rape. In the example above, others are spoken for; however, trans-exclusionary feminists often also speak for themselves, through heartfelt personal disclosures. The trans woman is evoked indirectly through statements about the healing value of "female-only space" (see, e.g., Hewitt) or directly through discussion of survivors' emotional triggers in relation to her body (see Kellaway; Zanin). The penis is the key object here, "stuck" to trans women through an invasive and violent obsession with their surgical status, but also imagined as a separate entity which is itself responsible for sexual violence rather than being, as Serano reminds us, merely someone's genital organ (31).

The idea of the penis as weapon was central to 1970s and 1980s radical feminism (see, e.g., MacKinnon 173). However, any useful sociological and political insights here about the co-constitution of masculinity and violence and the symbolic threat of the phallus appear to have been consumed by the debate over trans-inclusion and converted into a biologically essentialist preoccupation with this particular organ (which is always already coded as violence). The trans woman is automatically assigned with this organ (and thereby with violence), through the obsession with whether she has one or not. In 2014, a group of UK-based radical feminists started the Twitter hashtag #NoUnexpectedPenises during a trans-inclusion debate on social media. Narratives such as *"wanked ON at a Primal Scream gig. Didn't realise until we found the evidence on the back of our jeans"* were situated alongside declarations such as *"we want some time away from anyone with a penis."* One statement read, *"I've had men rub their erect penises against me on the tube ... But apparently if I say I don't want a penis around me I am a bigot. Fuck. That.*" The discussion reached its pinnacle in the question, "*Do people really not see that telling lesbians 'trans women are women' is promoting rape culture?*"

These narratives worked on multiple levels: deploying the rape experience as capital and constructing trans women as sexual predators through mobilizing the "sticky associations" (Ahmed 76) between the trans woman and the penis,[6] the penis and sexual violence. The use of the adjective "unexpected" also illustrates Ahmed's point about how bodies that threaten to "pass" can be especially fetishized as objects of fear (79). Furthermore, the phrase "no unexpected penises" evokes an organ with a life of its own, whose threat partly resides in the fact that it is not possible to tell whether it is there or not (perchance, like the stranger rapist, it might jump out from the darkness). This politics of fear uses the language of victimization and emotional triggers to great effect (or affect). However, while valid, painful, and real, triggers vary extensively and can sometimes be obscure (American Academy of Experts in Traumatic Stress), meaning they are not an adequate basis for policy and politics. Nevertheless, the rape experience is capitalized upon in order to put the surrounding politics beyond dispute: indeed, challenges to trans-exclusionary perspectives are often reinterpreted as a denial or politicization of the rape experience (see, e.g., Pennington), as though the latter has not already occurred. The claim to "ownership" of rape victimization by cisgender women, through the projection of violence on to trans women, further commodifies it and invisibilizes the experiences of trans women who have been subjected to violence and abuse.

MY PERSONAL IS *MORE* POLITICAL: EXPERIENCE WITHOUT STRUCTURE

In both the case studies above, experience is a form of capital invested to generate feeling and make political gains. This politics is quintessentially neoliberal, abstracting experience from its social context and deploying it in a competitive discursive arena in which historical dynamics, social contexts, and structural power relations are obscured. For example, the dialectic between oppression and empowerment that plays out over the "authentic" experience of the sex industry fails to acknowledge the ways in which repressive immigration policies and criminal justice systems produce particular personal narratives, and the location of commercial sexualities in a post-Fordist capitalist system with a service-based consumer culture, high unemployment, and shrinking social welfare. In the theatre of testimony, the figure of the victimized sex worker who must be rescued via criminal law upstages data on the links between criminalization and police and community harassment, susceptibility to infectious diseases, risk of violence, and access to health and social services (see, e.g., Krüsi et al.; Levy, *Criminalising*). In the emotive politics of fear, which aims to exclude trans women from women's spaces and services, disclosures of cisgender women's traumatic experiences prevent discussion of their privilege relative to trans women. This also gives no space to engage with the fact that trans women are particularly vulnerable to multiple violences, including domestic and sexual victimization, and are thus especially in need of nonjudgmental support services (see Whittle et al.; Roch et al.; National Coalition of Anti-Violence Programs).

In a competitive market, all experiences are equal: this reinforces the advantage of those who already have access to platforms (see also Ahmed 33), while masking their structural power. Indeed, there have recently been numerous incidences from both the UK and North America (with the election of Donald Trump being the most high-profile recent example) of privileged people successfully capitalizing upon narratives of marginality in response to the politics and claims of oppressed groups. Within feminist publics, academics and journalists with considerable institutional and media clout have echoed the refrain of the religious and libertarian Right in presenting themselves as victims of silencing and bullying by special interests and "political correctness," in response to sex workers' and trans people's demands for rights and space (see, e.g., Observer; Pollitt; Murphy; Glosswitch). Intra-feminist altercations are nothing new, and for Audre Lorde, defensiveness is an essential element of the power dynamics within the movement. However, the current context, with its abstraction of experience from structure, may facilitate the ability of privileged people to gain political advantage through wielding defensive personal narratives.

As the social and structural retreats, the relationships between experiences and political agendas instead begin to define them. Sex industry "survivors" have their stories validated by the powerful forces that co-opt them but can be depicted at the grassroots as coached by abolitionists into exaggerating their trauma.[7] Conversely, sex workers who advocate for labor rights are seen by much of mainstream feminism as having been duped by patriarchy into accepting their profession (Levy, *Criminalising* 47). This echoes the ways in which Muslim and ex-Muslim women who speak out about gendered oppression can be defined as imperialist "stooges," while feminists working within a religious framework and declaring attachments to Islam are diagnosed with false consciousness (Phipps; Kandiyoti).

These dynamics also flatten out lived realities, so they cannot be appropriated by the other side. If experience is capital, it can only be invested in particular currencies, which polarizes narratives and suppresses the possibilities in between. Those with differing experiences of the same phenomenon are unable to coexist, and there is also little space within the individual for mixed or ambivalent feelings to endure. For example, in much the same way as the complexities of ending a pregnancy may be underplayed by pro-choice individuals and groups wary of reinforcing pro-life agendas (Hess; Lyon; Webster), sex workers admit that they may deemphasize, hide, or even deny difficult experiences in resistance to the radical feminist definition of their work as abuse (Ray; Suzyhooker; Crow). Scott argues that politics based on experience has always had a tendency to essentialism, being concerned with difference and not the conditions that produce it (see also Mohanty, "Transnational Feminist Crossings"). Furthermore, in a context such as the one I have described, it seems there is a deliberate homogenization of narrative in order to compete.

Of course, there is no pure experience unmarked by the political (see Scott). However, this competitive arena, like the neoliberal context, is both suffused with emotion and rather callous: often, the first response to experiential narratives is, "Whose side are you on?" We then frequently discredit the experience, when we should be critiquing the associated politics. Pedwell highlights how empathy is mobilized to support dominant economic, political, cultural, and social relations, and it is certainly the case that the use of "survivor stories" in sex industry abolitionism and the rape experience in trans-exclusionary feminism aim to evoke an empathic response. However, another key factor here is that empathy is being withheld. This happens on all sides but is especially harmful to the already marginalized: the trans women, and the sex workers who advocate for labor rights, in the case studies above. We are asked to listen to "survivors": those who have exited the sex industry and those whose emotional triggers cause them to fear trans women's inclusion in women-only space. Yet the designation "survivor," and its associated claim on empathy, is withheld from the Others—dismissing their realities and invisibilizing their experiences of violence and abuse. The operation of experience as a form of capital, then, creates *selective empathies* granted only to those whose narratives have political use value.[8]

CONCLUSION

This does not mean, of course, that we should not theorize from experience; indeed, the "view from nowhere" with its attendant "voice of reason" can also be that of the oppressor and reeks of entitlement and privilege (I say this with an awareness that in writing this piece, I may reasonably be read that way myself). We must remain cognizant of the value of sharing our realities, in both personal and political arenas (see Hemmings, "Affective Solidarity"; Mazanderani, Locock, and Powell). However, if we could name and resist the commodification of experience, with its associated polarization and selective empathies, we might begin to articulate a politics that respects varied realities while allowing us to disagree. The idea of identity groups as coalitions of "heterogeneous commonality" (Collins, *Fighting Words* 224; see also Crenshaw; Carastathis), which characterized early attempts to theorize and use intersectionality, is useful here. To connect across difference is messy and painful, a process that must be continually made and remade (Calderón et al). Those of us with socioeconomic and cultural privilege must be prepared to surrender to this, acknowledging the fact that the dominant may be fearful of the mess that signifies a loss of control. The privileged must also give up the practice of "speaking for" and make sensible use of what Alcoff calls the "retreat response" (17): when the goal is mutual understanding, "speaking with" may be in order, but we also need to challenge ourselves, especially on public platforms, to "move over and get out of the way" (8).[9]

To use experience as capital is to misunderstand standpoint epistemology and assume that women's experiences automatically equal feminist politics (see also Scott 787; Hemmings, "Affective Solidarity" 156). In fact, experience must be grounded in an understanding of structural conditions in order to produce an emancipatory commitment (Brewer; Hemmings, "Affective Solidarity"; Nash). Some contemporary feminist forms of knowledge-making exemplify this: for instance, the social movement organizing of women of color melds issues of identity with socioeconomic analysis (Chun et al. 923) and the sex workers' labor rights activism that documents the harms of criminalization through linking experiences of oppression with specific laws and practices (see, e.g., Mensah and Bruckert; Nine; Levy, *Swedish Abolitionism*; Feministire). These politics filter experience through intersectional analyses of power, in contrast to its deployment in my case studies, by those *in power* to reinforce the status quo.

I conclude with the acknowledgment that all experiences are valid, and with a reminder that they are also asymmetrically situated. The injuries felt by those who are more privileged, while certainly painful, are not commensurate with the experience of oppression.[10] Ventriloquizing another's personal story is an act of power, especially when the oppression of this Other is wielded against another Other with whom one disagrees. Disclosing one's experience of violence in a bid to construct and exclude the Other is violence in itself. Especially when personal stories become capital in political debates, they must be understood in relation to dynamics of privilege and marginality; these also grant the advantaged few more access to narrative platforms than the rest. There is a fine line to walk here: between engaging in selective empathies and situating experiences structurally/appraising the uses to which they are put. Mindful of this, we must neverthe-less ask whose personal becomes *more* political, and why.

ACKNOWLEDGMENTS

I would like to thank my colleagues Catherine Will and James Hardie-Bick for their comments on early drafts of this piece. I am also very grateful to the two anonymous ref-erees from Feminist Theory for their detailed and constructive input.

This chapter was originally published as an article in *Feminist Theory* (Phipps, Alison, "Whose Personal Is More Political? Experience in Contemporary Feminist Politics," *Feminist Theory* 17.3 (2016): 303–21). I am grateful to the editors of *Feminist Theory* for their permission to reprint, and to Robin Truth Goodman for the opportunity to be featured in this wonderful collection.

NOTES

1 See also Rentschler for an important rebuttal of Brown's argument from the perspective of the victims' rights movement.
2 As Gorton explains, "Some argue that emotion refers to a sociological expression of feelings whereas affect is more firmly rooted in biology and in our physical response to feelings; others attempt to differentiate on the basis that emotion requires a subject while affect does not; and some ignore these distinctions altogether" (334).
3 Carrie Rentschler provides an important counterpoint to this in her exploration of the polit-ical value of victimization discourse.
4 I am not necessarily comfortable with the term "industry," since this does not seem particu-larly apt to the impoverished women's sector and also suggests a homogeneity of motive (in the form of a self-serving orientation), which seems a little harsh and overly simplistic.
5 This often happens regardless of the content of this grassroots politics, much of which does highlight experiences of violence caused by criminalization. Although, as I will point out later in the chapter, the competitive nature of the debate also means that sex workers' rights activists can be driven to minimize trauma to avoid giving fuel to abolitionists (and in a ter-rible epistemic injustice, they then become trapped in the designation of their narratives as inauthentic).
6 Of course, many trans women choose not to undergo genital surgery, which in no way invalidates their womanhood: the point here is that the assignment of the trans woman with a penis is used to construct her as a threat.
7 My evidence for this comes from a number of statements that have been made about prom-inent sex industry survivors who support abolitionist politics; some of these are available online, but I will not provide references as they contain personal details and allegations about these individuals.
8 This is linked to Berlant's analysis of the relation between compassion and sadism (9–11) but appears to be a deliberate, rather than an instinctive or conditioned, turning-away (although it may incorporate both these reactions).
9 Note that Alcoff herself does not necessarily endorse this approach.
10 Of course, an intersectional analysis allows that one may experience marginality and privilege on different axes: however, this does not mean that all social locations (and all experiences) are equivalent.

WORKS CITED

Agustín, Laura María. *Sex at the Margins: Migration, Labour Markets and the Rescue Industry*. London: Zed Books, 2007.

Ahmed, Sara. *The Cultural Politics of Emotion*. New York: Routledge, [2004] 2012.

Ahmed, Sara, and Jackie Stacey. "Testimonial Cultures: An Introduction." *Cultural Values* 5.1 (2001): 1–6.

Alcoff, Linda. "The Problem of Speaking for Others." *Cultural Critique* 20 (1991): 5–32.

American Academy of Experts in Traumatic Stress. *Post-Traumatic Stress Disorder in Rape Survivors*. Report, 2014. http://www.aaets.org/article178.htm.

Baker, Joanne. "Claiming Volition and Evading Victimhood: Post-Feminist Obligations for Young Women." *Feminism & Psychology* 20.2 (2010): 186–204.

Baldwin, Andrea. "Feminist Aliens, Memoirs from the Margins. A Caribbean 'Feminist's' Experience in Western Feminism." *Theoretical Practice* 10.4 (2013): 17–40.

Beck, Ulrich, and Elisabeth Beck-Gernsheim. *Individualization: Institutionalized Individualism and Its Social and Political Consequences*. London: SAGE, 2002.

Belenky, Mary Field, et al. *Women's Ways of Knowing: The Development of Self, Voice, and Mind*. New York: Basic Books, 1986.

Berlant, Lauren. "Introduction: Compassion (and Withholding)." *Compassion: The Culture and Politics of an Emotion*. Ed. Lauren Berlant. New York: Routledge, 2004, pp. 1–14.

Bernstein, Elizabeth. "Militarized Humanitarianism Meets Carceral Feminism: The Politics of Sex, Rights, and Freedom in Contemporary Antitrafficking Campaigns." *Signs* 36.1 (2010): 45–71.

Brah, Avtar, and Ann Phoenix. "Ain't I a Woman? Revisiting Intersectionality." *Journal of International Women's Studies* 5.3 (2004): 75–86.

Brewer, Rose M. "Black Women's Studies: From Theory to Transformative Practice." *Socialism and Democracy* 25.1 (2011): 146–56.

Brown, Wendy. "American Nightmare Neoliberalism, Neoconservatism, and De-Democratization." *Political Theory* 34.6 (2006): 690–714.

Brown, Wendy. *States of Injury: Power and Freedom in Late Modernity*. Princeton, NJ: Princeton UP, 1995.

Bumiller, Kristin. *In an Abusive State: How Neoliberalism Appropriated the Feminist Movement against Sexual Violence*. Durham, NC: Duke UP, 2008.

Calderón, Dolores, et al. "A Chicana Feminist Epistemology Revisited: Cultivating Ideas a Generation Later." *Harvard Educational Review* 82.4 (2012): 513–39.

Carastathis, Anna. "Identity Categories as Potential Coalitions." *Signs* 38.4 (2013): 941–65.

Carle, Robert. "Who Is Ayaan Hirsi Ali?" *Public Discourse*, April 25, 2014. http://www.thepublicdiscourse.com/2014/04/13075/. Accessed March 2, 2015.

Chun, Jennifer Jihye, George Lipsitz, and Young Shin. "Intersectionality as a Social Movement Strategy: Asian Immigrant Women Advocates." *Signs* 38.4 (2013): 917–40.

Code, Lorraine. "Ignorance, Injustice and the Politics of Knowledge." *Australian Feminist Studies* 29.80 (2014): 148–60.

Collins, Patricia Hill. *Fighting Words: Black Women and the Search for Justice*. Minneapolis: U of Minnesota P, 1998.

Collins, Patricia Hill. "Learning from the Outsider Within: The Sociological Significance of Black Feminist Thought." *Social Problems* 33 (1986): Supplement 14.

Congdon, Jason. "Speaking of 'Dead Prostitutes': How CATW Promotes Survivors to Silence Sex Workers." *openDemocracy*, November 26, 2014. https://www.opendemocracy.net/

beyondslavery/jason-congdon/speaking-of-%E2%80%9Cdead-prostitutes%E2%80%9D-how-catw-promotes-survivors-to-silence-se. Accessed March 2, 2015.

Crenshaw, Kimberlé Williams. "Mapping the Margins: Intersectionality, Identity Politics, and Violence against Women of Color." *Stanford Law Review* 43.6 (1991): 1241–99.

Crow, Eithne. Arguing Right(s). *Cup of Crow*, June 18, 2015. https://eithnecrow.wordpress.com/2015/06/18/arguing-rights/. Accessed August 2016.

Cvetkovich, Ann. *An Archive of Feelings: Trauma, Sexuality, and Lesbian Public Cultures.* Durham, NC: Duke UP, 2003.

Egan, Danielle, Frank, Katherine, and Johnson, Merri Lisa. *Flesh for Fantasy: Producing and Consuming Exotic Dance.* New York: Thunder's Mouth Press, 2006.

End Demand. "Survivors Archive." *End Demand UK*, 2015. http://enddemand.uk/survivors/. Accessed March 2, 2015.

Equality Now. "Survivor Stories." *Equality Now*, 2015. http://www.equalitynow.org/survivorstories.

Equality Now. "United Nations: Listen to Survivors—Don't Jeopardize Efforts to Prevent Sex Trafficking." *Equality Now*, 2015. http://www.equalitynow.org/take_action/sex_trafficking_action511.

Feministire. "An Open Letter to Tom Meagher, from St Kilda Street-Based Sex Workers." *Feminist Ire*, May 16, 2015. http://feministire.com/2015/05/16/an-open-letter-to-tom-meagher-from-st-kilda-street-based-sex-workers/. Accessed May 30, 2015.

Giddens, Anthony. *Modernity and Self-identity: Self and Society in the Late Modern Age.* Stanford, CA: Stanford University Press, 1991.

Global Commission on HIV and the Law. *Risks, Rights and Health.* Report, 2012. http://www.hivlawcommission.org/resources/report/FinalReport-Risks,Rights&Health-EN.pdf.

Glosswitch. "Universities Won't Be a Safe Place for Women Until They're a Safe Place for Feminism." *New Statesman*, October 15, 2014.

Glynn, Kevin. *Tabloid Culture: Trash Taste, Popular Power, and the Transformation of American Television.* Durham, NC: Duke UP, 2000.

Gorton, Kristyn. "Theorizing Emotion and Affect." *Feminist Theory* 8.3 (2007): 333–48.

Hanisch, Carol. *The Personal Is Political.* Written in 1969: Archive text available from http://www.carolhanisch.org/CHwritings/PIP.html. Accessed September 2, 2018.

Haraway, Donna. "Situated Knowledges: The Science Question in Feminism and the Privilege of Partial Perspective." *Feminist Studies* 14.3 (1988): 575–99.

Harvey, David. *A Brief History of Neoliberalism.* Oxford: Oxford UP, 2005.

Hemmings, Clare. "Affective Solidarity: Feminist Reflexivity and Political Transformation." *Feminist Theory* 13.2 (2012) 147–61.

Hemmings, Clare. "Invoking Affect: Cultural Theory and the Ontological Turn." *Cultural Studies* 19.5 (2005): 548–67.

Hesford, Victoria, and Lisa Diedrich. "Experience, Echo, Event: Theorising Feminist Histories, Historicising Feminist Theory." *Feminist Theory* 15.2 (2014): 103–17.

Hess, Amanda. "Regretting an Abortion Doesn't Make You Pro-Life." *Slate*, July 12, 2013. http://www.slate.com/blogs/xx_factor/2013/07/12/abortion_regret_it_s_not_just_for_pro_life_women.html. Accessed April 8, 2015.

Hewitt, Rachel. "When I Was Raped, It Was Female-Only Spaces That Helped Me Recover." *New Statesman*, February 24, 2015.

Hochschild, Arlie Russell. *The Managed Heart: Commercialization of Human Feeling.* Berkeley: U of California P, 1983.

Huber, Janice, Vera Caine, Marilyn Huber, and Pam Steeves. "Narrative Inquiry as Pedagogy in Education: The Extraordinary Potential of Living, Telling, Retelling, and Reliving Stories of Experience." *Review of Research in Education* 37.1 (2013): 212–42.

ITV News. "New Campaign Launches in Kenya and The South Bank Today." *ITV News*, October 10, 2014. http://www.itv.com/news/london/update/2014-10-10/new-campaign-launches-in-kenya-and-the-south-bank-today/. Accessed March 2, 2015.

Jessen, Liv. "Prostitution Seen as Violence against Women." *Sex Work, Mobility and Health*. Ed. Sophie Day and Helen Ward. New York: Routledge, 2004, pp. 201–14.

Johnson, Tia. "You Are the CEO of Your Life!" *Huffington Post*, September 10, 2014. http://www.huffingtonpost.com/tia-johnson/you-are-the-ceo-of-your-l_b_5956316.html. Accessed January 21, 2016.

Kandiyoti, Deniz. "The Triple Whammy: Towards the Eclipse of Women's Rights." *openDemocracy*, January 19, 2015. https://www.opendemocracy.net/5050/deniz-kandiyoti/triple-whammy-towards-eclipse-of-women%E2%80%99s-rights. Accessed February 23, 2015.

Kellaway, Mitch. "Michigan Woman Sues Planet Fitness over Trans-Inclusive Locker Room." *Advocate*, March 25, 2015.

Keller, Jessalynn Marie. "Virtual Feminisms: Girls' Blogging Communities, Feminist Activism, and Participatory Politics." *Information, Communication and Society* 15.3 (2012): 429–47.

Krüsi A., et al. "Criminalisation of Clients: Reproducing Vulnerabilities for Violence and Poor Health among Street-Based Sex Workers in Canada—A Qualitative Study." *BMJ Open* 4.6 (2014): 1–10.

Lamm, Kimberly. "Modern Spectacle and American Feminism's Disappointing Daughters: Writing Fantasy Echoes in *The Portrait of a Lady*." *Feminist Theory* 15.2 (2014): 179–96.

Levy, Jay. *Criminalising the Purchase of Sex: Lessons From Sweden*. New York: Routledge, 2015.

Levy, Jay. *Swedish Abolitionism as Violence against Women*. Sex Worker Open University Report, 2013.

Lewis, Helen. "Listen to the Sex Workers—But Which Ones?" *Guardian*, August 9, 2015.

Lorde, Audre. "The Uses of Anger." *Women's Studies Quarterly* 25.1/2 (1997): 278–85.

Loza, Susana. "Hashtag Feminism, #SolidarityIsForWhiteWomen, and the Other #FemFuture." *Ada: A Journal of Gender, New Media, and Technology* 5 (2014).

Lyon, Wendy. "(Hoping That) Women Hurt: Regret as a Tool of Advocacy." *Feminist Ire*, October 27, 2014. http://feministire.com/2014/10/27/hoping-that-women-hurt-regret-as-tool-of-advocacy/. Accessed February 12, 2015.

MacKinnon, Catharine A. *Toward a Feminist Theory of the State*. Cambridge, MA: Harvard UP, 1989.

MacKinnon, Catharine A., and Andrea Dworkin. *In Harm's Way: The Pornography Civil Rights Hearings*. Cambridge, MA: Harvard UP, 1997.

Massey, Alana. "Keeping Sex Workers Quiet." *Jacobin*, November 2, 2014. https://www.jacobinmag.com/2014/11/keeping-workers-quiet/. Accessed April 16, 2015.

Mazanderani, Fadhila, Louise Locock, and John Powell. "Biographical Value: Towards a Conceptualisation of the Commodification of Illness Narratives in Contemporary Healthcare." *Sociology of Health & Illness* 35.6 (2013): 891–905.

McGuire, Danielle. *At the Dark End of the Street: Black Women, Rape and Resistance—A New History of the Civil Rights Movement from Rosa Parks to the Rise of Black Power*. New York: Vintage Books, 2010.

Mensah, Maria Nengeh, and Chris Bruckert. *10 Reasons to Fight for the Decriminalization of Sex Work*. Social Sciences and Humanities Research Council of Canada, 2012.

Mohanty, Chandra Talpade. "Transnational Feminist Crossings: On Neoliberalism and Radical Critique." *Signs* 38.4 (2013): 967–91.

Mohanty, Chandra Talpade. "Under Western Eyes: Feminist Scholarship and Colonial Discourses." *boundary 2* 12.3 (1984): 333–58.

Molotch, Harvey. "What Do We Do with Disasters?" *Sociological Inquiry* 84.3 (2014): 370–3.

Moran, Rachel. "Buying Sex Should Not Be Legal." *New York Times*, 28 August 2015.

Munro, Ealasaid. "Feminism: A Fourth Wave?" *Political Insight* 4.2 (2013): 22–5.

Murphy, Meghan. "Kicking against Our Foremothers: Does Feminism Have an Ageism Problem?" *New Statesman*, February 26, 2014.

Nash, Jennifer C. "Home Truths on Intersectionality." *Yale Journal of Law and Feminism* 23 (2011): 445.

National Coalition of Anti-Violence Programs. *Lesbian, Gay, Bisexual, Transgender, Queer, and HIV-Affected Intimate Partner Violence in 2013*. New York: Anti-Violence Project, 2014.

New York State Anti-Trafficking Coalition. "A Survivor's Story." *Stop Human Trafficking NY*, 2015. https://stophumantraffickingny.wordpress.com/a-survivors-story/. Accessed March 2, 2015.

Ngai, Sianne. *Ugly Feelings*. Cambridge, MA: Harvard UP, 2005.

Nine. "Taking Ideology to the Streets: Sex Work and How to Make Bad Things Worse." *Feminist Ire*, November 23, 2012. http://feministire.com/2012/11/23/taking-ideology-to-the-streets-sex-work-and-how-to-make-bad-things-worse/. Accessed May 30, 2015.

Njambi, Wairimū Ngarũiya. "One Vagina to Go." *Australian Feminist Studies* 24.60 (2009): 167–80.

Park, Suey, and David J. Leonard. "In Defense of Twitter Feminism." *Model View Culture*, February 3, 2014. https://modelviewculture.com/pieces/in-defense-of-twitter-feminism. Accessed January 12, 2016.

Pedwell, Carolyn. *Affective Relations: The Transnational Politics of Empathy*. London: Palgrave Macmillan, 2014.

Pedwell, Carolyn. "Affective (Self)-Transformations: Empathy, Neoliberalism and International Development." *Feminist Theory* 13.2 (2012): 163–79.

Pedwell, Carolyn, and Anne Whitehead. "Affecting Feminism: Questions of Feeling in Feminist Theory." *Feminist Theory* 13.2 (2012): 115–29.

Pendleton Jiménez, Karleen. "'Start with the Land': Groundwork for Chicana Pedagogy." *Chicana/Latina Education in Everyday Life: Feminista Perspectives on Pedagogy and Epistemology*. Ed. Dolores Delgado Bernal, C. Alejandra Elenes, Francisca. E. Godinez, and Sofia Villenas. Albany: SUNY P, 2006, pp. 219–230.

Pennington, Louise. "Telling Rape Victims How They *Must* Process Their Rape Is Inherently Anti-Feminist." *My Elegant Gathering of White Snows*, February 28, 2015. http://elegantgatheringofwhitesnows.com/?p=2310. Accessed March 2, 2015.

Phipps, Alison. *The Politics of the Body: Gender in a Neoliberal and Neoconservative Age*. Cambridge, UK: Polity P. 2014.

Pilkington, Ed. "Ohio Transgender Teen's Suicide Note: 'Fix Society. Please'." *Guardian*, January 5, 2015.

Pollitt, Katha. "Who Has Abortions?" *The Nation*, March 13, 2015. http://www.thenation.com/article/who-has-abortions/. Accessed March 14, 2015.

Ray, Audacia. "Why the Sex Positive Movement Is Bad for Sex Workers' Rights." *Audacia Ray*, March 31, 2012. http://audaciaray.tumblr.com/post/20228032642/why-the-sex-positive-movement-is-bad-for-sex. Accessed March 30, 2015.

Rentschler, Carrie A. *Second Wounds: Victims' Rights and the Media in the US*. Durham, NC: Duke UP, 2011.

Rentschler, Carrie A., and Samantha C. Thrift. "Doing Feminism: Event, Archive, Techné." *Feminist Theory* 16.3 (2015) 239–49.

Roch, Amy, Graham Ritchie, and James Morton. *Out of Sight, Out of Mind? Transgender People's Experiences of Domestic Abuse*. Edinburgh: LGBT Youth Scotland, 2010.

Rousmaniere, Dana. "Project Manage Your Life." *Harvard Business Review*, February 10, 2015.

Rudulph, Heather Wood. "3 Survivors Reveal the Brutal Reality of Female Genital Mutilation." *Cosmopolitan*, April 25, 2014.

Scott, Joan Wallach. "The Evidence of Experience." *Critical Inquiry* 17.4 (1991): 773–97.

Serano, Julia. *Excluded: Making Feminist and Queer Movements More Inclusive*. Emeryville, CA: Avalon, 2013.

Spivak, Gayatri. "Can the Subaltern Speak?" *Marxism and the Interpretation of Culture*. Ed. Cary Nelson and Lawrence Grossberg. Basingstoke: Macmillan, 1988, pp. 271–313.

Steele, Catherine Knight. "Blogging While Black: A Critical Analysis of Resistance Discourse by Black Female Bloggers." *Selected Papers of Internet Research* vol. 1, 2012. http://spir.aoir.org/index.php/spir/article/view/31. Accessed January 23, 2015.

Suzyhooker. "Outcasts among Outcasts: Injection Drug-Using Sex Workers in the Sex Workers' Rights Movement, Part 1." *Tits and Sass*, September 2, 2013. http://titsandsass.com/outcasts-among-outcasts-injection-drug-using-sex-workers-in-the-sex-workers-rights-movement-part-1/. Accessed March 30, 2015.

Observer letter. "We Cannot Allow Censorship and Silencing of Individuals." *Observer*, February 15, 2015.

Turn Off the Red Light. "Testimonies and Case Studies." *Turn Off the Red Light*, http://www.turnofftheredlight.ie/learn-more/testimonies/. Accessed March 2, 2015.

United Nations. "UN News—FEATURE: 'I'm Not Whole'—Female Genital Mutilation Survivor Speaks Out." *UN News Service Section*, 2015. http://www.un.org/apps/news/story.asp?NewsID =50024#.VPR70bOsVrp. Accessed March 2, 2015.

United Nations Development Programme. *Sex Work and the Law in Asia and the Pacific*. UNDP report, 2012. http://www.undp.org/content/dam/undp/library/hivaids/English/HIV-2012-SexWorkAndLaw.pdf.

Webster, Hayley. "I Had an Abortion and Didn't Talk About It ..." *HayleyWebster.com*, April 1, 2015. http://www.hayleywebster.com/1/post/2015/04/i-had-an-abortion-and-didnt-talk-about-it.html. Accessed April 8, 2015.

Whittle, Stephen, Lewis Turner, and Maryam Al-Alami. *Engendered Penalties: Transgender and Transsexual People's Experiences of Inequality and Discrimination*. Manchester: Manchester Metropolitan U, 2007.

Wilkins, Amy C. "Becoming Black Women Intimate Stories and Intersectional Identities." *Social Psychology Quarterly* 75.2 (2012): 173–96.

Zanin, Andrea. "If Trans Women Aren't Welcome, Neither Am I." *Transadvocate*, September 25, 2013. http://www.transadvocate.com/if-trans-women-arent-welcome-neither-am-i_n_10232.htm. Accessed January 13, 2016.

CHAPTER TEN

Intersectionality

AÍDA HURTADO

Since the 1960s, the concept of intersectionality has been invoked in many areas of public life. Below I provide three snapshots of intersectionality illustrating the theory's origins in the legal arena and its widespread implementation in other sectors, including public art and political mobilization.

Intersectionality is a term used to describe intersections between identities in the modes of their oppression. A good example is in the legal field when in 1975, Ruth Bader Ginsburg, now Supreme Court Justice and recently anointed feminist icon, presented to the US Supreme Court the case of *Weinberger v. Wiesenfeld*. Stephen Wiesenfeld was a single father whose wife, the breadwinner in the family, had died in childbirth. Wiesenfeld, in seeking to raise his own son, was unable to collect his wife's benefits that she had earned as a school teacher. Early in their marriage he and his wife had agreed he would stay at home to care for their son and she would be the primary breadwinner, employed as a teacher and paying into Social Security. At the time, the law stipulated that only widows could receive "mother's benefits" (Carmon and Knizhnik 70). Bader Ginsburg, who was working for the American Civil Liberties Union (ACLU) at the time, filed for sex discrimination, which she eventually argued before the Supreme Court. In the brief, she laid out her case for why sex discrimination affected not only women but men as well. Her conceptualization of men as subject to sex discrimination was not only novel but also revolutionary. Her argument underscored the unfairness of sex segregation according to "norms" or sex stereotypes. According to Bader Ginsburg, the law "reflects the familiar stereotype that, throughout this Nation's history, has operated to devalue women's efforts in the economic sector," and simultaneously, the father "is denied benefits that would permit him to attend personally to the care of his infant son, a child who has no other parent to provide that care" (Carmon and Knizhnik 70–1). Ultimately, the unfairness of the law creates yet another victim when it "includes children with dead fathers, but excludes children with dead mothers" (71). Arguing thus, Bader Ginsburg used an intersectional approach to the analysis of sex beyond the binary of male/female to examine the intersections of gender with class.

In true feminist fashion, however, Bader Ginsburg did not take credit for the not-yet-coined intersectional approach she employed. Instead, she acknowledged that this legal concept was actually the brain child of Pauli Murray, an African American lawyer, and Mary Eastwood, founder and director of the organization *Human Rights for Women*. In an influential, and now classic, 1965 law review article "Jane Crow and the Law: Sex Discrimination and Title VII," they laid out the legal consequences in the workplace of the intersection of sex and race. Bader Ginsburg, again displaying her feminist commitment, publicly acknowledged the groundwork in this article, which argued the notion that a sex analysis alone was not sufficient for women to gain true equality (Carmon and Knizhnik).

Forty-two years later, in 2017, a local newspaper in a small college town in Northern California reported on the painting of a set of murals at a local community center. The murals were designed with the help of local youth. The central concept of the murals is intersectionality, and the work is titled "Unify, Decolonize, Thrive" (York). The news-paper article states, "the murals will delve heavily into a term known as 'intersectionality,' coined by law professor Kimberlé Crenshaw,[1] as a way to reveal limitations of single-issue anti-discrimination laws" (York 2). Jamie Joy, youth program coordinator for the county's Diversity Center, elaborated on the project's implementation of the concept of intersectionality:

> The kids that I work with, they hold multiple identities; they're not just thinking about the fact that they're gay or trans or gender non-conforming. They're thinking about their families' citizenship status and they're also thinking about their class status and their mental health and they're thinking about other issues that affect them also.... . The way that I understand intersectionality is just being aware of multiple identities and how they impact someone's privilege or lack of privilege in the world. I think the kids that we work with understand that on a deeper level than I did when I was 14 or 15 years old. (York 4)

Another powerful example of the implementation of the concept of intersectionality occurred during the Women's March on Washington, DC, of January 21, 2017. Carmen Pérez, one of the main organizers for the march, together with the many individuals involved in planning this historic event, agreed to use intersectionality as the guiding principle for the march's political and social agenda, as well as for the roster of speakers. Pérez explained why intersectionality had been such a useful concept in structuring the Women's March:

> My expertise has been in criminal justice for the past twenty years. But as women or just as human beings, we are not one-dimensional. We are intersectional human beings. We live in poverty; if we get deported we don't have access to reproductive justice rights, if we are incarcerated we don't have access to quality education. We have to be intentional about being intersectional; about stepping outside our issue expertise and finding our liberation bound [up] with others—whether it is climate change, repro-ductive justice, immigration reform, criminal justice reform, indigenous rights, these things impact us all. Instead of working in silos we have to coordinate our efforts a little bit better and be more intentional about intersections. (Hurtado, video of Pérez)

In this chapter, I present a brief historical overview of the concept of intersectionality, followed by discussions of recent developments in the expansion of the theory. I finish by outlining the advantages of using intersectionality in scholarship and political organizing.

BRIEF HISTORICAL OVERVIEW OF INTERSECTIONALITY

At the time of *Weinberger v. Wiesenfeld*, Bader Ginsburg could not fully articulate from a legal standpoint why women's experiences in the workplace or in the home did not fit existing legal doctrine. There were no legal frameworks in place that could accommodate the contingent categorizations of disadvantage based on race and gender that operated simultaneously in structural systems of oppression. Forty-two years later, however, the

Diversity Center coordinator Jamie Joy and the Women's March organizer Carmen Pérez could reference the legal doctrine published in 1989 by law professor and African American scholar Kimberlé Crenshaw in the article "Demarginalizing the Intersection of Race and Sex: A Black Feminist Critique of Antidiscrimination Doctrine, Feminist Theory and Antiracist Politics." As Crenshaw's writings elucidate, the consideration of gender and race, and how these categories intersect, is critical to understanding that women in the United States and around the world are subjected to multiple sources of oppression. Crenshaw's intervention was part of the growing chorus in feminist scholarship and feminist organizing asserting that the feminisms developed by such influential figures as Betty Friedan and Gloria Steinem could not be applied without modification to all groups of women. For example, women in Africa suffer from starvation as well as rape and other gender-specific oppressions resulting from political upheavals, historical circumstances, and economic and cultural oppression (White).

Crenshaw's pioneering work on intersectionality exposed the inadequacies of the legal system in handling multiple sources of discrimination experienced by African American women. Like Murray before her, Crenshaw demonstrated that in the case of employment discrimination, African American women were forced to bring legal suits either as women or as blacks. The courts would not accommodate black women's claims, fearing that the expansion of another protected category would open the possibility of endless discriminatory subgroupings:

> The legislative history surrounding Title VII does not indicate that the goal of the statute was to create a new classification of "black women" who would have greater standing than, for example, a black male. The prospect of the creation of new classes of protected minorities, governed only by the mathematical principles of permutation and combination, clearly raises the prospect of opening the hackneyed Pandora's box. (cited in Crenshaw, "Demarginalizing the Intersection of Race and Sex" 142)

In addition to employment discrimination, Crenshaw applied intersectionality to the legal analysis of rape. The law's archaic assumptions of white women's chastity[2] led to more punitive punishment for interracial rape when committed by black men. In addition, black women's rape was less often prosecuted than white women's when it was committed by men of any race. Similarly, in domestic violence cases, excessive punishment was handed down by the criminal justice system to black men. The treatment of black men by the criminal justice system led to the perhaps not-so-unintended consequence of black women underreporting physical abuse by the men in their lives. Crenshaw also outlined the consequences of intersectionality for political behavior ("Mapping the Margins"). Black women were pressed to join political movements aimed at ending racism or to join feminist movements aimed at ending sexism—they did not feel free to join both. Crenshaw did not explicitly examine other social categories that oppress women, such as class and sexuality, but the application of intersectionality to race and gender became central to examining multiple sources of oppression within feminist analysis.

While Crenshaw focused on the previously unexplored legal injuries of intersectional subordination, Patricia Hill Collins focused on the nonlegal societal structures that produce similar outcomes. According to Collins, "intersectionality is an analysis claiming that systems of race, social class, gender, sexuality, ethnicity, nation, and age form mutually constructing features of social organization, which shape Black women's experiences and, in turn, are shaped by Black women" (299). Collins posits that societal structures are formed and sustained to exert power over people of color in general and African Americans in particular. From Collins's perspective intersectionality "emerged from the recognition … that inequality could not be explained, let alone challenged, via a race-only, or gender-only framework" (82). Furthermore, macro-level systems of oppression are interlocking and affect individuals at different class and race intersections (82).

Cultural critic Rosa-Linda Fregoso applies intersectionality to the categorical differences between women in different nation-states. In particular, Fregoso scrutinizes the tendency of "First World Feminists" to apply the human rights paradigm to women globally. Fregoso calls attention to the error of "claiming a singular transnational identity for women" (23), noting the differences among women even within one nation-state. Her call is for "framing women's international human rights within very complex and specific cultural contexts" (23). As her key example, she uses intersectionality as a lens in understanding why young, working-class, dark-skinned Mexican women rather than wealthy, light-skinned Mexican women were the victims of "feminicide" in the border city of Ciudad Juarez (across from El Paso, Texas). Fregoso identifies variations among the Mexican victims based on class and race, which can give rise to a more penetrating analysis of the murders than the one provided by human rights discourse alone.

In earlier academic work, intersectionality had been used to analyze intersections of multiple subordinate positions, but recently, intersectionality has been applied to contradictory intersections as well. So, for instance, in the case of black men, one social category confers privilege (male gender), while another social category is the basis for subordination (being of color). Expanding intersectionality in this manner facilitates the analysis of the position of men of color (Hurtado and Sinha, White). White achieves incisive results using intersectionality to understand the lives of twenty African American men who identify as feminist and the different life paths that led to this level of gender consciousness. Sinha and I use intersectionality to analyze the paths that led young, educated Latino men to identify as feminist. In both instances, male privilege is affected by men of color's vulnerabilities due to race, class, and sexuality.

I turn now to the latest expansion of intersectionality by specifying which social categories might be useful to consider in intersectionality by integrating social psychologist Tajfel's social identity theory (1981). I continue by proposing that Anzaldúa's borderlands theory, and the writings on intersectionality by other Chicana feminists, explicate a *mestiza consciousness*, an intersectional identity that privileges the positive aspects of multiple identities as leading to a deeper understanding of oppression and the constructed nature of social reality.

SOCIAL IDENTITY THEORY, BORDERLANDS THEORY, AND INTERSECTIONALITY

Many social psychologists make a distinction between *personal identity* and *social identity*, which together form a person's integrated sense of self (Baumeister). Personal identity is that aspect of self-composed psychological traits and dispositions that gives rise to personal uniqueness (Tajfel). Personal identity is primarily socialized within families, varying in composition based on culture, language, class, and historical moment, among other factors (Hurtado, "Understanding Multiple Group Identities"). All human beings have personal identities that involve such activities as loving, mating, doing productive work—activities that are considered universal components of self. The self, however, is filtered through language, culture, historical moment, and social structures and social context (Reicher).

Tajfel describes the following dynamics in the construction of social identities. *Social identity* is that aspect self-derived from the knowledge of being part of social categories and groups, together with the value and emotional significance attached to those group formations. Social identities are created through *social categorization* based on social or physical characteristics that are meaningful socially, and many times politically, in particular social contexts. Among these categorizations are: nationality, language, race, ethnicity, gender, sex, ethnicity, and skin color. The meaning of an individual's social identities is derived through *social comparison*. That is, a group's status, degree of affluence, or other characteristics achieve significance *in relation to* perceived differences and their value connotations from other social formations—its value is largely based on the presence and significance of other social formations in the environment. When the social identities are stigmatized or do not bring an individual a positive sense of self, the individual has to do *psychological work*, both cognitive and emotional, to achieve a positive sense of self. Individuals strive to be different from other groups, but the difference has to be positive.

The social identities that are disparaged (including "invisible" identities, such as sexual orientation), those that have to be negotiated frequently because of their visibility (physical attributes, such as dark skin color), and those that have become politicized by social movements require psychological work to overcome the negative aspects attributed to group affiliation. Stigmatized social identities are powerful psychologically; they are easily identifiable to individuals (everyone knows if they are a man or woman) and they matter to individuals (there is an emotional attachment to either being a man or a woman), likely to be salient across situations, and likely to function as schemas, frameworks, or social scripts (Gurin et al., "Group Contacts and Ethnicity"; Hurtado and Gurin). For example, a lesbian African American adolescent with a physical disability is more likely to reflect heavily on her social identities than is a middle-class, white, heterosexual adolescent with no physical impediments.

According to Tajfel, socially valued group memberships that are accorded privilege, or are indistinguishable to others, may not even become social identities. Until the emergence of whiteness studies and men's studies, being racially white and male was not the subject of inquiry as problematic categories and is still not widely thought of as a social identity (Fine et al.; Hurtado and Stewart). The advantages accrued because of the racial benefits of whiteness and male gender are not easily articulated by its possessors, regardless of class, because white race privilege and male privilege is considered the norm in the United States (McIntosh; Connell). Although there are class variations among different groups of whites—poor whites versus middleclass whites—there is still no universal stigma that applies to this racial category.

Personal and social identity are not entirely independent of each other, but neither are they one and the same. The theoretical distinction between these two aspects of self is helpful in averting *dispositionalism*—the tendency in the field of psychology, and in the general population, to over-attribute causes for behavior to personality or to personality traits such as self-esteem or grit. Dispositionalism also leads individuals to underestimate the influence on behavior of social context and structural variables (Haney and Zimbardo). Distinguishing between personal identity and social identity makes apparent that personal identities are less monitored socially, so that a person can demonstrate effervescence one day and depression the next without a perception of incoherence. In comparison, an individual's social identities as embodied in gender, race, ethnicity, and socioeconomic class are immediately assessed in most social contexts and without extensive social inter-action. Therefore, the presentation of self is regulated through these group belongings in most social contexts such that coherence is a necessary prerequisite for social functioning. For example, an individual categorized as a man cannot dress as a woman one day and as a man the next without social (and sometimes violent) consequences.

The section "Master Statuses and Intersectionality" focuses on the specific social identities that sociologists enumerate under the category of master statuses because of their social, political, cultural, and persistent influence over individuals' lives and liveli-hood. These social identities are central to the theoretical framework of intersectionality (Collins and Bilge; Hurtado, "Intersectional Understandings of Inequality").

MASTER STATUSES AND INTERSECTIONALITY

In my work, intersectionality refers to the *master statuses* (Hughes) of class, race, sexu-ality, gender, ethnicity, and physical ableness (Hurtado, "Intersectional Understandings of Inequality"). This constellation of social identities is the primary basis for power distribu-tion *and* for stigmatization that is used to impose subordination (Hurtado, "Intersectional Understandings of Inequality"). Master statuses are used in most countries to make value judgments about group memberships and to allocate political, social, and economic power (Reicher). All measures of inequality such as education, income, and accumulated wealth are affected by these master statuses. Conversely, individuals holding privileged master statuses must negotiate the psychological effects of devalued group memberships if and when that privilege becomes problematized. Social identity theory (Gurin et al., "Group Contacts and Ethnicity"; Hurtado, "Understanding Multiple Group Identities") provides a framework for understanding both unproblematic and stigmatized group affiliations, especially those based on master statuses.

Reicher and Hopkins indicate that "the particular social identity that is salient in a given context will determine who is seen and treated as similar and who is rejected as an alien" (385–6). The meaning of particular social categories can only be fully understood in context, as the meaning changes when circumstances change (Turner and Onorato). Intersectional identities are those stigmatized social identities that intersect in particular contexts. A fitting metaphor for intersectional identities is an amorphic, fluid amoeba that changes shape as it moves through its surroundings, making one (or more) social iden-tities especially salient depending on the context. Each social category is porous and over-lapping others, with boundaries that are not rigid or fixed. From a social psychological point of view, intersectionality refers to a particular constellation of social identities based on master statuses, which are the primary basis for stigmatization and for allocation of privilege (Hurtado, "Intersectional Understandings of Inequality").

Personal identity is influenced by an individual's social identities, and stigma must be negotiated. Social identity theory as embodied in master statuses facilitates the examin-ation of the social process of intersectional social identity assignations by others versus the private self-perceptions of an individual's personal identity. A poor African American lesbian with physical disabilities will be treated in many social contexts according to her *visible stigmatized social identities* rather than her *personal identity*, which quite pos-sibly may include being a kind, gentle, and intelligent human being. Intersectionality as embodied in stigmatized social identities allows for an agile analysis of the different social contexts in which certain stigmatized social identities are more salient and likely to be used to oppress (Hurtado and Cervantez).

Intersectionality can illuminate when there are contradictory intersections of subordination and privilege, for example, being male and Latino (Hurtado and Sinha). Intersectionality also elucidates the benefits and consequences of privilege when master statuses are aligned to benefit individuals. Master statuses can confer privilege protecting an individual's personal identity from stigma and oppression. The application of intersectionality to the problematics of privilege, however, has yet to be fully developed. In sum, an intersectional social identity framework allows the examination of this complexity in various social spheres, in different life cycles, and across historical moments and experiences of social and economic inequality.

BORDERLANDS THEORY

Identification is defined as individuals seeing themselves as belonging to certain social categories, say, for example, ethnic, gender, and class groups (Gurin et al., "Stratum Identification and Consciousness" 30). Consciousness is defined as individuals becoming aware that the social groups they belong to hold a certain status (either powerful or not powerful) in society. Consciousness about one's place in society permits individuals to decide (or possibly to feel compelled) to take action to change their status, not just for their own benefit but for others in the group as well. Consciousness about the power and privilege of one's social belongings may also motivate individuals to maintain their status and actively act against others who may challenge their accrued benefits. Thus, having a characteristic that could potentially become a social identity, such as being female, may not turn into a social identity; some awareness of the political and social implications of category membership is necessary for identity constructions to become *conscious* and lead to political mobilization to fight inequality. In my work I integrate Gloria Anzaldúa's borderland theory to theorize about a particular type of consciousness (Gurin et al., "Stratum Identification and Consciousness") in which multiple social subjectivities (Hurtado, "Multiple Subjectivities") contribute to political understandings of various social statuses that in turn influence individuals' intersectional identities and their potential commitment to social justice.

Chicana feminist scholars have been at the forefront of the work on intersectionality since the 1980s and 1990s (Alarcón; Castillo; Moraga and Anzaldúa). The thrust of their work is to build multiple feminisms that center in their analysis: culture, class, sexuality, race, ethnicity, and, most recently, racialized masculinities (Hurtado and Sinha). A pivotal theoretical addition to Chicana feminisms has been the work of Gloria Anzaldúa—writer, public intellectual, and one of the first Chicanas to publicly claim her lesbianism (Moraga and Anzaldúa). The geographical border between the United States and Mexico is the source of Anzaldúa's theorizing. Borderlands theory expands on W. E. B. Du Bois's idea of double consciousness[3] by examining the experiences of Chicanas growing up in South Texas on the border between the United States and Mexico. The border between these two countries becomes a metaphor for the crossings necessary to exist in multiple linguistic and cultural contexts, including crossings between geopolitical boundaries, sexual transgressions, social dislocations, and in intellectual and literary production—fiction, poetry, memoir, auto-historia (auto-history), self-ethnography, among others.

Anzaldúa declares the border as the geographical location (*lugar*) that created the aperture for theorizing about subordination from an ethnically specific Chicana/mestiza consciousness. From her perspective, the history of conquest, which layered the new country over a preexisting one, was evidence of the temporality of nation-states (Klahn). The political borderline dividing the United States from Mexico did not correspond to the experiential existence on the border where many individuals lived, worked, and socialized in both countries without much contradiction (Anzaldúa). Living in the borderlands creates a third space between cultures and social systems that leads to coherence by embracing ambiguity and holding contradictory perceptions without conflict. *La frontera* (the border) is a geographical area characterized by hybridity, because it is neither fully of Mexico nor fully of the United States. La frontera is where you "put chile in the borscht/eat whole-wheat tortillas/speak Tex-Mex with a Brooklyn accent" (Anzaldúa 195). The borderlands, however they are defined, provide the space for antithetical elements to mix, not to become homogenized or incorporated into a larger whole but to become combined in unique and unexpected ways (Hurtado, *Voicing Chicana Feminisms*).

Borderlands theory was born out of Anzaldúa's experiences as the daughter of farmworkers living in extreme poverty in South Texas. However, the theory can be applied to many types of social, economic, sexual, and political dislocations. Anzaldúa's insights help us theorize the experiences of individuals who are exposed to contradictory social systems and develop *la facultad* (ability or gift)—the notion that individuals (primarily women) who are exposed to multiple social worlds (as defined by cultures, languages, social classes, sexualities, nation-states, and colonization) are able to perceive and challenge linear conceptions of social reality. Other writers have called this ability "differential consciousness" (Sandoval), perception of "multiple realities" (Alarcón), "multiple subjectivities" (Hurtado, *Multiple Subjectivities*), and a state of "conscientización"[4] (Castillo). Anzaldúa presages the concept of intersectionality by attributing Chicanas's subordination to patriarchy and to the intersection of multiple systems of oppression. Borderlands theory does not rank oppressions nor does it conceptualize them as static; rather oppressions are fluid systems taking on different forms and nuances depending on the context. Individuals can experience multiple oppressions and forms of resistance that are not easily accessible through traditional methods of analysis and measurement (Torre and Ayala).

Anzaldúa's borderlands theory delineates the experiential aspects of Tajfel's social identity theory. Tajfel did not explore the psychic cost of stigma to individuals, let alone to women. The burden is especially heavy when individuals have no control over the social categorization imposed on them by others. Tajfel's theorizing also did not directly address individuals' coping skills when confronted with the incongruence between their private self-perceptions (as competent, intelligent, logical individuals) and others' negative perceptions shaped by the individuals' stigmatized social identities (as lazy, stupid, incompetent). Anzaldúa's theory proposes that one possibility among many is to use the contradiction to one's advantage, rising above the negative assignation to develop a complex view that she called *mestiza* (hybrid) *consciousness* and that I call intersectional identities.

The development of a mestiza consciousness that simultaneously embraces and rejects contradictory realities to avoid excluding what it critically assesses is the result of individuals living in many liminal spaces (Lugones). A mestiza consciousness permits individuals to perceive multiple realities at once (Barvosa). Anzaldúa's work integrates indigenous Aztec beliefs and epistemologies that circumvent linear, positivist thinking that does not allow for hybridity, contradiction, and, ultimately, liberation from existing social arrangements (Hurtado, *Voicing Chicana Feminisms*). Borderlands theory is particularly important for social action and coalition building. There are no absolute "sides" in conflict; instead, there are contingent adversaries whose perceptions can be understood by examining (and empathizing) with their subjectivities. Because oppression is context dependent, no one is exempt from contributing to oppression in different social spheres (Perez). For example, a woman prison warden can surely impose repression in a prison populated by male inmates. Self-reflexivity and seeing through the "eyes of others" become essential in obtaining a deeper consciousness than staying within one's social milieu.

In my work I apply borderlands theory to intersectionality through social identity theory. The fluidity and context-dependent nature of intersectional identities result in "social travel" between social systems, cultural symbols, and cognitive understandings, ultimately creating a nonnormative consciousness of the arbitrary nature of social reality. Stigmatized social identities based on master statuses are not additive; they do not result in increased oppression with an increased number of stigmatized group memberships. Instead, individuals' group memberships are conceptualized as intersecting in a variety of ways, depending on the social context forming intersectional identity constellations (Hurtado and Gurin), many of which have the potential for liberation.

CONCLUSION

Like many feminist theoretical contributions, intersectionality was birthed from the necessity to address inequality based on sex, gender, sexuality, race, class, and ethnicity. Most recently, physical ableness has been added as another possible axis of inequality. Feminist organizing is committed to fighting for equality for all, not eliding difficult issues of representation. The commitment to social justice has pushed feminist writers and activists to extend the boundaries of the conceptualization of the intersections that contribute to inequality. When Ruth Bader Ginsburg litigated to persuade the Supreme Court that sex discrimination was not confined to women, but that all individuals that did not fit the roles assigned by the gender binary of male/female were affected, she and her colleagues saw the wisdom of defending Stephen Wiesenfeld against his oppression based on his gender nonconforming behavior. The principle applied by Bader Ginsburg in *Weinberger v. Wiesenfeld* in 1975 was derived from another feminist activist from a prior generation, Pauli Murray, who also argued that the gender binary applied in the law denied justice, in this instance, to black women fighting for equality in the workplace. The labor of these early feminists and many others has come to fruition, as has the concept of intersectionality as one of many feminist contributions that has entered the everyday experiences of people. Developing from its earliest theoretical formulation, intersectionality can now be applied to political organizing, whether it be on the local scale as in a community mural or on an unprecedented global scale as in the historic Women's March that took place on January 21, 2017.

NOTES

1 Kimberlé W. Crenshaw is a law professor and legal scholar who is credited for coining the term intersectionality in 1989 in what is now considered a classic essay titled "Demarginalizing

the Intersection of Race and Sex: A Black Feminist Critique of Antidiscrimination Doctrine, Feminist Theory and Antiracist Politics."

2 According to Crenshaw's analysis, historically there were no institutional efforts to regulate black women's chastity because they were not perceived as "true women," but rather they were "licentious," always desirous of sexual encounters (Crenshaw 35). In contrast, laws were developed to protect white women's chastity and rape by black men, which was the ultimate violation often punishable by lynching (Wriggins). Because the legal system's underlying assumptions about who possessed chastity and who did not, "black women could not be victims of forcible rape" (Crenshaw 35).

3 In *Souls of Black* Folks published in 1903, Du Bois wrote about blacks in the United States as experiencing a "double consciousness" as follows:

> It is a peculiar sensation, this double-consciousness, this sense of always looking at one's self through the eyes of others, of measuring one's soul by the tape of a world that looks on in amused contempt and pity. One ever feels his two-ness, an American, a Negro; two souls, two thoughts, two unreconciled strivings; two warring ideals in one dark body, whose dogged strength alone keeps it from being torn asunder. The history of the American Negro is the history of this strife—this longing to attain self-conscious manhood, to merge his double self into a better and truer self. In this merging he wishes neither of the older selves to be lost. He does not wish to Africanize America, for America has too much to teach the world and Africa. He wouldn't bleach his Negro blood in a flood of white Americanism, for he knows that Negro blood has a message for the world. He simply wishes to make it possible for a man to be both a Negro and an American without being cursed and spit upon by his fellows, without having the doors of opportunity closed roughly in his face. (2–3)

4 Castillo expands Freire's notion of concientización to include gender. Paulo Freire in the 1970s proposed that the genesis of individual behavior is not in the intrapsychic processes of the mind, but rather that behavior comes from individuals operating within oppressive and alienating social structures. Liberation theology was also central to the process of concientización.

WORKS CITED

Alarcón, Norma. "The Theoretical Subject(s) of This Bridge Called My Back and Anglo-American Feminism." *Making Face, Making Soul: Haciendo Caras*. Ed. Gloria Anzaldúa. San Francisco, CA: Aunt Lute Books, 1990, pp. 356–69.

Anzaldúa, Gloria E. *Borderlands—La Frontera: The New Mestiza*. San Francisco, CA: Spinsters/ Aunt Lute, 1987.

Barvosa, Edwina. "Mestiza Consciousness in Relation to Sustained Political Solidarity: A Chicana Feminist Interpretation of the Farmworker Movement." *Aztlán* 36.2 (2011): 121–54.

Baumeister, Roy F. "The Self." *The Handbook of Social Psychology*, vol. 1. Ed. Daniel T. Gilbert et al., Oxford: Oxford UP, 1998, pp. 680–740.

Carmon, Irin, and Shana Knizhnik. *Notorious RBG. The Life and Times of Ruth Bader Ginsburg*. New York: HarperCollins, 2015.

Castillo, Ana. *Massacre of the Dreamers: Essays on Xicanisma*. Albuquerque: U of New Mexico P, 1995.

Collins, Patricia H. *Black Feminist Thought: Knowledge, Consciousness, and the Politics of Empowerment*, 1st edn. New York: Routledge, 2000.

Collins, Patricia H., and Sirma Bilge. *Intersectionality*. Cambridge, UK: Polity P, 2016.

Connell, Raewyn. *Masculinities*. Cambridge, UK: Polity P, 1995.

Crenshaw, Kimberlé W. "Demarginalizing the Intersection of Race and Sex: A Black Feminist Critique of Antidiscrimination Doctrine, Feminist Theory and Antiracist Politics." *University of Chicago Legal Foundations*, 1989, pp. 139–67.

Crenshaw, Kimberlé W. "Mapping the Margins: Intersectionality, Identity Politics, and Violence against Women of Color." *Critical Race Theory: The Key Writings That Formed the Movement*. Ed. Crenshaw et al. New York: New Press, 1995, pp. 357–83.

Du Bois, W. E. B. *The Souls of Black Folk*. Mineola: Dover, 1903.

Fine, Michelle, et al., eds. *Off White: Readings on Power, Privilege, and Resistance*. New York: Routledge, 2004.

Freire, Paolo. *Pedagogy of the Oppressed*. New York: Continuum, 1970.

Fregoso, Rosa-Linda. *Mexicana Encounters: The Making of Social Identities on the Borderlands*. Berkeley: U of California P, 2003.

Gurin, Patricia, et al. "Group Contacts and Ethnicity in the Social Identities of Mexicanos and Chicanos." *Personality and Social Psychology Bulletin* 20 (1994): 521–32.

Gurin, Patricia, et al. "Stratum Identification and Consciousness." *Social Psychology Quarterly* 43.1 (1980): 30–47.

Haney, Craig W., and Philip G. Zimbardo. "Persistent Dispositionalism in Interactionist Clothing: Fundamental Attribution Error in Explaining Prison Abuse." *Personality and Social Psychology Bulletin* 35 (2009): 807–14.

Hughes, Everett. C. "Dilemmas and Contradictions of Status." *American Journal of Sociology* 50.5 (1945): 353–9.

Hurtado, Aída. "Intersectional Understandings of Inequality." *Oxford Handbook of Social Psychology and Social Justice*. Ed. Phillip L. Hammack. Oxford: Oxford UP, 2017, pp. 157–72 .

Hurtado, Aída. "Multiple Subjectivities: Chicanas and Cultural Citizenship." *Women and Citizenship*. Ed. Marilyn Friedman. Oxford: Oxford UP, 2005, pp. 111–29.

Hurtado, Aída. *Personal Video of Carmen Pérez on Intersectionality*. Washington, DC, January 21, 2017.

Hurtado, Aída. "Understanding Multiple Group Identities: Inserting Women into Cultural Transformations." *Journal of Social Issues* 53.2 (1997): 299–338.

Hurtado, Aída. *Voicing Chicana Feminisms: Young Women Speak Out on Sexuality and Identity*. New York: New York UP, 2003.

Hurtado, Aída, and Abigail J. Stewart. "Through the Looking Glass: Implications of Studying Whiteness for Feminist Methods." *Off White: Readings on Power, Privilege, and Resistance*. Ed. Michelle Fine et al. New York: Routledge, 2004, pp. 315–30.

Hurtado, Aída, and Karina Cervantez. "A View from Within and from Without: The Development of Latina Feminist Psychology." *The Handbook of U.S. Latino Psychology: Developmental and Community Based Perspectives*. Ed. Francisco A. Villarruel et al. Los Angeles: Sage, 2009, pp. 171–90.

Hurtado, Aída, and Mrinal Sinha. *Beyond Machismo: Intersectional Latino Masculinities*. Austin: U of Texas P, 2016.

Hurtado, Aída, and Patricia Gurin. *Chicano/a Identity in a Changing U.S. Society ¿Quién Soy? ¿Quiénes Somos?* Tucson: U of Arizona P, 2004.

Klahn, Norma. "Writing the Border: The Languages and Limits of Representation." *Travesía: The Border Issue*, special issue of *The Journal of Latin American Cultural Studies* 3.1–2 (1994): pp. 29–55.

Lugones, Maria. *Pilgrimages/Peregrinajes: Theorizing Coalition against Multiple Oppressions.* Lanham, MD: Rowman & Littlefield, 2003.

McIntosh, Peggy. "White Privilege: Unpacking the Invisible Knapsack." *Peace and Freedom*, 9–10 (July/August, 1989).

Moraga, Cherrie, and Gloria E. Anzaldúa, eds. *This Bridge Called My Back: Writings by Radical Women of Color.* London: Persephone Press, 1981.

Murray, Pauli, and Mary O. Eastwood. "Jane Crow and the Law: Sex Discrimination and Title VII." *George Washington Law Review* 34 (1965–6): 232.

Perez, Emma. *The Decolonial Imaginary: Writing Chicanas Into History*. Bloomington: Indiana UP, 1999.

Reicher, Stephen. "The Context of Social Identity: Domination, Resistance, and Change." *Political Psychology* 24.6 (2004): 921–45.

Reicher, Stephen, and Nick Hopkins. "Psychology and the End of History: A Critique and a Proposal for the Psychology of Social Categorization." *Political Psychology* 22.2 (2001): 383–407.

Sandoval, Chela. *Methodology of the Oppressed*. Minneapolis: U of Minnesota P, 2000.

Tajfel, Henri. *Human Groups and Social Categories: Studies in Social Psychology.* Cambridge: Cambridge UP, 1981.

Torre, María Elena, and Jennifer Ayala. "Envisioning Participatory Action Research Entremundos." *Feminism & Psychology* 19.3 (2009): 387–93.

Turner, J. C., and R. S. Onorato. "Social Identity, Personality, and the Self-Concept: A Self-Categorization Perspective." *The Psychology of the Social Self.* Ed. T. R. Tyler et al. Mahwah, NJ: Lawrence Erlbaum, 1999, pp. 11–46.

York, Jessica A. "Santa Cruz Mural Artists, Youth Examine Discrimination." *Santa Cruz Sentinel*, http://www.santacruzsentinel.com/article/NE/20170802/NEWS/170809925. Accessed August 28, 2017.

White, Aaronette M. *Ain't I a Feminist? African American Men Speak Out on Fatherhood, Friendship, Forgiveness, and Freedom.* Albany: State U of New York P, 2008.

Wriggins, Jeniffer. "Rape, Racism, and the Law." *Harvard Women's Law Journal* 6 (1983): 103–41.

PART TWO

The Text

CHAPTER ELEVEN

Language

KYOO LEE

"No room! No room!" they cried out when they saw Alice coming.
"There's *plenty* of room!" said Alice indignantly,
and she sat down in a large arm-chair at one end of the table.
—Lewis Carroll, Chapter 7: A Mad Tea-Party, *Alice's Adventures in Wonderland*

"Say it" (or shut—the f***—up?), thus spake Antigone:

Leader: Tell us—who was your father?
Oedipus: God help me! Dear girl, what must I suffer now?
Antigone: Say it. You're driven right to the edge.
Oedipus: Then speak I will—no way to hide it now.
Leader: You're wasting time, the two of you. Out with it, quickly.
(Sophocles 296)

So again: "say it," says Antigone—say what?
. . .
yeah, I'm telling ya, as we speak
F-word,
Father?

What is it that you can't say? Can't you just say it? Like some New Yawka, if you see something, not just see it for yourself, but share it with folks, yeah, say somethin,' whateva.

Well, a little too complicated to explain it all here but enough to say just this, that

with practically everyone around her doubly (dis/mis)placed or queer incested—as the mother-grandmother (Jocasta)/father-brother (Oedipus)/brothers-uncles (Eteocles & Polyneices)/sister-aunt (Ismene)—all now already dead or absent, Antigone our dear sister (Lee, "Review of *Revivals*" 371–2)

Needing . . . needingly unable to say "it" for herself, now finds herself on (the) edge, right at the heart of the genealogical entanglement, the epic mess, this royal mass . . . game.

So by demanding, instead, that Oedipus, her fa-bro-ther, "say it," sort it out, she, Antigone, practically turns him into an impossible echo, kinda frightened little girl having to respond somehow to the contradictory call/law/dictate of the father who, here,

Oedipus himself, has come to embody, which must've been devastating to the King, kinda beyond "threatening":

> "Why do men feel threatened by women?" I asked a male friend of mine. (I love that wonderful rhetorical device, "a male friend of mine." It's often used by female journalists when they have to say something particularly bitchy but don't want to be held responsible for it themselves).... "They're afraid women will laugh at them," he said. "Undercut their world view." Then I asked some women students in a quickie poetry seminar I was giving, "Why do women feel threatened by men?" "They're afraid of being killed," they said. (Atwood 413)

One is afraid of being "laughed" at by the other, who would, therefore, have to be killed. Laughing? Who is? Ridiculous, you say? Ridiculously outdated? We will get back to that.

(In "a quickie poetry seminar," who wouldn't want that?)

For now, consider this fact in that fiction, something of a real faction in the quotidian constancy of life: keep in mind that the other stranger from ancient Thebes, on behalf of her old kingly fabro whose "shattered" (Sophocles 297) states the leader (or chorus) "cannot endure," (Sophocles 297) starts speaking, pleading, practically screaming ... I mean, anyone laughing here, or feel like?

> I beg you!—beg you for my father, beg you
> With eyes that still can look into your eyes.
> I implore you, look—
> Like a daughter sprung of your own blood,
> I beg that my shattered father find compassion.
> We throw ourselves on your mercy as on a god,
> In all our misery. Hear us! Oh say Yes— (Sophocles 297)

So you see, hear, that this other beggar or beginner, this other

> one goes on and on, announcing without announcing her object or objectivity except her (b*tchy) self, her recalcitrant singular-starred self on (the) edge: what could she do or undo? ... The meta-metonymic metabolism of Antigone who is not yet gone or yet to be gone, the timeless icon of feminist alterity or alter-native viability, could be found in its imaginal (imagination/imaginary-enabling) vitality including quasi-theological sublimity, and what sustains this discourse of matrixial allogos or translogos is her mammal body density and intensity topographically mythopoeticised as such. (Lee, "Review of *Revivals*" 372)

How to howl, you ask, well, ask the owl ... of Minerva—yeah, Hegel, get some sleep— not what she can do for you but what you can do for her and with her, or then why not them.

How?

Carry on then—shall we?—reading Antigone's anti-*gone*an anti-genealogical allegor-ical language at work, her proto-refusenik speech act. Note how she goes about, stretching herself, trying to make her case, consciously or not. At any rate, we see this thing she is confronting: "it," the phal*logos* (*law/language/logic*), let's say, of patriarchal sovereignty, of male or man-made or masculine control, violence, transcendence, impotent import-ance, and so on.

Let's also say, it's feminist *al*logos: that's what she's activating while speaking n+ writing and speaking n+ writing otherwise as if she were speaking or writing nothing or else nothing audible or legible. As Bette Davis is quoted as saying, "when a man gives his opinion, he's a man. When a woman gives her opinion, she's a bitch" (*The Telegraph*). Yeah, what a pitch.

So are you kinda or I'm just saying something like that there is a little too much to say or almost nothing else to say?! Who would buy such a pretext? At any rate, what had been promised, *par moi* (by me, yes), to our dear editor Robin, a good woman, what was supposed to be given to her, even in the abstract, isn't—well, I see this other one—coming and what I have been on about so far is positively not *this* one that may not be coming at all:

> How does language figure in feminist theory, why does it matter, and for whom? Focusing on the auto-critical creativity of feminist discourses, this chapter reframes a set of now-familiar meta-theoretical questions on the sobjectivity[1] of "feminist" *logos* (logic, language, law) or *allgos*, as well as its sociopolitical ontology and phenomenology, to highlight its enduring relevance to the vibrant inter- and trans-lingualism of feminism today, not simply multi-. From "a woman" who "I ain't?" (Sojourner Truth, 1851) to "(a) woman" "one becomes" (Simone de Beauvoir, 1949), from the one in need of "a room of one's own" (Virginia Woolf, 1929) to the one in a suffocatingly "subaltern" situation room (Gayatri Spivak, 1985/8), from one gendered "F" to "someone" whose gender remains troubled/troubling (Judith Butler, 1990) to the point of being undocumented/undocumentable (Dean Spade, 2008) now in increasingly internationalized legal contexts, all these ones finding themselves thus "housed" (Martin Heidegger, 1947) in or outside "*L'ecriture feminine*" (Hélène Cixous, 1976), are still searching for their own, and yet open-ended, languages—in transit—analog and digital alike. In this vein, the second half of this chapter will offer some theoretical notes towards interlingual and translingual feminism in the making, while articulating its theoretical topos in relation to the more readily recognized paradigms of intersectionality, transnationality, and transdisciplinarity.

You call this an abstract. You called it an abstract. You call this abstract? Yes, I did and now I, too, see this quite abstract, maybe too. A paragraph this abstract, while promising, I should now fess up, isn't what I should've tried. Not having kept my word, I seem to be abstracting something new from there, anyway, an old truth about me being nothing abstract, for real.

My abstract plan failed miserably concretely, beyond the line beyond which death is the only certainty, perhaps not unlike Heidegger's *Dasein*, the "there-being" constantly approaching its deadlines, quotidian or ontologician (a rhyme is not just for a musician), and as far as I am concerned, there was no Plan B as there is no (such a thing as) Plan B in my dictionary anyway that begins and ends at an A, so to speak. My excuse? I realize I didn't and don't have the diction I need to "say it" right as in I knew I didn't have it as in I actually don't need it, come to think of it. I mean if I were, as it were, some Monsieur des Cartes, I could have played my card and say OK I'm just still "thinking," OK? Fair enough, that -king said n done or gone already, whether it is still alive and kicking or still(-being-)born, that still is beside the point, for there still seems so much to say or nothing else to say, some sorta, some kinda conundrum of loud silence now talking to itself taken to Its Other Selves . . .

. . . in what sort of language, though?

She who enters and inhabits, while at times wandering around and across, the world of what, for instance, Helene Cixous calls "womanly writing" (*l'ecriture feminine*, my translation) (Cixous), laughingly into and out of a room of her own as if to keep from crying, often responds to something already said (*logos*) by trying to state something to be said by herself (too) or—and this could be more interesting—by not responding right or at all.

What's new, though?

True enough, this way or route of writing,

> basically fluid (milky, orgasmic, oceanic), not solid, which, in counter-masculinist gestures, recycles and reinscribes some archaic "menstrual" marks all over in one way or another, enacting a sort of literary Jackson Pollocking of menstrual blood, in some compensatory or recuperative modes. One can then, man or woman, easily fall into the trap of reactionary or retrograde gender essentialism or semio-capitalism, going all the way, and mainly one way, as if the meaning of the "the flow of body" were now, suddenly, irreversibly renaturalized. Yet it has also been genealogically concocted, culturally orchestrated, historically sedimented, already: "given how the human body sees and hears itself in its reversibility ... what remains quite mysterious here is how that mute world ever receives a structure, that is, is the body biological or psychological or cultural in its linguistic orientation?" (Olkowski, "The End of Phenomenology" 76), in its *linguistic* orientation, wonders Dorothea Olkowski, as I do here, with Maurice Merleau-Ponty of *The Visible and Invisible*. What would be that very connective tissue ("reversibility") for two-way relationality, which "borders the body and language (Olkowski, "Merleau-Ponty" 355)"? (Lee, "Just Throw Like a Bleeding Philosopher" 28)

So again, "she," Antigone for one, the screamatrix who at times "can't stop screaming" (Butler) at and out of contradictions, remains such a model (monster [menstrual]) minority for many, time after time, many turning into countless daughters and sisters of the nymph Echo, "the girl with no door on her mouth" (Carson 131) to cite Sophocles sighted by Anne Carson, who also notes,

> It is an axiom of ancient Greek and Roman medical theory and anatomical discussion that a woman has two mouths. The orifice through which vocal activity takes place and the orifice through which sexual activity take place are both denoted by the word *stoma* in Greek (*os* in Latin) with the addition of adverbs *ano* or *kato* to differentiate upper mouth from lower mouth. Both the vocal and the genital mouth are connected to the body by a neck (*auchen* in Greek, cervix in Latin). Both mouths provide access to a hollow cavity which is guarded by lips that are best kept closed. (131)

And so, if mum's the word indeed in deed, as Theresa Cha says or does in some novel ways,

> From the back of her neck she releases her shoulders free. She swallows once more.... Swallows with last efforts last wills against the pain that wishes it to speak. She allows others. In place of her. Admits others to make full. Make swarm. All barren cavities to make swollen. The others each occupying her. (Chapter 3)

So those otherwise mute bodies, with the q-fem "lipthinker" (Lee, "Lipthink. Anyone?" and "Toward a Moral Theory of Sex") here, are saying that "woman is that creature who puts the inside on the outside" (Carson 129), whose "definitive tendency to put the inside on the outside could" (Carson 136) turn (out) provocative, more evocative than necessary, or else smoother, depending on other neighboring factors, insofar as "the doubling and interchangeability of mouth engenders a creature in whom sex is cancelled out by sound and sound is cancelled out by sex" (Carson 136); then, all four lips given, or eight, or more, "how should one lip*think* with the other, not just sync?" (Lee, "Lipthink. Anyone?" 191), one wonders—how one could approach the book of some "womanly" nature, a "restless burial site, an unsettled grave" (Lee, "Lipthink. Anyone?" 122), to revocalize Lynne Huffer's apt description of her feminist queer lip book, *Are the Lips a Grave?* (Huffer).

Well, sound her out, who would weird you out; "In all our misery. Hear us! Oh say Yes—" again, like Antigone too. So you get the edge, if not exactly "the picture." You hear the double edge of the one, this strange one not gone who—remember!—also said, "father, I'll help you; calm now, easy ... step by step, our steps together, lean your aged body on my loving arm" (Sophocles 295). Hear the barely heard-of, see the terrifyingly abyssal, no, not abysmal, "foreignness" (Meltzer 171) of her Antigonean desire; "even the etymology of her name suggests that the foreign ... is tied to Antigone's love for her father" (Meltzer 171) ... a foreign mummy, then, love?

In sum? Such a naturally foreign, estrogeniously estranged woman "Antigone" not gone yet or gone elsewhere in outside, assuming that such other gene or countergenealogy must or else should be surviving the "shattered" family "somelsewhere," (Lee, "Review of *the Collected Poems of Barbara Guest*") in this space of a relatively quieter if no less melodramatic theoretical speech of some sort, we would want to stay tuned to the rings of murmurings, to what springs from the innards n+ the outskirts of feminist alter-native-languaging, finding our way across, since "our crooked fingers are soft, soft, all my parent's children" (White), as a poet says, applying her lotion poethically.

Then I was going to stop there, but then, Robin, as I was telling you the other day, I found myself called into another zone of femlang. Not abandoning our project—(no, never), trust me, Goodman—I just had to go writing elsewhere for a while with another friend Jamieson, a good psycho-analyricist, with another *moi* in you or you in another *moi*, in "metony#metoo" (Lee and Webster), the "poetics, power, primal" scene of it all still unfolding as we speak.

What goes into and comes out of all these feminist speech acts including silent interactions? The first winkers must have been feminists, I wonder, if the first wanker is ... God knows.

Writing to another deadline, *this* day finally on, I see, I am suddenly reminded of Mina Loy, a centrifu*gal* from the futural past, whose faces I feel compelled to see again here.

Welcome to the twenty-first-century transatlantic avant-garde modernist gypsy poet Mina. Her mad scribbles circa 1913–14 "on the eve of a devastating psychological upheaval," (Loy, "Feminist Manifesto" 153) reappearing in the "Feminist Manifesto" of Yes-and-No along with "Aphorism in Futurism" at the turn of the twentieth century, written *as* a counterdiscourse to the "*Ma*nifesto of Futurism" (1909, my emphasis) by F. T. Marinetti, remain curiously, concurrently, contemporary:

Is that all you want?
And if you honestly desire to find your level without prejudice—be Brave & deny at the outset—that pa-
thetic clap-trap war cry Woman is the
equal of man—

                                        for
She is NOT! (Loy, "Feminist Manifesto" 153)

DIE in the Past
Live in the Future.

THE velocity of velocities arrives in starting.
. . .
TIME is the dispersion of intensiveness.
THE Futurist can live a thousand years in one poem.
. . .
LOOKING on the past you arrive at "Yes," but be-fore
you can arrive upon it you have already arrived at "NO."
. . .
THUS shall evolve the language of the Future.

. . .
ACCEPT the tremendous truth of Futurism
Leaving all those

                                                    —Knick-knacks.

                              —Loy, "Aphorisms on Futurism" 149–51

So, woman, is she or is she "<u>NOT equal of man</u>"? Does she or does she not have her
"thing(y)"? Why are you saying her mouth is saying no and her (other) mouth is saying
yes? How can she and cannot speak? Or, if we need to ask again, can she, say, the sub-
intern today, speak? Why does she and does not exist? I mean, "ain't I a woman?," thus
asketh Soujourner Truth, already, a long long time ago, <u>INNIT?!</u>, and, listen, she is, we
are all, getting just too tired … of <u>ALL THAT</u> is not that jazzy, not even bunny funny. If
she is not dead (yet), when is she, that "second sex" (de Beuavoir), coming—and if yes,
is she second-coming like a white Christ or a black Jesus (Grant) or a gray someone or
an entirely different character, not just transitory or transitional but categorically transformative and transportable? Neither simply Hellenic or Hebraic—who among us still
thinks that those little alphabetic boxes explain and exhaust planetary beings including
underlings and "trimmings" (Mullen)?—such transcategorically kinetic, auto-formative,
novel women of the day seem to be springing ex-cross-binarily and n+dimensionally
from all over the world, from some "other" Continents or "third" world altogether at this
very moment. Do you need evidence, still?

Stop reading this word and stop rescuing the world just to excuse yourself for wanting
to feel good about yourself, but, more simply, not just in theory, roll again, with some odd
aunties like Loy, into this ambivalent, timeless future, yes-and-but-no, of the self-splitting,
self-exploring, self-exploding, trans-generative, self-confronting language of the auto-
altering *femme*, this endless, eternalized *fem* question of itself—or herself, her-selves.

Wave after wave, four times or five times or it really ain't matter, in such "F-words"
in whatever language, in those linguistic enablers and shapers of the evolving world of
feminism, is emerging an F-world, each time anew, each place a part of some others,
and on each occasion, each movement is emergent, corrective, theoretical and active,
all at once.

Right, why not saying it, saving it, *doran*slating it,[2] all those F-words with or without
flowers in your hair or bare head ok too—with, in any case, critical creativity n creative
concision, with a femmiotic swerve from phallogocentrifeudallfilosophers n a translingual
philos for all the SOPHIAs IN Y'All I.N.D.E.E.D., IN "deeds not words," ("Deeds, not

Words"). YEAH, WHY NOT, WHY BOTHER, BROTHER?! AT HOME n ABROAD & IN STREET n AT SCHOOL n ON SCREEN & IN TRANSIT & IN TRANSLATION & IN TRANS-GENRE n INTERGENRE n ALL GENRES say it, transphilopoetically, transphilopoethically, transphilopolitically, transpolipoetically, transpolipoethically, transphilopolipoethically as if in trance, yes, yes, I'm saying it, and I say, say it—to y'all—to say it more by saying it no more.

The revolution begins at home.

—Cherríe Moraga and Gloria Anzaldúa, *This Bridge Called My Back*

Appendix

UMMAnifesto 2018

North South East West No Matter Y'all Matter, Our Dear Mother KIM Il SOON Says

Transcribed by Q aka Kyoo Lee

Inspired by "UMMA: MASS GAMES—Motherly Love North Korea" Solo Exhibition by Mina Cheon aka KIM IL SOON Ethan Cohen Fine Arts, NYC, New York, October 20, 2017–January 11, 2018

1. *Aujourd'hui, maman est morte* (Today, *m* is dead), Albert Camus once said, but hon, don u ever be sad: LOOK, our *Umma* Koreana's here, to stay, for u, for us, today, tomorrow.

2. Ignore her not, however poor or sour she might look and sound: LISTEN Y'all, she could be a messenger from a certain future only an art of the possible could tell—perhaps.

3. The father and the son show and tell, show off and tell you off sometimes, yet the mother and daughter in them just play, play a game even you can play including THIS.

4. Follow me, says Kim Il SOON to appear in the *Umma*ssgame of sincerity and security that asks not what the country can do for you but what you can do for the country, yeah.

5. Our Dear Reader new neighbor leader scholar teacher mother speaker Kim could be our new Michael Jackson of the world for we R the world we R the children *oui n'est-ce pas?*

NOTES

1 "(S)object that exists in a perpetual procedural loop, a perpetual substantive eclipse" (Fitterman and Place 38).
2 "*Dorans*," an old-fashioned vernacular Korean pronunciation of "trans," refers to an electronic transformer; as a naturalized, although now antiquated, "foreign" word still circulated in everyday Korean, it shows an influence from "Japanese" (*dorans*cription, as it were, of) English, a curious postcolonial intercultural trace.

WORKS CITED

Atwood, Margaret. "Poems Twice Told." *Second Words: Selected Critical Prose. 1960–1982*. Toronto: House of Anansi P, 2000.

Butler, Judith. "Can't Stop Screaming." *Public Books*. A Review of Ann Carson's *Antigonick*, 2012. http://www.publicbooks.org/cant-stop-screaming.

Carson, Anne. "The Gender of Sound." *Glass, Irony, and God*. New York: New Directions, 1992.

Cha, Theresa Hak Kyung. *Dictee*. San Francisco: Tanam P, 1982.

Cixous, Hélène. "The Laugh of the Medusa." Trans. Keith Cohen and Paula Cohen. *Signs* 1.4 (Summer, 1976): 875–93.

de Beauvoir, Simone. *Le deuxième sexe*. Paris: Gallimard, 1949.

"Deeds. Not Words." https://blog.oxforddictionaries.com/tag/deeds-not-words/.

Fitterman, Robert, and Vanessa Place. *Notes on Conceptualisms*. New York: Ugly Duckling P, 2009.

Grant, Jacquelyn. *White Women's Christ and Black Women's Jesus: Feminist Christology and Womanist Response*. Atlanta, GA: Scholars P, 1989.

Huffer, Lynne. *Are the Lips a Grave? A Queer Feminist on the Ethics of Sex*. New York: Columbia UP, 2013.

Lee, Kyoo. "Just Throw Like a Bleeding Philosopher: Menstrual Pauses & Poses. Betwixt Hypatia & Bhubaneswari. Half-Visible. Almost Illegible." *Feminist Phenomenology Futures*. Ed. Dorothea Olkowski and Helen Fielding. Bloomington: Indiana UP, 2017.

Lee, Kyoo. "Lipthink. Anyone? On, Lips Apart, Disagreeing *with* You … For a Queer Feminist *Rect*ification?" *differences* 27.3 (2016): 119–31.

Lee, Kyoo. "Review of *the Collected Poems of Barbara Guest* by Barbara Guest." *Brooklyn Rail*. April 1, 2017. https://brooklynrail.org/2017/04/criticspage/Barbara-Guest-The-Collected-Poems-of-Barbara-Guest.

Lee. Kyoo. "Review of *Revivals: Of Antigone* by William Robert." *philo*SOPHIA 7.2 (2017).

Lee, Kyoo. "Toward a Moral Theory of Sex. Its Lipkinkiness: On Oral, Labial, Dental Caesura, Fermata, Aria." *Feminist Formations* 29.3 (2017): 172–8.

Lee, Kyoo, and Jamieson Webster. "The Formal Ethics of Metony#metoo: Poethics. Power. Primal Scene." *Public Seminar*, April 18, 2018. http://www.publicseminar.org/2018/04/the-formative-power-of-metonymetoo/.

Loy, Mina. "Aphorisms on Futurism." *The Lost Lunar Baedeker: Poems of Mina Loy*. New York: Farrar, Straus and Giroux, 2015.

Loy, Mina. "Feminist Manifesto." *The Lost Lunar Baedeker: Poems of Mina Loy*. New York: Farrar, Straus and Giroux, [1913] 2015.

Meltzer, Françoise. "Theories of Desire—Antigone Again." *Critical Inquiry* 37.2 (2011): 171.

Modern History Sourcebook: Sojourner Truth. "Ain't I a Woman?" December 1851. https://sourcebooks.fordham.edu/mod/sojtruth-woman.asp.

Mullen, Harryette. *Trimmings*. New York: Tender Buttons Books, 1991.

Olkowski, Dorothea. "The End of Phenomenology." *Hypatia* 15.3 (Summer 2000).

Olkowski, Dorothea. "Merleau-Ponty: the Demand for Mystery in Language." *Philosophy Today* 31.4 (Winter 1987).

Sophocles. "*Oedipus at Colonus*" *Sophocles: The Three Theban Plays*. Trans. Robert Fagles. New York: Penguin Books, 1984.

The Telegraph. "Feminist Quotes That Have Fuelled the Debate." https://www.telegraph.co.uk/film/suffragette/famous_feminist_quotes/.

White, Simone. "Lotion." *Harpers' Magazine*. August 2016. https://harpers.org/archive/2016/08/lotion/.

CHAPTER TWELVE

Writing

AIMEE ARMANDE WILSON

A student enrolled in a class titled "Writing by Women" could be forgiven for thinking this class is interchangeable with one called "Women in Literature." Yet, the subtle differences in title imply not-so-subtle distinctions in approach. "Writing by Women" suggests a focus on authorship. In other words, the author's gender is the primary criterion by which texts would be selected for inclusion or exclusion. The subject matter addressed by these texts is secondary. By contrast, "Women in Literature" implies a dual focus on both subject matter and author. This course would presumably address the depiction of women within works of literature by men and women, as well as literature written by women, and perhaps even the role of women in the literary profession. Both course titles rest on the assumption that "women" is an identifiable and valid category around which to build a course, an assumption challenged by poststructuralist critics. These titles and the methodological approaches they imply outline the main debates waged and questions asked about writing within feminist circles.

In sum, debates can be placed into three categories: those addressing "writing" as a literary tradition (recovery of writing by women as well as patterns in the depiction of female characters); those addressing "writing" as a gendered style (whether women write differently than men); and those questioning the validity or utility of gender as a concept for analyzing writing. Overlaps between categories exist, of course, and debates are often much messier in practice than these categories suggest, but this framework is nevertheless useful for understanding the broad strokes of feminist thinking about writing. This chapter will provide a historical overview of these three categories while also discussing, in turn, modern inflections of these debates as regards the most important factor affecting writing in the twenty-first century, the internet.

"Writing" in this context most often refers to literature—texts that are purposefully creative and imaginative—yet, the term occasionally, and increasingly, connotes texts produced for other purposes, such as communication, self-expression, or as an aid to memory. Examples of these other kinds of writing would be letters, diaries, and shopping lists. These genres are particularly relevant when addressing the subject of women writers since women have historically been less likely to produce creative texts and to have their lives written about by others. Theorists focused on authorship and subject matter increasingly value these varieties of ephemeral and private writing as important records of women's lives.

Poststructuralist conceptions of "writing" are more complex and deserve a brief explanation. Generally, poststructuralists reject the notion that writing is a straightforward means of communication or self-expression. For these theorists, a word does not signify directly, does not point to an object or idea in the world in a one-to-one correspondence. What one person means by "mother" can be quite different from what another person means, and even one person's use of the word "mother" can conjure several different concepts at the same time (this variability is key to much poetic language). Far from orderly systems, languages are highly variable and imprecise. The relationship between the word "dog," for example, and actual dogs is arbitrary; there is no reason why these particular animals should be labeled with the signifier d-o-g. In this line of thinking, words do not contain meaning in themselves but derive meaning from their position within the language. A young child's notion of "dog" may be so capacious as to include every animal that is soft and walks on four legs. Over time, however, the child learns that the signifier "dog" does not include animals with hooves nor animals that meow. The meaning of "dog" rests on its difference from "sheep" and "cat." Similarly, "woman" has historically been defined in patriarchal societies as the opposite, negative, or inverse of everything that defines "man": if men are strong, women are weak; if men are rational, women are illogical. The word "man" has meaning only by virtue of what is not man. This point has important implications for the concept of "women's writing" since, according to this line of thought, "women's writing" continues to define women against men. "Women's writing," then, is a category that inadvertently subjugates women because it continues, implicitly, to define writing produced by women as marginal, as somehow different from the patriarchal norm.

RECOVERY AND WOMEN'S LITERARY TRADITIONS

In 1979, Elaine Showalter argued for the importance of scholarship on writing produced by all women, not just the "great" authors. She claimed, "Before we can even begin to ask how the literature of women would be different and special, we need to reconstruct its past, to rediscover the scores of women novelists, poets, and dramatists whose work has been obscured by time, and to establish the continuity of the female tradition from decade to decade" ("Toward" 137). Showalter's argument echoed Virginia Woolf's well-known declaration on the subject of a female canon: "we *think back through our mothers* if we are women" (75). At the time Showalter was writing, feminist recovery efforts were well under way, having begun some twenty years earlier in the 1960s. Labeled "gynocriticism" by Showalter, feminists attempted to understand "women *as writers*, and its subjects are the history, styles, themes, genres, and structures of writing by women" ("Feminist" 248). The central questions asked by gynocritics are "how can we constitute women as a distinct literary group?" and "What is *the difference* of women's writing?" (248). The latter question highlights a principle that unifies gynocritics: writing produced by women is fundamentally different from that produced by men and therefore deserves its own canon, traditions, and methodologies for analysis. Showalter distinguished gynocriticism from feminist criticism, which she defines as scholarship concerned with demonstrating the ways in which literature and literary scholarship has demeaned, belittled, or otherwise maligned women. Today, however, few feminists maintain this distinction, siding in favor of "feminist criticism" as an umbrella term covering both types.

In an attempt to define a female literary tradition, scholars such as Showalter, Susan Gubar, Sandra Gilbert, Alice Walker, and Shari Benstock spearheaded efforts to recover— that is, bring to greater public attention—forgotten or overlooked women writers. The works of writers such as Kate Chopin and Zora Neale Hurston are in print today largely due to recovery efforts.[1] The need for recovery stems from multiple causes. First and most obviously, skilled women writers have always struggled to find publishers and audiences due to persistent efforts on the part of patriarchal societies to silence women. The issue is magnified for poor women and women of color. When women did manage to find publishers and audiences, their writing was routinely discounted as trivial or unsophisticated. In nineteenth-century America, for example, Nathaniel Hawthorne lamented the "damned mob of scribbling women" whose works were somehow not as good as his own ("scribbling") and, simultaneously, competed with his works for readers (Baym 64). Finally, for many years, scholars considered the writing most commonly produced by women—documents such as letters, diaries, and recipes—to be unworthy of scholarly attention. (Many critics implicitly hold this opinion still today.) Men also produce ephemeral and private writing, of course, but they were much more likely to also produce public documents that would "count" as important, if not in the literary realm than in the historical one. Recovery of women's literary contributions and ephemera is perhaps the most successful and influential endeavor of feminist literary criticism.

Nevertheless, these early efforts to understand women's writing—like Western feminism in general—were insufficiently attentive to the differences between women, particularly regarding race and class. For instance, Sandra Gilbert and Susan Gubar's *Madwoman in the Attic* was widely influential in and out of academia. In it, Gilbert and Gubar craft an argument about women and authorship that revises Harold Bloom's *Anxiety of Influence* from a feminist perspective. Throughout the book, Gilbert and Gubar implicitly assume that female authors share a common experience with regard to literary tradition and that all female readers react in the same ways to the books they read.

In the early 1980s, feminist critics began critiquing the idea of a common "sisterhood," of which *Madwoman* was but one expression among many. bell hooks, for one, argued that mainstream feminism paid little attention to the ways in which black women's experiences were different from those of white women, saying "the upper and middle class white women who were at the forefront of the movement" failed to grapple with racism (87) and, as a result, "the Sisterhood they talked about has not become a reality, and … the hierarchical pattern of race and sex relationships already established in American society merely took a different form under 'feminism'" (121). As Alice Walker's *In Search of Our Mothers' Gardens* made clear, black women's creativity in the United States is as much a product of gender as it is a product of slavery and the continuing existence of racism. Gloria Anzaldúa's proposed solution to the oversimplified "sisterhood" was to recognize and embrace differences. She argued that Mexican-American women are "atravesados," or people who make a home on the borders of geography and culture. Anzaldúa broadened this idea into a promotion of "mestizo" thinking which, she argued, eschews binaries and embraces mixed ethnicities, sexualities, and nationalities. Attention to difference is a central aspect of recovery efforts today, but it remains a difficult and incomplete project. Electronic recovery projects provide new opportunities for recovery because the internet is, in a sense, inherently mestizo, crossing geographic borders in an instant. Yet, as I will discuss, these efforts are only as diverse as their creators make them. Exclusionary practices are often replicated, not erased, from electronic forms of communication.

In the twenty-first century, recovery efforts continue to occupy the traditional publishing landscape but they have also moved online. For example, Persephone Books, based in London, publishes beautiful editions of "neglected fiction and non-fiction by mid-twentieth century (mostly) women writers" ("Welcome"). In the electronic realm, the *Orlando* Project is a compendium of biography and criticism on British women writers with a specific emphasis on recovering neglected authors ("Scholarly Introduction"). The Women Writers Project, based out of Northeastern University, is a similar resource for early modern women's writing.

It may come to pass, however, that recovery efforts in their current form are less necessary since so much writing is now electronic in the form of blogs, emails, and social media posts. These genres make writing by women more widely accessible than it has ever been. Instead of recovery, then, curation is likely to become paramount in electronic environments where the quantity of available information is overwhelming. The proliferation of voices online makes finding the most interesting, relevant, and thoughtful writing difficult, especially since the provocative tends to drown out the thoughtful. The work of people curating electronic-based writing needs to be a process of filtering *forward* quality writing, as opposed to filtering *out*, as in traditional publishing practices.[2]

Furthermore, all the prejudices that exist in traditional realms—sexism, racism, homophobia, classism, and so on—are, if anything, exacerbated by the anonymity allowed by the internet. The voices of straight, white, cis,[3] and Anglo-American writers overshadow those of women, people of color, and LGBTQ folks. Since 2010, the VIDA organization has tallied the bylines and book reviews in major literary publications to document gender disparities. As would be expected, men's voices dominated. Many of the outlets included in The Count have since improved their ratios—some drastically—but disparity still exists across the field. In 2015, the organization began including race and ethnicity, sexual identity, and ability in the count and found similarly dispiriting results.[4] Therefore, continued vigilance in the vein of hooks, Walker, and Anzaldúa is necessary. As always, the writing filtered forward will only be as diverse as the curator's determination to make it so. In 1983, when Gayatri Chakravorty Spivak asked, "Can the subaltern speak?"—a question interrogating the extent to which people on the margins of society can have their voices heard—the answer was no. Because access to the internet falls largely on economic lines, and power dynamics on the internet replicate many of the same inequalities that exist offline, the answer is still, to an extent, no. Yet, because of the relative democratization of the internet, writing produced by women, including marginalized women, has a greater chance of attracting a reading audience because of the ability to bypass the publishing industry.[5]

THE "WOMAN'S SENTENCE": GENDERED WRITING STYLES

In 2011, Nobel Prize winning author V. S. Naipaul said, "I read a piece of writing and within a paragraph or two I know whether it is by a woman or not. I think [it is] unequal to me." He went on to say that writing by women is, to his mind, hampered by their "sentimentality" and "narrow view of the world" (quoted in Fallon). The sexism in these comments is both shocking and deliberate; Naipaul surely knew they would feed into a long line of arguments discounting women's writing as too emotional. Galling as these comments are, they do raise a different, relevant question: is it inherently sexist to argue that writing produced by women is different from that produced by men? Virginia Woolf implicitly answered in the negative when, in 1929, she made a feminist argument in favor of women writers looking to other women for inspiration, arguing that there is "no common sentence ready for [a woman writer] to use" because "the weight, the pace, the stride of a man's mind are too unlike her own for her to lift anything substantial from him successfully" (*AROO* 75). In this way, she advocated for the delineation and definition of the "woman's sentence."

Many feminist critics have entered the debate over the existence of a "woman's sentence." For as many theorists arguing that such a sentence exists, and that identifying and valorizing it is a liberating project, just as many theorists argue against it on the grounds that such a pursuit is based on historically determined stereotypes about men and women rather than inherent qualities. For this latter group of theorists, such "inherent qualities," or traits that all women share, do not exist. There is simply too much variation among people who identify as women. Attempting to identify commonalities based on anatomy essentializes women and thereby operates in service of oppression rather than liberation. It is worth noting the dearth of discussion over the "man's sentence" or male writing. Rather, men's writing is assumed to be a reflection of patriarchal culture's positioning masculine values as neutral, standard, or the norm.

Among those critics arguing for the existence of a woman's sentence, disagreement arises over the origins of the difference from men's writing. Some critics argue that these differences stem from structural inequities in patriarchal societies that lead women to experience the world in identifiably different ways. In the 1980s, critics emphasized the mother-daughter relationship as key to understanding the distinctiveness of a female aesthetic (Showalter, "Introduction" 7). Barbara Smith argued that race as well as gender must be accounted for, stating, "Black women writers manifest common approaches to the act of creating literature as a direct result of the specific political, social, and economic experience they have been obliged to share" (174). She goes on to say that this common approach constitutes a specifically "Black female language" that is distinct and worthy of its own body of scholarship.[6]

In contrast to these experience-based theories, French feminists emphasized the role of the body in linguistic differences. The theories of Julia Kristeva and Hélène Cixous, in particular, have been enormously influential, giving rise to countless extensions and revisions. Kristeva's argument is rooted in linguistic structure. She claims that language is heterogenous, that is, composed of distinct but related functions, which she calls the *symbolic* and the *semiotic*. The *symbolic* is that which is colloquially thought of as language, writ large: the syllables, words, and grammar rules that constitute spoken and written language. For Kristeva, however, this definition of language is incomplete. Aspects of language, she argues, exist in excess of or outside the boundaries of this system, aspects that cannot be contained nor repressed by linguistic rules. These excesses are the "rhythms, intonations, glossalalais" of speech (158). They are not meaningful in the way that words, syllables, and phonemes are signifiers that point to a signified. Rather, the *semiotic* arises from the body, from its chaotic drives and functions. In scientific language, the *semiotic* is repressed in favor of the *symbolic,* but can never be repressed completely; poetry, conversely, gives precedence to the *semiotic* (160).

The *semiotic* is associated with the feminine, specifically the maternal, because it is the language infants use before learning the *symbolic*. Kristeva, who is also a psychoanalyst, argues that children begin to use *symbolic* language when they realize they are distinct from the Mother (understood as both an archetype and the individual person) and that the Mother does not always understand nor immediately satisfy the child's needs. Satisfaction of those needs requires communicating them; communicating them requires leaving the primary *semiotic* state and entering the *symbolic*. Kristeva links the *symbolic* to masculinity because it is associated with rules and prohibitions, with the law-giving function of the Father. The child's entrance into the *symbolic* realm—learning to use language—thus "constitutes itself at the cost of repressing instinctual drive and continuous relation to the mother" (Kristeva 161). The semiotic cannot be repressed entirely, however. These random and unavoidable interruptions of the *semiotic* into *symbolic* language give rise to new meaning. The ruptures, Kristeva argues, are revolutionary and generative. Without the *symbolic*, all signification would be babble or delirium. But, without the *semiotic*, all signification would be empty and lack sense in our lives (Oliver 153–4). Ultimately, signification requires both the *semiotic* and *symbolic*, the feminine and the masculine. As Kelly Oliver explains, these gendered associations have real-world implications for artists. If a woman identifies with the *semiotic* in her work, if she creates texts that are nonrepresentational and experimental, she risks not being taken seriously by the social order. Because men are more closely identified with structured, "civilized," *symbolic* language, they have more latitude to be experimental (155).

Like Kristeva, Cixous's theories about writing are rooted in the body. Yet, unlike Kristeva, who argues that all language is composed of feminine and masculine aspects, Cixous argues that certain types of language express the female body—what she calls *écriture féminine* or feminine writing—while most other types of writing manifest patriarchal values. Men are capable of creating *écriture féminine*, but women have easier access to it by virtue of their embodiment. Cixous begins with the long-standing tradition of characterizing the female body as leaky, messy, dirty, or impure because, as she argues, it is overflowing and multiple: menstrual fluid, breast milk, tears, laughter, and the potential for multiple orgasms. These very same aspects of the body, Cixous argues, are what make women potentially disruptive to oppressive regimes:

> Because the "economy" of her drives is prodigious, she cannot fail, in seizing the occasion to speak, to transform directly and indirectly *all* systems of exchange based on masculine thrift. Her libido will produce far more radical effects of political and social change than some might like to think. Because she arrives, vibrant, over and again. (264)

Women's difference from men, their leakiness, is powerful and generous rather than degraded and disgusting. What is needed is a reevaluation of the female body. As Cixous puts it, "You only have to look at the Medusa straight on to see her. And she's not deadly. She's beautiful and laughing" (267). The first step in this dramatic reevaluation of female embodiment is women writing in and through their bodies. The result is *écriture féminine*, writing that is anti-representational, complex, contradictory, and concerned with contingency rather than representation, with cooperation rather than mastery.

In contrast, masculine writing, according to Cixous, emphasizes linear argumentation that demonstrates mastery. It is singular rather than multiple (the "thrift" in the quote above, referring to single orgasm), reductive rather than overflowing (eliminating doubt and confusion), and closed rather than leaky (neatly presented argument with a definable beginning, middle, and end). Common to both Cixous's and Kristeva's theories is the notion that writing produced to suit patriarchal ends arrests the full potential of language, particularly those aspects of language based on play, enjoyment, rhythm, and humor. Writing the woman's sentence means bringing these aspects of language—so common in childhood—back into regular use.

Influential as Kristeva and Cixous have been, many feminists take issue with theories such as these. A main point of contention is the assumption that linearity, multiplicity, abstraction, and other such qualities are gendered in ways that are linked to the body. Critics argue that theories based on the body are essentialist and anti-feminist since attempts to define women by their biology have so often been used to oppress women (consider the way childcare has long been undercompensated on the grounds that such care work is "natural" to women). Moreover, even if multiplicity, circularity, and cooperation are reclaimed as powerful disruptive forces, the concepts of the "woman's sentence" or *écriture féminine* are still based on the idea that "woman" is a definable category. What happens with women who are not capable of childbearing, producing breast milk, or achieving multiple orgasms? Are they not fully women? What about transgender men who menstruate?

In the 1990s, theorists influenced by poststructuralism answered questions such as these in ways that challenged the very notion of "man" and "woman" as identifiable categories. In this vein, the work of Judith Butler, Jack Halberstam, and Eve Kosofsky Sedgwick became foundations on which the fields of gender studies and queer theory were built. For these theorists, gender is powerful but it is also a cultural construct rather than an immutable fact arising from the body. As Butler puts it, "because there is neither an 'essence' that gender expresses or externalizes nor an objective ideal to which gender aspires; because gender is not a fact, the various acts of gender create the idea of gender, and without those acts, there would be no gender at all. Gender is, thus, a construction that regularly conceals its genesis" (190). From this perspective, both gender and sex vary so widely, are such shifty categories, that attempts to identify a "woman's sentence," a style of writing common to all women, are pointless, and the terms "women" and "men" are so plastic as to be useless at best and, at worst, harmful to individuals who do not fit neatly into one category or the other.

The implications of these arguments on feminist criticism have been multiple and momentous. Indeed, they bring into question the validity of the entire enterprise of recovery because the very category of "women's writing" is suspect. What does it mean to delineate a tradition of women's writing if we can't even agree on a definition of "women"? For feminists in the twenty-first century who maintain the legitimacy of the endeavor in light of poststructuralist critiques, the answer to this question most likely references cultural differences. In other words, even if "woman" is a shifty, nonbiological category, people perceived to be female are treated differently in patriarchal societies than are people perceived to be male, and these differences affect writing styles in ways that merit study. These differences are not thought to be monolithic nor universal, but they are nevertheless present and significant.

In Naipaul's aforementioned comment, he criticized women's writing for being sentimental. This aspect of his comment needs further glossing. Writing produced by women is frequently characterized as emotional, private, and autobiographical; unlike in Cixous's *écriture féminine*, these aspects of "confessional" writing are seen as weaknesses rather than revolutionary strengths. In a word, writing by women is often labeled "confessional," a term that has become an assertion of power over women by delegitimizing their writing. Susan Gubar theorized that centuries of artists, implicitly male, positioning the female body as the subject of art or as the blank page on which the artist's creation is inscribed has led "many women [to] experience their own bodies as the only available medium for their art, with the result that the distance between the woman artist and her art is often radically diminished" (299). Gubar goes on to say that this close association of text and female body is what leads so many women artists to choose "personal forms of expression like letters, autobiographies, confessional poetry, diaries, and journals" (299). It is true that many women choose "personal forms of expression," but many others choose impersonal or public forms of writing, such as journalism or biography. These writers do not fit neatly into Naipaul's or Gubar's frameworks but they are not less "womanly" for their choice of genre.

Although the intensely personal, confessional style that characterizes most blogs and social media posts is practically synonymous with many people's understanding of "women's writing" (for right or wrong), blogs and social media posts are nevertheless designed to be public, and often with political intent. These genres therefore necessitate new answers to old questions about privacy, power, style, and gender. At the least, writing produced by women in the twenty-first century is likely to bring about a change in either the connotation of the term *confessional* or a reevaluation of what constitutes personal writing. Blogs, tweets, and posts have replaced diaries for many (though certainly not all), and the easy accessibility of these forms allows larger numbers of people to create written records of their private lives. Interestingly, research indicates that women have historically been heavier users of social media than men, but the gap is decreasing quickly. A study conducted by the Pew Research Center found that, by 2016, 72 percent of women in the United States used at least one form of social media, compared to 66 percent of men ("Social Media Fact Sheet"). As men increasingly engage in this kind of public, diaristic writing, the association between "confessional writing" and women will necessarily become more tenuous. This is not to say that women writers will cease to be delegitimized, but that the label "confessional" or "personal" is less likely to be the tool for that delegitimization.

Virginia Woolf argued that women are drawn to write novels because it is a newer genre than poetry and theater, less concretized by the weight of tradition and more amenable to new approaches such as those imagined by women writers (*AROO* 76). A century later, the same theory might apply to writing found on blogs and in social media. The short, episodic form of the blog/social media post is easier for caregivers to create (overwhelmingly women, still). Furthermore, these genres are low-stakes and take little start-up time and money, which means women—historically lacking in encouragement, role models, and resources for writing—can more readily try their hand at it without much risk in terms of money and time. Of course, most blogs and posts will never amount to more than momentary records of interest to a small audience, but a growing number of people receive book contracts after creating a successful blog or website that addresses intensely personal issues in a manner some might call confessional. "Mommy blogs" like Heather Armstrong's *Dooce* have been particularly lucrative, and Julie Powell's *The Julie/Julia Project*, in which Powell documents her attempt to cook every recipe in Julia Child's *Mastering the Art of French Cooking* in one year, is a well-known example of a popular blog-cum-book (and eventually movie). While these blogs address subject matters that would historically be classified as "women's issues," female bloggers deal with many other issues, of course. For instance, the writer behind *Baghdad Burning*, a blog that later became a book, is known only by the pseudonym Riverbend and, at the time of writing the blog, was a young Iraqi woman living in Baghdad. She began the blog in 2003 to chronicle her life during the US occupation (Ridgeway xi–xii). While Riverbend's gender is certainly important to the unfolding events, her subject matter ranges far beyond those issues typically called "women's." Indeed, war is considered by some to be a "man's" issue, but such labels imply that Riverbend either cannot or should not write about war, an implication that is facile and erroneous.

The public nature of such "confessional" writing is not without risks. The personal essay boom of the late aughts and early teens is a case in point. Essays that were personal, shocking, and often gross mushroomed in this era's clickbait culture. As Jia Tolentino points out, these essays were most often written by women: "an ad-based publishing model built around maximizing page views quickly and cheaply creates uncomfortable incentives for writers, editors, and readers alike … The commodification of personal experience was also women's territory: the small budgets of popular women-focussed [*sic*] Web sites, and the rapidly changing conventions and constrictions surrounding women's lives, insured it." Writers who produced essays of this sort often endured significant emotional tolls as reader reactions ranged from dismissal and teasing to outright scorn, disgust, and threats. "Placing a delicate part of your life in the hands of strangers didn't always turn out to be so thrilling," writes Tolentino. "Personal essays cry out for identification and connection; what their authors often got was distancing and shame." Whereas Tolentino argues that this toll helped to bring about an end to this particular iteration of the personal essay, Arielle Bernstein argues that it has simply passed into a new phase. She claims, "what we are instead experiencing is an evolution—of writers being encouraged to not simply mine personal feelings for a quick click, but to make connections between the personal and the political more explicit." Like the second-wave feminist mantra "the personal is political," these writers strive to show the ramifications of political actions on the individual's daily life. Increasingly, feminist critics are acknowledging that this kind of middle-brow writing is an important cultural artifact and worthy of scholarly attention.

The shaming experienced by bloggers is only a small aspect of the violence that often accompanies online writing. Cyberbullying and stalking are rampant, with women, people of color, and LGBTQ folks receiving death threats with disturbing regularity. For example, in 2012, Anita Sarkeesian, a feminist media critic, launched a KickStarter campaign to study gendered tropes in video games. Her campaign, while financially successful, also brought her a steady stream of death, rape, and bomb threats as well as other forms of harassment that continue today (Parkin). While many media outlets have promised to curb online harassment, it generally continues unchecked, due in part to a lack of ability or, at times, a lack of willingness to punish harassers as criminals (Sweeney). Sexism is also an issue behind the scenes of the internet. Numerous studies document the gender disparities in Silicon Valley (McGee). Those women who do enter the profession often endure hostile work environments. For example, a recent study by a Facebook engineer found that "code written by female engineers at the company gets rejected 35 percent more often than that written by their male peers" (Cauterucci). (The study's author attributed the discrimination to knowledge of the writer's gender, not to a difference in the way women write code.) Women's careers are thus hampered by the same gender bias evident in traditional publishing spheres.

Furthermore, Anne Balsamo notes that many hackers believe that "hackers are gender- and color-blind due to the fact that they communicate (primarily) through text-based network channels" (147). Balsamo refutes this claim, stating, "this assertion rests on the assumption that 'text-based channels' represent a gender-neutral medium of exchange, that language itself is free from any form of gender, race, or ethnic determinations. Both of these assumptions are called into question not only by feminist research on electronic communication and interpretive theory, but also by female network users who participate in cyberpunk's virtual subculture" (147). The technology might be new, but the cultural biases are old.

The complicated relationship between embodiment and identity online is usefully highlighted by electronic writing styles that are self-consciously literary and/or formally experimental. Electronic literature, also called e-lit, is " 'digital born,' a first-generation digital object created on a computer and (usually) meant to be read on a computer"; most definitions of e-lit "exclude print literature that has been digitized" (Hayles 3). Writers of electronic literature are increasingly taking advantage of the internet's affordances to play with form in ways that involve the body. As Hayles explains, authors are using sound and animated text; incorporating game elements; and constructing three-dimensional spaces in which users can interact with the words in a narrative (7–11). Another form of e-lit, called "locative narrative," takes advantage of mobile technology to tell stories as listeners follow a specified route (Hayles 11). The genre of locative narrative, like e-lit in general, will only become more immersive as the power and ubiquity of electronic technology increases. Already by 1984, Donna Haraway could persuasively argue that our bodies were hybrids of machine and flesh: "By the late twentieth century, our time, a mythic time, we are all chimeras, theorized and fabricated hybrids of machine and organism; in short, we are cyborgs" (150). Haraway contends that this border between machine and flesh has been a fraught, contentious one, "a border war" (150), similar to the ways in which identity is often a source of contention among feminists. This need not be the case, she argues. Focusing instead on affinities that exist across and between identity categories, including gender, offers a way around binaristic thinking (me/you, us/them, man/woman, white/black) that has historically organized Western societies. Immersive varieties of literature, along with other technological developments using the internet, will only intensify the fusion of machine and flesh; this, combined with the ease with which people can adopt and shed personae on the internet, makes it plausible to argue that the internet will hasten the dissolution of binaristic thinking, an eventuality that would surely be welcomed by poststructuralists.

Yet, in many ways, identity—or at least the stereotypes associated with an identity—is further entrenched, enacted, and defended online. Sherry Turkle, for example, shares numerous stories of people who adopt online identities with genders that are different than their "real life" identities. The ability to play with identity is lauded by many media theorists, yet, as Turkle notes, such gendered "passing" requires adopting and adhering to rigid gender codes, particularly as regards communication patterns. She states, "To pass as a woman [in an online chatroom] for any length of time requires understanding how gender inflects speech, manner, the interpretation of experience" (212). Turkle notes that some regular users make a game out of trying to guess the "real" gender of the person behind the online identity, and do so along stereotypical lines. For instance, one user judges others based on the assumption that men care more about physical appearance than women: "Pavel Curtis ... observed that when a female-presenting character is called something like FabulousHotBabe, one can be almost sure there is a man behind the mask" (211). As this example suggests, attempts to pass as a different gender often reaffirm stereotypes about gendered writing patterns rather than affording experimentation and novelty. In this sense, the "woman's sentence" risks being defined by stereotypes about women rather than the sentences women actually produce.

Neither moving away from binaristic thinking, as many poststructuralist critics desire, nor revaluing those binaries, as many other feminists hope to see, will be a quick process. The internet facilitates people's *ability* to play with identity, but having the ability to change one's identity does not mean people will want to do so, nor does it mean people will cease judging others based on the identities they assume. As with airplanes, stem-cell research, and other life-changing technologies, the capabilities afforded by the internet outpace ethical and legal decisions about the desirability of these capabilities. Feminist ideas about writing are an important aspect of this theorization, particularly as the relationship between bodies, identities, and writing is further stretched, tangled, and revised by technological developments.

NOTES

1 For more on Chopin's recovery, see Toth, pp. 402–6. On the recovery of Hurston, see West, pp. 229–48.
2 I draw the term "filter forward" from library and information sciences discourse, where it is often used in reference to the work of open access publishers such as the Public Library of Science.
3 Schilt and Westbrook explain that "*Cis* is the Latin prefix for 'on the same side'. It compliments *trans*, the prefix for 'across' or 'over'. 'Cisgender' replaces the terms 'nontransgender' or 'bio man/bio woman' to refer to individuals who have a match between the gender they were assigned at birth, their bodies, and their personal identity" (461).
4 For more information, see www.vidaweb.org.
5 I say "relative democratization" because large numbers of people across the globe—including portions of the United States—cannot access the internet on a regular basis.
6 While disagreeing with Smith on the existence of a "Black female language," Deborah E. McDowell agrees that literary criticism, including feminist literary criticism, has largely ignored or maligned black women writers.

WORKS CITED

Anzaldúa, Gloria. *Borderlands/La Frontera: The New Mestiza*, 4th edn. San Francisco, CA: Aunt Lute Books, [1987] 2012.

Balsamo, Anne. *Technologies of the Gendered Body: Reading Cyborg Women*. Durham, NC: Duke UP, 1995.

Baym, Nina. "Melodramas of Beset Manhood: How Theories of American Fiction Exclude Women Authors." *The New Feminist Criticism: Essays on Women, Literature, and Theory*. Ed. Elaine Showalter, 1st edn. New York: Pantheon Books, 1985, pp. 63–80.

Bernstein, Arielle. "The 'Personal Essay Boom' Is Dead. Long Live the Personal Essay!" *Salon*, June 11, 2017.

Butler, Judith. *Gender Trouble: Feminism and the Subversion of Identity*. New York: Routledge, [1990] 2006.

Cauterucci, Christina. "Analysis Suggests Code from Female Facebook Engineers Gets Rejected More Often than Code From Men." *Slate XX Factor*, May 3, 2017.

Cixous, Hélène. "The Laugh of the Medusa." *French Feminism Reader*. Ed. Kelly Oliver. Lanham, MD: Rowman & Littlefield, 2000, pp. 257–75.

Fallon, Amy. "VS Naipaul Finds No Woman Writer His Literary Match—Not Even Jane Austen." *Guardian*, June 1, 2011.

Gilbert, Sandra M., and Susan Gubar. *The Madwoman in the Attic: The Woman Writer and the Nineteenth-Century Literary Imagination*. New Haven, CT: Yale UP, (1979) 2000.

Gubar, Susan. "'The Blank Page' and the Issues of Female Creativity." *The New Feminist Criticism: Essays on Women, Literature, and Theory*. Ed. Elaine Showalter, 1st edn. New York: Pantheon Books, 1985, pp. 292–313.

Haraway, Donna. "A Cyborg Manifesto: Science, Technology, and Socialist-Feminism in the Late Twentieth Century." *Simians, Cyborgs and Women: The Reinvention of Nature*. New York: Routledge, [1984] 1991, pp. 149–81.

Hayles, N. Katherine. *Electronic Literature: New Horizons for the Literary*. Notre Dame, IN: U of Notre Dame P, 2008.

hooks, bell. *Ain't I a Woman*. London: Pluto Press, [1981] 1987.

Kristeva, Julia. "From One Identity to An Other." *French Feminism Reader*. Ed. Kelly Oliver. Lanham, MD: Rowman & Littlefield, 2000, pp. 158–65.

McDowell, Deborah E. "New Directions for Black Feminist Criticism." *The New Feminist Criticism: Essays on Women, Literature, and Theory*. Ed. Elaine Showalter, 1st edn, New York: Pantheon Books, 1985, pp. 186–99.

McGee, Suzanne. "Silicon Valley's Gender Problem Extends Beyond Pay Gap." *Guardian*, March 6, 2016.

Oliver, Kelly. "Maternity, Feminism, and Language: Julia Kristeva." *French Feminism Reader*. Ed. Kelly Oliver. Lanham, MD: Rowman & Littlefield, 2000, pp. 153–8.

Orlando Project. "Scholarly Introduction." Cambridge: Cambridge UP.

Parkin, Simon. Gamergate: A Scandal Erupts in the Video-Game Community." *New Yorker*, October 17, 2014.

Ridgeway, James. Introduction. *Baghdad Burning: Girl Blog from Iraq*. New York: Feminist P, 2005, pp. xi–xxiii.

Riverbend. *Baghdad Burning: Girl Blog from Iraq*. New York: Feminist Press, 2005.

Schilt, Kristen, and Laurel Westbrook. "Doing Gender, Doing Heteronormativity: 'Gender Normals', Transgender People, and the Social Maintenance of Heterosexuality." *Gender & Society* 23.4 (August 2009): 440–64.

Showalter, Elaine. "Feminist Criticism in the Wilderness." *Critical Inquiry* 8.2 (1981): 179–205.

Showalter, Elaine. "Introduction: The Feminist Critical Revolution." *The New Feminist Criticism: Essays on Women, Literature, and Theory*. Ed. Elaine Showalter, 1st edn. New York: Pantheon Books, 1985, pp. 3–17.

Showalter, Elaine. "Toward a Feminist Poetics." *The New Feminist Criticism: Essays on Women, Literature, and Theory*. Ed. Elaine Showalter, 1st edn. New York: Pantheon Books, 1985, pp. 125–43.

Smith, Barbara. "Toward a Black Feminist Criticism." *The New Feminist Criticism: Essays on Women, Literature, and Theory*. Ed. Elaine Showalter, 1st edn. New York: Pantheon Books, 1985, pp. 168–85.

"Social Media Fact Sheet." *Pew Research Center*, January 12, 2017.

Spivak, Gayatri Chakravorty. "Can the Subaltern Speak?" *Marxism and the Interpretation of Culture*. Ed. Cary Nelson and Lawrence Grossberg. Champaign, IL: U of Illinois P, 1988, pp. 271–313.

Sweeney, Marlisse Silver. "What the Law Can (and Can't) Do about Online Harassment." *Atlantic*, November 12, 2014.

Tolentino, Jia. "The Personal-Essay Boom Is Over." *New Yorker*, May 18, 2017.

Toth, Emily. *Kate Chopin*. New York: William Morrow, 1990.

Turkle, Sherry. *Life on the Screen: Identity in the Age of the Internet*. New York: Simon & Schuster, 1995.

"The Vida Count." VIDA.org. *VIDA: Women in Literary Arts*.

Walker, Alice. *In Search of Our Mothers' Gardens: Womanist Prose*. Mariner Books, [1983] 2003.

"Welcome." Persephone Books. London: Persephone Press.

West, M. Genevieve. *Zora Neale Hurston and American Literary Culture*. University Press of Florida, 2005.

Woolf, Virginia. *A Room of One's Own*. Ed. Susan Gubar, 1st Harvest edn. San Diego, CA: Harcourt, 2005.

CHAPTER THIRTEEN

Reading

NICOLE SIMEK

This essay examines the ways in which recent turns in literary criticism and the human-ities toward affect, objects, and surfaces impact the reception and status of reading in feminist theory. Sharing a certain fatigue with the linguistic turn and its preoccupations with representation, proponents of these varied postcritical or descriptive approaches seek to shift concern away from the questions of mediation, interpretation, and suspicion marking twentieth-century thought, questions that became closely intertwined with the term "reading" itself.[1] Taken as synonymous with critique or with French theory, reading has become a stake in struggles over the aims and methods of humanistic modes of inquiry. A desire to recapture reading, to reshape its meanings and wrest it from theory's alleged overinvestment in representation, skeptical negativity, and critical detachment motivates a number of efforts to supersede or supplement what became known after Paul Ricoeur as a hermeneutics of suspicion.[2] Sharon Best and Stephen Marcus's "surface reading," or "just reading," Franco Moretti's "distant reading," Toril Moi's "reading as a practice of acknowledgment," and Rita Felski's deployment of actor-network-theory in tandem with Eve Kosofsky Sedgwick's concept of "reparative" reading all reaffirm the centrality of reading to their differing projects, and focus debate on reading's relationship to critical thinking and progressive politics.

In the following pages, I want to question the perception that the concept of reading, in its poststructuralist inflections, became shackled by an overinvestment in mediation, interpretation, and epistemology. An investment in mediation need not presuppose a sov-ereign, masterful subject as the ground for critique, nor divorce language from affect and embodiment, or epistemology from ethics or ontology. Rather than oppose reading to the nonhumanist preoccupations of these new turns, this essay seeks to reactivate the emancipatory potential that reading continues to open up for feminism, showing how reading's suspicion of neutrality or bias-free description (along with the givenness of experience) continues to matter to the goals at stake within various postcritical and even anti-hermeneutic modes of inquiry today.

I begin with these latter, which, in embracing modesty, transparency, and neutrality, would seem to strike at the very foundations of feminist theory. Built on a commitment to political progress and social justice, feminist theory envisions scholarship as an activity necessarily implicated in politics, economics, and culture, rather than as a neutral or objective practice that can be separated from these other spheres of human activity. What is striking, then, is the convergence between many of the stated aims or motivations of this descriptive, "neutral" turn that postcriticality ushers in and those of proponents of critique put to the service of progressive politics. In privileging neutral description over prescriptive critique, surface readers, for example, argue that we need to correct for the critical overreach and hubris of a hermeneutics that assumes too much about the critic's masterful discernment and the direct political effects of critical analysis. In so doing, they aim to cultivate by very different means an ethic of respect for texts and readers that is not so far removed from critical theory's desire to root out instrumental rationality, or from feminism's goal of elucidating and reforming relations of domination and exploitation. In examining this convergence and divergence here, I hope to better draw out the contemporary problem-spaces—to borrow David Scott's term—that we find ourselves in as academics. What are the contours of our problem-spaces, the horizons of investment and struggle through which we come to take particular questions as most urgently in need of exploration and argument? Then, with the shape of these urgencies in mind, how might we advance a discussion of feminist theory's aims and possibilities in our contemporary moment?

The descriptive turn, following Heather Love's use of the term, refers to a climate rather than a defined school of thought, a shared interest in description over explanation observable in the work of thinkers whose approaches and objects of study still vary. Naming the descriptive turn a "turn" highlights certain continuities and breaks over others that we could also attend to, by bringing together, for example, ethnographers attuned to everyday practice and sociologists invested in phenomenological analysis, but also post-humanist scholars like Bruno Latour, who takes issue with the conceptions of human agency underpinning these other descriptive approaches. Accordingly, in focusing on work that moves reading away from a hermeneutics of suspicion, I give attention selectively and heuristically to three broad preoccupations, among others, in this writing: accountability and accounting; ethics and affects; and violence and politics. These concerns run through debates over reading, and the role reading should play in scholarship moving forward. Reading "reading" through and with these investments refocuses our attention on the relational dimensions of reading and subjectivity, the vulnerabilities of the reader affected by the reading process, and the implications of this affectability for feminist projects.

ACCOUNTABILITY AND ACCOUNTING

The unaccounted for, the excluded, haunt and motivate the turn away from depth hermeneutics, and in some sense, in arguing in favor of better accounts, of better critical accountability, surface readers, distance readers, and actor-network theorists use the terms of a hermeneutics of suspicion against itself. In their introduction to their 2009 coedited issue of *Representations*, "The Way We Read Now," Stephen Best and Sharon Marcus acknowledge the central role of Fredric Jameson's *Political Unconscious* in motivating and giving shape to surface reading, even as surface reading departs markedly from this predecessor. If depth hermeneutics seeks to account for hidden structures, for that which goes unaccounted for, obscured by ideology and habit, Best and Marcus's surface reading aims to account better for that which "eludes observation" because it parades in plain sight, to account for that which depth hermeneutics fails to notice (18). Such an accounting is designed to overcome "selectivity" and improve accuracy, to get critics closer to facts, to truth (17).

The vocabulary of objectivity and neutrality that Best and Marcus deploy in the service of inclusivity is certainly irksome to critics who have strenuously worked to show how description is not value-neutral but functions normatively and sometimes violently—in the power-knowledge relations linking colonial ethnography and colonial governance, for example. As Christopher Miller has put it, "Few undertakings have proven more prone to ethical pitfalls than the description of other peoples" (34). Yet, Best and Marcus's insist that surface reading aims, like depth hermeneutics, to increase freedom, and to serve rather than destroy critique. Such a claim can appear puzzling to critics alert to work by thinkers like Donna Haraway, who argued in favor of pursuing objectivity while acknowledging that all knowledge is situated, that there is no vision—even machine-assisted vision—that escapes historical contingency. The path to a feminist objectivity, to "faithful accounts of a 'real' world, one that can be partially shared and that is friendly to earthwide projects of finite freedom, adequate material abundance, modest meaning in suffering, and limited happiness," can and must start from situated, mediated positions (579). Disagreements over the ethical or political potential of description hinge in part on definitions—on what scholars mean to say in advocating or critiquing descriptive modes of reading. For computational scholars, describing or detecting statistical patterns is adjunct to modeling and analysis, the work of explaining relationships and evaluating their significance—work that description cannot obviate (Richard Jean So; Moretti). On Heather Love's account, social science-inspired modes of description today aim not at a pure mode of accessing the world, but rather at an expanded sensitivity to the complexities of that world. What interests Heather Love in Bruno Latour's work, for example, is his complaint that social scientists tend to "muffle their informants' precise vocabulary into their own all-purpose meta-language" (Love 376). Description here means attentiveness and openness to multiple vocabularies, an attempt to render detail, variety, and complexity rather than reduce it.

Best and Marcus deploy the term "description" similarly as a methodological corrective, but also stress its ethical dimensions, arguing in favor of a nonnormative or non-judgmental approach to objects of study, a mode of "bearing witness to the given," as they put it, citing Anne-Lise François (18). They take issue with what they view as an overly deterministic political agenda that dictates interpretation in advance, and they call for an attentiveness to texts that does not assume that ideology will take a particular form within them: "We think," they assert, "that a true openness to all the potentials made available by texts is also prerequisite to an attentiveness that does not reduce them to instrumental means to an end and is the best way to say anything accurate and true about them" (16). Such a claim indicts a kind of false openness to texts, a failure of openness that, in this instance, is really only an openness to that which in a text can verify, or be made to verify, prefabricated claims about the obfuscations of ideology, the force of hidden structures, or the authenticity of suppressed histories. No matter the motivation, to read in effect with an eye *only* for hidden meanings amounts to a failure to account for texts, to be accountable to their differences and their surprises.

Emily Apter and Elaine Freedgood pursue this line of thought in their "Afterword" to the volume, praising post-suspicious readings for their attentiveness to "local legibilities," to the kinds of particularities and resistance to falsely universalizing frameworks that feminist and intersectionality theorists have long combatted (140). More forcefully, Apter and Freedgood denounce the "heroic" position assumed by theorists as master knowers, and the ethnocentric, even "ethno-delusionary" privileging of a kind of reading that requires training, that elevates the skill of scholarly interpretation above everyday reading practices (141)—above the kind of vernacular theorizing that has gone undervalued in the canons of theory, as postcolonial scholars Françoise Lionnet and Shu-Mei Shih have argued in *The Creolization of Theory*.

Expanding the canon, accounting for the unaccounted for, insisting on the multiplicity of literacies and the need to remain accountable to texts and reading practices in their particularity—all of these aims sound anti-imperialistic, anti-instrumental, and anti-mechanistic. Yet, as the discussion turns to methodology, these goals are then paired with descriptive techniques and digital technologies that would seem to evacuate the ethical or political potential these reading practices otherwise embrace. Best and Marcus advocate, for example, a form of algorithm-assisted analysis that sounds more positivist than not, arguing that "where the heroic critic corrects the text, the nonheroic critic might aim instead to correct for her critical subjectivity, by using machines to bypass it, in the hopes that doing so will produce more accurate knowledge about texts" (17). Such an attempt to "ste[p] outside the subject altogether," as Carolyn Lesjak has put it (247), risks mistaking algorithms as neutral and objective, risks mistaking "counting" for accounting, for being accountable.[3] More significantly, when taken to the extreme, the flight from partiality toward impartiality and "minimal critical agency," as Best and Marcus put it (17), arguably results not in better politics but in a flight from the political itself. As a practice of attentive listening, impartiality—the suspension of judgment, the refusal to take sides in advance—does create an opening for surprise, for unpredictable outcomes and new thought. Yet the knowledge impartiality produces is not omniscience and does not in itself produce or authorize a specific course of action. The evacuation of partiality can instead lead to an apolitical *ataraxia*, the state of indifference embraced by the Stoics, or, as Pierre Bourdieu puts it, "an ethical state of nonpreference as well as a state of knowledge in which I am not capable of differentiating the stakes proposed" (116). To embrace impartiality is to risk abstaining from reading and from staking claims altogether, offering ethical withdrawal in place of political engagement.

ETHICS, AFFECTS, POLITICS

Best and Marcus's article has drawn wide response because it strikes at the claims scholars stake in scholarship itself, at our investment in our fields of study as worthwhile, and, often, as politically consequential. The debate can helpfully be characterized as revolving around different approaches to politics, with Best and Marcus coming down on the side of "political realism" over "utopian impulse," as Jeffrey Williams puts it in "The New Modesty in Literary Criticism." Their focus on accuracy and truth is driven in part by the fear that critique is losing its hold on reality and persuasion in a reality-challenged society. Yet, in specifying a threefold goal for reading—accuracy, truth, and openness to potentials—Best and Marcus locate their intervention at the conjunction between epistemology, ontology, and ethics. What is at stake in debates over modes of reading capable of accounting for reality are not only epistemological conclusions about objectivity or accuracy but also, and primarily, the ethics and politics of fidelity—of relations of care, authority, privilege, access, and exclusion.

More specifically, this debate revolves around the articulation or tension between ethics and politics, between, in this case, an ethics of receptivity grounded in impartiality—the suspension of judgment, the refusal to take sides in advance—and a politics of reading that begins from a position of partiality, in the sense of being partial to particular causes and judgments, to particular evaluative criteria underpinning judgment and action. In other words, a primary question at issue here seems to be the extent to which

the particular kinds of legibility produced by each—by ethical care and political care—
are at odds with one another. To answer this question, critics have increasingly turned
their attention to affect, which, in raising new questions about legibility, illegibility, and
relationality, seems to promise ways through or around such conflicts.

The critique of critique, of hermeneutics of suspicion, passes through its affects, and
revolves around accountability—the affects of theorizing, the ability of theory to account
for affect, and the democratic or authoritarian consequences of reading affect in particular ways. In the name of expanded access, theory has been indicted both as overly
invested in suspicion, in paranoid knowledge (to take up Eve Kosofsky Sedgwick's critique), and, conversely, as disaffected, as overly invested in dispassionate, critical distance.
These takes on theory's affects diverge in their diagnosis, but both lines of argument
invoke the exclusionary effects of theory's current orientation, faulting theory, and depth
hermeneutics in particular, for its omissions: Sedgwick argues that the negativity of paranoia excludes other positive affects that might serve as resources for knowledge and politics, while Rita Felski (like Emily Apter and Elaine Freedgood, among others) argues that
the "prototype" of the "detached critic," a critic who is, tellingly, described as "ironic,"
has precluded engagements with other sorts of readers and other forms of reading (Felski
740). For Felski, description is full of affect rather than affectless and provides an antidote to a critical detachment that raises the elite critic up while scorning the naive or
the everyday. Description, on her account, aligns better with empathy, while interpretation (defined as suspicious interpretation) leads to the kind of muffling denounced by
Latour—a muffling of the range and complexity of affects involved in the encounter with
texts and people, or even a deprivation of affect altogether. "Instead of stressing our
analytic detachment, we own up to our attachments, shrugging off the tired dichotomy
of vigilant critic versus naive reader," Felski asserts. "Instead of demystifying aesthetic
absorption," she continues, "we see that experience as a key to the distinctive ways in
which art solicits our attention" (741–2).

Felski is right, I agree, to argue that criticism is not an affect-free exercise of pure intellect, that "reason cannot be filtered out from the ebb and swirl of moods and dispositions"
(740). But for scholars like those in feminist traditions of critique who have long rejected
pretensions to cold neutrality, and have instead embraced the anti-authoritarian practice
of exposing their investments and perspectives, the argument lies less in distinguishing
between passion and dispassion, and more in examining the different forms affect takes,
the new understandings of subjectivity or materiality that emerge from attention to
affect, and, again, how an ethical responsiveness to affect can be articulated, or not, with
political goals.

Katherine Behar takes up this question in her introduction to object-oriented feminism (OOF), which takes an interest in affect as a material dimension of a human
subjectivity rethought as a shared condition of objectivity.[4] Noting that OOF sought
to "capitalize somewhat parasitically" on philosophies like speculative realism "while
twisting it toward more agential, political, embodied terrain," Behar proposes erotics
as a third category articulated with ethics and politics, and experimental praxis as a
mode for relating the three. Behar's ethics shares much with Best and Marcus's in that it
emphasizes critical "modesty" and attentiveness, and renounces the attempt to arrive at
"an ontologically 'correct' master theory" that could then be applied to other material in
some surefire way (3–4). It is similar, too, in emphasizing the extension of "sympathies
and camaraderie" to that which has been excluded from empathy, in this case, "nonhuman neighbors" (Behar 8). Yet Behar's approach differs from Best and Marcus's in

deploying this ethics alongside a politics that doubles down on the radical potential of art, while also giving ethics priority over accuracy. "OOF refuses to make grand philosophical truth claims, instead staking a modest ethical position that arrives at 'being in the right' even if it means being 'wrong,'" writes Behar. "Welcoming wrongness," she continues, "affords OOF a polyamorous knack for adopting multiple, sometimes contradictory perspectives" (3).

Reading, here, is displaced by or refigured as acts of giving attention, "fomenting," and interacting, in keeping with object-oriented ontology's and new materialism's interest in relating to or being with things, rather than interpreting them from a stance that reinscribes phallocentric notions of the subject's sovereignty and privilege over the object (15). It is provisional and inductive, invested in experimental testing and investigative co-creation, and erotic. This erotics—which embraces humor, eschews reverence for purity, and strives "to foment unseemly entanglements between things" (3)—relates ethics to politics by, in some sense, collapsing the two: a polyamorous practice of experimentation exercises ethical responsibility by "listening to things" (19) and by questioning ontology's (particularly object-oriented ontology's) exclusions, and it is understood as political insofar as its nonnormative, nonhierarchical "erotic fusion[s]" with objects is a form of political arrangement in itself, or at least paves the way for rearrangements: "Experimentation is always participatory, always both observationist and interventionist," Behar argues. "This allows for tinkering with received truths, priming us for alliances with hacked realities, investigative arrangements in living, and radical aesthetic practices in art" (14).

At the same time, bringing together an attentiveness to "political formations that need not include humans" (14) with a politics that "engages with histories of treating certain humans (women, people of color, and the poor) as objects" (3) points to what Behar describes as "OOF's fundamental tension between objectification and self-possession" (24). To retain the ability to make judgments about oppression, inclusivity, and violence, OOF requires "object-oriented" concepts of self-determination and assent to replace the politically useful but ontologically and ethically suspect "subject-oriented" terms of "control, consent, and coercion" that object-oriented feminists seek to dispel (24). The nonnormative enters into tension with the normative, as scholars grapple with ways to distinguish between better and worse modes of object-object relationality, between beneficial and harmful ways of "being wrong" (24).

In approaching these questions through Wittgenstein's ordinary language philosophy, Toril Moi reaffirms reading's ethical and political potential, while emphasizing that there is no single methodology feminists could apply, or calculus we could make, to prevent being wrong, to prevent failing. Focusing on the work the use of words does, work that can only be investigated through close attention to particulars, never subsumed under and explained by a single, unified theory or set of concepts, Moi argues that to use words is to "make a claim" on others (208), and to read ethically is to respond to that claim, to practice what Moi, after Stanley Cavell, calls acknowledgement. Acknowledgement, Moi argues, is not "a state of mind, or a particular mental content," but rather "a *response*, something we *do*" (207). To acknowledge the claims another makes on us is to attend carefully to words, and "to establish between us a community based on the recognition of our separateness" (208). A claim, as she puts it elsewhere, is "not an order, but an invitation," or "what Simone de Beauvoir would call an appeal to the other's freedom" (92). There is no single correct response to the claims made on me, yet I can nevertheless be wrong, or respond badly:

Different brilliant readings aren't competing to reveal the same (absolutely certain) knowledge, as if the text only offered us one truth ... Rather, different readings reveal different readers' different ways of acknowledging the text. To acknowledge the text *in the right way*, each reader needs to work out his or her own position in relation to it.... . Acknowledgement isn't just a matter of accounting for the work's concepts. It also requires us to understand our own position in relation to the work's concerns. *To articulate a just response, we must do justice both to the work and to ourselves.* (209, emphasis added)

For Moi, what it means to do justice—to a work of art, to a person, to one's own investments, or to a life experience alike—cannot be fully defined in advance, but it does mean to open ourselves up to being addressed, to having new, puzzling, or thrilling experiences, as well as to enter into "a conversation" and "to show I understand how it is with you" (208, 217). "It is perfectly possible," she adds, "to fail in our efforts to acknowledge the other. Or never make the effort at all" (220). Success and failure depend on judgment, which Moi contrasts with measurement: they cannot be reduced to rules, but the absence of universal formulas for conduct or of standardized measures of success does not mean that qualitative, evaluative distinctions disappear. Reading well is about making such judgments and maintaining a care for particulars, one that does not "reduce the difficulty of reality to the flat and flattening categories on a general questionnaire" (242). The "precise and attentive use of words," Moi concludes, is "an act of resistance" today, in "a world in which so many powerful persons and institutions have a vested interest in making us lose faith in language's power to respond to and reveal reality" (242).

VIOLENCE AND CONSENSUS

Part of reading well, for Moi, involves reading to understand: to understand "how it is with you," to take up the phrase quoted above, to "get clear on" a problem, or to understand (and sometimes to transform) ourselves, since we are neither transparent to ourselves nor unchanging. Understanding can never be absolute, but Moi's concern is to demonstrate that partiality is a condition for understanding—and living well together—rather than an obstacle to it. "Philosophy begins," she notes, "when we realize that your examples vie with mine" (94), and we might add that politics begins here too. The task that remains, as Moi sees it, is "to get clear on what the new examples imply; how or whether they affect the analysis of the old ones; what zones of agreement and disagreement they help us outline" (94). For Moi, who turns to intersectionality theory to draw out the challenges facing feminist thought today, this philosophical and political work must pass through the study of particulars, renouncing the "craving" for generalizations that will always and everywhere hold true—a craving whose flip side is the never-finished critique of terms and definitions—like the term "women"—that fail to attain total inclusivity. "We can't solve political problems by focusing exclusively on definitions," she asserts, arguing that feminist theory must guard against a tendency to abstraction. "To solve political problems we need to produce concrete analyses of specific cases, cases that genuinely trouble us" (110). Analyzing examples and appealing to others' experiences to test them is political work. Politics must admit disagreement, without, however, renouncing the goal of common understanding, and our task, as Moi sees it, is "to learn to express political judgments and persuade others to share them" (110).

The weight Moi gives to understanding stems from her assessment of the political problems at hand, which, for her, revolve around skepticism—skepticism about the validity of knowledge production—and its detrimental effects on communal relation and engagement. More precisely, at issue here is a corrosive skepticism that denies the validity of any meaningful ethics, politics, or ontology, a skepticism deployed as a cover for confirming one's preconceived beliefs. Following Latour and Sedgwick, Moi emphasizes the need "to recognize situations in which suspicion is *not* called for," in which "skepticism and suspicion will be less politically useful than admiration, care, and love" (176). In so doing, Moi recalls an important dimension of Sedgwick's work, which should not be overlooked in the search for alternatives to critique, which is that suspicious and loving modes of reading are intertwined, and the political problem is in determining how to engage them both. What Sedgwick highlights in her essay on paranoid reading and reparative reading are the ways that privileged modes of knowing can fail performatively, can fail to produce progressive effects regardless of the truths they uncover. Speaking of AIDS activism, and the critical energies one might devote to tracing out the structural inequalities and systemic forms of discrimination that led to the epidemic's spread, Sedgwick muses that "whether or not to undertake this compelling tracing-and-exposure project represents a strategic and local decision, not necessarily a categorical imperative" (124). Paranoia—the "terrible alertness" to danger and self-defensive anticipation of danger, of bad news—both reveals and overlooks truths (128). Paranoia, Sedgwick argues, "knows some things well and other things poorly" (130); the question facing critics is not whether or not paranoid reading can reveal truths, but rather whether these truths are the ones most urgent to know in a given place and time, in a given problem-space.

This sense of urgency and investment in the stakes of criticism comes from confrontations with violence and deep unsettlement about how to combat it. In hindsight Best and Marcus sound overly confident in their contention that the "demystifying protocols" of a hermeneutics of suspicion seem "superfluous in an era when images of torture at Abu Ghraib and elsewhere were immediately circulated on the internet," when "the real-time coverage of Hurricane Katrina showed in ways that required little explication the state's abandonment of its African American citizens; and many people instantly recognized as lies political statements such as 'mission accomplished' " (2). Yet, Sedgwick puts the point well when she notes that the mode of "vigilant scanning" deployed by feminists and queers enables us to engage some practices of violence better than others (132). Namely, exposing hidden violence is most efficacious, she argues, in a "cultural context … in which violence would be deprecated and hence hidden in the first place" (140). One problem we face today is that some forms of violence are "hypervisible," and the struggle against them is a struggle not, then, to make them visible and graspable, but "to displace and redirect … its aperture of visibility" (140). Moreover, the exercise of violence—both judicial and extra-judicial—is not always deprecated, does not always scandalize. In such a framework, a framework in which violence is desired or viewed with satisfaction, exposure of a violent practice itself may fail to surprise, disturb, or motivate.

For feminist critics invested in a mode of scholarship that aims to intervene in the world and effectuate sociopolitical change, the urgent task at hand, I would argue, is not simply to turn away from a hermeneutics of suspicion and to "give a certain kind of irony a rest," as Apter and Freedgood quip (140), but rather to work within and out of a mode of reading that we might describe as ironic in its structure and demands. Irony, in multiplying significations, involves at once making and unmaking meaning, negating, and recreating. As Sedgwick repeatedly stresses, reparative practices—practices of relating and

building up—"infuse" paranoid projects of critique; pleasure, and depression, following
Melanie Klein, are interdependent, and "paranoid exigencies" as Sedgwick writes, "are
often necessary for nonparanoid knowing and utterance" (129). The task at hand is to
inhabit and negotiate both of these positions, to draw from the resources of both.

There are several consequences to such an argument, and I want to end with some
reflection on where the ironic interplay between paranoia and reparation might take
reading in an age of alternative facts, when demystification seems both urgent and impotent, and susceptibility to others' suffering may well come with exposure to others' violence. On this question, Kenneth Saltman has argued compellingly in favor of a critical
pedagogy that addresses the alienation of facts from their context of production ("Anti-
Anti-Theory"; see also *Failure*). Such a pedagogy entails demystifying not in the sense of
masterfully displacing myth with authentic truth, but rather in the sense of engaging with
the production of observations, arguments, and evidence—the dialogical constitution of
shared understandings that we come to call truth.

The role of friction in this continual renegotiation is difficult to overstate in our
current moment. The interrelation of paranoid and reparative practices, of readings that
perform the dismantling or smashing work of taking apart, of analyzing, on the one hand,
and those that put together, relate, and join, on the other, does *not* mean that a happy
and static methodological synthesis awaits us just over the horizon. There is no sure-fire,
"mid-level" reading practice between the close and the distant, between the deep and
the shallow that could escape this dynamism or that we could rest on. Still less, I believe,
have we arrived at a moment in which criticism can annihilate itself, standing aside to
allow texts, objects, or data to speak for themselves, as if meaning could simply manifest, unmediated. Quite the contrary, interrelationality is also incommensurabilty, and
the persistence of difference, of the difference between making and unmaking, highlights
the dynamism and unpredictability of interpretation, the intricacies of shifting problem-
spaces. In what sorts of practices and modes of knowing efficacy lies should remain an
unsettled question, continually asked and asked again.

Unpredictability also involves very real affective risks. If paranoia seeks to avoid bad
surprises by anticipating them, countervailing relational practices involve accepting surprise, both good and bad. If one name for a reparative relation to one's objects of study is
love, this emphasis on positivity, on nonjudgmental attentiveness, or on the pleasures of
being susceptible rather than immune to a text's charms, risks covering over or neutralizing the susceptibility to violence that comes with vulnerability. This is a risk Emily Apter
and Elaine Freedgood run, for example, in arguing that what replaces the "recalcitrant,
mystified, out-of-control, and conflicted text of Marxist-psychoanalytic reading" are
"texts that are friendly, frank, generous, self-conscious, autocritiquing, and unguarded"
(139). "In our relation to such texts," Apter and Freedgood continue, "we can be susceptible, just, physically intimate, and statistically rough-and-ready" (139). But to be susceptible only to that which comforts is to negate susceptibility itself. Sedgwick's recognition
of the similarities between hope and trauma points to the interrelation of unsettlement,
fracturing, and creativity. To teach that openness brings only new friends and pleasant
intimacies is to do our students a serious disservice. The type of friendliness Apter and
Freedgood evoke, I think, represents not just an inclusive measure making warmth and
pleasure acceptable again in an atmosphere privileging cold, critical distance, but potentially a flight from politics in the guise of a more ethical form of sociability.[5] To insist that
we must always relate, must always be positive, must always give texts unconditional,
nonjudgmental openness is to deny the inescapability and productivity of friction. To

insist exclusively on the positive outcomes of relationality is just as dubious as it is, conversely, to insist, as Sedgwick puts it, "that the one thing needed for global revolution, explosion of gender roles, or whatever, is people's (that is, other people's) having the painful effects of their oppression, poverty, or deludedness sufficiently exacerbated to make the pain conscious (as if otherwise it wouldn't have been) and intolerable (as if intolerable situations were famous for generating excellent solutions)" (144).

Sedgwick writes from a position of pain and attentiveness to pain, in search of resources to aid in living better, to preserve a motivation and reason to go on, to pursue a different future in full light of that pain, of a terrible alertness to the pervasive foreshortening of queer futures. By contrast, Best and Marcus's comments in 2009 abstract from this insight, and jar uncomfortably in our present moment. "Eight years of the Bush regime," they wrote at the time, "may have hammered home the point that not all situations require the subtle ingenuity associated with symptomatic reading, and they may have also inspired us to imagine that alongside nascent fascism there might be better ways of thinking and being simply there for the taking" (2). What disturbs me in this sentence is not so much the contention that symptomatic approaches may fail to live up to their critical potential and may thus need revitalizing, but rather the juxtaposition of fascism and easiness, the implication that if we only got a little friendlier with our texts, we could "simply" reach out and grab what's there for the taking. To over-read the sentence, we might also wonder how to interpret the "alongside" here: what purchase on nascent fascism might these tantalizingly available modes of thinking and being have? The separation of the "alongside" betrays to my mind a refusal of entanglement, a perilous attempt to side-step friction and dissensus, to look to the side for solutions. Reading's irony accepts negation and unpredictability as part and parcel of the generative but also the exciting and joyful as part of the work of critique. Rather than embracing a more comfortable form of generosity that is generative in name only, this fractious, joyful, and disturbing form of entanglement strikes me as a richer resource for criticism and politics.

NOTES

1 Patricia Clough describes the turn to affect, for example, as a turn away from a dominant model of textuality overinvested in language at the expense of materiality: "The turn to affect did propose a substantive shift in that it returned critical theory and cultural criticism to bodily matter which had been treated in terms of various constructionisms under the influence of poststructuralism and deconstruction" (206).

2 In *Freud and Philosophy: An Essay on Interpretation*, Ricoeur identifies Marx, Nietzsche, and Freud as "masters of suspicion" who fundamentally shifted the way we think about interpretation by putting consciousness itself—and its production of meaning—into question: "The philosopher trained in the school of Descartes knows that things are doubtful, that they are not such as they appear; but he does not doubt that consciousness is such as it appears to itself ... Since Marx, Nietzsche, and Freud, this too has become doubtful. After the doubt about things, we have started to doubt consciousness" (33). Consequently, for these thinkers, the search for truth requires an "exegesis of meaning," a hermeneutics that can decipher what is hidden or masked from consciousness: "Beginning with them," argues Ricoeur, "understanding is hermeneutics: henceforward, to seek meaning is no longer to spell out the consciousness of meaning, but to *decipher its expressions*" (33).

3 Lisa Marie Rhody makes a similar critique of distant reading's investment in the spatial representation of measurable literary features through visual graphs and maps, for it presents reading as a matter of apprehending seemingly unmediated images, and reintroduces problematic notions of critical neutrality: "When we substitute looking for reading, we reorient the critical perspective from close to distant, introducing an epistemological and cultural shift in the observer's perspective as well. For the feminist scholar, the relocation of the critical gaze to a position of omniscient authority, combined with the dehumanizing scientific discourse that describes the separation of textual features from the whole, presents fundamental problems" (660). For a contrasting view of distant reading's continued reliance on close reading, see Armstrong and Montag.

4 Object-oriented feminism shares tenets with speculative realism and its subfield, object-oriented ontology, two philosophical schools that take issue with Kantian correlationism, or the view that we can only have access to thought about things, not things in themselves. Speculative realists seek to overcome what they see as post-Kantian philosophy's overinvestment in epistemology and mediation—that is, an obsession with the conditions for knowledge—by returning philosophy to the business of ontology, to knowing things themselves. Object-oriented ontology takes a particular interest in undoing human-centered paradigms, embracing a flat ontology in which humans are objects among others, without any particular priority.

5 As Diana Fuss writes in the PMLA issue devoted to Rita Felski's *The Limits of Critique*, "Forging links, a helpful reading practice that could apply to any text or subject, provides no guarantee that the critical tone will be any less moody than other forms of reading. Much depends on what is being interpreted. Reading the newspaper precisely to forge links and explore connections, I am reminded daily that some words and actions are so appalling that the only ethical response can or should be denunciation" (353).

WORKS CITED

Apter, Emily, and Elaine Freedgood. "Afterword." *Representations* 108 (2009): 139–46.

Armstrong, Nancy, and Warren Montag. "The Figure in the Carpet." *PMLA: Publications of the Modern Language Association of America* 132.3 (2017): pp. 613–19.

Behar, Katherine, ed. *Object-Oriented Feminism*. Minneapolis: U of Minnesota P, 2017.

Best, Stephen, and Sharon Marcus. "Surface Reading: An Introduction." *Representations* 108.1 (2009): 1–21.

Bourdieu, Pierre, and Loïc J. D. Wacquant. *An Invitation to Reflexive Sociology*. Chicago, IL: U of Chicago P, 1992.

Clough, Patricia T. "The Affect Turn: Political Economy, Biomedia, and Bodies." *The Affect Theory Reader*. Ed. Melissa Gregg and Gregory J. Seigworth. Durham, NC: Duke UP, 2010, pp. 206–25.

Felski, Rita. "Latour and Literary Studies." *PMLA* 130.3 (2015): 737–42.

Fuss, Diana. "But What about Love?" *PMLA* 132.2 (2017): 352–5.

Haraway, Donna. "Situated Knowledges: The Science Question in Feminism and the Privilege of Partial Perspective." *Feminist Studies* 14.3 (1988): 575–99.

Lesjak, Carolyn. "Reading Dialectically." *Criticism* 55.2 (2013): 233–77.

Lionnet, Françoise, and Shu-mei Shih, eds. *The Creolization of Theory*. Durham, NC: Duke UP, 2011.

Love, Heather. "Close but Not Deep: Literary Ethics and the Descriptive Turn." *New Literary History* 41.2 (2010): 371–91.

Miller, Christopher L. *Theories of Africans: Francophone Literature and Anthropology in Africa.* Chicago, IL: U of Chicago P, 1990.

Moi, Toril. *Revolution of the Ordinary: Literary Studies after Wittgenstein, Austin, and Cavell.* Chicago, IL: U of Chicago P, 2017.

Moretti, Franco. "Franco Moretti: A Response." *PMLA* 132.3 (2017): 686–9.

Ricoeur, Paul. *Freud and Philosophy: An Essay on Interpretation.* New Haven, CT: Yale UP, 1970.

Rhody, Lisa Marie. "Beyond Darwinian Distance: Situating Distant Reading in a Feminist *Ut Pictura Poesis* Tradition." *PMLA* 132.3 (2017): 659–67.

Saltman, Kenneth J. "Anti-Anti-Theory: The Resurgence of Radical Empiricism in Education." Society for Critical Exchange Winter Theory Institute, Victoria: TX: U of Houston-Victoria, February 10, 2017. Conference Presentation.

Saltman, Kenneth J. *The Failure of Corporate School Reform.* Boulder, CO: Paradigm, 2012.

Scott, David. *Conscripts of Modernity: The Tragedy of Colonial Enlightenment.* Durham, NC: Duke UP, 2004. *eDuke Books*, doi:10.1215/9780822386186.

Sedgwick, Eve Kosofsky. "Paranoid Reading and Reparative Reading, or, You're So Paranoid, You Probably Think This Essay Is about You." *Touching Feeling: Affect, Pedagogy, Performance.* Durham, NC: Duke UP, 2003, pp. 123–51.

So, Richard Jean. "All Models Are Wrong." *PMLA* 132.3 (2017): 668–73.

Williams, Jeffrey. "The New Modesty in Literary Criticism." The Chronicle of Higher Education (Online), January 25, 2015. Chronicle of Higher Education website, www.chronicle.com.

CHAPTER FOURTEEN

Realism

MARGARET R. HIGONNET

This essay opens a comparative window on "female realism," as Ellen Moers put the phenomenon in *Literary Women*. My goal is to raise questions about both of those words and to bring three relatively neglected writers and texts into view: Anna Barbauld, Isabelle de Charrière, and George Sand. Both terms are contested. For example, Raymond Williams modestly calls "realism" a "difficult" keyword (216) as he reviews some of its many meanings as a period, movement, genre, or subgenre. Is it a mode or style that claims "accuracy" of representation, across changing models of accuracy over time? Is it, as René Wellek suggests, an "epistemological problem" of the relation of art to writing (1963: 224)? In the words of Fredric Jameson, "Whenever you search for 'realism' somewhere, it vanishes" (233). One model for thinking about realism as a literary practice is the description by Jonathan Culler of five levels of *vraisemblance*, in which the "real" is constituted through social "texts" about the physical, social, and textual worlds. In a logical circle, he suggests that texts shape readers' expectations and public opinion, which in turn generate explanatory readings that seem "natural and legible" (138). If we focus on the ways women writers invoke other texts or the artificiality of their own texts, we find evidence of their attempts to unmask those conventions of "realism."

Helen Small has summarized three approaches of feminist theory to definitions of realism: an "Anglo-American" focus on the complicity of realist writers with the political ideology they represent, a Marxist focus on writers' alienation from the social order, and a psychoanalytic poststructuralist critique of representation itself (227–9), leading to Judith Butler's philosophic reflections. One direction taken finds that realist texts have a "sex" that hinges on the sex of the protagonist, as in a female Bildungsroman. As for "female" authorship, many today reject Moers's approach as potentially determinist. While Margaret Cohen "excavates" women writers of "sentimental social novels" as opposed to realism, she argues that such novels were also written by male writers (9, 120). In a similar argument, Naomi Schor rejects an "essentialist reading" of actual women as writers that assumes their "inborn affinity" for realist details (x). Here, I postulate that when women publish in a highly gendered economy, they encode layers of irony through their play with masculine pseudonyms and other rhetorical devices. Did nineteenth-century textual experiments with "everyday" or "quotidian" subjects vary according to the perceived experiences of men or women, whether the writers were male or female, and did they "deconstruct" gender, as Virginia Woolf argues in *A Room of One's Own*? What do we conclude from readers' uncertainty about whether anonymous or potentially pseudonymous writers were male or female? What are the effects of textual (as well as personal) cross-dressing? Although we cannot answer all these questions, we can attempt to remain sensitive to their subversive implications.

Each of the key terms in play here belongs to a "fuzzy" set: realism, accuracy, truth, and the "effect" of the real, on the one hand; female, woman, and of course feminist, on the other. This fuzziness or vagueness, like shifting sands, echoes the ever-changing purposes of the reader. The concepts are constructed in a multidimensional dialogue and many of these key terms overlap with topics addressed by other contributors to this volume, who remind us that the last fifty years have witnessed broad changes in theoretical approaches, critical assumptions, and even biology that have redrawn this terrain. One might speculate, for example, that the range of physiologies now studied in sports medicine is as broad as the range of narrative gender positions at play in women's (as well as men's) writings.

Critics today of nineteenth-century French realism may tacitly use criteria that exclude women. Thus Auerbach and more recent Marxists assume that realism addresses an audience familiar with current politics, rather than with the social context of female readers. My three examples suggest some ways a woman writer may signal her relationship to the conventions of literary realism and also deviate from them. That split stance calls for recognition as a possible feminist version of the mode of realism. Thus, my argument will have two sides to it: on the one hand, I want to underscore the explicit connections between certain women's texts and the mode of realism they found among their contemporaries; on the other hand, I want to show how they deliberately deviate within that mode of realism. We may seek out evidence from women themselves about their understanding of their gendered positions as "female" writers, where possible, as one of the tools that can allow us to open up interpretive possibilities in their texts.

In tackling this conceptual intersection, my goal is to rethink both realism and women writers' status within discussions of realism, pushing back to the end of the eighteenth century. My argument has several facets: (1) I expand the range of realism as a movement rather than as a sharply delineated period concept, by including a witty poem of 1787 by the Englishwoman Anna Barbauld, and an epistolary French novella of 1784 by Isabelle de Charrière, a cosmopolitan Dutch writer who had married a Swiss aristocrat. These figures are usually considered to be "romantic" because of their dates, yet may also be considered marginal, because they do not cultivate the sublime or the sentiments taken to lie at the core of romanticism. I seek to loosen paradigmatic boundaries that have effectively omitted women. (2) In the process, to resist the common focus of historians on realist prose narratives, especially the novel, I include poetry as well as prose in this brief overview. (3) While critics often emphasize the darker aspects of quotidian life in "realist" texts, I reintegrate social satire and the humor of the quotidian into this examination of realism. Such elements certainly figure in texts by Balzac, Dickens, and George Eliot, as well as a neglected writer such as Barbauld. Particularly for women like George Sand, ironic forms of expression or voice offered an avenue for social commentary and reassessment of their own situations as writers: comic stylization could become a tool to resist social stereotyping. (4) Finally, I address narrative form, since women's writings in a mode that we may consider "realist" are surprisingly self-conscious about their construction of texts, a self-consciousness that manifests itself through multiple framing layers, divided conclusions, and embedded poetics.

PERIODIZATION

Precisely because "realism" is a fuzzy term, it has been applied historically across centuries, a tendency encouraged by Erich Auerbach's monumental *Mimesis*, which ranged from a chapter on two "antithetical" views of representation in Homer's *Odyssey* and Genesis 22:1, to a chapter on blended consciousness in Virginia Woolf's *To the Lighthouse*. Yet, historians of realism have primarily focused on select French novelists of the nineteenth century who are discussed by Auerbach in his eighteenth chapter as exemplars of a "modern tragic realism" that addresses "everyday experience in a low social stratum" with "objective seriousness" (see 458, 474, 490). France, he argues, "played the most important part in the rise and development of modern realism" by Stendhal, Balzac, and Flaubert, followed by the Goncourt brothers and Zola (491). From 1830 onward, Auerbach found that novelists who wished to give dramatic immediacy to "real life" with its "everyday triviality, practical preoccupations, ugliness, and vulgarity" (480–1) turned to "free indirect discourse," a form in which we overhear the thoughts of characters. In such realist texts, a historicist dynamic unites the informed audience with the implicitly omniscient author's representation of the contemporary social and political world. More recently, Auerbach has been displaced by literary historians under the influence of Roland Barthes's concept of a "reality effect" (*effet de réel*), in which insignificant details compel our belief because they seem to lie outside the author's control (141–8). In part inspired by Barthes's distinction between a "legible" text (*lisible*), identified with a realism whose reader is passive, and a "writable" (*scriptible*) text that provokes the reader's participation, modernism displaced realism as a critical value. Realism was critiqued as a constraining (*lisible*) narrative model because it was identified with a consistent point of view and ideological control over the reader.

Such theorization of realism assumes that we can talk about realism and modernism as aesthetic practices that dominate in certain historical moments. However, Katie Trumpener's essay on periodization challenges the old assumption by literary historians that a period is composed of a "stable unit of time" (349) and proposes instead that we develop more nuanced scales of analysis and time that could accommodate cross-currents and undercurrents. Thus, one may draw on Claudio Guillen's more complex model of literary history using the metaphor of "currents" and cross- or counter-currents (497–9). A further tool to disrupt periodization is a comparative approach that reflects different historical and social contexts, including matters of gender, across national traditions. In England and in France, for example, differences of religion, political crises, and social class structures affected the distinct evolutions of the realist movement and gender ideologies. As Auerbach conceded, the practices of realism in England "began much earlier" than in France and continued into the Victorian era (491). Thus, in English literary history, Elizabeth Gaskell, Charlotte Brontë, and George Eliot have found a secure place, while in French and German histories women tend not to be perceived as "realists" (Cohen 8, 191).

FEMALE REALISM

Ellen Moers launched her study of "female realism" with a discussion of Jane Austen, who wittily emphasized the importance of money (and the lack of it) in women's lives. One tool that Ellen Moers used in her study was the surprising extent to which women themselves staked a claim to realism in their own writing by underscoring money and work, with documentary support. Charlotte Brontë, for example, opened her industrial novel *Shirley*, promising that the story to come would not be sentimental but would present "Something real, cool, and solid ... something unromantic as Monday morning"— starting when the working week begins (5). While Brontë was writing, she affirmed in March 1849 to her publisher's reader that "Truth is better than Art"; a few months later, she defended her novel against a review by G. H. Lewes, protesting to her publisher, "it is real" (xvi). Indeed, as Moers points out, Brontë read newspapers and quarterlies, including back issues of the Leeds *Mercury*, in order to gather information about the Luddite movement in Yorkshire (Moers, 82). The documentary impulse that drove Brontë was central to many writings that targeted social reform, such as Charlotte Elizabeth Tonna's *The Wrongs of Woman* (1843–44), which cites commissioners' reports to substantiate the conditions of female labor in factory towns. Elizabeth Barrett Browning prepared her protest ballad, "Cry of the Children," by reading R. H. Horne's report on child labor, and Harriet Beecher Stowe wrote *A Key to Uncle Tom's Cabin* that collected documents she had used, in order to support her indictment of slavery in *Uncle Tom's Cabin*.

Rather than Moers's emphasis on subject matter, narrative structure was the focus of Nancy Miller's essay "Emphasis Added: Plots and Plausibilities," about writing that resists social maxims and social scripts: "I am arguing that the peculiar shape of a heroine's destiny in novels by women, the implausible twists of plot so common in these novels, is a form of insistence about the relation of women to writing" (44). Miller pushes us toward metanarrative analysis: "the plots of women's literature are not about 'life' and solutions in any therapeutic sense, nor should they be. They are about the plots of literature itself, about the constraints the maxim places on rendering a female life in fiction" (46).

Poetry—Anna Barbauld

One of the prime assumptions about realism has been to identify codes of the everyday with prose, as well as with high seriousness. By contrast, my first case study presents poetic satire about the everyday as experienced by women. Anna Barbauld (1743–1825), who wrote on domestic as well as political topics, belongs to a larger group of witty British women poets to whom Stuart Curran called attention in his landmark essay, "Romantic Poetry: The I Altered." He held them up as predecessors of Dickens and Hardy, because of their "investment in quotidian tones and details" combined with "a portrayal of alienated sensibility" (203). Curran launches his thesis with a critique of "received history," claiming that it "has been written wholly, and arbitrarily, along a masculine gender line" (187). It was precisely their "quotidian values," he suggests, that led women poets to be "submerged" and overlooked (190). A surprising number of women poets wrote on topics that by some measures might be considered "realist," using stylistic strategies that would be at home later in Balzac or Dickens.

Although the focus here is on Barbauld, she can be read against a background of similar poetic experiments at the beginning of the nineteenth century, especially in England. As a research group in the Netherlands has shown, women in this revolutionary period exchanged ideas and texts, initiating a shared culture (Van Dijk). Germaine de Stael called attention in her *De la littérature considérée dans ses rapports avec les institutions sociales* to the contributions of women, whom she considered to have helped originate "an interest in domestic life" (2.232). It is women, she suggests, who find nuance in character and who have transformed literature since the Renaissance, as they acceded increasingly to civil equality. She attributes to women the modern interest in philanthropy and philosophical liberty (2.235). Numerous women wrote abolitionist poems that call upon readers to confront contemporary society and politics, but their emotional appeals and melodrama may seem to lack the objectivity (understood as a tone of neutrality) essential to later mid-century "realist" writers. Closer to Barbauld's range is Mary Robinson, herself a social satirist, who praised women for novels on "domestic life," while her own poems powerfully deploy montage and catalogue to capture the public arena. Robinson's pseudonymous *Thoughts on the Condition of Women and on the Injustice of Mental Subordination* (1799) praised a list of "female pens" who had contributed to this shared culture of women. Like Robinson and Mary Wollstonecraft, many women poets were drawn to secularization and science in the Enlightenment, and were politicized by the French Revolution. Elisabeth Moody, for example, wrote about Linnaeus and Marie Antoinette. Her satiric realism about the "economy" of the kitchen neatly fits Moers's thesis about women and labor. In a "prayer" addressed to "Economy" before a "fête," Moody exposed the parsimony and privation forced upon a housewife and her household staff. A burlesque describes abandoning the pleasures of reading her favorite Italian authors, in order to pursue the culinary seduction of a lover. This light composition about the lightest of pastries, their margins "printed" by the cook, ironically embraces the art of the authors she claims to be abandoning.

With a similar mockery of domestic tasks, Anna Barbauld elegantly aligns two kinds of quotidian, male and female, in her "Washing-Day," when the once-a-week laundry routines of the "red-armed washers" intersect with and interrupt the daily patterns of life for the men and children of the family (7–9). Barbauld invokes the world as seen by the "domestic Muse," who speaks a maternal vernacular "in slipshod measure loosely prattling on" (l. 8), talking about the orchard, milk curds, drowning flies, or a child's lost shoe. Her mock-heroic housewife must contend with the threats of rain, winds that might blow down drying aprons, and all the sequence of washing, starching, and ironing. Pleasant smiles and repose are banished, even from the garden, where cold wet sheets "flap" visitors in the face. The master of the house can scarcely hope to be fed, and his friend is brushed out of the house without dessert. The wit of the poem draws on the chaotic scene to evoke its metrics, and its metrics to evoke the chaos. The cooped-up children of the family tease their grandmother, whose potential reproach is repressed in a fragmentary line of ellipses, suggesting her indulgence. First a punning run-on line and then a dash marking a caesura neatly capture the feared disasters of "loaded lines at once / Snapped short—and linen-horse by dog thrown down" (ll. 6–7), in a metrical rupture that demonstrates the poet's mastery of her art.

The voice of the putatively coherent "authorial" narrator has been a key question for students of realism in prose narrative generally. Barbauld's mock-heroic poetic narrator invokes the muse and then the housewife who bends beneath "the yoke of wedlock," and who knows "full well" the scene (ll. 9, 10). Although such satiric references may mark the speaker as female, the narrator speaks from authoritative memory of experience as a puzzled child—an outsider, who might be of either sex, and whose lack of comprehension challenges the reader to ask "why washings were" (l. 79). The perch of the children enables them to challenge the rationale of the social status quo. At the conclusion of the poem, the children take the soapy waters of the washing day to blow bubbles, emblems of the vanity of life, and at the same time transcendent images of the poet's transformation of material life into the perfect shape of art. Thus, the children take over the action and enact a poetics of the real.

Critics have been baffled by the apparent contradictions of that ambiguous conclusion. These self-conscious references to the artist's own labors seem to trouble the controlled surface of an objective, neutral narrative, a structure typically thought to characterize realist fiction. Yet, the embedded bubble-metaphor is consistent with well-known passages in a later realist writer such as George Eliot, whose *Adam Bede* opens in the "workshop" of a carpenter, prefaced by Eliot's artistic metaphor of the "drop of ink at the end of my pen" that will mirror visions of the past (9). Although separated by sixty years, the two artists draw on similar tactics of reflexive meditation about the representation of everyday life. Albeit in somewhat different philosophic tones, both writers undercut their representations, a gesture that can be read as diffidence, but that also achieves a philosophical level of realism by subverting the possibility of absolute verisimilitude. Barbauld uses the traditional metaphor of the evanescent, iridescent bubble, itself a distorted, rounded mirror, and Eliot's narrator explains in the seventeenth chapter of her novel that she aims "to give a faithful account of men and things" as mirrored in her mind, even though "[t]he mirror is doubtless defective" (193). This ironic twist in the narrator's voice deviates from the omniscient claims of much realist literature. Yet, it plays a significant role, I suggest, in women's writing that stakes a realist claim, because it underscores the gendering of perspective and the instability of common perceptions of "the real."

Charrière

A particularly forceful, narrative presentation of the tension between two gendered perspectives can be found in Isabelle de Charrière's forty-page tale *Letters of Mistress Henley Published by Her Friend*, which was written as a reply to Samuel de Constant's *The Sentimental Husband*, a Swiss novel that lamented a marriage destroyed by the frivolity of a young wife and concluded by the husband's suicide. Charrière paradoxically creates an illusion of objectivity through Mistress Henley's passionate letters attributing her unhappy marriage to her own errors. Charrière juxtaposes the views of husband and wife, but inverts the positions of the couple in Constant's novel, her intertext. Mistress S. Henley surprises us through her insistence on her mistakes in petty decisions, by contrast to the rationality of her chilly husband. The paradox of the protagonist's manifest struggle to be objective in spite of her crushed sensibility calls upon us to respect her depiction of the simple events of daily life. As S. explains in her fourth letter, her uninteresting details about "little things" or trifles are necessary, since "I would think I was telling you nothing if I withheld anything" (Charrière 26). At each point, when she tries to accommodate her husband's preferences by reversing her own choices, she asks "Could I be wrong again, always wrong, wrong in everything?" (25). This display of self-erasure darkly echoes her husband's calm rationality. Twenty years later, Charrière recalled scandalous speculations by naïve readers, who had interpreted both novels (Constant's and her own) as records of "real" marriages (OC 6.559). Later critics were more sophisticated: Sainte-Beuve praised her natural, realist tone ("réel," "nature"), and in turn Henry James called her "the first of the realists," admiring her "delightful French style" and her "strength and truthfulness" (665). Describing her manuscript of *Henriette et Richard* as an "anecdote" (despite its length), Charrière explains that "my precision about dates, distances, localities, will I hope give this work the air of an anecdote rather than a novel" (OC 8.275). Her claim of precision or *exactitude* corresponds to her interest in realist effects, yet modern students of realism have overlooked her.

The originality of Charrière's fictive narrative voice corresponds to her use of the letters by S. to a nameless friend. Situated as the "you" of the letters, the reader is invited to assess the marital situation. *Mistress Henley* foreshadows Flaubert's *Madame Bovary* by depicting the bitter frustration of everyday provincial life. Charrière's "S. Henley" believes she has rationally chosen an ideal partner, a sensible widower in a well-endowed household with a child. In spite of her good intentions, she finds herself criticized by her husband first as a stepmother and then as a pregnant future mother. The one-sided sequence of letters shapes a series of mini-crises that suggest how fragmented Mistress Henley's experience of marriage is, as she plunges into despair about the impossibility of communication. Critic Gina Fisch suggests convincingly that Charrière interferes with "the rules of novelistic illusion" "so as to challenge readers to rethink their assumptions about the novel's subject" (1059).

As readers, we are empowered and impelled to weigh our interpretation of the last letter, which refuses to tell us what "happened." Charrière's novels are explicitly open-ended, a strategy that incites the reader to draw conclusions by plotting competing curves of plausibility. When silence follows Mistress Henley's despairing announcement that she is pregnant, but that her husband does not trust her maternal judgment, the reader may speculate which ending might foster narrative plausibility: for S. to die in child-birth, to find an emotional adjustment to her children and husband, or simply to wither under his indifference. Although Mistress Henley tells us she could not commit suicide, Charrière's readers assumed that the incomplete plot line signified a suicide. Charrière, however, plays with us, as if she were a puppeteer, always insisting that the fictive "real" is an illusion. Thus, *Mistress Henley* fits with a group of novels that Ellen Moers presents, where we do not follow a courtship romance that closes on marriage but a study of marriage itself as a test whose answers are left open.

The range of Charrière's play with representation passes from the banal details of everyday life ("dates and distances"), to the depiction of social (and political) concerns of her contemporaries in terms that they recognized, to her mimicry of literary conventions, but with an ironic twist, like the self-mocking touches of Jane Austen. Her sprightly mock-romance *The Nobleman*, published anonymously when she was twenty-two and then suppressed, continues after the elopement of her protagonists with the line, "let us not trouble ourselves any more about them" but then in fact recounts a later reconcili-ation (28). Such unsettled and unsettling conclusions are characteristic of her work. In a letter of August 7, 1793, Charrière boasted, "Up until now I have published novels that had no ending, I could print one that would have neither ending nor beginning" (OC 8.276). She was describing *Henriette et Richard,* which begins with a comic declaration of indifference to the narrative task. The narrator takes us into her confidence and sums up the career of Henriette's father in a single sentence about him as a social type: "Now that our heroine has been born, we will let her father enrich himself and live like others of his class without bothering about him until the moment when the Revolution changed his residence and his fortune" (OC 8.293). The high-handed narrator shortcuts readerly expectations, while summarizing the typical socioeconomic causalities of realism.

We must note that Charrière was not a feminist in a modern sense—unlike some of her contemporaries, she did not advocate the vote for women but rather sought social equality. She was surprisingly sensual, as she declared in her youthful autobiography, *Portrait de Zélide*. Like many women, she read herself as a mix of gender traits. At the age of twenty-two, in a letter of October 23, 1762, Charrière wrote, "You are not the first to regret that I am not a man; I myself have often done so, not that I would have been so admirable a man, but I would appear less out of place than I do now; my situation would lend greater liberty to my tastes; a more robust body would better serve an active mind" (OC 1: 142–3). Her self-conscious authorial "we" makes the reader complicit in the construction of both narrative and gender conventions. Tellingly, in *Henriette et Richard*, a manuscript novel of 1792–3 that she left incomplete at her death, a letter from Richard to Henriette describes gender, like nobility, as an arbitrary social convention: "The bourgeois invents the noble as you represent him to yourself. Man invents woman. Then we kneel before a chimera that we have invented" (OC 8.98). Richard's insight foreshadows new arrangements that might emerge from the revolution. But when it became clear that they would not, Charrière abandoned the manuscript rather than conform to narrative conventions.

SAND

Many elements of Charrière's oeuvre seem to foreshadow George Sand's forging nearly half a century later of a persona and a radical narrative form, in a new, puzzling version of realism. Her first novel, *Indiana*, has received intense attention in recent decades, celebrated, for example, in special issues of journals and in an MLA "Teaching" volume that explores its complexities as a hybrid of romantic and realist devices (Pasco 185–92). The novel opens on the deeply unhappy marriage of nineteen-year-old Indiana to an older, harsh military man, M. Delmare, in a variant on the situation of *Mistress Henley*. While Indiana and her cousin Ralph sit quietly with his dog on either side of the fireplace, her husband paces with annoyance that his wife is pretty, his country house is comfortable, and his factory a success, giving him nothing to complain about; he decides to complain about the dog (having killed Indiana's dog previously). In the second chapter, after M. Delmare has stepped out of their living room, Indiana laments to her cousin Ralph, "I must resign myself to never being right" (23). Far more intricate than Charrière's tale of marital disagreement, Sand's novel shifts narrative voice and tone, interrupting to address a male audience, and then shifting from an unreliable third-person account to a first-person letter writer. The most conspicuous difference between the two authors is that Sand rejects an identity as a female author: "Never call me a woman author [*auteur femme*]," she wrote to Charles Meure, January 27, 1832 (Sand 2.16). Famously, she cross-dressed in order to gain the freedom to walk with her colleagues in the evening. The experimental narrative close of *Indiana*, leading from the cousins' suicidal leap to an epilogue, was probably the most shocking feature of the text, as it dismantled every romantic and realist convention of closure.

George Sand's ironic narrative framing of *Indiana* has many layers, a technique that would be used as well by the Brontës in their novels. Her first layer of disguise was the pseudonym G. Sand, concealing her own identity, Aurore Dupin Dudevant. Sand's readers speculated whether G. was male or female—"Georgina" perhaps. With that ambiguous pseudonym in place, Sand presented the body of the narrative through an ostensibly omniscient male voice, who judges the characters as social types, but whose opinions are self-evidently unwarranted or will be overturned by events. In the epilogue, a traveler claims to pick up the thread in a letter reporting his encounter with the cousins and their destiny. That shift in narrative voice and form, from third- to first-person, constitutes another of the implausible ruptures that have mystified readers. In turn, the "Preface" of 1832 continues in an authorial male persona, to describe "his" modest aims as a realist writer, defending his neutrality as well as his depiction of his characters as types who represent the law, public opinion, illusion, and female passions. Just two years after Stendhal had used a mirror metaphor in *Le rouge et le noir*, Sand likewise declares, "The writer is only a mirror which reflects" social inequalities and maladies (5). Yet, two key bedroom scenes play out between mirrors and a doubling of the figures of Indiana and her maid Noun—a metaphoric allusion to the *mise en abime* in literary representations of the social order that destabilizes any simple notion of reflection. Likewise, a letter of February 28, 1832, claimed that her novel would be "neither romantic ... nor frenetic ... it is ordinary life. It is bourgeois realism [*de la vraisemblance bourgeoise*], but unfortunately, it is much more difficult than pompous literature" (Sand 2. 46–7).

While Margaret Cohen argues that Sand "defaults on the realist contract" (152), Naomi Schor has argued that the implied realist logic of the first narrative voice incorporates an appropriate focus on physical details, political events, and social change in the wake of the Revolution of 1830. Sand's sophisticated use of doubling, for example, juxtaposes the relatively passive heroine with her passionate servant and "soeur de lait," Noun, who when pregnant, commits suicide, having been rejected by her ignorant mistress. Sand's mentor Henri de Latouche first told her the manuscript was "a pastiche, school of Balzac," but on rereading proclaimed its superiority to Balzac and Mérimée (Schor xii). The "Preface" of 1832 claims "the writer has invented almost nothing"; the writer is "a machine" and need not apologize "if the impressions are correct and the reflection is faithful" (5). The first chapter in particular seems replete with effects of the real. M. and Mme Delmare disagree about a dog in the "trivial, commonplace incident" that typifies the disharmony of a domestic evening; the intensely detailed scene by the fireside is highlighted by a comparison to a chiaroscuro Rembrandt, in a subtle reference to conventions of realist "genre" painting (17–18). Sainte-Beuve in a review a few months later praised the novel for presenting a familiar world that was true and living.

Despite this insistence on codes of realism from the first, Sand presents the voice of the narrator with exuberant irony. By the end of the first page, he has praised Colonel Delmare as an "excellent master who made everyone tremble, wife, servants, horses, and dogs" (15). Sand further invokes realism by detailed mockery of a family portrait of Sir Ralph, Indiana's cousin, complete with dogs and an English horse that could have been painted by Stubbs. In a satire on realist effects, the narrator praises its "perfection of detail, all its trivia of likeness, all its commonplace minutiae. It was a portrait to make a nurse weep, to make dogs bark, and to make a tailor faint with joy. There was only one thing more insignificant than the portrait, it was the original" (67). Indiana, we must note, keeps the portrait under a double veil—just as Sand veils her own ironic narrative (Higonnet 272). Three years later, Balzac would introduce a novel that began tongue-in-cheek, "All is true."

While Sand's main irony is directed at the omniscient claims of the narrator, the male narrator's mockery in turn addresses the characters' self-delusions. He undermines the vain rake Raymond, a journalist-aristocrat who incarnates the observation that language is a "prostitute" queen, and who seduces himself with his own eloquence; he agrees with M. Delmare and Raymond that Indiana repeats "the exaggerated feelings she had acquired from books" written for lady's maids (85, 152). Similarly, he deflates Indiana's hope to die from disappointed love: "she was not even dangerously ill" (238). Realism trumps romantic convention. When the narrator observes about Indiana's deluded passion for Raymond that "Woman is naturally foolish [imbécile]" (192), his insulting generalization reminds us that one of the codes of realism for Roland Barthes is the social code of the familiar clichés about types and situations that the audience may be counted upon to read as "natural," as valid within a shared social context, or as appropriate to a literary genre. The 1832 preface confirms that each of the characters is a type and thereby exposes the romance tropes (7). But at another level of realism, we recognize the conventions whereby Indiana is entrapped not only in marriage but also in the social scripts that deprive her of a language of her own.

Sand's epilogue challenges both romance and the realist novel by "writing beyond the ending" in a rupture that has shocked many readers. In this extraordinary double ending, the planned joint suicide of Indiana and Ralph, dictated by the genre of sentimental romance, is followed by their implausible survival in a low-key, extramarital island paradise. Comically, the couple jump in the wrong direction, where their fall is cushioned by some bushes. There are many ways to read their subsequent economic situation, Indiana's muteness, and the cousins' modest idealist project of freeing a few sick slaves. The implausibility and open-ended suggestiveness of that world interpellate the reader to write the next act.

Each of these three authors invites us to consider what constitutes an objective narrator, in quite different ways that challenge conventional conceptions. Barbauld calls up the memory of a child; Charrière speaks in the voice of a woman who doubts herself; Sand ruptures the level of narration, interrupts the narrative to speak to the reader, and then jumps ship to land on an island with a new voice altogether. The questions they raise about reliability foreshadow later nineteenth-century realist texts that subvert dogma and convention. Through shifts in voice and perspective, they reopen notions about the neutral observation of social relationships and refuse conventional endings that in the authors' view would not be realistic. By incorporating directly into their texts issues and images of the act of representation, whether as an iridescent bubble, textual gaps, or mirrors, they reach beyond simple ideas of mimesis to interrogate the possibility of fixed representation. This short sketch of a few examples must serve to indicate the kinds of devices to which women writers turn, in order to undermine the conventions that confine the literary representations of women's lives. Layers of ironic framing serve to ward off censorship. A broader comparative study would be able to trace the different intersectionalities that characterize a work such as the Cuban Gertrudis Gómez de Avellaneda y Arteaga's *Sab* (1841), where the issues of race that Sand aligns with gender are much more fully developed. We need to pursue issues of class as well as race, such as those raised in Rebecca Harding Davis's *Life in the Iron Mills,* where the core symbol of an ironworker's artistic ambitions is a gigantic woman made of rough korl, the porous dross left over in iron smelting. Texts such as these compel us to recognize the complexity and sophistication with which women writers have tackled issues of representation.

WORKS CITED

Auerbach, Erich. *Mimesis: The Representation of Reality in Western Literature.* Trans. Willard R. Trask. Princeton, NJ: Princeton UP, 1953.

Barbauld, Anna Letitia. "Washing-Day." *Selected Poetry and Prose.* Ed. William McCarthy and Elizabeth Kraft. Peterborough, CA: Broadview P, [1797] 2002, pp. 143–7.

Barthes, Roland. "The Reality Effect." *The Rustle of Language*. Trans. Richard Howard. New York: Hill & Wang, 1986, pp. 141–8.

Brontë, Charlotte. *Shirley*. Intro. Lucasta Miller. London: Penguin, [1849] 2006.

Charrière, Isabelle de. *Letters of Mistress Henley, Published by Her Friend*. Intro. Joan Stewart and Philip Stewart, Trans. Philip Stewart and Jean Vaché. New York: Modern Language Association, 1993.

Charrière, Isabella de. "The Noble." *Four Tales*. Trans. S. M. S. New York: Scribner's, 1926, pp. 1–29.

Charrière, Isabelle de (Belle de Zuylen). *Oeuvres complètes*. Ed. Jean-Daniel Candaux, C. P. Courtney, Pierre Dubois et al., 10 vols. Amsterdam: van Oorschot. Cited as *OC*, 1979–84.

Cohen, Margaret. *The Sentimental Education of the Novel*. Princeton, NJ: Princeton UP, 1999.

Culler, Jonathan. *Structuralist Poetics: Structuralism, Linguistics and the Study of Literature*. Ithaca: Cornell UP, 1975.

Curran, Stuart. "Romantic Poetry: The I Altered," *Romanticism and Feminism*. Ed. Anne K. Mellor. Bloomington: Indiana UP, 1988, pp. 185–207.

Eliot, George. *Adam Bede*. Ed. Margaret Reynolds. London: Penguin, 2008.

Fisch, Gina. "Charriere's Untimely Realism: Aesthetic Representation and Literary Pedagogy in Lettres de Lausanne and La Princesse de Cleves." *MLN* 119.5 (2005): 1058–82.

Guillen, Claudio. "Second Thoughts on Currents and Periods," *The Disciplines of Criticism: Essays in Literary Theory, Interpretation, and History*. Ed. Peter Demetz, Thomas Greene, Lowry Nelson, Jr. New Haven, CT: Yale UP, 1968, pp. 477–509.

Higonnet, Margaret. "Realism: A Feminist Perspective." *The Force of Vision 3: Proceedings of the XIIIth Congress of the International Comparative Literature Association*, vol. 3, Tokyo: U of Tokyo P, 1996, pp. 267–75.

James, Henry. "Charles Augustin Sainte-Beuve." *Literary Criticism: French Writers, Other European Writers, The Prefaces to the New York Edition*. Ed. Leon Edel. New York: Library of America, 1984, pp. 664–95.

Jameson, Fredric. "The Ideology of the Text." *Salmagundi* 31–2 (1976): 204–46.

Miller, Nancy. "Emphasis Added: Plots and Plausibilities in Women's Fiction." *PMLA* 96.1 (1981): 36–48.

Moers, Ellen. "Money, the Job, and Little Women: Female Realism." *Literary Women*. Oxford: Oxford UP, 1976, pp. 67–89.

Pasco, Allan. "Romantic Realism in *Indiana*." *Approaches to Teaching George Sand*. Ed. David A. Powell and Pratima Prasad. New York : Modern Language Association, 2016, pp. 195–2.

Sand, George. *Correspondance*. Ed. Georges Lubin, vol. 2. Paris: Garnier, 1966.

Sand, George. *Indiana*, Trans. Sylvia Raphael, Oxford: Oxford UP, [1832]1994.

Schor, Naomi. *Breaking the Chain: Women, Theory and French Realist Fiction*. New York: Columbia UP, 1985.

Schor, Naomi. "Introduction." *Indiana*. Trans. Sylvia Raphael. Oxford: Oxford UP, [1832] 1994.

Schor, Naomi. *Reading in Detail: Aesthetics and the Feminine*. New York: Routledge, 1987.

Small, Helen. "Feminist Theory and the Return of the Real: 'What We Really Want Most out of Realism.'" *Adventures in Realism*. Ed. Beaumont, Matthew. Malden, MA: Blackwell, 2007, pp. 224–40.

Staël-Holstein, Germaine de. *The Influence of Literature upon Society*, 2nd edn. London: Colburn, (1800) 1812.

Trumpener, Katie. "In the Grid: Period and Experience." *PMLA* 127.2 (2012): 349–56.

Van Dijk, Suzan, Valérie Cossy, Agnese Fidecaro, Henriette Partzsch, eds. *Femmes écrivains à la croisée des langues / Women writers at the crossroads of languages 1700–1900*. Geneva: MétisPresses, 2009.

Wellek, René. "The Concept of Realism in Literary Scholarship." *Concepts of Criticism*. Ed. Stephen G. Nichols Jr. New Haven: Yale, 1963.

Williams, Raymond. *Keywords, a Vocabulary of Culture and Society*. New York: Oxford UP, 1976.

CHAPTER FIFTEEN

Poetics

CAITLIN NEWCOMER

In his foundational *Poetics*, Aristotle makes an argument about the positive social function and ethical utility of art, and especially poetry. This positive claim comes as a reaction to Plato's moral suspicion of poetry as a deceptive mode, requiring the expulsion of all poets from the ideal republic. Aristotle's text serves as a theoretical investigation of poetry, a philosophical meditation on its function and role.

Yet, nowadays such a theoretical and practical investigation of poetry represents only one possible variation of the concept of poetics. Poetics is both a discipline and a discourse, although in both cases it is flexible, even elusive. In a broad sense, the term denotes a theory of literary discourse, allowing for discussions of, say, the poetics of prose. More specifically, "poetics" often refers to a focus on poetry's (or a particular school/mode thereof) characteristic techniques, conventions, preoccupations, and strategies. One can thus speak of "neoclassical poetics," "postcolonial poetics," "aleatory poetics," "feminist poetics," and so on.[1] Yet, poetics can also describe a poet's own reflections on her praxis, as well as the set of compositional principles (whether implicit or explicit) by which a poet or poem operates.

More broadly, since at least the middle of the twentieth century, the term has increasingly designated a surveying function, linked to broad investigations of the conventions, structures, and devices of particular genres, discourses, or cultural systems. For example, a "poetics of space" (Gaston Bachelard), "poetics of culture" (Stephen Greenblatt), or "poetics of postmodernism" (Linda Hutcheon), to name just a few examples, none of which place poetry near the center of the argument. In all cases, however, there is the sense that "poetic language" is somehow different from everyday discourse, a special usage that challenges pure utility and moves us squarely into the realm of art and artistic making.

Nonetheless, the multiplicity of ways we talk about "poetics" raises questions about what discursive fields "poetics" can occupy, and what varied constellations its invocation might call to mind. For example, how do we distinguish poetics from literary criticism, from critical theory, from aesthetics, from creative praxis or self-reflection? Where do these fields overlap and where, if at all, can boundaries be drawn? Is poetics a written declaration or public statement? Is it a personal activity or dialogue with one's making? The weight given to such questions and answers constitutes one of the features that most clearly demarcates different conceptions of poetics from one another. "Poetics," then, has never and will never exist in isolation but always within an intricate web of associations and possibilities.[2] Thus, this chapter seeks to discuss a pragmatic rather than an ontological question, replacing the definitional "what is poetics" with the descriptive "what does (feminist) poetics do (and what might it do in the future)?"

Despite the seeming openness of the term, it remains nonetheless conceptually difficult (and ultimately undesirable) to take poetics away from poetry completely. As Linda Kinnahan notes, no matter how it is used, "the concept of poetics carries the traces of poetry's distinguishing quality as a genre—its concentrated, intensified meditation on operations, structures, forms, and organizations of language" (54). Often, competing definitions of the term can be traced back to differing assumptions about what poetry is and does. Theorizing a poetics, then, means necessarily occupying a poetic conceptual space. As a result, the broad usage of the term discussed above speaks both to a continued marginalization of poetry within broader cultural discourse as well as to the potential power, importance, and necessity of poetic making and theorizing to both the twentieth and twenty-first centuries. For this reason, I will confine my response to discussions of poetics as they pertain to innovations in poetic making, asking what new opportunities for feminist theory a feminist poetics can bring into being.

Such questions align with long-standing debates about the intersection of gender, literary production, and literary consumption (questions also discussed in the surrounding chapters). Rather than settle such questions, this chapter seeks to open up new avenues of inquiry and potential, moving through an investigation of the following questions: (1) What are some of the stories feminist theory and literary criticism tell in regard to poetics? Or, how have the intersection of feminism, poetry, and theory been configured and reconfigured within particular traditions of feminist thought? (2) How might we access the idea of a feminist poetics? and (3) What new articulations exist or may become possible through the languages created by feminist theorizer-poets?

FEMINISM, POETRY, AND THEORY: AN INVESTIGATION

In their 1994 collection *Feminist Measures: Soundings in Poetry and Theory*, editors Lynn Keller and Cristanne Miller describe how the book grew out of what they perceived to be the "inadequate critical attention" paid in the previous few decades to "the relation of poetry to recent theoretical and feminist discourses" (1). In Keller and Miller's formulation, there are two main reasons why this state of affairs came to be. For literary critics, on the one hand, a tendency to privilege fiction and drama and, on the other, a pervasive sense in the sixties and seventies that poetry was somehow antithetical to theory (54). Additionally, when poetry was discussed, the prevailing tendencies often privileged what Marjorie Perloff has called "the impasse of the lyric," a restrictive association of poetry almost solely with the expressive Romantic lyric that occurred in the latter half of the twentieth century (172). For feminist critics of the sixties and seventies, then, the prevailing tendency was to privilege first-person poems in the confessional mode that spoke clearly about some narrativizable or "accessible" facet of so-called "female experience."[3] Feminist criticism of such poetic work tended to focus on "thematic and socially oriented reading practices" and to "[stress] the political, communal relevance of representing private experience" (Keller and Miller 5). In other words, these decades tended to emphasize (and thereby privilege) recognizable and relatable content as the best expression of women's long-silenced voices and experiences. This perspective extended beyond critics to poets and publishers who sought to build a tradition around more direct expressions of experience and easily accessible narratives. For example, anthologies of the 1970s like *No More Masks! An Anthology of Poems by Women*, *Rising Tides: 20th Century*

American Women Poets, Psyche: The Feminine Poetic Consciousness, an Anthology of Modern American Women Poets, and the *Penguin Book of Women Poets* tended to aim, as the editors of the Penguin anthology put it, at "redressing the balance" (Cosman, Keefe, and Weaver 30) by correcting "a long neglect" (32) of women's contributions to poetry, a goal that participates in a broader feminist critical trend of recovery projects focused on bringing to light and revaluing overlooked and neglected writing by women. As the editors of *Rising Tides* put it, the anthology contains "poems which speak with a woman's voice, through a woman's perceptions, about a woman's experiences" (Chester and Barba xxvi).[4] Thus, the predominant conception of feminist poetics at this time focused on giving voice to the silenced and creating personal connections between reader and writer. Such a move often reflects directly political rather than theoretical goals by serving a connective, consciousness-raising function.

While I want to avoid the trap of dismissing women's more narrative or confessional writing as less interesting than other, more avant-garde models[5] (a move that participates in the pervasive devaluation of the daily and inner lives of girls and women at all levels of social and cultural life), this focus on "accessible" lyric modes had the dual negative effects of essentializing (claiming that there is such a thing as "female experience") and also limiting the possibilities for what models of feminist poetic theorizing and making were granted academic or publishing validity.[6] By valuing a clear-cut accessibility funneled through the loose structure of the Romantic lyric (a first-person speaker, a poem built around definable image and emotion), feminist critics and publishers worked to create aesthetic criteria for "feminist poetry" (and thereby feminist poetics), which set limits on what kind of poetics—and thereby what kind of poet—could be published and written about under that label. As Keller and Miller note, however, focusing conceptually on the idea of poetics might help to blur or interrogate perceived boundaries between "theoretical" and "literary" work (1) in order to open up new possibilities for both future theorizing and poetic practice. This orientation grew out of shifts in thinking about the role of feminist poetics that arose during the 1980s. During this era, the formation of outsider outlets like the journal *HOW(ever)* (and its later online renaissance, *How2*, launched in 1999) revealed a growing desire on the part of some experimental poets (informed by poststructuralism and interested in feminist theory) to bring together feminist literary critics and theorists with feminist-identified poets seeking to explore new pathways for poetry and poetics in order to explicitly create a space where feminist poetics and feminist theories could join in generative exploration, critique, and dialogue.

Interestingly, the creative impulses that *HOW(ever)* sought to promote were in many ways also an explicit return to experimental modernism, since the start of a specifically codified feminist poetics and feminist poetic tradition in Europe and the United States can be traced to the turn of the twentieth century. At this time, feminist approaches to poetry and poetic theorizing were strongly connected (although not exclusively) with experimental modernism. For example, modernist writers like Gertrude Stein and Mina Loy were among the first to "usher self-consciously feminist analysis into [English language] poetry" ("Feminist Approaches"). Stein's "Patriarchal Poetry," for example, explicitly articulates how patriarchal economic, sexual, psychological, and compositional practices negatively impact women's lives and creativity. Stein writes, "Patriarchal poetry and not meat on Monday patriarchal poetry and meat on Tuesday. Patriarchal poetry and venison on Wednesday Patriarchal poetry and fish on Friday" (572). Such mocking of patriarchal forms draws our attention to the regimented rules and requirements occasioned by "Patriarchal poetry," requirements that focus heavily on the domestic and spiritual duties that hamper the free expression of women's creativity and sexuality. Similarly, Mina Loy's "Feminist Manifesto" (not explicitly a poem, but potentially classifiable as a statement of poetics) calls for the total destruction of gender roles and conventions, arguing, "the only method is **Absolute Demolition**." In addition, African American poets like Gwendolyn Bennett and Helene Johnson and blues singers like Ma Rainey and Bessie Smith sought to counter prevalent cultural stereotypes of black women in order to both celebrate and create new possibilities for their lives and creative expression, an approach to poetics that emphasized explicit cultural critique and overwriting. All in all, the period saw concerted attempts to redefine poetic content, form, and praxis from a variety of feminist perspectives—goals that would also motivate the founding of HOW(ever) in the early 1980s. In fact, the journal made this connection quite explicit, framing its project as an inquiry into "modernist and contemporary innovative writing practices by women" (How2).

Kathleen Fraser and Frances Jaffer launched HOW(ever) in May of 1983. The print journal ran until January of 1992 (for a total of two dozen issues) and was later reincarnated online in 1999 as HOW2 (active roughly through the first decade of this century). In the inaugural issue of the print version, both Fraser and Jaffer responded (separately) to the question "WHY HOW(ever)?" Fraser's response, rhythmically modeled on the writings of Gertrude Stein, points to a sense of exclusion, a belief that formally experimental writing by women has been left out of the critical discussion, and that its re-inclusion may have the effect of a paradigm shift. She asks, "And what about the women poets who were writing experimentally? Oh were there women poets writing experimentally? ... But we hardly ever heard about their poems where I was sitting listening. You mean in school? I mean where poems were being preserved and thought about seriously and carried forward as news" ("WHY HOW(ever)"). Fraser's response also exhibits a potentially critical, possibly productive, not inherently necessary relationship to both historical and contemporary feminist theory and criticism:

> And the women poets, the ones you call experimentalist, were they reading Simone de Beauvoir? Firestone? Chodorow? Irigaray? Some were. They were reading and they were thinking backwards and forwards. They were writing to re-imagine how the language might describe the life of a woman thinking and changing. And the poetry they were writing wasn't fitting into anyone's anything because there wasn't a clear place made for it. ("WHY HOW(ever)")

Interestingly, the focus on "the life of a woman" persists here, but with the added sense (quite similar to modernist rhetoric earlier in the century) that the expression of "thinking and changing" required new strategies for poetic making. Two main factors occasioned the lack of space Fraser references: on the one hand, feminist poetry of the time (as discussed above) tended to privilege accessibility (as defined by clear and direct narrative, vocabulary, and image), and, on the other hand, the new experimental movements of the day (in the United States, at least), such as the Black Arts Movement and Language poetry, tended to be male-dominated and often overlooked women's contributions to the field. For Fraser, feminist poetics did not have a clearly defined relationship to prevailing modes of feminist theory, although theory could nonetheless aid in the process of developing one's own approach to poetics. A feminist poetics, then, could theorize ("thinking backwards and forwards") without constructing itself along lines of either pure self-expression or the enactment of an outside set of theoretical principles. In short, a feminist poetics need not have an essential relationship to the more codified genre of "feminist theory" although it was always also engaged in the act of theorizing, but it could also be product-ively informed, inspired, unsettled, and frustrated by it.

By the mid-1980s, particularly with the rise of poststructuralist French feminists such as Luce Irigaray, Helene Cixous, Julia Kristeva, and Monique Wittig, and the work of publications like *HOW(ever)*, an interest in the gendered nature of language itself, an emphasis on the role of language in constructing subjectivity, and an interest in a some-what broader range of modernist and contemporary experimental forms began to open up, thereby broadening the range of what might fall under the heading of "feminist poetics." Since the eighties, there exists a marked turn toward descriptions of poetics that are quite similar to many of the stated goals of this volume: a commitment to dis-ciplinary iconoclasm and proliferation, always necessarily dialogic, disruptive, unsettled, and multiplicitous as well as a belief that social transformations necessarily require (and are often preceded by) linguistic ones. Or, as poet/theorist Rachel Blau DuPlessis puts it in her foundational feminist essay collection *The Pink Guitar: Writing as Feminist Practice* (1990), the view that "[a] poetics gives permission to continue" (156).

GRANTING PERMISSION: TOWARD A FEMINIST POETICS

Perhaps the most well-known association of "feminist" and "poetics" comes from Elaine Showalter's 1979 "Towards a Feminist Poetics." In this essay, Showalter approaches feminist poetics as analogous with a specifically gendered approach to theorizing lit-erature, asking what a poetics of feminist criticism would and should mean. Although Showalter ultimately concludes that a poetics of feminist criticism "still awaits our writing," she argues that its goal is to "construct a female framework for the study of women's literature, to develop new models based on the study of female experience, rather than to adopt male models and theories." Showalter names this new approach "gynocritics." Gynocritics, rather than focusing on "woman as reader" (or what she terms "the feminist critique" which is primarily concerned with exploring "the ideo-logical assumptions of literary phenomena"), looks instead at *"woman as writer ...* with the history, themes, genres, and structures of literature by women." Thus, Showalter here uses "poetics" in the most general mode of literary criticism (a study of structures and approaches) while not applying it directly to poetry (in fact, the majority of the lit-erature she discusses as examples are novels, with the exception of the work of Elizabeth Barrett Browning). As a result, another variation on how we conceptualize feminist poetics might be to consider it, as Showalter does, in terms of how we approach acts of critical reading and response.

While Showalter's approach essentializes gender[7] (e.g., in her use of female versus male models), she insightfully links this new theoretical approach to the task of finding "a new language, a new way of reading that can integrate our intelligence and our experience, our reason and our suffering, our skepticism and our vision." The emphasis on newness, on crafting new approaches to languages and texts, also aligns Showalter's project (des-pite its other differences) with that of a feminist poetics seeking to find new means of granting "permission to continue" (to use DuPlessis's phrase again).

As noted above, Showalter discusses feminist criticism but not primarily poetry. Yet, for most critics interested in feminist poetics, the question of the relation between poetry and theory is of paramount importance. To return briefly to the classical age, Aristotle most closely aligns poetics with poesis, the act of composition or poetic making. This seemingly distinguishes poetics from theoria (theory) because of the primacy it grants the act of making. However, if poetics is synonymous with poesis, how does that connect to feminist theory or to the very act of theorization at all? Is poetics an articulation of theories that exist outside itself, or is it itself a mode of theorization? The truest answer, perhaps, is that poetics (and poetry) can be all of these things simultaneously. However, as we think about the intersection of the terms "feminist theory" and "poetics," as we move forward into the twenty-first century, I propose that the poetry that offers the most potential for feminist theorizing is poetry that itself is a mode of theoretical speculation, because it is in this vein that poetry and poetics can best offer new possibilities for feminist theory, rather than simply becoming an echo of what already exists. Historically, poetry and feminist theory join most explicitly at the level of poesis (making) via the pathways of innovation and experimentation, as articulated by the very existence of a space like *HOW(ever)*. As we saw previously, during the eighties (further intensified around the turn into the new century), the force of feminist poetics started to shift from content to form, leading to a contemporary moment where discussion of "feminist poetics" now tends to imply both formal experimentation and fluid theorization. This in turn raises questions about what the feminist poetics of the future will do—how will it be shaped by and in its own turn shape the theories just now coming into existence?

To some extent, then, the answer to the question of how we might intersect the terms "poetics" and "feminist" hinges on how we answer a previous one—what does poetry have to offer twenty-first-century feminist theory? Poetry as a medium has a unique transformative potential. Poetry both studies and activates new potentialities in language—constantly attuned to the ways in which language makes material intersecting webs of history and power. Poetry—because of its close attention to the ways language makes meaning—has the power to reflect and form our frames of consciousness and perception. Poetry, therefore, (especially poetry that questions the sociocultural operations of tradition, that seeks to break down boundaries at the level of both form and content), has the potential to shape and reshape our very conceptions of reality. In a linguistically mediated world, poetry—perhaps the literary genre most attuned to the intricacies of language and linguistically created meaning—offers a theoretical space from which paradigms have the potential to be re-made. A poetics of poetry, then (as Kinnahan also notes [54]), would most productively approach poetry as active theorization, and a poetics of poetry on the part of critics would seek to reveal and examine this theorizing. On the part of poets, poetics exists not just as a description of writing (as it is most commonly billed by current publication models) but as a means of questioning, investigating, testing, and changing writing praxis.

For me, specifically feminist poetics often takes cues from an intertwining of DuPlessis's assertion of the necessity of giving "permission to continue" with the British poet and critic Robert Sheppard's assertion that "Poetics is born of crisis—the need to change" ("Necessity"). One might hear an echo of Virginia Woolf's famous dictum on modernism here: "On or about December 1910 human character changed." Such a connection is revealing: the need to change brings with it the need to find new tools, to work without models, to question, to speculate, and to hypothesize. We might apply such origins to feminist theories as well—born of crisis, seeking change in order to grant various forms of permission. As a result, to think about the role of the "now" in terms of both poetry and poetics requires that we necessarily recalibrate the questions we are asking, and perhaps even the positions from which we ask them. The poetics of the now and the future, then, does not seek to describe writing (as might be said of literary criticism) but to change it (and perhaps, by extension, the way we see the world as well).

If poetics, then, can function not merely as a retrospective description of the writing process or as an articulation of theories that already exist (putting theory into praxis), then a space opens up for thinking through feminist poetics as an action, behavior, or orientation. In other words, the experience of poetic making brings new visions for theorization into being. Interestingly, certain avant-garde formulations of poetics already hold within them many of the stated goals of this volume—for example, Language poet Charles Bernstein has characterized poetics as "an activity that is ongoing, that moves in different directions at the same time, and that tries to disrupt or problematize any formulation that seems too final or preemptively restrictive" (150). Poetics in this vein, then, is always necessarily dialogic, disruptive, unsettled, and multiplicitous. Yet an internal tension sometimes arises when we try to relate poetics to theory: "when poetics stops it becomes theory, retrospective rather than speculative, definitive rather than open to infinitude" (Sheppard). Such a statement frames theory as something undesirable or even antithetical to poetics. While I think such a statement mischaracterizes theory, framing it as something stagnant and always behind the fact, it nonetheless puts forward a common thread in discussions of innovative poetics: it cannot stop but must constantly speculate, shift, and change shape. Statements of and about feminist poetics tend to also draw on this sense of openness rather than enclosure, of keeping to a constantly unsettled state, rather like the shark who must move continually in order to keep water flowing over its gills. As Sina Queyras notes, despite the difficulty of fixing any one definition to such a mercurial term, the idea of not "corralling, closing and excluding, but opening and including is central for a feminist poetic" (114).

In *Woman, Native, Other: Writing Postcoloniality and Feminism*, Trinh Minh-ha makes a similar case for theory, stating that "theory no longer is theoretical when it loses sight of its own conditional nature, takes no risk in speculation, and circulates as a form of administrative inquisition. Theory oppresses, when it wills or perpetuates existing power relations" (42). Here, then, we see an alignment between poetics and theory, a way to overlap poetics and theorization in speculative endeavor. When we also apply her statement to poetics, it privileges innovation, the constant awareness of capitalism's relentless capturing and commodifying of culture (to reference Simon Critchley) and the way that language shapes possibilities for subjectivity. She continues, "it is still unusual to encounter ... instances where the borderline between theoretical and non-theoretical writings is blurred and questioned, so that theory and poetry necessarily mesh, both determined by an awareness of the sign and the destabilization of the meaning and writing subject" (42). Building on this statement, then, we might argue that poetry and poetics offer a means of keeping theory active, alive, full of risk, and open to failure (and therefore inherently anti-authoritarian). One of the things a focus on poetics can offer feminist theories is a space specifically dedicated to openness, to a perpetual state of becoming, a blurring of boundaries and lines that question arbitrary disciplinary, generic, and philosophical divides. This begs the question, how close have we come to arriving at a moment where feminist poetics and feminist theory can be one and the same? How might the boundaries between poetry and theory be broken down or challenged, and what might be the result? Is such a breakdown possible or even desirable?

EXPLORING THE UNTRIED: SOME (FURTHER) THOUGHTS ON TWENTY-FIRST-CENTURY FEMINIST POETICS

What does (a) feminist poetics of the twenty-first century do? Or, "What is the state of feminist poetics? … How does one embody a feminist poetic?" (Queyras 109). Or, "What challenges do feminist poetics face today? What role do they envision for the cultural?" (Capperdoni 34). In *The Pink Guitar: Writing as Feminist Practice*, DuPlessis argues (like Queyras) that "crucial to the feminist project" is "freedom for speculation, for voices, for innovative structures, for inter-generic, experimentalist modes" (viii). While *The Pink Guitar* was published in 1990, DuPlessis's statements nonetheless helped to lay the groundwork for twenty-first-century explorations of the possibilities to be found in the intersection of "feminist" and "poetics." And yet, while late-twentieth-century articulations of feminist poetics tend to focus heavily on new possibilities for form (and therefore for female subjectivity), in general our present articulations, while keeping such questions still very much in view, tend to imagine a more explicit role for the cultural and the political (Claudia Rankine's *Citizen*, e.g., which contains lists of victims of police violence while also pushing against the boundaries of genre). Perhaps, after a pendulum swing into experimentation motivated by the directly personal and accessible models of feminist poetics prioritized in the sixties and seventies, a new arc has begun—a continuation of our past coupled with the new territories or perspectives inherent in perpetual motion. Or, as Capperdoni more concretely puts it, "What is the relationship between a poetics engaging the materiality of language as a site of deconstruction of patriarchal structures and a re-articulation of gendered and sexed subjectivity [what DuPlessis most explicitly calls for] … to the work of younger generations of poets loosely associated with [or in some way influenced by] language writing, a poetics generally understood in terms of its engagement with the effects of global capital and its impact on bodies and identities, labor relations, rural and urban spaces?" (35). Capperdoni here raises the question of how contemporary feminist poets' positions in various social margins (and/or their desire to write in some way about those margins) manifests these social prerogatives at the level of poetic genre. One answer might be to see the political/cultural not just as a subject for poetry (as the more narrative or confessional feminist poetry of the sixties and seventies did), and not just in terms of the materiality of language (as more Language-influenced poets did), but as both a subject for investigation and a "direct engagement" with language and form (Queyras 111). In other words, perhaps feminist poetics (keeping in mind the necessary plurality of the term) can have its cake and eat it too. Perhaps an emerging feminist poetics can marry both form and content so that expression and subject share more equitable importance.

In addition, one unique facet of our current moment is the plethora of earlier feminist models easily available to younger poets interested in the intersection of feminist theory, politics, and poetics. The explicit connections made during modernism between theorizing gender and power and innovating with poetic form mean that thinking about the term "poetics" in the context of the twenty-first century has the force and weight of at least a 100 years of explicitly connecting theories of poetics with various constellations of feminist theory. It also means that both poets and critics have a plethora of possible models on offer. As Deborah Mix has noted, "Generic form is a kind of vocabulary," (27) which provides readers with a set of roadmaps and biases for what a given work might be and do. It follows, then, not only that experimentation with genre works to alter such familiar conventions as gender and patriarchy but also that a critical attention to such experimentation provides us with new "vocabularies" for thinking about genre and its connections with broader social categories like race, class, and sexuality. Similarly, earlier models create their own vocabularies, both theoretical and stylistic. The fact that feminist poetics now has a long history of such models, encompassing multiple aesthetic, political, and theoretical commitments, means that we are in the midst of a particularly rich moment for expanding, combining, recombining, and rethinking creative possibilities. This seems one of the most exciting paradoxes of our contemporary poetic moment: the ability to use and reuse earlier and potentially competing traditions without being beholden to any particular one. In other words, such a poetics privileges active development rather than settled inheritance. It is alive, attuned to both the world before it and the world around it. To attempt to describe the "spirit" (Sheppard) of such a poetics means an emphasis on permission, experiment, play, on the "active production of speculative discourses" (Sheppard), an ongoing process or practice that constantly plays court to change.

Such a poetics not only asks what can be renewed and what must be invented but also asks how the very genre boundaries between poetry and theory might be broken down or challenged, and what this breakdown of boundaries would mean toward a breaking down of oppressive social conventions. Texts like Claudia Rankine's *Citizen: An American Lyric* (2014), for example, blur the lines between genres in order to create out of a hybrid poetics. *Citizen* has been awarded or shortlisted for prizes in poetry, political writing, criticism, and creative nonfiction. Its sections alternate between prose, lineated forms, lists, art prints, photographs, and on and on. Texts like *Citizen* reflect the stance that a poetics need not be either/or: that perhaps poetics might both describe and speculate, argue and enact. As Ben Lerner notes, the combinatory poetics that writers like Rankine[8] espouse "are engaged with demonstrating how the uncritical acceptance of voice and narrative conventions *as well as* their 'wholesale' disavowal by certain avant-garde writers can preserve racist and sexist ideologies" ("Beyond Lyric Shame"). Such a stance helps to move us beyond the binary of "accessible narrative" versus "formal experimentation" which has dogged much of the recent history of feminist poetry and poetics. Thus, one possible way of thinking through new directions for the intersection of feminism and poetics may manifest in the impulse to unsettle demarcated genre lines in order to create new "vocabularies" (to quote Mix again) for an increasingly boundary-less world. If we accept that poetics can produce theory (rather than simply enact it) than we necessarily give an increased validation to the need for poetry and poetics in the twenty-first-century feminist landscape. Poetics, then, does not just explain an already existent approach or theory; it can also open up new pathways for theory itself.

NOTES

1 All are entries in *The Princeton Encyclopedia of Poetry and Poetics*, a canonical list if ever there was one.

2 Those interested in historical definitions of the term are advised to begin by consulting the entry on "Poetics" in *The New Princeton Encyclopedia of Poetry and Poetics* (1993).

3 In fact, this privileging lasted well beyond the sixties and seventies, certainly through the eighties and even into the nineties. I would argue that it was not until the early 2000s that a solid body of scholarly work on (predominantly Anglo-American) feminist experimental writing (or more broadly innovative writing by women) came into being. For example, consider Kathleen Fraser's *Translating the Unspeakable: Poetry and the Innovative Necessity*, Linda Kinnahan's *Lyric Interventions: Feminism, Experimental Poetry, and Contemporary*

Discourse, Elisabeth A. Frost and Cynthia Hogue's *Innovative Women Poets: An Anthology of Contemporary Poetry and Interviews*, Laura Hinton and Cynthia Hogue's *We Who Love to Be Astonished: Experimental Women's Writing and Performance Poetics*, as well as Lynn Keller's *Forms of Expansion: Recent Long Poems by Women*, Ann Vickery's *Leaving Lines of Gender: A Feminist Genealogy of Language Writing*, Deborah Mix's *A Vocabulary of Thinking: Gertrude Stein and Contemporary North American Women's Writing*, and Elisabeth A. Frost's *The Feminist Avant-Garde in American Poetry*. The roots of this flowering trace back to projects like *How(ever)*, which made dialogue between experimental feminist poets and feminist critics and theorists an explicit goal.

4 The seventies also saw a small swell of critical output on Anglo-American women poets and feminist poems, the two most important being Suzanne Juhasz's *Naked and Fiery Forms: Modern American Poetry by Women, a New Tradition*, the first feminist book of essays on multiple women poets, and Sandra Gilbert and Susan Gubar's *Shakespeare's Sisters: Feminist Essays on Women Poets*. These works participated in recovery projects as well, drawing critical attention to under-seen writers and texts, but also worked to create an emerging body of feminist literary criticism.

5 If we adopt Alicia Ostriker's influential assertion in *Stealing the Language: The Emergence of Women's Poetry in America* (1986), that women poets of whatever stripe exist as "thieves of language," one counter-assertion might be that all poetry that speaks openly from the position of marginality (whether due to gender, race, class, sexual orientation, and so on) is always already operating from a position of marginal radicalness, that its assertion of exist-ence and importance is itself an avant-garde act. However, the counter response might be that without the addition of formal or linguistic experimentation one risks reproducing the very power structures that create one's own marginalized status.

6 The lyric/anti-lyric debate is more than a formal one. It centers on debates over subjectivity, about whether poetry is synonymous with the expression of a speaking self, or whether this expressive subjective function could somehow be emptied out. In the poetry world, the most notorious dismissers of subjectivity were the (mostly male) practitioners of the Language movement. However, there is a possible middle path here—one can keep the self-expressive functions of lyric while still experimenting with the formal strategies by which this self is expressed. Clarity, in other words, need not be a necessary precursor as it was for much "mainstream" feminist poetry of the seventies and early eighties. More recently, the "new lyric theory" has done much to broaden our understanding of what the lyric has been, is, and could be, recuperating it for the twenty-first century and for more radical and experimental poetics. For those interested in further exploration, *The Lyric Theory Reader: A Critical Anthology*, edited by Virginia Jackson and Yopie Prins, provides a useful introduction to modern theories of the lyric.

7 See Aimee Armande Wilson's chapter in this volume on "Writing" for more on this long-standing debate.

8 Lerner also discusses Maggie Nelson and Juliana Spahr, and I would add to that provisional list writers like Carrie Lorig and Khadijah Queen, although this is only the tip of the iceberg.

WORKS CITED

Aristotle, *Poetics*. Trans. S. H. Butcher. *The Internet Classics Archive*. http://classics.mit.edu/Aristotle/poetics.html. Accessed June 4, 2017.

Bernstein, Charles. *A Poetics*. Cambridge, MA: Harvard UP, 1992.

Capperdoni, Alessandra. "Feminist Poetics as Avant-Garde Poetics." *Open Letter* 14.3 (2010): 33–51.

Chester, Laura, and Sharon Barba, eds. *Rising Tides: 20th Century American Women Poets.* New York: Pocket Books, 1973.

Cosman, Carol, Joan Keefe, and Kathleen Weaver, eds. *The Penguin Book of Women Poets.* New York: Viking Books, 1978.

DuPlessis, Rachel Blau. *The Pink Guitar: Writing As Feminist Practice.* New York: Routledge, 1990.

Fraser, Kathleen. "Why HOW(ever)." *HOW(ever)* 1.1 (1983), http://www.asu.edu/pipercwcenter/how2journal/archive/print_archive/0583.htm. Accessed August 29, 2017.

Juhasz, Suzanne. *Naked and Fiery Forms: Modern American Poetry by Women: A New Tradition.* New York: Octagon Books, 1976.

Keller, Lynn, and Cristanne Miller. "Feminist Approaches to Poetry." *The Princeton Encyclopedia of Poetry and Poetics.* Ed. Roland Green and Stephan Cushman, 4th edn. Princeton, NJ: Princeton UP, 2012.

Keller, Lynn, and Cristanne Miller. "Soundings in Poetry and Theory." *Feminist Measures: Soundings in Poetry and Theory.* Ed. Lynn Keller and Cristanne Miller. Ann Arbor: U of Michigan P, 1994, pp. 1–14.

Kinnahan, Linda A. "Feminist Poetics: First Wave Feminism, Theory, and Modernist Women Poets." *Literature and the Development of Feminist Theory.* Ed. Robin Truth Goodman. Cambridge: Cambridge UP, 2015, pp. 54–68.

Lerner, Ben. "Beyond Lyric Shame: Ben Lerner on Claudia Rankine and Maggie Nelson: Two Fresh Investigations of the Prose Poem." *LitHub,* November 29, 2017, http://lithub.com/beyond-lyric-shame-ben-lerner-on-claudia-rankine-and-maggie-nelson/. Accessed November 29, 2017.

Loy, Mina. "Feminist Manifesto." *Andrew Pilsch.com: Mina Loy Online,* https://oncomouse.github.io/loy/feminist.html. Accessed September 19, 2017.

Mix, Deborah M. *A Vocabulary of Thinking: Gertrude Stein and Contemporary North American Women's Innovative Writing.* Iowa: U of Iowa P, 2007.

Ostriker, Alicia. *Stealing the Language: The Emergence of Women's Poetry in America.* Boston, MA: Beacon P, 1987.

Perloff, Marjorie. *The Dance of the Intellect: Studies in the Poetry of the Pound Tradition.* Evanston, IL: Northwestern UP, 1996.

Queyras, Sina. "Nothing Simply This Way Comes: Contemporary Feminist Poetics." *Open Letter* 12.9 (2009): 109–19.

Rankine, Claudia. *Citizen: An American Lyric.* Minneapolis, MN: Greywolf P, 2014.

Sheppard, Robert. "The Necessity of Poetics." *Pores: A Journal of Poetics Research,* 1, http://www.pores.bbk.ac.uk/1/index.html. Accessed June 4, 2017.

Showalter, Elaine. "Towards a Feminist Poetics." 1979. *Women Writing and Writing about Women.* Ed. Mary Jacobus. New York: Routledge, 2012, pp. 22–41.

Stein, Gertrude. "Patriarchal Poetry." *Stein: Writings 1903–1932.* New York: Library of America, 1998, pp. 567–607.

Trinh, T. Minh-ha. *Woman, Native, Other: Writing Postcoloniality and Feminism.* Bloomington: Indiana UP, 1989.

CHAPTER SIXTEEN

Translation

LUISE VON FLOTOW

Feminist translation as a practice, and later a theoretical concept of the twentieth century, came to the fore in certain parts of North America in the 1980s. A local movement at first, it soon developed in wide-ranging directions. It consisted, early on, of two main lines of approach: one, in which the translator with a feminist ethics rejects and changes the misogynist or otherwise disrespectful, unsavory patriarchal aspects of a text she is translating, and the other, in which the translator innovates language, creates feminist meaning, is free to express herself or himself with some (political) abandon though always with reference to a specific source text, and proudly draws attention to their deliberate textual manipulations.

Feminist translation came as a disturbance in a field that had not paid much attention to the political aspects of translation or recognized the considerable political clout that translation can wield, and was regarded as a strangely political aberration. It upset a discourse that for years had turned around the "art" and the "craft" of translation, usually in regard to literary texts. The idea that there could be such a thing as "feminist translation" was both perturbing and interesting. And while feminist translation of the 1980s was largely a field in which university professors were active and excelled, and which they promoted, it came to play an important role in changing the tone around translation—from artsy or erudite considerations about the meanings and translated versions of foreign texts to a politicized and scholarly understanding and rendering of contemporary works that challenged the patriarchal status quo—in universities, publishing houses, and cultural settings more broadly.

This chapter retraces these early developments, and then examines some of the more important translation strategies put in place as feminist translation initiatives. It discusses some of the translation studies research projects set in motion by this new discourse, and explores the rifts that opened up over the course of the 1990s between different feminist perspectives on politicized text manipulation. In regard to more recent developments, it explores the gaps between the "west/east" and "north/south" vectors that are being addressed in transnational feminist work more generally since the early 2000s and also touch current translation studies.

RE-TRACING THE BURGEONING "FEMINIST TRANSLATION" MOVEMENT

It may be difficult today to recreate or reimagine the enthusiasm and the energy that was present in the 1980s around feminist thinking, feminist activity, and the feminist translation innovations deriving from these, or to understand the righteous anger that bolstered this energy. Certain statements dating from this period may, however, provide a feel of the times: Canadian Susanne de Lotbinière-Harwood, a vocal figure in the early days of feminist translation, for instance, opens her 1991 book *Re-belle et infidèle/The Body Bilingual* with a political statement about translation: "Parler n'est jamais neutre," écrit Luce Irigaray. Traduire non plus" (11). In this emphatic opening assertion that translation, like speech, is always partial/partisan, and with her reference to Irigaray, one of the "French feminists" revered in North America, De Lotbinière-Harwood announces the political direction of her work. And she goes on to show and explain how she, as a working feminist translator, sees this partisan aspect of translation: "Feminism," she writes,

> disturbs the patriarchal scheme of things. Our infidelity is to the code of silence imposed on women since pre-"historical" times, and to the way the story tradition-ally is told. In speaking out, feminists have moved beyond "a woman's place," and have made our alien's language heard for the first time. Like writing in the feminine, feminist translation collaborates in this subversion by crashing the language line and voicing what was muted. (95)

In this excerpt, some of the subversive pleasure found in being disruptive is palp-able: "the patriarchal scheme of things" is set up as the enemy; "infidelity" rather than pious, weak or simply well-behaved fidelity is the order of the day, especially as fidelity has traditionally meant women's silencing; women having an "alien" language is presented as a fact, and subsequently often described as requiring translation into "male-speak," and feminist translation is paralleled with "writing in the feminine" as a strategy that breaks down conventional, patriarchal language and makes audible what has long been inaudible.

These are ideas that pervaded the times, in which "subversion" becomes an important term in academic and broader feminist discourse (Levine). Feminist scholars view the patriarchy as a powerful force that can and must be subverted, and feminist translation as one of the tools. Similarly, utopian ideas about fidelity in translation¹are rejected as illusory, if not pious and hypocritical, given the fact that research on translation easily reveals how relative such fidelity has always been. The first English version of Simone de Beauvoir's *Le deuxième sexe* is, of course, an irrefutable case in point; its system-atic "infidelity" has been documented since the early 1980s. But, perhaps even more telling, "fidelity" in translation is undermined by work such as Lori Chamberlain's art-icle "Gender and the Metaphorics of Translation," which traces how this concept has traditionally been linked to the sexual roles assigned to women in patriarchal societies (Chamberlain, reprinted in Venuti), thus linking fidelity to misogyny, and emphasizing women's reproductive role in patriarchy. And so "infidelity" becomes a buzzword of fem-inist translation, along with subversion, creativity, performance, and later, with Barbara Godard, "transformance" ("Performance/Transformance").

The strongly Canadian aspect of early theorizing about feminist translation comes out of the merging of several cultural and political moments over the course of the 1970s: among them, the daily practice of translation that had become the norm in Canada due to official bilingualism in French and English, and the attempts by English- and French-speaking women writers and thinkers to break through the linguistic barriers maintained by this bilingualism and talk to each other, read each other, and communicate beyond official channels. The "Women and Words" conference held in Vancouver in 1985 provided an important meeting point of the two language sectors and gave rise to numerous translation projects. Further, given that Quebec writers/thinkers had immediate access to contemporary French philosophers such as Michel Foucault, Hélène Cixous, Luce Irigaray, and Jacques Derrida, all of whom theorized on language and discourse as instruments of power, these ideas had entered Quebec literary theory and literature much more directly and much earlier than in English Canada or in the United States, where a ten-year translation gap is the norm. A sensitivity toward the details of language quickly became an important aspect of Quebec women's writing: the silent 'e' in French, for instance [le e muet], which marks the feminine grammatical gender, was viewed as a symbol of women's silence, and the fact that the masculine form of pronouns, adjectives, and past participles ostensibly includes any females, but actually hides them from linguistic view and naming, reinforced feminist attitudes on patriarchal language. Neologistic, highly experimental texts by authors such as Louky Bersianik, Nicole Brossard, and France Théoret developed in response and evoked women's civil and psychosocial status in terms that strongly reflected their exclusion from conventional language and the institutions that control it. Such work was new, bold, and subversive, cutting to the quick of the cultural power wielded by patriarchal language, and such work was underdeveloped in English Canada. Translation—and very soon, feminist translation—became necessary for the English side to read the French feminist innovations.

Toward the end of the 1980s, after a good fifteen years of feminist translation praxis, Godard produced the most trenchant theorizing of feminist translation. In the journal *Tessera* (reprinted in Bassnett and Lefevere), which was devoted to "Translating Women/ La traduction au féminin," she published a wide-ranging text that develops the parallels between feminist discourse and writing and (feminist) translation, and ends with the now famous assertion that the "feminist translator" replaces the "modest, self-effacing translator" and "*womanhandles* the text" (50). Godard gets to this point by arguing that feminist discourse is already a doubled language that needs to engage with and yet differentiate itself from the "monologism of the dominant order" (45). She parallels the production of this discourse with translation, since women writers need to "translate" their way "into subjective agency" (45), "into existence" (46). In this theory of feminist discourse, "translation is, therefore, *production, not reproduction*" (47, my emphasis), she asserts, and goes on to attack the theory of equivalence in translation which is (and remains) dominant in many minds. She asserts that ideas about the equivalence that translation might or should produce depend on a belief in the transparency of meaning, which is groundless, especially in regard to feminist discourse, which is itself translation. Moreover, such theory renders invisible the "translator-function." Feminist translation theory, on the other hand, emphasizes the polyphony of the translated text and foregrounds the self-reflexive elements of the translator's discourse, flaunting this work, flaunting its textuality.

Godard's argument rests on a resistance to patriarchal monologism and on the need for women to write their way out of the conventions and traditions that have oppressed them, by translating their language and their experiences in the process. She is referring in large part to feminist work from Quebec that she, herself, had been translating over the past decade: Nicole Brossard's *L'Amèr, ou le chapitre effrité,* which became *These Our/ Sour Mothers* as well as her *Amantes / Lovhers,* and a selection of texts by France Théoret that were published as *The Tangible Word.* Her view of feminist translation as productive comes in part from her work interpreting these hermetic, experimental texts for the English-speaking readers, and so in the literary world of the 1980s Godard, the feminist translator, affirms "her critical difference," "her delight in interminable re-reading and re-writing"; she discerns and assigns meaning, and aware of the provisionality of her practice, she pays "self-reflexive attention" to this practice. Finally, she "flaunts her signature in italics, footnotes—even in a preface" (50). In other words, this translator is aware of the contingency of meaning, its links to time, and place, and politics, and of the power of the translator to set the text in a certain way for a certain purpose. And an important part of this power lies in explicating the text, an art that Godard, the university professor, practiced extensively in translator's footnotes and prefaces as well as scholarly articles.

STRATEGIES OF FEMINIST TRANSLATION

Many different strategies are available to deal politically with texts, and feminist politics in translation has deployed them all and may need to devise more. They range from macro-strategies such as non-translation, retranslation, and strategic text selection to micro-strategies such as omission, addition, supplementing, and the development of various stylistic, grammatical, or neologistic innovations that work on the details of the text itself.

MACRO-STRATEGIES

Translators' Notes, Prefaces, Explanations

Since any feminist work is highly sensitive because it puts into question traditional heteronormative, patriarchal, and usually sexist social orders, a common strategy in the translation of feminist writing is to preface such translations with explanations, often including political or literary theory and text examples. These prefaces help explain and justify the "intellectual activism" of feminist translation (Ergun), which mobilizes new ideas and seeks to make them accessible to new readers. Translator prefaces provide the space for a discussion of feminist principles, histories, and ideas as well as specific translation problems. They provide the translator with a space where this traditionally silent and invisible text purveyor becomes visible as an active and highly skilled producer of knowledge. Similar purposes are served by translators' footnotes in feminist translation projects: they point to and discuss specific difficulties of linguistic transfer, and again signal the translator's presence and involvement. These strategies allow translators and editors to draw attention to the feminist aspects of the translation and/or the original text, explain their approach to it, discuss translation difficulties, and inform readers of their intentions and the texts' challenges. More recently, such strategies have been demonstrated in both prefaces and academic articles by Hala Kamal, regarding her work translating *The Encyclopedia of Women and Islamic Culture* into Arabic (2008). Unlike the interventions found in conventional translations and their paratexts, which are normally left unmarked and therefore invisible—for instance, in Borges's Spanish translations of Virginia Woolf (Leone) or in the paratexts introducing Sei Shônagan's 1,000-year-old *Pillow Book* (Henitiuk)—translators/translations with a feminist agenda openly present their politics and the textual strategies these deploy. They do not hide them.

In cultures and locations where feminism is seen as a deleterious foreign import, often a factor of the west to east problematic when "western" feminism is translated into various Asian cultures, other strategies have been devised: Kanchuka Dharmasiri in Sri Lanka, for instance, describes how she embeds translations of relevant excerpts from

Beauvoir or Wollstonecraft into existing, local texts, dating from the fourth century bce and written by Buddhist nuns, which are not labelled feminist but show striking parallels with the ideas of Anglo-American and European women writers. She thereby counters the effects of Buddhist nationalist ideology in contemporary Sri Lanka, and not only makes available feminist materials but emphasizes the overlap between these materials and local, even folkloric, texts by and about women.

Non-translation and Strategic Text Selection

From a feminist perspective, not every text merits translation. A useful strategy to block unwanted material is to simply not translate. This is how Canadian De Lotbinière-Harwood justifies her decision to translate no more male poets: "I realized with much distress that my translating voice was being distorted into speaking in the masculine" ("Geo-Graphies" 63–4). This silencing strategy is, however, countered by the argument that it is wise to know what "the other side" is publishing, and to translate its writings too.

More proactive strategic text selection promotes the translation of specific works that are deemed useful, inspirational, and informative for feminism. The rush of Anglo-American feminist work into Russian (Barchunova, "A Library of Our Own?") and other East European languages from the 1990s onward is one example of selective, though not always successful, translation. Similarly, the translation of progressive and informative materials such as the American women's reproductive health manual *Our Bodies, Ourselves* (1971ff) into Arabic or Serbian or Chinese (Davis; Bogic; Bessaih; Bogic and Bessaih; Li) has set out (and perhaps served) to undermine some sexist cultural oppression by providing hitherto unavailable medical information and ways of looking at women's bodies.

Feminist Publishing, Reviewing, Critiquing

The establishment of feminist publishing houses that ensure the translation and dissemination of feminist materials has been an important strategy along with the cultivation of networks of politically motivated and supportive publishers, editors, scholars, reviewers, and critics. Feminist/women's publishers established in the 1980s such as Virago Press in London, Frauenoffensive in Munich, Remue-ménage in Montreal, and The Feminist Press at the City of New York in the United States have produced many translations of women's/feminist work. Both sympathetic and scandal-creating reviews have helped disseminate information about new translations and new ideas, and combat the silencing technique that feminist writers struggle against. Such collaborative strategies have their historical moments, however, and depend on contexts, political environments, and grassroots movements rather than official top-down initiatives (see Des Rochers 122–4).[2] They have also amassed considerable criticism, even from within feminist circles: Gayatri Spivak's accusation that casts white Anglo-American feminism as a self-serving, neo-colonial movement producing "translationese" versions of an undifferentiated hodge-podge of women writers from developing countries is perhaps the most aggressive. But other postcolonial critics such as Chandra Mohanty concur in milder terms, pointing out that it is not enough to translate women writers; what counts is how they are read, understood and located institutionally. Similar criticisms are now being voiced in Eastern Europe and Russia after the 1990s glut of translation of feminist materials from western

Europe and North America that often misunderstood and mistranslated this work, since not only were translators unprepared (Barchunova,"Gender and Translation"; Slavova) but selections were made at random and without chronological ordering.

Retranslation

The strategy of retranslating works deemed important for the cultural and political history as well as the social development of women has led to interesting alternatives as old texts are read from new perspectives and translated for new audiences. Retranslations of biblical texts and of the Quran have revealed many possible new meanings and messages. The translation of *Genesis*, by Mary Phil Korsak, for example, shows how retranslation from the ancient source language removes layer upon layer of patriarchal interpretation, translation, and adaptation that had established the human female as not only the secondary but the originally sinful part of the human equation. Korsak's retranslation questions and revises this interpretation, showing how the first sexed human—a female called Hawwa [Life], whose name is traditionally transliterated as Eva—is created from the "groundling, the adam." In other words, the story of a gentleman named Adam, whose rib serves to create the first woman, Eva, thereby forever putting women in the Judaeo-Christian mythology into second place, is a deliberate misunderstanding and mistranslation of the ancient text. Korsak's thoughtful paratexts explain the linguistic choices and decisions that lead to these conclusions. Similarly, new translations of the Quran by learned Muslim women provide other versions of the text, which has been equally distorted by hundreds of years of patriarchal interpretations (Hassen).

Retranslation is not always successful, however. The second English version of Simone de Beauvoir's *Le deuxième sexe* is a recent example. It was published in 2009, to replace and correct the first English version (Beauvoir, 1953), that had been under fierce attack for making extensive and unmarked cuts in the French text, especially in regard to exceptional women in history, and misinterpreting/mistranslating much of Beauvoir's philosophical discourse, making it (and her) appear incoherent. Given the importance of Beauvoir for second-wave feminism, this 1953 translation, from which many others were forged—into Chinese, into Hindi, and so on—needed a new English version. The second translation, a rather literal piece of work that sought to represent Beauvoir's discourse, voice, and style more clearly and directly, set off a storm of criticism and controversy, and disappointed many of those who had lobbied and hoped for a version that would do Beauvoir justice. Far too literal for many readers (Bauer), it was criticized for its wooden language, "mangling of syntax" and "mishandling of key terms for gender and sexuality" (Moi). This translation raised great hopes, and dashed them.

Gratis Translation

A little acknowledged and somewhat shameful strategy in feminist translation is gratis translation work. Translators are often politically motivated enough to do this highly skilled labor for free or for a very low rate of pay, thus helping to create and disseminate new information on culturally and socially sensitive questions that might otherwise remain silent. Countless translators can attest to this macro-strategy in feminist translation.

MICRO-STRATEGIES

Micro-strategies in any translation include omission, addition, supplementing, and various forms of modulation or manipulation. While these serve to accommodate and adapt the text to its new cultural/linguistic environment, certain strategies have been devised and deployed to make texts more feminist in translation than they may be in the source version. The most important are the following:

Stylistic/Grammatical Adjustments

Making the feminine visible in language is perhaps the most important contemporary feminist micro-strategy and is carried out through grammatical and stylistic means. Given the tendency in numerous languages to assume that the masculine form of words/pronouns and other referents include women, without actually mentioning or naming them, one strategy consists of deliberately using only the feminine plural forms or devising odd juxtapositions of masculine/feminine forms. This disrupts conventional reading practices and awakens readers to the grammatical imbalance of conventional language. In Canada, feminist translators working on Quebec texts have often deployed this strategy, with Susanne de Lotbinière-Harwood, the English translator of Lise Gauvin's *Lettres d'une autre/Letters from an Other*, setting out her agenda in the preface: "My translation practice is a political activity aimed at making language speak for women ... make the feminine visible in language" (9). Her strategies include the creation of less usual collocations such as "women and men," the addition of scare quotation marks for irony or an extra "e" added to a noun to mark it as feminine (voyeure), and so on. In a similar vein, twenty years later, Hala Kamal carries out adjustments in Arabic; she translates the term "women" as in "women's studies" or in the title of the *Encyclopedia of Women and Islamic Culture* into an unexpected plural in Arabic: thus "women's studies" becomes "al-Dir s t al-Nis'iyya," rather than "Dir s t al-Mar'a," the phrase that is more commonly used (261). This counteracts "the singular form's implications that perpetuate an understanding of women within a monolithic formula" (262), and draws attention to the difference between "woman" (the singular form) as some kind of essential construct and "women" (in the plural) referring to many different versions of a human female.

Interestingly, in Japan, the need to defeminize literary language for feminist purposes has been extolled by Hiroko Furukawa. She explains how the excessive feminization of literary language used to represent (and in some ways normalize) women's speech in literary translation and in literary products generally needs to be addressed in both theory and practice in order to get rid of a stereotype that makes women very visible in language, but negatively so. Furakawa's work draws attention to the importance of transnational feminist work in translation, and the focus on the difference between cultural representations of women that must be taken into account.

Creative/Neologistic Translation

The translation of neologisms in any text is a problem. Feminism, like any other political movement, has produced its share of specific terms and expressions—one very pertinent example is the word "gender"—and has promoted the coining of new words in literary, poetic, and artistic work that express the heretofore inexpressible. Feminist translation of such terminology is often innovative and equally neologistic.

To take the example of the word *"gender"*: it was developed by second-wave Anglo-American feminists in the 1960s and 1970s, borrowed, somewhat controversially, from medical writings of the 1950s on intersex children and their transition to male or female identity (Germon), which had originally borrowed the term from grammatical gender: masculine and feminine. Since then, it has become "so thoroughly naturalized into the English language that today it seems indispensable" (Germon 1). However, it presents huge challenges for translators in other languages (Flotow and Scott) and has led to many new words being created. In Arabic, Kamal, for example, opts for the term *"al-jender"* in her translations of Anglo-American feminist theory, justifying this theoretically and historically ("Translating Feminist Literary Theory," 68–9); in Bulgarian, Kornelia Slavova created the term "socio-sex," and other languages have seen similar invention. But the neologisms found in feminist writing itself have also presented enormous difficulties and room for creativity in translation, since such writing often ironically deconstructs conventional "malestream" language, mocking it, making space for feminist innovation, and drawing attention to the need for other language to express women's interests and perspectives. Barbara Godard's creative renderings of innovative and ironic French may mark a high point in translating feminist neologisms (*These Our Mothers* 1983) while Erika Wisselinck laments that the wordplay in Mary Daly's *Gyn/Ecology* (1977) (Flotow) is beyond contemporary German which has not yet created the "Frauensprache" [women's language] necessary to deal with her neologisms. This causes a failure to translate. The upshot seems to be that in facing the difficult "parler-femme"/"woman-speak," the most important strategy is to immerse oneself in that world: "to translate feminists you have to read feminists" (De Lotbinière-Harwood, *Letters* 11).

RESEARCH AND RIFTS

As in other disciplines, the rise of feminism, and especially of the subversive idea of feminist translation in the late twentieth century, triggered numerous research projects on women: these included work on women translators over the ages, which sought both to identify such translators and to examine/highlight the feminist aspects of their work, on women writers and the translations of their works, on important 'key' texts (such as the Bible or the Quran or Beauvoir's writing) whose translations and interpretations have substantially influenced women's lives and thinking. And so Margaret Hannay's collection entitled *Silent but for the Word* traces Tudor women's influence as patrons, translators, and writers of largely religious works, and shows how their influence is palpable in this period, and a collection of essays entitled *Translating Slavery. Gender and Race in French Women's Writing, 1783–1823* (Kadish and Massardier-Kenney) presents heretofore "forgotten" abolitionist writings by a number of French women intellectuals from the late eighteenth century. In an approach sometimes termed "gynocriticism," which places emphasis on the social and historical conditions of women's literary endeavors and on women's difference, women translators in eighteenth- and nineteenth-century England have been unearthed, literally (Stark; Agorni; Hosington), Germany (El-Akramy; Adamo; Brown), Italy (Sanson), and an archaeology of their work has been undertaken. Many of these studies show that women translators in the early modern period of Europe resorted to translation as a way of participating in intellectual life, often restricting themselves to the appropriately feminine subject of religion, but we know that women also reached out into other areas,[3] either by subverting their source texts to assert their own agency or by developing quite different interests: travel-writing, for example, in which they "translate" in a more metaphorical sense (Agorni), or the translation of scientific texts.

The study of women translators of science rather than literary or religious material dates from the early 2000s with Michele Healy, one of the first to explore the work of English women translators of science—from Aphra Behn in the 1600s to Elisabeth Sabine in the 1800s. She shows how women translators were instrumental in promoting, explaining, and disseminating scientific knowledge, with Ada Lovelace,[4] for example, not only translating but also prefacing and annotating a French report on the calculating machines developed by Charles Babbage, the so-called "father of computer science," with whom she collaborated in many different ways (Healy 246ff.). Healy calls for much more work in this area, suggesting, for instance, that studies of the work of influential European midwives—whose texts circulated in translation before "orthodox medicine asserted control over the birthing process" (291)—would be of great value. Contemporary interest in the translation of texts on women's reproductive health has recently focused on the multiple translations of the American feminist classic *Our Bodies, Ourselves*, and more recently, the natural childbirth movement in the Middle East (Susam-Saraeva).

The point throughout this type of research is to lay open and bring to light long lost, neglected, or deliberately ignored information that details women's competence, scholarship, interests and needs, their skill at multilingual communications at various points in history and their work in moving important ideas and concepts across linguistic and cultural boundaries despite severe sociopolitical restrictions at certain times and in certain places, which include deliberately inadequate education. Farzaneh Farahzad, for instance, traces the striking development of women translators working in Iran, from a situation in which 90 percent of all Iranian women were illiterate in 1900, to the early 2000s, by which time Iranian women had translated hundreds of books (Farahzad). While such research has garnered considerable academic interest and exposure, and has stimulated more work well beyond Anglo-American/European circles, it has also encountered problems and faced rifts that, for some time, stymied further development.

These have stemmed from one important realization: women's diversity. The universalizing aspects ascribed to certain types of feminism, which neglect the cultural, historical, experiential, and ideological differences between women and the cultures they live in, led to considerable rifts in the movement. They also affected translation. One such rift became visible when the French abolitionist women of late-eighteenth-century France— Mme de Stael, Olympe de Gouges, Madame de Duras—were translated into 1990s North America, almost 200 years later (Kadish and Massardier-Kenney). This project divided the translators of the French discourse into two camps, those with a US background for whom the source texts were reminiscent of white supremacist language and thus too racist to be translated into contemporary English, and those with European backgrounds who hardly noticed the racist intonations of the source texts and were focused on resurrecting important women intellectuals. This showed that far more was involved than a US version of feminist politics of translation.

A related problem was noted by Mirella Agorni in her work on eighteenth-century English women producing translations from Italian as well as travel-writing about Italy; she warns of the risks in identifying a "tradition of female writing"—and translating—(7), which puts more emphasis on the common aspects of women's experiences than on their diversity. This diversity, she writes, is "best exemplified by their manifold relations to such constitutive elements as time, place, class, race and culture" (6–7), in other words by today's theories of intersectionality (Crenshaw), which call for the recognition and expression of the local, contextual, and sometimes individual features of texts by translators who keep in mind the diversity of their writers and their readers. Universalizing statements about women can be un-helpful if not condescending or just plain mistaken—except perhaps in reference to the presence and power of patriarchal systems that continue to be in place—and have led to tremendous criticism of Anglo-American and European feminisms and any tendency to speak for, or draw conclusions in regard to "everywoman." A particularly emphatic version of such critique argues for "polyphony in feminist translation" (Reimóndez 48), accusing feminist translation theory of failing "to propose strategies to reduce the representational gaps of non-hegemonic languages in the so-called 'transnational' conversation" (49). The author demands trans-lation projects well beyond the realm of the "hegemonic languages," which can however be put to use as pivot languages, and goes on to describe one such project that translates feminist materials from Tamil into Galician.

While the problem of language hegemony in feminist translation initiatives dates from Gayatri Spivak's essay "The Politics of Translation," another more recent issue has been identified as undermining transnational feminism: the rise, since the mid-1990s, of "gender" terminology and so-called "gender-mainstreaming," or what J. Devika refers to as "governmentalized feminism" (582), which makes the "gender expert stand in the place of the feminist, essentially shorn of oppositional charge" (582). The increas-ingly normative international development discourses around gender have been seen to drown out feminist voices, initiatives, and interests (Tiessen; Descarries), especially in non-anglophone environments, where the concept of gender enters via (mis)trans-lation, and writers, researchers, academics, teachers, and intellectuals are increasingly dependent not only on a term that rarely translates easily but also on "structures outside their social framework" (Descarries 565). When "gender" is translated from English into other languages, feminist aspects (can) simply disappear, or be annihilated. This is where more work in feminist translation and feminist translation studies must come in, in the form of transnational feminism.

TRANSLATION AND TRANSNATIONAL FEMINISM

Given the globalized, postcolonial formations in which we function today, where know-ledge and all kinds of borders (geographic, economic, political, cultural, libidinal, among others) are being remapped, "we are witnessing an ever-growing need for feminists to engage in productive dialogue and negotiations across multiple geopolitical and theoret-ical borders," write Costa and Alvarez (557). This productive dialogue requires transla-tion and translation criticism, and the translation strategies need to be feminist, promoting social change, creativity, and critiques of established paradigms (Descarries 569).

Translators and scholars of translation studies with feminist leanings have been busy in this field for some time: in Eastern Europe and Russia, for instance, they have shown how the influx of Western feminist materials in the 1990s was not a great success, with the sometimes undifferentiated and poorly prepared selection and translation of texts deemed useful for feminist purposes even undermining the intent of the translation projects. Tatiana Barchunova ("A Library of Our Own?") argues that "naïve" (i.e., under-paid, under-educated, "Soviet") translators of the 1990s render texts by Joan Scott, Nancy Fraser, or Judith Butler incoherent, or at best, unuseful. Kornelia Slavova and Anna Bogic study the problems that develop as feminist work moves unsystematically from "west to east," subject to the vagaries of funding, the whims of publishers, and the abilities and willingness of translators to understand and render terminology such as "empowerment," "agency," or "gender." As Slavova points out, the resulting conceptual confusion around gender issues in the postcommunist world means that "logical and historical connections between layers of meaning have been lost" (41), for example, as excerpts are translated and circulated outside the logical chronology, Butler before Scott, Haraway before Beauvoir. Further, the nuances in sex/gender distinctions often disappear, bringing about "a certain simplification and universalization of ideas—as if all feminist theory is monolithic and unified" (Slavova 41).

And while the term "translation" is often used metaphorically in the area of transnational feminism (Alvarez et al.), two recent books and a number of articles have begun to address the question in terms of translation "proper" (Jakobson). In an inclusive move designed to open up feminist translation studies to voices from beyond English-language Translation Studies, *Translating Women. Different Voices and New Horizons* (Flotow and Farahzad) presents work from different parts of the world, written in English by scholars from beyond the Anglo-American Eurozone: on the history of women translators in Iran, on Western women converts' translations of the Quran, on the sociocultural and political difficulties around translating Anglo-American and European feminist texts in Colombia, Turkey, Japan, China, and Serbia, on the translatability of other feminisms, from Cuba or Saudi Arabia, into the Anglo-Euro scene, and on feminist translation initiatives in Mexico, Morocco, and Sri Lanka. This first attempt at inclusive feminist translation studies is, of course, open to the usual criticisms about the "hegemonic" use of English—which involved an enormous labor of editing and rewriting to produce—but it is wise to remember that in cultures where feminism is not a welcome perspective at university or at more popular levels, such work would hardly be published or circulated locally. Publishing in English makes it available and its authors visible, and expands feminist translation studies. It is one practical response to the challenges of transnational work. The second recent publication, *Feminist Translation Studies. Local and Transnational Perspectives* (Castro and Ergun), has extended this initiative into theorizing on the risks of the west/east and north/south problematic of hegemonies, the ongoing discussions around universalisms versus local situatedness, and on the translation of queer and LGBTQI+ materials. Questions of "feminist translation in transnational solidarity" (Castro and Ergun 104) abound.

These are the important feminist translation initiatives of our time, a time where the enthusiasms and creative work of the struggle against patriarchy in the 1970s and 1980s have given way to much broader geopolitical challenges. Addressing them via feminist translation practices and theories provides endless opportunities for cross-cultural and transnational feminist initiatives of the most diverse kind. These are differently heady times.

NOTES

1 "Fidelity in translation" is a double-edged, problematic concept: on the one hand, it can refer to the translator being faithful to the source language and on the other hand (usually simultaneously) it refers to the translator being faithful to the target language. Friedrich Schleiermacher's 1813 lecture (reprinted in Venuti 2012, 43–63) lays out the problem and seems to decide on the side of the source language while fully aware of how a translator's reputation can suffer in the target language. Contemporary translation theorists who continue

to debate the issue in terms of ethics, politics of translation, social activism in translation, and professionalism seem to have come to terms with the impossibility of fidelity to either source or target, and agree that translation solutions are contingent on time, place, political and social contexts, and finances. See also Emmerich (2017).

2 Des Rochers discusses the lack of feminist influence of an official women's institution such as that set up in Cuba after the Revolution and headed by Vilma Espin, Castro's sister-in-law.

3 The translations of Mary Wollstonecraft are interesting in this regard. In the 1780s and 1790s she produced what would be called feminist translations today, adapting and adjusting texts quite deliberately to her pedagogical feminist purposes (Kirkley).

4 Lovelace, the daughter of Lord Byron, was a gifted mathematician, and translated and introduced Babbage's work from French-language summaries and accounts of it.

WORKS CITED

Adamo, Sergia. "Übersetzungsgeschichte als Geschichte der Frauen. Überlegungen zur Rolle der Frauen als Leserinnen und Übersetzerinnen im 18. Jahrhundert." *Übersetzung aus aller Frauen Länder*. Ed. Sabine Messner and Michaela Wolf. Graz: Leykam Buchverlagsgesellschaft, 2001, pp. 77–87.

Agorni, Mirella. *Translating Italy for the Eighteenth Century: Women, Translation, and Travel Writing, 1739–1797*. Manchester: St. Jerome, 2002.

Alvarez, Sonia, et al. *Translocalidades/Translocalities: Feminist Politics of Translation in the Latin/a Americas*. Durham, NC: Duke UP, 2014.

Barchunova, Tatiana. "Gender and Translation." *Translation of "Western" Feminist Texts into Russian (Post-1990)*. Presentation at University of Ottawa's Symposium, November 7, 2017.

Barchunova, Tatiana. "A Library of Our Own? Feminist Translations from English into Russian." *A Canon of Our Own? Kanonkritik und Kanonbildung in den Gender Studies*. Ed. Marlen Bidwell-Steiner et al., *Gendered Subjects*, Band 3, Innsbruck: Wien Bozen, 2006, pp. 133–47.

Bauer, Nancy. "The Second Sex." *Notre Dame Philosophical Reviews*. Notre Dame, IN: University of Notre Dame, August 2011, https://ndpr.nd.edu/news/the-second-sex.

Beauvoir, Simone de. *The Second Sex*. Trans. Constance Borde and Sheila Malovany-Chevallier. New York: Alfred A. Knopf, [1949] 2009.

Beauvoir, Simone de. *The Second Sex*. Trans. and ed. H. M. Parshley, London: Jonathan Cape, 1953.

Bersianik, Louky. *L'Euguélionne*. Montreal: Stanké, 1985.

Bessaih, Nesrine. "Gender and Translation." *Intersectional Translated Narratives about Intimacy and Relationships*. Presentation at the University of Ottawa's Symposium, November 6, 2017.

Bogic, Anna. *Our Bodies, Our Location: The Politics of Feminist Translation and Reproduction in Post-Socialist Serbia*. Doctoral Dissertation. Canada: U of Ottawa, 2017.

Bogic, Anna, and Nesrine Bessaih. "'Nous les femmes' de 1970 à 2017 à travers les traductions et adaptations de *Our Bodies, Ourselves* en français." *TTR : Traduction, Terminologie, Rédaction* 29.2 (2018): 43–71.

Boston Women's Health Book Collective. *Our Bodies, Our Selves*. Boston: New England Free P, 1971.

Brossard, Nicole. *L'Amer ou le chapitre effrité*. Montreal: Quinze, Reprint (1988), Montreal: L'Hexagone. Trans. Barbara Godard (1983). *These Our Mothers or: The Disintegrating Chapter*. Toronto: Coach House Press, 1977.

Brossard, Nicole. *Lovhers*. Trans. Barbara Godard. Montreal: Guernica Editions, 1987.

Brown, Hilary. "Rethinking Agency and Creativity: Translation, Gender and Collaboration in Early Modern Germany." *Translation Studies* (2017): 84–102, http://dx.doi.org/10.1080/147 81700.2017.1300103.

Castro, Olga, and Emek Ergun. *Feminist Translation Studies. Local and Transnational Perspectives.* New York: Routledge, 2017.

Chamberlain, Lori. "Gender and the Metaphorics of Translation." Reprinted in *Translation Studies Reader*. Ed. Lawrence Venuti, London: Routledge, 1988/2000, pp. 314–29.

Costa, Claudia de Lima, and Sonia E. Alvarez. "Dislocating the Sign: Toward a Translocal Feminist Politics of Translation." *Signs. A Journal of Women in Culture and Society* 39.3 (2014): 557–63.

Crenshaw, Kimberlé. "Demarginalizing the Intersection of Race and Sex: A Black Feminist Critique of Antidiscrimination Doctrine, Feminist Theory and Antiracist Politics." *University of Chicago Legal Forum* 140 (1989): 139–67.

Davis, Kathy. *The Making of Our Bodies, Ourselves. How Feminism Travels Across Borders.* Durham, NC: Duke UP, 2007.

De Lotbinière-Harwood, Susanne. "Geo-Graphies of Why." *Culture in Transit. Translating the Literature of Quebec.* Ed. Sherry Simon. Montreal: Véhicule P, 1995, pp. 55–68.

De Lotbinière-Harwood, Susanne. *Letters from an Other.* Translation of Lise Gauvin's *Lettres d'une autre* (1984). London: Women's P, 1989.

De Lotbinière-Harwood, Susanne. *Re-Belle et Infidèle/The Body Bilingual.* Toronto-Montréal: Women's Press/Les éditions du Remue-ménage, 1991.

Des Rochers, Arianne. "The Travels of a Cuban Feminist Discourse. Ena Lucia Portela's Transgressive Writing Strategies in Translation." *Translating Women: Different Voices and New Horizons.* Ed. Luise von Flotow and Farzaneh Farahzad. New York: Routledge, 2017, pp. 120–37.

Descarries, Francine. "Language Is Not Neutral: The Construction of Knowledge in the Social Sciences and Humanities." *Signs: A Journal of Women in Culture and Society* 39.3 (2014): 564–9.

Devika, Jayakumari. "Getting beyond the Governmental Fix in Kerala." *Signs: A Journal of Women in Culture and Society* 39.3 (2014): 580–4.

Dharmasiri, Kanchuka. "Voices from the *Therīgāthā*: Framing Western Feminisms in Sinhala Translation." *Translating Women. Different Voices and New Horizons.* Ed. Luise von Flotow and Farzaneh Farahzad. New York: Routledge, 2017, pp. 175–93.

El-Akramy, Ursula. "Caroline Schlegel-Schelling: Salonniere und Shakespeare-Ubersetzerin." *Ubersetzung aus aller Frauen Lander.* Ed. Sabine Messner and Michaela Wolf. Graz: Leykam Buchverlagsgesellschaft, 2001, pp. 71–6.

Emmerich, Karen. Literary Translation and the Making of Originals. London: Bloomsbury, 2017.

Ergun, Emek. "Reconfiguring Translation as Intellectual Activism: The Turkish Feminist Remaking of Virgin: The Untouched History." *Trans-Scripts* 3 (2013): 264–89.

Ergun, Emek, and Olga Castro. "Pedagogies of Feminist Translation. Rethinking Difference and Commonality across Borders." *Feminist Translation Studies. Local and Transnational Perspectives.* Ed. Olga Castro and Emek Ergun. New York: Routledge, 2017, pp. 93–108.

Farahzad, Farzaneh. "Women Translators in Contemporary Iran." *Translating Women. Different Voices and New Horizons.* Ed. Luise von Flotow and Farzaneh Farahzad. New York: Routledge, 2017, pp. 3–16.

Flotow, Luise von. "Mutual Pun-ishment? Translating Radical Feminist Wordplay: Mary Daly's *Gyn/Ecology* in German." *Traductio: Essays on Punning and Translation.* Ed. Dirk Delabastita. Belgium: Presses universitaire de Namur, 1998, pp. 45–66.

Flotow, Luise von, and Joan W. Scott. "Gender Studies and Translation Studies: 'Entre braguette'—Connecting the Transdisciplines." *Border Crossings. Translation Studies and Other Disciplines.* Ed. Yves Gambier and Luc van Doorslaer. Amsterdam: John Benjamins, 2016, pp. 349–73.

Flotow, Luise von, and Farzaneh Farahzad. *Translating Women. Different Voices and New Horizons.* Ed. Luise von Flotow and Farzaneh Farahzad. New York: Routledge, 2017.

Furukawa, Hiroko. "De-Feminizing Translation: To Make Women Visible in Japanese Translation." *Translating Women. Different Voices and New Horizons.* Ed. Luise von Flotow and Farzaneh Farahzad. New York: Routledge, 2016, pp.76–89.

Germon, Jennifer. *Gender: A Genealogy of an Idea.* Basingstoke: Palgrave Macmillan, 2009.

Godard, Barbara. "Performance/Transformance." *Tessera* 11 (December 1991): 11–18. ISSN 1923–9408, http://tessera.journals.yorku.ca/index.php/tessera/article/view/24929.

Godard, Barbara. "Theorizing Feminist Discourse/Translation." Reprinted in *Translation, History and Culture.* Ed. Susan Bassnett and André Lefevere, London: Pinter, 1989/1990, pp. 87–96.

Hannay, Margaret P. *Silent But for the Word: Tudor Women as Patrons, Translators and Writers of Religious Works.* Kent, OH: Kent State UP, 1985.

Hassen, Rim. "Negotiating Western and Muslim Feminine Identities through Translation: Western Female Converts Translating the Quran." *Translating Women. Different Voices and New Horizons.* Ed. Luise von Flotow and Farzaneh Farahzad. New York: Routledge, 2017, pp. 17–38.

Healy, Michele. Doctoral Dissertation. *The Cachet of the "Invisible" Translator: Englishwomen Translating Science (1650–1850).* Canada: U of Ottawa, 2004.

Henitiuk, Valerie. "Prefacing Gender: Framing Sei Shônagan for a Western Audience, 1875–2006." *Translating Women.* Ed. Luise von Flotow. Canada: U of Ottawa Press, 2011, pp. 239–62.

Hosington, Brenda M. "Women Translators and the Early Printed Book." *A Companion to the Early Printed Book in Britain 1476–1558.* Ed. Vincent Gillespie and Susan Powell. Cambridge: Brewer, 2014, pp. 248–71.

Irigaray, Luce. *Parler n'est jamais neutre.* Paris: Éditions de Minuit, 1985.

Jakobson, Roman. "On Linguistic Aspects of Translation." *On Translation.* Ed. Achilles Fang et al. Cambridge, MA: Harvard UP, 1959, pp. 232–9.

Kadish, Doris Y., and Françoise Massardier-Kenney. *Translating Slavery. Gender and Race in French Women's Writing, 1783–1823,* vol. 1. Kent, OH: Kent State UP, 1994.

Kamal, Hala. "Translating Women and Gender. The Experience of Translating the Encyclopedia of Women and Islamic Cultures into Arabic." *Women's Studies Quarterly* 36.3 & 4 (2008): 254–68.

Kamal, Hala. "Translating Feminist Literary Theory into Arabic." Philological Studies at the Jan Kochanowski University 29 (2016). http://www.ujk.edu.pl/ifp/studia_filologiczne/?page_id=730.

Kirkley, Laura. "'Original Spirit': Literary Translations and Translational Literature in the Works of Mary Wollstonecraft." *Literature and the Development of Feminist Theory.* Ed. Robin Truth Goodman. Cambridge: Cambridge University Press, 2015, pp. 13–26. http://dx.doi.org/10.1017/CBO9781316422007.

Korsak, Mary Phil. *At the Start. Genesis Made New. A Translation of the Hebrew Text.* New York: Doubleday, 1993.

Leone, Leah. "A Translation of His Own: Borges and A Room of One's Own." *Woolf Studies Annual* 15 (2009): 47–66.

Levine, Suzanne Jill. *The Subversive Scribe: Translating Latin American Fiction.* Minneapolis, MN: Gray Wolf, 1991.

Li, Boya. "Gender and Translation." *Translating Feminism in "Systems": The Representation of Women's Sexual and Reproductive Health in the Chinese Translation of "Our Bodies, Ourselves."* Presentation at University of Ottawa's Symposium. November 7, 2017.

Maier, Carol. "A Woman in Translation, Reflecting." *Translation Review* 17 (1985): pp. 4–8.

Mohanty, Chandra Talpade. *Feminism without Borders: Decolonizing Theory, Practicing Solidarity.* Durham, NC: Duke UP, 2003.

Moi, Toril. "The Adultress Wife." *London Review of Books* 32.3 (February 2010).

Reimóndez, María. "We Need to Talk … to Each Other. On Polyphony, Postcolonial Feminism and Translation." *Feminist Translation Studies. Local and Transnational Perspectives.* Ed. Olga Castro and Emek Ergun. New York/London: Routledge, 2017, pp. 42–55.

Sanson, Helena. *Women, Language and Grammar: Italy 1500–1900.* Oxford: Oxford UP, 2011.

Schleiermacher, Friedrich. "On the Different Methods of Translating." Reprinted in *The Translation Studies Reader.* Ed. Lawrence Venuti. London: Routledge, 1813/2012, pp. 43–63.

Slavova, Kornelia. "'Gender' on the Move: Shifting Meanings between Western and Non-Western Worlds." *Comment faire des études-genres avec de la littérature: Masquereading.* Ed. L'Harmattan Guyonne Leduc. 2014, pp. 31–44.

Spivak, Gayatri Chakravorty. "Politics of Translation." Reprinted in *The Translation Studies Reader.* Ed. Lawrence Venuti. New York: Routledge, 1992/2004, pp. 369–88.

Stark, Susanne. "Women and Translation in the Nineteenth Century." *New Comparison* 15 (1993): 33–44.

Susam-Saraeva, Sebnem. "Whose 'Modernity' Is It Anyway? Translation in the Web-Based Natural-Birth Movement in Turkey." *Contemporary Perspectives on Translation in Turkey,* special issue of *Translation Studies.* Ed. Elif Daldeniz. vol. 3, no. 2. London: Routledge, 2010, pp. 231–45.

Théoret, France. *The Tangible Word.* Trans. Barbara Godard. Montreal: Guernica Editions, 1991.

Tiessen, Rebecca. *Everywhere/Nowhere: Gender Mainstreaming in Development Agencies.* Bloomfield, CT: Kumarian P, 2007.

CHAPTER SEVENTEEN

Genre

MIHOKO SUZUKI

To sing of wars, of captains, and of kings,
Of cities founded, commonwealths begun,
For my mean pen are too superior things.

Anne Bradstreet, "The Prologue," The Tenth Muse (1650)

Subtile Calliope, the Gods delight,
And Mankinds recreation, guide me right
That I may the desired goale attaine
And crownes of glory, by thy conduct gaine.

Lucy Hutchinson, Translation of Lucretius, De rerum natura (1675)

GENRE REGENDERED: EARLY MODERN WOMEN AND EPIC

It is the shared etymological origin of "genre" and "gender"—from the Latin *genus*, meaning birth/origin or race/family—that leads us to surmise that gender is one of the constitutive elements of literary genres as vehicles of ideology, and that ideology has been predominantly patriarchal.[1] Twentieth-century feminist criticism took great strides to make manifest the at times covert ways in which genre encodes and affirms patriarchal ideology: a prime example being Nancy Vickers's influential, now canonical, feminist interpretation—and demystification—of the Petrarchan blazon, which had until then been taken at face value to express the poet's celebration of the beloved's beauty. Vickers demonstrated that the blazon was not what it appeared to be—but a dismemberment of the woman's body and fetishization of each part. To this end, she argued that Ovid's account in the *Metamorphoses* of Actaeon being torn apart by his dogs—upon being transformed into a stag as punishment for surprising the naked Diana—underlies the poet's defensive and anxious projection of this violence onto the body of the beloved.[2]

Although Vickers's theory has generated productive understandings of women's writing in the form of Petrarchan lyric—by, for example, Louise Labé, Veronica Franco, and Mary Wroth (see Jones)—one literary genre that still remains underexamined by feminist scholars, even in the twenty-first century, is women's authorship of epics. I suggest that this absence of reflection on women's contribution to the epic arises from the prevailing assumption that as the most prestigious literary genre it was the preserve of males, and that women dared not aspire to write in the form.

In my 1989 book on the figure of Helen in classical and Renaissance epic by canonical male authors, I stated that the genre of epic was "one that takes as its subject the founding, ordering, and defending of cities and the bequeathing of responsibility and prerogative from father to son" (*Metamorphoses* 1). It therefore did not occur to me to discuss any examples of the epic by female authors. The publication of Margaret Atwood's *Penelopiad* (2005) and Mary Zimmerman's *The Odyssey: A Play* (2006), however, provided me with the impetus to reflect upon contemporary women writers' challenge to the patriarchal ideology of classical epic (see "Rewriting"). And through my teaching, I also came to realize that early modern women did indeed work in the epic genre, bringing innovation to the form. Most notably, *The Book of the City of Ladies* (c. 1405), which I now consider to be the first epic by a woman in the Western tradition, comes into being through Christine de Pizan's radical strategy of revising previous epics.[3] Other examples, such as Moderata Fonte's *Floridoro* (1581), Anne Bradstreet's *The Tenth Muse* (1650), and Lucy Hutchinson's *Order and Disorder* (1679), indicate that Christine's was not an isolated example. My discussion in this chapter on the regendering of the genre of epic will focus on the strategies Christine de Pizan and Moderata Fonte used in order to challenge the ideology of the form of male-authored epic that represented women as obstacles to the epic project and scapegoats to be sacrificed, as I previously argued. Rather, Christine and Fonte bring women to the fore of city-building and government, as well as claim the authority of writing in this prestigious form that heretofore excluded women as both hero and author.

CHRISTINE DE PIZAN AND EPIC

Christine de Pizan (c. 1364–c. 1431), the daughter of the royal counselor at the French court of Charles V, recounts in *The Book of the Mutability of Fortune* (1403) that she inherited her father's learning in the form of "two precious stones of great value" (32)—which carry strong associations with male generation. This association is confirmed when she claims that the stones became "brighter ... and grew greatly" (48) upon the death of her husband: "I sensed that my limbs were much stronger than before ... my voice much fuller, and my body harder and quicker ... I found my heart strong and bold ... I felt that I had become a true man" (47). This momentous transformation led her to take up the male profession of writer and political counselor; in that capacity, she produced a large number of works on statecraft for her royal and aristocratic patrons, exhorting them to maintain peace in the face of ongoing civil war between the Armagnacs and Burgundians.

Her *Book of the City of Ladies* was highly influential in both France and England for at least a century after her death; its modern English translation was published in 1982—during second-wave feminism, and notably preceding its modern French edition. Although the work has generated a large amount of scholarship since then, it has not been systematically considered as an epic. I suggest that Christine was consciously writing the *City of Ladies* as an epic, hybridizing it with elements of autobiography, as did her most proximate predecessor in the form, Dante. The tripartite structure of the *City of Ladies* closely hews to that of Dante's *Divine Comedy* (1320); and Christine's dividing her City into three parts, each devoted to rulers, wives, and saints, corresponds to Dante's designating his three canticles as *Inferno*, *Purgatorio*, and *Paradiso*, with their respective inhabitants. In addition, Christine's opening "scene of instruction," in which she finds herself despondent after reading a misogynist text, recalls Dante finding himself lost in "a dark wood" (*Inferno*, canto 1, l. 2). To Dante's assistance comes Virgil, who will be his initial guide through *Purgatorio* where Beatrice will take him into *Paradiso*; to Christine's rescue come three ladies—Reason, Rectitude, and Prudence (Figure 17.1). The works

FIGURE 17.1 Cité des Dames Workshop, *c.* 1410. Reason, Rectitude, and Justice appear to Christine; Reason helps Christine build the City. British Library Harley MS 4431, fol. 290. © British Library Board.

themselves, Christine's *City of Ladies* and Dante's *Divine Comedy*, are the result of this fictional encounter of the writer's alter ego with these counselors and guides.

If Christine insistently refers to Dante in fashioning the structure of her work—even as she notably revises the masculinist focus of Dante's epic—she also insistently challenges the patriarchal ideology of the classical epic tradition, in particular the representations of female characters, by offering alternative interpretations. Because the Homeric epics themselves were not available to her, she focuses her critique on Virgil's *Aeneid*, most saliently in retelling the stories of Dido, the obstacle to Aeneas's quest to found Rome, and Lavinia, the vehicle for attaining his goal.[4] She divides Dido's story in two parts and focuses in the first part on her successful establishment of and rule over Carthage, praising her "prudence" and "her exceptional constancy, nobility, and strength" (91). By deliberately fragmenting the narrative, so that Dido's accomplishment as a ruler is separated from her demise as a lover, Christine contests Virgil's version that undercuts and diminishes Dido's public role by subsuming it to her suicide after Aeneas abandons her. Moreover, while Virgil largely blames Dido for abrogating her duty as ruler—at the same time expressing sympathy by repeatedly calling her "infelix" (unhappy)—Christine places the blame squarely on Aeneas, who "departed at night, secretly and treacherously, without farewells and without her knowledge" (189). Through this revision of Virgil, Christine in effect offers a strong alternative interpretation of Dido's story.[5] In the case of Lavinia, Christine supplements the *Aeneid* by picking up Virgil's epic at its conclusion after Aeneas's killing of Turnus: she thereby challenges Virgil's representation of Lavinia as a cipher and prize who never speaks in the *Aeneid*, by depicting her as an able ruler after Aeneas's death until her son Ascanius attains majority (96–7). In both these cases, Christine's innovation—in fragmenting Dido's story, and continuing the narrative beyond Virgil's conclusion—bespeaks a challenge to the ideology of Virgil's epic form.[6]

Christine had earlier mounted such a challenge in *Othea's Letter to Hector* (c. 1400), one of the most widely disseminated of her works.[7] As an avatar of Christine, Othea—an invented name that can be understood as "O théa," an (epic) invocation of the goddess— serves as guide to the fifteen-year-old Hector, who corresponds to the dauphin Louis d'Orléans, the dedicatee (Figure 17.2). By identifying Othea as the goddess of prudence, Christine calls attention to a woman's wisdom and her ability to guide Hector, to whom the French traced their origins, through his son Francio, the founder of France—just as Aeneas had founded Rome. This motif of the founding of European nations by Trojans who dispersed after the fall of their city became a widespread convention in Renaissance national epics, such as Ronsard's *Françiade* (Seznec 24). The prominence of Othea as the authoritative exemplar of wisdom and prudence finds counterparts in the body of the work in the importance of Minerva and Pallas Athena as well as the female warrior Penthesilea.[8]

As the title of the first printed edition of the text *Les histoires de Troye* (1499)— published in English translation as *The hundred stories of Troy* indicates, *Othea* appears to be a "mythographic text" (see Chance 25–32); yet, if we focus on its *form*, rather than its *content*, *Othea* can be read as another instance of Christine's radical reconception of epic.[9] Susan Noakes has characterized *Othea* as a "dismemberment" of the story of Troy, in which hermeneutic, rather than narrative, concerns are brought to the fore (113). I suggest that Christine challenges the ideology of epic by disrupting its unity of form: the 100 discrete units of Text–Gloss–Allegory that Christine assembles in *Othea* forgo narrative coherence. For example, the death of Achilles not only *precedes* the Judgment of Paris but also the wedding of his parents Peleus and Thetis. This disruption of epic narrative parallels Christine's subversion of the received idea of epic heroines that we saw in the *City of Ladies*. Christine further disrupts narrative consistency and coherence through the discrepancy between the introductory and concluding frames: the introduction features Othea instructing Hector, though at the work's conclusion they have been replaced by the Sibyl instructing Augustus.

Noting the distinctive page layout of the *Othea*, Nancy Freeman Regalado has called attention to Christine's treatment of Pasiphae (ch. 45)—in which the "dissolute" mother of the Minotaur is allegorized as "the soul having returned to God" (pp. 79–80)—as an instance of "astonishing, even willful, discrepancy between the topic of *texte* and *glose* and the interpretation proposed in the *allegorie*" (228). I suggest that a similarly notable discrepancy between text and image can be found in Christine's representation of Circe and Odysseus' men, a well-known episode from the *Odyssey*. The text provides a rather conventional, moralizing account of the Circe episode: "You should avoid the port of Circe / Where Ulysses' knights / Were all changed into pigs. / Remember her ways" (Text 98, p. 128); "We can interpret the port of Circe as hypocrisy, which the good spirit should avoid above all other things" (Allegory 98, p. 128). However, the accompanying miniature appears to contradict this conventional message (Figure 17.3): here, Circe is shown as a goddess and a princess, clad in blue—a color closely associated with Christine herself in the authorial portraits among the miniatures she commissioned—much larger and more prominent than Odysseus' men. The boars look up at her adoringly as if they are eager to please her; she is neither sinister nor malevolent, but appears gentle and benign.[10] Similarly, in a miniature illustrating chapter 39, Christine had earlier presented "the sorceress" Circe

FIGURE 17.2. Othea and Hector. British Library Harley MS 4431 fol. 95v. © British Library Board.

in the same chapter (and miniature) with the medical authority, the "very wise scholar" Aesculapius; while the allegory states that "Thou shalt not kill" (75), the miniature shows Circe spearing frogs, thus rendering her offense ironic. Sandra Hindman has shown that Christine closely directed the illumination of her works (75–6); we can therefore suggest that Christine purposefully transvalued Circe—at least in the visual representation—in a way that anticipates Moderata Fonte's similar revision, as we shall see.

FIGURE 17.3 Circe and Ulysses' Men. British Library Harley MS 4431 fol. 140. © British Library Board.

Just as the Cumaean Sibyl directed Aeneas's journey through the underworld, Othea proposes to guide Hector in the beginning and a Sibyl presents Augustus with a vision of the Virgin and the Christ child at its conclusion, thus framing *Othea*, as I have already mentioned. The Sybil points out to Augustus that the *pax romana* was attributable not to him, but to God, "who had created everything ... [and] who should be worshipped" (Gloss 100, p. 130). Here, at her work's conclusion, Christine makes reference to the final canto of the *Paradiso* that concludes with the Godhead, "the Love which moves the sun and the other stars" (canto 33, l. 145).

The prominence of Othea and the Sybil exemplifies Christine's authorial self-construction throughout many of her works as a political counselor. In addition, the figure of the Sybil—as an authoritative figure of prophecy that is closely associated with poetry—enables Christine to legitimate her own political and poetic authority. It is fitting, therefore, that Christine considered this work to be particularly suitable for rulers: in addition to dedicating it to Louis d'Orléans, she commissioned customized manuscripts for Queen Isabeau of Bavaria; Jean, duke of Berry; Philip, duke of Burgundy; and even the English king Henry IV, whose invitation to join his court she declined. Comparing herself to the Sibyl and the reader/ruler to Augustus,[11] Christine claims and affirms her own authority by pointing to the Godhead as a being superior to the temporal ruler. Christine fittingly casts this work as an epic, the most elevated and prestigious literary form, although deploying the epic to practical, political ends. While the explicitly stated goal of the *Aeneid* and its successors in the epic tradition was praise—*encomium*—and its aim to instruct the ruler remained implicit or oblique, Christine forgoes praise to speak truth in providing guidance to the ruler. In doing so, Christine exemplifies the importance of the figure of counselor, whose truth-telling (*parrhesia*) Michel Foucault identified as the foundation of Western political thought (69–71 and *passim*).

In addition to the *City of Ladies* and *Othea* that most directly derive from and that she places most explicitly in the epic tradition, Christine includes in her other works references to epic form and aspects of previous epics. For example, she begins the *Life of Charles V* (1404)—which Natalie Zemon Davis considered to be one of the earliest works by a female historian (157–60)—with a prominent epic invocation to God. Milton is considered to have been the first to repurpose the classical epic by invoking the Holy Ghost instead of the Muse at the beginning of *Paradise Lost*; Christine precedes Milton by more than two centuries in invoking the Christian God as her Muse.

In *The Book of the Mutability of Fortune*, Christine recounts her transformation into a man upon the death of her husband, whom she likens to the pilot of a ship (45–6). She thereby casts her husband as Palinurus, the pilot in the *Aeneid* whose death marked the arrival at his destination of the epic's hero, Aeneas. Christine's likening herself to Aeneas, and her likening of her arrival at authorship to the founding of Rome, suggests that her sense of her own androgyny emboldened her to take on the masculine, privileged form of epic. Most saliently, Christine self-consciously remade the quintessentially patriarchal form of epic in her "city" of ladies. In *Othea*, she innovated the form by fragmenting the epic narrative into discrete episodic fragments—a strategy of *briocolage*, which anticipates the postmodern practice of radical breaking and remaking. She thereby challenged the ascription of a unified body to the tradition of classical epic. Furthermore, she uses epic conventions or markers in her other works to affirm her status as a writer of the first order. In these texts we can see Christine de Pizan's theory and practice of creating female epics that enable her to claim authorship and authority in a genre that had largely relegated women to an object to be possessed and exchanged or a disruptive obstacle to masculine epic order.

MODERATA FONTE, *FLORIDORO*

My second example is *Tredici canti del Floridoro* (Thirteen cantos of Floridoro) by the middle-class Venetian, Moderata Fonte (1555–1592), whose actual name was Modesta Pozzo; she explained in the dedicatory letter that she assumed an "imagined name" because she was "a young marriageable woman and, according to the customs of this city, obligated in many respects" (49).[12] She later wrote a posthumously published protofeminist dialogue, *The Worth of Women* (1600). While Christine did not have access to the Homeric epics, Fonte had access to their translations into Italian by fellow Venetian Ludovico Dolce: the *Iliad* in 1570 and the *Odyssey* in 1573.

While scholars mainly discuss *Floridoro* as a chivalric romance, Fonte's predecessors, such as Ariosto, self-consciously placed their works in the epic tradition, as does Fonte.[13] Repeatedly referring to Ariosto's *Orlando Furioso* (1516), she also calls attention to her divergence from the conventional epic romance by overshadowing the title character Floridoro by her female hero, Risamante. Introducing the unnamed Risamante, Fonte writes, "A knight in search of adventure ... / ... / seemed vigorous and brave / in appearance, and daring over all others" (canto 2, stanza 4, p. 89). Twenty-two stanzas later, Fonte reveals the knight to have been all along a "most noble maiden" with "blonde tresses," eyes like "two stars," and "fresh, rubicund cheeks" like "lilies and crimson roses," and her hand "whiter than snow" (stanza 25–6, p. 96). The Petrarchan blazon—in which the male poet praises the body parts of his beloved—is embedded in this narrative context where the object of the gaze has proven herself to be an "expert warrior" capable of overcoming her "ferocious" male opponent; therefore, the blazon does not work to objectify Risamante, as it does in male poets' use of the trope, as Vickers has shown. Fonte demonstrates that beauty does not disable her epic heroine, since it is not revealed to the reader until we have seen the prowess that enables her to overcome a furious giant.

In view of this strategy, the manner in which Fonte introduces her eponymous (male) hero—much later in the narrative, three cantos later—is equally significant:

> His splendid white and vermilion complexion
> made every eye eager to contemplate him.
> Every part of him, except his speech,
> appeared that of an illustrious and beautiful girl. (canto 5, stanza 46, p. 180)

Fonte here deploys the familiar Petrarchan trope of the "white and vermilion" that combine in the beloved beauty's complexion to introduce Floridoro; accordingly, she explicitly compares her hero to a "beautiful girl." It may be unexpected, then, that she later describes him challenging to combat "ferocious Marcane" and his brother, about to abduct Floridoro's beloved Celsidea (canto 11, stanza 59–62, p. 323). This sequence reverses the way in which Fonte introduced Risamante, first representing her as a male knight and then unveiling her feminine beauty. By indicating that she clearly does not consider feminine beauty in her eponymous male hero to disable him as a warrior,[14] Fonte challenges the *Iliad*'s assumption that male beauty and prowess are incompatible—as exemplified in the dichotomy between the brothers Paris and Hector. Through the androgyny of both Risamante and Floridoro, then, Fonte questions the strict division of masculine and feminine—a central feature of classical epic—in both her central characters.

The epic simile is one of the most well-known conventions and markers of the genre. Fonte deploys a pair of these similes to emphasize the heroic nature of Risamante's victory over Macandro:

> As from a high mountain an internal spring
> issues furiously, and descends violently
> in a twisted path down the rocky cliff face,
> and leads to the river and widens it in the plain,
> just so from the living and animate mountain

that Macandro resembles, the blood
spreads and stretches out eagerly and furiously,
and makes a lake appear in the sand. (canto 2, stanza 10, p. 91)

But just as a lofty and firmly rooted tree,
against which a mighty wind employs its every force
(which however does not uproot it or snap it at the base,
but bows down and bends somewhat the high branches),
once that furor has ceased, with just as much
strength straightens up and spreads its foliage to the sky,
just so the warrior, after the blow Macandro
struck made him bend down, soon rose again. (stanza 15, p. 92)

These similes recall those in the *Iliad* that compare warriors and their confrontations with one another to natural forces and phenomena, thereby calling attention to the larger-than-life encounter between Risamante and Macandro. However, Fonte's similes also demonstrate her innovation in the genre. The first emphasizes the massive size of the giant by likening him to a mountain and the serious injury inflicted on him by a woman warrior by comparing the blood issuing from his wound to the gushing of spring water down the mountain. The second helps the reader visualize the nimble recovery of Risamante from Macandro's blow by comparing it to the flexibility of "a lofty and firmly rooted tree." The two together indicate the contrast between the two warriors—one massive and static, and the other majestic but agile; they also serve to explain the victory of Risamante over Macandro.

Rather than quest to establish a city (like Aeneas) or to regain his patrilineal family (like Odysseus), Risamante seeks to recover her property rights—to the kingdom of Armenia—after her father had disinherited her in favor of her more conventionally feminine twin sister, Biondaura:

Daughters of the king of Armenia both the one and the other,
they are equal in everything between them as the heavens pleased,
except that one is soft and delicate,
and the other goes armed as a warrior. (canto 2, stanza 30, p. 97)

We learn that Risamante had been "stole[n] ... from her father" by the wizard Celidante, who raised her in "skill and valor" and "in arms"; the king subsequently "bequeathed this royal burden / to her [Biondaura] alone, and did not even name the other" (stanza 35, p. 98). Thus, the father designates as heir the conventionally feminine daughter instead of the one who disrupts gender expectations; and Biondaura refuses to accede to Risamante's message that "since heaven / had made them born of one father and so much alike, / in dominion as well they should be equal" (stanza 33, p. 98). Fonte validates Risamante's "just anger" by praising her "excellent heart" and her "good deeds" (stanza 36, p. 99). By defining Risamante's quest in this way, Fonte challenges the epic form's ideology of institutionalizing the patrilineal family. The challenge is particularly salient, because, as Valeria Finucci points out, Fonte herself had to legally assert her right to a portion of her father's assets against her older brother (120–1).

One of the established epic conventions is the Descent to the Underworld (*katabasis*): Odysseus meets and converses with the dead Achilles, Agamemnon, and his mother; Aeneas meets Dido and the Trojan warrior Deiphobus from his past and is shown his future progeny, including Augustus. Fonte in her version also has Risamante learn about her descendants, as Ariosto's Bradamante does. Virginia Cox points out that Fonte departs from Ariosto in having a "beautiful fairy" take over the role of Ariosto's Merlin in overseeing the revelation to her heroine; she also departs from Ariosto in the prediction that Risamante will give birth to a daughter, Salarisa—rather than a son (*Prodigious Muse* 180). But perhaps what is of more interest in Fonte's reconception of the epic is her refashioning of the actual descent to the underworld in ways that parallel the Cave of Montesinos in Cervantes's *Don Quixote*; since Part Two of Cervantes's work in which the episode appears was published in 1615, after *Floridoro*, the two episodes indicate different—but related—ways in which early modern writers of romance epic reimagined the epic convention of the Descent to the Underworld.

In this episode, Risamante falls into a "dark tomb" after she encounters a serpent guarding its entrance. The tomb is in fact a womb-like space that portends protection and birth, rather than death and decay: it houses "a noble matron and a handsome boy," protected by a "noble fay." Fonte's depiction, without blame, of the queen of Phrygia, who committed adultery resulting in the birth of the boy—like Floridoro, characterized by a feminine grace, "fresh and beautiful / as a lily" (stanza 22, p. 125)—is exceptional in its matter-of-fact quality. She gives voice to the mother's affirmative perspective on the birth of her son, albeit illegitimate: "when I look at this beautiful fruit / that was born of it, I am even more sluggish to repent" (canto 31, p. 128). By contrast, Fonte represents the jealous husband's "unceasing persecution" as excessive; indeed, the fay, "moved to pity … / helped and counseled [her]" (stanza 33, p. 129) and places a serpent at the mouth of the tomb to protect her. The fay further prophesies that at the moment the serpent is vanquished by a "noble virgin," the husband will die and the woman and her son "will be free from this prison" (stanza 36, p. 130). Risamante has, therefore, contributed to their liberation by killing the serpent; she enters the tomb and learns the woman's story, as well as her own genealogical future from the fay, "who loved her dearly / [and] embraced Risamante like a daughter" (stanza 38, p. 130). The account of her descendants concludes with Fonte's dedicatee, Bianca Capello, whose "virtue" and "valor" Fonte emphasizes before going on to praise her beauty—as she did with Risamante; she concludes the encomium with a celebration of her "wisdom" and "eloquence" (stanza 65, p. 140).

This episode challenges the prohibition against women's extramarital sexual relationships, especially adultery, through characters who inhabit a tomb that exemplifies the prison-like space of the patriarchal marriage for women. At the same time, this space is also womb-like in its generative aspect: the mother and her son, pursued by her vengeful husband, can begin their lives anew in accordance with the protective plan of the fay and its valorous execution by Risamante—two women who act on behalf of a third. Along with the woman-centered genealogy that the fay imparts to Risamante as the epic heroine, the episode that is advanced by the three female characters and the feminine boy is a notable revision of the patrilinearity of the epic, as exemplified by the emphasis on the relationship between fathers and sons, both literal and figurative: Achilles and his father figures Agamemnon and Priam; Odysseus and his adolescent son Telemachus as well as his elderly father Laertes; Aeneas, his father Anchises, and his son Ascanius.

In a major revision of an influential episode for the epic tradition from the *Odyssey*, Fonte fashions Circetta, the daughter of Circe, as "so learned and so perfect a sorceress, / … honest and marvelously wise, / most graceful, sensible, and charming" (canto 7, stanza 52, p. 230); the mother educated her daughter in the salutary, rather than the baleful use of her magic.[15] According to Circetta, after Circe gave birth to their daughter, and after "she made every science plain to her lover," Ulysses, "cunning ... / ... stole away without saying a word" (canto 8, stanzas 14, 16, p. 237). Fonte's reinterpretation of Circe's sinister feminine magic in the *Odyssey* as knowledge desirable to Ulysses, as well as of Circe as a loving but ultimately abandoned lover, recalls Christine's similar revision in the *City of Ladies* of the sorceress Medea as well as her revision of the relationship between Dido and Aeneas in the *Aeneid*. Moreover, Fonte suggests that the *Odyssey*'s account of Circe's transforming Odysseus' men into animals was a literal representation of the metaphorical transformation the men brought on themselves: "Each man is so good a magician with his own form / ... / now this one, now that one / often takes on the semblance of a greedy wolf, / others of the muddy and filthy animal, / others of the stolid bear, fell and treacherous" (stanzas 4–5, p. 233).

Fonte not only revises the traditional representation of this heterosexual relationship, but also reverses the intense emphasis on male friendship and/or homoeroticism that characterizes the epic tradition: in the *Iliad*, between Achilles and Patroclus; in the *Aeneid*, between Aeneas and Achates as well as Nisus and Euryalus. In *Floridoro*, Fonte follows this tradition by including "a love so powerful and so vigorous" between Floridoro and Filardo, which she introduces by a proem on the importance of the "dear union of true friends" (canto 9, stanzas 6, 1, pp. 256, 254). However, as a counterpoint to this expected relationship in epic between men, Fonte fashions an explicitly lesbian, mutually loving relationship between "the beautiful ladies"—the one womanly, Celsidea; and the other valorous, Risamante.

> Already Celsidea so loved and appreciated her
> that she wanted to spend the night with her,
> and so they went together to their repose
> until the fresh dawn appeared in the sky. (canto 2, stanza 39, p. 100)

This relationship is publicly recognized without a hint of censure or opprobrium: "grieving and sad" as Risamante is about to depart after their night together, Celsidea "pleaded with the king to entreat her / to remain with her for three days yet" (stanza 40, p. 100).[16]

Near the end of the epic, Fonte provides an epic catalogue of contemporary Italian poets, in which she includes herself, unnamed, at the end as

> a solitary young woman . . .
> [who] did not dare come out with others into the light,
> quite ashamed that she, too bold,
> aspired to the way which leads to heaven,
> having as low and dull a mind
> as her design was clear and sublime.
> . . .
> This damsel had no caption
> . . .
> for the sculptor who fashioned her portrait
> did not wish that her name be known. (canto 10, stanzas 36–7, p. 288)

Like her pseudonym, "Moderata Fonte"—a virtual oxymoron juxtaposing "moderate" and "fountain" (of inspiration)—these lines combine pride and modesty by placing Fonte at the end of a series of notable male poets without naming her. To the same end, Fonte seeks to temper her self-assertion ("aspired to ... heaven"; "clear and sublime") with self-deprecation ("low and dull a mind").

Fonte ends *Floridoro*, if not in midsentence or stanza, but after having announced "What happened next elsewhere I'll sing, / for now of Celsidear I want to tell you somewhat" (canto 13, stanza 70, p. 389). In light of this abrupt ending, most scholars characterize *Floridoro* as "unfinished" or "incomplete" (Cox, *Women's Writing* 150; *Prodigious Muse* 164, 168; Finucci 118; Kolsky 167); yet, since the work was published during Fonte's lifetime, it is reasonable to assume that this truncated ending was how she intended to conclude it.[17] Indeed, I suggest that through this open-endedness, Fonte deliberately diverges from the closure that characterizes the *Divine Comedy*, or *Orlando Furioso* with the poet's nautical homecoming.[18] A similar open-endedness marks Marguerite de Navarre's *Heptameron* (1558), though published posthumously. Unlike Boccaccio's *Decameron* (1353) that decisively concludes with the completion of the promised 100 tales and an author's epilogue, the *Heptameron* breaks off in a way that deliberately calls attention to its lack of closure: "Well, I have a story ready to tell you ... So please all listen carefully" (543). These endings, I suggest, signify a carefully crafted refusal of closure—a refusal through which Marguerite de Navarre and Moderata Fonte challenged the ideology of masculine form.[19]

Fonte's multifaceted achievement as an epic poet is a considerable one. What is also remarkable is that Fonte's was only one of three epics that were written by women of her time: the Roman Margherita Sarrocchi's *Scanderbeide* (1606) and her fellow Venetian Lucrezilla Marinella's *Enrico* (1635)—both romance epics in the tradition of Tasso's *Jerusalem Delivered* (1581). All three feature androgynous heroines, indicating that just as Christine de Pizan's "transformation" into a man upon her husband's death enabled her entry into the epic tradition, so Fonte, Sarrocchi, and Marinella deployed androgynous protagonists who made successful forays into the battlefield as an analogy and license to themselves as epic poets.[20] At the same time, Fonte and Sarrocchi dedicated their epics to female patrons. Although Fonte also addressed Bianca Capello's husband Francesco de' Medici, she emphasized to a greater degree her connection with her fellow Venetian Capello. Sarrocchi dedicated her epic to Giulia d'Este, whom she praised for her "princely lineage ... foremost among kings and heroes," as well as for her "virtues" and "wisdom" that "surpass[ed] Minerva's merits" (76). Fonte and Sarrocchi therefore found actual women who could take the place of traditionally male patrons, as counterparts to their fictional heroines.

CONCLUSION

I began this chapter with an epigraph from Anne Bradstreet (1612–1672), writing in colonial Massachusetts. While the title of the collection of her poems, *The Tenth Muse*, indicates her ambition (or the ambition of the male relatives who brought the manuscript to London to be published), the poetry included in this volume, including the *Four Monarchies*, has been neglected in favor of the poetry addressed to her husband and children.[21] Thus, she was constructed as a "domestic" poet, whose ambition as an epic poet has not been acknowledged and given its due, despite her secure place in the canon of American literature. In the opening lines to the Prologue of *The Tenth Muse* (see epigraph), she adroitly denies and asserts her epic ambition, by putting "under erasure" her quotation of the first line of the *Aeneid*, "I sing of arms and the man" (Arma virumque cano), by the final line of the tercet, which claims that such subjects "[f]or my mean pen are too superior things."[22] She thereby deploys the rhetorical trope of *occupatio*, in which the writer pretends to deny what is in fact affirmed.

In the final lines of the Prologue she reassures the male poets who would exclude her on the basis of her sex:

> Give thyme or parsley wreath, I ask no bays,
> This mean and unrefined ore of mine
> Will make your glist'ring gold but more to shine. (4)

While stating that she does not seek the poet's laurel ("bays"), and is content with the kitchen herbs thyme and parsley, she calls attention to the fact that the bay leaf is also a kitchen herb, to which she, as a woman, would be entitled to lay claim. In light of this distinction that she deftly collapses, the final couplet calls into question the hierarchy between the male poets' "glist'ring gold" and her "unrefined ore"—in that while the former may be superficially impressive, the latter is more substantial, holding greater potential.[23]

Bradstreet's case exemplifies scholars' reluctance to recognize women as writing in the epic tradition, based on assumptions about epic as a masculine genre and the most prestigious in the hierarchy of genres. Paying close attention to how writers such as Christine de Pizan and Moderata Fonte use the literary conventions of epic through which they proclaimed and affirmed their participation in the epic tradition enables us to recognize that early modern women did indeed go beyond prescribed boundaries of gender and genre. In doing so, these writers critically engage with the ideology of the epic form—most notably, the emphasis on and affirmation of patriarchal lineage and relations, as well as the strict division between the sexes and their spheres of activity. To that end, they use epic conventions such as the simile and the catalogue to mark their divergence from their (male) epic predecessors. In addition, they innovate and inject new energy into the epic by hybridizing it with other genres; this hybridity has made it at times difficult to see the importance of epic form in these works. They also challenge the authority of previous epics by reinterpreting and revising characters and episodes.

The recent, and substantial, recovery of early modern women's writing by feminist editors has made possible this reassessment of the received notion that women did not arrogate to themselves the privilege of writing in the prestigious (and hence masculine) form of epic. Indeed, another example of a female epic poet is Bradstreet's contemporary Lucy Hutchinson (1620–1681), who translated Lucretius's *De rerum natura* (On the Nature of Things), from which my second epigraph is taken. Here, Hutchinson's voice comes together with Lucretius's invocation of Calliope, the Muse of epic poetry, enabling her to carve a space for herself in the epic tradition. She went on to write a biblical epic based on Genesis, *Order and Disorder*, which included passages not only from her Lucretius translation, but also near-translations and imitations of the *Aeneid* and the *Metamorphoses* (see Suzuki "Lucretius"). As feminist scholars investigating these newly edited texts as well as asking new questions of those more familiar (like Bradstreet's), we can now give proper due to the literary ambition and creativity of early modern women, whose works are now beginning to join the ranks of the epic tradition—assumed, as recently as the late twentieth century, to have been a male preserve.

NOTES

1 I thank the members of the Interdisciplinary Research Groups on Antiquities and Early Modern Studies at the Center for the Humanities, University of Miami, especially Anne J. Cruz, Jennifer Ferriss-Hill, Laura Giannetti, Guido Ruggiero, Hugh Thomas, and Barbara Woshinsky, for their suggestions that made their way into the final version.

On the "ideology of literary form," the notion that literary genres carry ideological meanings, see Jameson.

2 Another example of a theoretical intervention in the 1980s on the question of gender and genre—also focused on the woman's body—can be found in Patricia Parker's "Literary Fat Ladies," where she argues for the "association of the dilation of romance narrative with the figure or body of the female enchantress" (10). The texts she discusses as exemplary of this theory are those by canonical male authors, such as Ariosto and Shakespeare.

3 Scholars such as Quilligan have examined Dante's importance for Christine but without explicitly considering her relationship as an author of epic to the prior tradition of the genre (18–28).

4 On Dido and Lavinia as sacrificial scapegoats to the epic project of Aeneas's founding of Rome, see Suzuki, *Metamorphoses* (103–34).

5 On the importance of Dido for Christine's self-fashioning as an author, see Desmond chap. 6; Ferguson argues for Dido as an exemplum for Christine's appropriation of "metaphorical territories and textual treasures" (187). On Dido in the *City of Ladies*, see also Quilligan (102–3, 171–3).

6 Ovid, in his letter from Dido to Aeneas in the *Heroides*, casts blame on Aeneas—in the voice of and from the perspective of Dido; the love elegy focuses on Dido as a lover and not as a ruler. *Le Roman d'Enéas* (*c.* 1160) gives Lavinia a larger role than does Virgil, but as a woman in love with Aeneas, rather than as a political agent.

7 Forty-nine manuscripts are extant; there were four early print editions; and three English translations were produced between 1440 and 1540. On Othea as a figure for Christine, and Hector as a figure for Louis d'Orléans, see Hindman (42–3). Consequently, the Trojan narrative shadows the political situation of the French monarchy (55–63).

8 On Christine's Minerva as mother, author, and protector, see Chance (121–33, esp. 124–7).

9 Focusing on *Othea*'s allegorical form and its "textual and *visual* polyphony," Ignatius concludes that Christine creates "an object of contemplation, and not a didactic treatise" (138–9, emphasis in original). Desmond and Sheingorn also read the *Othea* through its visual program, which they liken to cinematic montage, "in which meaning is derived from unexpected juxtapositions" (6).

10 For another, "queer," reading of Circe in the *Othea*, see Sheingorn, 144–5.

11 In the *Path to Long Study* (1402), Christine is led by the Sibyl of Cumae to witness allegorical ladies in council discuss the world's troubles and their possible solutions; she returns to counsel the French princes. On the figure of the Sibyl, who first appears in *Othea*, as an exemplum for the author, see Fenster (116–19).

12 Cox translates the last phrase as "obliged to be more circumspect" (*Women's Writing* 331n). According to Cox, since Fonte's younger contemporary, Lucrezia Marinella (also unmarried), published under her own name, Fonte's pseudonym can be understood in the context of the earlier social climate that was less hospitable to the female writer. Both Fonte and Marinella were *cittadine* (citizens—a Venetian status between the patricians and the people), and thus it was more acceptable for them to publish their works than it was for patrician women (146).

13 Cox states that "*Floridoro* … falls squarely into the genre of romance as practiced by Ariosto," while also pointing out her departures from Ariosto (*Prodigious Muse* 165, 179–81). Kolsky, however, discusses the work as "an *epic* in the style of Ariosto" (emphasis added); and investigates the reasons for her incursion into "such a male-dominated domain" (165, 166). Yet, he emphasizes the constraints of the genre rather than Fonte's innovation in it, stating that she only "makes seemingly minor variations" (173)—a reading I strongly contest.

14 Kolsky essentializes gender difference in considering Floridoro to represent society's "feminine conscience"; he ultimately assesses the titular hero's feminine character negatively, claiming that it leads to a "parody of knightly behavior" (178, 179).

15 On Fonte's departure from Ariosto's Alcina as well as Homer's Circe, see Cox, *Prodigious Muse* (184). By contrast, Kolsky characteristically considers Circetta to be "tied down by the history of the epic," and that Fonte merely repeats "the same scenario as that between Circe and Ulysses … as if time had stopped still" (170, 174). I am suggesting, rather, that through Circetta Fonte critiques the received representation of Circe. In *The Worth of Women*, Fonte parodies Penelope's dream of the eagle's slaughter of the geese (representing Odysseus and her suitors) when Leonora recounts her dream of "a battle between my little cat and a troop of valiant mice, of which she had made mincemeat," which purportedly represents herself "fighting hand in hand with some of those dreadful men of yours … hacking them to pieces and massacring so many of them that they were all put to flight" (119).

16 For another reading of this episode, see Finucci's commentary to her edition (100n13). In Fonte's revision of Ariosto, Finucci does not discern "sexual implications" in the relationship between Celsidea and Risamante.

17 In the dedicatory letter to Francesco I de Medici, Fonte states, "I have permitted the printing of these thirteen cantos," and that "the work is already totally plotted, and will reach better than fifty cantos" (49). In the "Life of Moderata Fonte" that introduced *The Worth of Women*, her uncle, Giovanni Niccolò Doglioni, states that "she wrote the *Floridoro* (not just the cantos that appeared in the published edition, but others that have not yet been published" (36). I am arguing that this information concerning Fonte's composition of further cantos that were never published does not diminish the significance of her pointedly choosing to end the published version in a manner that withholds closure.

18 For another, psychoanalytic, reading of this lack of closure, see Finucci. Kolsky considers the "unfinished nature" of the work in primarily negative terms: "a lack of commitment … a loss of interest … a realization of the fundamentally 'male' properties of the epic poem" (169).

19 Parker's theory of narrative dilation and deferral of closure as associated with women's *bodies* in male-authored texts is of relevance here; as female *authors*, Fonte and Marguerite de Navarre refuse closure altogether.

20 The three were preceded by Ariosto whose Bradamante celebrated his patron Isabella d'Este, but I am suggesting that for female poets, an androgynous heroine and a female patron carry different, enabling significances.

21 I discuss this reception of Bradstreet in "What's Political."

22 Compare Bradstreet's lines here with Horace's humorous self-deprecation in *Satires* 2.1.12–15 and *Epistles* 2.1.250–57, where he states that he cannot write epic verses; but in his case, he is choosing to write in lyric and satire, rather than epic, in perfect epic verses.

23 Compare with Fonte's similar reflection in *Floridoro* on women's worth: "Gold which stays hidden in the mines / is no less gold, though buried, and when it is drawn out and worked, / it is as rich and beautiful as other gold" (canto 1, stanza 3, p. 145).

WORKS CITED

Alighieri, Dante. *The Divine Comedy*. Trans. Charles Singleton. 3 vols. Princeton, NJ: Princeton UP, 1970.

Bradstreet, Anne. *The Tenth Muse Lately Sprung Up in America*. London: Stephen Bowtell, 1650.

Chance, Jane. "Introduction." *Christine de Pizan's Letter of Othea to Hector*. Trans. Jane Chance. Newburyport, MA: Focus, 1990.

Cox, Virginia. *The Prodigious Muse: Women's Writing in Counter-Reformation Italy*. Baltimore, MD: Johns Hopkins UP, 2011.

Cox, Virginia. *Women's Writing in Italy, 1400–1600*. Baltimore, MD: Johns Hopkins UP, 2008.

Davis, Natalie Zemon. "Gender and Genre: Women as Historical Writers, 1400–1820." *Beyond Their Sex: Learned Women of the European Past*. Ed. Patricia H. Labalme. New York: New York UP, 1984, pp. 153–82.

Desmond, Marilynn. *Reading Dido: Gender, Textuality, and the Medieval Aeneid*. Minneapolis: U of Minnesota P, 1994.

Desmond, Marilynn, and Pamela Sheingorn. *Myth, Montage, & Visuality in Late Medieval Manuscript Culture: Christine de Pizan's Epistre Othea*. Ann Arbor: U of Michigan P, 2003.

Fenster, Thelma. "Who's a Heroine? The Example of Christine de Pizan." *Christine de Pizan: A Casebook*. Ed. Barbara K. Altmann and Deborah L. McGrady. New York: Routledge, 2003, pp. 115–28.

Ferguson, Margaret W. *Dido's Daughters: Literacy, Gender, and Empire in Early Modern England and France*. Chicago, IL: U of Chicago P, 2003.

Finucci, Valeria. "When the Mirror Lies: Sisterhood Reconsidered in Moderata Fonte's Thirteen Cantos of Floridoro." *Sibling Relations and Gender in the Early Modern World*. Ed. Naomi J. Miller and Naomi Yavneh. Aldershot: Ashgate, 2006, pp. 116–26.

Fonte, Moderata. *Floridoro: A Chivalric Romance*. Ed. Valeria Finucci and trans. Julia Kisacky. Chicago, IL: U of Chicago P, 2006.

Fonte, Moderata. *The Worth of Women: Wherein is Clearly Revealed Their Nobility and Their Superiority to Men*. Ed. and trans. Virginia Cox. Chicago, IL: U of Chicago P, 1997.

Foucault, Michel. *The Government of Self and Others: Lectures at the Collège de France 1982–1983*. Ed. Frédéric Gros and trans. Graham Burchell. New York: Palgrave Macmillan, 2010.

Hindman, Sandra L. *Christine de Pizan's Epistre Othéa: Painting and Politics at the Court of Charles VI*. Toronto: Pontifical Institute of Medieval Studies, 1986.

Hutchinson, Lucy. *Order and Disorder*. Ed. David Norbrook. Oxford: Blackwell, 2001.

Hutchinson, Lucy. *Translation of Lucretius*: 2 Parts. *The Works of Lucy Hutchinson*. vol. 1. Ed. Reid Barbour and David Norbrook. Oxford: Oxford UP, 2012.

Ignatius, Mary Ann. "Christine de Pizan's *Epistre Othéa*: An Experiment in Literary Form." *Medievalia et Humanistica* n.s. 9 (1979): 127–42.

Jameson, Fredric. *The Political Unconscious: Narrative as a Socially Symbolic Act*. Ithaca: Cornell UP, 1981.

Jones, Ann Rosalind. *The Currency of Eros: Women's Love Lyric in Europe, 1540–1620*. Bloomington: Indiana UP, 1990.

Kolsky, Stephen. "Moderata Fonte's *Tredici Canti del Floridoro:* Women in a Man's Genre." *Rivista di studi italiani* 17 (1999): 165–84.

Marinella, Lucrezia. *Enrico; or, Byzantium Conquered: A Heroic Poem*. Trans. and ed. Maria Galli Stampino. Chicago, IL: U of Chicago P, 2009.

Navarre, Marguerite de. *The Heptameron*. Trans. P. A. Chilton. London: Penguin, 1984.

Noakes, Susan. *Timely Reading: Between Exegesis and Interpretation*. Ithaca: Cornell UP, 1988.

Parker, Patricia. "Literary Fat Ladies and the Generation of the Text." *Literary Fat Ladies: Rhetoric, Gender, Property*. London: Methuen, 1987, pp. 8–35.

Pizan, Christine de. *The Book of the City of Ladies*. Trans. Earl Jeffrey Richards. New York: Persea, 1982.

Pizan, Christine de. *The Book of the Mutability of Fortune*. Ed. and trans. Geri Smith. Toronto: Iter, 2017.

Pizan, Christine de. *Othea's Letter to Hector*. Ed. and trans. Renate Blumenfeld-Kosinski and Earl Jeffrey Richards. Toronto: Iter, 2017.

Quilligan, Maureen. *The Allegory of Female Authority: Christine de Pizan's Cité des Dames*. Ithaca: Cornell UP, 1991.

Regalado, Nancy Freeman. "Page Layout and Reading Practices in Christine de Pizan's *Epistre Othea*: Reading with the Ladies in London, BL. MS Harley 4431." *Founding Feminisms in Medieval Studies: Essays in Honor of E. Jane Burns*. Ed. Laine E. Doggett and Daniel E. O'Sullivan. Cambridge: D. S. Brewer, 2016, pp. 219–33.

Sarrocchi, Margherita. *Scanderbeide: The Heroic Deeds of George Scanderbeg, King of Epirus*. Ed. and trans. Rinalda Russell. Chicago, IL: U of Chicago P, 2006.

Seznec, Jean. *The Survival of the Pagan Gods: The Mythological Tradition and its Place in Renaissance Humanism and Art*. Trans. Barbara Sessions. Princeton, NJ: Princeton UP, 1953.

Suzuki, Mihoko. "Lucretius and Lucy Hutchinson." Review of *The Works of Lucy Hutchinson*, vol. 1: *Translation of Lucretius. The Classical Review* 63.1 (2013): 279–81.

Suzuki, Mihoko. *Metamorphoses of Helen: Authority, Difference, and the Epic*. Ithaca: Cornell UP, 1989.

Suzuki, Mihoko. "Rewriting the *Odyssey* in the Twenty-First Century: Mary Zimmerman's *Odyssey* and Margaret Atwood's *Penelopiad*." Special Issue: Reading Homer in the 21st Century. *College Literature* 34.2 (spring 2007): 263–78.

Suzuki, Mihoko. "What's Political in Seventeenth-Century Women's Political Writing?" *Literature Compass* 6.4 (2009): 927–41.

Vickers, Nancy. "Diana Described: Scattered Woman and Scattered Rhyme." *Critical Inquiry* 8.2 (Winter 1981): 265–79.

CHAPTER EIGHTEEN

Archive

LAURA HUGHES

> This archive is a living reminder, a rebuke to the currently fashionable "post" thinking on questions of theory and feminism. It is a post-post institution. It marks not the exhaustion or the death of feminist theory, but its continuing vitality.
>
> —Joan W. Scott (143)

In the epilogue to *The Fantasy of Feminist History* (2011), Joan Wallach Scott draws attention to the power of feminist potential arising from archives. Focusing, in particular, on the Feminist Theory Archive at Brown University's Pembroke Center, Scott locates in the archives a vital impetus capable of reminding, rebuking, and marking: feminist theory is here, it continues to assert its relevance, and it does so not by harking back to the past but by animating the present and the future. Both as archival institution and as archived material, the Feminist Theory Archive actively participates in the life of feminist theory. As Scott suggests, archives are a way for feminism to continue to live on: not just to document the history, to preserve the past against those who would seek to eliminate its traces; but a place from which feminism, and in particular feminist theory, can have continued effects, and can produce archival events.

Expanding the various avenues for feminist activism, the archival work of feminist movements has put the past to use in the present and for the future. Put differently, the archive can be reactivated to fuel new feminist practice and thought. This chapter will explore the nuances of these two statements, showing how archival work and the archive, understood broadly, have reverberated throughout contemporary feminist thought. Although feminist theory and archival studies have been seen as two increasingly important albeit largely separate fields of inquiry in the past decades, the two are nevertheless, and will continue to be, in important dialogue about questions of institution, materiality, and temporality. The echoes of these dialogues can be traced through overlaps of scholars working between the two fields, and through contributions made to archive studies by feminist thought and practice.

Feminist theory intervenes within a field dominated by patriarchal, phallogocentric views on archives. Archives have long been understood as ways of categorizing and controlling—even creating—knowledge and information. Concepts such as provenance, access, and original order, dependent on patriarchal and phallogocentric concepts of legacy, the subject, and temporality, are foundational to archival practices and inform standards developed by national archival associations such as the Society of American Archivists.[1] This follows a nationalistic precedent that can be traced to the establishment of state archives,[2] a view of the archive's patriarchal authority that is underwritten by the Ancient Greek etymology of *arkhe* and *archon*, which Jacques Derrida traces in *Archive*

Fever (2). Along with Derrida, Michel Foucault's archival thought is a critical consideration of the modern archive; cited together, they form a theoretically legitimate bridge between archival science and critical theory, one that has been significant in the so-called archival turn in humanities and social sciences since the 1990s.

Yet, the notion of an archival "turn" is questionable: though it is informed by changes in technology and the influence of neoliberalism, the scope and longevity of archive studies does not fit neatly into narratives of disciplinary evolution or generational concerns within academia. Archive studies has provided a source of critique and material for disciplines that have grown in importance alongside it, including gender, queer, and women's studies, and feminist theory. In parallel, feminist theory has continued to reinvest archive studies with importance. Since Ann Cvetkovich's *An Archive of Feelings* made a major intervention into the joint areas of feminist queer theory and archive theory, other studies have explored the interstices: Kate Eichhorn's *The Archival Turn in Feminism*, Patrick Keilty and Rebecca Dean's *Feminist and Queer Information Studies Reader*, and the special issue "Critical Archival Studies"—particularly Marika Cifor and Stacy Wood's article "Critical Feminism in the Archives"—are at the forefront of feminist archival studies. With its analysis of time and generation, the institution, material and matter, feminist theory's dialogue with archives continues, changing the way archival science and archive studies are thought about and carried out.

Feminist work in archives—seen both in the archival work and research of feminist scholars, archivists, and librarians as well as in theoretical interventions into archival concepts—has caused important shifts in archival studies. Yet it is counterproductive to separate the theoretical and the practical when it comes to archives. My intent here is to look at the conjunction of archives and feminist theory to show how theory is irrevocably linked to the physical archive, and how in many cases theory arises from the archive—as a discursive event that demonstrates the vitality of both the archive and of theory. This chapter foregrounds collections in order to show how major theoretical considerations of feminism over the past few decades—alongside and sometimes in conjunction with the rise in archival studies—dovetail with developments in archival collections, archival theory, and practice. Feminist theory has had explicit and implicit effects on archival theory and practice. How in turn have archives served to illustrate, complicate, or advance major concepts of contemporary feminist theory?

DOCUMENTING FEMINISM IN ARCHIVAL COLLECTIONS

Feminist theory and practice (along with other critical discourses) have challenged the patriarchal stronghold on archives, recognizing the silences and erasures in historical, political, and literary archival records and reading these for the patriarchal, phallogocentric biases and faults that they represent, as well as by inventing alternative methodologies that look beyond the conventional practices of a discipline to integrate additional knowledge and materials. They have also created new archives of materials from which to write alternative histories. Initiatives in Europe and the United States such as the World Center for Women's Archives and the International Archives for the Women's Movement, both of which took root in the 1930s and 1940s and underwent periods of turbulence and dormancy, show that archiving feminism is not solely a contemporary concern but arises periodically alongside feminist activism.[3] Yet the histories of these archives also belie their own silences and erasures; the understudied development of collections by black women such as Mary McLeod Bethune serves as an example of the exclusions committed within feminist archiving and its history (Coller-Thomas). While Cifor and Wood advocate for "moving beyond representational politics" (2), the overwhelmingly Western- and Anglo-centric nature of the collections cited in studies about feminist archives must be addressed in order to realize what Cifor and Wood call "the transformational potential of feminism for archives and of archives for dismantling the heteronormative, capitalist, and racist patriarchy" (1). At stake here is the issue of institution and the complex relationship feminist archives have had with traditional institutions throughout their histories.

The section that follows considers three types of archives with different institutional attachments, focusing on collections that are emblematic of each: grassroots archives (the Lesbian Herstory Archives), group collections within institutions (the Feminist Theory Archive), and single-author literary archives (the Gloria Anzaldúa, Hélène Cixous, and Monique Wittig papers). My hope is that the specificity of these three types of collections will give a sense of their vibrancy and their potential for activating feminist theory for the future, illuminating a range of ways of addressing issues of institution, materiality, kinship, and temporality.

Grassroots Archives

The desire to document the history of political activism and community life—and to preserve materials attesting to this in the face of likely abandonment by established cultural institutions—led to the rise of grassroots collections such as the Lesbian Herstory Archives (LHA). These collections are often set up outside institutions, recognizing sexist and homophobic practices embedded in traditional collections. This is the case for many of the archives documented in *Women's Collections*, as well as for collections of activist movements like ACT UP/NY (AIDS Coalition to Unleash Power, now housed at the New York Public Library), the Gay and Lesbian Historical Society of Northern California (renamed the Gay, Lesbian, Bisexual, and Transgender Historical Society of Northern California), the riot grrrl and punk zine culture of third-wave feminism, or the June L. Mazer Lesbian Archives.[4] Many of these began as private collections, often in domestic spaces, before developing various relationships with cultural institutions such as libraries and universities. By setting up collections outside institutions and in opposition to them, these organizations question the foundational principles of archival work. As Cifor and Wood note, archivists have enfolded concepts and strategies from feminist praxis into writing about their profession: those concerned with social justice in the archival field have drawn on concepts of "collective rhetoric," "consciousness-raising," and "ethics of care"; these are just some ways in which "feminist theory can contribute to archival discourse and practice, critiquing concepts that have remained unquestioned, such as community and organization" (10).

The opposition to the institution in turn has the potential to affect change within the institution: the traditional archive must shift, if ever so slightly, to account for what it does not or cannot contain, and respond to the innovations made outside its walls. The position of the LHA staunchly outside and separate from traditional archival institutions points to the failings of the inside, exposing the vulnerabilities of traditional archives.[5] Begun in 1973, the LHA eventually settled in a Brooklyn brownstone, spreading out over multiple floors and a variety of spaces as eclectic as the materials it contains. As a counter-archive, the LHA produces its own ways of archiving in the absence of the institution.[6] Although the archives "bear the imprint of professional archivists" (Corbman 13), choices such as "non-hierarchical object-placement" (Cooper 532) suggest a willful overriding of conventional archival practice, "challeng[ing] conventional concepts of information collection, legacy, and community" (526).

The LHA fosters a community, thriving on access to materials and participating in their preservation. The all-over organization, described by some as confusing, also promotes "self-discovery and browsing"; patrons often find inspiration in the materials after familiarizing themselves with the archives' organization; consulting the materials becomes a form of self-exploration meant for "everyday users" through repeated idiosyncratic visits, not scholars with a specific agenda (Cooper 536, 526). The Archives' community aspect is reinforced through the physical conditions of consultation. In the LHA, the reader is not separate from the materials or from other readers; the reading rooms are set up to facilitate involvement that extends beyond the individual, placing the researcher in a wider community across time and space. The LHA's alternative archival practices of organization, preservation, and access illuminate and enhance the vitality of the archived materials in ways that traditional archival institutions do not.

Furthermore, the LHA revises the archival concept of place by creating an overlap between the archive and life beyond it spatially: the caretaker of the archive lives in the archive. According to Cooper, this "home-like" setting is essential to the exploratory consultation method encouraged by the LHA. The idea of "home" is reinforced through the regular event "At Home with the Archives."[7] If the archive as place is at its core linked to the notion of domesticity and domiciliation (Derrida 2–3; Stoler 24), and if this space has traditionally been male-dominated, organized on principles of patriarchal authority, the LHA's reconfiguration of the archive's home and of the archive *as* home represents a significant shift in understanding genealogy and kinship through the archive. Altogether, the LHA provides a reflection on temporality, community, materiality, and on the institution, devising new ways of archiving that are better suited to feminist and lesbian concerns.

Group Collections within Institutions

Can feminist archives effect similar change from within institutions? Many grassroots archives documenting feminist movement have made their way into public and private libraries and special collections, often associated with institutions of higher education: Hildenbrand's volume features such collections at Smith College, Radcliffe College, Texas Woman's University, and the University of Waterloo; others at Barnard College and Duke University include important collections of feminist zines and documentation of feminist public culture.[8] These collections are varied in their scope, content, and mission, and while they have a mostly representational impetus they have also served as spaces for rethinking what materials can be archived and how best to preserve and access them; this is particularly the case for the zine collections at Barnard and Duke. The Feminist Theory Archive (FTA) at Brown's Pembroke Center poses particular challenges to the conventions of archiving as a self-reflexive, community-based feminist collection centered on the common generic designation of "theory."

Founded in 2003 by Elizabeth Weed, the FTA serves as a repository for scholars' papers, processed as individual collections. Naomi Schor's papers were the first to be made available, and the Archive has expanded rapidly: at the time of writing the papers of over forty individuals are available for consultation. The FTA's website lists over 150 donors; all have contributed to feminist thought and diverse understandings of gender, but the names range widely across academic disciplines. The FTA's significance comes from the vast number of people involved, not from any one figurehead. The inaugural donation of Naomi Schor's papers seems to serve as an example and an impetus, not as the capstone of a hierarchy.[9] This sets the FTA apart from groupings of theorists, such as the Critical Theory Archive at the University of California-Irvine, which features the papers of nine "major figures," or the IMEC, whose holdings include Althusser, Guattari, and Derrida, as well as Foucault and Barthes before their transfer to the Bibliothèque nationale de France. The sheer number of individual voices included makes the FTA the largest and most comprehensive archives of critical theory in the world.

The issue of institution is significant for the FTA beyond the material and financial resources it finds at an Ivy League University: higher education is a pervasive concern of the Archive. The donors' involvement in academia underwrites a focus on pedagogy, and on the potential for feminist pedagogy revealed in the donors' materials (including syllabi, course notes, curricular design, and potentially audio/video recordings), which highlight the classroom as a venue for feminist thought and practice alongside publication endeavors. The FTA's focus on pedagogy can be seen further in its collective archival mission to preserve a variety of feminist perspectives and approaches. The implications for notions of legacy, generation, and temporality reverberate with respect to archives in general, suggesting a pedagogical function of archives and opening avenues of inquiry about the scope of feminist pedagogy's impact within cultural institutions such as archives, libraries, and universities.

Single-Author Collections

Single-author collections such as the Gloria Anzaldúa papers at the University of Texas-Austin's Benson Latin American Collection, the Hélène Cixous papers at the Bibliothèque nationale de France, and the Monique Wittig papers at Yale University's Beinecke Library form a third category of archiving feminist theory. Archived separately from other feminist theorists and theory collections such as the FTA, the Anzaldúa, Cixous, and Wittig papers could be seen as enhancing the writers' status as "figureheads," which would seem to run counter to the anti-hierarchical trend of feminist archives. More than this, however, their institutional presence speaks to the overlap between theory and literature. That these writers' papers are treated as literary artifacts speaks to the emphasis feminist theory—and critical theory more generally—has placed on writing, on overriding generic distinctions, and on challenging the authority of language and phallogocentrism. In this sense, we can compare individual feminist theory archives to those of writers such as Sylvia Plath and Emily Dickinson, whose papers have received extensive attention in regard to literary archives and manuscript study within a feminist context.[10]

Questions of categorization and material preservation at the heart of Anzaldúa's, Cixous's, and Wittig's work can indicate new methods of archival processing and researching, whether by theories developed in published texts or by the material idiosyncrasies of archived artifacts.[11] Notions of the materiality of language and the body are illuminated in archival work, whether in archiving or consulting. Cixous in particular reflects on the archival process in her writing, at times alongside the actual archiving of her papers; in this way she elaborates an archival theory concurrently with preparing her writing for an archival afterlife.[12] How must archival practice shift when faced with such self-reflective feminist archives?

The creation of these grassroots, collective, and single-author collections—whether by institutions; individuals who collect materials after an event, or posthumously; or by those who created the materials—is itself a feminist act, redressing narratives of exclusion and countering ongoing marginalization of feminist thought and issues of gender and sexuality. In addition to ensuring that feminist voices are included in a historical or literary record, the presence of feminist voices in or alongside the institutions actively changes them.

BETWEEN ARCHIVE THEORY AND FEMINIST THEORY

If we can see, through the work of Cifor and Wood, as well as of Cvetkovich and Eichhorn, that feminist theory has made important contributions to revitalizing and transforming archival work, can we also affirm that the archive as metaphor and methodological resource has enriched feminist theory? If, per Anne E. Fernald, the term archive is not "sustainable without feminist theory" (231), can the inverse also be true?[13] That many of the writers instrumental to archive theory have fueled feminist theory indicates more than an overlap of shared concerns. Feminist theory has shaped archive studies; in turn, working with archives and thinking about the archive compels feminist thought. As it sits at the hinge of theory and practice, of past, present, and future temporalities, and as it illuminates issues of materiality, the archive is a fruitful metaphor and resource for feminist theorists.

Voices, Methods, Process

Casting the development of archival collections as a historiographic move, Cifor and Wood note that "self-representation and self-historicization" (2) can be critical acts. The work of feminist historians poses challenges to the strictures of universities, government, and cultural institutions, both by pointing out the failures or weaknesses of a specific collection and, more significantly, by developing critical methodologies for working with materials as varied as legal documents of the Revolution (Farge), sixteenth-century royal correspondence (Zemon Davis), and colonial records (Stoler, Kolsky, Arondekar). Because the gaps and absences of the materials they consult speak volumes about the original institutions or authorities that collected them, these scholars highlight the power of institutions as seen through the archive, opening up to a critical archival approach.

Arlette Farge and Natalie Zemon Davis, who worked together on *A History of Women in the West*, have separately developed new ways of approaching archival research and understanding the researcher's role in the archives. Zemon Davis's book *Women on the Margins* opens with a prologue in which the author stages an imagined conversation with the three women whose lives she explores in the book, foregrounding a methodology that gives women's voices pride of place. In *The Allure of the Archives*, Farge elaborates a research method by describing in sensuous detail the process of sifting through France's National Archives, emphasizing physical contact with materials (62, 69). This attention to and interaction with materials allows the artifacts themselves to dictate the pace and objectives of the researcher's approach. Accepting "how slow work in the archives is, and how this slowness of hands and thought can be the source of creativity" (62), Farge rejects "scientific method" (69) in favor of idiosyncratic, adaptable processes through which "a new object is created, a new form of knowledge takes shape, and a new 'archive' emerges." (62) This puts documents and researcher on the same level, eschewing hierarchies of knowledge and attention, notions of passivity and activity, and sharp divides between thought and practice.

In their research in colonial archives, Ann Laura Stoler and Anjali Arondekar draw out what archival materials communicate and perform beyond what appears to be clear, visible, and on the surface. Stoler's method of reading "along the archival grain" (in her book of the same name) considers how traces of archival processes reveal colonial anxieties and expose the failings inherent in a dominating system. In *For the Record*, Arondekar proposes a new theory of reading archival materials not for truth-value but to examine the "limits of visibility" that constrain sexuality and bodies in colonial archives. In her criticism of feminist approaches to the colonial archive that "hold on to the idea of an archive that will somehow yield proper subjects of study" (6) and demonstrate an "archival movement from secrecy to disclosure," Arondekar challenges the ways conventional archival research upholds heteronormative binaries (7–8).

Diana Taylor's exploration of the binary opposition of written to spoken or lived (22–5) draws attention to the ways archiving authorities have relied on the power of the written word to consolidate their authority over other forms of knowledge and experience. A focus on the "scenario" would, according to Taylor, allow for other voices to emerge, such as the colonized or feminine voice repressed by rigid patriarchal, writing-based archival power (28ff.). Joan W. Scott's take on the FTA is emblematic in this regard, proposing a form of critique that rewrites a common myth of the archive as inert, stagnant, and related to the past, foregrounding instead the interaction between people and artifacts, which has the potential to reactivate an archival *jouissance* that could "issue forth without end" (148). This archival work is the driving force of archival vibrancy, of critique, and of theory. Scott's alternate view has implications for considerations of temporality, genealogy, and materiality in the archive: shared by feminist reflection and archive studies, these nodal points are explored in the following two sections.

Temporality and Genealogy

As we have seen in Scott's and other feminist, anti-colonial, and anti-patriarchal reworkings of archival methodology, the question of the archive is a question of temporality: rather than conceiving of archives as retrospective and mournful, other temporal configurations are at play. Certainly, archiving can legitimize, bury, memorialize, or resuscitate past concerns newly relevant; it can also facilitate periodization, establishing genealogies and generations. Temporality is wrapped up in the question of the archive from the very start of Eichhorn's book *The Archival Turn in Feminism*: the "the archival turn" of her title implies a before and an after, linked for Eichhorn to third-wave feminism's rapid "migra[tion] to archives and special collections" (15) and for Cifor and Wood to a "collecting and partnership focus for archives" since the late 1990s (13). The recent interest of third-wave feminism in archiving would indicate a desire to tap into the work of feminist pasts to renew feminist movement in the present and future. In this sense, the "turn" also alludes to a semi-circular directionality that veers into feminist temporalities since the seventies, including Kristeva's notion of "women's time," differently driving successive generations of feminist struggle, and Irigaray's "temporality of the female imaginary," as Ewa Plonowska Ziarek puts it (61). Sara Ahmed's, Claire Colebrook's, and Elizabeth Grosz's discussions of temporality in relation to narratives of feminist genealogy and feminist political goals are also significant in this regard. Emily Apter's "Women's Time in Theory" links the feminist concern with genealogy and periodicity to historical forgetting and recovering what is considered "démodé," untimely, and out of time (9). Apter calls this "an aesthetic function of women's time," but I see it as an archival impulse as well—particularly for feminist archives that explicitly and implicitly complicate trans-generational kinship and harness it for feminist movement.

In describing the potential the archive offers to feminism, Eichhorn links the authority of the archival institution to an understanding of archival temporality and genealogy, both of which "strengthen contemporary feminism" (15–16). Genealogy authorizes and legitimizes as well, forging connections and kinship between individuals and giving relationships a narrative structure in time. Conversely, if the archive authorizes these works, something that the publishing industry cannot do, beholden as it is to the forces of capitalism (Eichhorn 15–16), it is because the archive has the power to confer value and to mobilize this value in service of social cohesion. For feminism in particular, the archive is important in establishing a genealogical politics (a point Eichhorn, Cifor, and Wood all make through the work of Wendy Brown), but this genealogy is also complicated by the ways in which narratives of feminist history have articulated ruptures, disavowals, and affinities. When it focuses on historicizing, narrativizing, and archiving feminist activism, feminist theory and praxis adopts an archival sense of time and generation, discussed in Clare Hemmings's *Why Stories Matter*. Notions of temporality from queer scholars (such as Elizabeth Freeman's *Time Binds*), especially in relation to the archive, offer alternative configurations of kinship and affinity.[14] These connections may arise through archival research, or through the creation of archival collections understood broadly.

Archives of feminist theory and archives documenting feminist work in and out of institutions establish an alternative record, often resulting in collaborative, trans-generational configurations of the history of feminism.[15] In parallel, new archival techniques illuminate non-patriarchal relationships between thinkers and within communities, drawing from radical cataloguing initiatives, such as those of Jenna Freeman at Barnard, and from encoding initiatives at the Critical Theory Archive at UC-Irvine and between the Beinecke and Houghton Libraries.[16] In conjunction with queer theory and archives, these strategies and methods could be further developed by feminist theory and practice to illuminate yet unexplored connections between feminist thinkers, writers, and activists.

Materials, Materiality, Body

In providing a space for voices to be recognized and communities to form, the archive still retains authorizing mechanisms that inhere in any institution. What is the status of the material that is "authorized" by the archive and the status of the bodies in that place? How do the archive's temporal and genealogical functions bring together human and non-human bodies? What is the relationship between the archived artifacts and the people who created them: are artifacts extensions of the bodies or "voices" of their creators? How does the archive account for physical traces such as hair and stains? These archival metaphors and actual archived components are complicated by notions of materiality and the body within feminist theory, as addressed by Judith Butler, Ann Cvetkovich, Elizabeth Grosz, and Luce Irigaray.[17] Their conceptions of matter's vitality and agency challenge conventional notions of archival research as an extractive process, an adventurous mining or heroic foray performed by an active researcher on passive materials.[18]

This view of archival research relies on an understanding of matter as inert and inexpressive, compounded by a pervasive division between body and mind that is foundational to Western philosophy, and which has contributed to an understanding of women (as well as colonized people) as corporeal, linked to nature, and beyond the scope of reason and civilization: a divide between nature and culture and mind and body that has reinforced racist patriarchal domination, and which has been challenged by much of feminist theory in the twentieth and twenty-first centuries. Elizabeth Grosz's work on embodiment contributes to overriding mind/body dualism by turning attention to the question of matter and rehabilitating it into ontological and epistemological schemas. Butler also confronts this divide, arguing that matter is not fixed but only appears to be so through the process of materialization. Irigaray's *This Sex Which Is Not One*, crucial to both Butler and Grosz, is instrumental in putting the body back in philosophy, a move that foregrounds the materialist turn of the 1980s and 1990s in which archive studies emerged.[19] Wittig's work on materialism provides an alternate view that has long been sidelined in the study of feminist theory. A feminist material approach would also mean a revision of what "matter" is and its capacity for vitality and agency. The work of Karen Barad, following on Donna Haraway, on the nature/culture divide and its implications for feminist thought has been significant in this regard, as has Gail Weiss's *Body Images*. Crossing boundaries between archive science and metaphorical archives, this scholarship hearkens to work being done through digital humanities and to new technologies of creating and archiving.

Feminist materialisms open up new ways of thinking about how physical bodies—artifacts and researchers—interact in the archive. As we have seen, this challenges the ways we think about the role of the researcher faced with the expressiveness of gaps and absences in the archive; it also evokes issues of accessibility and attention to the importance of rethinking what counts as archival material. Ann Cvetkovich's *Archive of Feelings* brings together a variety of objects of study to understand the affective component of archives, looking beyond conventional archives and "incorporating objects that might not ordinarily be considered archival" (243–4). Cvetkovich's attention to cultural documents not usually considered archivable relates to historiographic methods of reading silences and absences, though Cvetkovich is more concerned with filling up those gaps and thereby expanding the notion of what are considered "archives." Determining whether that archive is a "real" brick-and-mortar institution with trained archivists, or a "metaphorical" archive as a virtual collection or without a physical presence, seems to me to assume a false binary that makes the institution the primary concern. Taking an expansive view of the archive is necessary to rethinking what a "real" archive is and does. For Cvetkovich, the archive is not based on recognizable, legible supports or institutional value but coheres, instead, around an affective archival charge that "lives not just in museums, libraries, and other institutions but in more personal and intimate spaces, and significantly, also within cultural genres" (243–4). This moves beyond a representational view of feminism in archival institutions, showing how archives articulate the relationship between material and immaterial, a crucial theoretical lever for feminist concerns of matter and body, foregrounding the potential of virtual archives for feminist theory and practice.

CONCLUSION

At the conjunction of the material and the immaterial, the virtual feminist archive is not the converse of physical archives—these are instead the condition of the virtual archive's existence. By widening the archival net, Cvetkovich brings in a catch that it is more materially diverse and more emotionally charged. Her approach draws on collections such as the Lesbian Herstory Archives which themselves "propose that affects—associated with nostalgia, personal memory, fantasy, and trauma—make a document significant" (243–4) through their collecting and processing practices. Affect, along with "ephemeral evidence, spaces that are maintained by volunteer labors of love rather than state funding, challenges to cataloging, [and] archives that represent lost histories," confirm for Cvetkovich "the status of the archive as a practice of fantasy made material" (268).

Cvetkovich's mention of fantasy here recalls Scott's *Fantasy of Feminist History*, which concludes by imagining the archive as a utopian space of possibility. I wish to echo Scott's claim that the archive offers an ideal venue for continuously renewed, critical feminist thought, especially as the archive's material dynamism counters any facile characterization of theory as abstract, idealizing, or impractical. Indeed, Eichhorn describes her *Archival Turn* as a coda to *An Archive of Feelings*—an academic convention that establishes a genealogy of scholarship on feminist theory and archives. By moving Cvetkovich's focus on lesbian public cultures toward feminism, Eichhorn upends narratives of feminist theory's evolution towards queer theory, which would eventually replace it. Similarly, critical feminist theory must expand horizontally in dialogue with other critical theories of the archive to fully grapple with its own silences, anxieties, and processes of self-archiving.

NOTES

1 On these archival concepts, see the SAA's online glossary.

2 See Azoulay's "Archive."

3 See Hildenbrand's "Introduction" (1–9) and Eichhorn's "The 'Scrap Heap' Reconsidered" (25–54).

4 On ACT UP/NY and the GLBTHS, see Cvetkovich (244–51). On third-wave feminism and zine collections, see Eichhorn, especially chapters 2, 3, and 4; and Cifor and Wood (12). On the Mazer Lesbian Archives, see Cifor and Wood (13).

5 See also Moore and Pell.

6 The term "counter-archive" was coined by Paula Amad.

7 On the LHA website and mentioned in Cooper (18).

8 See Eichhorn on Barnard (chapter 4) and Duke (chapter 2).

9 See the FTA website, as well as Weed's "History."

10 See Helle on Plath and Loeffelholz on Dickinson.

11 See Bost on Anzaldúa's archives.

12 See especially Cixous's *Manhattan* and *Double Oubli*; as well as my essay "Escaping Matter."

13 Cifor and Wood cite Fernald (16).

14 See, in particular, Carolyn Dinshaw's *Getting Medieval* and *How Soon Is Now?*, as well as J. J. Halberstam's *In a Queer Time and Place*.

15 See, in particular, Eichhorn's chapter on "Archival Regeneration" (55–84).

16 On Freedman, see Eichhorn's "Radical Catalogers and Accidental Archivists: The Barnard Zine Library" (123–53). See Seltzer, Bisio, and Liu, "Deconstructing the Critical Theory Archive at UCI" and Harvard Library Lab's "Connecting the Dots" for encoding initiatives.

17 See also Kumbier and Murray on textual materiality in queer and feminist contexts, respectively.

18 See Arondekar (9), quoting Stoler on "extractive" desire and method.

19 Particularly "When Our Lips Speak Together" (205–18) and "The 'Mechanics' of Fluids" (106–18).

WORKS CITED

Ahmed, Sara. "The Other and Other Others." *Economy and Society* 31.4 (2002): 558–72.

Amad, Paula. *Counter-Archive: Film, the Everyday, and Albert Kahn's Archives de la Planète (1908–1931)*. New York: Columbia UP, 2010.

Apter, Emily. "Women's Time in Theory." *differences* 21.1 (2010): 1–18.

Arondekar, Anjali. *For the Record: On Sexuality and the Colonial Archive in India*. Durham, NC: Duke UP, 2009.

Azoulay, Ariella. "Archive." *Political Concepts: A Critical Lexicon*. http://www.politicalconcepts. org/issue1/archive/16. November 30, 2017.

Barad, Karen. *Meeting the Universe Halfway: Quantum Physics and the Entanglement of Matter and Meaning*. Durham, NC: Duke UP, 2007.

Bost, Suzanne. "Messy Archives and Materials That Matter: Making Knowledge with the Gloria Evangelina Anzaldúa Papers." *PMLA* 130.3 (May 2015): 615–30.

Brown, Wendy. *Politics Out of History*. Princeton, NJ: Princeton UP, 2001.

Butler, Judith. *Bodies that Matter: On the Discursive Limits of Sex*. London: Routledge, 1993.

Butler, Judith. *Undoing Gender*. New York: Routledge, 2004.

Cifor, Marika, and Stacy Wood. "Critical Feminism in the Archives," in "Critical Archival Studies," ed. Michelle Caswell, Ricardo Punzalan, and T-Kay Sangwand. Special issue, *Journal of Critical Library and Information Studies* 1.2 (2017).

Cixous, Hélène. *Manhattan: Lettres de la préhistoire*. Paris: Galilée, 2002.

Cixous, Hélène. *Tours promises*. Paris: Galilée, 2004.

Colebrook, Claire. "Stratigraphic Time, Women's Time." *Australian Feminist Studies* 24.59 (2009): 11–16.

Coller-Thomas, Bettye. "Towards Black Feminism: The Creation of the Bethune Museum-Archives." *Women's Collections*. Ed. Suzanne Hildenbrand. New York: Haworth P, 1986, pp. 43–66.

Cooper, Danielle. "Welcome Home: An Exploratory Ethnography of the Information Context at the Lesbian Herstory Archives." *Feminist and Queer Information Studies Reader*. Ed. Patrick Keilty and Rebecca Dean. Sacramento: Litwin Books, 2013, pp. 526–41.

Corbman, Rachel F. "A Genealogy of the Lesbian Herstory Archives, 1974–2014." *Journal of Contemporary Archival Studies* 1.1 (2014): 1–16.

Cvetkovich, Ann. *An Archive of Feelings*. Durham, NC: Duke UP, 2003.

Derrida, Jacques. *Archive Fever: A Freudian Impression*. Trans. Eric Prenowitz. Chicago, IL: U of Chicago P, 1996.

Dinshaw, Carolyn. *Getting Medieval: Sexualities and Communities, Pre- and Postmodern*. Durham, NC: Duke UP, 1999.

Dinshaw, Carolyn. *How Soon Is Now?* Durham, NC: Duke UP, 2012.

Eichhorn, Kate. *The Archival Turn in Feminism*. Philadelphia, PA: Temple UP, 2013.

Farge, Arlette. *Le Goût de l'archive*. Paris: Seuil, 1989.

Farge, Arlette, and Natalie Zemon Davis. *History of Women in the West, Vol. III*. Cambridge, MA: Harvard UP, 2000.

Fernald, Anne E. "Women's Fiction, New Modernist Studies, and Feminism." *Modern Fiction Studies* 59.2 (2013): 229–40.

Freeman, Elizabeth. *Time Binds: Queer Temporalities*. Durham, NC: Duke UP, 2010.

Grosz, Elizabeth. *In the Nick of Time: Politics, Evolution, and the Untimely*. Durham, NC: Duke UP, 2004.

Grosz, Elizabeth. *The Incorporeal*. New York: Columbia UP, 2017.

Grosz, Elizabeth. *Time Travels: Feminism, Nature, Power*. Durham, NC: Duke UP, 2005.

Grosz, Elizabeth. *Volatile Bodies: Toward a Corporeal Feminism*. Bloomington: Indiana UP, 1994.

Halberstam, Judith Jack. *In a Queer Time & Place*. Durham, NC: Duke UP, 2005.

Haraway, Donna. *Simians, Cyborgs and Women: The Re-invention of Nature*. London: Free Association Books, 1991.

Harvard Library Lab. *Connecting the Dots: Using EAC-CPF to Reunite Samuel Johnson and His Circle*. https://osc.hul.harvard.edu/liblab/projects/connecting-dots-using-eac-cpf-reunite-samuel-johnson-and-his-circle. November 30, 2017.

Helle, Anita, ed. *The Unraveling Archive: Essays on Sylvia Plath*. Ann Arbor: U of Michigan P, 2007.

Hemmings, Clare. *Why Stories Matter: The Political Grammar of Feminist Theory*. Durham, NC: Duke UP, 2010.

Hildenbrand, Suzanne, ed. *Women's Collections: Libraries, Archives, and Consciousness*. New York: Haworth P, 1986.

Hughes, Laura. "Escaping Matter: The Fonds Cixous as Virtual Archive." *Cixous after/depuis 2000*. Ed. E. Berglund-Hall et al., Amsterdam: Rodopi, 2017.

Irigaray, Luce. *Speculum Of the Other Women*. Trans. G. C. Gill. Ithaca: Cornell UP, 1985.

Irigaray, Luce. *This Sex Which is Not One*. Trans. C. Porter, with C. Burke. Ithaca: Cornell UP, 1985.

Keilty, Patrick, and Rebecca Dean, eds. *Feminist and Queer Information Studies Reader*. Sacramento: Litwin Books, 2013.

Kolsky, Elizabeth. *Colonial Justice in British India*. Cambridge: Cambridge UP, 2011.

Kristeva, Julia. "Le temps des femmes." *34/44: Cahiers de recherche de science des textes et documents* 5 (1979): 5–19.

Kumbier, Alana. *Ephemeral Material: Queering the Archive*. Sacramento, CA: Litwin, 2014.

Lesbian Herstory Archives. http://www.lesbianherstoryarchives.org/. November 30, 2017.

Loeffelholz, M. "Networking Dickinson: Some Thought Experiments in Digital Humanities." *Emily Dickinson Journal* 23.1 (2014): 106–19.

Moore, Shaunna, and Susan Pell. "Autonomous Archives." *International Journal of Heritage Studies* 16 (2010): 255–68.

Murray, Simone. *Mixed Media: Feminist Presses and Publishing Politics*. London: Pluto P, 2004.

Pembroke Center. *Feminist Theory Archive*. Providence, RI: Brown U. http://www.brown.edu/research/pembroke-center/archives/feminist-theory-archive/. November 30, 2017.

Scott, Joan W. "Epilogue: A Feminist Theory Archive." *The Fantasy of Feminist History*. Durham, NC: Duke UP, 2011, pp. 141–8.

Seltzer, Sara Renée, Alexandra Bisio, and Shu Liu. "Deconstructing the Critical Theory Archive at UCI: An Experiment with EAC-CPF and Linked Open Data." *Journal of Western Archives* 5.1 (2014): http://digitalcommons.usu.edu/westernarchives/vol5/iss1/8. December 30, 2014.

Society of American Archivists. *A Glossary of Archival Records and Terminology*. https://www2.archivists.org/glossary. November 30, 2017.

Stoler, Ann Laura. *Along the Archival Grain: Epistemic Anxieties and Colonial Common Sense*. Princeton, NJ: Princeton UP, 2009.

Taylor, Diana. *The Archive and the Repertoire: Performing Cultural Memory in the Americas*. Durham, NC: Duke UP, 2003.

University of California-Irvine Libraries. *Critical Theory Archive*. https://special.lib.uci.edu/collections/critical-theory-archive. November 30, 2017.

Weed, Elizabeth. *History*. Pembroke Center. https://www.brown.edu/research/pembroke-center/sites/brown.edu.research.pembroke-center/files/uploads/Notes_PC_History_Final.pdf. November 30, 2017.

Weiss, Gail. *Body Images: Embodiment as Intercorporeality*. New York: Routledge, 1999.

Wittig, Monique. *The Straight Mind and Other Essays*. Boston, MA: Beacon P, 1992.

Zemon Davis, Natalie. *Women on the Margins*. Cambridge, MA: Harvard UP, 1995.

Ziarek, Ewa Plonowska. "Toward a Radical Female Imaginary: Temporality and Embodiment in Irigaray's Ethics." *Diacritics* 28.1 (1998): 59–75.

CHAPTER NINETEEN

Critique

EWA PŁONOWSKA ZIAREK

FEMINIST "GENRES" OF CRITIQUE VERSUS THE POSTCRITICAL TURN

Can we imagine feminist theory in the twenty-first century without critique? This hardly seems possible given the crucial role of critique in feminist articulations of multiple overlapping forms of oppression, ranging from racism, sexism, white supremacy, and heteronormativity; to economic exploitation, neoliberalism, imperialism, and colonialism. Even the most cursory glance at just a few selected titles testifies to the centrality of critique in diverse feminist inquiries: *Inessential Woman: Problems of Exclusion in Feminist Thought*; *Feminist Studies/Critical Studies*; *The Feminist Critique of Language*; *Conflicts in Feminism*; *Disputed Subjects*; *Killing Rage: Ending Racism*; "Women and Development: A Critique"; *Feminism Beside Itself*; *Feminism without Borders: Decolonizing Theory, Practicing Solidarity*; *A Critique of Postcolonial Reason*, "Critique, Dissent, Disciplinarity"; and *Learning to Unlearn: Decolonial Reflections from Eurasia and the Americas*. As some of these titles already suggest, the role of feminist critique is not limited to diagnosis, calling into question, or opposition. Although it begins with the contestation of domination, critique has also played a major role in feminist re-formulations of such key issues as liberation, coalitions, equality, difference, freedom, community, citizenship, democracy, experience, subjectivity, sexuality, race, gender and transgender, power, language, affectivity, materialisms old and new, embodiment, dissidence, ontology, epistemology, ethics, pedagogy, aesthetics, and artistic practices. In other words, as I have argued elsewhere,[1] feminist critique is not simply negative but reaches beyond its oppositional stance toward formulations of alternative modes of being, relations of feeling, knowing, and acting in the world.

In addition to these feminist contestations of an unjust world and articulations of the political and cultural alternatives to the status quo, there is also a robust tradition of internal critiques of feminism from within. Such intramural questioning of feminism is a matter not only of methodological disagreements but also of political, theoretical, and ethical accountability. Contesting the often gendered and racialized hierarchical divisions between theory, practice, and experience (McDowell 105–7), numerous feminist critiques—advanced by women of color, non-Western, and working-class, queer, and transgender theorists—have pointed out false generalizations, limited solidarities, and exclusions perpetuated by feminism itself, and time and again have called mainstream feminists to account for their own complicity with racism and power. As bell hooks writes in *Feminist Theory*, "though I criticize aspects of feminist movement as we have known it so far, a critique which is sometimes harsh and unrelenting, I do so not in an attempt to diminish feminist struggle but to enrich, to share in the work of making a liberatory ideology and a liberatory movement" (15). This call to accountability for feminism's complicity with domination cannot be dismissed as a typical hypervigilant self-reflexivity of critique, as Felski and Anker argue (9), because it originates from experiences of marginalization and desire for the creation of richer, more diverse feminist theories and practices. Furthermore, as Deborah McDowell suggests, what is also at stake in these internal critiques within feminism is the contestation of unequal access to "knowledge production" (113) and its dissemination.

Nonetheless, in the last twenty years, feminist critics (such as Sedgwick and Felski, among others) have called the efficacy of critique—feminist critiques included—into question. Lumping together Marxist ideology critique, deconstruction, psychoanalysis, and poststructuralism, these theorists rename critique by other, less salutary terms: a hermeneutics of suspicion (Felski), symptomatic reading (Best and Marcus), paranoid reading (Sedgwick), or even worse, as Bruno Latour suggests, as an elevated academic conspiracy theory. Such "name calling" is usually a first step toward deflating the "prestige" and radicalism of critique. For example, by extending Ricoeur's characterization of the legacy of Nietzsche, Marx, and Freud as a hermeneutics of suspicion to all forms of critique, including feminist ones, Felski treats critique as a "genre" characterized by typical conventions, rhetoric, styles, and moods (32–3). Like Sedgwick before her, Felski defines these generic conventions of critique as a demystification and exposure of hidden "truths." Motivated by suspicion, critique is faulted for its naïve faith in the efficacy of the demystification of global systems of oppression and for conflating the exposure of power with political agency (Felski 7). Thus, part of the allure of critique is that it allows its practitioners to assume the role of the expert and radically progressive intellectual, driven by a desire to diagnose hidden operations of power by which everyone else is duped.

No doubt, this genre of critique is readily recognizable and rightly questioned. But who is the subject of critique characterized in this manner? Does the reconstruction of a "genre" of critique suffer from overgeneralization produced by the exclusion of diverse feminist voices and modes of criticism? Feminists arguing against marginalization and exclusion of alternative modes of knowing certainly do not need suspicion to know the racist and gender domination, violence, and everyday micro-aggression experienced in individual and collective lives. Instead of the demystification of common sense, the starting point of such critiques is articulation of women's everyday experiences of domination and resistance. As McDowell, for example, writes, one of the distinguishing features of black feminist theory is the assertion of "the significance of black women's experience" (104), together with the refusal of the gendered and racialized hierarchy between experience and theory (104–6). The standpoint theory proposed by Patricia Hill Collins is just one powerful instance of critical black feminist epistemology. In this tradition of critique, suspicion of ordinary language and knowledge does not make sense because the valorization of women's quotidian experiences and vernacular cultures becomes the grounds for contesting exclusionary academic knowledge and its politics of willed ignorance. Furthermore, the theorization of marginalized collective experiences, cultures, and histories confronts time and again—and yes, diagnoses and puts into question—what Spillers calls "sexist" and "racist" passions, which not only block such discursive articulations on institutional levels but also treat them as "objects of revulsion and fear" (xii).

As these remarks suggest, a generic description of critique—demystification, suspicion, expert knowledge—proposed by proponents of the postcritical turn is too narrow, too white, and gender neutral. Thus, although critics of critique rightly point to critique's

Eurocentric bias (Anker and Felski 13), such a bias is also reproduced by their gestures of defining critique within the narrow scope of what counts as the representative genre of critique in the humanities today (especially if its genealogies are limited to the legacies of Marx, Freud, and Nietzsche). And nowhere is this exclusionary account of critique more visible than in Bruno Latour's influential essay, "Has Critique Run Out of Steam" (2004), in which feminism and critical race studies simply do not exist.

PARANOID CRITIQUE AND THE FEMINIST QUEER REPARATIVE TURN

If the characterization of critique as a hermeneutics of suspicion is too narrow to reflect diverse feminist critical practices, does the renaming of critique as a paranoid reading fare any better? The characterization of critique as paranoid has been inspired by selective readings of Eve Kosofsky Sedgwick's essay, "Paranoid Reading and Reparative Reading" (2003). Also referring to Ricoeur, Sedgwick renames critique as a strong paranoid theory of negative affect and she includes her own previous work, in particular, *The Epistemology of the Closet*, in this genre. In so doing, she is one of the first feminist queer critics to question the efficacy of demystification and to expose the relation between critique and negative affect. However, Sedgwick adds that a paranoid drive for demystification is anticipatory and defensive: its relation to the future is characterized by the avoidance of any unpleasant surprise. Although disastrous events cannot be avoided, they can be predicted by a vigilant critical practice.

Such a broad characterization of the legacy of critique as a paranoid reading is also limited and raises a series of questions. In our present context of the brutality of state instruments of violence against African-Americans, immigrants, Muslims, and refugees, can we ever be paranoid enough? Do not racist violence, Islamophobia, and anti-immigration populist movements in the West exceed paranoid fantasies? Sedgwick anticipates these questions and, in contrast to proponents of the postcritical turn, her exploration of the limits of critique occurs in the context of the unrepairable: dying with breast cancer, the Aids epidemic, and living and dying in the context of pervasive racism. Furthermore, she is attentive to the different trajectories of paranoid readings in different political and historical contexts. For instance, in the context of queer theory, the inter-rogation of complex associations between homosexuality, paranoia, and homophobia has a long intellectual history from Freud to Hocquenghem. Furthermore, rather than rejecting paranoid reading altogether, Sedgwick—as Heather Love rightly points out—transforms it into a weak local theory, which can coexist with a number of other inter-pretive approaches (238). Thus, Sedgwick does not limit the range of critical practices to the paranoid/reparative binary but proposes another interpretative possibility—one among many—of reparative reading animated by affective appreciation of artworks and formations of alternative queer communities, based on love and friendship.

It is important to remember the existential and historical weight of the unrepairable as we assess the reparative turn in feminist queer studies, inspired by selective readings of Sedgwick's work. In her "The Times We're In: Queer Feminist Criticism and the Reparative 'Turn,'" Wiegman characterizes "the reparative turn" in queer feminist schol-arship (Cvetkovich, Love, and Freeman, among others) as seeking relations to the objects of study based upon "affection, gratitude, solidarity and love" rather than on critique, "correction, rejection and anger" (7), all of which are associated with paranoid critique. Inflected with attention to everydayness, reparative reading cultivates a different kind of ethos based on more life-affirming queer communities, love, and hope despite domination and inspires belief that a painful and traumatic past could have happened differently. As Jackie Stacey points out, reparative reading assumes that affective proximity to the loved object might "nurture both critic and reader" (46). Such an affective thinking with, rather than against, one's objects of study—which in fact has always been at work in the feminist recovery of forgotten figures and archives in history, philosophy, and literature—creates new resources for queer survival and community. Nonetheless, despite this concern with community, the call for reparative readings has rarely been understood as a demand for economic and political reparations for the dispossessed groups.

Most feminist critical reassessments of the reparative turn point to the bracketing of ambivalence, unconscious fantasy, and aggression, all of which are confined to paranoid reading. Questioning the critic's desire for reparation as a compensation for the lost "authority of critique" or the humanities in general, Wiegman concludes that the objective of such a reading is to repair the devalued "agency of interpretive practice itself" (7). Stacey and Love are also wary that the exclusive focus on reparation as nurturing and loving relation forgets the unconscious phantasy and ambivalence characterizing all object relations. Gail Lewis cautions about the possible omnipotent, manic, and narcissistic character of reparative fantasies, which do not necessarily enhance our relations to others, in particular in the context of racism and domination (36–7). Her worry is that by failing to address the "toxicity of racism, misogyny, homophobia, class hatred and disablism," the interpreter herself becomes the beneficiary of reparative practices rather than collectivities (31). Stacey also questions the "slippage" between psychoanalytical mechanisms and cultural interpretations inherent in the call "to abandon interpretation in the name of reparation" (43). Perhaps to avoid this confusion between psychoanalytic and cultural interpretations, we might, as Lewis does,[2] return to Klein herself, whose theory of the paranoid position and reparation has been a source of influence for Sedgwick as well as for several critics, who, like Muñoz, engage with the reparative turn in the context of artistic practices by women of color.

RETHINKING KLEIN'S AMBIVALENT LEGACIES IN FEMINIST QUEER STUDIES

This return to Klein confronts us with a stunning contrast between a "strong" paranoid critique, diagnosed by Sedgwick, and a psychoanalytic theory of the paranoid-schizoid position characterizing the most vulnerable beginnings of psychic life. Instead of a critique, we are confronted with the infant's earliest inscriptions of preverbal, bodily inflected, heterogeneous fantasies and affects, for which any interpretive or cultural practice cannot fully account, but from which it can never purify itself either. Everything in the Kleinian universe at this stage—proto-psyche, its part proto-objects, bodily sensations and organs, anxieties and drives—is in flux and in bits and pieces. In other words, nothing could be more different from the paranoid critique than Klein's own formulation of the schizoid/paranoid position at the inception of psychic life. And it is an open-ended question as to how the antithesis between a strong paranoid theory and the most vulnerable beginnings of psychic life, between the expert and the infant, is to be understood. Perhaps what Sedgwick diagnoses as a strong paranoid critique is a very sophisticated defense mechanism—or what Kristeva calls a rigid counterphobic construction—against overwhelming preverbal infantile anxieties of disintegration and annihilation characteristic of the paranoid-schizoid position. As Kristeva notes in *Powers of Horror*, such a counterphobic construction is "a defensive, over-coded discourse that knows too much and manipulates its object wonderfully well" (41–2).

Since schizoid splitting and the fragility of infancy are bracketed in Sedgwick's translation of the paranoid position into a hegemonic, "strong" critique, I would like to return to the earliest schizoid mechanisms analyzed by Klein in her 1946 essay "Some Notes on Schizoid Mechanisms." Klein formulates the paranoid-schizoid position belatedly—in fact, ten years after she elaborates the processes of reparation in her 1937 paper "Love, Guilt, and Reparation." What is poignant in Klein's work, and what is not examined in our contemporary rejection of strong paranoid critical theory, are the fantasmatic, anxiety-ridden, and catastrophic aspects of the paranoid-schizoid position: the overwhelming sense of "the catastrophe" of the internal and external world, which has to be separated at all cost from the object of love and the good parts of the psyche (24). As Kristeva notes, anxiety is as fundamental for Klein as libido is for Freud or desire for Lacan. Klein argues that an overwhelming anxiety is an unavoidable psychic consequence of the Freudian discovery of the death drive. For Klein, the duality of drives—the death drive and the life drive—accompanies the emergence of the psyche and its most rudimentary fantasies. What is felt by the infant as the primordial anxiety of annihilation arises from psychic inscriptions of "the operation of the death instinct," exacerbated by the trauma of birth, non-satisfaction of bodily needs, as well as a hostile external environment (4). Because of the intensity of this anxiety, the earliest psychic life has "a tendency toward disintegration, a falling into bits" (4). Fragmentation is both the first psychic inscription and defense against the negativity of the death drive, which, as Kristeva points out, "generates a *series of fantasies*: sadistic, paranoid-schizoid, manic, and depressive" before creating the capacity of symbolization (*Klein* 142). In response to such an overwhelming anxiety of annihilation, which, in the Kleinian world, precedes and has a far more important role than castration anxiety, the first infantile defenses against the schizoid fragmentation arise: "the result of splitting is a dispersal of the destructive impulse which is felt as the source of danger" (5). These defense mechanisms not only fragment the nonintegrated proto-self but also separate love from hate, dissipate aggression, and splinter proto-objects, which, through the projection of the dispersed death drive, are felt to be threatening both from within and without. In oral sadistic fantasies, not only is the bad part-object separated from the good proto-object (the maternal breast), but it is also devoured and torn into pieces.

What characterizes the Kleinian schizoid/paranoid position is the incessant flow back and forth of the split part of objects, drives, sensations, as well as the bits and pieces of the psyche, organs, and somatic substances: they are projected, re-introjected, and projected again and again. As Klein puts it, "the projection of a predominantly hostile inner world which is ruled by persecutory fears leads to the introjection—a taking back—of a hostile external world; and *vice versa*" ("Notes" 11). A crucial part of this fluid process is played by the defensive mechanism of projective identification, through which the infantile psyche expels, together with its aggression, dangerous parts of the self and somatic substances, first onto the breast and later into the inside of the maternal body. Although it can become a prototype of aggressive relations to others, the schizoid splitting and projective identification has a double valance: it is both an origin of pathological symptoms and the first step toward creativity and thinking; it is the beginning of the differentiation of sensations and qualities (good and bad) and of the unstable perception of the inside/outside boundary, which, far from being a theoretical construction, is steeped in aggression and pain (*Klein* 64, 71). Finally, projective identification—the expulsion of painful affects and bad body parts—enables a heterogeneous elaboration of the quasi-object—"an *amalgam* of representations, sensations, and substances" (63). By calling these part objects/expelled parts of subject "abject," Kristeva emphasizes not only the instability and permeability of the border from which future subjects and objects will have to be separated but also "the privative sense of the prefix 'a,'" the not yet subject not yet object from which subject and object will differentiate themselves (72).

However, when mediated and mobilized by religious, cultural, and political practices, projective identifications—the expulsion of one's own aggression onto external objects, which subsequently appear to persecute us from without—are at work in fantasmatic collective constructions of hostile racialized others, from the white child's phobic construction of blackness analyzed by Fanon to the political mobilization of Islamophobia and the fear of refugees and immigrants, so skillfully manipulated by right-wing populist movements in Europe and in the United States. And indeed, critique and facts are all too frequently powerless against this discourse if fantasies, mobilizing defense mechanisms against the infantile dread of annihilation, are not addressed and worked through.

Another defensive mechanism characterizing the paranoid-schizoid position that I want to stress in the context of feminist investments in the reparative turn is the tendency toward idealization of the gratifying part objects and denial of the persecutory anxieties. As manifestations of infantile omnipotence, such idealization of a good object is a psychic flight from internal and external distress. This idealization creates the fantasmatic Manichaean dualism of "extremely good" and "extremely frightening" quasi-objects. The tendency toward idealization (or exaggeration) of good objects, which provide both gratification and defense against anxieties of annihilation, persists as cultural and political phenomena. Klein's diagnosis of the mechanisms of idealization and projective identification traces, therefore, a genealogy of the Manichaean investments in good and bad objects, friends and enemies, proceeding from the earliest infantile anxieties and defenses, and persisting in modified forms in adult relations and social institutions. The intensity of passions and aggression we are willing to invest in the defense of our good objects is in the last resort a narcissistic defense against the infantile dread of annihilation. Consequently, both the over-idealization of the theoretical reparative turn and the rejection of critique repeat this Manichaean configuration of the paranoid-schizoid position.

So far, I have discussed the bracketed schizoid and idealization mechanisms of the paranoid position; now I want to stress not only the depressive counterpart of the drive toward reparation but also its coexistence with aggression, loss, and the earlier schizoid anxieties and defenses. As both Sedgwick and Kristeva note, the Kleinian paranoid and depressive positions are neither developmental stages nor linguistic structures, but "structures of emotional life" that coexist in the unconscious (*Klein* 67). The precondition of the depressive position, which has also been frequently discussed in contemporary feminist and race theory in more general terms of mourning and melancholia, is a working through of the resistances of schizoid and paranoid fantasies and defenses in order to overcome the Manichaean separation between good and bad parts, love and hate. Thus, the paradoxical "achievement" of the depressive position is that of ambivalence, or the discovery of the interaction between love and aggression addressed to the same object which is both good and bad. Ambivalence arising out of working through the schizoid paranoid splitting might be another precondition for overcoming rigid gender and racial hierarchies, which are ultimately based on the division between good and bad and the separation of love from hate. This tendency toward integration, which produces the ambivalence of love and hate, gives rise to a different kind of anxiety: an intense anxiety of loss and guilt for the damage inflicted on the loved object.

The sense of the whole object thus arises from the possibility of its loss and destruction, which also means the death of the psyche. The proto-psyche could not experience such loss in the paranoid-schizoid position because absence has been felt only as persecution by bad objects. Consequently, what cannot be extricated from the drive for reparation is the experience of loss, the repeated waves of depression, and the sense of guilt arising from the confrontation with one's own hatred and aggression. Working through loss and aggression is thus inseparable from the so-called reparative turn in infantile and adult life. Even though, as Sedgwick rightly points out, the tendency toward reparation is intertwined with love, sublimation, gratitude, and creativity, it cannot be separated from psychic conflicts, aggression, anxiety, and depression. Anxiety over the loss of the object characteristic of the depressive position can all too often reinforce the schizoid mechanisms of splitting and projective identification. By contrast, the unconscious loss and guilt lead toward reparation, that is, toward undoing in fantasy the damage inflicted on the loved object by hatred, when the psyche is supported by the gratification of loving and being loved by others. Only by bearing in mind this painful counterpart of reparation, which, if too intense, causes a vicious circle of recurrent melancholic and schizoid mechanisms, can we avoid the idealization of reparation and the denial of conflict, aggression, and ambivalence.

TOWARD A "KLEINIAN" GENEALOGY OF CRITIQUE: PHANTASY, PLAY, AND OTHER THEORETICAL "DEFICIENCIES"

As we have seen, both the paranoid-schizoid position and psychic phantasies of reparation are modes of relationality characterized by fragility, love and hate, different modes of anxiety, and the ambivalence of the death drive. Therefore, any strong opposition between paranoid critique and reparative reading seems to reenact the schizoid splitting between bad and good on the level of intellectual practice. Furthermore, what for Klein enables the emergence of any intellectual interpretative practice—whether the hermeneutics of suspicion, paranoid critique, or reparative reading—is the often-underscored phenomenon of play, which allows the child and the adult alike to work through unconscious phantasies and inhibitions. Both play and phantasy can be sources of creativity as well as of the affective, embodied, and heterogeneous registers of intellectual activity.

Let us return then to the question of phantasy, which plays a key role in Klein's theory of both paranoid-schizoid and depressive positions. As she suggests, our earliest unconscious fantasies are not only defense mechanisms but also the source of imagination, which at the beginning is inseparable from hallucination or from the capacity to imagine and create what is not there: the early phantasy "later develops into the more elaborate workings of imagination" (Klein, "Love" 308). Although Klein does not offer a strong theory of fantasy, her notion of fantasy should be of interest to contemporary feminist theorists of affect and materiality. Most discussions of phantasy (spelled with ph) in Klein's work quote Susan Isaac's formulation that phantasies are the primal "psychic representatives" of drives that precede words: "There is no impulse, no instinctual urge or response which is not experienced as unconscious phantasy" (Isaac 83, quoted in Kristeva, *Klein* 138). For Kristeva, the striking features of phantasy in Klein's school are the "binary expression" of the drive through "sensation/affect" and its part objects as well as the key role of negativity in its formation (*Klein* 142). This means that primal phantasies can be limited neither to the visual apparatus nor to linguistic structure, because they are "mixtures" of radically heterogeneous registers: psychic inscriptions of bodily sensations, drives, affects; gestures, bodily functions, movements; bodily substances, fluids, and organs; "concretizations" (the indistinction of words and things); and eventually memory traces of perceptions and words (141). These phantasies have strong bodily elements, although the body in question and its organs are irreducible to organic functions. Can Klein be regarded as the first theorist of bodies without organs in the process of becoming? To emphasize this irreducible heterogeneity (frequently confused with empiricism), Kristeva suggests that Klein offers us an "incarnated metaphor" (141–4) rather than a theoretical "logic" of fantasy, and that she invents a broader, nonvisual sense of the imaginary, which, in addition to the visual register, refers to emotions, affects, nonvisual perceptions of taste and touch, bodily movements, and so forth.

As Kristeva points out, women analysts stress diverse registers of fantasy in the process of the formation of knowledge and interpretation, while male analysts—Winnicott, Bion, and Lacan—"curb" this heterogeneity by subjecting it to the visual order inscribed in the symbolic. Needless to say, Kristeva's characterization of the heterogeneity of Klein's fantasy is implicitly or explicitly critical of Lacan's formula of fantasy ($\lozenge$ a). As Darian Leader suggests, Lacan's turn to mathematical symbols offers a "structural solution" to the contra- dictory preverbal and transverbal elements of the fantasy, which could not be inscribed in a linguistic sentence or philosophical proposition (95). By contrast, rather than transcending nonverbal, bodily semiotic elements of fantasy through algebraic formulation, Kristeva's emphasis on the incarnate metaphor argues that the primary processes of condensation and displacement operate in broader transverbal registers (affect, taste, touch perception) whether in the case of an infant, a phobic child, an adult, a feminist critic, or an analyst. Consider, for example, Kristeva's analysis of the phobic object in *Powers of Horror* as a defective metaphor "in want of metaphoricalness": "incapable of producing metaphors through means of signs alone, he (the phobic child) produces them in the very material of drives—and it turns out that the only rhetoric of which he is capable is that of affect" (37). Furthermore, such a metaphor is charged with indexicality of the "unknowable": "the phobic object is ... *the hallucination of nothing*: a metaphor that is the anaphora of nothing" (*Powers* 42). It is precisely this semiotic heterogeneity and impurity of the earliest fantasies and their unconscious persistence in individual lives and in social mechanisms that is erased when we translate the schizoid paranoid position into paranoid critique.

As Kristeva and Sedgwick agree, Klein can hardly be regarded as a proponent of rigorous, strong theory; on the contrary, she has been criticized for her theoretical deficiency, for her "crude" interpretations, and for an impure mixture of "visceral" empiricism and the- oretical insight. One of the most controversial and creative of Klein's discoveries is not a strong theory but a therapeutic play technique with young children. As Kristeva observes, for Klein, play "was the royal road to the unconscious" just as the dream was for Freud (*Klein* 48), and it is through play that she wanted to confront "an enigmatic knowledge that characterizes the fantasy" (40) but that resists rationality and critique, the twin legacy of Enlightenment philosophy. Klein's intersubjective play technique—which deploys and interprets diverse semiotic registers of gestures, body movements, affects, toys, space/time coordinates, the processes of condensation and displacement—translates fantasies into games in order to work through them and to overcome unconscious resistances, staging a creative psychodrama/transference between the analyst and the child.

Not limited to analytic technique, play phenomenon is a part of ordinary experiences, ranging from the child's interactions with others, to artistic practices, intellectual activities, and social relations. What is unique to Klein is her emphasis on the semiotic heterogeneity and interpersonal character of play, which is often missed in criticisms focused exclusively on her overly sexualized symbolizations of child's play. For Kristeva, however, Klein's engagement with multiple registers of play cannot be limited to symbolic interpretations alone, even though such interpretations make important interventions. In fact, focusing on Klein's "theoretical deficiencies" ignores the key point of play technique, namely the importance of the attentive analytic responsiveness to the specificity of child's play, through which unconscious knowledge appears. Klein's interactive interpretations of the child's unconscious fantasies, enacted through play, engage all the diverse registers of fantasy and play itself. As Kristeva puts it, since the child has limited access to speech, or no access at all, "not only did Klein work *on* the imaginary (of the child) *in* the imaginary (of the analyst) but her work was so deep and intense that the interaction between the two imaginaries ... as they focus on bodies and their acts can only give the impression that we are digging into our guts in the manner of 'an inspired gut butcher' as Lacan once quipped" (*Klein* 148). This visceral quality of Klein's work is an effect of her listening "as close as possible to *frustration*—rather than to *gratification*" (Kristeva, *Klein* 148). Klein's acknowledgment of the child's negative transference—for instance, fear and anxiety directed to the analyst—in the context of play allows the child to release aggression and death drive in order to initiate the process of working through defenses, pain, and inhibitions. By encouraging negative transference onto the analyst, who positions herself or himself as the "maternal" receptacle of the child's anxiety and aggression, Klein alleviates these preverbal anxieties and encourages their translation into play and subsequently into words and stories.

According to Kristeva, Klein believed that by "freeing up the death drive" through play and interpretation she could encourage thinking, especially as the child's position shifts in the process of analysis from inhibition and suffering to creative collaboration/invention of games and participation in the narration of fantasy. The play technique transforms, therefore, preverbal phantasies, enacted in play through sensations, relations to objects, and body movements, into a co-creation of imagination, meaning, and thinking. This transition from preverbal to symbolizable phantasies is coextensive with a desire for meaning—which emerges "through pain and despite pain" (*Klein* 44). Thus, in contrast to the expert's diagnosis—or symptomatic reading, associated by Felski and Anker with psychoanalytic critique (4)—the analyst, according to Klein, plays the role of a supportive participant in the collaborative process of play, storytelling, and interpretation. Such a co-creation of meaning and relational character of thinking is ultimately the greatest achievement not only of psychoanalytic interpretation but also of artworks, intellectual activities, and supportive social interactions. And I would submit that this desire for meaning despite pain, which manifests itself in child's play, also motivates feminists' critiques and manifold interpretations of culture and politics.

I began this essay by questioning whether the hermeneutics of suspicion, demystification, and even paranoid reading can reflect diverse feminist critical practices. Consequently, rather than embracing a postcritical turn in feminist studies, I have called for just the opposite; namely, for a more careful and nuanced reconstruction of diverse methods, styles, and affects of feminist critiques. Such a reparative recovery of a more representative archive of feminist critiques is one of the collective tasks of feminist theory in the twenty-first century and, therefore, lies beyond the limited scope of this essay. My contribution to feminist theories of critique has been more modest: through my engagement with feminist queer studies, I have attempted to enlarge the feminist archive of critique through the legacy of Melanie Klein. Klein enables us to construct at once a more playful and a more painful relational version of critique, dedicated to a fragile co-creation of meaning, and, at the same time, she diagnoses psychic and social mechanisms—such as loneliness, inhibitions, infantile omnipotence—which block such creation. Despite Klein's preoccupations with the death drive, anxiety, vulnerability, and aggression in individual and social relations, her theory manifests nonetheless a concern for life and meaning. And I would argue that this concern for life: one's own and the lives of others, precisely at the moment when this life is most threatened or devalued, manifests itself in the work of feminist critics that I admire: Sedgwick, Spillers, Butler, hooks, Kristeva, and Crenshaw, among others. Rather than suspicion, this concern with the creation of more capacious meanings and more just political relations in the world is at the core of different genres of feminist critique.

NOTES

1 See *Feminist Aesthetics and the Politics of Modernism* (Ziarek *Feminist Aesthetics* 1–7) and "The Stakes of Feminist Aesthetics: Transformative Practice, Neoliberalism, and the Violence of Formalism" (Ziarek "The Stakes of Feminist Aesthetics").

2 In contrast to Lewis's referring to Klein through the work of Bion (33–5), my return to Klein is mediated through Kristeva.

WORKS CITED

Anker, Elizabeth S., and Rita Felski, eds. *Critique and Postcritique*. Durham, NC: Duke UP, 2017.

Best, Stephen, and Sharon Marcus. "Surface Reading: An Introduction." *Representations* 108 (Fall 2009): 1–21.

Butler, Judith. "Critique, Dissent, Disciplinarity." *Critical Inquiry* 35.4 (Summer, 2009): 773–95.

Cameron, Deborah, ed. *The Feminist Critique of Language: A Reader*. 2nd Edn. New York: Routledge, 1998.

Elam, Diane, and Robin Wiegman, eds. *Feminism beside Itself*. New York: Routledge, 1995.

Felski, Rita. *The Limits of Critique*. Chicago, IL: Chicago UP, 2015.

Flax, Jane. *Disputed Subjects: Essays on Psychoanalysis, Politics and Philosophy*. New York: Routledge, 1993.

Hirsch, Marianne, and Evelyn Fox Keller, eds. *Conflicts in Feminism*. New York: Routledge, 1990.

Hirshman, Mitu. "Women and Development: A Critique." *Feminism/Postmodernism/Development*. Ed. Marianne H. Marchand and Jane L. Parpart. New York: Routledge, 1995, pp. 42–55.

hooks, bell. *Feminist Theory: From Margin to Center*. New York: South End P, 1984.

hooks, bell. *Killing Rage: Ending Racism*. New York: Henry Holt, 1995.

Isaac, Susan. "The Nature and Function of Phantasy." *Developments in Psycho-Analysis*, by Melanie Klein, Paula Heimann, Susan Isaac, and Joan Riviere. London: Hogarth P, 1952, pp. 67–121.

Klein, Melanie. "Love, Guilt and Reparation (1937)." *The Writings of Melanie Klein, Volume I: Love, Guilt and Reparation and Other Works, 1921–1945*. New York: Free P, 1975, pp. 306–43.

Klein, Melanie. "Some Notes on Schizoid Mechanisms (1946)." *The Writings of Melanie Klein, Volume III: Envy and Gratitude and Other Works, 1946–63*. New York: Free P, 1975, pp. 1–24.

Kristeva, Julia. *Melanie Klein*. Trans. Ross Guberman. New York: Columbia UP, 2001.

Kristeva, Julia. *Powers of Horror. An Essay on Abjection*. Trans. Leon S. Roudiez. New York: Columbia UP, 1982.

Latour, Bruno. "Has Critique Run Out of Steam? From Matters of Fact to Matters of Concern." *Critical Inquiry* 30.2 (2004): 225–48.

de Lauretis, Teresa, ed. *Feminist Studies/Critical Studies*. Bloomington: Indiana UP, 1986.

Leader, Darian. "Phantasy in Klein and Lacan." *The Kleinian–Lacanian Dialogues*. Ed. Bernard Burgoyne and Mary Sullivan. New York: Other P, 1999, pp. 83–95.

Lewis, Gail. "Not By Criticality Alone." *Feminist Theory* 15.1 (2014): 31–8.

Love, Heather. "Truth and Consequences: on Paranoid Reading and Reparative Reading." *Criticism* 52.2 (2010): 235–41.

McDowell, Deborah. "Transferences: Black Feminist Discourse: The 'Practice' of 'Theory'." *Feminism Beside Itself*. Ed. Elam, Diane, and Robin Wiegman. New York: Routledge, 1995, pp. 93–118.

Mohanty, Chandra Talpade. *Feminism without Borders: Decolonizing Theory, Practicing Solidarity*. Durham, NC: Duke UP, 2003.

Muñoz, José Estaban. "Feeling Brown, Feeling Down: Latina Affect, the Performativity of Race, and the Depressive Position." *Signs* 31.3 (2006): 675–88.

Sedgwick, Eve Kosofsky. "Paranoid Reading and Reparative Reading, or, You Are So Paranoid, You Probably Think This Essay Is about You." *Touching Feeling: Affect, Pedagogy, Performativity*. Durham, NC: Duke UP, 2003, pp. 123–52.

Spelman, Elizabeth V. *Inessential Woman: Problems of Exclusion in Feminist Thought*. Boston, MA: Beacon P, 1988.

Spillers, Hortense J. *Black, White, and in Color: Essays on American Literature and Culture*. Chicago, IL: U of Chicago P, 2003.

Spivak, Gayatry Chakravorty. *A Critique of Postcolonial Reason: Toward a History of the Vanishing Present*. Cambridge, MA: Harvard UP, 1999.

Stacey, Jackie. "Wishing Away in the Balance." *Feminist Theory* 15.1 (2014): 39–49.

Tlostanova, Madina V., and Walter D. Mignol. *Learning to Unlearn: Decolonial Reflections from Eurasia and the Americas*. Columbus: Ohio State UP, 2012.

Wiegman, Robyn. "The Times We Are In: Queer Feminist Criticism and the Reparative 'Turn.'" *Feminist Theory* 15.1 (2014): pp. 4–25.

Ziarek, Ewa Płonowska. *Feminist Aesthetics and the Politics of Modernism*. New York: Columbia UP, 2012.

Ziarek, Ewa Płonowska. "The Stakes of Feminist Aesthetics: Transformative Practice, Neoliberalism, and the Violence of Formalism." *differences* 25.2 (Fall 2014): 101–15.

PART THREE

The World

CHAPTER TWENTY

World

MASOOD RAJA

Worlding has a long lineage following Martin Heidegger but becomes a prominent concept after Gayatri Spivak employs it in "The Rani of Simur: An Essay in Reading the Archives," one of her earlier feminist critiques of colonial history and the process of historymaking. The concept of worlding of the world appears first in this Spivak essay about the emergence, and eventual disappearance, of Rani of Simur from colonial narratives. In this essay, Spivak broaches three various stages of worlding the colonized spaces through the acts of epistemology, or knowledge-making. What happens to the figure of the native woman in this act of worlding happens to be a crucial point of inquiry for Spivak and for feminist theory. It becomes important for feminist theory because it traces not only how the colonial space is worlded for the natives but also how the female-gendered subject fares in this worlding.

In this chapter I will first discuss Spivak's usage of worlding, especially as it concerns the subaltern and postcolonial women, and then go on to discuss the role of world literature in our classrooms. I will conclude my discussion with the role of world literature in contemporary academia and then hazard a few opinions about a more nuanced world literature pedagogy that focuses on issues of feminism.

Spivak discusses the term worlding while describing the three layers of inscription of native female figure within the epistemic and legal narrative of empire. Spivak first discusses a report prepared by Captain Geoffrey Birch, who in Spivak's words is "advancing his career, riding about in the Hills with a single native escort—a slight romantic figure if encountered in the pages of a novel or on the screen" (253). In this process the act of worlding the native world to the natives is inextricably connected to an act of cathectation by the native and also with the power of the master to inscribe and shape this response. Spivak describes this outcome of the encounter and the mastery of landscape as follows:

> He is actually engaged in consolidating the self of Europe by obliging the native to cathect the space of the Other on his home ground. He is worlding their own world, which is far from mere uninscribed earth, anew, by obliging them to domesticate the alien as Master. The worlding of a world on uninscribed earth alludes to Heidegger's essay "The Origin of the Work of Art." (Spivak, "The Rani of Simur" 253)

It is important to first discuss, briefly, cathectation itself as a concept. Even though Freud uses the term in one of his lectures, in the current context the term loosely denotes the practice by the natives to invest their desires into the actions and pronouncements of the colonizers. Thus, in the act of cathectation, natives see the world around them with the sensitivities, preferences, and prejudices of their colonial masters. It is this act of cathectation that worlds the native world for the natives, as they start seeing their own physical space through the eyes of their colonial masters.

"The Rani of Simur" thus uses a layered recovery of the account of a native female historical figure from three archival sources: The report by the field agent, the pronouncements of his immediate superiors, and the account of Rani's history in the colonial archive. Captain Geoffrey Birch, during his journey over the Indian landscape, includes the following instructive passage in his letter to his superiors:

> I have undertaken this journey] to acquaint the people who they are subject to, for as I suspected they were not properly informed of it and seem only to have heard of our existence from conquering the Goorkha and from having seen a few Europeans passing thro' the country. (qtd. in Spivak, "The Rani of Simur" 254)

Thus, Spivak opines, through this movement of the colonial subject over the native land-scape, accompanied by his native servant, "the figure of the European on the hills is being reinscribed from stranger to Master" (254). For the purposes of this chapter, this account of a native officer consolidating the self of Europe through traveling over and recording the native geography should suffice. Worlding, thus, can be understood as that epistemological sense by which the colonial masters not only establish themselves, and thus by extension their laws and their perceptions of the world as the norm, but in the process also ensure that the very natives whom they govern also must see their own world through the eyes of their masters.

This worlding is not accidental. In fact, one could argue (and Spivak does), that the entire colonial project depends on this worlding, and it is achieved through law, admin-istration, and also through the educational system. The entire argument of Thomas Babington Macaulay's (in)famous minute on Indian education rests on this power to invest the native desire in the colonial project itself. In his speech, Macaulay asserts,

> We must at present do our best to form a class who may be interpreters between us and the millions whom we govern; a class of persons, Indian in blood and Colour, but English in taste, in opinions, in morals, and in intellect. To that class we may leave it to refine the vernacular dialects of the country, to enrich those dialects with terms of science borrowed from the Western nomenclature, and to render them by degrees fit vehicles for conveying knowledge to the great mass of population. (Macaulay 130)

The worlding of the world for the colonial masses, thus, is ideally achieved when a local, native elite cathects the role of the empire and invests their energies in making this pal-atable to the larger segments of the population. This worlding, thus, cannot be achieved without colonial educational system and the legal apparatus that established the hege-monic writ of the empire. On the role of colonial education in establishing the self of Europe in the colonies, Ngugi Thiong'O probably has the most acute understanding. In tracing the impact of colonial education, Ngugi provides the following account of how this education restructures the imagination of native children, in other words worlds their own world for them:

> Since culture does not just reflect the world in images but actually, through those very images, conditions *a child to see the world* in a certain way, the colonial child was made to see the world where he stands in it *as seen and defined by or reflected in the culture of the language of imposition.* (17, emphasis added)

Thus, the colonial educational system plays an important role in worlding the native space for the natives so that they see their own world from the point of view of their colonial masters. This is the ultimate hegemonic victory of colonial system of law and education: it worlds the native world for the natives and encourages them to see it from the point of view of their oppressors. In terms of gender relations, by focusing on patriarchal customs and traditions, the colonial system also ossifies the gender roles and ends up sanctioning and promoting a more restrictive role for the colonized women. Note that Spivak considers the colonial women as the ultimate subaltern subject. Just as the Rani of Simur disappears from the colonial archive, so do other women disappear from colonial histories, or even when they do appear, they are already spoken for. Another good example of this historical treatment of subaltern women in India is included in Spivak's most famous essay "Can the Subaltern Speak." Even though the British law against Sati was promulgated to "save" Hindu women from self-immolation, in the historical records of these widow sacrifices "as one goes down the grotesquely mistranscribed names of these women, … one cannot put together a 'voice' " (Spivak, "Can the Subaltern" 93). It seems, even when these women enter the colonial history, they are inserted into history only because of their utilitarian value to the project of empire and there is no space in colonial histories for their own voices to be heard or discerned.

Furthermore, in India, for example, since the stability of the empire was necessary for revenue collection, the colonial powers often worked in concert with the local elite and hence, in return for stability, often encouraged and even solidified the premodern gender hierarchies. In some cases, even the prevalent cultural norms that would have otherwise favored women, were also reversed through a symbiotic relationship with the local elites. Chandra Mohanty[1] provides the following account of gender hierarchies enabled and structured by the colonial system itself. In the Haryana's rural culture, the widows traditionally had the right to inheritance, but in order to keep the land within the family, "there was considerable restriction placed on whom they could marry" (62). Thus, even when the widows "challenged the patriarchal custom" (62), "the colonial state sanctified the custom by depending on a 'general code of custom" (62) that allowed the rural elders to keep coercing the women to marry within the family. Of course, all of this was done because the "colonial state" had "an economic interest in seeing landholding stable (to ensure revenue collection)" (62).

There are also indirect implications for the rights of women under colonial regimes, especially when it comes to articulating "proper" womanhood as juxtaposed against "Western(ized)" women. Thus, while the colonial system itself creates a secondary role for women, the native elite, despite their symbolic investment in the West and in the process of worlding their own world with this investment in their masters also develop a sort of reactionary narrative that impacts the rights and roles of women within the colony and in the postcolony as well. Partha Chatterjee explains the impact of colonial experience on gender roles by discussing the native division of the colonial space into *ghar* [home] and *bahir* [outside] as follows:

> It was [outside] a place of oppression and daily humiliation, a place where the norms of the colonizer had to perforce to be accepted.… . But in the entire phase of the national struggle, the crucial need was to protect, preserve, and strengthen the inner core of the national culture, its spiritual essence. No encroachments by the colonizer must be allowed in that inner sanctum. In the world, imitation of and adaptation to

Western norms was a necessity; at home, they were tantamount to annihilation of one's very identity. (121)

In such a scenario, then, inscribing women in more traditional roles, in opposition to their Western(ized) counterparts, becomes a major part of the nationalist struggle. Hence, according to Chatterjee, in the nineteenth- and twentieth-century Bengali plays, the figure of a westernized woman is often offered as a comical character and "what made the ridicule stronger was the constant suggestion that the Westernized woman was fond of useless luxury and cared little for the well-being of the home" (122). This tendency to constantly inscribe women in more traditional, domestic roles develops also in an overwhelming majority of liberation movements in the Islamic countries, of which Algeria is a good example. Thus, it seems that the question of women becomes central to the national struggles and, as the natives attempt to transcend the worlding of their world by the colonizers, they constantly look for precolonial models of female-gendered performance and, in the process, women are reinscribed into more traditional and domestic roles.

Coming to world literature and its appearance in the metropolitan academy, one could pose some interesting questions about the kind of worlding of the developing world the world literature offers to metropolitan students. It is important to note that most world literature courses were introduced in the universities as a replacement for what used to be Continental Literature, and the argument in favor of this shift is often utilitarian in nature, which connects the study of world literatures to the students' need to know the complex, interconnected world in which they will eventually seek jobs. As I have argued elsewhere, the world, as we know it "must be taught" (Raja 1), and world literature attempt to do just that. The question here, of course is, does world literature really teach the world, or does it need to be taught a certain way to accomplish this mission? There is no scholarly consensus about the possibilities and transformative impact of world literature. Emily Apter, while highlighting the "untranslatability" of world literature, opines as follows about the world literature classes:

> Severed from place, thrown into the maw of the global culture industry or survey course, and subject to pedagogical transmission by instructors with low levels of cultural literacy and nonexistent knowledge of a translated work's original language, local or native literature relinquishes its defining self-properties once it is exported and trafficked like an artifact. (326)

I would argue that this is the case not only in translated works but also in the works by native authors that might have been written in metropolitan languages, for even when written in the metropolitan languages, the texts cannot be fully understood without a clear knowledge of the meaning-making processes and storytelling techniques of the particular culture that these works represent. The problem is aggravated because most of these survey-level courses are either taught by graduate students or by lecturers who are underpaid, over worked, and not necessarily trained as world literature instructors. As a result, the most likely problem that happens is that the instructors reduce the texts and make them intelligible using the meaning-making process that they are used to. This would lead to, at worst, complete misreading of the other cultures and thus a failure of the very mission of world literature. Not only do the teachers need to be trained in teaching world literature critically, but they also need to understand that literary texts alone cannot inform the students about the world and at times can completely solidify their stereotypical views about the non-Euro American cultures, especially if these texts are read from a purely Western point of view.

Thus, at least a basic knowledge of the cultures of the global periphery is necessary to teach world literature effectively. Considering that most postcolonial/world literature texts are still littered with the expected tropes of the metropolitan market, the need for informed critical pedagogy, a pedagogy that is aware of the meaning-making processes of the global periphery and that does not consider Western feminism as a universally uncontested practice, is even more urgent. Usually, suggests Aijaz Ahmad, one sees "representations of colonialism, nationhood, post-coloniality, the typology of rulers, their powers, corruptions, and so forth" (124). If this is the repertoire of representations, then these texts are more likely to confirm the preexisting stereotypes, especially if taught by the instructors who are neither trained in teaching world literature nor have the time to learn on their own as they are also often overworked.

There are, of course, some viable strategies that can make the learning and teaching of world literature transformative. For example, Mark Bracher offers a strategy of teaching world literature in a way that it actually makes our metropolitan students more empathetic to their global counterparts. Discussing the cognitive structures behind our views of our global others, Bracher discusses "two basic forms in which out-groups are perceived to deviate from the category of the Human" (35):

> The most common form involves denying that the other possesses uniquely human qualities (UH) that distinguish humans from other animals ... The other form of dehumanization denies that the Other possesses certain qualities that are central to human nature (HN) such as interpersonal warmth, drive, and vivacity. (35)

These beliefs in the nature of being human, then, create certain schemas and prototypes that inform a Western reader/student's perception of his or her global others. Bracher suggests that in order to alter these schemas more than "simply having the students read" (41) the texts about their global others is needed. In other words, world literature by itself, if uncritically taught, can have no lasting transformative impact on our students. If our prejudices are based in our internalized prototypes, then altering those protoypes is a necessary first step toward creating a more emphatic human subjectivity, and Bracher suggests the following toward that end:

> One of the most basic things teachers can do to promote these corrective processes [processes that alter prejudicial schemas] is to select texts that provide multiple corrective exemplars for each of the prototype categories (i.e., prototypic individuals, prototypic body images, episode scripts etc.). (41)

Furthermore, Bracher also suggests that teachers should focus their teaching on these exemplars—that complicate the prototypic and stereotypic assumptions—and incorporate them in their discussions of the texts and in their assignments to the students. Thus, a combination of effective texts and informed pedagogy, in the end, might be able to mobilize world literature in becoming transformative and in creating the kind of transnational global understanding of each other.

A great example of the use of critical pedagogy in reading and teaching the world of global periphery is Robin Goodman's response to Hernando De Soto's empirical work on informal markets in relation to an African novel about the semi-employed. Robin Goodman offers a critique of neoliberal economics for creating suffering and poverty and in making the plight of the poor even worse. She does that by performing an acute reading of Buchi Emecheta's 1979 novel *The Joys of Motherhood*. Let me first suggest how an underpaid world lit instructor might teach this novel as narrating the individual will and struggles of an African woman. If taught uncritically, the novel will confirm to our students the brutal nature of African urban cultures and may further sanctify their views about the superiority of their own culture. Goodman, however, by connecting the fate of Nnu Ego to the forces of global neoliberal capital, makes the metropolitan complicit in the project of poverty in the Third World. She argues,

> *The Joys of Motherhood* centers on how Nnu Ego loses her identity during a time of national transition into a wage economy set up to keep labor costs low and public obligations minimal in order to ensure profitability for foreign investments and war. (101)

Thus, what happens to Nnu Ego during the course of the novel cannot just be taught as a narrative of struggle by an African woman against the native patriarchy, but it should be taught as the experiences of a human subject whose choices are overdetermined by the very system of economics that defines the value of human life in the global periphery. Now, teaching the novel with these insights would require a deeper understanding of Nigerian culture as well as a good understanding of the impact of neoliberal capital. Without these two knowledges, the novel would end up being yet another tale of victimhood of an African woman within a patriarchal African culture, and hence the novel, instead of transforming our students' views about the world, would end up solidifying their previously held stereotypes about Africa.

Overall, one could also argue that, just as the colonial law and narratives worlded the world for the native inhabitants, world literature, depending upon how it is taught, has the power of worlding the world for our students. If taught uncritically, without accounting for what Apter terms its "untranslatability," world literature is more likely to solidify previously held stereotypes and prejudices about the global Others. But if taught with the insights provided by critical pedagogy and if mobilized toward reshaping our students' imaginations, then world literature can be a powerful tool for teaching the world.

NOTE

1 Note that here Mohanty is relying on the primary research of Prem Chowdhry. For details, see Chowdhry, "Customs in Peasant Economy: Women in Colonial Haryana," in *Recasting Women: Essays in Colonial History*, ed. Kumkum Sangari and Sudesh Vaid (New Delhi: Kali Press, 1989), pp. 302–36.

WORKS CITED

Ahmad, Aijaz. *In Theory*. London: Verso Books, 1992.

Apter, Emily. *Against World Literature*. London: Verso Books, 2013.

Bracher, Mark. "Educating for Cosmopolitanism: Lessons from Cognitive Science." *Critical Pedagogy and Global Literature: Worldly Teaching*. Ed. Masood Raja, Hillary Stringer, and Zach Vandezande. New York: Palgrave Macmillan, 2013, pp. 25–46.

Chatterjee, Partha. *The Nation and Its Fragments*. Princeton, NJ: Princeton UP, 1993.

Goodman, Tobin Truth. *World, Class, Women*. London: Routledge, 2003.

Macaulay, Thomas Babington. "Minute on Indian Education. *Postcolonialisms*. Ed. Gaurav Desai and Supriya Nair. New Brunswick, NJ: Rutgers UP, 2005, pp. 121–31.

Mohanty, Chandra Talpade. *Feminism without Borders*. Durham, NC: Duke UP, 2003.

Raja, Masood A. "Introduction." *Critical Pedagogy and Global Literature: Worldly Teaching*. Ed. Masood Raja, Hillary Stringer, and Zach Vandezande. New York: Palgrave Macmillan, 2013, pp. 1–5.

Spivak, Gayatri C. "Can the Suablatern Speak." *Colonial Discourse and Postcolonial Theory*. Ed. Patrick Williams and Laura Chrisman. New York: Columbia UP, 1994, pp. 66–111.

Spivak, Gayatri C. "The Rani of Simur: An Essay in Reading the Archives." *History and Theory* 24.3 (1985): 247–72.

Thiong'O, Ngugi Wa. *Decolonising the Mind*. Oxford: James Currey, 1986.

CHAPTER TWENTY-ONE

Environment

SHANNON DAVIES MANCUS

Temporally and ideologically, the environmental movement and second-wave feminism are linked. *Silent Spring* and *The Feminine Mystique* were published less than five months apart, and many scholars involved in both movements engaged in intersectional activism throughout the 1970s noted the ways in which the oppression of animals and the so-called natural world mirrored the oppression of women, people of color, and the poor. These scholars and activists decided that the two problems—one of which was spurred in part by a recognition of "silence," and the other originally identified as having no name—needed to be theorized together to disrupt the larger ideology that structured the violences of both.

The term "ecofeminism"—a term that has gone in and out of favor, in ways that will be explored below—is widely considered to have been first used in France in 1974. Feminist Francoise d'Eaubonne is credited with having minted the term "ecological feminisme" in her forcefully named essay "Le féminisme ou la Mort" in order to theorize the intersection of the two movements. The same year, Susan Griffin began working on her enduringly influential work *Woman and Nature: The Roaring inside Her* (1978). Griffin's text examines the ways in which the feminine and the "natural" have been constructed and sutured in order to codify a gradation of value that has remained an ontological constant in Western philosophical thought and cultural traditions. She concludes that in the "hierarchical geography" of such thought, "not only are human beings elevated above the rest of nature, but men are closer to heaven than women. In short, the idea that women are close to nature is an argument for the domination of men" (xv).

Griffin's work was influenced by other feminist texts in terms of both content and style. *Woman and Nature* is part prose, part poetry, and its structure was impacted by proto-deconstructionist author Julia Stanley Penelope. Penelope's work influenced Griffin to note and imitate "the wide use of the passive voice in analytical writing by male experts," which she believed allowed her to show "that this syntax obscured who said or did or thought what to or about whom and therefore concealed inherent structures of power" (xi).

This voice results in a series of rhetorical moves that emphasize the assumption of the "naturalness" of ideology, predicated on the twinned forces of androcentrism and anthropocentrism:

> "It is decided that the existence of God can be proved by reason and that reason
> exists to apprehend God and Nature." (8)
> "It is observed that women are closer to the earth.
> That women lead to man's corruption.

Women are 'the Devil's Gateway,' it is said." (9–10)
"It is decided that matter cannot know matter.
That matter 'is but a brute thing and only capable of local motion.'
That matter has no intellect and no perception." (16)
"That Adam is soul and Eve is flesh." (19)

Griffin's text was at the forefront of an explosion of ecofeminist writing and activism, which explored the ways that concepts like fecundity, cultivation, and rape functioned in the nexus of gendered and environmental politics. Ecofeminists and other feminists concerned with environmental justice frequently argue that the domination of women and the earth are linked, and the liberation of one depends on the liberation of the other. Disrupting entrenched patterns of thought and cultural hierarchical constructions that have led to the oppression of both is the key to a more just world by breaking what Adams and Gruen have called "mutually enforcing logics of domination" (7).

This essay will begin by tracing a brief intellectual history of the intersection of feminism and environmental activism before turning to examine the 2017 Darren Aronofsky film, *mother!*, which was inspired by Griffin's *Woman and Nature*. In tracing this trajectory, I will address the politics around the term "ecofeminism," a category of theory which fell out of favor in the early twentieth century due to a widespread and mostly apocryphal assumption that the field primarily sought to argue that women were naturally more peaceful and attuned with nature than men. While this type of writing certainly did exist, the majority of scholarly ecofeminist writing, like Griffin's, fought to disrupt the binaries and hierarchies inherent in such assumptions. Through examining *mother!* and the director's purported relationship with ecofeminist theory, I will argue that the charges of essentialism often misattributed to the field are more a testament to the persistence of cultural conceptions of gender than to a widespread presence of essentialism in the canon of ecofeminist writing. The enduring nature of the perceived feminization of "nature" and the "naturalization" of "women," far from being endemic to the field, is instead a powerful testimony to the necessary persistence of methodologies like ecofeminism that critique narratives that naturalize binaries and hierarchies of all kinds. The most recent writing by scholars attending to the nexus of feminism and the environment are attuned to the ways different forms of violence, such as sexism, racism, colonialism, and heterosexism are linked. Their scholarship can help us imagine new narratives and cultural scripts that disrupt insidious hierarchies and allow for the envisioning of a more just world.

Early ecofeminist theorists and their fellow travelers critiqued and called for disruptions of androcentric and anthropocentric hierarchies. Many early ecofeminist authors sought to denaturalize what they saw as a patriarchal, hierarchical, and instrumental view of both women and the environment in order to enact a fundamental shift in understanding of our place in the environment as ontological. Ecologically minded feminists excavated for the insidious concepts that contributed to systematic oppression. Through their work, they came to different, but related, diagnoses of cultural malignancy.

One strain of embodied ecofeminism that proved impactful—both in terms of popularity and in terms of lending credence to charges of essentialism—was the rise of the theories and practices of goddess feminism. On Halloween day in 1979, two important books that linked the practices of feminism, ecological awareness, and paganism were published on opposite US coasts. Starhawk's *The Spiral Dance: A Rebirth of the Ancient Religion of the Great Goddess* was published in San Francisco, while Margo Adler's *Drawing*

Down the Moon: Witches, Druids, Goddess-Worshippers and Other Pagans in America was printed in New York City. Though differing in scope and scale, both attempted historical and theoretical interventions that linked the advent of patriarchal religion to the domination of both women and nature, and sought to trace a lineage of underground goddess-driven religions from antiquity to the modern era.[1] Paganism, they argued, could be a transforming force for American and global cultures.

Though looked upon skeptically by modern theorists, these books circulated widely and went through reprints, including tenth-, twentieth-, and twenty-fifth-year anniversary editions.[2] Additionally, their terminology and theoretical aspects served as handy references for scholars, such as Riane Eisler, who largely agreed with the sentiments behind goddess feminism even if they didn't advocate for the practices. Using the imagery of pagan tools that have come to represent female and male energies, Eisler argued in *The Chalice and the Blade: Our History, Our Future* (1987) that the current model of claiming dominion over the natural world—the "blade"—had been and could be otherwise, outlining a "chalice" approach that stressed partnership.

While goddess feminists and other scholars were identifying the ways in which androcentric religious hierarchies instantiated violent practices, others focused on the ways in which the concepts of enlightenment and rationality justified instrumental views of nonhuman, nonmale life. Carolyn Merchant's *The Death of Nature: Women, Ecology, and the Scientific Revolution* (1980) argued that notions of technological progress justified and encouraged the exploitation of both nature and women, while Val Plumwood's *Feminism and the Mastery of Nature* (1993) traced the genealogy of intellectually justified domination much further back to Classical Greek philosophers and the concept of rationalism. In all cases, the authors identified carefully scaffolded hierarchies that served to bolster male power at the expense of women and nonhuman nature.

The research that identified hierarchies, however, was often subjected to criticisms (fairly or unfairly) for ossifying the false dualisms that the hierarchies were built upon, and charges of gender essentialism continue to haunt those theorists who endeavor to work at the intersection of environmentalism and feminism. Many of the authors who followed these scholarly excavators of oppressive philosophy stressed the need to disrupt binary thinking writ large while still taking the heterogeneous effects of ecological devastation into account.

The 1990s saw an outpouring of self-identified ecofeminist texts that were inflected by their authors' awareness of third-wave feminism and increased attention to intersectionality. A cluster of scholars who focused on colonialism, racism, and international issues brought attention to the cultural and geographical heterogeneousness of the consequences of environmental degradation.[3] A separate but linked set of scholars focused on the problem that even while hierarchies and essentialist constructions of gender were being disrupted, many binaries remained in place, particularly cis-normative assumptions of gender/sex associations and divisions between the human and nonhuman.[4] However, even though many of the most consistent, nuanced, and lauded voices from the movement were vocal about the need to de-essentialize gender and disrupt sex-based binaries and hierarchies of all sorts, some texts either carelessly naturalized the categories and assumed characteristics of "man" and "woman," or were speciously accused of doing so in ways that persuaded those outside the field of a lack of radical progressive thought within ecofeminist circles. As a result, charges of essentialism stuck to the term "ecofeminism" within the academy, and the label became almost taboo, with anecdotes abounding of scholars being advised to strike the term from their scholarship to protect their careers.

While prominent scholars, particularly in the field of Animal Studies, have recently mounted solid defenses for the term and advocated for the redeployment of "ecofeminism,"[5] other scholarly clusters arose that eschewed the term and participated in broader theoretical turns to focus on the intersection of sex, gender, and ecology. Queer Ecology and Material Feminism share intellectual genealogies and theoretical interests with ecofeminism while trying to disrupt real and perceived binaries in ecofeminist scholarship.

Greta Gaard's "Toward a Queer Ecofeminism," Stacy Alaimo's *Undomesticated Ground: Recasting Nature as Feminist Space*, and the multiple writings of Catriona Sandilands contributed significantly to the establishment of the field of queer ecology. As defined by Sandilands, the field of Queer Ecology "is a form of cultural, political, and social analysis centrally focused on interrogating the relations between the social organization of sexuality and ecology, akin to environmental justice scholarship on race and ecofeminist thinking about gender … I understand queer ecology to be allied with, but not subsumed by, such currents as ecofeminism and environmental justice" ("Lesbian Separatist Communities," 133).[6] The contemporaneous and complementary turn to materialist feminism includes scholars who seek to continue the critiques of scholars that had examined the disparate material effects of environmental devastation on subaltern populations. It also disrupts the assumption of complete anthropocentric dominance by upending a human/nature binary and identifies entanglements that diffuse nonhuman agency. Alaimo describes the project of what she calls "new materialisms" as "emphasiz[ing] materiality as agential" and "stressing the entanglements and interactions between humans and the nonhuman world" ("Your Shell on Acid," 101–2).[7]

Though the term "ecofeminism" and its attendant methodologies fell out of favor in academia because they were tarnished by the brush of essentialism, the type of narratives they critiqued continue to thrive. The most recent visible example of this is Darren Aronofsky's *mother!*, one of the most controversial films of 2017. What is particularly ironic about this is that the film was directly influenced by the director's contact with Susan Griffin's canonical 1978 ecofeminist text *Woman and Nature: The Roaring inside Her*. A closer examination of the film and the media surrounding it proves demonstrative of the ways in which radical writing can get misinterpreted in a reactionary way, and it provides a paradigmatic example of how ecofeminist writings have been misinterpreted through a cultural lens of calcified essentialist tropes.

Very little was known about the film prior to screenings, as the studio and director sought to capitalize on anticipation of Aronofsky's latest work; Paramount went as far as to move the screening of the film by two months to attempt to keep the themes and content of *mother!* from leaking prior to its release. The marketing campaign for the film purposefully added to the air of mystery, and invited those familiar with the psychological nature of Aronofsky's other films (such as *Requiem for a Dream* and *Black Swan*) to seek subliminal messages and clues as to the theme of his new movie in the few pieces of footage and artwork that were released for public consumption.

Two radically different posters were disseminated featuring aesthetically disparate pictures of the two leads. On one, Jennifer Lawrence stands in an Edenic, verdant space that is dominated by mossy greenery and exotic flowers, though the colors are muted and the entire image looks like a painting captured through a Vaseline lens, like a delicately bizarre artistic love child of a Gauguin and a Monet. In the center, gazing beatifically upward and outward, stands Lawrence looking like a Grecian bride in a gossamer white dress. In contrast to the nearly pastel palate of her surroundings the center of the image is dominated by a vibrant gaping red wound in Lawrence's chest; she has pulled out her

heart and offered it to the viewer, and the blood flowing from the afterbirth of her sacrifice has stained her garment. This image was cropped for the cover art of the DVD; in that
circumscribed image, Lawrence's ethereal expression is the focus of the artwork, and the
only evidence of the violent act depicted in the poster is the top of the wound that crests
over the bottom edge of the image. This cropping emphasizes the vaginality of the cavity
that occupies the space where the titular character's heart should be, by giving the viewer
a closer look at the outer fold of skin, the inner fold of muscle, and the dark red recess of
the interior of the mother's chest. This disturbing and conspicuous aspect of the artwork
equates the female biological sex with emotional vulnerability and marks the character
from the outset as carrying the weight of noxious cultural imperatives about femininity
and motherhood.

The aesthetics of the poster featuring Javier Bardem, the other lead of the film, stand in
stark contrast to the artwork featuring Lawrence. Bardem, sitting in a chair in a nondescript
blue outfit, occupies the center of an image that is otherwise entirely consumed by stylistic-
ally rendered red flames. Whereas Lawrence's hands reach out toward the viewer with her
heart in her hands to comprise an offering gesture, Bardem also reaches out to the viewer,
but with his palm upturned in a gesture that implies that the viewer should give *him* something. With the other hand, he possessively clutches a gold globe against his chest.

Eagle-eyed Aronofsky fans noticed a lighter, stamped with the image of fish, hidden
in both images. Some correctly speculated that this Christian symbol might indicate that
the director was returning to an exploration of Judeo-Christian themes.[8] The idea that
Jennifer Lawrence might be a personified version of Mother Nature was confirmed by
the last teaser of subject matter before critics were allowed to see the screening of the
film: "prayer cards" featuring an "adapted" version of the Lord's Prayer adapted by
Rebecca Solnit, which read,

> mother's prayer
>
> our mother who art underfoot,
> hollowed be thy names,
> thy seasons come, thy will be done,
> within us as around us,
> thank you for our daily bread, our water, and our lives and so much beauty;
> lead us not into selfish craving and the destructions
> that are the hungers of the glutted,
> but deliver us from wanton consumption
> of thy vast but finite bounty,
> for thine is the only sphere of life we know,
> and the power and the glory, forever and ever,
> Amen

When these cards were distributed, many tweets from critics noted that they seemed to
be attempting to add to the spooky marketing of the film as a psychological thriller.[9]
However, when taken in context of the film, the prayer seems almost alarmingly sincere.

mother!, though it may share some DNA with horror and thriller films, is an avant-
garde allegory. This was confirmed in interviews that Aronofsky gave after the film
opened that stated explicitly that he intended the "mother" from the title to be Mother
Earth, and for Bardem's character to be an avatar for the grand patriarch of Judeo-
Christian religions. It was in these interviews that Aronofsky revealed that he took direct

inspiration for the subject matter of the film from encountering and reading *Woman and Nature*, and that he spoke with Susan Griffin during filming and asked her to give feedback at an early screening.

In an interview with the *New York Times* shortly after the film's release, Aronofsky said of the work: "[I]t weaves together ideas about men and women and the roles we've historically been assigned: man battling nature, woman in tune with it" (Ryzik). In an interview with *Collider*, Aronofsky was quoted as saying that "the structure of the film was the Bible, using that as a way of discussing how humans have lived here on Earth ... I sort of wanted to tell the story of Mother Nature from her point of view" (Chitwood). This commitment to point-of-view storytelling is borne out by the cinematography; Lawrence is shot in close-up for nearly sixty-six minutes of a roughly two-hour-long movie.

The film, confusingly, opens with a shot of an unknown woman on fire. As she stares defiantly at the camera, a single tear rolls down her face, recalling another essentialized eco-avatar: that of the so-called Crying Indian of the "Keep America Beautiful" ads of the 1970s. A quick cut implying cause and effect introduces Bardem's character as he sets what appears to be a fist-sized, oddly shaped precious jewel into a pedestal in a room destroyed by fire. He sighs and the evidence of the destruction of the fire retreats as the house creaks back to life.

The movie then radically shifts in tone to a seemingly verisimilitudinous portrait of domestic life. Jennifer Lawrence wakes up in the unburnt house and begins to search for Bardem. The titular character is the young partner of a frustrated writer named in the credits as "Him," but referred to by other characters as "the poet." She is contentedly repairing the house. He is trying to produce a new work, unsuccessfully. However, directly after a moment in which the poet finally seems inspired to write, a man appears at the back door. The poet, without consulting the mother, invites the man to stay and the two men spend the night drunkenly carousing. The evening culminates in the mother stumbling upon the man shirtless and vomiting in a toilet while the poet attempts to hide from the mother a wound that spans the back of the man's rib cage. The next day the man's wife appears at the door.

The two prove distressingly bad house guests, repeatedly ignoring the mother's pleas for them to not smoke in the house, using resources and not cleaning up after themselves, and ultimately entering the writer's office (after repeatedly being asked not to) and breaking the heart/jewel that restored the house at the very beginning of the film. The mother pleads for the poet to cast them out of the house entirely, but he merely boards up his office and allows them to stay. Shortly after, the man and woman's sons appear. One violently murders the other, and though the mother gets a respite from intruders while everyone else is at the hospital, Bardem soon returns to reveal that the son has died and that he has invited the family and friends of the man and the woman to gather to memorialize the son at their house.

Throughout the rest of the film, Bardem invites a parade of strangers into the house who destroy Lawrence's domestic work. This culminates in a sequence which flashes forward in time to a day when Lawrence is nine months pregnant and the poet has released his finished text. In a sequence described by the cast and the production crew as "the nightmare," adoring fans of the poet overrun the house, and Lawrence, who goes into labor, has to fight through the worst violences of humanity to try to find her way to a safe space to go through labor, including avoiding execution-style killings and crawling through mass graves to get to the writer's office. There, she gives birth, but when the poet makes it clear he still will not cast out the people wrecking their house, she refuses to let him hold the baby. He waits until she falls asleep, takes the baby, and gives it to the crowd. She wakes up in time to see the crowd murder and eat their child. She flies into a murderous rage while Bardem pleads that she forgive the occupants of their house. She fights her way to the basement furnace, punctures it, and lights the oil spilling from it on fire. As the house incinerates, the shot from the beginning repeats, this time with Lawrence as the burning woman. Bardem, unscathed, carries her burnt body up to his charred office. He asks for her heart, and she gives it to him. As she turns to ash, he crushes the heart into a new jewel. He places it on the pedestal and the house breathes back to life. The shot that introduced Lawrence is repeated with a new woman. The film ends.

Aronofsky's purports to use the retelling of biblical events (the creation of Adam and Eve, the story of Cain and Abel, the birth and death of Christ and the sharing of his body as communion) to articulate ecofeminist theories, and on some level, it is not only Griffin's theoretical musings but also her specific artistic vision that seems to seep through into the film. Griffin's imagistic writing can almost be seen to transfer directly into Aronofsky's avant-garde vision of parts of *mother!* In the section "This Earth (What She Is to Me)," Griffin presages the circular nature of the film and the affectual branding of the mother:

> Each time I go to her I am born like this. Her renewal washes over me endlessly, her wounds caress me; I become aware of all that has come between us ... She is as delicate as I am; I know her sentience; I feel her pain and my own pain comes to me, and my own pain grows large and I grasp this pain with my hands, and I open my mouth to this pain, I taste, I know, and I know why she goes on, under great weight, with this great thirst, in drought, in starvation, with intelligence in every act does she survive disaster. (221)

Aronofsky's conception of "the mother" reflects the tropes that Griffin identifies as entwining discursive conceptions of nature and femininity. "Mother earth," as defined both by Griffin's writing and by Aronofsky's film, is a constantly renewing figure whose existence between her cyclical destruction is marked by a pain that is coded as distinctly "feminine." The incendiary nature of the cycle and the constant threat of encroaching charred matter that is present in the film also seems to be described almost directly by Griffin. In the chapter "His Cataclysm: The Universe Shudders," under the subsection "Pollution," Griffin describes the reoccurring cycle of the creation of pollution, but the prose seems to have inspired the recurring cycle of mayhem and incineration that Bardem's character creates every time he restarts the sequence with a new mother:

> Every attempt to destroy this matter brings it back again.... . For every head cut off a new one grows. Every particle ignited, the least bit of dust blown away, what rises in the air expanding, bursting into flame, incandescent, seeming to vanish, be gone forever, returns, returns, always comes back to him, unmercifully. What he has sent into the rivers comes back, blackens the shore, enters the land, feeds his crops, enters his mouth, festers in him. What he has burned gathers in the air, hangs in space, yellows his vision, stings his eyes; he creates it. What he has worked out of the ground and transformed darkens the skies, gives out an odor he cannot forget, wherever he turns.... . At his hands, the molecules change, and changed and changing they enter his skin, hide in what he eats, secrete themselves in his tissue, alter the molecular structure of his body. He goes inside the heart of life, he says(136)

In addition to seeming to visually reference prose from Griffin's text, *mother!* illustrates Griffin's critique of the androcentric hierarchies by illustrating the connection between various technological violences, arrogance, and the destruction of the earth with the worship of the divine male figure. It also illustrates the way in which the feminine and the "natural" are both material and devalued.

Lawrence's character's needs and desires are ignored throughout the film as others assume her function is to serve and support them. However, it is not only the mother's wishes that are repeatedly ignored but also her warnings. People heedlessly take what doesn't belong to them and carelessly destroy the house until she reaches a proverbial "tipping point" and burns the house down, embodying a trope that has been employed frequently by climate change activists: that of the angry earth perpetrating revenge-disasters such as wildfires against a populace that continues to ignore her warnings. However, even in this, *mother!* complicates the idea of natural limitation with lasting consequences by implying that the biosphere can undergo destruction and then heal itself. The scenario of the film resonates with the Gaia hypothesis: the idea that "nature" is a closed, self-regulating, "perfect" system, and that it is only human folly that disrupts it. This poses a few problems in terms of scripting environmental politics; if the presence of humans is the root cause of the problem, potential solutions are rightfully unpalatable. Additionally, the repeating cycle of the film implies inevitability; if there is no chance of things being otherwise, there can be no solution that can be scripted by the narrative.

In an interview with Entertainment Weekly, about the "F" rating the film received from CinemaScore, Aronofsky explained that the film's tone is a reflection of his feelings about climate change: "It scares me, and it's time to start screaming," he added. "So I wanted to howl. This was my howl, and some people are not going to want to listen to it. That's cool" (Coggan). In crafting his "howl," however, it is significant that Aronofsky ensured that the actual cries of outrage in the film are projected through an essentialized female body. It is Lawrence who bears the responsibility of emoting, and that gendered outsourcing of emotional labor had physiological consequences. One of the most notorious stories to come out of the filming of *mother!* can be interpreted as a violent but pertinent phenomenological manifestation of the subtitle of Griffin's book. During the climax of the film, when the mother has finally had enough of the intrusion, mayhem, and destruction, she hits a breaking point that causes her to "roar" in anguish and rage. Lawrence lost herself so completely in the moment that she hyperventilated severely and tore her diaphragm, and Aronofsky had to calm her down by repeatedly reminding her that the specific scenario wasn't real. Many feminist film critics, however, have noted the material corollaries between Lawrence's experience and that of her character, which gives the lie to Aronofsky's soothing protestations: At the time, Aronofsky, the creator of the scenario (a kind of poet, even), was Lawrence's lover. The parallels between the relationship between the director and the leading actress and the two main characters extended to the way each male figure outsourced affectual responsibility onto Lawrence, and the gendered burden that was placed upon her could not be confined to the fictional narrative and therefore had tangible, real-world effects. This is, ironically, the main point of Griffin's intellectual project as well as that of many other writers that concern themselves with feminism and ecology: that essentializing "women" and "nature" as natural resources that are instrumentalized as "motherly" and "emotionally volatile" leads to dire material consequences for both.

There are other obvious problems with calling this text feminist. Lawrence's character is literally a domestic goddess, and both her character name and the title of the movie reduces her to her reproductive role. Her heart and her vagina are imagistically linked before the film begins, and her only desires seem to be to have a child, to be alone with her husband, and to take care of the house. All of the women in the film are created by the poet, and in the repeating cycle the male creator has a stable identity where the role of the mother can be fulfilled by interchangeable women. This affirms an old politics of male creationary power being agential and evidence of an individualized genius and female creationary power as interchangeable and altruistic.

This illustrates the problem of the perception of ecofeminism in larger intellectual circuits. Whereas Griffin was *critiquing* duality and essentialism, Aronofsky selectively interpreted her writing in a way that fails to make that critical distinction; in many ways *mother!* seems to confirm many of the most noxious stereotypes that caused scholars to turn away from pursuing ecofeminist lines of query. Griffin was pointing out that the linking of the concept of woman with the concept of the environment was part of a larger ideological project that justified the domination of both. Aronofsky, seemingly uncritically, links "nature" and the feminine in a way that codifies the insidious discourses that Griffin was trying to disrupt. Aronofsky stated in an interview with the *Guardian* that for him, his filmic statement on environmentalism and climate change is ultimately about "a woman who is asked to give and give and give until she can give nothing more" (Kermode). Griffin, however, emphatically argues *against* personifying nature as female, insisting that "[b]y imagining women as closer to nature, it becomes possible to imagine men as farther away from nature. And in this way, both men and women can indulge in the fantasy that the human condition can be free of mortality, as well as the exigencies and needs of natural limitation" (xvii). Whereas Griffin presents the binary between man/divinity and woman/nature in order to emphasize its constructed nature and suggest that that particular ideological formulation served to justify the domination of women and the nonhuman world, Aronofsky reifies these connections while simultaneously crediting Griffin for his ideas.[10]

Of the use of the singular noun in her title, Griffin wrote, "The book is titled *Woman and Nature* instead of 'Women and Nature' for a reason. Though I describe women's experiences, the subject of the book is the *idea* of *woman*, produced by a culture bent on the domination of both women and nature" (xiii). Recent ecofeminist writing seeks to disrupt the other assumption that is built into Griffin's title: the *idea* that human beings and "nature" are separate. Feminist authors such as Donna Haraway have proposed alternative conceptions of human and nonhuman relationships. Texts like Phillips and Rumens's *Contemporary Perspectives on Ecofeminism* (2015), Claxton's *Heidegger's Gods: An Ecofeminist Perspective* (2017), and Gaard's *Critical Ecofeminism* (2017) all unapologetically use the formerly eschewed term in their titles, and all address ways to disrupt the discursive binaries and hierarchies that have led to global systems of oppression and our current environmental crises.

As humanity grapples with the declaration of the Anthropocene, this upwelling of writing that searches for new narratives that disrupt deeply engrained systems of domination in our cultural discourses is critical. Scholars and scientists examining current environmental catastrophes have noted that our greatest problems are not caused by a lack of relevant technology but rather by a failure to create compelling narratives that assist in the imagining of a more sustainable relationship between the human and nonhuman world. Narratives that not only position humans in a dominant hierarchical position in relation to "the environment" but also fail to take into account the ways in which humans and the nonhuman world are hopelessly entangled do not provide a structure that can possibly capture the nature of the scale and invidiousness of our current ecological problems. Ecofeminist theory and related disciplines that are attentive to intersectional violences are therefore critical for understanding the ways that linked binaries and hierarchies have material effects on lived reality and can provide Anthropocene-era scholars critical tools to envision a less violent and oppressive future.

NOTES

1 Many of the historical assertions made in the books are now largely considered to be based on apocryphal research; the authors drew on Margaret A. Murray's *The Witch-Cult in Western Europe* (1921) and texts by Merlin Stone including *When God Was a Woman*. Starhawk, however, has defended stories in the book in more recent interviews citing a distinction between mythology and history.

2 Texts that purport to empower millennial women through the reclaiming of the title of "witch" have been recently resurgent, with titles like *Jailbreaking the Goddess: A Radical Revisioning of Feminist Spirituality* (Allen), *Woman Most Wild: Three Keys to Liberating the Witch Within* (Dulsky), *Basic Witches: How to Summon Success, Banish Drama, and Raise Hell with Your Coven* (Saxena and Zimmerman), and *Witches, Sluts, Feminists: Conjuring the Sex Positive* (Sollee) recently hitting the market.

3 See, for example, The 1994 collection *Ecofeminism: Women, Culture, Nature* edited by Karen J. Warren, which included diverse voices and chapters that focused on the synthesis of anti-colonialist and ecofeminist lenses, the intersection of race, gender, and environmental justice, and the importance of listening to indigenous and international voices; Rosemary Radford Ruether's *Women Healing Earth: Third World Women on Ecology, Feminism, and Religion;* and Noël Sturgeon's *Ecofeminist Natures: Race, Gender, Feminist Theory, and Political Action*. Other texts that have been inspired by feminism's turn toward anti-colonial and socialist politics include Shiva's *Biopiracy: The Plunder of Nature and Knowledge* (1997) and Ariel Salleh's *Ecofeminism as Politics: Nature, Marx and the Postmodern* (1997).

4 Carol Adams's *The Sexual Politics of Meat: A Feminist-Vegetarian Critical Theory* (1990) and Greta Gaard's *Ecofeminism: Women, Animals, Nature* (1993) were particularly influential texts in this regard.

5 For discussions of the politics of using the label "ecofeminist" and for spirited defenses of the term, see especially Gaard, "Ecofeminism Revisited: Rejecting Essentialism and Re-Placing Species in a Material Feminist Environmentalism," (2011), and the first chapter of Adams and Gruen's *Ecofeminism: Feminist Intersections with Other Animals and the Earth* (2014).

6 Recent major works in Queer Ecology include the writings in Mortimer-Sandilands and Erickson's edited volume *Queer Ecologies: Sex, Nature, Politics, Desire* (2010) and Nicole Seymour's *Strange Natures: Futurity, Empathy, and the Queer Ecological Imagination* (2013).

7 Other important texts in the materialist vein include Karen Barad's *Meeting the Universe Halfway: Quantum Physics and the Entanglement of Matter and Meaning* (2007), Stacy Alaimo's *Bodily Natures: Science, Environment, and the Material Self* (2010), Jane Bennet's *Vibrant Matter: A Political Ecology of Things* (2010), Elizabeth A. Grosz's *Volatile Bodies: Toward a Corporeal Feminism* (2011), Mel Chen's *Animacies: Biopolitics, Racial Mattering, and Queer Affect* (2012), Timothy Morton's *Hyperobjects: Hyperobjects: Philosophy and Ecology after the End of the World* (2013).

8 Aronofsky had previously drawn on the Bible as subject matter with his 2014 epic *Noah*.

9 This marketing backfired spectacularly, with audiences who saw the first screenings of the film feeling like the studio had pulled a genre-based bait-and-switch. The film made headlines when CinemaScore audiences gave it an F, a rare event for the review website.

10 For Griffin's reaction to Aronofsky's film, see Kilkenny.

WORKS CITED

Adams, Carol J. *The Sexual Politics of Meat: A Feminist-Vegetarian Critical Theory*. 25th anniversary edn. London: Bloomsbury, 2015.

Adams, Carol J, and Lori Gruen, eds. *Ecofeminism: Feminist Intersections with Other Animals and the Earth*. New York: Bloomsbury, 2014.

Adler, Margot. *Drawing Down the Moon: Witches, Druids, Goddess-Worshippers, and Other Pagans in America*. Rev edn. New York: Penguin Books, 2014.

Alaimo, Stacy. *Bodily Natures: Science, Environment, and the Material Self*. Bloomington: Indiana UP, 2010.

Alaimo, Stacy. *Undomesticated Ground: Recasting Nature as Feminist Space*. Ithaca, NY: Cornell UP, 2000.

Alaimo, Stacy. "Your Shell on Acid: Material Immersion, Anthropocene Dissolves." *Anthropocene Feminism*. Ed. Richard Grusin. Minneapolis: U of Minnesota P, 2017, pp. 89–120.

Allen, Lasara Firefox. *Jailbreaking the Goddess: A Radical Revisioning of Feminist Spirituality*. Woodbury, MN: Llewellyn, 2016.

Aronofsky, Darren. *mother!*. Hollywood, CA: Paramount Pictures, 2017.

Barad, Karen. *Meeting the Universe Halfway: Quantum Physics and the Entanglement of Matter and Meaning*. Second printing edn. Durham, NC: Duke UP, 2007.

Bennett, Jane. *Vibrant Matter: A Political Ecology of Things*. Durham, NC: Duke UP, 2010.

Carson, Rachel. *Silent Spring*. Anniversary edn. Boston, MA: Houghton Mifflin, 2002.

Chen, Mel Y. *Animacies: Biopolitics, Racial Mattering, and Queer Affect*. Durham, NC: Duke UP, 2012.

Chitwood, Adam. "Darren Aronofsky Confirms What 'Mother!' Is Really About." *Collider* (blog). September 18, 2017. http://collider.com/darren-aronofsky-explains-mother-movie/.

Claxton, Susanne. *Heidegger's Gods: An Ecofeminist Perspective*. London: Rowman & Littlefield, 2017.

Coggan, Devan. "'Mother!' Director Darren Aronofsky Responds to F CinemaScore." *Entertainment Weekly*, September 21, 2017. http://ew.com/movies/2017/09/21/mother-director-darren-aronofsky-responds-to-f-cinemascore/.

Dulsky, Danielle. *Woman Most Wild: Three Keys to Liberating the Witch Within*. Novato, CA: New World Library, 2017.

Eaubonne, Françoise d'. *Le féminisme ou la mort*. Paris: P. Horay, 1974.

Eisler, Riane. *The Chalice and the Blade: Our History, Our Future*. Updated edn. New York: HarperOne, 2014.

Friedan, Betty. *The Feminine Mystique*. 1st edn. New York: W. W. Norton, 2013.

Gaard, G. "Ecofeminism Revisited: Rejecting Essentialism and Re-Placing Species in a Material Feminist Environmentalism." *Feminist Formations* 23.2 (2011: 26–53).

Gaard, Greta, ed. *Ecofeminism: Women, Animals, Nature*. Philadelphia, PA: Temple UP, 1993.

Gaard, Greta. "Toward a Queer Ecofeminism." *Hypatia* 12.1 (1997): 114–37.

Gaard, Greta. *Critical Ecofeminism*. Lanham, MD: Lexington Books, 2017.

Griffin, Susan. *Woman and Nature: The Roaring inside Her*. Reissue edn. Berkeley, CA: Counterpoint, 2016.

Grosz, Elizabeth. Volatile Bodies: Toward a Corporeal Feminism. Bloomington: Indiana UP, 2011.

Haraway, Donna J. *Staying with the Trouble: Making Kin in the Chthulucene*. 1st edn. Durham, NC: Duke UP, 2016.

Kermode, Mark. "Mother! Review: A Complicated Labor for Jennifer Lawrence." Guardian, September 17, 2017. https://www.theguardian.com/film/2017/sep/17/mother-review-a-full-house-of-horrors-darren-aronofsky-jennifer-lawrence.

Kilkenny, Katie. "A Conversation With the Ecofeminist Who Helped Inspire 'Mother!'." Pacific Standard, September 20, 2017. https://psmag.com/social-justice/a-conversation-about-mother-with-susan-griffin.

Merchant, Carolyn. The Death of Nature: Women, Ecology, and the Scientific Revolution. Rev edn. San Francisco, CA: HarperOne, 2008.

Mortimer-Sandilands, Catriona, and Bruce Erickson. Queer Ecologies: Sex, Nature, Politics, Desire. Bloomington: Indiana UP, 2010.

Morton, Timothy. Hyperobjects: Philosophy and Ecology after the End of the World. Minneapolis: U of Minnesota P, 2013.

Murray, Margaret Alice. The Witch-Cult in Western Europe: A Study in Anthropology. London: Forgotten Books, 2012.

Phillips, Mary, and Nick Rumens. Contemporary Perspectives on Ecofeminism. London: Routledge, 2015.

Plumwood, Val. Feminism and the Mastery of Nature. London: Routledge, 1993.

Ruether, Rosemary Radford, ed. Women Healing Earth: Third World Women on Ecology, Feminism, and Religion. Maryknoll, NY: Orbis Books, 1996.

Ryzik, Melena. "Making 'Mother!,' the Year's Most Divisive Film." New York Times, September 19, 2017, sec. Movies. https://www.nytimes.com/2017/09/19/movies/jennifer-lawrence-darren-aronofsky-mother-explained.html.

Salleh, Ariel. Ecofeminism as Politics: Nature, Marx, and the Postmodern. 2nd edn. London: Zed Books, 2017.

Sandilands, Catriona. "Lesbian Separatist Communities and the Experience of Nature: Toward a Queer Ecology." Organization and Environment 15.2 (2002): 131–63.

Saxena, Jayna, and Jess Zimmerman. Basic Witches: How to Summon Success, Banish Drama, and Raise Hell with Your Coven. Philadelphia: Quirk Books, 2017.

Seymour, Nicole. Strange Natures: Futurity, Empathy, and the Queer Ecological Imagination. 1st edn. Urbana: U of Illinois P, 2013.

Shiva, Vandana. Biopiracy: The Plunder of Nature and Knowledge. First paperback edn, used edn. Boston, MA: South End P, 1999.

Sollee, Kristen J. Witches, Sluts, Feminists: Conjuring the Sex Positive. Berkeley, CA: ThreeL Media, 2017.

Starhawk. The Spiral Dance : A Rebirth of the Ancient Religion of the Great Goddess. 20th anniversary edn. New York: HarperOne, 1999.

Stone, Merlin. When God Was a Woman. New York: Harcourt, 1976.

Sturgeon, Noel. Ecofeminist Natures: Race, Gender, Feminist Theory and Political Action. New York: Routledge, 1997.

Warren, Karen J., ed. Ecofeminism: Women, Culture, Nature. 1st edn. Bloomington: Indiana UP, 1997.

CHAPTER TWENTY-TWO

Anthropocene

ALISON SPERLING

INTRODUCTION

Around the turn of the twenty-first century, a group of scientists declared that human-kind had become the most dominant geological force on Earth, a force whose history of burning of fossil fuels now registers as black carbon, inorganic ash, and spherical car-bonaceous particles in recent geological strata around the world. This residue, which will be the geologic legacy of the human, designates what has been unofficially termed the "Anthropocene" and remains a hotly contested term in both scientific circles and the humanities. Necessitated by the Anthropocene's increasingly urgent and unequal effects of climate change, feminist thought has long been theorizing the political and ethical responsibilities that this new geological epoch compels. In fact, as this chapter will show, much of the cultural engagement with and critique of the Anthropocene and its uneven effects has come from feminist theory and practice across disciplines. Posing a collective challenge to masculinist rationality and knowledge production, feminism in the Anthropocene insists on the myriad ways in which culture must inform scientific thought, in order to gain fuller understanding of, as well as to think up possible reparations for, what is nothing short of global ecological catastrophe.

This chapter will attempt to lay out some of the ways in which feminist theory has engaged with ecological questions and catastrophes in the last few decades, a genealogy that will help us to arrive at an understanding of the Anthropocene through feminism. As a relatively recent term with which theorists in the humanities have engaged, the Anthropocene is young yet, though has already been taken up with fervor across dis-ciplines. Though unevenly felt, the overwhelming environmental effects of climate change—warming and acidifying oceans, increasingly toxic air, and species extinction at unprecedented rates—have become of the utmost importance to feminism. Although the proposed "Anthropocene," comes to us as a term from the geological sciences, fem-inist interventions in discussions of the Anthropocene help to further develop the term in humanistic discourses. Feminist theory of the Anthropocene has therefore developed in relation to other fields like postcolonial studies, indigenous studies, and science studies, and it takes numerous directions, like essentialist and anti-essentialist arguments about sex and gender, deconstructive readings, artistic expression, and calls for political action. These varying feminist interventions in the Anthropocene have proven vital to its continued examination.

[handwritten margin note: What anthropocene 13/]

PLACING THE GOLDEN SPIKE

Though already in use by biologist Eugene Stoermer in the 1980s (Steffen, Crutzen, and McNeill 843), the term "Anthropocene" began to more formally circulate following Paul J. Crutzen's article "The 'Anthropocene,'" coauthored with Stoermer in the *International Geosphere-Biosphere Programme Newsletter* in 2000. Unofficially named as the successor to the Holocene, which spanned the last 12,000 years or so, the proposed "Anthropocene" names the current geological epoch after humanity, now the most dominant geological force on the planet.[1] As Crutzen and Stoermer detailed nearly two decades ago,

> During the past 3 centuries human population increased tenfold to 6000 million, accompanied e.g. by a growth in cattle population to 1400 million (6) ... In a few generations mankind is exhausting the fossil fuels that were generated over several hundred million years. The release of SO_2 ... is at least two times larger than the sum of all natural emissions ... more than half of all accessible fresh water is used by mankind; human activity has increased the species extinction rate by thousand to ten thousand fold in the tropical rain forests (9) and several climatically important "greenhouse" gases have substantially increased in the atmosphere: CO_2 by more than 30% and CH_4 by even more than 100%. (17)

This great acceleration, caused by the numerous actions and events Crutzen lists off, has caused unprecedented change in global environmental systems. Such change is harmful for living and nonliving systems alike, and, without an enormous collective will, human impacts will continue to degrade the environment in countless and irreversible ways.

Despite Crutzen and Stoermer's claim in 2000 that "To assign a more specific date to the onset of the 'anthropocene' seems somewhat arbitrary" (17), in a follow-up article of 2002 Crutzen writes,

> It seems appropriate to assign the term 'Anthropocene' to the present, in many ways human-dominated, geological epoch, supplementing the Holocene ... [it] could be said to have started in the latter part of the eighteenth century, when analyses of air trapped in polar ice showed the beginning of growing global concentrations of carbon dioxide and methane. This date also happens to coincide with James Watt's design of the steam engine in 1784. (Crutzen 211)

For this pair of pioneering scientists of the Anthropocene, carbon and methane emissions turned deposits, dating to the latter half of the eighteenth century, are the primary elements that mark the new epoch. Due to this sudden increase in exploitation of fossil fuels in that period, human energy use rose sharply, consuming four to five times more energy than their agrarian predecessors (Steffen, Crutzen, and McNeill 848). But other possibilities of origin are also acknowledged: the beginning of humankind, the discovery of fire, the date of the first nuclear testing, and a somewhat more popular contender, the advent of agriculture. The debate about when, where, and with whom the Anthropocene began (and is accelerated) matters to feminist inquiries into the Anthropocene, as does the project of naming this new epoch. Feminist theory across disciplines has presented significant challenges to purely technoscientific narratives that inform the Anthropocene and has opened up for questioning which dominant scientific, historical, and cultural factors and peoples are privileged in naming of the Anthropocene as such.

Jill Schneiderman's essay "The Anthropocene Controversy," briefly charts the extent to which disagreements and tensions undergird the naming of the Anthropocene. How, for example, can an epoch be named after a species that is not equally responsible for its conditions throughout history? Might the Anthropocene represent the Anthropos[2] as an inaccurately undifferentiated species, thereby eclipsing the responsibility that may lie more with one group of humans in one place and time than another? As feminism continues to argue, sediment formation across the planet exposes the proposed geologic epoch as forming in uneven and patchy ways. Human activity has not been equally reflected in strata samples, in part because areas of the world were cultivated later than others (Schwägerl and Bojanowski, cited in Schneiderman, *Spiegel* online). Schneiderman writes,

> Much is at stake in this controversy, for unlike other geological units of time, the name and definition of this one will have consequences outside the geological sciences. If the epoch were to be viewed as starting with the use of fire, culpability for global climate change would rest with all of humanity. In contrast, if the epoch were to be seen as beginning with industrialization, then responsibility for the global environmental crisis would reside historically with Europeans and North Americans. (189)

Her framing of the stakes as a matter of culpability certainly makes sense considering the ways in which some populations have had little or nothing to do with the so-called great acceleration of the twentieth century, an acceleration and exhaustion of fossil fuels that have been largely responsible for the warming of the planet, rising ocean levels, and acidification of the oceans. For Schneiderman and others, language is therefore crucial to the descriptive unfolding of the Anthropocene; it names who and what are responsible for its arrival.

Postcolonial thinkers have been vital to feminist theory of environment, engaging the question of responsibility through interconnected systems of exploitation and oppression. Dipesh Chakrabarty's foundational interventions on the Anthropocene, especially the momentous essay "The Climate of History: Four Theses," have considered simultaneous historical lines that arrive at the current ecological moment, including the history of "man" as a species, but also "humanity's" current imbrications in systems of global capital: "Whether we blame climate change on those who are retrospectively guilty—that is, blame the West for their past performance—or those who are prospectively guilty (China has just surpassed the United States as the largest emitter of carbon dioxide, though not on a per capita basis) is a question that is tied no doubt to the histories of capitalism and modernization" (218). Chakrabarty's complex framing of guilt for bringing about the Anthropocene suggests that regardless of whom and when we blame climate change, the rise of capitalism and industry are inextricable from its history. After a career of postcolonial critique spent rejecting universal histories of "man," Chakrabarty asks: "How do we relate to a universal history of life—to universal thought, that is—while retaining what is of obvious value in our postcolonial suspicion of the universal?" (219). Though insisting on the history of capital as central to the Anthropocene, his ultimate refusal to reduce our current crisis to a story of capitalism (221) leaves him ruminating on the possibilities of thinking the universal on the scale of the human species, suggesting perhaps that climate change calls for a "global approach to politics without the myth of a global identity" (222). Feminist thinkers have much to offer in response to Chakrabarty's often-cited universalizing gesture here, as the project of disentangling man from the human has been a central one to feminist theory in the Anthropocene. Stacy Alaimo has recently briefly charted some of these responses, including the work of Sylvia Wynter, Alexander G. Weheliye, Claire Colebrook, herself, and others, who have in one way or another disputed the fact that the term "Anthropocene" requires a new sort of univocal "man," especially at the level of environmental activism and social justice movements which emerge from "particular, local formulations of the human" (Alaimo, "Shell" 100).

Non-Western and indigenous formulations of and responses to climate change, for example, are particular examples that demand attention to the local rather than the universalized "man." Environmental change driven by centuries of colonial projects has driven indigenous peoples from lands across the planet, which has led indigenous scholar Kyle Whyte to call climate change a form of "intensified colonialism" (2). As Whyte points out, indigenous peoples and, especially, indigenous women are the groups most severely affected by climate change,[3] already constituting the first global "climate refuges" in areas like the Arctic that is warming at twice the global rate, causing sea level to rise and warm rapidly.[4] These projects of intensified colonialism are also highly gendered, as Whyte and others have argued. Mary Thomas and Kathryn Yusoff, drawing from a report by Kandi Mossett, a member of the Indigenous Environmental Network, has shown, for example, that "violence against women has increased by 168 percent since fracking technologies opened up vast oil reserves in the Bakken Formation [or North Dakota] in the 2000s" (Mossett and Goodman, quoted in Thomas and Yusoff 131). As they explain, this increased violence against women in the area is due largely to the increased number of men working there, as well as the "violent social-sexualized relations that characterize the social reproduction of labor" (131). It is difficult to think of a feminist, universal "Anthropos" when indigenous and other non-industrial, non-Western cultures, while not contributing to climate change, are at the highest risk of violence from the effects of projects (such as fracking) that continue to exacerbate environmental degradation as well as of the increasingly violent social relations that accompany these projects. Feminist environmental justice work and activism therefore cannot only focus on the universal level of the "Anthropos" but must also, as Alaimo suggests, be attuned to local and particular groups that feel unjustly oppressed and exploited under the stresses of climate change and its many diverse causes.

"Placing the Golden Spike" recalls an art exhibition of the same name, cocurated by Sara Krajewski and Dehlia Hannah at the INOVA gallery in Milwaukee, Wisconsin, in 2015.[5] The golden spike is the name of the symbolic marker of geological epochs, driven into the rock layers at an exemplary site designated by the International Union of Geological Sciences. This particular art exhibition and its installations challenged visitors to cast a critical eye toward where (and when) we might drive this spike, where and when we situate the Anthropocene. Eve Andreé Larameé's video, *The Uranium Daughters*, overlaid thermographs and spectrographic maps of the Fukushima Daiichi nuclear reactor meltdown on top of landscapes of the Mojave Desert and the Nevada nuclear test site N2S2. Yevgeniya Kaganovich's series of durational installations *grow* places small plant-like formations made of plastic in "unused and overlooked places" (Hannah 38), which are taken from discarded plastic to accumulate and "grow" into unwieldy plastic bodies. And Natalie Jeremijenko's *Signs of (Intelligent) Life* and *Phenological Clock* adapted outdoor commercial signs into planters for native species meant to improve and diversify local ecosystems. Different propositions and proliferations of the placement of the golden spike tell different stories. Does the dawn of the atomic age mark the Anthropocene, as Laraméé's work suggests? The invention of commercial plastics in 1907? The advent of agriculture in the early phases of the Holocene, to which Jeremijenko's installation may allude? Or perhaps it is some other moment, like the beginning of the slave trade in the sixteenth century, or much earlier, at the moment of the first human life?

Feminism's plurality of epistemic possibilities of the Anthropocene are crucial to its intervention—"[i]t matters what thoughts think thoughts, it matter what stories tell stories" (Haraway, *Staying* 39). Feminist engagements with the Anthropocene—its manifestations, origins, science, populations, data, methods, histories—are as imaginative as they are varied. It is this openness to epistemological and ontological questions that the Anthropocene insists on, that feminist histories of accounting for and naming the Anthropocene are marked by. As Schneiderman asks, "[w]hat do we obscure and what do we privilege with such a choice [of 'Anthropocene']"? (176) Recently, an array of plausible alternatives to the term Anthropocene have been proposed across disciplines in the humanities from the Chthulucene to Capitalocene and the "racial Capitolocene," the Plasticene, the Misanthropocene, and the Petrolcene. Feminisms such as those charted in the next section have served (and continue to serve) as a challenge to the earth sciences that we must "acknowledge that the concept of the Anthropocene requires cultural as well as geological involvement" (Schneiderman 187).

FEMINISM GOES PLANETARY

In the introduction to the edited collection *Anthropocene Feminism*,[6] Richard Grusin poses the book's central set of questions that serve to frame this section as well: "What does feminism have to say to the Anthropocene? How does the concept of the Anthropocene impact feminism," and "[h]ow can feminism help to historicize, challenge, or refine the current understanding of the Anthropocene?" If "thinking the Anthropocene must come from feminism" (Grusin x), how does feminist theory face the seemingly impossible task of thinking deep time, subjectivity, or the future of the planet, *after* the human? How can feminism "develop planetary and very long term perspectives in a geocentered and not anthropocentric frame?" (Braidotti 27), and how has feminism already been doing this work? When did feminism "go planetary?" (Braidotti 29). This set of questions about feminism's role in the Anthropocene suggests a spatial and temporal dimension to feminist thought as well as an inherent impossibility: how to think about a your world after you are gone, after all of humans are gone. Feminism's contribution to thinking about the Anthropocene in the twenty-first century has been the way in which feminism has theorized our responsibilities not only toward other humans but also to nonhumans as well. Feminism has long refused the centrality of humans in the cosmos and demands political and ethical orientations to the environment not merely for the sake of humans or their brief time on earth, but for the preservation of an earth long after humans are gone. Feminism has both long anticipated and overwhelmingly responded to an urgency of the Anthropocene that has arguably been urgent for quite some time.

Though there are undoubtedly multiple (longer) genealogies of feminist thought that arrive at the theorizing of the current ecological moment,[7] three particular though loosely defined strands emerging in the latter half of the twentieth century might be woven together to account for the development of a distinctly feminist studies of the Anthropocene: ecofeminism (and much ecocriticism that followed) and feminist studies of science and technology (FSTS) and feminist posthumanism(s), within which one might place new materialisms. I will discuss the overlappings between ecofeminism and feminist science studies in this section and, in the next section, I'll briefly discuss feminist posthumanism. While feminist environmental thought of the 1970s begins with diversely interrogating, celebrating, and/or challenging the complexities of women's long history of being equated with "Nature," ecofeminism, as an extremely varied field, also importantly has argued for linked histories of capitalism, colonialism, and the joint, global subjugation of women and nature. The 1980s, in presenting present feminist studies of science, not only cover a lot of ground, including the study of women scientists and their work, but also explore the presumed objectivity of scientific study, thereby posing key challenges to scientific methods themselves. Feminism in and of the Anthropocene draws from these collective theoretical histories of feminism to continue to forge new forms of affective, aesthetic, political and ethical relations with the nonhuman world.

Though often omitted in histories of ecocriticism (DeLoughrey and Handley 14), ecofeminism emerged primarily in US contexts in the 1970s[8] and 1980s from "the intersections of feminist research and the various movements for social justice and environmental health," with critiques of racism, speciesism, and colonialism at its core (Gaard, "Ecofeminism Revisited" 28). Ecofeminists like Val Plumwood and others also questioned environmental philosophy's engagement with the rationalist tradition, one in which Plumwood argued was inherently masculine and inimical to both women and nature. Some earlier ecofeminists suggested that women were in fact biologically attuned to nature in a way that further connected women and the environment. This particular mode of ecofeminist thought therefore garnered sustained criticism for proposing an essentialist vision of women as intrinsically tied to nature, often presented in early accounts as a kind of mysticism,[9] and many environmental feminists moved away from their identification with the field.

Although Maria Mies and Vandana Shiva's foundational intervention *Ecofeminism* of 1993 did not entirely escape this critique, their work was a significant departure from some ecofeminism in that their foundational claim was that it was global capitalism that destroys women and the environment alike, and that this shared experience under capitalist structures of domination must be rejected in favor of local, diverse, self-sustaining communities of production (Sandilands 97). Despite the many critiques of ecofeminism, some feminist philosophers have revisited ecofeminism for Anthropocene studies, especially for its important contributions to contemporary feminist theory about environmental crises.[10] Claire Colebrook, for example, has recently written that ecofeminism is "no minor off-shoot of feminist thought but structures its genealogy" (Colebrook, *Sex after Life* 8, quoted in Williams). Key works of ecofeminism by Plumwood and Carolyn Merchant, for example, have been revived in contemporary feminist thought as having been unfairly judged as essentialist. A. E. King's work, for example, theorizes an intersectional ecofeminism for young women in rural India, and Greta Gaard's proposed queer ecofeminism in "Ecofeminism and Climate Change" relies on what Gaard identifies as "[t]he shift [in ecofeminism] from *women as individuals* to *gender as a system* structuring power relations" as "an important development in feminist responses to climate change" (22). Her important inclusion of LGBTQ populations in ecofeminism and climate justice, and her vegan-ecofeminist challenges to posthumanism (Gaard, "Posthumanism") distinguishes her work as a valuable addition (and corrective) to the historically contested field.

Donna Haraway, whose 1984 "A Cyborg Manifsto" was published more contemporaneous with canonical ecofeminist ideas, developed quite a different figure as a way to refute the problem of essentialism that has long haunted feminist environmental thought. Haraway develops the notion that we are all cyborgs, hybrids of machine and organism, which "skips the steps of original unity, of identification of nature in the Western sense" (292). In speculating toward a world without gender and drawing primarily from women of color feminisms, Haraway advocates for the dissolving of boundaries between dualisms, between the technical and the organic. But instead of linking women to some natural organic past, Haraway refuses essentialism in favor of technological hybrids, no longer able to separate oneself from the nonhumans and technologies that are both unavoidable and necessary for survival. As I will briefly chart in the next section, feminist thinkers of the Anthropocene are much indebted to Haraway's cyborg figure, and have done much to reformulate the terms of embodiment that is required of the Anthropocene subject.

In "Science Fiction Feminisms, Feminist Science Fictions, & Feminist Sustainability," authors Joan Haran and Katie King remark that there is ample evidence of "the proximity, if not always coincidence, of ecofeminism and feminist science studies." Indeed, they seem to have developed alongside one another, with not much evidence of cross-pollination. Yet, although not explicitly or solely tied to nature, the field of feminist science studies shares many concerns and tenets central to the long arc of ecofeminism. Gaard has claimed that just as Val Plumwood argues that rationalist traditions and dualism are masculinist methods, scholars of feminist science studies begin with a foundational interrogation of masculinist modes that have dominated scientific knowledge.

Feminist science studies have worked to challenge the concept of scientific objectivity and the notion of value-neutral science and hold instead that science is a discourse and activity that is informed by cultural factors, biases, and norms. Donna Haraway, for example, argues for knowledges of "location, positioning, and situating, where partiality and not universality is the condition of being heard to make rational knowledge claims," and argues for situated-ness "from a body, always a complex, contradictory, structuring, and structured body, versus the view from above, from nowhere, from simplicity" ("Situated" 589). Knowledge for Haraway must be embodied, though for Haraway, the terms of the body are radically redefined, in part by the body's inseparability from technological systems that are integral to its operation. Haraway would come to reject the dualism of the nature/culture divide often perpetuated in the science by developing "naturecultures" (Haraway, *Companion* 33), and Karen Barad, physicist and feminist theorist of science and technology, would continue to develop an agential notion of matter itself as "produced and productive, generated and generative" (Barad 137). Feminist theory of the environment is largely indebted to the rethinking of the relationship between humans and nonhumans, and the radical redefinition of nonhuman matter as having its own agential force, effectively challenging both Nature and Women's supposed linked histories as passive bodies.

Feminist studies of science and technology (FSTS), and their intertwined history with ecofeminism, are therefore integral to the study of the Anthropocene, within which predominantly men have come to define its terms as well as develop the kinds of technologies intended to "fix" it. As Greta Gaard has noted, these techno-scientific solutions of the problems of climate change, like geoengineering, effect half of the world's population (women), and yet women represent only a minute fraction of those actually working on these developments. Though not always rejecting geoengineering possibilities entirely, FSTS warns of the dangers inherent in technological utopian impulses in response to the Anthropocene, as well as reminds us of the decades of its attachments to the military-industrial complex that is largely responsible for many of the actual causes of the planetary crisis we currently find ourselves in (the history of military biochemical spraying, for example, which pollutes the lower atmosphere [and its inhabitants, of course] at multiple levels with the goal of managing solar radiation) (Von Werlhof 118). Often relayed by feminism as a domineering and masculine approach to the problems of climate change, geoengineering is a highly gendered and racialized mode that FSTS scholars attempt to engage and temper. In the face of such drastic measures already in effect across male-dominated scientific fields, feminist critique that is critical of technology but does not universally demonize it (Haraway, "A Cyborg Manifesto" 316) is of crucial importance.

FEMINIST POSTHUMANISM AND THE ANTHROPOCENE SUBJECT

As one reviewer of Rosi Braidotti's seminal 2013 book *The Posthuman* breathlessly remarks, "It will be impossible to do justice to the posthuman, literally. It is impossible to review the possibilities that the ever more haunting 'figure' of the posthuman contains" (Herbrechter 1). In her contribution to *Anthropocene Feminism*, Braidotti persuasively argues that the last thirty years of feminist thought demonstrate a shift in feminism itself, claiming that "feminism is *not* a humanism" (21). In part, her claim is grounded in the fact that the human has historically been equated with a *he*: white, Western European, heterosexual, and able-bodied (Braidotti 23). The epistemic violence that inheres in this normative model has historically cast anything other than this white, masculine figure as inferior, as less-than-human. Feminist, anti-racist, and postcolonial theory, an "antihumanist feminist generation" beginning in the 1970s, "embraced the concept of difference with the explicit aim of making it function differently" (Braidotti 24). Posthuman feminism rejects Eurocentric humanism toward a "shift in our collective sense of identity ... not only the critique of species supremacy—the rule of the Anthropos—but also the parameters used to define it" (Braidotti 25–6). Revisions to humanism that are offered by feminist critiques have worked for decades to decenter "Man," the Anthropos, by challenging the very nature of human subjectivity and bounded individualism. The result in feminist theory in and of the Anthropocene has been a posthumanism that considers nonhumans, life and nonlife, as central to its thought and politics.

In her essay "Four Theses on Posthuman Feminism," Braidotti lists a long genealogy of posthuman feminism, including Franz Fanon, Edward Said, Michel Foucault, Patricia Hill Collins, Etienne Balibar, Vandana Shiva, and others. Beginning in the 1990s, feminist texts mention the "posthuman," converging, according to Braidotti, on the issues of climate change and information technologies (28). What Braidotti calls "matter-realist" feminists like Jane Bennett and Stacy Alaimo make up a lively node of contemporary posthuman feminism for the Anthropocene. Keeping with posthumanism's project of denaturalizing "man" through a critique of human species supremacy is at the core of feminist materialisms (Alaimo and Hekman) and new materialisms (Coole and Frost). With a more level ontological field of "mattering," objects, systems, nonhuman animals, bacteria, and affects are imbued with vibrancy and agency that serve to challenge the boundedness of the human subject. Stacy Alaimo's concept of "transcorporeality," Nancy Tuana's "vicous porosity," and the many toxic embodiments theorized in the Anthropocene due to environmental degradation all call attention to the porous vulnerability and nonhuman makeup of the so-called human subject.

While interspecies intimacies are brought to the fore in Haraway's *Companion Species Manifesto* and in Eva Hayward's recent concept of "tranimalities" to name just two of these innovations, Heather Davis demonstrates that all bodies are composed of some fraction of plastic in what she calls "the Plastisphere," and Myra Hird's study of teeming bacterial worlds continue to push us to think beyond human exceptionalism. This theoretical line through posthuman toxicity in the Anthropocene can be traced alongside queer posthumanisms,[11] as well as disability studies,[12] which have worked to chart flows of Anthropogenic material across bodily and disciplinary boundaries, disrupting any previously held distinction between human and nonhuman bodies.

SPECULATIVE FEMINISM, IMAGINATIVE FUTURES

In their introduction to the concept of "Anthropocene Feminism" in a special issue of *PhiloSOPHIA* in 2016, Claire Colebrook and Jami Weinstein write that "feminism is not simply another issue that ... supplements the Anthropocene ... feminism is at once a critique of the force of 'man,' contesting everything that seems self-evident, unified, present, and inescapable in what counts as human, *while also being the imagination of something that would no longer be man as such*" (175, emphasis mine). That feminism is not just an addendum but a vital theoretical and methodological mode of the Anthropocene unites the feminist theory presented in this chapter. Further, their definition of Anthropocene feminism as an "imagination" emphasizes the centrality of speculative futures that feminist thought attempts to make possible in seemingly impossible times.

As this chapter has demonstrated by means of entangled feminist genealogies leading us into the Anthropocene, collective imaginings of futurity in the midst of crisis necessitate a look back. What can feminism do to retrieve and recover amidst the march of masculinist scientific drives toward the myth of pure rationality and objectivity in the production of knowledge?

In a special issue of *Extrapolation* on Indigenous Futurisms, Anishinaabe scholar Grace Dillon identifies in the movement the "sense that Western science has lost something vital by isolating itself from spiritual origins in a quest to achieve objectivity" (6). She writes of the mode of Indigenous speculation: "Futurisms offer new ways of reading our own ancient natures" (6). Indigenous futurisms have much to offer the study of the Anthropocene, its complex temporalities, its violent histories of colonialism and empire, and its deep attunement to the nonhuman world. Indeed, as scholars already mentioned have pointed out, the project of decolonializing the production of knowledge has long been central to indigenous scholarship. Paired with new scholarship on indigenous temporalities,[13] indigenous studies and indigenous futurisms offer fruitful possibilities for collaboration with feminist theory in the Anthropocene.

Intersectional "Futurisms" attentive to race, ethnicity, sexuality, gender, disability, and class prove especially welcome to a feminist study of the Anthropocene: Indigenous Futurism, Afrofuturism, ChicanX Futurism to name only a few cross-sections. Circulating recently, for example, have been articles with titles like "To Get Ready for Climate Change, Read Octavia Butler" (LeMenager). A key figure for Afrofuturism, Butler's fiction draws from Sixties Black Power and Black Feminism and "forecasts a multi-racial social movement" which emerges from widespread economic and climate collapse" (LeMenager). The resurgence of afrofuturism and other speculative world-building in the twenty-first century is one of the most lively sites for feminist climate critique and tools for collective survival, even flourishing. It imagines futurity (ecological and otherwise) not as a rehearsing of white European male domination but as futures wherein blackness is ever present and celebrated while retaining elements, aesthetics, and values of a shared African past.[14] These distinct forms of speculation are, as Colebrook and Weinstein suggested of feminism, "*the imagination of something that would no longer be man as such.*"

These forms of imaginative political engagement may assist in beginning to respond to Françoise Vergès's recent question: "Is the Anthropocene racial?" Responding to what she feels is a lack of scholarly engagement with race in the Anthropocene, she asks,

> What methodology is needed to write a history of the environment that includes slavery, colonialism, imperialism and racial capitalism, from the standpoint of those … whose … bodies [were treated] as objects renewable through wars, capture, and enslavement, fabricated as disposable people, whose lives do not matter? (online)

Feminist scholarship, especially cross-disciplinary work toward social and environmental justice, has begun to address this set of questions, with perhaps much work to be done.[15] Feminism of the Anthropocene must reconstruct pasts and imagine futures that do not isolate a single thread but that expose their intertwined histories (and presents) with violently oppressed peoples and nonhumans. These respective histories are crucial to coming to understand and represent the Anthropocene, as they continue to constitute the exacerbation of its effects on these populations.

Rosi Braidotti writes of the "posthuman feminist … a complex assemblage of human and nonhuman … remains committed to social justice" (Braidotti 29). Situated in this way, feminism in the Anthropocene might heed Colebrook's call that feminism retains its singularity in a way that generates an "impossible multiple" ("We Have Always" 9). Uniting feminism in the Anthropocene is the overwhelming singular question that feminism cannot stop asking: "*whose* Anthropocene?" (10), a question to which there is a multiplicity of responses. The question not only forces us to reexamine what constitutes the very boundaries of the human in the Anthropocene; it also continues to structure feminism in the Anthropocene as committed to an orientation toward projects that further social justice. These projects increasingly require our urgent attentiveness to the changing climate. Feminism's vital contributions to the study of the Anthropocene attest to the fact that what is needed are not only historical, social, and scientific accounts but, just as importantly, and not in isolation from the others, imaginative speculation.

NOTES

1 The International Commission on Stratigraphy (ICS) has yet to officially designate the epoch of the Anthropocene with the placement of a golden spike, a geologic signifier of historical epochs in accordance with particular stratal sections and their material components. The ICS stratigraphy chart is updated here: http://www.stratigraphy.org/ICSchart/ ChronostratChart2017-02.pdf.

2 "Anthropos" is Greek for "human." I use it throughout this chapter encompassing both humans as a universal species and as a species that now operates as a dominant geologic force, hence its role in the popularized term of our new geologic epoch, the "Anthropocene." I occasionally use quotes around "Anthropos" because it is precisely its universalizing function that is central to feminist critiques of the Anthropocene and the very possibility of the "Anthropos."

3 Here, Whyte sites the US National Climate Assessment and Intergovernmental Panel on Climate Change Fifth Assessment.

4 Julie Koppel Maldonado et al., "The Impact of Climate Change on Tribal Communities in the Us: Displacement, Relocation, and Human Rights," *Climatic Change* 120, no. 3 (2013).

5 The exhibition, Placing the Golden Spike: Landscapes of the Anthropocene, was held at INOVA: Institute of Visual Arts at the University of Wisconsin-Milwaukee, from March 26 to June 13, 2015.

6 *Anthropocene Feminism* is an edited collection of essays many of which were presented at the conference of the same name, held by the Center for 21st Century Studies at the University of Wisconsin-Milwaukee in May, 2014.

7 For instance, DeLoughrey and Handley's *Postcolonial Ecologies* traces ecological thought and ecocriticism through postcolonial theory, which they demonstrate has been long concerned with ecologies that "place the human in nature" (26) through a critique of empire. Such perspectives are inflected with different concerns than American environmentalism. Though postcolonial thought has contributed enormously to ecological thought, broadly speaking, I have chosen to focus on specifically feminist threads here, which as will be clear, are often indebted to and engaged with postcolonial critique.

8 Ecofeminism was first introduced in Francoise D'Eaubonne's *La Feminisme ou la Mort* (1974), but appeared in the United States for the first time in Rosemary Radford Ruether's *New Woman, New Earth: Sexist Ideologies and Human Liberation* (1975).

9 See, for examples of these critiques, Bina Agarwal's "The Gender and Environment Debate: Lessons from India," *Feminist Studies* 18(1): 119–158 (1992), Christine J. Cuomo's "Unraveling the Problems in Ecofeminism," *Environmental Ethics* 14(4): 351–363 (1992), or Victoria Davion's "Is Ecofeminism Feminist?" in Warren K.J. (ed) *Ecological Feminism*. New York, Routledge, 8–28 (1994).

10 I am indebted here to Susanna Williams's willingness to share with me a section of her unpublished work in progress, which charts the legacy of ecofeminism in the development of ecocriticism and in ecological postcolonial theory.

11 See, for example, Heather Davis's work on plastics, Kathryn Yusoff's queer genealogy of coal, and Mel Y. Chen's queer and racialized transnational mobility of lead. Though not explicitly queer, Stacy Alaimo's chapter on silica in *Bodily Natures* as well as Stephanie LeMenager's book *Living Oil* contribute to this feminist and queer attention to the *stuff* of the Anthropocene.

12 It is impossible to think of a feminist posthuman subject of the Anthropocene without looking to the field of disability studies, especially those theorizing specifically environmental disabilities and their intersection with race, gender, and sexuality. I'm thinking of the work of Nancy Tuana, Michelle Murphy, and Mel Y. Chen. I also think that animal crip studies like Sunara Taylor's book *Beasts of Burden* importantly captures the ways in which factory farming practices (a huge contributor to Anthropogenic climate change) serve to disable nonhumans as well.

13 See, for example, Mark Rifkin's *Beyond Settler Time: Temporal Sovereignty and Indigenous Self-Determination*, Duke University Press, 2017.

14 Scholars and artists of Afrofuturism typically mark its formation in the 1970s, though the term was first coined in Mark Dery's essay "Black to the Future" in 1994.

15 See, as some specific examples of intersectional work on race and climate change, essays on the aftermath of Hurricane Katrina, for example, Nancy Tuana's "Viscous Porosity: Witnessing Katrina," or Rebecca Solnit's "Reconstructing the Story of the Storm: Hurricane Katrina at Five."

WORKS CITED

Alaimo, Stacy. *Bodily Natures:Science, Environment, and the Material Self*. Indiana UP, 2001.

Alaimo, Stacy. "This is Your Shell on Acid: Material Immersion, Anthropocene Dissolves." *Anthropocene Feminism*. Ed. Richard Grusin. Minneapolis: Minnesota UP, 2017, pp. 21–48.

Alaimo, Stacy, and Susan Hekman, eds. *Material Feminisms*. Bloomington: Indiana UP, 2008.

Barad, Karen. "Posthumanist Performativity: Toward an Understanding of How Matter Comes to Matter," *Signs: Journal of Women in Culture and Society* 28.3 (Spring 2003): 801–31.

Braidotti, Rosi. "Four Theses on Posthuman Feminism." *Anthropocene Feminism*. Ed. Richard Grusin. Minneapolis: Minnesota UP, 2017, pp. 21–48.

Chen, Mel Y. *Animacies: Biopolitics, Racial Mattering, and Queer Affect*. Durham, NC: Duke UP, 2012.

Coole, Diana, and Samantha Frost, eds. *New Materialisms: Ontology, Agency, and Politics*. Durham, NC: Duke UP, 2010.

Colebrook, Clair. *Sex After Life: Essays on Extinction, Vol. 2*. London: Open Humanities P, 2014.

Colebrook, Clair. "We Have Always Been Post-Anthropocene." *Anthropocene Feminism*. Ed. Richard Grusin. Minneapolis: U of Minnesota P, 2016, pp. 1–20.

Colebrook, Claire, and Jami Weinstein. "Introduction: Anthropocene Feminisms: Rethinking the Unthinkable." *philoSOPHIA* 5.2 (Summer 2015): 67–78.

Crutzen, P. J. "Geology of Mankind." *Paul J. Crutzen: A Pioneer on Atmospheric Chemistry and Climate Change in the Anthropocene*. 2016, pp. 211–15.

Crutzen, P. J., and E. F. Stoermer. "The 'Anthropocene'." *IGBP Newsletter*, 41, pp. 17–18, 2000.

Davis, Heather. "Toxic Progeny: The Plastisphere and Other Queer Futures." *PhiloSOPHIA* 5.2 (Summer 2015).

Dillon, Grace. "Introduction: Indigenous Futurisms, Bimaashi Biidaas Mose, Flying and Walking Towards You." *Extrapolation* 57 1.2 (Spring-Summer 2016): 1–6.

ElizabethDeLoughrey, and George B. Handley, eds. *Postcolonial Ecologies: Literature of the Environment*. Oxford: Oxford UP, 2011.

Gaard, Greta. "Ecofeminism and Climate Change." *Women's Studies International Forum* 49 (March–April 2015): 20–33.

Gaard, Greta. "Ecofeminism Revisited: Rejecting Essentialism and Re-Placing Species in a Material Feminist Environmentalism." *Feminist Formations* 23.2 (Summer 2011): 26–53.

Gaard, Greta. "Posthumanism, Ecofeminism, and Inter-Species Relations." *Routledge Handbook of Gender and Environment*. Ed. Sherilyn MacGregor. New York: Routledge, 2017, pp. 115–30.

Grusin, Richard ed. *Anthropocene Feminism*. Minneapolis: Minnesota UP, 2017.

Hannah, Dehlia, and Sara Krajewski, ed. "Placing the Golden Spike: Landscapes of the Anthropocene." Published on the occasion of the exhibition at INOVA (Institute of Visual Arts) U of Wisconsin-Milwaukee (March 26–June 13, 2015). Curated by Sara Krajewski and Dehlia Hannah. https://www.academia.edu/12438747/Placing_the_Golden_Spike_Lanscapes_of_the_Anthropocene_Exhibition_Catalogue_.

Haraway, Donna. *The Companion Species Manifesto: Dogs, People, and Significant Otherness*. Chicago, IL: Prickly Paradigm P, 2003.

Haraway, Donna. "A Cyborg Manifesto: Science, Technology, and Socialist-Feminism in the Late Twentieth Century." *Simians, Cyborgs, and Women: The Reinvention of Nature*. New York: Routledge, 1991, pp. 292–324.

Haraway, Donna. "Situated Knowledges: The Science Question in Feminism and the Privilege of Partial Perspective." *Feminist Studies* 14.3 (Fall 1988).

Haraway, Donna. *Staying with the Trouble: Making Kin in the Chthulucene*. Durham, NC: Duke UP, 2016.

Haran, Joan, and Katie King. "Science Fiction Feminisms, Feminist Science Fictions & Feminist Sustainability." *Ada: A Journal of Gender New Media and Technology* 3 (November 2013). Online.

Hayward, Eva, ed. "Tranimalities," a special issue of *TSQ: Trans Studies Quarterly*, vol. 2, issue 2. Durham, NC: Duke UP, May 2015.

Herbrechter, Stefan. Rosi Braidotti. *The Posthuman*. *Culture Machine*. Reviews, April 2013, pp. 1–13. www.culturemachine.net.

Hird, Myra. "The Phenomenon of Waste-World-Making." *Rhizomes: Cultural Studies in Emerging Knowledge*, issue 30, 2016.

LeMenager, Stephanie. "To Get Ready for Climate Change, Read Octavia Butler." *ElectraStreet*, November 2017. http://electrastreet.net/2017/11/to-get-ready-for-climate-change-read-octavia-butler/.

Kings, A. E. "Intersectionality and the Changing Face of Ecofeminism." *Ethics and the Environment* 22.1 (2017): 63–87.

Plumwood, Val. *Feminism and the Mastery of Nature*. New York: Routledge, 1993.

Sandilands, Catriona. Ecofeminism by Maria Mies and Vandana Shiva. *Economic Geography* 72.1 (January 1996): 96–9.

Schneiderman, Jill S. "The Anthropocene Controversy." *Anthropocene Feminism*. Ed. Richard Grusin. Minneapolis: U of Minnesota P, 2016, pp. 169–95.

Schwägerl, and Axel Bojanowski. "Do Humans Deserve Their Own Geological Era?" *Spiegel Online*, July 8, 2011. www.speigel.de. Accessed November 2017.

Solnit, Rebcca. "Reconstructing the Story of the Storm: Hurricane Katrina at Five." *The Nation*, 2010. http://www.thenation.com/ article/154168/reconstructing-story-storm-hurricane-katrina-five.

Steffen, Will, Paul J. Crutzen, and John R. McNeill. "The Anthropocene: Are Humans Now Overwhelming the Great Forces of Nature?" Royal Swedish Academy of Sciences, *Ambio* 36.8 (December 2007).

Taylor, Sunara. *Beasts of Burden: Animal and Disability Liberation*. New York: New P, 2017.

Thomas, Mary, and Kathryn Yusoff. "Geology." *Gender: Matter*. Macmillian Interdisciplinary Handbooks, Ed. Stacy Alaimo. Farmington Hills, MI: Macmillan Reference USA, 2017.

Tuana, Nancy. "Climate Change through the Lens of Feminist Philosophy." *Meta-Philosophical Reflection on Feminist Philosophies of Science*. Ed. M.C. Amoretti and N. Vassallo. Switzerland: Springer, 2016, pp. 35–53.

Tuana, Nancy. "Viscous Porosity: Witnessing Katrina." *Material Feminisms*. Ed. Stacy Alaimo and Susan Hekman. Bloomington: Indiana UP, 2008, pp. 188–213.

Vergès, Françoise. "Racial Capitolocene." *Futures of Black Radicalism*. Ed. Gaye Theresa Johnson and Alex Lubin. New York: Verso Books, 2017. https://www.versobooks.com/blogs/3376-racial-capitalocene.

Weheliye, Alexander G. *Habeas Viscus: Racializing Assemblages, Biopolitics, and Black Feminist Theories of the Human*. Durham, NC: Duke UP, 2014.

Whyte, Kyle. "Indigenous Climate Change Studies: Indigenizing Futures, Decolonizing the Anthropocene." Forthcoming 2017 in *English Language Notes*. https://static1.squarespace.com/static/55c251dfe4b0ad74ccf25537/t/5893be5246c3c41105f6dc8c/1486077523702/Indigenous_Climate_Change_Studies_Indige.pdf.

CHAPTER TWENTY-THREE

The Political

MARIOS CONSTANTINOU

ANTIGONISMS

In attempting to think through the feminist quest for the political, I recall Hannah Arendt's discussion of metaphors in the *Life of the Mind*. Arendt suggests that metaphors enable analogical thinking, like threads by which the mind holds on to the world, giving us bearings lest we stagger blindly when our senses and the relative certainty of knowledge cannot guide us through (109). I therefore want to preface this essay by considering four proper names as instructive metaphors of the political. Together they epitomize abiding divisions and suspensions of the political that will be unpacked in the rest of the essay. They are not cultic personas of an archaic age but perennial signifiers of the *ungovernable*, dramatizing the foundational role of gender metaphors in the enactment of the political.

First, Antigone, the *femina sacra* of civil disobedience is not only an evocative source of insights into the political but also an original metaphor of its contentious promise. Doing justice to the political is doing justice to this living metaphor. Attending the political becoming of Antigone, her *antigonism* as an embodiment of justice, we gain a perspective on woman as a figure of the universal, of a mode of life that is also a mode of struggle. In Sophocles' *Antigone*, what at first sight appears as a private funeral duty, the last rite owed to a blood relative, escalates into political antagonism in the Schmittian sense (detailed below). In a momentous reversal of functions, the state's ruling which proscribes the fulfilment of burial duties, although seemingly defending public legality, opposes the underlying natural law of the city and is thus reduced to private vice. In effect, Creon, "the ruling one," is rendered *apolis* (cityless), bereft of political bearings, whereas Antigone's disobedience to the ruling obtains the public dignity of the political. "While I live, a woman shall not rule," says Creon (525). No woman will be allowed to become a "ruling woman," or to initiate in the Arendtian sense a new political beginning by rewriting State law: "Is not the city thought to belong to the ruler?" Creon asks. Haemon, a political midway point between his father Creon and his fiancée Antigone, responds thus: "you will be a fine ruler over a deserted city" (739). I single out three peak moments that immortalize Antigone as a universal metaphor of revolt against patriarchy, exposed as anti-political tyranny: (a) when Haemon warns Creon about the "silent advancing" of the city which stands by Antigone's side, claiming respect and honor for her daring act (690–5); (b) when Creon accuses Haemon of "fighting on the woman's side," charging him as "contemptible and inferior to woman" (746); (c) when, finally, Antigone turns indignantly against "the rich men of the city": "I am being mocked! Why do you insult and abuse me while I am still visible?" (838–9). Antigone has been, still is, and shall be the potential answer to any sophistic appropriation of the political by the rule of state and capital. *Antigonism* transforms the political beyond them, keeping the promise of justice alive by living through it. The neology I suggest points to a body that is both traumatized and natural as well as a source of the political becoming of freedom.

Second, Euripidean Medea, heroine of incarnate disorder, defies both family and state loyalty, striking a dissonant chord at the heart of our contemporary sense of the social and the political. Woman as a stateless outsider, betrayed and exploited, allegedly barbarian, and demonized as infernal, manic, and insane. Medea, the "reproductive demon" of the folk archetype, haunts the feminist imagination with her anti-patriarchal revolt by taking the very lives she gives birth to. Medea's otherness interweaves all the contemporary strands of the biopolitical standing out as an exception to the reproductive and behavioral norms of the social, to the rules of the maternal and the unmaternal. She is a living metaphor of the enormous adversity under which a foreign woman labors, after having disowned country and kinsfolk and after renewed exile. What I sustain from Medea is her prayer on the occasion of Jason's violation of the oath and the intervention of the nurse invoking the justice of Zeus as the "guardian of men's oaths" (*Medea* 160–70).

Third, Aristophanes' *Lysistrata* shifts the terrain of the political from the tragic pursuit of immortal glory and imperial power to the comic performance of political blame: the gaiety of speaking and acting in truth. According to this plot, the first comic heroine of the political, whose very name in Greek literally means disbander (*lysi*) of armies (*strata*), leads a panhellenic women's movement to put an end to the civil war between Athens and Sparta which fight for hegemony over the Greek cities. The women's movement encroaches on the public space of the male polis, (a) politicizing the private sphere by means of a conjugal strike that unifies the domestic front across the warring states, and (b) mobilizing elder women to occupy the Acropolis, thus cutting off male access to the war funds stored at the shrine-treasury of Athena. In the manner of a comic fantasy of the political, the tables are turned in both spheres, ending temporarily brutal confrontations between sexes and citizens.

Finally, Praxagora in Aristophanes' *Assembly Women*, bears a name of Arendtian aura, which signifies simultaneously speech and deed and literally means *female action in public*. It is a metaphorical enactment of Arendt's worst nightmare. The terminal crisis and loss of their Empire in 404 bc forced the Athenians to rethink the design of their political institutions, including the participation of women. Against this background, Praxagora goes a step further than Lysistrata who achieved only a provisional conciliation between sexes and citizens. Heading a new women's movement to save Athens from abusive male rule, Praxagora and the Athenian women occupy the assembly, vote for a transfer of power and actually replace the polis with a kind of household communism writ large. "The rise of the social," Arendt's bête noire, is thus realized by economic and sexual ordinances that decree the abolition of private property and family, provide for common dining halls and sexual freedom on the condition that the young and beautiful copulate first with the old and ugly. Wealth, age, and beauty as sources of social inequality are wiped out, although slaves are excepted from this equalizing allowance and will still do farming and manual labor.

Arendt wouldn't disagree with Aristophanes' critical satire of Athens' theoretical fancy and taste for communist experiments that liquidate the political into the social. Yet the *Assembly Women's* household communism was incorporated with some modifications by Plato into his *Republic*. Although the latter is considered as a paradigmatic treatise of the political, its programmatic commitment to eugenic breeding points already in the direction of the biopolitics of "social race." Thus biological life itself becomes the site for the fashioning of "the political." Nonetheless, the conceptual core of this fourfold metaphorical operation, namely justice, mutual pledge, household economics, and social movements became a critical referent of Arendt's lifelong theorization of the political and feminism's political imagination.

BIOPOLITICS: A FAUSTIAN PACT

The feminist movement is inextricably entangled in the vortex of the biopolitical upheaval illustrated above, which also explains Arendt's forbidding aloofness to the challenge it represented in the twentieth century. Feminism's biopolitical predicament is marked by the following dilemma. It either respects the boundaries between the public, the private, and intimate spheres, amplifying women's autonomy in each of them sep-arately by institutional means, at the cost that is of its character as a movement with mobilizational force, or it merges and politicizes the three spheres whose boundaries are so porous that sustaining them is superfluous. The trouble is that both dimensions of the dilemma have been effectively subjected to inverse politicization. While late-twentieth-century feminism moved along the lines of the biopolitical Left, opposing established conservative power in the name of bodies and rights, it was eventually over-taken by the double surprise of institutional right-wing biopolitics and the emergence of grassroots, "right-to-life" movements with their own rival conceptions of the good and the right and in the name of which restricting rights is assumed to be a superior form of the good life. That the biopolitical enfolding of feminism was already under cross fire by opposed visions of the social was evident in the 1973 US Supreme Court ruling over abortion (*Roe v. Wade*). In her reading of the ruling, Mary Poovey highlights the implications of subsuming a woman's right to terminate her pregnancy under the "right to privacy" as defined by the first clause of the Fourteenth Amendment of the US Constitution. The ruling predicates this right upon "safeguarding the woman's health … and in protecting potential human life." Since no pregnant woman can remain isolated in her pregnancy as she carries an embryo and a fetus and by her biological con-dition she is never really alone, it follows that her right to privacy must be accordingly measured against other interests. Hence the state may regulate the abortion procedure by *deciding* what the other interests are and at what time they get involved (Poovey, "The Abortion Question" 244–5).

On Carl Schmitt's account, all the biological ambiguities of pregnancy, sociological and moral arguments concerning privacy, choice, and rights, have been decided and settled by a constitutional state's sovereign decision. In effect, woman's reproductivity becomes a site of exception which occasions the disclosure of sovereignty: "sovereign is he who decides on the exception" (*Political Theology* 5). Ironically too, "choice, privacy and rights invert effortlessly into their opposites … " (Poovey, "The Abortion Question" 249). They become a rallying point for the counterattack of the far right. Biopolitics is no more left than right and no more feminist than statist and patri-archal. In fact, Penelope Deutscher argues that the exceptions that defined the ruling of *Roe v. Wade* duplicate the state of emergency regarding civil liberties ("Inversion of Exceptionality" 61). They share the same structure of exceptionality. Although in *Roe v. Wade,* the state cannot override the pregnant woman's right, it does assert a legitimate interest in protecting both "woman's health and the potentiality of human life" she carries. She is considered a reproductive demon à la Medea and hence as "a potentially murderous competing sovereign whose self interest" intervenes with the interest of state sovereignty (66).

The malleable scope of biopolitics is further indicated by Aihwa Ong's examination of logics of exception as they are applied to migrant women who are unprotected by labor laws in Southeast Asia. Interestingly, Ong argues that migrant women outside the boundaries of citizenship are not necessarily reduced to bare life. NGOs, settled on grants, regulate their state of exception through constant negotiation and reevaluation of their morally deserving humanity (*Neoliberalism as Exception* 24). As "practitioners of humanity," NGO missions administer states of exception created by global neoliberalism "aligning the bodily integrity of migrant women with their availability as a cheap labor" (199). Although Ong's framework of conceptualizing exception operates explicitly in a post-Schmittian direction which is presumably post-sovereign too in order to accommodate NGO counterpolitics of survival at the intersections of labor markets and moral edification (5, 25), she does acknowledge that they are "not postnational enough" or nongovernmental as they claim since their leverage power derives from becoming "a subcontracting party or subject to national agendas and capitalist interests" (216). This nexus does not sound post-Schmittian at all. Even Church-controlled NGOs teach self-discipline to foreign domestic workers, adjusting their moral economies to the neoliberal agenda for cheap and mobile labor markets, not to political citizenship. By linking their health insurance to their flexibility as "free economic agents" NGOs ensure their availability for overseas contracts (210–17). So much for "biowelfare" humanism. In order to make full sense of the Faustian pact with counterpolitics and be able to think through alternatives, we need to revisit Hannah Arendt.

THE ACTUALITY OF THE POLITICAL, THE EXCESS OF THE SOCIAL, AND THE STAKES OF INTIMATE REVOLT

On Arendt's account what we currently call biopolitics is the social conditioning of the political. The social echoes the biological, hence the devious mode of biopolitics which is literally a *state of necessity,* a permanent state of emergency contingent upon Schmitt's concept of decision that encompasses women's precarity as outlined above. In order to make out how neoliberalism thrives on the state of exception and in effect on women's vulnerability we should read Schmitt and Arendt in tandem, something that, despite all its merits, Ong's analysis refrains from doing. Thus the scarcity of thinking the autonomy of the political.

Arendt states clearly that necessity is a *prepolitical phenomenon*, which, in order to be mastered, requires coercion and violence. She explains that ruling over slave labor and women's labor became a historical condition of male freedom from necessity (*Human Condition* 31, 72). Both, man's labor to provide nourishment and women's labor in giving birth, are "born of necessity and necessity rules over all activities performed in it" (30). Ong's analysis of neoliberal exception remains anchored in this interchangeable logic of performing safe-unsafe labor as necessity. There is nothing beyond that. The political, however, asserts its autonomy against the biopolitical necessity of vegetating on sheer survival. The political is Arendt's rallying cry against humanity's reduction to biological life and women's slavery in particular. It is therefore enacted and saved by its own actuality, for the virtues of political self-realization, of self-disclosure through deeds, and words of exemplary nobility are actualities in themselves and not sheer means (206–7).

Women in this sense, as well as men, have lost what distinguishes them from *animal socialis*, that is, their unique political virtues, their capacities for new political creations through action and speech, precisely because this logic of the biosocial has risen to prominence "banishing them into the sphere of the intimate and the private" (49). Arendt talks about a ban on the political, its proscription and suppression in the intimate and private spheres where it can spend its outlawed creativity. This prompts me to think that feminist thinking on the political is justifiably a return of the repressed, mixed with an eventual recovery of alienated possibilities of action, of ostracized speech and exiled writing. For women's intimate revolt did not originate as the opposite of the political, but in opposition to the social, challenging the "polite society" which typifies behavioristic norms of propriety, and civility. Emphatically, Julia Kristeva has engaged this promising work of revolt against both feminist conformity and the clinical work of psychoanalytic normalization. Working on intimate revolt, she keeps alive the spirit of political anti-conformity in the sense of semeiotic spontaneity and psychic curiosity. Kristeva pleads for a feminism that neither retires on old gains and values nor celebrates the unquestioned positivity of the new (*Intimate Revolt* 6–7). A revolting intimacy is intrinsic to the actuality of the political and its passionate thinking as it sustains the nerve and resolve of recommencements against social inertia. It keeps alive the "possibility of the appearance of great works," even at the price of errors and impasses (6, 13). What, then, are the sources of the social that deplete the political and call for intimate revolts which for Arendt at least were both appealing and threatening?

First, Arendt implicates Political Economy, the leading "social" science of the seventeenth- to eighteenth-century Absolute Monarchy. Although a contradiction in terms, Political Economy became the *raison d'état* of a national economy with imperial designs, turning issues of housekeeping into matters of public business for the sake of "rapid and constant growth" (*Human Condition* 29). Hannah Pitkin points out that Arendt engenders the rise of the social as feminine, given traditional feminine concerns with the household and the centrality of female reproductive power for its sustenance and growth (*Attack of the Blob* 168). In my view, Arendt exposes the pathologies of both, overprotective matriarchal tyranny and patriarchal state despotism reflected in expanding administrations. Both undermined the spontaneity and creativity needed for the initiation of political beginnings.

Second, the social is epitomized by the fusion of courtly and salon elites. Status-seeking, lifestyle elites routinely perform their "social labor," consumed by conformist rituals of etiquette, intrigue, and diplomatic perfidy. This is indeed the nerve center of Arendt's dissection of the social: "vices surrounded by riches." The diplomatic frontage of "respectable society" was only a cover for "broken promises and oaths" and a forerunner of a universal species "whose capacity for consumption [was] accompanied by the inability to judge" (*On Revolution* 105; *Between Past and Future* 199). The logic of the social points to "a perverted form of 'acting together' by pull and pressure and the tricks of cliques," which brings to the fore those "who know nothing and can do nothing" (*Human Condition* 203). Reducing the political to politesse kills spontaneous action, the judging and revising norms by imposing innumerable status-oriented "make-behave" rules as exemplified by the polite society of the salon (*Human Condition* 40).

A major stake in this loss of political actuality is the false appearance of female emancipation. Arendt's historical biography of *Rahel Varnhagen* is an unmatchable narration of the rise of the social and its disastrous consequences on Jewish pariah women who pursued *parvenu* strategies of assimilation. What they in fact had joined was Germany's "high society," at the cost of their femininity, individuality, and Jewish identity. The social space of the salons and lodges fostered an atmosphere of oppressive conformity, turning public matters into issues of private gossip, dissolving intimacy into theatrical courtship, necessitating self-denials of Jewish identity, name changes, baptisms, opportunistic marriages, and so on. For Arendt, the social bond between the pariah-turned-parvenu and the "polite society," glossed over by a veneer of female emancipation, was sustained by an altered reality of self-delusion, false equality, and fraudulent assimilation. It could not and did not forestall the catastrophe of the German Jewry; it foreclosed political action, preempted a political change of mind and a standpoint of conscious pariahood in solidarity with pariahs. *Rahel Varnhagen* demonstrates that the social is not embodied only by the polite elites of "high society," but consists in an entire system of status hierarchy to which status-seekers also aspire (Pitkin, *Attack of the Blob* 32): "Unable to distinguish between friend and enemy, compliment and insult, seeking acceptance from those they despise," the parvenu must learn to identify with the oppressors, begging from those he ought to be fighting, becoming one of the props which hold up the social order that excludes them (Arendt, *Jew as Pariah* 87, 107; *Rahel Varnhagen* 224) Deprived of political sense, the parvenu woman is unable to make such Schmittian distinctions, which Arendt wants to turn against Schmittian masters. Indeed, the political question for the feminism of our age is how to redeem the Rahel Varnhagens of the world, because ours too is an age driven by an "irresistible necessity in motion," a neoliberal revolution by rich elites and humanist patrons, a real moving force that sustains the imperial blob to which we surrender as "organic bodies subject to a natural process" (*On Revolution* 114).

Arendt's third point regarding the growth of a social form of politics is the most controversial. She considers the French Revolution as an accelerator of the social, because it completed the turn to Political Economy that was left unfinished by the Old Regime. If the "respectable society" of the courtly elites and salon cliques undermined the autonomy of the political by prescribing its decadent lifestyle of intrigue and perfidy as a public standard, the social revolution of the poor instigated by bourgeois demagogues, instrumentalized the political into a social apparatus. By usurping rather than using efficient administrative means to resolve the poverty crisis, the revolution opened the floodgates to mass society and laid the groundwork for totalitarian movements. Thus, the commanding opinion of the crowd, driven by material necessity, replaced the political conflict of opinions.

Doubtlessly, Arendt's political elitism is resonant and outspoken. Only competent and inspired elites of the political reflecting the public spirit of the republic can withstand the demoralizing pressure of social excess from above and below (*On Revolution* 278–80). Bracketing for a while Arendt's elitism, we nonetheless gain a valuable perspective on the evolving pathologies of the social as they plague our confused present. We may recall that the confluence of bourgeois elites and the mobs had set in motion social Bonapartism, imperialism, and the totalitarian movements of the last two centuries. This apolitical conjunction of salon society and mob rule, of deprived crowds and status hungry elites, is a prime example of social conformity appearing as oddball Bohemia. It is also an example of necessity and lack, prefiguring the contemporary fate of the political in the hands of interest groups, expert consultants, corporate advocates, think tanks, radical chic NGOs, and academic entrepreneurs who turn inside out whatever critical idea is generated by resistance and struggle. Is not what is presently called *Empire* a pathological evolution of "social movements" into "non-governmental rule," fully accommodated by the nexus of state and capital? What else is a neocommunist feminist like Jodi Dean denouncing when she interrogates the new hybrid elite power that lacks political sense and basic concepts of action? If Arendt charged the French Revolution for politicizing poverty, Dean turns on the neoliberal counterrevolution which privatizes the plight of poor women and their reproductive health in a "purely economic frame of post-democratic governmentality, where everything depends on a competitive funding environment"; a situation that privileges "mobile, global, frictionless" NGOers whom she aptly designates as "consumer-participants." Dean talks about a new form of feminist passivity "suggesting engagement and disengagement simultaneously, as shopping and political commitment are manifest in one and the same action of signing, clicking, or registering as a member" ("Feminism, Communicative Capitalism" 229). Thus, legitimacy, accountability, and political antagonism are replaced by NGO network, "contract-based projects, multistakeholderism, expertise and reputation management ... which suggest not only a retrenchment from feminist politics but also a more disturbing overall delegitimation of feminism" (229, 231).

ROSA LUXEMBURG AS A JEWISH ANTIGONE: OUTSIDER-FEMININITY, COUNCIL REPUBLICANISM, AND THE ROAD NOT TAKEN

Arendt searched eagerly for strong republican moments between the status and money-dominated high society and the social class-war of revolution. Her quest was controversially framed as a theory of judgment. In the above discussed context, Rahel Varnhagen dramatized feminism's overall difficulty to cope with the incorporation of token women into the social circles of salon elites. It reflects the upstart's anxiety that comes to bear on fake beginnings and the forgery of a new life on the precarious ground of Jewish exception. It revealed the ambivalent transition of the aspirant outsider that makes the move into civil society precisely because she has abdicated judgment and political sense or rather taste. In rethinking such high-handed social conformity which prefigured the social fascism that destroyed European Jewry, I propose considering Kristeva's subject of intimate revolt in tandem with Arendt's eager concern for beginnings. After all, for Arendt, the question of the political bears on words and deeds that epitomize a second birth of the body. It largely conveys intimate revolt rather than Lacanian lack or foreclosure of the subject. I believe that this perspective remains a submerged possibility in Arendt's work.

Admittedly, the main thrust of Arendt's thought points to judgment, bearing overtones of "culture" and "taste," overlooking judgment-enabling or disabling conditions. Culture and politics are thus aligned, not in order to validate truth but to imagine politics as a *decision* about "what manner of action is to be taken in it ... what kind of things are to appear" (*Between Past and Future* 223). For judging "is not valid for those who do not judge, or for those who are not members of the public realm where the objects of judgement appear" (221). Gillian Rose rightly points out that judgment is analogical to a *culture* of judgment which, however, defines the social not the political. It implies "a culture without risk, without struggle, pain or death," marking a retreat to ecclesiology and the sociability of aspirant saints "at a remove from the judged and unloved world" (*The Broken Middle* 233).

Arendt's insightful congeniality with Rosa Luxemburg indicates, I want to believe, a more resilient perspective on judgment, which adds nuance to her elitism. For Arendt, Luxemburg was neither part of Germany's social-democratic nomenclature nor an insider of Bolshevism's disciplinarian elite, but "a rather marginal figure with relatively brief moments of splendor and great brilliance, whose influence in deed and written word can hardly be compared to her contemporaries" like Lenin, Trotsky, Bebel, and Kautsky (*Men in Dark Times* 34). Ironically, Arendt quotes the last lines of *Antigone* where the chorus responds to the crushed sovereign and contrite Creon: "keen judgement and sharp sense are the highest in importance and the core of happiness ... The *great words* of boasters are always punished with great blows, and as they grow old teach them wisdom" (*Antigone* 1348–53; *Human Condition* 25). And yet, despite Sophocles' warning, Arendt enshrined great deeds and words into the political canon. In the case of Luxemburg, however, she is fascinated by her marginality, lack of leverage, and lack of prominence.

Luxemburg captivates Arendt's thought because she exemplifies her concept of the self-conscious pariah who defies the parvenu option, stakes herself politically in revolt, only to meet Antigone's fate. And although she put her trust on work with the oppressed and engaged with the world, she kept the social at a distance. To this effect, Arendt affirms the ethical code of Luxemburg's revolutionary peer group and her Jewish family background as the "hidden equalizers of those who always treated one another as equals and hardly anybody else ... a childhood world in which mutual respect and uncondi-tional trust, a universal humanity and a genuine almost naïve contempt for social and ethnic distinctions, were taken for granted"; sharing in common "moral taste which is so different from moral principles" (*Men in Dark Times* 41). Arendt considers Luxemburg as being "self-consciously a woman," while tellingly underscoring "her distaste for the women's movement to which all other women of her generation and political convictions were irresistibly drawn ... In the face of suffragette equality, she might have been tempted to reply *Vive la petite difference.* She was an outsider, not only because she was and remained a Polish Jew in a country she disliked and a party she came soon to despise, but also because she was a woman" (44–5).

The marginal condition of the "outsider with moral taste" who enjoys a "hidden equality" affords Luxemburg a spontaneous sensibility in revolt and enables her to "judge" Lenin on republican grounds regarding the decline of public freedom in Soviet Russia, "more afraid of a deformed revolution than an unsuccessful one" (53) and also to formulate her original theory of imperialism contra Marx. Ultimately, Arendt praises accordingly Luxemburg's singular insight into the nature of political action which "she had learnt from the revolutionary workers' councils, that good organization does not pre-cede action but is the product of it, that the organization of revolutionary action can and must be learnt in revolution itself; that revolutions are 'made' by nobody but break out spontaneously; *and that the pressure for action always comes from below*" (52). A road not taken.

EQUIVOCATIONS OF THE POLITICAL: LAPSES OF JUSTICE, MISCONCEPTIONS OF EMPIRE

Does Arendt's uncompromising critique of the social imply an evasion of justice? Pitkin strongly believes that justice does not figure in Arendt's political horizon. Hence, Pitkin looks for actionable transitions between private and public linkages, between social and political questions geared to justice. There is no political sense in grieving deeply about the politicization of poverty by the housewives in the French Revolution, as Arendt does when she regrets the substitution of the canonical republican opposition between oppressors and oppressed by the cataclysmic uprising of the poor against the rich. In opposition to Arendt, Pitkin suggests that what in this case becomes a political force is a part of humanity not simply a part of nature. What is more, the political becoming of humanity enlists selfless passion as a capacity for suffering and solidarities under the principle of Justice (Pitkin, "Justice" 282). Instead of depersonalizing suffering and poverty which are readily manipulated and administered by the lust for power, Pitkin insists that a housewife can activate transitions from private association to public responsibility by nurturing principles of justice effectively. Lenin in fact posited a similar indicator for the withering away of the state apparatus when he associated this prospect directly with the capacity of emancipated housewives to engage in soviet rule. For Arendt, instead, the French mothers marching to Versailles were involved in an uprising "whose end is impotence, whose principle is rage and whose conscious aim is not freedom but life and happiness" (*On Revolution* 112–13). This lapse of justice inflects the basic concepts by which she thinks the political. For Pitkin, the constitutional metaphors of "founding" and "beginnings" are not only suffused with idealized Roman imperial imagery but are also conceived as profound denials of mothers and bodies. A metaphor of political beginning that denies the maternal body "is bound to distort whatever it was meant to illuminate" (Pitkin, *Fortune Is a Woman* 281–2).

Indeed, dematernalized natality, "the human condition" of new beginnings by virtue of birth which is otherwise consonant with the natural and prepolitical sphere of the private household, is elevated by Arendt to "a central category of political thought" (*Human Condition* 9). Foundings and refoundings embody new births and rebirths akin to the theological paradigm of virgin birth, "the miracle of natality that saves the world," in which the political faculty of action is ontologically rooted. Arendt, therefore, identifies the political faculty of beginning something new with the "power of performing miracles in faith" (247). America's constitutional miracle, however, neither appeared on virgin ground nor floated on quicksand. It was facilitated by the inheritance of preconstituted political bodies, articles of confederation and a slave economy that reinscribed a merciless hierarchy within natality.

Likewise, Arendt recalibrates Rome's method of expansion, quite indifferent for the imperial biases of the concepts she reappropriates. This method is assimilated into the concepts of augmentation and new beginning which appear to fulfill and stretch imperial benevolence rather than menace and cunning. As a consequence, Arendt overpassed Jewish and Greek responses to the expansion of *imperium Romanun* that even in her own terms exemplified a vicious embodiment of the social, besides material gain and vain glory, "which with its armed forces and grandiose ideas, wiped out all republics and all their civic institutions" (Machiavelli 279). Instead of inquiring into the imperial condition of the slave spectacle, of arenas of performing lethal gaiety and patron-client relations that reinforced the conformist power of the social and the parvenu spirit of collaborationism, Arendt depicts imperial augmentum "as a means by which [the Romans] recognized both themselves and their opponents ... When the battle was over ... they gained something new, a new political arena secured by a peace treaty, according to which yesterday's enemies became tomorrow's allies. In political terms, it allows a new world to rise up." (Arendt, *Promise of Politics* 178). Thus, Pax Romana becomes the *augmentum corporis* of Empire. Imperial peace first imposed on the vanquished and, then turning them into clients, grows into an essential augmentum of the imperial axis. Performing the augmentum corporis of Empire as a peace treaty that legalizes the subservient and deferential status of the client comes to be the ultimate condition of the political.

IMPERIAL BLOB: PERFORMATIVE CONTRADICTIONS OF THE POLITICAL IN THE AGE OF NEOLIBERAL LUMPEN POWER

Remarkably, the scruples and objections of feminist scholarship, including arguments of Arendtian inspiration such as Bonnie Honig's against the shrinkage of the horizon of the political, have already been less tactfully but consistently articulated by Carl Schmitt: "The political can derive its energy from the most varied human endeavors ... It does not describe its own substance, but only the intensity of an association or dissociation of human beings whose motives ... can effect at different times different coalitions and separations" (*Concept of the Political* 38). In this sense any antithesis emerging from the ranks of the social can evolve into a political antagonism "if it is sufficiently strong to group human beings effectively according to friend and enemy. The political does not reside in the battle itself which possesses its own technical, psychological and military laws, but in the mode of behavior which is determined by this possibility" (Schmitt, *Concept of the Political* 37). For instance, some possibly secondary antitheses between transgender and transsexual vanguards may be transformed, as has currently happened, into a political intensity resonant with what Schmitt calls "mutual negations": "The enemy is a negated otherness" (63). Present and future feminist forms of intersectionality may be taken as attempts to overcome issues of "negated otherness" that Schmitt enlists in his definition of the political. Without explicit reference to Schmitt, Honig reiterates this insight in the context of her own theory of the proliferation of spaces of performative freedom: "But not everything is political in this mended account; it is simply the case that nothing is ontologically protected from politicization, that nothing is necessarily or naturally or ontologically *not* political. The distinction between public and private is seen as the performative product of political struggle, hard won and always temporary" (Honig 121–2).

While not being unheedful of Arendt's profound concern about the rules and disciplines of the social in producing docile subjects and instrumentalized politics, Honig thinks that Arendt's excessive formalization of political action based on inelastic boundaries between private and public is ultimately as self-defeating as its permeability and amorphousness. Both ways lead to the occlusion of the political. Instead, she suggests taking the political not as a reference to a specific site but as a metaphor for a variety of spaces, both topographic and conceptual, where ordinary sequences may be disrupted and conventions contested, ranging from "God, nature, technology capital, labor, and work to those of identity, gender, race, and ethnicity. We might then be in a position to *act*—in the private realm" (Honig 121). All the same, it remains uncertain whether the political as an aesthetic metaphor of proliferating acts that perform contestation can indeed mandate forms of radicalization with emancipatory content, or whether it will further radicalize obscurity by swelling "activist" bubbles.

The Arendtian imaginary of the political keeps engaging twenty-first-century feminist theory, remaining a horizon against which new feminist thinking sustains its innovative impetus. One such animating reembodiment that modifies the political scope of Arendtian concepts comes from Judith Butler. Butler dilutes the Arendtian space of appearance of its aristocratic aura of excellence reflected in speech and deed. Alternatively, she foregrounds gender performativity which rehearses plural embodiments of the political as it breaks through, freely moving along, strolling the streets, wandering in public without threats of violence or censorship (Butler 18, 52).

Butler acknowledges that gender choosing and gender norming are equal, though contradictory, possibilities. She does realize that norms are active prior to both will and enacting speech acts, with the effect that their mere consideration creates corporeal vulnerability. However, Butler now takes this as a domain of susceptibility, as a realm of being receptive and affected, hence as a condition where gender swerves can always happen. Under this condition, new forms of gendered life many begin "by breaking with citational chains of gender normativity" (64). Paradoxically, new gender beginnings can take place any time but appear more daring and courageous under the current neoliberal condition of vulnerability and precarity. This condition must be added to the mixture of the social as it evolves in the light of anti-austerity movements. Pressed under the neoliberal condition, Butler reiterates the Arendtian mode of the political within its own "exclusion zone" so to speak, maintaining that the neoliberal onslaught on life itself makes the very claim to a livable life an embodied political demand "that shows us the simultaneity of being precarious and acting" (156).

A complication, however, arises when precarity and vulnerability morph into opportunistic rituals of performative defeat as the Greek case of the Syriza government indicates. Certainly, a new round of performances calling the lie on truth is possible and might serve as a bittersweet comfort, keeping despair temporarily at bay. But it cannot rearticulate either labor or gender power with the political capacity of interrupting catastrophic accumulations of capital. Performatives alone cannot provide alternatives at the macro-historical level where neoliberalism sums up all prior beginnings of capitalism by repeating the monstrosity of original accumulation ad infinitum. Arendt herself is aware of the social perversion of beginnings which turns original accumulation into a perpetual principle of the future: "letting loose the old expropriation process" eliminates the political and founding force of mutual covenants as a possibility (*Crises* 212). Empty speech over bare biological life is what happens to politics when it abdicates its oath-bearing force in the face of overwhelming economic brutality. Performativity alone cannot account for the incapacity effected by large-scale expropriation. Here, *conditions* of performativity matter immensely, reinforcing neoliberal patronage over the expropriated and destroying the force of effective speech that is embodied in the political action of a just oath (*On Revolution* 215; *Human Condition* 243–7). In this context, the conjunction of vulnerability and precarity, as Pitkin argues, defines people as pariahs and then seduces them into becoming parvenus with client status: "but it also disguises this action as a natural, inevitable process beyond human power" (*Attack of the Blob* 76). Following Pitkin, my conceptualization of the imperial blob imagery exposes this mystified scene of dependency, featuring nongovernmental rule on pay, stressing agency—not freedom—while rendering people politically powerless, first coating them, then consuming them (*Attack of the Blob* 4, 6).

The challenge, then, for twenty-first-century feminist politics is to resist effectively imperial modes of *lumpen* governance, of patronized vulnerability and precarity that "reinstate and naturalize relations of inequality" (Butler 142). Neoliberal lumpen power is essentially the effect of a New Political Economy of social pariahdom. It brings within its disciplining range, precaritized and atomized masses of the poor, refugees, women, queer, transgendered and transsexual people, reperforming nineteenth-century Victorian philanthropy as emergency charity in the void of decimated public services, instilling individualistic responsibility "as the demand to become an entrepreneur of oneself under conditions that make that dubious vocation impossible" (15).

Equally challenging is Butler's amplification of this argument in the collateral context of Empire, which is the defining condition of the social in our age. Although not framed in explicit Arendtian terms, Butler's description of Palestinian precarity and vulnerability is resonant with Arendtian overtones. We figure from what she writes below that Palestinian women experience Israeli occupation as an extreme manifestation of the social. Rather than pulsing with Arendtian visions of natality and expectations of new beginnings, they face an uncanny, interim form of caretaker imperialism which forecloses political possibilities. This imperial form allows only for the management of life as necessity in an extreme context which illustrates the political crisis of feminism. It replaces the antithesis of the social and the political with the parasitical relation of pariah and client parvenu. In the Palestinian territories the infrastructural conditions of life are habitually destroyed by routine-like military operations carried out by Israeli security forces. Once the first round of operations is completed by bombing schools and hospitals, "by water rationing, the uprooting of olive groves and the dismantling of irrigation systems," security forces withdraw, allowing at intervals Empire's light-troops to step in for repair jobs at subsistence level: "NGO interventions presume that the destruction will continue, and understand their task as ameliorating those conditions between bouts of destruction. A macabre rhythm develops between the tasks of destruction and the tasks of renewal or reconstruction (often opening up temporary market potential as well) all of which supports the normalization of the occupation" (Butler 13). Echoing the discussion of *Antigone* at the beginning of the essay, we should recall that when the Chorus asks Creon about his death plan he replies in very much the same terms. He decides to vanish her off, still living, in a rocky cavern, believing that if he supplies Antigone with a token quantity of food he and the city may escape the contagious *miasma*, the moral plague caused by homicide (773–6). Creon's biopolitical opportunism aims at wiping off antigonism by speculating on humanitarian death at subsistence level. This is precisely what is rehearsed by NGO relief imperialism. Rendering itself self-servingly necessary and ingratiating to "both sides," it keeps Palestinian population ratios in balance, while preempting thoroughgoing opposition to the occupation. Butler's intervention alerts us to an imperial form of social patronage as embodied by neo-lumpen NGOs which set up their upwardly mobile business upon regimes of necessity within zones of precarity and vulnerability.

The logic of Empire as an advanced jellyfication of the social is further underscored by Jaspir Puar. Along with other Jewish as well as non-Jewish combative scholars, she argues strongly against the pinkwashing of occupation. Pinkwashing exemplifies yet another occasion of what Arendt calls abdicated judgment and conformist adjustment to the blob pressure of social and State interest. What she means is the functionalization of queerness within Israel's culture war machine, which brands the state of Israel as "gay friendly" and "queer tolerant" as opposed to a homophobic, illiberal, and backward Palestine. This is arguably a new stake in the social patronage of the politics of emancipation. Queering Empire or implicating its gender anxieties and its transgender avatars in global culture wars involves what Jasbir Puar refers to as a "dirty bargaining" between their own safety and countenance of the continued oppression of Palestinians (Puar 287). As if the two are convertible and as if the Israeli state occupation and the Palestinian oppression of queerness are equivalent and contiguous (288–9).

But how new is that stake after all? The paternalistic assumptions entertained by contemporary imperial queerness recall to mind an important lesson that Angela Davis has drawn regarding the continuity between the two "feminist centuries." Davis evokes in tandem the white entourage of US feminists visiting Iran after the 1979 Islamic Revolution that overthrew the Shah dictatorship, seeking to instruct Iranian women into the feminist track, along with George and Laura Bush posing as liberators of oppressed Muslim women "explaining that this was one of the motivations for invading Afghanistan" (Davis 63–4). This is a durable lesson to keep: "a victory is not so much to secure change once and for all, but rather to create new terrains for struggle" (18). As a matter of fact, no new critical globalisms or transnational aspirations and alliances are possible unless both feminist and leftist perspectives take up the challenge of their own de-imperialization. No thought is safe from the resounding ironies of our age. Butler's *Notes toward a Performative Theory of Assembly* was set forth in the thick of a global assembly line. Global sweatshops "link us in ways contingent on exploitative practices of production and consumption. In the Global North we purchase the pain and exploitation of girls in the Global South, which we wear everyday on our bodies … the challenge is, as Marx argued long ago, to uncover the social relations that are both embodied and concealed by these commodities" (Davis 22–3).

UNRULY NEEDS AND THE QUESTION OF HEGEMONY

Nancy Fraser, fully attentive to these hazards, has taken issue with the neutralizations of the political, providing long-missing and long-lasting insights into the ironic dialectic between feminist politics and depoliticization. In this context, Fraser encountered Habermas's revised Critical Theory which, despite its practical intent to clarify the emancipatory potential of contemporary struggles, remained untouched by the "outpouring creativity in feminist theory." Habermas's sense of the political fell prey to a fateful dualism, reflecting androcentric biases through its categorical dichotomies which counterposed "lifeworld" to "system," "public" to "private," "symbolic" to "material reproduction," thus enclaving childrearing from the rest of social labor, not realizing that systemic media (money, gender, power, law) were already steering their way through "the everyday" and "the private" (*Unruly Practices* 122).

Unavoidably, then, Fraser was obliged to settle accounts with the legacy of Arendt as well. As she did with the case of Habermas, Fraser opposed Arendt's mutually exclusive dichotomies between the social and the political, the private and the public, which she found untenable and depoliticizing. Conceptualizing need as a political idiom became her major point of dissent with Arendt. For Fraser "needs are irreducibly interpretive and need interpretations are in principle contestable," "subject to critique" and denaturalization. Rather than taking for granted the social as an improper violation of the public-private boundary, she problematizes the instrumental reason by which administrative apparatuses institutionalize the social (*Unruly Practices* 160). Needs are privatized and depoliticized by technocratic discourses clustered around the managerial state. Social policy moralizes the poor differentially, feminizes poverty by discriminating between qualified male social security contributor-recipients and female dependent clients who still need to qualify with the "Juridical-Administrative-Therapeutic" apparatus (JAT) (155, 160).

Yet, drawing variably from neo-Marxist state-theory, Fraser explains that JAT is neither the unequivocal master of the social nor a uniform political agent, reflecting, instead, volatile hegemonic equilibria which are condensed outcomes of struggles and compromises over public redefinitions of needs that broke away from economic and domestic spheres. The social then is a three-dimensional arena where (a) JAT need discourses propounded by social planners and professions of therapeutic engineering cross ways with (b) oppositional need interpretations and "newly politicized groups" casting off "natural, prepolitical interpretations," and (c) reprivatization claims articulated by neoliberal think tanks and New Right constituencies (157). On this account, the political reflects antagonistic need interpretations that gain or lose political status, are "validated as a matter of legitimate political concern," or are delegitimized and reprivatized as nonpolitical. The scope of the political expands or contracts accordingly (164).

Fraser is at great pains balancing a Gramscian notion of hegemony articulated as "a concatenation of different publics that together construct the 'common sense' of the day" (167) with a Habermasian notion of validity which is a ground of legitimacy whereby opponents are mutually engaging in seminar style undistorted communication over needs. Habermas aside, Fraser approximates Chantal Mouffe's neo-Gramscian perspective. Her notion of contestatory needs does encompass struggles for a cultural hegemony "which allows for the possibility of radical democratic social movements: broad, informally organized, collective formations wherein politics and poetry form an unbroken continuum as struggles for social justice shade into the unleashing of creativity" (107).

In contrast, Chantal Mouffe argues that whatever the poetic imagination of a hegemonic bloc, it does involve democratic equivalence. She is advocating for a transformation of existing subject positions, converging in affect and passion on a new hegemonic identity and "not on the need for argumentation and publicity" (*Return of the Political* 86). The radical democratic challenge for Mouffe is to stake out feminist claims, values, and concerns within the context of a wider articulation of struggles against multiple forms of subordination, expanding the social imaginary, transforming relevant subject positions, thus materializing democratic equivalence between oppressed groups (*Return of the Political* 88). Mouffe makes plain that (a) the transformation of subject positions entails subversion and overdetermination of one or a number of them by others. The ensuing totalization temporarily at least, halts the interminable dispersion and decentering of subject positions which defines postmodern variants of anti-essentialism; (b) for democratic equivalence cum hegemony to be possible, *exclusion is necessary*, for no fully inclusive community is possible, no full realization of democracy is attainable and no political sense of a "we" is feasible without a constitutive exterior (Laclau and Mouffe, *Hegemony*; Mouffe, *Return of the Political* 85).

Besides being inflected by Carl Schmitt, Mouffe's thinking of the political carries across strong Arendtian intuitions that go against the grain of maternalist feminism (Sarah Ruddick) and sexual contract theory (Carole Pateman). In this respect she amplifies the insights of Arendtian scholars (Mary G. Dietz), arguing that whatever the merits of maternal virtues, the unequal relation between mother and child cannot qualify as a model of citizenship (Mouffe, *Return of the Political* 80). Indeed, Mouffe reinforces Arendt's hypothesis considering that every situation is an encounter between private and public insofar as the former is never insulated from the public condition of citizenship (84). At her most civic-republican, Mouffe sees no obvious reason to justify the relevance of sexual difference in all social relations. Although still pertinent, she argues, there is no ground why sexual difference should be sustained perpetually, especially in the domain of politics: "sexual difference should not be a valid distinction" (82).

DISAVOWALS OF THE POLITICAL: ILLUSIONS OF INCLUSION AND INFLUENCE

Although Mouffe's model draws its main thrust from convergent civic republican and communitarian visions of virtue and the common good, Iris Marion Young has voiced strong doubts about a neglected undertow of her theory, namely pluralism. Young objects as follows. The struggle for democratic equivalence which implies aggregation of claims, identities and policy preferences, all effectively totalized by a hegemonic recomposition of the majoritarian bloc that wins the policy battle, leaves no room for a normative evaluation of its legitimacy in terms of justice and rightness. What underlies Mouffe's theory of the political is an aggregative paradigm of hegemonic coalition analogous to "a model of interest group competition in which aggregated might makes right," reducing any normative justification claims to mere ideology (Young, *Inclusion* 51). Instead, Young's revised Habermasian alternative emphasizes deliberative democracy premised on fair, open and mutual communicative engagement whereby "disorderly, disruptive, annoying or distracting means of communication are often necessary or effective elements to engage others in debate over issues and outcomes" (50). Thus, a public sphere qualifies as such if it functions as a terrain of opposition where powerful agents are exposed and shamed, held accountable and influenced to change policy orientations (173).

But the global scope of influence and the boundary of political contestation are confined to bargaining leverage, purchasing power, lobbying targeted states, corporations, parliaments, and UN fora. Young partly follows Jean Cohen and Andrew Arato's dualistic theory of collective action by which they retrace reflexively the US feminist trajectory in terms of new social movement politics. Their dualistic synthesis first identified an "offensive" feminism operating with strategic/instrumental modes of action, aiming at inclusion and policy reform, pressing for an Equal Rights amendment and lobbying for influence on Congress, courts, and government. Accordingly, the militant dispositions of feminism were filtered institutionally and balanced by a self-limiting radicalism. By integrating the strategy of indirect influence into its methods, US feminism avoided the risk of self-bureaucratization and political elitism, respecting the lifeworld-system boundary rather than acting directly on the subsystems of political and economic power. Thus, by filtering militancy and replacing direct political action with influence, the feminist movement triggered a process of institutional learning that redefined the relations of the social and the political (Cohen and Arato, *Civil Society* 561). Second, partial routinization and institutionalization of the feminist charisma "neither excluded, nor substituted for mass collective action, grassroots associations, autonomous self-help organizations or identity-oriented politics" (557–8). Duly, the "defensive" aspect of the feminist movement involved self-organization, preserving and developing communicative infrastructures, solidarity networks, self-improvement, consciousness raising and so on (531).

What remained unclear in Cohen and Arato's 1990s dualistic conception of the feminist movement was an unforeseen possibility of neoliberal duplication which presently demonstrates that the "social movements" Young still has in mind do not stand simply for participation, inclusion, and political reform. Unshakeable evidence ever since indicates that the "social movements" as a descriptive and normative term explaining social change have become so flabby and shifty that, though qualifying for Young's programmatic platform of global reform, still require an "equitable financing that draws not only on the resources of states but also on private economic powers" (Young, *Inclusion* 274).

RECKONING WITH THE POLITICAL CRISIS OF FEMINISM

Interestingly, the latest work of Nancy Fraser, at least in its diagnostic aspect, makes no allowances for postpolitical clichés and neoliberal platitudes. Read against the grain, it is a heretical epitaph on older and newer tales of feminist novelty and its neoliberal doubling. Reflecting on this cunning of feminist progression, she wonders: "Was it mere coincidence that second-wave feminism and neoliberalism prospered in tandem? Or was there some perverse, subterranean, elective affinity between them?" (*Fortunes of Feminism* 218). Fraser's response is shaped by an acute awareness of the long durée of feminism's restless duality. Cold war feminism operated with a dual framework that played civil and political rights off against social and economic rights, privileging the register of recognition over redistribution. Its transnational spin off, enmeshed in new funding regimes of global governance, emphasizes excessively issues of violence, sexual trafficking, and reproduction as opposed to structural crises of imperialism and pauperization. Fraser spotlights what is concealed by "the feminist hoopla" of project-capitalism, namely, the fact that it sets in motion and intensifies "the NGO-ification of feminist politics, widening the gap between professionals and grassroots," whose effect is "to depoliticize the grassroots and to skew the agendas of local groups in directions favored by First-World funders. By its very stopgap nature, moreover, NGO action did little to challenge the receding of public provision or to build political support for responsive state action" (221–3). Fraser realizes that major components of feminist critique originally addressed to welfare bureaucratic paternalism, to the sexist family wage, to the sovereign nation-state as an obstacle for engaging global injustices, along with the claim to the recognition of identity and difference "now appear fraught with ambiguity, susceptible to serving the legitimation needs of a new form of capitalism" (223). Hence, the need to respecify the political, to reactivate the emancipatory promise of feminism by reconnecting its critical force to the critique of neoliberal capitalism "and thereby reposition feminism squarely on the Left" (225). But if "feminism" is already enframed by its uncanny doubles of flexible capitalism and imperial governmentality, this is no less the case with the NGO-ified "Left," a desideratum at best that is more hazardly supposed than confirmed in the brave new-nothing condition of Empire. In respecifying the political, Fraser circumvents the deep ambivalence of the Left, a sensible victim of neoliberal horror as well as a pragmatic henchman.

Absent of a hegemonic signifier of the Left, Fraser falls back on "public opinion," aiming at a "dialogic theory of justice," in which she integrates representation as a third dimension besides recognition and redistribution. Since representation is now the fundamental question of the political, Fraser foregrounds misrepresentation and misframing along with maldistribution and misrecognition as issues of justice. The political in this sense is a constitutional condition of boundary-setting, structuring the contours of contestation, participatory parity or disparity, inclusion, and so on. The political condition stipulates the subject and method of claim-making and adjudication (*Fortunes of Feminism* 195). Predictably, she postulates a transnational civil society driven by a democratizing process of frame-setting, complemented by global enforcement apparatuses able to translate public opinion into binding decisions (205). In order to sustain a semblance of consistency for the political, Fraser experiments with accountability schemes in global governance regimes, mixing nongovernmental, governmental, and transnational institutions ("Publicity" 152–3). Reasonably too, one may wonder whether the assumed civil society track assorted diversely by the global poor, Occupy, Wikileaks, World Social Fora, for example, can (a) endure by transforming their multiplicity into collectivity, (b) cope with selective pressures of redirection, patronized representation, with becoming a discrete object of divisive policy discourse, or (c) can indeed afford a dialogical transformation of technocratic, elite-dominated enforcement apparatuses, Transnational Advocacy Networks, and academic think tanks. To reuse Fraser's own words, the bar is lowered to a point where this final scenario of the political fails to take into account the necessary tension between fact and norm ("Publicity" 139).

CROWDS, PEOPLE, AND PARTY: THE BREAST-VALUE OF THE POLITICAL

Representation is a bridge-concept that draws together the political impulses and repressions of the last two centuries. Fraser's late focus on representation reflects the same complication which grew out of Hannah Pitkin's landmark treatment of the issue back in 1967 (*Concept of Representation*). Pitkin had raised the question of popular representation, underscoring not only popular consent to the representatives' decisions, but also the good reasons people might have for consenting (110–11). Pitkin did not consider the possibility of these reasons being constituted through representation itself. She failed to distinguish between a manipulated popular will and a popular constitution of political will. She thought that the reasons for accepting representation laid outside the range of representation. Fascism exemplifies an extreme case where reasons lay within representation but, Ernesto Laclau argues, a radical Leftist populism may resignify the people in a more equivalent and egalitarian direction. For Laclau, the crisis of representation and hence the impasse of the political is owed precisely to this populist deficit. Populism is not a movement but the hegemonic logic of the political. Against the mainstream demotion of populism to the irrational realm of the unthinkable, Laclau reinforces its logic as a master principle of the political. On the whole, any political project claiming a generic importance is necessarily populistic to some extent. Why? "Because the political always entails the construction of a 'people'" (*Populist Reason* 153). Here, we may retrace our earlier discussion at the crossroads of Schmitt and Arendt. The political is the anatomy of the social. Its Gramscian moment, however, points to the hegemonic logic of a horizontal populism. On Laclau's account, the people as a political subject is generated in terms of equivalence which reinscribes existing social particularities and new heterogeneous differences on a hegemonic surface (154). The operation of equivalence that articulates social particularities into a totalizing hegemonic force of representation constitutes a nodal point which exceeds by far its heterogeneity, obtaining indeed a psychoanalytic status which Joan Copjec calls "the surplus breast value of the milk" (Copjec, *Imagine* 60). Operating in this obscure terrain, between redemptive jouissance and pragmatism, the task of the party is to constitute or perform a "people" (Laclau, *Populist Reason* 182). And yet, identifying libidinal drive and political calling may entail a dramatic oversimplification of the popular, an underestimation of the divisions which preempt popular unity, displace or fake militancy, supplant or dilute political articulation, and confuse antagonistic frontiers.

In the wake of Laclau's populist theory of the political, which sublimates Gramsci and Lacan, Jodi Dean adds a more hardboiled mix of Elias Canetti and Roberto Michels, making indeed virtue of vice, of substitutionism, of the iron law of oligarchy and the like: "The crowd lacks capacities of endurance, implementation and execution. Without mediation, that is to say, absent a transferential relation to another space, it doesn't know what it desires. The crowd doesn't have a politics. It is an opportunity for politics ... The very idea of a politics of everyone is a debilitating fantasy that denies the constitutive feature of the political: division goes all the way down" (Dean, *Crowds* 160). Jodi Dean conceptualizes a new communist party, operating as an opening that will empower Canetti's crowd to perceive itself and be perceived as a people. The new party enables a people to appear politically in the rupture of the crowd event. Against participatory democrats and radical pluralists of inclusion, Dean crosses the noted diagonal Schmitt-Arendt. All those who hint at the possibility of a Left politics without "judgement," "condemnation," "exclusion," and "discipline," desiring the benefits of a people's collectivity without its effects, those in other words who are "unwilling to talk about the party should not talk about political transformation" (153–4). It is tempting to receive this statement as a reflexive continuation of Leninism by postfeminist means. But it is less and more than that. Dean's is a Lacanian party in excess of itself, of its errors and betrayals; it is impure; it is not, should not and cannot be infallible and may even "turn its immense energies on itself. If we cannot bear it, we aren't the Left, the communists we need" (154). It is less formidable than it sounds since the avatars of this transferential regroupment that Dean has in mind are either evolutionary hybrids of the New Media–New Left constellation repeating performatively routine betrayals and ritual defeats like the Greek Syriza, or "political openings" by reasonable fellows such as Bernie Sanders in the United States and Jeremy Corbyn in the UK (22).

What Dean proposes may be promising in the following sense. Rather than repeating *ad nauseum* critiques of totalizing visions, or embracing "civil society movements" and networked clicktivism, or highlighting oppression and exclusion based in sex, gender, race, ethnicity and so on, or deconstructing logics of normalization or joining the creative industries with cultural studies, or rallying at global summits with covered expenses by NGOs, she turns the tables by asking a vital question, requiring also an indispensable answer: How can we imagine the political under crowdsourcing conditions of communicative capitalism? The point is that diverse resistances, isolated campaigns, and victories or individual acts of subversion are either reduced to criminality or to mere opinion, circulated in social media networks, easily sidelined by new content and feeds. On their own they cannot endure and cannot amplify. New media *crowdaffect* simply displaces the need for long-term political commitment and endurance, neutralizing it by an addictive connectivity that depletes the resources of the political: "Capital uses every *state, non-state and interstate* resource to advance its position. A Left that refuses to organize itself in recognition of this fact will never be able to combat it" (153, emphasis added). Maybe we do need to bend the stick on the other side, again, but now aware that a party is sustained by organs which sometimes double those of Oedipus and other times those of Octopus.

WORKS CITED

Arendt, Hannah. *Between Past and Future: Exercises in Political Thought*. New York: Meridian Books, 1954.

Arendt, Hannah. *Crises of the Republic*. San Diego, CA: Harcourt Brace Jovanovich, 1972.

Arendt, Hannah. *The Human Condition*. Chicago: Chicago UP, 1958.

Arendt, Hannah. *The Jew as Pariah: Jewish Identity and Politics in the Modern Age*. Ed. Ron H. Feldman. New York: Grove, 1978.

Arendt, Hannah. *The Life of the Mind*. San Diego, CA: Harcourt Brace Jovanovich, 1978.

Arendt, Hannah. *Men in Dark Times*. San Diego, CA: Harcourt Brace, 1968

Arendt, Hannah. *On Revolution*. London: Penguin Books, 1963.

Arendt, Hannah. *The Promise of Politics*. New York: Schocken Books, 2005.

Arendt, Hannah. *Rahel Varnhagen: The Life of a Jewish Woman*. Trans. Richard and Clara Winston. San Diego, CA: Harcourt Brace Jovanovich, 1974.

Aristophanes. "Assemblywomen." *Frogs, Assemblywomen, Wealth*. Ed. and trans. Jeffrey Henderson. Cambridge, MA: Harvard UP, 2002, pp. 237–411.

Aristophanes. "Lysistrata." *Birds, Lysistrata, Women at the Thesmophoria*. Ed. and trans. Jeffrey Henderson. Cambridge, MA: Harvard UP, 2000, pp. 253–441.

Butler, Judith. *Notes toward a Performative Theory of Assembly*. Cambridge, MA: Harvard UP, 2015.

Cohen, Jean, and Andrew Arato. *Civil Society and Political Theory*. Cambridge, MA: MIT P, 1992.

Copjec, Joan. *Imagine There's No Woman: Ethics and Sublimation*. Cambridge, MA: MIT P, 2003.

Davis, Angela. *Abolition Democracy: Beyond Empire, Prisons, and Torture*. New York: Seven Stories P, 2005.

Dean, Jodi. *Crowds and Party*. New York: Verso Books, 2016.

Dean, Jodi. "Feminism, Communicative Capitalism, and the Inadequacies of Radical Democracy." *Radical Democracy and the Internet: Interrogating Theory and Practice*. Ed. Lincoln Dahlberg and Eugenia Siapera. Basingstoke: Palgrave Macmillan, 2007, pp. 226–45.

Deutscher, Penelope. "The Inversion of Exceptionality: Foucault, Agamben, and 'Reproductive Rights'." *The Agamben Effect*, special issue of *The South Atlantic Quarterly*. Ed. Alison Ross. 107.1 (2008): 55–70.

Euripides, "Medea." *Cyclops, Alcestis, Medea*. Ed. and trans. David Kovacs. Cambridge, MA: Harvard UP, 1994, pp. 283–427.

Fraser, Nancy. *Futures of Feminism: From State-Managed Capitalism to Neoliberal Crisis*. New York: Verso Books, 2013.

Fraser, Nancy. "Publicity, Subjection, Critique. A Reply to My Critics." *Transnationalizing the Public Sphere*. Ed. Kate Nash. Cambridge: Polity P, 2014, pp. 129–56.

Fraser, Nancy. *Unruly Practices: Power, Discourse and Gender in Contemporary Social Theory*. Minneapolis: U of Minnesota P, 1989.

Honig, Bonnie. *Political Theory and the Displacement of Politics*. Ithaca: Cornell UP, 1993.

Kristeva, Julia. *Intimate Revolt: The Powers and Limits of Psychoanalysis*, vol. 2. Trans. Jeanine Herman. New York: Columbia UP, 2002.

Laclau, Ernesto. *On Populist Reason*. New York: Verso Books, 2005.

Laclau, Ernesto, and Chantal Mouffe. *Hegemony and Socialist Strategy: Towards a Radical Democratic Politics*. New York: Verso Books, 1985.

Machiavelli, Niccolo. *Discourses*. London: Penguin Classics, 1983.

Mouffe, Chantal. *Return of the Political*. New York: Verso Books, 1993.

Ong, Aihwa. *Neoliberalism as Exception: Mutations in Citizenship and Sovereignty*. Durham, NC: Duke UP, 2006.

Pitkin, Hannah Fenichel. *The Attack of the Blob: Hannah Arendt's Concept of the Social*. Chicago UP, 1998.

Pitkin, Hannah Fenichel. *The Concept of Representation*. Berkeley: U of California P, 1967.

Pitkin, Hannah Fenichel. *Fortune Is a Woman: Gender & Politics in the Thought of Niccolò Machiavelli*. Chicago, IL: Chicago UP, 1999.

Pitkin, Hannah Fenichel. "Justice." *Hannah Arendt: Critical Essays*. Ed. Lewis P. Hinchman and Sandra K. Hinchman. New York: SUNY P, [1981] 1994, pp. 261–88.

Poovey, Mary. "The Abortion Question and the Death of Man." *Feminists Theorize the Political*. Ed. Judith Butler and Joan W. Scott. New York: Routledge, 1992, pp. 239–56.

Puar, Jasbir. "Citation and Censure: Pinkwashing and the Sexual Politics of Talking about Israel." *The Imperial University: Academic Repression and Scholarly Dissent*. Ed. Piya Chatterjee and Sunaina Maira. Minneapolis: Minnesota UP, 2014, pp. 281–97.

Rose, Gillian. *The Broken Middle: Out of Our Ancient Society*. Oxford: Blackwell, 1992.

Schmitt, Carl. *The Concept of the Political*. New Brunswick, NJ: Rutgers UP, 1976.

Schmitt, Carl. *Political Theology: Four Chapters on the Concept of Sovereignty*. Trans. George Schwab. Cambridge, MA: MIT P, 1988.

Sophocles. "Antigone." *Antigone, the Women of Trachis, Philoctetes, Oedipus at Colonus*. Ed. and trans. Hugh Lloyd-Jones. Cambridge, MA: Harvard UP, 2002, pp. 1–127.

Young, Iris Marion. *Inclusion and Democracy*. Oxford: Oxford UP, 2000.

CHAPTER TWENTY-FOUR

Political Trauma

JOY JAMES

INTRODUCTION: CAPTIVE MATERNAL THEORIZING

For black feminist theorist Barbara Christian, theory is a verb, not a noun. For those sharing the political persona of the "captive maternal," theory becomes a shield and weapon: armor against capture, and tool for liberation. Captive maternals are ungendered protectors and nurturers of besieged communities, embodied here in black female form (see James, "Afrarealism," "Captive," "The Womb"). Captive maternal freedom struggles are the provenance of liberator not predator theories. Christian mapped the place of theory for those assumed by Western/non-African thought to have little capability within it:

> For people of color have always theorized-but in forms quite different from the Western form of abstract logic. And I am inclined to say that our theorizing (and I intentionally use the verb rather than the noun) is often in narrative forms, in the stories we create, in riddles and proverbs, in the play with language, because dynamic rather than fixed ideas seem more to our liking. How else have we managed to survive with such spiritedness the assault on our bodies, social institutions, countries, our very humanity? And women, at least the women I grew up around, continuously speculated about the nature of life through pithy language that unmasked the power relations of their world. (Christian, 68)

Despite its increasing prominence or commoditization, black feminist theorizing counters academic theory and canonical hierarchies in Western theory through its focus on and channeling of progressive activism. Theorizing, if related to liberation, functions as a verb. Embodied in the captive maternal, it is a site of production (work) and reproduction (labor). While theory may manifest as leisure for elites, for captives it resonates in struggle. Black feminist theorizing seeks to undo the appropriation of captive maternals' generative powers and nurturing for "the community of slaves" (Davis). Paradoxically, the more captive maternals nurture, the more the recipients of their care are cushioned from and better able to tolerate bondage or emboldened to rebel against it.

The struggle for black feminist theorizing is how to leverage its analyses, which can be and often are appropriated and used for purposes other than the empowerment or liberation of black communities. The origins of square dancing in the United States offer a template for considering the "race for theory." The state dance in thirty-one of the fifty United States, square dancing is considered to be an almost exclusively white cultural formation. However, enslaved people of African descent were forced to develop this musical and dance form to soothe and please their white enslavers. After emancipation, blacks were largely ousted from a "whitened template"; yet some maintained pleasure in their mastery over an art form that they were forced to craft, one (re)fashioned through black enslavement and claimed as largely white property (Blakemore; Jamison).

"[U]masking the power relations of their world," black women theorists as activists command a stage as "callers." From a platform, with an elevated view, they can instruct the Promenade of democratic culture. The dismissal that captive maternal articulations through art, print, performance, and rebellions are limited in scope, or a self-serving lens lacking universal application for the greater good, ignores how black feminized labor is invested in most democratic structures in the Americas or nations in which black enslavement was a foundational pillar for the development not only of a political economy but also of a white-dominated democracy. With contributions that are considered fit for cultural, political, and theoretical appropriations or theft, the "raw material" for theory from the Western womb (discussed below) originates with a captive maternal. Black feminist theorizing has created movements that altered the trajectory of democracy, moving it from predatory to emancipatory, with an expansion of civil and voting rights. The 1977 Combahee Collective political treatise by black lesbian feminist activists organized against rapes and murders of young black women and girls in Boston, tragedies that police and the black community (perceiving the girls and women as sex workers) largely ignored. Following the 2013 acquittal of Trayvon Martin's executioner in Florida, and the 2014 police killing of Michael Brown in Ferguson, as NYPD choked the life out of Erica Garner's father, Eric, on a Staten Island street, captive maternals mobilized into multiple formations contesting police and social violence. They used their voices to call for formations and to give directions in movements that were choreographed and spontaneously invented. The theorizing of captive maternals forged by racial captivity and gendered labor altered the practice of democracy and the evolution of democratic thought. The polis as racial-sexual restrictive arena became the site for transformation into an anti-racist, ungendered commons.

"Western forms of abstract logic," as conventional theory, are insulated from evolutionary change and historically have been hostile to the agency of theorizing from captive maternals. Where Western theory presents the black and indigenous as less than human and intellectually impaired (by culture or biology), it attempts to secure the stage with a white-dominant official caller, bringing order to a fray that conquest and enslavement orchestrated. Even when talking about "race" and "racism," theorists can avoid a confrontation with critical perspectives in anti-black racism. The womb of Western theory gave birth to captive maternals as it produced philosophy and theory—and engineered a command performance with a whitened square dance.

Where theories and philosophies from the "civilized" Western womb trend as hostile and predatory toward captive maternals, there is a pitted battle over the power of the caller to share or monopolize agency in theory and philosophy. It is not just political philosophy that is politicized. All theory is political; just as there is theorizing for liberation, there is theorizing for domination. Sometimes both coexist in the same time and space frame. The propertied white male founders of US democracy blended counterrevolution against abolitionist gradualism, fear of black rebellions in Haiti and the colonies, and Enlightenment philosophes' platforms to form their democratic republic; its homage to the Athenian polis constructed a border for a frontier democracy where public and private realms were walled off but engineered so that the public sector restricted to white male rule fed upon the labor and consumption of the private sector—children, women, poor and enslaved men, all buttressed by enslaved people of African descent, who were themselves supported by black captive maternals. "Originalists" interpret the US Constitution to restore control over the female, child, and racially fashioned captive, stripping them of agency. Historically, free (white) males of property were presumed to inherit a unique capacity for contemplating the universal, the timeless, and the sublime. That rationalized their concentration of power as domination. In reality, they disproportionately benefited from rape, violence, and terror as political phenomena. The theft of time, the trauma of rape and enslavement, the resulting incapacitations of body and mind, the debilitation of spirit—all are appended to predatory theory's hierarchies and contested by liberatory theory's battle to call forth theory that does not reduce the experiences of captive maternals to raw resources mined for capital, or narratives that become theory only after they are translated into Western abstract logic. When the capacity to create theory is restricted to the Western abstract mind, only those who take that route to the stage are certified to become callers who determine the steps and movements that produce art, pleasure, and enlightenment. Assertions that captive maternals are incapable of producing theory about reality that their labor cocreated solidify the dominant role of the captor as structure, boss, interpreter, and warden. Captors in their own race for dominance reengineer theorizing to mask the traumas of captive maternals, and the theft of their time and labor. Predatory "theorizing" renders the captive an "edible," a "delectable negro[/negress]" that black queer theorist Vincent Woodard describes as cannibalized by the benevolent/malevolent master/mistress.

Arguably, captive maternals exist in all societies. Nonetheless, those forged in European/white settler democracies that amassed racial capital bear the scarification of slavery and rape. Intergenerational losses through time, theft, and trauma alter the wombs of captives (Hurley). Democracy's promised evolutionary trek toward a humanitarian destiny depended upon exploitation and consumption of captive maternals. Hence, Christian's "race for theory" is a response to the democratic and the dictatorial that stepped over captive maternals scrubbing floors without comprehending that their forced labor and organic theories could seek to democratize a racial democracy through civil and human rights campaigns.

Predatory democracies developed a black matrix as the underbelly of their institutions: the labor and the work that builds social platforms also enables production and performance. The captives' unexpected ability to theorize changed the nature of captivity as they sought to abolish it. The black matrix inside the Western womb functions as a fulcrum to leverage power against predatory democracies. Atop that fulcrum sits a spectrum whose bandwidth reflects diverse political ideologies. Both the fulcrum's leverage and the spectrum's conflicting ideologies can tilt toward freedom or repression.

MATERNALS AS MAROONS

During the "new world" enslavement era in the Americas, captive maternals defended maroon camps established by enslaved African runaways and indigenous peoples staving off genocide. They protected and nurtured flights and fights that ensured natality: the rebirth of family, kin, community, and culture. Their maroon societies theorized and defined the borders and boundaries of democracy. In defiance of abstract logic and predatory tendencies in Western thought concerning who was human and who was not, theorizing as a verb led to a feminist maroon philosophy to counter a racist democracy terrorizing diverse populations. The maroon camp is an oppositional site seeking to define democracy, an independent site or alternate state in which freedom is defined by the captive and war is a structural possibility.

Maroons are not refugees; their camps become their alternate states and sanctuaries. Refugee camps are also comprised of captive maternals in flight. However, refugee camps exist on the largess and under the management of hosting nations and international funders that structure and police them. In Myanmar, authorized by the head of government, former political prisoner and Nobel peace laureate Aung San Suu Kyi, Buddhist military leaders, and their soldiers terrorized, raped, and murdered Rohingya babies, children, youth, men, and mothers. Using the epithet of "black niggers" in their terrorism, they hunted the Muslim Rohingya out of Myanmar. That genocide led to a refugee site in Bangladesh where journalists recorded tortured Muslim mothers of slain and wounded children stating that they would drink poison rather than return to Myanmar. Journalists and international aid organizations offer few accounts of the mothers moving beyond survival and traumatized existence. In the narratives of Western media, their refugee camps are unable to exist as maroon camps.

Even if camps exist for decades, people as refugees hold temporary time in exile as it becomes a permanent fixture of their identities. Having survived a war of ethnic cleansing and/or genocide, they are often depicted as without political agency and political will. Their trauma and escape from it become the defining aspects of their past, present, and future; their time will be counted as "before" and "after" trauma, and transformational time within rebellion is assumed to have been removed from their existence. They become encased in the identity of survivors of torture, of outliving their relatives, including their children, who were not supposed to precede them in death. With the child-rape endemic in Australia's camps on Naru, refugees are portrayed as having rights that were violated, or as apolitical noncombatants fleeing combatants and (para)militaries.

A refugee camp is not identical to a maroon camp, but it can harbor one. Maroon sites bordered antebellum slave democracies and contained defenders of freedom who were portrayed as combative criminals. Those inhabitants have historically been criminalized and hunted as fugitives who possessed the power to destabilize slavery and predatory existential and material capital. To become maroon and theorize as such, register(ed) as a crime punishable by torture and death. From the first captive maternals legally branded by race in the seventeenth-century colonies to the captive maternals trapped in mass incarceration in the twenty-first century, enslaved or contained black females have spent centuries theorizing escape routes in the "new world" (and the "old" under Arab enslavement of Africans).

In democracy, monarchy, dictatorship, and totalitarian regimes, theorizing appears everywhere captive maternals labor, and with that appearance maroonage manifests. Western democracy forced captive maternals to labor to realize its boasts of superiority, only to watch said maternals engineer a black matrix-as-womb within the Western womb of abstract logic, and through that matrix build a fulcrum beneath a political spectrum that ranges from the revolutionary to the counterrevolutionary. The gradualism of inclusivity in liberal democracy allowed de jure citizenship regardless of race, gender, age, or "disability." In theory, all are empowered against predatory utility and consumption, and disposability. In reality, captive maternals, as maroon philosophers or prisoners, could not rend the Western womb sufficiently to prevent its adaptability and capacity to take the generative powers of the slaves it birthed.

Tracing the idealism of democracy to the Athenian polis that she heralds as the antidote to totalitarianism, Hannah Arendt fails to acknowledge the creation and subjugation of captive maternals as a *political phenomenon* and the maternals' reactive, protective theorizing and confrontations as polis-building. Critiques of the democracy organized to steal time and labor while inflicting (racial) pain (de Tocqueville; Guinier; Harris) seem provocative. Yet, white supremacist or nationalist democracies are artificially made through forced breeding, which becomes over time "naturally" reproduced by the conformity of the captives themselves. The violence required to stabilize chattel slavery, corporate-state convict prison leasing, Jim Crow, mass incarceration, police killings, cointelpro and political assassinations of black activists—from Fred Hampton to Marielle Franco—is cultivated alongside theories that idolize democracy. In a racist democracy, whether the United States or Brazil, the chasm between white freedom and black existence is black freedom. Existence is tolerated, freedom is denied. *Maroonage*, a political alternative created when democracy spawned racial slavery, not only defines the territorial reach of antiblack captivity but also measures the distance between the desire to survive and the desire to thrive. Christian's "theorizing" is an antidote to the Western womb only when a black matrix that can resist emerges from that womb.

Conventional theory restricts maternal captives to reproductive labor. Yet, the maternals constantly move or flee beyond constrictions. Their praxes mix political desire, emotional intelligence, and experiential knowledge. From the Latin "breeding female animal" and "mater" or mother, a "matrix" of origins can repurpose black female captivity; the mythologized American founding fathers gestated a revolution out of black captivity to create an imperial democracy.

The black matrix-as-fulcrum leverages theory into political power. Against Western womb theory, a sovereign captive maternal theorizes maroonage as revolutionary rather than escapism. The black matrix can also turn the generative powers of the antirevolutionary captive maternal on the political spectrum: from the revolutionary ethos of former black panther Assata Shakur through the liberalism of FLOTUS Michelle Obama to the reactionary conservativism of Condoleezza Rice, who backed the Supreme Court nominee Brett Kavanaugh, the spectrum stabilized by captive maternals reflects varied ideologies that confront or ignore political trauma inflicted on marginalized peoples. Emotional and physical labor can reproduce black captives who stabilize a tyrannical democracy or black captives who revolt against tyranny. Repression does not inevitably lead to rebellion; rebellion is not inherently transformational. The captive's work and labor can unseat the master/mistress or serve them tea.

The *black matrix* as a fulcrum can leverage against the Western womb. Negatively viewed by some as the terrain of criminality and violence, a site that produces the antisocial and the criminal, terrorism is practiced against the birth site of maroon philosophy, which nonetheless functions to liberate democracy. The captive maternal was born not in nature but in ectogenesis, in an artificial environment of imperial and racial capital, femicide, and forced breeding. The violence of Western womb theory is tied in part to its manufacturing of the artificial and the predatory. Maroonage theorizing, using Audre Lorde as a reference, (1) escapes an artificial womb of pornographic violence, (2) seeks erotic powers in a black matrix partial to freedom, and (3) steals self into maroonage philosophy. If the raison d'être for the captive maternal is to seek her own survival and pleasure in freedom and the flourishing of family, kin, and community, then the "mammy," resilient citizen, and revolutionary all have escaped the confinement of Aristotle's deliberative faculties that sought to rival nature by creating an ectogenetic womb.

WESTERN WOMB THEORY

The deliberative faculty of the soul is not present at all in the slave; in a female it is present but ineffective.

—Aristotle, Politics

Aristotelian predations shape Western theory. Patriarchal enslavement places Aristotle's "deliberative faculty of the soul" as the apex for philosophy and theory. The capacity for consciousness to think critically and comprehensively is attributed solely to those who are neither captive nor female; the signifier of the awakened mind is the sine qua non that defines the fully human. Told that they lack such intellectual capacity, slave and female are forewarned that their tenuous links to "human"—in a world dominated by humans—will be their demise in social and political life. If there must be a "master," then there must be a "slave." This seems a recurring theme in Western womb theory.

In *Introduction to the Reading of Hegel*, Kojeve writes, "Hegel says that the being that is incapable of putting its life in danger in order to attain ends that are not immediately vital—i.e. the being that cannot risk its life in a Fight for Recognition, in a fight for pure prestige—is not a truly human being." Kojeve fails here to see how the "slave" as female racial captive risks the lives of self and progeny.

Embedded and embodied in Aristotle's legacy is a womb for theory for Western philosophers. As a site legitimizing and structuring violence and trauma, it transfers labor and time from the captive maternal to consumers and "superior" humans, the master/slave dynamic. Aristotle's three-part construct is as follows: theorist is free male-as-human; non-theorist is slave-as-antihuman; and defective-theorist is nonslave female-as-semi-human. The "natural order" ignores that (1) action is part of theorizing—the "slave" is created by an act of *enslaving* (not by biology or ontology); (2) ungendering the slave veils power differentials among the enslaved. "Black" often means "black males"; "black females" often refers to cisgendered females; violence disproportionately targets black transgendered women and girls. Adult dominance over children rarely enters the discussion of theory. Violence is not solely traceable and attributed to the Western womb (see Sun Tzu below). But Western womb theory as an empire at war with its shackled issue has the capacity to make violence not only otherworldly but also a testimony to the shining achievements of democracy-as-capital consumption.

The Western womb incubates violence alongside idealism for democracy as an emancipatory and expansive project. The authoritarian womb makes no pretense of its predations and the expendability of populations. Both feed on trauma and time theft from the captive maternal, but only one is supposedly designed to evolve for her protection. Aristotle's three-tier humanity is not only a blind spot; it is also the height of the psychological "illusion of knowledge" in which one's view of the world is a projection of one's need to feel confident within it. The world is not a safe space or place, particularly for captive maternals.

The free theorist—propertied, leisured, empowered—accumulates the time, space, and pleasure of captives. "Lesser humans" are deemed to have a limited capacity for consciousness and thus are relegated to reproductive labor in the private realm of field, factory, household, garden, and nursery. Underground culture is sought out to feed civic democracy, yet stripped of its revolutionary chaos. For as Western womb theory sutures racial-sexual violence to organize social and political development, it channels disruptive chaos or fugitive flight with trauma. Forced labor, rape, enslavement, and genocide continue to build worlds where "slaves" and "females" create the space and leisure for sovereigns. Aristotle's fractured humanity of fully human (free male), partially human (free female), and antihuman (ungendered slave) masks all agency by naturalizing erasure. Aristotle's theory-as-noun meets Christian's theory-as-verb; if "terrorism" is understood from the perspective of the act of terrorizing, not just the experience of suffering, then there is a clash of civilizations of theory. Aristotelian "slaves" lacking deliberative faculties were defeated in war that is terror. In Plato's cave, perhaps hiding from capture, watching the shadow play inside means lost opportunities to dialogue with captive maternals fighting to create alternative worlds outside the cave. It is the prohibition of alternative that safeguards the interests of captive maternals that damages liberatory theory.

Contemporaneous to Aristotle, thirteenth-century Chinese militarist Sun Tzu's *The Art of War* describes executing the emperor's two favorite concubines for jeopardizing his employment due to their coquettish recalcitrance to lead captive women in battle field exercises. Sun Tzu had boasted that he could turn the women into soldiers; his double homicide (femicide) had the tacit approval of the emperor. Chastened by the murders, the remaining women impeccably performed their drills. Impressed by their training, the emperor hired rather than beheaded Sun Tzu. Noting that self-knowledge is a prerequisite for battle, *The Art of War* gives no indication that surviving women turned grief and trauma into deliberations on revenge or flight. The women's telling of time would reasonably become altered by the violence they witnessed and survived. The stealing of captive time and the traumatizing of survivors are key features of political domination and trauma.

TIME THEFT AND TRAUMA

Extraction of resources from the captive maternal is a form of evisceration. The captive maternal herself is probably viewed as a natural resource; assaults on black female anatomy and psychology, what philosopher Janine Jones describes as "plunder," seek to consume captive maternal capacity and autonomy.

The "state of nature" is a state of war, in a Hobbesian sense, until a social contract is established to civilize all parties. No such contract was offered in good faith to ungendered captive maternals. The accumulation of captives and territory produced trauma that altered the balance of power as the promissory for life itself. Imprisonment and captivity dog the lives of all captive maternals. Some live under slave status (caged till the date of emancipation or demise of their "owner"), penal status (duration of legal sentence from conviction until pardon, escape, or death), or maternal status (the duration of the neediness of those one nurtures and their post-mortem life span memorialized as slain children or kin). Wealth supposedly improves health outcomes, but black mothers face increasing maternal and infant mortality rates regardless of income status.

If the #MeToo campaign redresses the sexual assault and violence of powerful white males by focusing on the victimization of influential white females, the rapes in Libya, Italy, Niger, and Sudan against black females, perpetrated by Arabs, Europeans, and Africans, barely register in the national or global press.

Movements against racial captivity and rape are continually created by the women and girls most affected. Such women were traumatized after the legal abolition of slavery when the thirteenth amendment codified slavery or involuntary servitude through conviction and incarceration; then the fourteenth amendment, which was to guarantee civil rights for freed blacks, was gradually repurposed by the Supreme Court to grant political personhood to corporations that often tended to disenfranchised black masses; the fifteenth amendment, the right to vote, was eviscerated through felon disenfranchisement, poll taxes, gerrymandering, and voter ID laws. Like the lost ark, the "lost amendment" US prisoners struck for during the 2016 election—a law to abolish the thirteenth amendment's legalization of slavery—entails the legal right to theorize rebellion, an endeavor outlawed and punished from the founding fathers to the FBI and Homeland Security (whose new "black identity extremist" index delegitimizes black freedom from captivity and deflects from white-supremacist violence).

The economies of pleasure and domination in democracy are tied to bondage of various forms facing the captive maternal. With power understood in its pornographic rather than erotic forms, to use the distinction established by Audre Lorde, the captive maternal necessarily has to reinvent herself in the world through struggle and theorizing.

Part of the struggle is the sexual fetish that encases her in democracy. In the mid-twentieth-century south, Vernon Johns, the fiery forerunner and mentor of Martin Luther King Jr., who was removed as pastor from Dexter Avenue Baptist Church because of his confrontations with white supremacy and more conservative black middle-class parishioners, confronted white police officers raping black women and girls. Johns allegedly placed on Dexter's church marquee in bold letters the title of his forthcoming Sunday sermon, after a heinous rape of one of his parishioners: "When the Rapist Is White." Captive maternal trauma would expand the title: "When the Rapist Is the State."

Trauma is also found in the violation of black female fertility through surrogacy rulings (Allen) and antiblack abortion advocacy. Former secretary of education William Bennett under President Ronald Reagan responded on his 2005 Morning America Talk Show to a caller's query that to "abort black babies before they are born" is the most efficient way to end crime; Bennett admitted in the same conversation that his "final solution" or genocide would be unethical (he failed to note that to end crimes against racial captives and rapes of most whites would require aborting white babies). Yet, political fertility is also a factor to consider.

Captive maternal theorizing about trauma is less about keeping time or score and more about inculcating meanings into life. Captive maternals' labor creates the meanings and measures of time as captive maternals manufacture time for others, providing respite, space, and quiet to think, while captives undertake the mundane chores and deprivations tied to survival of structure. Western theory created the captive maternal to transfer time through appropriation and theft from the laborer to the consumer-captor.

Time is critical in the accumulation of capital and the distribution of punishment. The captive permits the enslaver to be free of reproductive labor, of menial chores and domesticity, of soiling and washing and soiling again hands in garbage, toilets, food production, and sanitation (what the largely unseen cadres of workers perform daily on campuses).

For communities, black time exists as captive time and nonblack time as free time. The prison language of doing hard time while black reflects the racial horrors of incarceration but also suggests the precarities of captive maternals crossing in and out of formal incarceration. Penal culture reflects society; the social order mirrors prisons.

When time and trauma are interwoven into political resistance, captive maternals will alter the former using time to derail mechanisms of trauma and terror. A black mother with a child lynched by the police or state will tell time differently—counting from before the murder and after the murder. A black mourning mother who becomes an active protagonist to minimize state violence will layer another form of counting time upon their loss—before resistance and after resistance began. Decades before the killing of Trayvon Martin, Sandra Bland, Tamir Rice, John Crawford, Michael Brown, and Eric Garner and the acquittals of their killers, black captive maternals in defiance mobilized against self-deputized police who were licensed to murder with impunity. Mamie Till held a 1955 open casket funeral for her lynched fourteen-year-old Emmett. Several months later, Rosa Parks's arrest following her refusal to relinquish a seat on a segregated Montgomery, Alabama, bus created a movement that chose Martin Luther King Jr., a young, obscure pastor, to be its titular leader. In 1976, Soweto maternals buried their massacred black South African school children who were gunned down while chanting and singing refusals to learn the dead white language of Afrikaans from their captors. The anti-apartheid movement that continued to grow was amplified by captive maternals. The movements sparked by black captive maternals across the globe transform trauma and time theft into political power. This act of grace relates to but may differ from the religious expression of grace as sacrifice and forgiveness. The community of captive maternals bringing comfort to grieving mothers, families, and communities is not a "church" codified in state power or canon.

CONCLUSION

The Western womb created a feminized captive caretaker it could not fully control. Captive maternals with the tools and risk-taking willingness to build a fulcrum would leverage theory toward independence. In the December 2017 Alabama senate race, 98 percent of black women and 93 percent of black men, subjugated in a southern state run by white elites, voted to elect Doug Jones with a slim percentage of white voters. Jones had prosecuted the Klan murderers of young maternal activists in the civil rights movement, and four black girls were killed in the 1963 Sixteenth Street Baptist Church bombing in Birmingham, Alabama. In that close election, 63 percent of white women and 72 percent of white men voted for an accused pedophile, the Republican candidate Roy Moore, endorsed by President Donald Trump, despite the credible public testimonies of white women who wept while stating that they had been preyed upon by Moore when he was a district attorney and they were high school students.

In determining the outcome of one of many elections by tilting democracy toward civil rights and away from predator politics, captive maternals have served society despite the fact that the greater democracy would not easily seek solidarity with captive maternals.

WORKS CITED

Allen, Anita. "Surrogacy, Slavery and the Ownership of Life." *Harvard Journal of Law & Public Policy* 13.1 (1990): 139–49.

Blakemore, Erin. "The Slave Roots of Square Dancing." *JSTOR Daily*, June 6, 2017.

Christian, Barbara. "The Race for Theory." *Feminist Studies* 14.1 (Spring, 1988): 67–79.

de Tocqueville, Alexis. *Democracy in America*. Trans. Henry Reeve. London: Saunders and Otley, 1840.

Davis, Angela. "Reflections on the Black Woman's Role in the Community of Slaves." *Black Scholar* 3.4 (December 1971): 2–15.

Freud, Sigmund. *Aetiology of Hysteria*. London: Hogarth P, 1896.

Guinier, Lani. *Tyranny of the Majority*. New York: Free P, 1995.

Hurley, Dan. "Grandma's Experiences Leave Epigenetic Mark on Your Genes," *Discover Magazine*, May 13, 2013. http://discovermagazine.com/2013/may/13-grandmas-experiences-leave-epigenetic-mark-on-your-genes.

Harris, Cheryl. "Whiteness as Property." *Harvard Law Review* 106.8 (June 1993): 1707–91. https://sph.umd.edu/sites/default/files/files/Harris_Whiteness%20as%20Property_106HarvLRev-1.pdf.

Jamison, Philip A. "Dance Calling: The African-American Connection." *Journal of Appalachian Studies* 9.2 (Fall 2003): 387–98.

Kojeve, Alexander. *Introduction to the Reading of Hegel: Lectures on the Phenomenology of Spirit.* Ithaca: Cornell UP, 1969. https://archive.org/stream/pdfyxPoejl7ruL9jyW3_/KOJEVE%20introduction%20to%20the%20reading%20of%20hegel_djvu.txt.

James, Joy. "Afrarealism and the Black Matrix." *Black Scholar* 43.4 (Winter 2013): 124–31.

James, Joy. "Captive Maternal Love." *Literature and the Development of Feminist Theory*. Ed. Robin Truth Goodman. New York: Cambridge UP, 2015.

James, Joy. "The Womb of Western Theory." *Carceral Notebooks, Pt. III, Carceral Logic Today*, vol. 12, 2016.

Lorde, Audre. *Uses of the Erotic: The Erotic as Power*. New York: Crossing Press/Out and Out Books, 1978.

Morrison, Toni. *Playing in the Dark: Whiteness in the Literary Imagination*. Cambridge: Harvard UP, 1993.

Smith, Barbara, et al. "The Combahee River Collective Statement." 1977. https://wgs10016.commons.gc.cuny.edu/combahee-river-collective-black-feminist-statement/.

Tzu, Sun. The Art of War. http://classics.mit.edu/Tzu/artwar.html, translated by Lionel Giles.

Woodard, Vincent. *The Delectable Negro*. New York: New York UP, 2015.

CHAPTER TWENTY-FIVE

Labor

SUSAN FERGUSON

INTRODUCTION

Labor has long been a concern of feminist theory. As early as 1792 in the *Vindication of the Rights of Women*, Mary Wollstonecraft affirms the value of maternal and wifely labors and proposes that the equal education of women would benefit their work as physicians, shopkeepers, and in other professions. Feminists ever since have returned to the topic, often advancing a more critical, nuanced, and complex understanding of what constitutes labor, who labors, under what conditions, and how the value of labor is to be measured. And for more than two hundred years they have proposed strategies for women's emancipation grounded in new ways of imagining women's work.

Within this rich and variable history of feminist thinking about labor, two broad analytic approaches can be discerned. While each identifies the societal devaluing of and restrictions on the work women do as defining features of women's inequality and oppression, they differ in their conceptualizations of social power and, relatedly, in their political projects for women's emancipation. The first focuses on the sexual division of labor, which refers to the social conventions assigning responsibility for physiological reproduction, childrearing, and "domestic work" to women across class societies, while assigning other "productive" tasks to men. This line of criticism condemns the hardships of women's lot thus defined, and the injustice of men's advantageous social and economic position. The nature of women's work and the conditions under which women labor are critically examined against the nature and conditions of the work men do. The sexual division of labor is generally (though not always) rejected as unnatural or unjust. And because freedom is imagined to reside in women's economic independence from men, the main political strategy is the integration of women into the paid workforce on equal footing with men.

The second analytic approach focuses on the ways in which the patriarchal control of women's labor is implicated in the ongoing reproduction of capitalist society. It is not the sexual division of labor itself that explains women's oppression but the fact that it is grounded—in contradictory and partial ways—in the essentially dehumanizing logic of capitalist accumulation. Labor in this reckoning is also conceived broadly, and the value of women's domestic work is affirmed. That value, however, is assessed not only on a moral scale (for its worth in ensuring a good and just society). It is analyzed in political-economic terms (for its worth in securing the continuation of a *capitalist* society). Freedom is here imagined as a total reorganization of *all* labor in order to disrupt capitalism's tendency to privatize and dehumanize the production processes involved in meeting subsistence needs.

This chapter reviews the historical trajectories of these two analyses, hereafter referred to as "equality feminism" and "social reproduction feminism." It reaches back in a necessarily cursory fashion through the past two centuries to highlight their related-yet-distinct understandings of the significance of labor in feminist thought. The chapter also critiques the individualism and class limitations of the lens through which equality feminism views the world of women's work—limitations that, I suggest, the social reproduction feminist approach pushes beyond.

EARLY FEMINISM: LABOR'S EQUALIZING POTENTIAL

What women *do*—and, what they have been *prevented from doing*—constitutes much of their actual experience of oppression. So it is not surprising that "work" features as a prominent concern in early feminist theorizing. Writing at the beginning of the first industrial revolution, many feminists accepted the gendered division of labor that cast women as naturally suited to running households and childrearing. Yet, they nonetheless called for reforms to address women's and men's unequal relationship to labor. In *Vindication*, for instance, Wollstonecraft argues that opening up education in the classics to women "of the middle rank" and "the superior class" will both prove and improve women's capacities to apply rational and moral principles to their domestic duties (which she sees as their natural calling), as well as to their occupations (she mentions physician, nursing, midwifery, and running a shop or a farm) (ch. 4). Other radical democrats of the 1790s ventured more direct critiques of women's position in the labor market. Olympe de Gouges advocates for men and women to share equally in all "positions, employment, offices, honors, and jobs" (art. XIII), while Mary Anne Radcliffe cites men's usurpation of waged work as the "grand cause" of women's poverty and their consequent turn to thieving and prostitution (86). Rather than think ill of those who have no choice but "to seek bread in the paths of vice," she urges, society should offer charity and work (46).

In all these accounts, labor itself is viewed positively. Useful, rational work is proposed as a corrective to women's degradation and inequality, as well as to the corruption of their character wrought by society's ill treatment of them. In fact, Wollstonecraft and Radcliffe suggest that wealthier women have something to learn from the "industriousness" of their poorer, working sisters. Neither considers the servile nature and hardships of women's domestic or other menial work a feminist issue. Wollstonecraft makes this point most clearly in her portrayal of equal and free relations between the sexes, a scene in which the wife depends upon "merely a servant maid to take off her hands the servile part of the household business" (ch. 9). Equality, it seems, is to be achieved on the condition that an industrious poor woman is available to scrub the floors and change the diapers.

In other words, early feminist contemplations of women's relation to labor rest on a *naturalization* of capitalist class relations.[1] This is a theme that runs through the equality feminist analytic for the next two hundred years. Two further—more progressive—themes are also apparent in these early accounts. First, while relatively indifferent to domestic labor, these feminists offer some critical insight into the sexual division of labor in the paid workforce, with Radcliffe explicitly challenging the naturalization of gender roles barring women from certain occupations. Second, Radcliffe specifically positions financial independence as a feminist goal. The path to equality and freedom, she suggests, lies in improving women's access to paid work. This emphasis on labor's equalizing potential is, as we will see, embraced not just by later liberal feminists, but also by many socialist feminists.

THE PROBLEM OF DOMESTIC LABOR

A more critical approach to theorizing labor finds its roots in the nineteenth century when feminists began to pay more attention to childrearing and maintaining a household. Rather than a matter of women's duty, they proposed that such activities were not inherently uplifting even if socially valuable. Their analyses led to some surprisingly modern-sounding proposals for easing the burdens of domestic labor and refashioning what women's independence might look like. They also opened the door to criticizing the class contours of women's labor.

That door opened most widely in 1820s Britain. In their 1825 treatise, Utopian Socialists William Thompson and Anna Wheeler describe women's domestic enslavement in admonishing tones, referring to the home as "the eternal prison-house of the wife" (79).[2] But they move beyond moral condemnation to a political-economic critique. The key, if not fully developed, insight they advanced is that capitalism is not simply sustained by the exploitation of waged labor; it also crucially depends upon the *privatization* of (women's) domestic labor, and thus on women's oppression. That is, the economic system is, at heart, also a system of gender oppression precisely because domestic labor is, in capitalism, a private affair.

Although this insight inspired experiments in communitarian living arrangements for many years to come, it remained undeveloped as a *theory* of women's oppression.[3] In his 1884 book, *The Origin of the Family, Private Property and the State*, Frederick Engels instead explains that the historic shift from communally held property to private property concentrated wealth in men's hands, causing them to take "command in the home," while women were "degraded and reduced to servitude" (120–1). But because workers do not own property under capitalism, he reasons, patriarchy lacks a material foundation within their class. In his estimation, (as in Marx's), women should join the waged labor force to gain the independence needed to confront whatever vestiges of patriarchy remain in their homes. As waged workers, they can then take part in the collective struggle to overturn capitalism (and with it, the materialist basis—private property—of women's oppression).[4] Rather than develop the idea that women's domestic labor is a cornerstone in the capitalist edifice, Engels advanced a variation of the theory of the equalizing potential of women's paid labor.

Engels's position dominated the Marxist Left for the following century, with the question of domestic labor surfacing periodically. Two classic histories of women's work reveal two divergent perspectives: Alice Clark's 1919 *Working Life of Women in the Seventeenth Century* and Ivy Pinchbeck's *Women Workers and the Industrial Revolution 1750–1850*, published eleven years later. Tracking the shift from agrarian household to piecework to factory production, Pinchbeck presents a triumphalist picture in which the hardships of women's paid work gradually diminish as technology, capitalist concessions to organized labor, and state regulations coalesce to improve their lot. By the end of the industrial revolution, she insists, single women could count on financial independence, and "the emancipation of working women had definitely begun" (314). Clark, on the other hand, is much less optimistic. Capitalist industrialization, she argues, undermined women's "productive capacity" (290) making life much harder for working-class women, in part because they were now concentrated in the lower paid jobs. Along with being among the first to clearly articulate the ghettoization of women's waged labor, she raises the question of the relationship between women's paid and unpaid labor, proposing that the latter is equally productive as paid work.

Whereas much of the organized socialist Left tended to shun arguments about domestic labor, considering them irrelevant to their political project, liberal feminists embraced them. Instead of inquiring into how cooking and cleaning sustain capitalism, however, they adopted and extended a moral, individualist critique leading to strategies to release women from housework's drudgery. Their numerous proposals range from advocating that men share in "the common household burdens" (Blackwell 155) to imagining technological advances in cleaning and waste disposal. Others insightfully drew a direct line between unpaid and paid labor, and proposed that standards and regulations that applied in industry also be instituted in homes. Rather than wait for men to do women's work, Charlotte Perkins Gilman suggests that the work of "heating, lighting, feeding, clothing and cleaning" be organized into a "large, well-managed business combination ... [ensuring] regular hours of labor and free time of rest." She also advocates "liberal payment for each grade of service" (177–8). Decades later, Edith Stern extends this line of reasoning. The housewife is the "Forgotten Worker" who enjoys no minimum wage, no health and safety standards, no mandated periods of rest, she laments. "Free individuals, in a democracy perform personal services for themselves or, if they have cash, pay other free individuals to wait on them" (353).

Instead of disrupting the competitive system, these feminists believed that women's freedom could be secured through improving it. Capitalistically produced goods and services and the absorption of domestic labor into regulated capitalist production relations would release women from the bondage of the home. While their critiques assert the social value of unpaid housework and childrearing, however, they never question why the division between paid and unpaid work exists in the first place. And neither do they acknowledge the specific oppressive experiences of the class of workers who will produce the goods and services that will supposedly emancipate women, most of whom are also women. Rather, waged labor and Stern's "free individual," available to either pay for it or perform it, are held up as the model and means of independence and freedom.

The insufficiently theorized relation of paid and unpaid work continued to haunt the feminist agenda in the post–Second World War era. A sustained growth in productivity and expanding social security provisions led to many—though not all—workers enjoying higher wages and an improved standard of living. This relative affluence, which was disproportionately enjoyed by white, male-headed households in North America and Western Europe, permitted certain working-class women to opt out of paid labor.[5] Full-time (unpaid) mothering and "housewifery" came to be the model of womanhood for increasing numbers of women. Yet, while the idea that women's oppression was grounded in domestic labor's drudgery and isolating effects resonated with many housewives, it eclipsed the experiences of millions of immigrant and black women. These were the women who mopped the floors and wiped the children's noses in homes other than their own—in *white* homes—for very, very low pay and little control over the conditions of their labor. As Angela Davis eloquently writes about black American women, "While they have seldom been 'just housewives' they have always done their housework" (231).

Indeed, Claudia Jones, writing in 1949, points out that along with tending to their own homes, black women in the United States were twice as likely as white women to work for a living—and to do so for less than half the wages. Domestic labor for these women was thus neither a marker of middle-class status nor an isolating experience. Rather, *paid* domestic labor indicated poverty *and* racism. And this is Jones's central point. Calling out the "super-exploitation" and "degradation" of black women, Jones presages later black feminist theorizations of "intersecting" oppressions by insisting that the "Negro woman ... [faces] special oppression ... as Negro, as woman, and as worker" (7). What's more, Black women's *unpaid* housework and childrearing has its own distinct history and meaning.

Jones introduced considerable complexity to the feminist understanding of women's labor and social power. While (like her Communist Party brethren) Jones saw the key to (black) women's emancipation as fighting for the betterment of their wages and conditions, she moved beyond them in arguing that labor isn't just an "economic" issue. She insisted that, because the American workforce is so thoroughly racialized, there can be no improvement for all until racism is also confronted and destroyed. This is a radical and important innovation. It situates women's paid labor as inextricably tied not only to sexism but also to racism, raising the specter of—if not fully analyzing—a wider systemic logic. Sadly, it surfaced only to be quickly passed over. The Communist Party of the United States and the labor movement to whom Jones made her plea failed to build upon these insights, while mainstream feminists ignored them.

The latter did address women's double burden of paid and unpaid work, but without acknowledging all the rich complexity of racialized women's work. The National Organization for Women (NOW) 1966 "Statement of Purpose," for instance, proposes that technology can liberate women from domestic duties—which the authors describe as "a most important part" of women's lives. Rejecting the notion that women should choose between motherhood and career, it proposes "partnership" marriages, childcare centers, and job retraining—echoing the individualist and market-based policies of an earlier era's feminism. Such measures promote women's economic independence, helping to move them out of poorly paid service-sector jobs. The Statement authors observe, but do not analyze or draw any political conclusions from, the racialized nature of the workforce.

In these 150 years of feminist thinking about labor, then, we see a continued assertion of the social value of domestic labor and a growing willingness to critically inspect the conditions under which women perform household work. Thompson and Wheeler identify its significance in the reproduction and expansion of capitalism in the 1820s, but most later socialists do not pursue this nascent political-economic analysis. Instead, they elaborate a moral critique and advance a variation of equality feminism. Similarly, Jones's effort to racialize the analysis of paid and unpaid labor is not sustained. Rather, by the 1960s, women's emancipation is largely defined in terms of the freedom to choose between different types of work: motherhood or career, or both.

Arguably, the vision of paid labor as emancipatory has dominated the liberal feminist agenda ever since. It informed feminist development analyses and initiatives in the 1970s and 1980s that sought to integrate women in Global South countries into the formal economy (Rathgeber; Reeves and Baden). And despite critics, the United Nations and many nongovernmental agencies continue to work within this paradigm, most recently in its neoliberal guise which promotes the extension of microcredit to poor women to finance their entrepreneurial ventures (Rankin). Access to higher education, professional jobs, and executive boardrooms is the key strategy of today's mainstream feminism in the Global North as well. Whether it is politicians like Hillary Clinton whose Twitter feed rhapsodizes, "To every little girl who dreams big: Yes, you can be anything you want—even president," or business leaders like Sheryl Sandberg, author of *Lean In*, "corporate feminism" (Burnham) today picks up on this one strand of feminist critique—the argument that women's freedom requires equalizing their chances in an unequal labor (and corporate executive) market.

Such a feminist vision does not escape the contradictions associated with equality feminism of centuries past. However important it is for women to be treated equally alongside men in the workforce, the vast majority of women—in the Global South and North—cannot truly choose between motherhood and career, or even just a job. And most of them work at jobs too far removed from company boardrooms for "leaning in" to be meaningful. They also know too well that women's oppression does not stop at the factory gates or office lobby. For those who do have well-paying jobs, choosing motherhood regularly depends upon other (and generally *otherized*, e.g., racialized) women being available to take on the drudgery of domestic labor—the twenty-first-century equivalent of Wollstonecraft's "mere servant maid" tending to the "servile part of the household business."

A POLITICAL ECONOMY OF WOMEN'S LABOR

This is what makes the twentieth-century revival of the Utopian Socialist insight about domestic labor so important and inspiring today. That story begins with the publication in 1969 of "The Political Economy of Women's Liberation" by Margaret Benston. With this article, Benston moved beyond a moral-political critique of housework as isolating and oppressive to develop a socio-materialist analysis of it, and in so doing laid the groundwork for a theory of capitalism's intrinsically patriarchal nature. Using Marxist concepts, she proposed that domestic labor is *economically (and thus capitalistically) productive* labor.[6] That is, household tasks women perform to prepare their husbands and children to be present and future workers are essential to capitalist processes of value creation.[7] This is because the products of domestic labor—the food, clothing, and care of bodies—ensure an ongoing supply of the human labor power required to generate *economic* (or *exchange*) value for capital. In other words, women's domestic labor *socially reproduces* labor power for capital.[8]

Yet, organized in private households and undertaken by women who perform it not for pay but because the patriarchal gender relations demand as much, domestic labor is not something whose value can be measured capitalistically. It is therefore deemed *unproductive* (both in Marxian economics and in mainstream estimations of a society's economic activity, such as the Gross National Product).[9] Similarly, presumed a private affair, it is granted little cultural recognition. So long as domestic work is organized in this fashion, Benston argues, women cannot be free: "Equal access to jobs outside the home, while one of the preconditions for women's liberation, will not in itself be sufficient to give equality for women; as long as work in the home remains a matter of private production and is the responsibility of women, they will simply carry a double work-load" (21).

An international feminist political and intellectual community enthusiastically greeted Benston's article, debating and further developing its premises (Miles). For the better part of the decade, feminists grappled with the questions: what is the relationship between domestic labor and value-productive labor? Does the former directly create surplus value or not? How precisely does the patriarchal organization of housework intersect with the capitalist organization of productive labor? More than just an academic debate, the "Domestic Labor Debate" fueled the International Wages for Housework (IWHW) campaign, launched in 1972 (Katsarova). Campaign cofounders Mariarosa Dalla Costa and

Selma James argued (against Benston who proposed housework comprises a distinct noncapitalist mode of production) that domestic labor is, in the capitalistic sense, productive labor. And since it is directly creative of surplus value, they reasoned, women who perform it are entitled to a wage.

While the IWHW campaign effectively politicized domestic labor, its critics raised different concerns. Some noted that payments for housework would extend capitalist exploitation to the domestic sphere, while others interpreted the campaign, and social reproduction feminism more generally, as universalizing women's experiences of oppression, reductively assuming all women share the isolation devaluation and invisibility of the middle-class housewife (Weeks; Molyneux). Meanwhile, Marxist-Feminism was losing ground as an intellectual current. Heidi Hartmann famously criticized it for politically and theoretically subsuming women's issues in class struggles, and failing to address men's purported material interest in women's oppression. Meanwhile, a revived black feminism pointed to its failure to theoretically engage with issues of racism (Mohanty; Davis). By the 1980s, an aggressive ruling-class offensive had effectively beaten back the labor and social movements that had earlier galvanized dissent, and the project of articulating a comprehensive theory of patriarchal capitalism based upon a political economic critique of women's reproductive labor lost traction.

Yet, as most Left feminists abandoned Marx for Derrida and Foucault, some continued to develop the social reproduction feminism paradigm (see Bezanson and Luxton). One important advance came with the publication in 1983 of *Marxism and the Oppression of Women: Toward a Unitary Theory*. Its author, Lise Vogel, takes up where the Domestic Labor Debate left off, but points to a path beyond its political and theoretical impasses. She argues (*with* Benston, and *against* Dalla Costa and James) that domestic labor produces use values (not exchange value). And she further proposes (*against* Benston and *with* Dalla Costa and James) that domestic labor does not constitute a mode of production outside of capitalism. Rather, Vogel advances an understanding of capitalism as comprising intertwined and contradictory economic and extra-economic dynamics. In her reading, patriarchy and capitalism are not two distinct-yet-intersecting systems, but form an inseparable—unitary—system, one in which neither form of domination is reducible to the other. As I suggest elsewhere, Vogel thereby moves the analysis of capitalism onto more dialectical terrain, one that positions its parts (e.g., labor/capital relations and gender relations) as integrally related aspects of a capitalist totality while sustaining and reproducing difference or particularity within that totality (Ferguson). All this she accomplishes by engaging with and extending a theory of the duality of social reproductive labor, insisting that it is both useful and abstract, both inside and outside the direct labor/capital relation, and both in contradiction with and essential to the reproduction of capitalism.

A point of clarification should be made before leaving the discussion of Vogel's contribution. It may appear that she is simply re-asserting the white middle-class preoccupation with women's housework because the focus is still on unpaid domestic labor. She is not. Vogel's key theoretical advance is to locate women's oppression not in domestic labor per se, but in the gendered relations of biological and social reproduction of people, and specifically in the contradictions that characterize the relation of social reproduction to paid waged labor. Because women are—by virtue of the social organization of their biological capacities to give birth and nurse infants—situated at the crux of that contradiction, Vogel posits this relationship as furnishing a socio-material logic to the ongoing oppression women experience under capitalism. This is not the same thing as saying that all women's experiences as domestic laborers are inherently oppressive. Rather, the point is that capitalism's incessant and powerful need for workers—for the ongoing (re)production of life—leads it to incorporate any and all practices, institutions, and relations to meet those ends. The privatized family and women's domestic labor therein has been, and continues to be, a primary means of producing labor. But it is not the only one (think of the role schools, hospitals, daycares, restaurants, and prisons play in this regard).[10] Nor is the family always organized along patriarchal lines: single-parent, female heads of households are still oppressed, for example, despite their domestic labor not benefitting any particular adult men.

CAPITALISM'S COMPLEX SOCIAL REPRODUCTIVE LABOR

Another way of thinking about all this is to consider that the bodies of workers are not accidental to the capitalist process of accumulation. They must be disciplined and differentiated—to be workers certainly, but also to be different sorts of workers. Some— *many*—must be workers willing (or who have no choice but) to perform dangerous, arduous jobs at irregular hours for low pay. They must be, in other words, workers *who can reproduce themselves and others in ways that keep their costs of social reproduction as low as possible*. A focus on global capitalism suggests that bodies, and their insertion into social reproductive processes, are not only differentiated biologically. They are also spatially and socially located in a global capitalist terrain marked by national borders and imperialist power relations (see Ferguson and McNally). These hierarchical geo-social relations create opportunities for the systemic cheapening of some lives, a process that draws upon and reinstates racist, colonialist (as well as sexist and hetero-sexist) practices and institutions. This dynamic comes to light when examining labor's social reproduction across socio-spatial difference—by tracking, for instance, regimes of migration within nations or across international borders. Such regimes are found throughout capitalism's long history, from the great wave of Irish workers who landed jobs in Britain's nineteenth-century textile mills, blast furnaces, and bourgeois homes, and the millions of bonded Africans toiling on American plantations, to the present-day 200-million-plus international migrant workers who mind other people's children, harvest and process farm produce, and mine the earth's riches in countries other than those they hold citizenship in.

Hardly a matter simply of the "free" movement of "free" labor, the arrival at capital's doorstep of a relatively cheap, already racialized and/or colonized workforce is a result of forces of domination and coercion. The coercive underbelly of capitalism's global labor market involves, in the first instance, state-sanctioned dispossession of indigenous communities, small landholders and craft workers, and the undermining of domestic production units (Mies; Federici). It also involves reliance on various forms of unfree labor, from outright slavery to debt bondage to so-called temporary migrants denied basic rights of citizenship (LeBaron; Banaji).[11] It is exercised through a global framework of wars, borders, trade and investment agreements, surveillance, and policing—mechanisms ensuring that capitalists don't just get any labor power, but that they get workers who are racialized, colonial subjects. And as labor is ever cheaper to reproduce, it becomes in fact "disposable" (Wright). That is, there is a point at which labor is socially reproduced at the barest minimum costs, at which the simultaneous reproduction of human life and labor power is no longer so much of a contradiction. For, at this point, Alessandra Mezzadri suggests, "capital can consume workers' bodies without major concerns for profitability.

After all, upon the depletion of some, others can be made available at the same cheap rates" (161).

To most fully grasp the differential dehumanization of laboring bodies that occurs as part of sustaining capitalist social relations, however, we need to look not only to Marxism and social reproduction feminism, but also to feminist traditions focused on problems of difference, culture, and identity.

Robin Truth Goodman does just this in her 2013 book, *Gender Work: Feminism after Neoliberalism*, tracing a line of thinking about "women's work" running through certain poststructuralist accounts of the subject. She proposes that "women's work" (the work of care, service, affect, and socialization) comes to play the role of language in organizing the social (most fully in Aihwa Ong's account of the cultural logic of global capitalism). Yet, its signifying powers break down precisely because, as Kristeva insists, life exceeds representation. Subjects are thus formed in relation to both work and to "a nonconceptual imaginary, where we are more than what we do within the global productive matrix and its enterprises" (Goodman 108). Goodman then relates this culturalist concern with subject formation to the production/reproduction contradiction that inhabits capitalism, following Michael Hardt's and Antonio Negri's critique of neoliberal capitalism's tendency to subsume life to work. She emphasizes that the "so-called feminization of work" Hardt and Negri identify is neoliberalism's mechanism for *intensifying* exploitation (171). It is not just any laboring subject that is of value to capital; it is the laboring subject who is devalued by their prior and ongoing feminization. Melissa Wright provides a compelling example of this tendency in her study of women workers at a Mexican television factory. In her 2006 book, *Disposable Women and other Myths of Global Capitalism*, she draws on Butler's theory of embodied subjectivity to show how feminized *mexicanas* are valued as maquiladora workers precisely because their (mythic) "third world and female corporality" (14) marks them as "perpetually unskilled and untrainable" (47)—bodies to be used up and disposed of when their value to capital is depleted.

But even as "women's work" is internal to capitalism, observes Goodman, it remains separate from it. This is because the reproduction of life—producing to meet human needs that will sustain this and future workforces—is not reducible to the rhythms and pace of capitalistic production. It demands a different temporality. The work of biological reproduction, caretaking, serving, and socialization that is involved in producing laboring subjects creates and fulfills needs and desires that are "excessive to capital, uncontainable, or untranslatable by it" (160). As such, "women's work" constitutes the creative grounds to move beyond capitalism.[12]

Rosemary Hennessy approaches this same point about the contradictory interplay of cultural and economic value in producing laboring subjects by engaging discussions in queer theory about "the materiality of affect." While agreeing that affects (the sensations and emotions that register in the body) are multiple and open-ended, she also proposes that their "indeterminacy is grounded in the historical organization of the social relations that support life" (44) or, more precisely, that produce and meet human needs. Given the systemic pressure to reduce the costs of the wages and social services on which the working class's very survival depends in order to increase profitability, capitalist "historical organization" is characterized by the systemic production of *unmet* human needs. Reproductive labor, Hennessy argues, thus constantly negotiates a dominant "affect-culture" that calls for disciplining expansive sensations and feelings in the service of creating value for capital (50). Moreover, because workers sell part of themselves (their human capacities) to capital for a wage, they all wear what she calls "a second skin"—an embodied (degraded) identity that appears natural but that is in fact changeable, "open to history … [and thus becomes] sites of struggle" (126). And those workers who tend to people's most intimate needs for bodily and emotional caretaking—the paid and unpaid work of feeding, child and elder care, and housework—bear particularly feminized, sexualized, and/or racialized second skins.

CONCLUSION

Goodman, Wright, and Hennessy extend the social reproduction analytic to account for the particularity of the laboring subject. Mindful of the cultural dynamics and embodied processes of subject formation, their contributions grapple with the complexities involved in theorizing labor as a concrete, lived capitalist reality. This is a concept of labor that identifies common capitalist conditions of dispossession and accumulation, and the contradictory relationship between capitalist production and reproduction, but also recognizes that labor is differentiated in and through the racialized, sexualized, and gendered relations inflecting those conditions. It is, as well, a concept of labor that foregrounds the generative, creative aspect of people's everyday practical human activity—activity that holds within it the potential to create new worlds in new ways. Thus, a social reproduction feminist approach invokes and mines a rich theoretical terrain, one that moves well beyond equality feminism's optimistic assessment of paid labor as the site of women's equality and freedom and the contradictions associated with that position. It suggests that it is the capitalist organization of work—paid and unpaid—that perpetuates gendered (as well as racialized, heterosexualized, and colonized) unfreedom, seeing in social reproductive labor the systemic thwarting of meeting life's needs. And it counsels a rejection of that organization, and a refiguring of labor relations in ways that align with and meet human needs.

NOTES

1 1790s radical democrats, in general, criticized *inequality*, not *capitalism* and *class* dynamics.
2 The *Appeal* bears Thompson's name, but he attributes the ideas in it to Wheeler.
3 See Hayden, and also Siegel for discussions of US experiments in socializing domestic work.
4 Engels saw the end of capitalism as also involving the socialization of housekeeping, childcare, and education. But nowhere did he suggest these tasks are integral to capitalism's ongoing reproduction.
5 Not only did African Americans and other immigrants share unequally in the prosperity of the era, racist eligibility criteria for public assistant measures such as Aid for Dependent Children in the United States (later known as Aid for Families with Dependent Children) also prevented many from drawing on state resources to the same degree as white families (Nadasen).
6 "Productive" labor, in the Marxist lexicon, refers to that which directly generates surplus value for capitalists. Benston, and many other social reproduction feminists, often confusedly move between this specific analytic meaning of the term and a more conventional definition.
7 Benston assumes a heterosexual, nuclear family.
8 Benston, however, did not use the term socially reproductive labor.
9 The Marxian concept of productive labor is designed to reveal the logic of capital, whereas mainstream economics uses it to measure output.

10 See Picchio, and also Seccombe for discussions about the role of the state in social reproduction.

11 Banaji suggests that, historically, capitalist labor is better characterized by varying degrees of unfreedom.

12 For more on this point, see Hennessy; Weeks.

WORKS CITED

Banaji, Jairus. "The Fictions of Free Labour: Contract, Coercion and So-called Unfree Labour." *Historical Materialism* 11.3 (2003): 69–95.

Benston, Margaret. "The Political Economy of Women's Liberation." *Monthly Review*, September 1969, pp. 13–27.

Bezanson, Kate, and Meg Luxton. "Introduction: Social Reproduction and Feminist Political Economy." *Social Reproduction: Feminist Political Economy Challenges Neo-Liberalism*. Ed. Kate Bezanson and Meg Luxton, Kingston: McGill-Queen's UP, 2006, pp. 3–11.

Brown Blackwell, Antoinette. "Relation of Women's Work in the Household to Work Outside." *Up from the Pedestal: Selected Writings in the History of American Feminism*. Ed. Aileen S. Kraditor. New York: Quadrangle Books, [1873] 1975, pp. 150–9.

Burnham, Linda. "1% Feminism." *Open Democracy*, April 13, 2013. https://www.opendemocracy.net/5050/linda-burnham/1-feminism. Accessed August 1, 2017.

Clark, Alice. *Working Life of Women in the Seventeenth Century*. New York: Routledge, [1919] 1992.

Clinton, Hillary. "To Every Little Girl Who Dreams Big: Yes, You Can Be Anything You Want—Even President. Tonight Is for You.—H." *Twitter*, June 7, 2016, 6:08 p.m. https://twitter.com/HillaryClinton/status/740349871073398785.

Dalla Costa, Mariarosa, and Selma James. *The Power of Women and the Subversion of the Community*. Bristol: Falling Wall P, 1973.

Davis, Angela. *Women, Race and Class*. London: Women's P, 1982.

De Gouges, Olympe. *Declaration of the Rights of Women and Citizens*. 1791. http://www.fmyv.es/ci/in/women/3.pdf. *Fundación Márgenes y Vínculos* (Margins and Links Foundation). Accessed August 1, 2017.

Engels, Frederick. *The Origin of the Family, Private Property and the State*. New York: International, [1884] 1972.

Federici, Silvia. *Caliban and the Witch: Women, the Body and Primitive Accumulation*. New York: Autonomedia, 2004.

Ferguson, Susan. "Intersectionality and Social-Reproduction Feminisms: Toward an Integrative Theory." *Historical Materialism* 24.2 (2016): 38–60.

Ferguson, Susan, and David McNally. "Precarious Migrants: Gender, Race and the Social Reproduction of a Global Working Class." *Socialist Register 2015: Transforming Classes*. Ed. Leo Panitch and Greg Albo. London: Merlin P, 2014, pp. 1–23.

Goodman. Robin Truth. *Gender Work: Feminism after Neoliberalism*. New York: Palgrave Macmillan, 2013.

Hartmann, Heidi. "The Unhappy Marriage of Marxism and Feminism: Towards a More Progressive Union." *Capital & Class* 3.2 (Summer, 1979): 1–33.

Hayden, Dolores. *The Grand Domestic Revolution: A History of Feminist Designs for American Homes, Neighborhoods, and Cities*. Cambridge, MA: MIT P, 1982.

Hennessy, Rosemary. *Fires on the Border: The Passionate Politics of Labor Organizing on the Mexican Frontera*. Minneapolis: U of Minnesota P, 2013.

Jones, Claudia. *An End to the Neglect of the Problems of the Negro Woman!* Political Affairs. National Women's Commission, CPUSA. University of California Digital Library, June, 1949, p. 5. http://purl.flvc.org/FCLA/DT/1927554. Accessed August 1, 2017.

Katsarova, Rada. "Repression and Resistance on the Terrain of Social Reproduction: Historical Trajectories, Contemporary Openings." *Viewpoint Magazine*, issue 5, October 31, 2015. https://www.viewpointmag.com/2015/10/31/repression-and-resistance-on-the-terrain-of-social-reproduction-historical-trajectories-contemporary-openings/. Accessed August 1, 2017.

LeBaron, Genevieve. "Unfree Labor beyond Binaries: Social Hierarchy, Insecurity, and Labor Market Restructuring." *International Feminist Journal of Politics* 17.1 (2014): 1–19.

Mezzadri, Alessandra. *The Sweatshop Regime: Labouring Bodies, Exploitation, and Garments Made in India*. Cambridge: Cambridge University Press, 2017.

Mies, Maria. *Patriarchy & Accumulation on a World Scale: Women in the International Division of Labour*. London: Zed Books, 1998.

Miles, Angela. "Margaret Benston's 'Political Economy of Women's Liberation: International Impact." *Canadian Women's Studies/Les cahiers de la femme* 13.2 (1993): 31–5.

Mohanty, Chandra Talpade. "Under Western Eyes: Feminist Scholarship and Colonial Difference." *boundary* 2.12–13 (1984): 333–58.

Molyneux, Maxine. "Beyond the Domestic Labor Debate." *New Left Review* 116 (1979): 3–27.

Nadasen, Premilla. *Welfare Warriors: The Welfare Rights Movement in the United States*. New York: Routledge, 2005.

Perkins Gillman, Charlotte. "Economic Basis of the Woman Question." *Up from the Pedestal: Selected Writings in the History of American Feminism*. Ed. Aileen S. Kraditor. New York: Quadrangle Books, [1898] 1975, pp. 175–8.

Picchio, Antonella. *Social Reproduction: The Political Economy of the Labour Market*. Cambridge: Cambridge University Press, 1992.

Pinchbeck, Ivy. *Women Workers and the Industrial Revolution 1750–1850*. London: Virago P, [1930] 1985.

Radcliffe, Mary Anne. *The Female Advocate: Or an Attempt to Recover the Rights of Women from Male Usurpation*. London: Vernor and Hood (Printed for Vernor and Hood, No. 31, Poultry), 1799. http://ota.ox.ac.uk/text/5092.html. Accessed August 1, 2017.

Rankin, Katharine N. "Governing Development: Neoliberalism, Microcredit, and Rational Economic Woman." *Economy and Society* 30.1 (2001): 18–37.

Rathgeber, Eva M. "WID, WAD, GAD: Trends in Research and Practice." *The Journal of Developing Areas* 24.4 (1990): 289–302.

Reeves, Hazel, and Sally Baden. *Gender and Development: Concepts and Definitions*. London: Institute of Development Studies, 2000.

Seccombe, Wally. *Weathering the Storm: Working-Class Families from the Industrial Revolution to the Fertility Decline*. New York: Verso Books, 1993.

Siegel, Reva B. "Home as Work: The First Women's Rights Claims Concerning Wives' Household Labor, 1850–1880." *Yale Law Journal* 103 (1993–4): 1073–217.

"Statement of Purpose." *National Organization for Women*, 1966. http://now.org/about/history/statement-of-purpose/. Accessed August 1, 2017.

Stern, Edith. "Women Are Household Slaves." 1949. *Up from the Pedestal: Selected Writings in the History of American Feminism*. Ed. Aileen S. Kraditor. New York: Quadrangle Books, 1975, pp. 346–53.

Thompson, William. *Appeal of One Half the Human Race, Women, Against the Pretensions of the Other Half, Men, to Retain Them in Political, and Thence in Civil and Domestic Slavery.* London: Longman, Hurst Rees, Orme, Brown & Green, 1825.

Weeks, Kathi. *The Problem with Work: Feminism, Marxism, Antiwork Politics, and Postwork Imaginaries.* Durham, NC: Duke UP, 2011.

Wollstonecraft, Mary. *Vindication of the Rights of Women.* Boston: Peter Edes, 1792; *Bartleby.com*, 1999. http://www.bartleby.com/144/. Accessed August 1, 2017.

Wright, Melissa. *Disposable Women and Other Myths of Global Capitalism.* New York: Routledge, 2006.

CHAPTER TWENTY-SIX

Commodity

ROBIN TRUTH GOODMAN

In business, as in life, nothing is ever handed to you.

—Ivanka Trump

A core argument in feminist theory centers on the connection of women and commodities in exchange. This chapter revises the way feminist theory has understood the relationship between gender and the commodity by situating the commodity within the culture of the neoliberal state which profits from the marketability of private life and the reproductive economy.

Traditionally, the relationship between women and commodities has been understood through an "exchange of women" narrative, borrowed from the French structuralist anthropologist Claude Lévi-Strauss, where women are exchanged between groups of men, creating an alliance between those men. "The duality that appears within societies under one form or another," writes, for example, Simone de Beauvoir in her inaugural feminist text, *The Second Sex*, "opposes a group of men to a group of men; women constitute a part of the property which each of these groups possesses and which is a medium of exchange between them" (70–1). As the formative and communicative link in the social bond, women are seen to strengthen the identity of the community and transmit it over time: as Beauvoir continues, "The community sensed its unity and desired a continued existence beyond the present; it recognized itself in its children, recognized them as its own; and in them it found fulfillment and transcendence" (67). In this "tribal" scenario that feminism projects onto premodern social relations to explain the cause of modern women's oppression, women—because they are so embedded in the intimacies at the heart of cultural life, as identity—maintain a connection to the community from which they are traded, a connection they bring to the community they are married into. This gives them an essential value "ready" for exchange.

Furthermore, this "exchange of women" has become one of the motifs for discussions in feminism about the status of gender and sexuality in relation to the Symbolic. As Judith Butler summarizes this link, "the regulated cultural mechanism of transforming biological males and females into discrete and hierarchized genders, is at once mandated by cultural institutions (the family, *the residual forms of 'the exchange of women,'* obligatory heterosexuality) and inculcated through the laws which structure and propel individual psychic development" (*Gender Trouble* 100, my emphasis). Following Sigmund Freud's and Claude Lévi-Strauss's treatment of the "exchange of women" as a prohibition against incest that results in cross-tribal filiation or, in Freud's case, peaceful reconciliation and psychic balance, the "exchange of women" has become a formative site for analyzing "gender" as a cultural and historically stabilizing phenomenon that does not refer directly to specific meanings, bodies, or desires but, instead, to a set of institutionalized rituals through which we identify and through which we reproduce social norms.

Prior to production, the "exchange of women" is a scenario in which the meaning of gender relies on women being taken out of their social context (reproductive kinship relations) and circulated as Signs. The "exchange of women" thesis also relies on an assumption that, because women are so embedded in their social contexts, their transfer over to an alternative group connects the old forms to the new in a new alliance. It demands a pre-alienated existence. The shortcoming of this assumption for interrogating women's oppression is that, in order to attribute meaning and order bodies, it universalizes a version of tribal blood kinship whose most basic appearance would be the nuclear family and confines oppression to the top-down organization of the patriarchal family rather than, as Judith Butler has highlighted, taking into account a "number of kinship relations [that] exist and persist that do not conform to the nuclear family" ("Is Kinship Always Already Heterosexual?" 102). In addition, the "exchange of women" thesis introduces kinship as prior to or outside alienation. In contrast, Judith Butler has challenged this version of kinship by showing kinship to combine "practices ... that emerge to address fundamental forms of human dependency" (103) with practices that dispossess, pathologize, and delegitimate social relations. She also treats kinship politically, as it is used by the state and non-state powers to impose and intensify restrictive norms of family belonging. Yet, because Butler sticks with the model of kinship (even if constructed) for understanding gender as a mainstay of the Symbolic, gender is always at least partially in the sphere of reproduction in her account. If gender is alienated, it is alienated because symbolic systems disrupt primary, fundamental social relations, forms of dependency and belonging. The limitations of kinship for an analysis of gender is that it projects an area of social activity outside of production and alienation. It cannot show that production is already alienating kinship relations from the inside.

The alienability of gender introduces not just an abstraction where women, as exchangeable units, are turned into calculable value, but also the possibility of markets in gender, where gender acts like financial currency. That is, like credit default swaps, gender can be broken down into attributes, personality forms, and bodily sensibilities, repackaged and sold on the open market. Speaking of developing her new fashion brand Women Who Work, for example, Ivanka Trump proclaims, "there was an enormous disconnect between how professional women looked, how we lived, how we spent our time and sought to express ourselves, and the apparel and accessories that were available to us ... I was really proud of the fact that my collections captured a femininity and a sense of fashion that working women hadn't been able to express even a decade before" (*Women Who Work* 6). Ivanka's company Woman Who Work (the brand name also used as the web address and the title of her book) broke down an image of the contemporary woman entrepreneur into multiple life moments, activities, parts, and moods, each with its own style and affordable product line, the travel sections linked to the Trump hotels and resorts. Ivanka describes her company as built to earn profits by responding to women's entrepreneurial needs, from flexibility to lifestyle integration and team-focus. "Feminine" traits—such as "interpersonal skills," "communication management" (492), and "technology of sexiness" (441)—are solicited by firms, says Ann Gray who studies seminars, image consultants, and weekend conferences where women learn how to construct their personalities, their postures, and their gestures *as women* according to the framework of the femininity valued in job markets. Such self-reconstruction demands *for gender* a constant self-surveillance on outer appearances, including wardrobe and surgery, as well as on interior life, including projecting confidence and modifying home and gardens but extending as well to dating, hygiene, sex, and childcare, all of which can be approached through training.

Not only is femininity a product, but as a product it is considered as the packaging of a set of social relations that can organize the activities of entrepreneurial production better than ever. As Wendy Brown puts it, neoliberalism mobilizes a set of features, including "an emphasis on ... teamwork" (4), which integrates "stakeholders" toward "consensus-driven managerial solutions to problems" (6). The lateralization of such seeming "power-sharing" is "configured as practices of self-investment where the self *is* an individual firm; and work as well as citizenship are configured as modes of belonging to the business ('team')" (3). Ivanka professes this affective integration into the life of the firm through teamwork as a particularly women's contribution to the firm's value because women are nice, respectful, engaged, motivated, communicative, optimistic, and resilient. Women's management offers this effective and profitable change to corporate culture, she suggests: "Rather than police your team, populate it with like-minded A+ talent at every level, and trust them to act responsibly and in the company's best interest" (*Women Who Work* 173). She goes on: "I want my employees to think of the greater organization; to support the smartest, most innovative ideas ..., and to help their colleagues.... . I expect my team to be known for its honesty and directness" (*Women Who Work* 174). Women are emotive, sympathetic, sharing, honest, and kind, and those traits lead them to better business practices and better profit. Because feminist theory has focused predominantly on the "exchange of women," the commodification of feminine aspects and the circulation of pieces of the feminine Symbolic as entrepreneurial brands are tendencies that raise questions for future directions in feminist thought.

The subordination of the commodity—in this case, women—to its role as an object in exchange bypasses Marx's central question that guides him toward his analysis of commodities: how are they alienated and fetishized? The formula expected of exchange—where commodities in the market find their equivalents in money which finds its equivalent in a different commodity—does not explain, says Marx, why money increases when it passes through the commodity in the next phase of exchange (when money is exchanged for a commodity which is again exchanged for money)—why are there profits? In other words, if I have money that I exchange for a commodity, why can I sell that commodity for more than I paid—how does capital grow? Marx's answer is that the variability of social relations—including in the reproductive sphere—influences the exchange value of an object. The number of work hours necessary to make the object is dependent on the social organization, for example, the level of technology and the forms of social life: "this ultimate money-form of the world of commodities," Marx summarizes, " ... actually conceals, instead of disclosing, the social character of private labour, and the social relations between the individual producers" (50). The commodity in exchange erases by absorbing what Marx calls the "social character" of the object. "To them [the workers]," notes Marx, "their own social action takes the form of the action of objects, which rule the producers instead of being ruled by them" (49). The commodity is the form taken by the alienation of the social relations that brought it into being. Though Marx does not consider gender explicitly, gender can now be understood as a symbolic object, available to exchange for profit, that produces value by absorbing and concealing the social relations in which it is made. Our kinship and social relations are being taken apart and sold back to us in the branded image.

THE "EXCHANGE OF WOMEN" AND THE COMMODITY

Anthropologist Gayle Rubin was the first feminist to use the "exchange of women" to explain the universal oppression of women as a problem of the Symbolic. In her 1976 groundbreaking article "The Traffic in Women," Rubin dismisses Marxist thinking on commodity production as an answer to the question of the genesis of sexism because, she says, the commodity is too historically specific to the age of industrial capitalism. In contrast, she claims, women's oppression occurs "in societies which can by no stretch of the imagination be described as capitalist" (163), in other words, in societies organized around unalienated kinship relations. Rubin reviews what she understands as Marx's critique, concluding that women's work, or reproductive labor (i.e., housework, childcare, food preparation), is outside (i.e., surplus, free additional labor) the driving history of commodity production that men workers performed in factories. Though she agrees that this history does take into account women's devaluation under capitalism, it does not grant the single cause that she is looking for that effects oppression's universality. She finds this Marxist explanation insufficient to explain, for example, why women are the ones delegated reproductive labor in the first place, or why they are oppressed in ways unrelated to commodity production, as with foot-binding practices, sexual aggression, or restrictions on women's sexuality. For this, she needs to turn to anthropology, to look toward the "primitive" and the "economy" of gift-giving for the primal cause. Like Simone de Beauvoir, she borrows from Lévi-Strauss who concludes, "The emergence of symbolic thought must have required that women, like words, should be things that were exchanged" (496).

The move toward the anthropological does not just allow Rubin (an anthropologist) to envision a peeling away of layers of modernity in order to reveal the most basically human, or natural kinship, as the singular origin of culture. In addition, the anthropological turn allows Rubin to veer away from Marx and toward Engels, whose idea of capital formation challenges Marx's in his 1884 tract, *Origin of the Family, Private Property, and the State*. For Engels, capital accumulation precedes the commodity: when human communities became sedentary and the wealth of families and clans increased, communities persisted through a division of labor within the family (patriarchy), male labor became more necessary, and men needed a way to determine inheritance in order to ensure that their tools and other belongings were passed down to their own children. The relatively recent development of the monogamous family, says Engels, "is based on the supremacy of man, the express purpose being to produce children of undisputed paternity; such paternity is demanded because these children are later to come into their father's property as his natural heirs" (33). The nuclear family is a historical afterthought as well as historically out-of-date. In accordance, what Rubin coins as the "sex/gender system"—"a set of arrangements by which the biological raw material of human sex and procreation is shaped by human, social intervention and satisfied in a conventional manner" (165)—served as controls over the organization of sexualities for the purpose of maintaining private property and inheritance. Thus, the rise of patriarchy coincides with the oppression of women and takes place prior to or outside of the productive mechanisms of industry that Marx describes, in the sphere of the Symbolic or ideology, or reproduction. For feminism, Rubin's analysis led in two directions: one toward linguistic theory and psychoanalysis, with gender operating as the grand signifier of difference that structures arbitrary assignments of meaning, and the other toward Althusserian ideology, with gender "calling" subjects, via the Unconscious, into identification with their place in the system of accumulation and production. Mixing Althusser with Lévi-Strauss's analysis of kinship and exchange, Juliet Mitchell, for example, reads the problem of ideology analysis to be its focus on the productive economy, a focus which separates it from patriarchal ideology where the "exchange of women that defines human culture is reproduced" (413) in the nuclear family.

Rubin's formulation of the sex/gender system informed a generation of feminist debate. "The society we know, *our* own culture," Luce Irigaray begins her essay "Women on the Market," "is based upon the exchange of women" (170). Irigaray equates the exchange of women to commodity production. Her idea here is similar to her inspirational ideas about how women are represented in philosophy, ethics, and psychoanalysis, where women appear as the inverse of men—as their absence—in order to shore up men's absolute and material presence, to ensure against their loss of identity and control. "*Commodities,*" she writes, "*are a mirror of value of and for man*" (177, Irigaray's emphasis). For Irigaray, exchange turns women into values that mirror each other, emptying them of their own expressions and qualities in order to use them as symbolic equivalencies, like money, that give value to men. "It is thus not as 'women' that they are exchanged, but as women reduced to some common feature—their current price in gold, or phalluses—and of which they would represent a plus or minus quantity" (175). Without having to be explained as having been made, commodities here are reduced to only exchange. Whereas Marx addresses the mechanisms of exchange as a pivot or entry-way to interrogate deeper the productive system that creates the conditions of such equality in value between very different objects, Irigaray's project tells the story of exchange as the whole story of value. In this, she erases production and labor, situating the oppression of women as prior to commodity production and projecting the "exchange of women"—or kinship and reproduction—in tribal societies as the origin of capitalist culture.

There is more to say about Irigaray, particularly, for example, about how the "exchange of women"—women as a mirror of value—is linked to Freudian castration, or the idea that something can disappear under somebody's gaze and needs therefore to be secured in its representation. Women have already been castrated, just as money has no substance outside of its value-representation in other money, so that women are exchanged as mirrors of male value, not as themselves. The problem, however, of placing the "exchange of women"—or barter—at the dominant center of feminist critiques of women's oppression or of patriarchy is not only, as we have learned from anthropologist David Graeber, that: "there's no evidence that [barter] ever happened, and an enormous amount of evidence suggesting that it did not" (28). Indeed, Graeber says that women would not have been alienated from their communities and their social contexts except *after* money was established as an apparatus of trade, at which point organized violence could demand women and children as payments for debt. The "exchange of women" is not a mechanism for producing equalities, kinship, and alliance but rather a system of accumulation by force. For Graeber, the modern discipline of economics had to project an origin story about barter in order to instantiate a field of economic activity that was autonomous from other social arrangements and so could be studied in itself. This raises the question of whether or not feminist theory's emphasis on kinship and exchange has been doing the same thing, and if placing the "exchange of women" at the core of feminist philosophical thinking on women's oppression or on the Symbolic function tends to obscure some of the features of commodity production—particularly its violence—that underlie our moment of gender today.

ENTREPRENEUR OF THE SELF

When Ivanka Trump tells us in the first line of her first book that "In business, as in life, nothing is ever handed to you" (*The Trump Card* 1), she is not necessarily denying her privilege, which she freely admits. Rather, as she goes on to teach us, what she means is that she learned from her parents how much hard work it took to make herself into the Trump she was born as. *Believe me, it takes a lot of work to be so great.* Her parents, she boasts, expected a lot from her and her brothers, and she had to work hard to receive what was coming to her anyway. She is not a product of her social circumstances or social connections but rather of her own individual efforts—completely on her own, without help. Both her books—*The Trump Card* in 2009 as well as *Women Who Work* in 2017 (completed before her father assumed the presidency but written during the campaign)—perform just that: they show her making Ivanka Trump as a Trump. That is not all. The books also aspire to show you the rules, that is, to make you, its reader, into a Trump, to produce more Trumps in her image. "Just as we search for the best location and the finest materials and develop the most innovative design before breaking ground on a new project," she informs her readers, "I look to stand on the strongest possible foundation as an individual" (*The Trump Card* 130). Ivanka is a construction project of the Trump Corporation and you can be too! Ivanka never tells us *what* exactly she does to fill her time, but we know she is always engaged in endless fervent passionate activity, staying up late at night to answer e-mails and getting up before the crack of dawn. She is the perfect example of what Byung-Chul Han has called the subject of "Burnout Society" or "achievement society":

> The reaction to a life that has become bare and radically fleeting occurs as hyper-activity, hysterical work, and production. The acceleration of contemporary life also plays a role in this lack of being. The society of laboring and achievement is not a free society. It generates new constraints.... In this society of compulsion, everyone carries a work camp inside.... One exploits oneself. (19)

The achievement subject, says Han, is not obedient but rather free, expecting more and more pleasure in its cumulative repetitions. Like Ivanka, it indicates "an excess of stimuli, information, and impulses" (12), or rather, "an *excess of positivity*" (41, original emphasis). Aside from cute little anecdotes—like how her whole family cut their teeth building with LEGOS as infants, establishing the "Trump" brand as integral and exclusive to her consciousness— Ivanka's books are primarily filled with empty platitudes, celebra-tory optimism, excited busyness, and inspirational quotes that at the same time manage to make this reader, at least, feel inadequate for *only aspiring* to build myself up to the perfection of a Trump.

Even though her success is part of being a Trump but only available to her through her hard work, she feels guilty, she says. Her books are a type of confession, a saving-face. Her first book *The Trump Card* starts out responding vituperatively to imagined critics who might "dismiss my success in our family business as yet another example of nepotism" (1). She wants to convince you, her reader, that her privilege is not guilty of such nepotism or of getting anything that she has not deserved through her own self-starting, resilient efforts at self-building. These would-be doubters attribute guilt to her, she says, because they do not understand the burden of her privilege. In fact, she faced a great challenge when seeking a job at her family's corporation because she had to prove her value, "to sit around a conference table with a group of middle-aged men—some of whom, I'm sure, would be wondering what the hell I was doing here" (*The Trump Card* 2). Because she struggled so hard to get the job that was already hers, she wants to share the knowledge she acquired. So, she is handing it out. She writes her book, she says, because she wants to teach you to share her privilege that you do not have and will never have. This means that anyone can be a Trump by becoming the Trump she, alone in her knowledge, already is and they will never be.

Ivanka's books are a mix between self-help, confessional, and autobiography, where the address to "you" is interspersed with first-person anecdotes from Ivanka's repertoire of stories about her development as the Trump she already was, as though "you" and "I, Ivanka," were part of the same assembly. Ivanka is calling to you. The path toward Trump-ness is an assimilation into the brand: as we follow the pedagogical path that she outlines, we construct ourselves as Trump—we become part of the architecture; we follow her example as she (who is sometimes you) builds herself up from blueprints that she writes (*Women Who Work*, e.g., 27, 44, 84, 105, 107), as though she were a project site for a new Trump building that she (and so you, too) would become; in her words, we architect our lives (*Women Who Work*, e.g., 11, 12, 27, 38, 111). This book, she says, "evolves my personal mission and that of the brand I've built into a new worldview—a one-life men-tality [between work and home]—to aid you in navigating the different challenges and opportunities you face now, and in the years to come" (*Women Who Work* 13). "[W]e embody the mission of the brand" (*Women Who Work* 83), she boasts.

My intention here is not to review Ivanka's book, as *Women Who Work* and its author were already panned by critics. Comedian Samantha Bee on *Full Frontal* called her a "feckless c***" for posting an image of herself holding her baby son on the same day that the Trump administration authorized taking immigrant children in detention away from their parents (she later apologized for the vulgar language). Samantha Bee also lambasted Ivanka for using "architect" as a verb over and over; for lifting quotes from the work of other authors and stamping her name on it in a true Trump tradition; and for assuming that all women can take a day off to care for a sick child and not lose their jobs. She also cites Whoopi Goldberg who reacts with repulsion to Ivanka's trivializing Toni Morrison's novel about freedom from slavery, *Beloved*, by comparing its use of the word "freedom" to the freedom from having your time taken up by menial work-tasks like responding to email: for freedom, Ivanka writes, all you need is "proactive planning" (*Women Who Work* 113), setting goals and priorities and managing your time effectively. Noting the book's vapidity, Jia Tolentino in *The New Yorker* skewers Ivanka for writing a so-called book that reads like a store catalogue "as a way to make Ivanka products more market-able," with "random advertisements for Trump companies, like this one: 'Scion Hotels offer energized social experiences and shared work spaces designated to bring people together to exchange ideas and create.'"

Rather, I trace a line of feminist thinking that considers the commodity as one of the dominant forms femininity takes within neoliberalism. Lisa Lowe argues that Victorian commodities "mediated colonial labor and imperial trade as social conditions occluded in the production of 'value'" (83). Extending this analysis would suggest that the gender-commodity is also the product of present-day imperializing relations and occluded neo-liberal power impositions. Lowe, though, maps the commodity and its imperializing power as the background behind images as they appear in literary texts, whereas the commodity is actually integral to social relations and often out-in-the-open as their organizing prin-ciple. The gender-commodity is a form of address in which the culture demands that we affirm oppressive relations by affirming ourselves, by signing in or performing ourselves as commodities in the performance of our individualities. Media scholar Rosalind Gill, for example, observes that advertising is promoting the personality of the super-empowered woman as an agent who can make a difference by choosing to buy. "[W]hat kind of feminist politics," she asks, "follows from a position in which all behavior (even following fashion) is understood within discourse as free choice and autonomy?" (435). How is it, she continues, that applying beauty products is felt as "really, truly deeply our own, felt not as external impositions but as authentically ours?" (436). Such "entrepreneurial actors," she observes, are "rational, calculating and self-regulating" (443), meaning that change or political commitment is an individual practice, applied only to improvements to make the self more beautiful by using the right kind of cosmetics. Similarly, British cultural theorist Angela McRobbie has read a popular fetishization of girls who succeed, where girls' "capacity, success, attainment, enjoyment, entitlement, social mobility and participation" (721) have all become export values proving economic resilience in neoliberalism's ideology of self-reliant meritocracy. "Nowadays," she reflects, "the young woman's success seems to promise economic prosperity on the basis of her enthusiasm for work and having a career" (722). Girls, in other words, are targeted as good, neoliberal investments, made to please.

Though, in *Women Who Work*, husband Jared Kushner plays a somewhat shadowy figure who occasionally enters into proximity to Ivanka in order to be nice to their kids, Ivanka could not be called an object of exchange. She gives us no tales of romance, weddings, or sex—nor tales of alliance, like a meeting between the boards of directors of the Trump and Kushner real estate corporations (for example)—, these being outside of the range of autobiographical experiences that she identifies as important to her entrepreneurial subjectivity. Instead, as a full-fledged billboard for neoliberal authenticity, she is a woman of "capacity," self-regulating and autonomous. She is all alone, bursting out of her own head with the wisdom of Athena and the energy of Hercules. As a woman who had nothing handed to her, she did it all herself—she made herself and thinks you can too, or at least encourages you to, if you set your goals, order your priorities, are authentic to yourself, embrace challenges, keep a good to-do list, and work like crazy. Femininity is the self-sustaining part of that. The demands of femininity allow you to see how much self-control you have, how much of a master you are of your own situation. There need be no separation between work and private life, no balance, no boundaries, but, instead, you should do what you love, follow your passions, be resilient, and everything, she assures us, will fall into place.

Though Ivanka does everything for her work, self-maintenance, and family life herself (because nothing is ever handed to her)—including taking time for the self-care of massages, taking classes, meditation, evenings with friends, recreational travel, rest, Sabbath observance, date nights with Jared, and gym workouts—there are moments when the logic of her description points to something unmentioned but necessary: "Sometimes when things get crazy at work," she laments, "it's not always easy to carve out the time you'd like to spend with your children" (*Women Who Work* 151). So who, a reader might ask, does the housework when things get crazy? "I can't possibly do everything or I wouldn't be able to meet all my professional aspirations and obligations," she confesses, "... I don't do afternoon pickup from school. I don't take Joseph to the sports playgroup in the middle of the day" (*Women Who Work* 132). The caring hands that *do* take Joseph to the sports playgroup—the invisible ones—are *not* the ones Ivanka is addressing in the "you"—the selves that are helped. These hands are *not* the ones invited to the therapy session, that would be helped by flexible work-time, more teamwork or more authenticity in the work process. Invisible are the social relations that sustain Ivanka's work ethic: the quasi-discernible traces of the workers who make and care for the Trump, who enable Ivanka to focus her time on producing her exemplary self-sustaining entrepreneurial female self, the perfect picture of individual, self-managed, well-dressed success. Though motherhood gives Ivanka's enterprising women their sensitivity that benefits teamwork, honesty, and other horizontal relations in the innovative firm, that same motherhood is sustained only through the vertical relations of neoliberal corporatism.

In a pervasive media culture like ours, Ivanka is far from aberrant. What *is* exceptional about this particular appearance of the gender commodity is that it marks an instance where the gender commodity has merged into the neoliberal state. As early as 1970 in his *The Consumer Society*, Jean Baudrillard was prophesizing the advent of a state that adopts the techniques of advertising, alerted to the way gender was integral to such campaigns. "[A]n entire society," he remarks, "is homogenized by incessant daily acculturation to the silent and spectacular logic of fashion" (166)—the shop window is the essential point where politics coincides with solicitude, or what Baudrillard calls the "*beneficent,* maternal *ambience*" (192). What you are engaging as you stand in front of the fashion display, through the transparent glass, is a conditioning into a world where social relations are on display that "are produced in the same way as objects" (172), where you are asked to make choices, to affirm social codes and moralities, by unthinking assent, for the sake of mother love. Being "absorbed in the contemplation of multiple signs/objects" you are, as well, "absorbed into the order of signifiers of social status" (192)—Ivanka is happier than you because she knows what to wear! Follow her lead; wear her line! "We know better than you do about yourselves" (169), mocks Baudrillard. The fashion display comes to stand in the place of politics: "advertising, fashion, human and public relations can be interpreted as a kind of *perpetual referendum*—in which citizen consumers are entreated at every moment to pronounce in favor of a certain code of values and implicitly to sanction it" (168). This kind of solicitude (the care of the state in its "maternal *ambience*"), where you are taken care of by choosing the objects that you buy—this "dimension of 'solicitude,' in the 'caring,' 'favouring,' 'mothering' sense" (168), where you are told what you need to be happy—camouflages "the spectre of fragility" (174) that saturates an uncaring and violent society. In the place of actual supports, you are granted advice, therapy, and boundless optimism, to solve depressive states, anxiety, dissatisfaction, malaise, neurosis, and radical alienation.

Baudrillard is addressing the "society of affluence" of the late 1960s, where "the proliferation of caring agencies" (177) settles into a "totalitarian ethic" (176)—the imperative to be absorbed passively "*in the joyful conformity to the system* of the 'dynamic' young manager, bright-eyed and ... ideally fitted to continual activity" (183). Today, in our age of austerity, when service and work are slashed out of the picture, the "*satisfaction without end*" (177) brings nothing but dissatisfaction. The satisfaction that these agencies once promised—offering "soothing, guilt-dispelling balm and smiles ..., psychological lubricants ..., [e]nzymes for gobbling up anxiety ..., tranquillizers, relaxants, hallucinogens and therapies of all kinds" (177)— is for you to take responsibility for, to choose and to purchase on your own in an existential assent to the authority of the self-made mother-manager.

"PHARMACO-PORN" POLITICS

Michel Foucault developed a concept of neoliberalism as care of the self that can partly explain Ivanka's self-stylization. What Foucault analyzes as neoliberalism—not so different from classical liberalism—is the work of the state to reduce its areas of governance in the name of free enterprise. "The Rule of law," he notes in his lectures, "... formalize[s] the action of government as a provider of rules for an economic game in which the only players, the only real agents, must be individuals, or let's say, if you like, enterprises" (173). These entities or individuals are intended to be self-governing, do-it-yourself, while the art of government is to figure out an administrative logic of self-regulation that would leave the economic actor to its own devices. Significantly, Foucault has been criticized for interpreting the neoliberal state as plotting its own reduction and sidelining from the field of economic action. Instead, as Beatriz Preciado exhibits in her own brilliant autobiography *Testo Junkie*, the field of economic action is constituted through the excesses of the commodity, particularly the commodity of gender, under the force of the corporate state. State action is not removed from the field of economic activity but integrated inside of it in the form of the commodity.

Testo Junkie is a mix of anecdotal vignettes of the sex life and drug use of someone addicted to testosterone with scholarly reflections on the current state of cultural theory. The narrator (presumably, the author) experiments with drug use as a way of experimenting with gender. For example: "Our first contact is very clear: she's the whore; I'm the transsexual ... Now I think of my own nipples under my sweater, my completely shaved pubes, a cut at my right side, the alchemy of testosterone coursing through my blood. I take turns imagining myself with and without a cock ..." (88–9). The drugs intensify and transform the experience of gender in various ways: biological, psychological, sexual, and phenomenological. The narrator's intention is to reach a stage where conventions of gender do not apply, where narrative does not even apply. She knows that the drugs could shorten her life, make her sick or, eventually, dysfunctional, but the experiment of challenging the control exercised by economic power on her body is worth physical deterioration. As a sometimes sex worker, she knows that her experiment does not free her from such power, as the power is pervasive and the methods she uses to play with power just end up pushing her deeper into addiction to its pleasures, even as it is killing her. Her experiment stretches the order of gender and sexuality to the point where it is exposed as the death-dealing framework of modern alienation.

The purpose of the experiment is to take control of the fashioning of the self, buying the drugs both legally and illegally. Yet, the author/narrator is well aware that the self-fashioning is manipulated by the controllers of the new forms of panoptical power and the "sexopolitical" regime embedded in the commodity. One of these is the pharmacological industry which trades in sex and gender:

> If architecture and orthopedics in the disciplinary society served as models for understanding the relation of body to power, in the pharmacopornographic society, the models of body control are microprosthetic: now, power acts through molecules that incorporate themselves into our immune system; silicone takes the shape of our breasts; neurotransmitters alter our perceptions and behavior; hormones produce their systemic effects on hunger, sleep, sexual arousal, aggressiveness, and the social decoding of our femininity and masculinity. We are gradually witnessing the miniaturization, internalization, and reflexive introversion (an inward coiling toward what is

considered intimate, private space) of the surveillance and control mechanisms of the disciplinary sexopolitical regime. (78–9)

The drug-taker is neither outlaw nor transgressor; now the drug-taker is the norm, the buyer of commodities transformed into the commodity itself, a new stage of architecture beyond Foucaultian discipline, craving normal emotional responses only induced in medicated states.

One prevalent example of the regime is the birth control Pill. The Pill infuses us with hormones that create gender in us by producing—forcing—traits, rules, desires, and behaviors that Freud used to call "secondary" sexual characteristics as seemingly natural. Instead of tagging the autobiography with a birth, as in classics like *David Copperfield*, or with a parental line that positions the developing story line within a kinship context, Preciado traces the history of her origin through the history of hormonal manufacture, the fabrication of technology for gender construction and planning. The birth control Pill stands in the place of the mother, the one who calls out to the interiorized model of the hormonal blueprint, creating the gendered subject as junkie. The circular box that holds the Pill, which disciplines users for daily dosage on a twenty-eight-day cycle, is modeled on Jeremy Bentham's architectural plan for the Panopticon: the Pill is the Panopticon that we swallow. "We can think of the Pill as a lightweight, portable, individualized, chemical panopticon with the potential to change behavior, program action, regulate sexual activity, control population growth and racial purity, and redesign the sexual appearance (by refeminizing it synthetically) of the bodies that self-administer it" (205). Like Ivanka, Preciado understands herself as self-made, architected; unlike Ivanka, she is also aware that, because she can make herself for gender (even craves it), she is an industrial product, an effect of pharmacological therapy that administers the chemical modifications ingested to discipline the body of the producer/consumer.

Drugs are not the only mechanism of gender (read, social) control that Preciado identifies. Also, gender and sexuality are activated through the "masturbatory virtual device" (265) of pornography. Like drugs and hormonal ingestibles, pornography stimulates chemical reactions in pleasure centers that prompt desire, a kind of desire that pornography can direct into types of sex and gender conduct. For Preciado, pornography is not an illicit act only to be found on the social margins. Rather, pornography is the organizational principle of the contemporary economy. "[T]here is no work," she quips, "that isn't destined to cause a hard-on, to keep the global cock erect ... The only authentic surplus value is the index of the cock's elevation, its hardness and rigidity, the volume of its spermatic ejaculations" (293). Pornography names such practices as copyright—which produces nothing but controls through patents the reproduction of desire and ideas, "the conversion of life into information" (278)—entertainment, communications, the internet, the culture of the spectacle, digitation, licit and illicit drug sales, biotech, genome, and sex work, where anything that is public is marketable.

Preciado's favorite example of the pharmocopornographic power of the commodity is the disinherited heir to the hotel empire–turned reality TV star, Paris Hilton. As the ultimate sex worker, Hilton managed to make her idleness and vice appear in the media as *hard work* because of the work involved in displaying them, hard work meant to arouse the desire of her viewers: "her entire life and sexuality are being transformed by devices of extreme surveillance, into work—into digital images that are transferable worldwide. Her triumph is having known how to recover her body and her sexuality as ultimate values on the global-exchange market of pharmacopornographic capitalism" (280). As the heir of the commodity, Preciado is Ivanka's twin, yet unlike Ivanka, Preciado turns convention on its head, exposing that what seems on the fringes of normality is the pinnacle of mainstream commodity culture. Did not Ivanka likewise understand her body as her work and her work as making available for public, marketable consumption her self-construction? In Ivanka's terms, her pornographic narrative attributes to maternal femininity internal, private traits like communication, affective connection, and sexiness while branding and selling them as a work ethic, "teamwork," or corporate capacity. As provocation to pleasure, Ivanka's self-made self-display refers to a private, intimate, psychological, and personal formation as though there exists a place of pure, natural reproduction, kinship, and social belonging prior to production. Yet, she sells this entire package as a transparent public display of the pieces of the global commodity's ideological cover: maternal ambience offering a smiling solicitude for exchange.

In the glow of that smile, Ivanka has tried to hijack the future of feminism. At the time of this writing, the first proposed Trump budget supports her initiative to federally fund six weeks of family leave with $25 billion over a decade. Yet, the family planning provision is an unfunded mandate that pushed the costs onto the states, primarily paid for by state unemployment insurance, and left the decision of whether to implement the federal policy up to the states themselves. In the meantime, Ivanka asked for a meeting with Cecile Richards of Planned Parenthood. During this meeting, at a Trump-owned New Jersey golf course, Jared Kushner pressed Richards to quit providing abortions in exchange for increased funding for Planned Parenthood, and Ivanka, according to Richards, only piped in to say that her father was pro-life, inferring that women's legal right to abortion was no longer worth defending because of the president's will. Though family leave was touted by the Administration as an aid to the most needy, the Trump budget proposal also included a $1.4 trillion cut to Medicaid, cuts to programs for nutritional support for pregnant women and infants, cuts to after-school programs, cuts to education at every level, and a $193 billion cut to food stamps. In the following year, things got even worse. The tax bill passed at the end of 2017 will give relief to the most wealthy and allow a "tax holiday" for repatriating money that was sent offshore at the expense of American workers while giving an excuse to cut much needed public and social safety net spending because of the resulting escalation in the deficit. For example, citing their concern over projected deficits resulting from the tax bill, Republicans in the House decided to cut the Children's Health Insurance Program (CHIP). In addition, under the guidance of the Independent Women's Forum (see my prior article "The Independent Women's Forum"), another Ivanka initiative—part of a deal to sell $110 billion in arms to Saudi Arabia, even while Saudi is engaged in a years-long aerial bombardment of Yeman that has killed tens of thousands of civilians—corrals the Saudi royals and the United Arab Emirates into putting $100 million into a World Bank account to support women entrepreneurs worldwide (we can always count on the Saudi rulers to take the lead on feminism!) In fact, during the October 2016 presidential debate, Donald Trump himself pointed out the Saudis' abominable record in women's rights, when he said about the Clinton Foundation's $25-million donation from Saudi Arabia, "You talk about women and women's rights? These are people that push gays off business, off buildings. These are people that kill women and treat women horribly and yet you take their money." He then demanded that Clinton return the money.

Feminist theory of the twenty-first century needs to develop a serious framework for interrogating the lineage of the commodity in gender's contemporary appearances. Such an account would extend from anthropologies of exchange to analyze the control commodity culture exerts by absorbing our bodies and desires into its forms, injecting its power into our molecular and sensory material. It would account for how reproduction itself has been commodified as part of the neoliberal productive apparatus and ideology. In their self-promotion, such commodities give us an image of kinship that, while shining happiness and healing upon us, disinvests and destroys social relations and care. More than ever, the marketplace displays offers of gender-products that dress up and bejewel the exploitive social relations that produce them, and the neoliberal state has followed suit in becoming an extension of such products' advertisements and promotional strategies. The social relations whose image sets the neoliberal state aglow with optimism, efficiency, and activity, bolstering its credibility, are the very ones that find themselves dispossessed and bound on the chopping block, ready for slaughter. As Beatriz Preciado concludes, "Gender must be torn from the macrodiscourse and diluted with a good dose of micropolitical hedonist psychedelics" (397). We must find ideas and practices that allow us to dis-identify with the items on display to which we are addicted, to pull them mortally apart and put them together differently, in order to imagine gender's reworked politicization for feminism's future.

WORKS CITED

Baudrillard, Jean. *The Consumer Society: Myths & Structures*. Trans. George Ritzer. London: Sage, 1998.

Bee, Samantha. "Ladies Who Book." *Full Frontal*, May 10, 2017. https://www.youtube.com/watch?v=JFq77o0hYjg&t=337s. Accessed May 21 2017.

Brown, Wendy. "Sacrificial Citizenship: Neoliberalism, Human Capital, and Austerity Politics." *Constellations* 23.1 (2016): 3–14.

Butler, Judith. *Gender Trouble: Feminism and the Subversion of Identity*. New York: Routledge, 1990, 1999, 2006.

Butler, Judith. "Is Kinship Always Already Heterosexual?" *Undoing Gender*. New York: Routledge, 2004, pp. 102–30.

de Beauvoir, Simone. *The Second Sex*. Trans. H. M. Parshley. New York: Vintage Books, 1989.

Engels, Friedrich. *Origin of the Family, Private Property, and the State*. Trans. Alick West. 1993, 1999, 2000. Marx/Engels Internet Archive. https://www.marxists.org/archive/marx/works/download/pdf/origin_family.pdf.

Foucault, Michel. *The Birth of Biopolitics. Lectures at the Collège de France 1978–1979*. Ed. Michel Senellart and trans. Graham Burchell. New York: Palgrave Macmillan, 2008.

Gill, Rosalind. "Culture and Subjectivity in Neoliberal and Postfeminist Times." *Subjectivity* 25 (2008): 432–45.

Goodman, Robin Truth. "The Independent Women's Forum: Teaching Women's Rights in the 'New Iraq.'" *Schooling and the Politics of Disaster*. Ed. Kenneth J. Saltman. New York: Routledge, 2007, pp. 219–32.

Graeber, David. *Debt: The First 5,000 Years*. Brooklyn, NY: Melville House, 2011, 2012, 2014.

Gray, Ann. "Enterprising Femininity: New Modes of Work and Subjectivity." *European Journal of Cultural Studies* 6.4 (2003): 489–506.

Han, Byung-Chul. *The Burnout Society*. Trans. Erik Butler. Stanford, CA: Stanford UP, 2015.

Irigaray, Luce. "Women on the Market." *This Sex Which Is Not One*. Trans. Catherine Porter with Carolyn Burke. Ithaca: Cornell UP, 1985, pp. 170–91.

Lévi-Strauss, Claude. *The Elementary Structures of Kinship*. Ed. Rodney Needham and trans. James Harle Bell and John Richard von Sturmer. Boston, MA: Beacon P, 1969.

Lowe, Lisa. *The Intimacies of Four Continents*. Durham, NC: Duke UP, 2008.

Marx, Karl. *Capital: A Critique of Political Economy. Volume I*. Ed. Frederick Engels and trans. Samuel Moore and Edward Aveling. Marx/Engels Internet Archive. https://www.marxists.org/archive/marx/works/download/index.htm.

McRobbie, Angela. "Top Girls? *Cultural Studies* 21.4–5 (2007): 718–37.

Mitchell, Juliet. *Psychoanalysis and Feminism: A Radical Reassessment of Freudian Psychoanalysis*. New York: Penguin Books, 1974.

Preciado, Beatriz. *Testo Junkie: Sex, Drugs, and Biopolitics in the Pharmacopornographic Era*. Trans. Bruce Benderson. New York: Feminist P, 2013.

Rubin, Gayle. "The Traffic in Women: Notes on the 'Political Economy' of Sex." *Towards an Anthropology of Women*. Ed. Rayna R. Reiter. New York: Monthly Review P, 1976, pp. 157–210.

Tolentino, Jia. "Ivanka Trump Wrote a Painfully Oblivious Book for Basically No One." *The New Yorker*, May 4, 2017. http://www.newyorker.com/books/page-turner/ivanka-trump-wrote-a-painfully-oblivious-book-for-basically-no-one?intcid=mod-latest. Accessed May 21, 2017.

Trump, Donald. "The Final Trump-Clinton Debate Transcript, Annotated." *Washington Post*, October 19, 2016. https://www.washingtonpost.com/news/the-fix/wp/2016/10/19/the-final-trump-clinton-debate-transcript-annotated/?noredirect=on&utm_term=.f59bbea0f4a7. Accessed April 11, 2018.

Trump, Ivanka. *The Trump Card: Playing to Win in Work and Life*. New York: Touchstone Books, 2009.

Trump, Ivanka. *Women Who Work: Rewriting the Rules for Success*. New York: Portfolio/Penguin, 2017.

CHAPTER TWENTY-SEVEN

Matter

EMANUELA BIANCHI

The gendered stakes of matter are visible and audible in the very word: matter—*materia-mater*—mother. Taking this equivalence at its word, we see that matter signifies a kind of source or origin, one with a specifically feminine sign: matter as mother, the maternal origin, accompanied, no doubt, by all the fantasies of existential solace, terror, and mystery that the maternal origin may be capable of conjuring. Matter, as philosopher Luce Irigaray, among others, first brought to our attention in the 1970s, is as a philosophical term inseparable from what it has been opposed and subordinated to in the Western philosophical tradition as first conceived in Ancient Greece: it thus takes its place in a chain of well-known equivalences—matter is opposed to form as body is opposed to mind or soul, as nature is opposed to culture, as sensible is opposed to intelligible, as feminine is opposed to masculine.

Hélène Cixous, writing around the same time as Irigaray, begins her essay *Sorties* with just this series of oppositions, and adds another through which they might all also be understood: passivity/activity (63–4). The first term is ineluctably subordinated to the second, and functions as its other, its undergirding and support, providing not simply an infrastructure but also a kind of reflected glory in which the superordinate term might bathe. Such a conceptual grid is indeed an all-too-familiar commonplace of twentieth-century feminist thought. For Irigaray, from her early critical-feminist philosophical analyses in *Speculum of the Other Woman* and *This Sex Which Is Not One* (both first translated into English in 1985), the facticity of the origin of all of us in a maternal body, and the radical notion that this mother is also a woman, becomes in the masculinist discourses of philosophy a frozen site, incapable of reciprocity, functioning only as a mirror for the male. In particular, at the level of an investigation into substance and being inaugurated in the Western philosophical tradition, the advent of "matter" in Aristotle's thought as a term of Western metaphysics marks in a profound way the appropriation and evisceration of the maternal-feminine: red blood becomes white blood (*le sang blanc*) as factical, corporeal origin is transformed into its French homonym, mere reflective surface and semblance (*le semblant*) (*This Sex* 77, 186–8, 192, 197; *Speculum* 216, 221). Nonetheless, Irigaray insists that there is a profound power for feminism to be sought in the "elsewhere of matter," since "mother-matter-nature must go on forever nourishing speculation," even if such matter is typically expelled as excess waste, if not madness, in the phallic order (*This Sex* 76–7).

At the same time, "matter" has also appeared in feminist thinking as a referent of "materialism" within the materialist feminist tradition. "Materialism" here, however, signifies less matter as a term within Western metaphysics, but denotes, rather, the range of human activities by which the means of human subsistence are produced and reproduced. Materialism in this Marxist sense thus refers to a field that includes material conditions of production, relations of production, forces of production, and the various activities of human labor through means of which humans act upon, transform, and reproduce their material and human worlds. The mode of production in which we find ourselves is determinative for Marx of our mode of life, and the "nature of individuals" will also depend on the material conditions of production in which they find themselves (150).

While "matter itself" is not a key term or element in this field, materialist feminists such as Silvia Federici have emphasized how traditional Marxism has excluded or downplayed the labor power represented by the corporeal dimensions of human existence undertaken by women: the labor represented by provision of sexual services (paid or unpaid), pregnancy, childbirth, breastfeeding, caretaking, food preparation, housework, household management, and other labor, mostly falling to women, that functions in capitalism primarily to reproduce the workforce. In her analysis of the transformation under capitalism during sixteenth- and seventeenth-century Europe of the body of the worker into a mechanical instrument of production, and the body of woman in turn into a machine for reproduction of the workforce, Federici raises parallels with the transformations in conceptions of the body itself in the thought of early modern philosophers such as Descartes and Hobbes (see, especially, 133–61). For these thinkers, the body itself, its corporeal and material nature, is newly understood according to the causal, calculative, and productive logic of the machine. If the body is rendered in these philosophies akin to something dead, an automaton, a tool or an instrument without liveliness in itself, what then provides the impetus and the energy for its movement? Here, we can see how the concerns of materialist feminism dovetail with the "matter" of Western metaphysics. As the rise of capitalism intensifies the dependence of women on employers and on men, the body becomes not just that which must be transcended and overcome, but it is further hypostatized as the passive receptacle, instrument, and reflector of something else. What is this but a certain force that now resides firmly on the side of the masculine, the state, and capital's economic power, and which provides the animating, motive, and now productive principle through which it might be operated and governed?

In bare bones, then, these are two lines of thinking which reveal how and why matter comes to "matter" for feminist thought (see Meißner). Irigaray, too, pays attention to the "materialist" side of mattering, insofar as she emphasizes how women within patriarchal kinship structures and capitalist markets function as objects of exchange that work to consolidate masculine subjecthood (*This Sex* 170–97, see also Rubin). In modernity, then, we must add the "object" opposed to the "subject" to our chain of equivalences. Clearly, it would be all too easy for this study to become an investigation of all that lies upon one side in this chain of associative oppositions: matter, nature, the sensible, the body, the object, all of which may be gathered under the sign of the feminine. But while they are all interlinked and connected, and in a certain sense form an inseparable complex insofar as they are all bound to the "feminine," "matter" *as such* has a particular history, a particular genealogy, and a particular set of resonances.

For the explicit thematizing of matter for twenty-first-century feminist theorizing, we must at this juncture turn to a pair of key texts, Judith Butler's *Bodies That Matter* and Elizabeth Grosz's *Volatile Bodies*, both written in the early 1990s, that in tandem reckon with, on the one hand, the force of matter as productive activity, as what "comes to matter," and, on the other, the philosophical reduction of matter to a remainder or reserve, to what has been rendered static and passive in Western thought. While both these texts principally foreground the body, they together also insist that matter as such must be transvalued, rendered inseparable from force, movement, and history. In bringing this newly animate matter to center stage, they mark a decisive shift in feminist theorizing and arguably also lay the groundwork (along with the key work of feminist science studies scholar Donna Haraway) for movements in the wider theoretical humanities such as posthumanism, speculative realism/object-oriented ontologies, affect theory, and critical animal studies.

For feminist thought, an array of contemporary threads emanate from this moment, including the feminist new materialisms, developments in environmental philosophy and ecocriticism, philosophy of technology, philosophical engagements with neuroscience, gender and transgender theorizing, and critical race theory, especially in the proximity of matter with black life asserted by the early-twenty-first-century US racial justice movement, Black Lives Matter. However, before we turn to the contemporary scene, it will be necessary to get as clear as possible on our terms through tracing a genealogy of the concept of matter in Western thought. It is my contention that in twenty-first-century feminist thought "matter" is rarely precisely articulated, and it is often presented as variously interchangeable with other concepts such as "body," "the real," "nature," "flesh," "object," and so on. Its originary articulation still has a great deal to tell us about what is at stake in this concept.

As is well known, the "dawn" of Western philosophy is marked by a turn away from mythology toward naturalistic explanations for the origin and substance of the phenomenal world. Greek mythology and tragedy clearly grapple with the corporeal and material facticity of human life: mortality; origins and genealogy (in which mortals and divinities both play a part); and coming to be, with thematics of sex and gender insistently in the foreground. The first philosophers, by contrast, look to naturalistic explanations, turning to what we now call the "elements" as ways to account for cosmic origins and constitution. We may well ask: what becomes of sexual difference in this turn? Thales names the *archē*—origin and principle—as water, and Anaximenes designates air. Heraclitus looks to *logos* as a figure of unity, but his fragments on the physical world emphasize the agonistic transformations among the elements, foremost of which will be fire in its destructive action. Empedocles will, in turn, speak of the "four roots" (not elements, as per frequent mistranslations), and these are given the names of divinities as well as earth, air, fire, and water, while Anaxagoras will propose a cosmos made up of a mixture of seeds and portions of different stuffs, set in motion and ordered by *nous* or mind, a pure and fine stuff that is forever separate from the mixture of the other materials (but not yet a true dualism). The atomists Leucippus and Democritus offer the *atomos*: the uncuttable and miniscule unit of being, characterized only by shape, position, size, and arrangement, that is contrasted with void. While these varied conceptions swirl in the territory of what we now call "matter," describing the stuff of the physical universe, the concept of matter *as such* has not yet arisen on the scene.

In terms of the fate of sexual difference in these early, post-mythical conceptions of the physical world, the question remains relatively open. Irigaray, once again, has shown herself attuned to the possibilities of symbolizing a forgotten or as-yet-unthought feminine through her reclamations of the "elemental" in works such as *Elemental Passions, Marine Lover of Friedrich Nietzsche*, and *The Forgetting of Air in Martin Heidegger*. Irigaray's call for thinking the complexities of a phenomenology of fluid dynamics that might correspond to a specifically feminine corporeity and feminine sexual pleasure constitutes a feminist response to Nietzsche and Heidegger, philosophers who have themselves sought to go back beyond and behind the reign of Western metaphysics installed by Plato and Aristotle. For them, this return to the beyond or hither-side of Plato signals the possibility of reclaiming a conception of being as inherently motile—for Nietzsche, this is conveyed by the Dionysian side of life expressed in the tragic age of Greece: corporeity, music, rhythm, upsurge, loss of boundary, dissolution, ecstasy.[1] For Heidegger, it portends a thinking of Being as essentially in movedness, one in which the movement of emergence into the open is inseparable from a recession into the hiddenness of the root (227). For Irigaray, responding to these philosophers by thinking with water and air opens on to different conceptions of ethics, a sexuate ethics that signifies proximal modes of relationship to the other, and specifically the sexual other, that are a far cry from the rigid separations and easily calculable dynamics given by solid mechanics. Water and air give life and breath, place, containment, movement, freedom, and nourishment to subjects, and yet according to Irigaray are forgotten, just as the maternal body with its life- and oxygen-giving function is likewise eclipsed. Even though Nietzsche and Heidegger push through and beyond metaphysics, their ignorance of the fluid, nourishing, dimension of the elemental is of a piece with their inability to countenance sexual difference.[2]

Read in a certain light, Empedocleanism, with its emphasis on the always-double movement of separation and joining of the four elemental roots in love and strife without any need for the lack or absence that is void, the ever generative/destructive cyclicity of his cosmos, and his insistent metaphorics of flow and counterflow, may be the most Irigarayan of the Presocratic philosophies (see J. E. Butler). Ancient atomism, again, might be said to bear a rather ambivalent relationship to the question of sexual difference: on the one hand it deals purely in the mechanics of solids: atom penetrates void. On the other hand, atomism offers the prospect of an endlessly open, productive, proliferative and evolutionary cosmos: the endless combinatory power of atoms is indeed aligned with feminine generativity, as in Lucretius's *De Rerum Natura*, from the invocation of the goddess Venus at the start of the poem, to the later images of a feminized earth giving birth from her wombs to boundless living forms (*De Rerum* 1, 1–49, 5, 795–827).

With Plato, everything changes. While the battle of the earthly, war-loving Giants and the peace- and form-loving Gods in the *Sophist* conveys the ontological hierarchy between earth and forms quite clearly, it is in the *Timaeus* that the nascent, albeit still inarticulate, thought of "matter as such" first arises. This latter dialogue is Plato's narrative of the creation and constitution of the cosmos, the story of how the realm of being, that of the forms, eternal, ideal, and perfect, comes to be instantiated as the world of becoming, that of generation and passing away. A significant innovation here is the figure of the *dēmiourgos* or divine craftsman (there is no creator God heretofore in Greek religion or philosophy), who binds layers of the same and the different together, and creates a cosmos in motion, akin to a self-sufficient living creature. And yet, precisely halfway through the dialogue, we stall, and hear a call for another beginning. What is called for is a "third kind," in addition to being and becoming, and yet this is something hard to think about or speak about: the call gives rise to a tumbling surfeit of figures, even though we are also told it must always be called by the same name, because it never departs from its own proper potential even as it receives the many things that enter into it (*Timaeus* 50c). It is neither being as such, nor a temporal being of the realm of becoming, and it is only knowable, as Plato says, via a kind of "bastard reasoning" (*Timaeus* 52b). We are clearly no longer in the territory of paternal authorization, of legitimate naming or language. Some names and figures that arise in the face of these provisos are as follows: third kind, errant cause, mother, nurse, the scent-free substrate for a fragrant ointment, the gold out of which a statue is made, a wax tablet that receives imprints. Receptacle, space, place. *Hupodochē, chōra, topos.*[3] The thought at work here is that if being is to be instantiated, there must be something for it to be instantiated *in*. Father (being) and son (becoming), after all, require a woman, a mother and a nurse, in order to effect the passage from one to the other: that which receives.

Importantly, Timaeus makes clear that the receptacle is *in motion*. It receives the static mathematical forms, triangles, the two-dimensional planes out of which the elements, three-dimensional figures, will be constructed: tetrahedron, octahedron, icosahedron, and cube compose (respectively) the building blocks of fire, air, water, and earth, and shakes and winnows them out, in a proto-separation and proto-ordering of the cosmos (*Timaeus* 53a). With Plato, the physical story told by earlier thinkers gives way to a metaphysical ontology, and we are newly party to the passage from being to becoming via this strange, errant, and definitively feminine "third kind." And yet, although we are on the way, we will still not quite have arrived at "matter."

Matter *as such* first emerges in the thought of Aristotle, where it is called *hulē*, a word that means wood (archaically, a living forest, but in Aristotle's time principally dead wood, ready for fashioning by the carpenter). We are used to thinking of it as simply contrasted with form—in the case of the bronze sphere, the bronze is the matter, the sphere is the form. The scene of matter's emergence, however, is rather more complex. At the start of the *Physics*, Aristotle is concerned with how an entity comes to be. He agrees with his Eleatic predecessors that being cannot emerge from non-being—an existing thing must come from something else that pre-exists it. Aristotle has no time for origin myths, the infinite regress does not bother him and he simply accepts the idea of a temporal perpetuity. But nonetheless, things that never existed before do come into being, whether through the workings of art (*technē*) or simply by nature (*phusis*). Introducing his way of thinking, he asks us to consider a man learning the art of music (*Physics* I.7). In such a process, the man's prior nonmusicality gives way to his musicality. In a manner of speaking, something *has* come from nothing—musicality has come from nonmusicality, A has resulted from not-A; a positive state has come from its absence or privation. But this is only possible because something has been there all along, namely the man, to ground this process as "something which lies under"—a substrate that undergoes a change. But in this case, we've simply seen a preexisting being, the man, undergo a change in relation to a nonessential attribute (the man is still essentially himself before and after learning music).

What about the case of the coming to be of an entity itself, qua entity? Here, the structure is the same but the terms change. A non-sphere becomes a sphere. Not-A becomes A, but what allows this coming to be to take place is the *matter* that underlies the change. This is a three-term structure: there is the privation, the form, and the matter that persists through the change. The form-matter composite is nothing more than the endpoint of a three-term teleological process, hence an *entelecheia* or *energeia*, a being at the end, or being in completion (translated as actuality and activity in the Latin scholiasts) (*Physics* I.9). In a sense, matter might also be understood as a kind of potential or *dunamis*, or in Heideggerian terminology something that is "appropriate for ..." the given thing it will become (thus clay is appropriate for the pot, bricks are appropriate for the house, menstrual blood is appropriate for the mammal), but it encompasses lack, it is able to take on form, and it undergoes this change passively, acted upon always from elsewhere. But note: in the first case, the man is self-evidently the subject, substance, and substrate of the change. In the second, the "substance" or "the being itself," is really the end-term or result, and matter relegated to "mere" substrate-hood that enables its appearance. I will propose, then, that the thought of matter is haunted by this originary paternal fullness—that of the primary substance—the man himself, whose place it took—now transposed to the status of an ontological destiny, rendering matter now as mere potentiality and lack.[4]

Given matter's status as a kind of enabling placeholder, whose only determinacy derives from the thing it is destined to become, the answer to the question "what is the matter" of a thing can be difficult to state. In the case of the sphere, it is certainly the bronze, but one might further decompose this into an element, in this case water. The four elements can, for Aristotle, also transform into one another, leading us to speculate that some ultimate matter must underlie them, but this is not something he ever explicitly considers. Matter remains ever evasive: it cannot be seen, touched, understood, pointed to, as evidenced especially in Aristotle's anti-atomistic belief in the indefinite decomposability of things (*Physics* 207a 33–5). In the case of living things, there is a further difficulty—we can give a "static" decompositional sense, the "matter" of a man is his flesh, bone, tissues, and blood, but in another sense, a "genetic" sense, it is the matter he was originally derived from, that is, his mother's menstrual blood.

Here, then, sexual difference returns. The female provides the matter as menstrual blood; the male supplies the form as sperm. Not only that, but the sperm also supplies the "source of motion." The matter provided by the female is thoroughly identified with the passive substrate that *undergoes* change initiated by the male seed. But immediately a problem arises: whence the female offspring? The famous answer: she is the result of an error in the reproductive process, a mild form of monstrosity. Despite its designation as dead wood, as passive, as molding material, this matter is, for Aristotle, *also* a source of errancy, exemplified by the female offspring as the error which is also necessary, thus symptomatic.[5] Sexual difference thus fundamentally anchors Aristotle's metaphysics of form and matter, ensuring that in the case of sexually differentiated natural generation matter and form are paradigmatically separated, so that they might reunite in the womb. The masculine principle conveyed in the sperm here is set to act much as a craftsman upon the "dead wood" of the matter, initiating motion and imparting form. And Aristotle does in fact use in this context the locution "primary matter," referring to the menstrual blood (*Gen. Anim.* 729a 33).[6] Aristotle thus repeats Aeschylus's famous edict spoken by Apollo at the close of the *Eumenides*, namely, that the mother is no real parent to the child, but they are merely strangers to one another (657–61). The paternal appropriation and dispossession of the mother in tragedy is granted full scientific and philosophical imprimatur. And yet, things can go astray … the feminine matter turns out not be quite as "appropriate" as its designation would indicate, harboring obscure motions that may work *against* nature's aims as well as for them. Or indeed, in the case of the feminine offspring, it represents the symptomatic and paradoxical situation in which nature's aims are both fulfilled and disrupted at the same time (see Bianchi).

The Latin translation of *hulē* as *materia* thus maintains and linguistically enshrines the fundamental relationship of matter and femininity, grounded in the birth of metaphysics and consolidated in the philosophy of Aristotle. Matter, as we have seen, maintains its feminine associations in the atomism of Lucretius, this time in a positive and light of burgeoning entities and flourishing, though Lucretius also refers to atoms as seeds or *semina*, as well as *primordia*, first things. However, matter begins to take on an increasingly venal aura in the syncretisms with monotheistic Christianity of Neoplatonism, its indeterminacy accruing explicit associations with darkness and evil.

The Aristotelian conception of matter, its indeterminacy now tinged by evil, largely prevails throughout the medieval era both in Europe and in the Arab world, though the alchemy practiced in the Arab world, entering into Europe through Spain, with its empirical investigation into the transmutation of metals and its reliance on the highly malleable notion of *prima materia*, also begins to bear on conceptions of the physical constitution of things. Here, too, gendered conceptions persist: some elements are associated with masculinity and the sun, others with the feminine and the moon.[7] Paracelsus speaks of certain principles as *semina*, after Lucretius, and the alchemists and early chemists also refer to solvents as *menstrua*, substances capable of dissolving and taking apart other more noble kinds of matter (here the venal femininity can be strongly detected, even as the ultimate *menstruum* was the subject of intense research). In Renaissance and early modern Europe, then, figures like Giordano Bruno, Robert Boyle, Pierre Gassendi, and Walter Charleton begin to revivify atomistic theories, with Bruno turning Aristotle radically on his head, arguing in Epicurean-feminist style that *mater-materia* is essential and fundamental, while form is merely a transient guest that occupies it and departs, utterly ephemeral.

From here, theories of matter begin to proliferate. Descartes, for example, believed not in atoms and void but in a plenum in which infinitely divisible parts of matter flow past one another without any gap, an unlikely advocate, perhaps, of a form of fluid mechanics, given his more famous dualist scheme in which mind is definitively separated from the extended world. But this dualism also has the effect of consolidating the dead mechanicity of matter, which must then receive force or motion from without, for Descartes originally supplied by God (II, §36, 240). Newton's laws establish motion as intrinsic to matter through the concept of inertia, though Newton still asserts God as an "active power" in the universe (*virtus activa*, a scholastic conception derived from *vir*, man, also held by Aquinas to reside in male semen), substantially coterminous with all things (Newton 587; Aquinas 1a, Q118, A1, ad. 4). But Newton indeed makes *change* something different again, requiring a mathematically precise causal account. Force, velocity, and acceleration are rendered separate from the bodies they affect, a body being a collection of matter: matter understood as both mass and volume, and mass understood as resistance to acceleration and an index of gravitational attraction. Matter thus becomes, in Newtonian physics, associated with a kind of resistance to force and is therefore opposed to it, and yet, according to Newton's second law, it is something also mathematically inextricable from and even derivable from force, movement, and time: $f = ma$. Rearranging for mass, Mass equals Force divided by Acceleration. Temporality, here, is buried in acceleration, and matter is thus rendered fully knowable, calculable, predictable, and incapable of representing any kind of alterity or offering anything new.

Amongst the burgeoning atomisms, monads, and idealisms of early modernity, the most thoroughgoing materialism of the period is, perhaps unsurprisingly, to be found in the thought of a woman, Margaret Cavendish. For Cavendish, not only does motion inhere entirely in matter, and not in a separate or separable concept like force, but mind and thinking are also thoroughly material phenomena—the physical world is a plenum of active, vital, perceptive, thinking matter. Cavendish, then, may be genuinely designated the true foremother of the feminist new materialisms.

Scientific advances including atomic theory, the periodic table, and Hertz's theory of electromagnetism, with its insoluble disjunction between waves and particles (see Schürmann 28–30), emerge solidly in the nineteenth century only to be supplanted by subatomic particles, relativity, and quantum theory in the twentieth century. In the face of these increasingly complex conceptions of the interrelations between matter and energy, the weight of feminized materiality seems to recur, again and again, for example, as a consistent trope throughout Simone de Beauvoir's *The Second Sex*, in whose existentialist parlance women are weighed down with excessive being-in-itself, unable to transcend themselves in the activity of the for-itself that characterizes the freedom of men. It appears this philosophical habit is hard to shake, and perhaps, indeed, it is a consequence of philosophical questioning itself. In his recent *The Thought of Matter*, Richard Lee indicates that in Aristotle's critique of Thales, a definitive shift to a philosophical understanding of the physical takes place, in that Aristotle requires not simply that an assertion about the fundamental nature of the world be made, but a *reason* given for that nature (12). In other words, a question is raised about the *source* of the given things that would count as a philosophically adequate explanation, a "why" of it. For Lee, matter cannot be approached philosophically except through the thought of it, through an account which would seek to answer the question of why something is. But does this very gesture of demanding a source, a principle, or explanation that goes beyond the given phenomena also have the effect of divorcing motion from matter and thus rendering it passive? Aristotle will, in his famous theory of the four causes in *Physics* II, designate the *source of motion*, the motive cause or *archē kinēseōs*, as "a father or an advisor"—a masculine subject-presumed-to-know. Is part of the very gesture of philosophical questioning destined to separate force, explanation, thought, and movement, all at once, from matter, and with it instantiate and consolidate the active-passive binary, the soul-body binary, the form-matter binary, the mind-extension binary, the force-matter binary, the transcendence-immanence binary, so amenable to metaphorizing through sexual difference because of the no-doubt existentially resonant mechanics of heterosexual fucking?

The turn to matter and materialism in recent feminist thought thus both grapples and fails to grapple with these fundamental questions. Judith Butler's *Bodies that Matter* responds to the problemetic posed by matter for her performative theory of gender by rendering it as *materialization*, that is, as a product and effect of a kind human activity, thus retaining the problematic of mediation that concerns Lee. This activity is that of performativity, which is not reducible to the notion of a conscious act or action that *acts upon* an already constituted passivity, but rather refers to a constant repetition of acts that necessarily conform and fail to conform to standards of normativity they also serve to constitute. Such activity has a regulatory force that impels certain materializations and not others, renders some kinds of bodies intelligible, legible, legitimate, and renders other bodies abject. Certain kinds of matter (typically, human bodies possessing the attributes straight, white, male, able-bodied, etc.) come to *matter* (and exert legislative power) while others fall outside the regulatory limits of legibility, of recognizability, and consequently fail to matter, are foreclosed, suffering a fate that aligns with that of the traditional philosophical conception of matter as unconstructed, inaccessible, indeterminate, and abyssal. In a sense, then, Butler accounts for the force implicit in the philosophical question Lee identifies, one which effects the very normative-abjecting splitting it sets out to explain.

Butler's thought is often contrasted with that of Grosz (e.g., by Cheah). The former is seen as concerned with the human activities of language, norms, and world-making, while the latter is seen as concerned with "real matter" and its ability to push back against and act upon the social, insofar as it is not merely passive and acted-upon, but also must be understood as unruly, restless, and volatile. And yet Butler's emphasis on *force* and its effects also dovetails with Grosz's turn in *Volatile Bodies* toward a Deleuzian-Spinozist ontology of forces and intensities, which leaves the stases, the resistances, the very weight of matter behind. In one sense, then, this resolution of matter into a field of forces and intensities, powers, impulsions, and compulsions has the salutary effect of expanding the field of activity, animacy, or agency, to cover all of being, everything that is or may come to be, in effect to reinstitute motion at the heart of matter and materialization. This is the fundamental move upon which the entire field of the feminist new materialisms is staked.

What does, or really what *can* matter *do* in and for contemporary feminism, if it can indeed be recast as encompassing what it has traditionally been contrasted with: not form, spirit, or mind (so easily cast as mystifications), so much as motion, force, activity, wave, vibration, intensity, animacy, agency, signification (see, e.g., Alaimo and Hekman; Barad; Bennett; Chen; Clough; Colebrook; Hinton and van der Tuin; Kirby; Pitts-Taylor). The feminist political force of transvaluing matter as lively, even as *agentic*, is on one level utterly clear and urgent: that which has been historically cast as passive, feminine, objectal, now is newly understood as harboring the capacity to *act*, to *act with*, to *act upon*, to feel, to initiate events, including events of liberatory political change. No more shall any entity, human or otherwise, physical or metaphysical, be rendered purely passive. The agency traditionally denied to women is reinstalled not only at the level of the human but also at the level of fundamental metaphysics.

What is more, the *new materialisms* signify the renewed possibility of a productive feminist relationship with the natural and physical sciences—from quantum physics to neurobiology and the biology of sex and sexuality, to agriculture, and environmental science—in the wake of a purported earlier feminist avoidance of biology on the grounds that it is already infused with sexist assumptions and cannot but carry with it the threat of essentialism.[8] Recasting matter, and really the whole realm of nature, as immanently in motion, actively self-organizing (De Landa) rather than fixed and determinate, renders it a participant in the unfolding of history rather than as a threat of stasis, and renders possible a whole range of liberatory feminist engagements that were previously barred.

On the other hand, we might want to ask to what extent such transvaluation can be sustained, given the drag of matter's philosophical legacy, that is to say, its passive, dead weight; its indeterminacy and abjection. Matter certainly remains a continuing problem in contemporary physics: the recent search for the fundamental mass-granting particle, the Higgs boson, giving rise less to answers than to further speculations about yet more obscure particles, dark matter, antimatter, and so on. If matter is foreclosed, passive, feminized, abject, abyssal, it also retains a feminized power of fascination, the magnetic enticement of a lure, as a feminist optic is uniquely able to disclose. Might it be the case that this turn to animate matter also covers over the *effect* of an inquiry into matter, forgetting once again the foreclosed remainder of the force of materialization described so vividly by Butler. In closing, then, I will raise some brief concerns arising from the "new materialist" moment.

One of the most widely cited contemporary renderings of matter for feminist new materialisms is the "agential realism" of Karen Barad. In *Meeting the Universe Halfway* Barad turns to quantum physics in order to argue that human knowers and the matter they set out to investigate *both* participate, performatively, in the determination of the being of things. According to her Bohrian model, the results of experiments that track a quantum particle in its diffraction cannot be observed without losing sight of the state of the apparatus itself. No choice is possible between tracing the path of a particle or observing interference effects, thus giving rise to the notions of intra-action and entanglement between observer and observed. Quantum entanglement, further, refers to a dynamic among particles themselves, in which one responds to another, its copy, mysteriously, at a distance. Barad develops the notion of a *phenomenon* as mutually constituted by ontological and epistemological intra-actions—both matter and knowers engage in performative activity—as well as intra-actions among non-human entities. Barad's terms here—entanglement, diffraction, intra-action—transposed from the quantum level and applied to everyday relations among humans and their worlds, have seen avid uptake in the contemporary critical humanities. Yet the power of the discourse of ultimate science is still evidently at work here: quantum physics is offered as a master discourse with the power to deliver an account of ultimate reality through empirical means (Barad 35). While the uptake of these terms in the literature often draws on their metaphorical or poetic power, a certain authority also accrues from the status of physics as arbiter of ultimate reality. Moreover, Barad intends this quantum discourse to provide a literal underpinning rather than an analogical model for the appearance of both entities and our knowledge about them (24).[9] Entities, for Barad, then come to be as a result of "agential cuts" in complex intra-active systems, for which we are in part ethically responsible, providing a compelling link between fundamental ontology and the ethico-political.

Nonetheless, her theory runs into problems. Not only does it require ultimate reliance on physics as a master-discourse (a stance critiqued by feminist epistemologists and philosophers of science, including Harding [43–8], and Haraway who calls the fantasy of a totalizing scientific view the "god-trick" [581–2]). It also extends quantum phenomena, such as the entanglement of particles at a distance, to our everyday, macro world, when, clearly, these do not and cannot occur in this domain.[10] What is more, it assumes a standpoint in which the philosopher stands not outside the matter as observed by the scientist, but, in order for the truth claims made to actually hold, outside the whole performative system of the matter, the apparatus, *and* the scientist who constructs it, in order to gain an "objective" view of these onto-epistemological processes and the "phenomena" which thereby emerge (see Calvert-Minor). In order to accept Barad's position, we must deny our own enmeshment in the scene as a whole. Finally, and importantly, Barad simply fails to account for the effects discussed earlier, articulated most trenchantly by Butler, in which *materialization* as such—an irreducibly (if not solely) human activity, irreducibly accompanied by human responsibility—has been seen to inevitably produce a remainder, something abject, something abyssal, something venal and feminized: matter.[11]

Nowhere, it seems, is this production of remaindered, abject, feminized, matter more vividly articulated than in US Black Studies' focus on the black body, especially captive black body in slavery, whose living legacy is brought to consciousness in contemporary history in the movement called Black Lives Matter. The racial dimensions of matter/mattering have been explored in a new materialist idiom by Chen, and in a postcolonial feminist context by Roy and Subramaniam, and yet the history of modern slavery offers an acute and monstrous vision of a fundamental ambiguity that persists in Western history and thinking between people and matter, and of the mattering of bodies.

It is a philosophical commonplace that slavery renders subjects as objects, turns humans into commodities to be exchanged and put to use, and that this racialized splitting in modernity also inseparably produces white subjectivity as supremacy as both cause and effect of this colonial legacy. But a powerful strand in Black Studies—comprising Hortense Spillers, Saidiya Hartman, Jennifer Morgan, Donna Jones, Alexander Weheliye, Fred Moten, Zakiyyah Iman Jackson, Christina Sharpe, Amber Musser, Diana Leong, among many others—moves away from the violence of this abstraction to bring into focus the *materializations* undergone and experienced by black people. Spillers describes the enslaved, captive body rendered as flesh, or as matter: abducted, processed, shipped, raped, whipped, lacerated, broken, and experimented upon—what she calls the "atomizing of the captive body" (68). As she notes, this set of systematic operations destroyed not only individual bodies but also all material, generational, and nominal bonds between parents and children, annihilating not just kinship on the symbolic level and thus gender itself in any legible constitution, but, also, profoundly for this thinking of matter/*mater*, the possibility of any material/maternal reproductive connection or continuity (see also Morgan; Jackson). Black bodies, even after emancipation ("in the wake" of slavery as Sharpe puts it), continue to be materialized as systematically immiserated, terrorized, differentially housed, employed, medicalized, and educated, surveilled, policed, judged, incarcerated, expendable, and, of course, killable without accountability: these are the conditions of contemporary black life in the United States, as the Black Lives Matter movement has brought so starkly into relief.

Here, the "new materialist" move in which abjected and objectified matter is now newly understood as encompassing force, motion, vitality, vibrancy, and agency would seem to be a salutary development, just as it has been for feminism and political theory. And given the litany of passive verbs appearing in the previous paragraph, it would be hard to argue with the value of a newly animate and agentic conception of matter with which to counter the many social and physical violences inflicted by whites and by white supremacy upon black people. Not only, as Leong argues, does the "new materialism" fail to account for, and is far from able to dismantle, a highly persistent oppressive arrangement (2017), but the association between black bodies (as "matter"), black cultural practices, and a certain vitality also has a long and much theorized history that significantly precedes this "new" movement. Zora Neale Hurston's poetic and performative engagement in black religious practices such as Obeah, for example, foregrounds the slippage of the boundary between animate and inanimate that harnesses the power of things as a "tactic for gaining power" (Biers 173). The *Négritude* poets, especially Leopold Senghor and Aimé Cesaire, in turn, articulated an immanentist ontology of force that may be read in concert with the life philosophies of German Romanticism, Nietzsche, Bergson, and even, *avant la lettre*, Deleuze and Guattari: Donna Jones relates that they "imagined themselves a carriers of positive difference and affirmed the productivity of their own desire," with Césaire in particular fully cognizant of the *breaks* in duration imposed by the Atlantic slave trade, denied by Bergson's conception of an unbroken *durée*, as well as a "polymorphous and incessantly creative nature" harking back to Heraclitus (Jones 170, 176).

Another strand in this tradition also emphasizes the extent to which black bodies have also been produced, through slavery and its aftermath, as precisely motile, vital, and vibrant, as pleasurable spectacle, as a seemingly bottomless affective resource for whites— an intrinsic element of white supremacy and capitalism's antiblack racializing consumerist calculus.[12] Hartman describes how slaves were made to dance, sing, and "step it up lively" on demand for white owners and buyers, in the coffle, at the market, and on the plantation. Weheliye, in turn, develops Spillers's notion of *pornotroping* in representations of slavery, in which the sexualized and violated black body is enjoyed in the very excess of its embodied reaction to violence, as the "heartrending shrieks" of the whipped and suffering person, especially as rendered in film, are both testament to horrific violence and yet also libidinally invested (104). Arguably, the black body has always already been produced, spectacularly so, for white supremacy as the very "vibrant matter" touted so guilelessly by the new materialisms: productive, reproductive, creative, musical, rhythmical, physically vital, and endlessly resilient.

The binds persisting here for the modern black subject have been perhaps most famously explored by Franz Fanon in *Black Skin, White Masks*, for whom all the resources of African life and culture, so richly represented by the *Négritude* poets, are inevitably processed through the violent hierarchies of white supremacy. Ambiguities, remainders, and difference do not, however, fail to persist: matter's trace? Fred Moten attunes us to the alchemical and poetic possibilities incipient in black performance, in mourning, in the voice where "the shriek turns speech turns song," (*In the Break* 22) and yet also remains wary of any discourse of possible transcendence, "unless transcendence is understood as immanence's fugitive impurity" (*In the Break* 755).[13] Zakiyyah Iman Jackson in turn reads the black mater(nal), foreclosed by ontology, as holding the potential to destabilize or rupture the reigning order (in a way that mere "vibrant matter" could not) (5; see also Leong).

If, as Moten claims, blackness is indeed "prior to ontology ... ontology's anti- and ante-foundation, ontology's underground, the irreparable disturbance of ontology's time and space," ("Blackness" 739) might there be space also, here, for a thought of matter? Not one that yearns for paternal and metaphysical substantiality, nor that confidently proclaims atoms and void, nor that trusts that modernity's scientific tools or twenty-first-century philosophical designations can deliver its truth and determine its onto-logical place. Rather, such a thought never stops attending to how matter is remaindered, discarded by philosophical thinking as thought's absence, a thinking that represents less an ontological *other* (bound to reappear as abyss, or lure, or flesh—sign of European can-nibal consumption) than an *otherwise* of thought. The philosophical call that evoked it is the call for an origin (*archē*), something elemental (less something compositional, but, in Empedoclean parlance, roots or *rhizomata*, common to all things). Mattering, the gerund that signifies temporality, is still far from an "idle pun" (J. Butler 7), but discloses a certain fugitivity, a call to consciousness and responsibility that evades—endlessly—all claims to knowledge, sense, definition, and determination.[14]

NOTES

1 What is less well known is that Nietzsche owes his conception of the Dionysian to J. J. Bachofen, for whom the conception is fundamentally associated with the feminine.

2 Arguably, Heidegger's reliance on vegetal metaphors in his rendering of *phusis* aligns with a similar emphasis on vegetality in Irigaray's recent work (see Irigaray and Marder).

3 The subsequent tradition, both ancient and modern, will foreground the name of *chōra*: space, field, position, territory, land, countryside, but *chōra* is just one of the many names given by Plato to this third kind.

4 Claire Colebrook (2008) will revalue this lack in potentiality as virtuality, and a powerful source for feminist politics; to my mind it is overdetermined by the substantial fullness it is destined toward (Aristotle says matter reaches out to form just as the female reaches out to the male [*Physics* I.9, 192a, 16–18, 23–4]).

5 See Bianchi. Something of Plato's designation of the "third kind" as "errant cause" may per-sist here, though Aristotle does address Plato's receptacle in the *Physics*, stating that Plato believes that matter (*hulē*) and space (*chōra*) are the same, and place (*topos*) and space (*chōra*) are also the same (*Physics* 209b 13–17).

6 This locution can, in other contexts, refer to the most immediate or "proximate" matter something is made out of—the bricks for a house, for example—but in this context there are grounds for understanding it in a more fundamental sense. See Bianchi, 37.

7 Parallels may also be found in ancient Chinese alchemy (see Cooper 137–9).

8 On these renewed engagements, see Franklin, Chen. A genealogical debate has ensued as to whether twentieth-century feminism truly failed to engage with the sciences. The claim is perhaps made most firmly by Alaimo and Hekman (*Introduction*), thrown into question by Ahmed, and defended by Davis.

9 It is worth noting that the same ambiguity between analogy and literal, material, basis is found in Lucretius, when he invokes the atomic swerve or *clinamen* as the explanation for human free will.

10 See Lee Smolin, *Time Reborn*, 162. For an excellent overview see Seely, esp. on Derrida and matter as radical alterity or *différance*.

11 For Barad, matter is constituted by a "congealing of agency ... a stabilizing and destabilizing process of iterative intra-activity" (151), but there is no strong account of the philosophical and political mechanisms by which such congealings themselves are produced, and which produce their hierarchizing effects in turn.

12 See Ngai, esp. chapter 2, "Animatedness."

13 James critiques the sonic dimensions of new materialism—its reliance on notions such as vibration and resonance—from a Black Studies perspective as inherently neoliberal and exclusionary.

14 Such a formulation both does and does not go beyond Derrida's consideration of matter as radical alterity and thus as *différance* (64), also discussed by Seely (11).

WORKS CITED

Ahmed, Sara. "Imaginary Prohibitions: Some Preliminary Remarks on the Founding Gestures of the New Materialism." *European Journal of Women's Studies* 15 (2008): 23–39.

Alaimo, Stacy, and Susan Hekman. "Introduction: Emerging Models of Materiality in Feminist Theory." *Material Feminisms*. Bloomington: Indiana UP, 2008, pp. 1–20.

Alaimo, Stacy, and Susan Hekman, eds. *Material Feminisms*. Bloomington: U of Indiana P, 2008.

Aquinas, Thomas. *Summa Theologiae: Questions on God*. Ed. Brian Davies and Brian Leftow. Cambridge: Cambridge University Press, 2006.

Bachofen, Johann Jakob. *Myth, Religion, and Mother Right*. Trans. Ralph Manheim. Princeton, NJ: Princeton UP, 1967.

Barad, Karen. *Meeting the Universe Halfway: Quantum Physics and the Entanglement of Matter and Meaning*. Durham, NC: Duke UP, 2007.

Behar, Katherine, ed. *Object-Oriented Feminism*. Minneaplis: U of Minnesota P, 2016.

Bennett, Jane. *Vibrant Matter: A Political Ecology of Things*. Durham, NC: Duke UP, 2010.

Bianchi, Emanuela. *The Feminine Symptom: Aleatory Matter in the Aristotelian Cosmos*. New York: Fordham UP, 2014.

Biers, Katherine. "Practices of Enchantment: The Theatre of Zora Neale Hurston." *TDR: The Drama Review* 59.4 (2015): 67–82.

Bruno, Giordano. *Cause, Principle and Unity, and Essays on Magic*. Ed. Richard J. Blackwell and Robert de Lucca. Cambridge: Cambridge University Press, [1584] 1998.

Butler, James Eric. "Effluvia: Empedocles Studies." *Epochē* 9.2 (2005): 215–31.

Butler, Judith. *Bodies That Matter: On the Discursive Limits of "Sex."* New York: Routledge, 1993.

Calvert-Minor, Chris. "Epistemological Misgivings of Karen Barad's 'Posthumanism.'" *Human Studies* 37.1 (2014): 123–37.

Cavendish, Margaret. *Observations upon Experimental Philosophy*. Ed. Eileen O' Neill. Cambridge: Cambridge University Press, 2001 [1668].

Cheah, Pheng. "Mattering." Review of *Bodies That Matter: On the Discursive Limits of "Sex"* by Judith Butler. Volatile Bodies: Toward a Corporeal Feminism by Elizabeth Grosz. *Diacritics* 26.1 (1996): 108–39.

Chen, Mel Y. *Animacies: Biopolitics, Racial Mattering, and Queer Affect*. Durham, NC: Duke UP, 2012.

Cixous, Hélène. "Sorties: Out and Out: Attacks/Ways Out/Forays." *The Newly Born Woman*. Ed. Hélène Cixous and Catherine Clément and trans. Betsy Wing, Minneapolis: U of Minnesota P, 1986, 63–132.

Clough Patricia, Ticineto with Jean Halley, eds. *The Affective Turn:Theorizing the Social*. Durham, NC: Duke UP, 2007.

Colebrook, Claire. "On Not Becoming Man: The Materialist Politics of Unactualized Potential." *Material Feminisms*. Bloomington: Indiana UP, pp. 52–84.

Cooper, Jean. *Chinese Alchemy: Taoism, the Power of Gold, and the Quest for Immortality*. San Francisco, CA: Weiser Books, 2016.

Davis, Noela. "New Materialism and Feminism's Anti-Biologism: A Response to Sara Ahmed." *European Journal of Women's Studies* 16.1 (2009): 67–80.

de Beauvoir, Simone. *The Second Sex*. Trans. Constance Borde and Sheila Malovany-Chevallier. New York: Vintage Books, 2011.

De Landa, Manuel. "Nonorganic Life." *Incorporations*. Ed. Jonathan Crary and Sanford Kwinter. New York: Zone Books, 1992. 129–67.

Derrida, Jacques. *Positions*. Trans. Alan Bass. Chicago, IL: U of Chicago P, 1981.

Descartes, René. "Principles of Philosophy." *The Philosophical Writings of Descartes*. Trans. John Cottingham, Robert Stoothoff, and Dugald Murdoch. New York: Cambridge University Press, [1649] 1985.

Fanon, Franz. *Black Skin, White Masks*. Trans. Charles Lam Markmann. New York: Grove P, 1967.

Federici, Silvia. *Caliban and the Witch: Women, the Body, and Primitive Accumulation*. Autonomedia, 2004.

Franklin, Sarah. "The Cyborg Embryo: Our Path to Transbiology." *Theory, Culture & Society* 23.7–8 (2006): 167–87.

Grosz, Elizabeth. *Volatile Bodies: Toward a Corporeal Feminism*. Bloomington: Indiana UP, 1994.

Haraway, Donna. "Situated Knowledges: The Science Question in Feminism and the Privilege of Partial Perspective." *Feminist Studies* 14.3 (1988): 575–99.

Harding, Sandra. *The Science Question in Feminism*. Ithaca: Cornell UP, 1986.

Hartman, Saidiya V. *Scenes of Subjection: Terror, Self-Making, and Slavery in Nineteenth-Century America*. Oxford: Oxford UP, 1997.

Heidegger, Martin. "On the Essence and Concept of Φύσις in Aristotle's Physics B,1." Ed. William McNeill and trans. Thomas Sheehan. *Pathmarks*. Cambridge, MA: Cambridge University Press, 1998, pp. 183–230.

Hekman, Susan. *The Material of Knowledge: Feminist Disclosures*. Bloomington: Indiana UP, 2010.

Hinton, Peta, and Iris van der Tuin. "Preface." *Women: A Cultural Review* 25.1 (2014): pp. 1–8.

Hinton, Peta, and Iris van der Tuin, eds. "Feminist Matters: The Politics of New Materialism." Special issue of *Women: A Cultural Review* 25.1 (2014).

Hird, Myra J. "Feminist Matters: New Materialist Considerations of Sexual Difference." *Feminist Theory* 5.2 (2004): 223–32.

Irigaray, Luce. *Elemental Passions*. Trans. Joanne Collie and Judith Still. New York: Routledge, 1992.

Irigaray, Luce. *The Forgetting of Air in Martin Heidegger*. Trans. Mary Beth Mader. Austin: U of Texas P, 1999.

Irigaray, Luce. *The Marine Lover of Friedrich Nietzsche*. Trans. Gillian C. Gill. New York: Columbia UP, 1991.

Irigaray, Luce. *This Sex Which Is Not One*. Trans. Catherine Porter. Ithaca: Cornell UP, 1985.

Irigaray, Luce. *Speculum of the Other Woman*. Trans. Gillian C. Gill. Ithaca: Cornell UP, 1985.

Irigaray, Luce, and Michael Marder. *Through Vegetal Being*. New York: Columbia UP, 2016.

Jackson, Zakiyyah Iman. "Sense of Things." *Catalyst: Feminism, Theory, Technoscience* 2.2 (2016): 1–48, http://catalystjournal.org/ojs/index.php/catalyst/article/view/74/212. Accessed December 21, 2017.

James, Robin. *The Sonic Episteme*. Durham, NC: Duke UP, forthcoming.

Jones, Donna V. *The Racial Discourses of Life Philosophy: Négritude, Vitalism, and Modernity*. New York: Columbia UP, 2010.

Kirby, Vicki. *Telling Flesh: The Substance of the Corporeal*. New York: Routledge, 1997.

Lee, Richard A. Jr., *The Thought of Matter*. Lanham, MD: Rowman & Littlefield, 2017.

Leong, Diana. "The Mattering of Black Lives: Octavia Butler's Hyperempathy and the Promise of the New Materialisms." *Catalyst: Feminism, Theory, Technoscience* 2.2 (2016): 1–35, http://catalystjournal.org/ojs/index.php/catalyst/article/view/100/203. Accessed December 21, 2017.

Marx, Karl. "The German Ideology, Part 1." *The Marx-Engels Reader*, 2nd edn. Ed. Robert C. Tucker. New York: W. W. Norton, 1978, pp. 146–200.

Meißner, Hanna. "New Material Feminisms and Historical Materialism: A Diffractive Reading of Two (Ostensibly) Unrelated Perspectives." *Mattering: Feminism, Science, and Materialism*. Ed. Victoria Pitts-Taylor. New York: New York UP, 2016, pp. 43–57.

Morgan, Jennifer L. *Labouring Women: Reproduction and Gender in New World Slavery*. Philadelphia: U of Pennsylvania P, 2004.

Moten, Fred. "Blackness and Nothingness (Mysticism in the Flesh)." *South Atlantic Quarterly* 112.4 (2013): 737–80.

Moten, Fred. *In the Break: The Aesthetics of the Black Radical Tradition*. Minneapolis: U of Minnesota P, 2003.

Musser, Amber Jamilla, *Sensational Flesh: Race, Power, Masochism*. New York: New York UP, 2014.

Newton, Isaac. *The Principia: Mathematical Principles of Natural Philosophy*. Trans. I. Bernard Cohen, Anne Whitman, and Julia Budenz. Berkeley: U of California P, [1687] 1999.

Ngai, Sianne. *Ugly Feelings*. Cambridge, MA: Harvard UP, 2005.

Pitts-Taylor, Victoria, ed. *Mattering: Feminism, Science, and Materialism*. New York: New York UP, 2016.

Roy, Deboleena, and Banu Subramaniam. "Matter in the Shadows: Feminist New Materialism and the Practices of Colonialism." *Mattering: Feminism, Science, and Materialism*. Ed. Victoria Pitts-Taylor, New York: New York UP, 2016, pp. 23–42.

Rubin, Gayle. "The Traffic in Women: Notes on the 'Political Economy' of Sex." *Toward an Anthropology of Women*. Ed. Rayna Reiter. New York: Monthly Review P, 1975, pp. 157–210.

Schürmann, Reiner. *Broken Hegemonies*. Trans. Reginald Lilly. Bloomington: Indiana UP, 2003.

Seely, Stephen. "The Spirit of (the) Matter: Deconstruction, Meta/Physics, and the "New" Feminist Materialism," *philoSOPHIA: a Continental Feminist Society 9th Annual Meeting*, Conference Presentation. Paper on file with the author, May 16, 2015, Atlanta, GA: Emory U.

Sharpe, Christina. *In the Wake: On Blackness and Being*. Durham, NC: Duke UP, 2016.

Smolin, Lee. *Time Reborn: From the Crisis in Physics to the Future of the Universe*. Boston: Mariner Books, 2013.

Weheliye, Alexander. *Habeas Viscus: Racializing Assemblages, Biopolitics, and Black Feminist Theories of the Human*. Durham, NC: Duke UP, 2014.

Zinkernagel, Henrik. "Niels Bohr on the Wave Function and the Classical/Quantum Divide." *Studies in History and Philosophy of Modern Physics* 53 (2016): 9–19.

CHAPTER TWENTY-EIGHT

Technology

ANNE CONG-HUYEN

INTRODUCTION

In September of 2017, news publications worldwide reported that Samantha, an anatomically female robot who made her debut at the Ars Electronica Festival in Linz, Austria, had been retired so that she could be repaired, after significant damage had been visited upon her body at the electronic arts exhibition. According to the London-based UK publications the *Mirror* and the *New Statesman*, the "sex doll was so heavily molested by eager men it broke," "was left heavily soiled," and "two fingers were broken in the melee" by men who behaved "like barbarians." (Barrie, Norris). The episode, for many, reflected the deeply ingrained misogyny and toxic masculinity of the tech industry, but it also reinforced the problematic imagery that abounds within the high tech industries that feature feminized figures that exist only to serve and please (male) users. To some, like Norris of the *New Statesman*, the proliferation of these figurations only serves to exaggerate unrealistic ideals of femininity while also "inviting" and "normalising" violence onto female bodies (or machines that resemble female bodies). Sadly, what many critics have noticed is that the violence made hypervisible in this episode is not an aberration. In fact, gendered violence is not restricted to robotic bodies, nor is it unique to the tech industry.

Although the above example is a dramatic one, the cultural criticism presented here was published in mainstream publication, which made it notable. This effort, however, is not new. Such popular criticism owes a great debt to the work of feminist scholars of technology who have laid the foundations for gendered analyses of science and technology fields. What it points to, in particular, is an unspoken relationship between technological innovation, its conflation with computation, and its visualization in the form of feminized (normative yet exaggerated female) bodies. In general, it comes down to men making techie things that look or sound like women, though the technological thing is not made *for* women. As many, like Lisa Nakamura, have observed, "[T]echnology has narrowed to really mean *computing*, which is a field that de facto excludes women of color, and women generally" ("Feminism, Technology, and Race" 2:51–3:28) The confusion of "technology" for "computers" has become a common one and is a phenomenon that can be observed across popular media and journalism, where the "Technology" section of any publication will include coverage of the newest releases from major tech companies (phones, gaming consoles, computers, apps, etc.), in-depth investigative pieces about labor practices of e-retailers, or breakthroughs in green energy. This smattering of examples, for instance, comes from a single perusal of the "Technology" subsection of a popular news aggregating site.

If we turn to reference texts that define and give us common understandings of the term, major mainstream reference texts, for example, define technology as follows:

Technology, the application of scientific knowledge to the practical aims of human life or, as it is sometimes phrased, to the change and manipulation of the human environment. (*Encyclopedia Britannica*)

The branch of knowledge dealing with the mechanical arts and applied sciences; the study of this. (*Oxford English Dictionary*)

the practical application of knowledge especially in a particular area: engineering, medical *technology*. (*Merriam-Webster*)

According to these definitions from general reference texts, technology is about scientific knowledge, mechanical arts, practical application, and engineering. These definitions align neatly with Nakamura's observation that generally, in the United States, when we think of "technology," we are thinking of computers. Even in higher education, literature and research for educators about "technology in the classroom" almost exclusively refers to the integration of electronic, digital, or computational tools in the classroom. Pedagogical models used by educational technologists, such as the Technological Pedagogical Content Knowledge (TPACK) framework or the Substitution Augmentation Modification Redefinition (SAMR) model, are designed to help teachers determine how and when to incorporate computers into teaching. EDUCAUSE, one of the largest ed-tech (educational technology) organizations, refers to itself as "a higher education technology association" that includes "the largest community of IT leaders and professionals committed to advancing higher education." In terms of the "higher education industry," or what some might call the "educational industrial complex," educational technology becomes synonymous with Information Technologies (e.g., computers and telecommunications).

In both general terms, and even in the more niche language of higher education, "technology" refers to specialized machines and tools produced and serviced by highly trained individuals or engineers. For many, as evidenced by both dictionary definitions and the more corporate EDUCAUSE, the terms "technology" and "feminism" would seem unrelated, even oppositional. These are all topics and professional fields that should be gender neutral, based solely on one's training, education, and skill, right? So, what does technology have to do with feminism? And what does feminism have to do with technology? As feminist scholars of Science and Technology would argue, *everything*. Rhetoric about technology, at its best, aspires toward neutrality, but historically it has proven to be deeply gendered and racialized.

Prior to this collection, "technology" was seldom included in anthologies and reference texts about feminist theory. Generally, if it makes an appearance, "technology" emerges in chapters or articles about Science and Technology Studies (STS) more broadly. Lynda Birke and Marsha Henry's contribution to the second edition of *Introducing Women's Studies* is one of the few examples we have, and their chapter provides a thorough introduction to feminist scholarship about technology. Their essay from 1997, "The Black Hole: Women's Studies, Science and Technology," provides one of the earlier overviews of feminist approaches to science and a somewhat shallow dive into feminist critiques of technology. Like many collections about feminist technology that would come later, their chapter places an emphasis on reproductive technologies that affect the female body (e.g., the Pill, Depo-Provera, IUD). Though helpful as a starting point, this article also points to the importance of specialized collections dedicated to gender and science and technology as sites that curate this work in isolation from the larger work of feminist scholarship. These more specialized collections also tended to address the topics of gender gaps in scientific and technological industries, cyberfeminism, or techno-feminism. By consulting canonical and general feminist theory and philosophical texts, however, it would appear that technology has been of little importance to women and feminists.

The elision of the term "technology" in many feminist reference texts does not accurately reflect the field, however, as feminist scholars in the Anglophone Global North have been theorizing, publishing, and organizing about technology, the gendered body, labor, and related experiences since the mid-1980s and earlier. Despite a surge of such scholarship emerging in the mid-1990s and into the 2000s, in fields such as cultural studies, film and media studies, STS, labor studies, and others, feminist technology studies is reflected only to a limited degree in these larger reference texts. If reflected at all, technology is likely to take the form of chapters on "cyborgs," rather than ones on "technology."[1] The figure of the cyborg, most famously theorized and developed by Donna Haraway as a symbol for hybridity, contradiction, and resiliency (and which will be discussed in further detail shortly), is indeed significant and powerful for the development of feminist approaches to technology, and has led to a proliferation of different, yet related, identities and practices for feminists engaging with technology as both object of study, as praxis, and as structure for community formation and action.

This chapter, in an attempt to capture the breadth of feminist engagements with technology, offers both a condensed historical overview of the term "technology," while also providing a broad overview of the breadth of feminist technological scholarship. The following sections unpack the fundamental questions at the heart of feminist approaches to technology and explores their emergence and complexity in a range of fields, from literature, to humanistic inquiry and social scientific studies of technology. Outside of scholarly practice, feminist engagement with technology also takes on other forms: artistic production, community organizing, collective resource making, and even feminist blogging. Despite the range or forms that these activities take, the tensions at the heart of feminist technology studies are threaded throughout this disparate array of work, a broad interdisciplinary field of practice that likely began with Mary Shelley's *Frankenstein; or, The Modern Prometheus*. The product of a nineteenth-century teenage girl participating in a wager between friends, *Frankenstein* offers a narrative that seriously contemplates the potential for science and technology is made real to horrific effect. This story effectively created a new genre, science fiction, where science meets technology and imagines possible presents and futures. Donna Haraway would later trouble the relationship Shelley represented between the obsessive Dr. Frankenstein and his spurned monstrous progeny with her image of the cyborg, who rejected this patriarchal formula and instead emerges as a figure untethered from her past and symbolizes feminist potential and power. This monstrous yet beautiful lineage takes shape today in both the academic and journalistic critiques of digital spaces and labor systems *and* the collective work of groups such as FemTechNet or FemBot.

HISTORY

As many historians and philosophers of technology will point out, the word "technology" is notoriously difficult to define, and many working in the field do not bother to define it. They instead take it as a given. The general public tends to think of "technology" as devices, tools, *things* that make our life easier, and "high tech" as industries that require high levels of education, expertise, and knowledge. But this usage of the term did not become common until quite recently and is generally dated to the period following the Second World War, which saw dramatic cultural shifts in labor, production, and knowledge.

The *Oxford English Dictionary* traces early usage of the word "technology" to the seventeenth century, when it was used as a term that meant a "discourse or treatise on an art or arts." By 1706, Edward Phillips's *The New World of Words: Or, Universal English Dictionary*, was already defining "Technology" as "a Description of Arts, especially the Mechanical" ("technology"; Casaubon; Phillips 649), drawing a material distinction between "technical arts" and other ones. But George Wilson, in 1855, argued that " 'Technology' literally signifies the Science of the Arts, or a Discourse or Dissertation on these," and continued "Its object is not Art itself, *i.e.*, the *practice* of Art, but the principles which guide or underlie Art," suggesting that *practice* and *application* were not of paramount importance in defining technology (Wilson 5). In his *Keywords: A Vocabulary of Culture and Society*, Raymond Williams's definition of "Technology" emphasizes the nineteenth century as the moment of cultural shift, where technology went from the notion of a "study of the arts" to the eventual "practical arts":

> **Technology** was used from C17 to describe a systematic study of the arts (cf. ART) or the terminology of a particular art. It is from fw *tekhnolgia, Gk,* and *technologia,* mod. L. a systematic treatment. The root is *tekne,* Gk,—an art or craft ... It was mainly in Mc19 that **technology** became fully specialized to the 'practical arts'; this is also the period of **technologist**. The newly specialized sense of SCIENCE (q.v.) and *scientist* opened the way to a familiar distinction between knowledge (*science*) and its practical application (**technology**), within the selected field. (292)

> Though communicated as early as the 18th century, the weight placed on the mechanical and practical expertise would not become pronounced and commonplace until the mid-20th century. By the 1920s and 1930s, "technology," according to Colleen A. Dunlavy, was understood in an anthropological sense as 'useful knowledge' but confined to the largely male preserves of industry and engineering. [Thorstein] Veblen and others also stressed the machine-like, autonomous nature of the emerging "industrial system" (which they believed engineers were uniquely suited to head).

Dunlavy cites this period as the emergence of the engineer, a group who strove to be professionally identified with technological work, meanwhile espousing a definition of the term "technology" that emphasized it as an "applied science" that is closely related to "science" as we know it today.

As Jentery Sayers describes so succinctly, "During the twentieth century, the meaning of 'technology' gradually expanded to include both the processes of a system and the physical devices required of that system." After the Second World War, the United States saw this abrupt shift, and by the mid-century it became an adjective used to distinguish certain sectors of the economy (e.g., "high tech") related to the manufacture and maintenance of complex machines.

It would appear that at this time the term "technology" took on a superficially gender-neutral, though ostensibly masculine character. Ruth Oldenziel makes that very argument in *Making Technology Masculine.* She writes,

> There is nothing inherently masculine about technology. The representation of men's native and women's exotic relationship with technology elaborates on a historical, if relatively recent and twentieth-century Western tendency to view technology as an

exclusively masculine affair. The public association between technology and manliness grew when male middle-class attention increasingly focused its gaze on the muscular bodies of working-class men and valorized middle-class athletes, but disempowered to bodies of Native Americans, African Americans, and women. (10–11)

This gendering of technology can be traced much earlier, however, and can be seen even in those early-seventeenth-, eighteenth-, and nineteenth-century texts, all written by men and extolling the achievements of men. Our historical records, as reflected in reference texts like the *Oxford English Dictionary* or *Merriam-Webster*, reinforce the belief that even before technology was about high tech tools or the work of engineers, it was about the Art, science, and the work of brilliant and privileged men.

Technology and machines, especially in an industrial context, have been an important cultural issue for much longer than this brief history would have us believe, and ambivalence toward technology is a long-recorded phenomenon. The Industrial Revolution of the nineteenth century, for instance, saw the rise of Luddite rebellions of textile workers who felt threatened by changing labor practices that brought in new machines that were affecting the production of fabric and clothing. Over time, this movement would come to be widely known (incorrectly) as having a technophobic relationship to new machines, versus the technophilic tendency of factory owners. A similar dynamic materializes at different moments, today taking the form of those who want to "get off the grid" or "put technology in its place," a stance that stands in opposition to early adopters, hackers, or free speech activists who have embraced the power and potential in digital. Likewise, many scholars have observed the gendering of this relationship toward technologies, with men, especially white men, depicted as being inclined toward the high tech, while women and girls are portrayed as being disposed to arts, the aesthetic, toward feelings, and social endeavors as opposed to technological advancement. This is a common trope reinforced in everything from popular movies (e.g., *Desk Set*, *War Games*) and advertisements for high tech devices, and has had important effects on the way women and people of color have been viewed in relation to technology.

The transformation of technology from knowledge of an art to a synonym for computation has had the effect of gendering and racializing technology as white and male, but as scholars of gender, race, and technology such as Judy Wajcman, Anne Balsamo, Lisa Nakamura, Wendy Chun, and others have shown, gender and race *themselves* have become technologies of control and containment for unruly and disobedient populations.

FEMINIST APPROACHES TO TECHNOLOGY

In general, much of the available writing about technology has a tendency of falling into certain traps: technological determinism, technological instrumentalism, technological positivism, and technological essentialism.[2] Feminist approaches to the study of technology, on the other hand, avoid the snare of being reductionist, positivist, and essentialist (Faulkner). Scholars coming from this perspective, informed by the work of Sandra Harding and Donna Haraway, tend to refute simplistic notions that would accept technologies as being ideologically neutral or that assume technological innovation as the answer to all global crises and problems. At the core of feminist approaches to the study of technology is this notion of situated knowledge, which demands that scholars, educators, and artists question and problematize narratives surrounding technological objects and those very objects themselves. This disparate and wide-ranging body of work has benefited from, and contributed to, the strong feminist work done in the fields of fiction (namely science fiction), American studies, cultural studies, film and media studies, STS, and any number of related fields. This work has laid the foundation for deeply evaluating the social, cultural, economic, and ideological dimensions of technology.

In 1988, Donna Haraway posed a major challenge to the so-called impartial nature of science by privileging the concept of "situated knowledges," or "Feminist objectivity." With "situated knowledges," she emphasized embodied experience over "objectivity" and the omniscient eye of Western science ("Situated" 581). For Haraway and other feminist social scientist scholars of science, "situated knowledge" was a method for revealing objectivity as a concept that is socially constructed and upheld in science as practice, a practice that is exclusionary and entrenched with patriarchal political significance. Favoring situated knowledge, with its embodied, complicated, and active sight, over what was commonly accepted as objective observation, problematizes that which is culturally viewed as neutral, but also encourages multiple perspectives, including that of the subjugated and marginalized, rather than the mainstream, because they "are least likely to allow denial of the critical and interpretive core of all knowledge" (584). They are, by their nature, more critical.

Considering the existing histories of technology up until this point, the work of feminist scholars, then, has been to complicate this historical record, which itself perpetuates the problematic power dynamics embedded in systems of knowledge production and distribution, and which further elide the voices and contributions of women, the LGBTQIA*, and people of color. Feminist historians and cultural critics, for example, have recuperated histories that exclude the accomplishments of women. Rozsika Parker and Elizabeth Wayland Barber, for instance, questioned this record of technology as the application of practical and mechanical arts. This formulation of technology privileges certain practices that are gendered masculine (e.g., scientific inquiry, working with machines, inventing tools), while other kinds of practical arts or domestic handicrafts and decorative arts such as weaving, sewing, or embroidery are trivialized as "women's work" and "crafts," rather than "Art." Even with the Arts and Crafts Movement of the nineteenth century, which elevated handicrafts and decorative arts, it was primarily the achievements of men like William Morris or Frank Lloyd Wright that were valued, and not the work of women like May Morris or Candace Wheeler, who were still excluded from the Arts and Crafts Guilds (Dačić; Zipf).

These cultural politics are reinforced even as new industries emerge in more recent eras. Lisa Nakamura, in a similar vein, uncovered the history of Navajo women and their work producing semiconductor chips for Fairchild Corporation in the 1960s and 1970s, and Karen Hossfield showed the ways that Silicon Valley companies exploited brown female laborers. This recent work focuses a light on the way technological work has long been gendered but also racialized, highlighting the confluence of gender, race, and class as technologies in and of themselves to produce and perpetuate systems of power, control, and subjugation. Work examining gendered labor politics is indebted to the work done in feminist labor studies (Boris; Hochschild and Machung) and also informs the more recent scholarship on digital labor and affective labor (Arcy; Terranova; De Kosnik; Vora).

At the same time, the work of feminist scholars in related fields has expanded the critical nature of studying technology: media studies, feminist techno-science, STS, human–computer interaction, and digital humanities. These fields have pushed feminist technology studies beyond the important work of recuperating feminist histories. The work in these areas demonstrates a desire to recognize power inequities entrenched in our tools, systems, and infrastructures; to uncover the values reflected in our technologies and their mediation; to critique the invisibility of women in technological fields and yet their visibility as specters informing design and intent; and to develop solutions for patriarchal structures that marginalize and exploit queer people, people of color, women, children, and the disabled. Such activity spans topics as broad as industrial labor, automatons, clockwork jewelry, eugenics, Siri, sexbots, surveillance, and much more. Though this work is interdisciplinary and diverse, in general it coheres around an emphasis on situated knowledge, embodied experience, and feminist resistance to patriarchal norms.

CYBORGS

Perhaps no figure is more important to feminist technology studies than that of the cyborg. Coined in 1960 by US scientists Manfred Clynes and Nathan S. Kline in the article "Cyborgs and Space," the "cyborg" is a cybernetic organism, an organism whose body "incorporates exogenous components" through cybernetic feedback loops that help extend the function of the organic body (27, 74). In their original theory, the external elements would help a human body to adapt its regulatory functions to life in space. Popular culture seized on this concept to provide futuristic human-high tech hybrids from Robocop and the Bionic Woman to Darth Vader in *Star Wars*. Whether in science fiction literature, television, or movies, the figure of the cyborg is a fraught fusion of material technologies and organic human bodies that resist being overtaken by that external technology. The risk of being incorporated into the technological other is one of the core tensions that drives fictional narratives of cyborgs.

In 1985, Donna Haraway reclaimed the cyborg as a feminist symbol when she published "A Cyborg's Manifesto" in *Socialist Review*. This wide-reaching essay and declaration has since become one of the most important texts for the fields that would emerge around feminist technology studies, and the cyborg has become the icon around which feminist theorists, practitioners, and artists have rallied around. In this essay, Haraway appropriated the figure of the "cyborg" to "build an ironic political myth faithful to feminism, socialism, and materialism" (4). For her, "cyborg" is not only "a cybernetic organism, a hybrid of machine and organism" but is also a creature of narrative, "a creature of social reality as well as a creature of fiction" (4). Haraway's cyborg is important as a being that unsettles boundaries: namely those between human and animal, organism and machine, and physical and nonphysical. These three boundaries blur the lines between self and other, genders and races, and public and private. The cyborg is the symbol of that which is hybrid, fragmented, and which cannot be essentialized. It is the very thing that resists classification and control. As Haraway declares,

> The cyborg is resolutely committed to partiality, irony, intimacy, and perversity. It is oppositional, utopian, and completely without innocence ... Cyborgs are not reverent; they do not re-member the cosmos. They are wary of holism, but needy for connection—they seem to have a natural feel for united-front politics, but without the vanguard party. The main trouble with cyborgs, of course, is that they are the illegitimate offspring of militarism and patriarchal capitalism, not to mention state socialism. But illegitimate offspring are often exceedingly unfaithful to their origins. (9–10)

Embodying Haraway's feminist, situated approach to technology and science, the cyborg is a creature that is a product of her context, and she is critical of her very roots. She is othered, racialized, gendered, and a laboring body that also desires affinity and "connection" outside of prescribed organic families. She is complicated, transgressive, dangerous, and full of potential. She represents possible futures and endings. Because of her power, the cyborg has become iconic for feminist scholars and technologists who critique notions of womanhood and of technology that are exclusionary, essentialist, and limiting.

FEMINIST TECHNOLOGY STUDIES

Where the cyborg was born as a symbol for female, queer, and racialized affinity and resilience, "cyberfeminism" materialized in the 1990s as a theory invested in feminist liberation through the affordances of the internet, simultaneously developed by British theorist Sadie Plant and Australian activist art collective VNS Matrix, who are both cited as having coined the term in 1991, and both influenced by the pervading techno-utopian ideals emerging with the rise of the internet or "Cyberspace."[3] For cyberfeminists, technology, especially the internet, had the potential to ultimately liberate women from patriarchal control, and it also served as a tool to critique the misogyny of cyberpunk texts like those of William Gibson. As VNS Matrix declared in "A Cyberfeminist Manifesto for the 21st Century," a pirate digital art installation, "The clitoris is a direct line to the matrix," a reference, according to Plant, to "both the womb—*matrix* is the Latin term, just as *hystera* is Greek—and the abstract networks of communication which are increasingly assembling themselves" (Plant 59). This universalizing tendency of early cyberfeminists is problematic, however, as theorists such as Maria Fernanadez have argued, since it implicitly centers white feminism and fails to recognize racial and sexual differences. According to Fernandez: "Despite the rhetoric of equality and disembodiment that prevails in discussions of cyberspace, racism is alive in digital spaces in overt and invisible forms. If mind and body are inextricably connected, digital representation, textual and visual, must be affected by embodied practices" (41). Likewise, recent feminist scholars attuned to queer, marginal, non-Western, and poor communities have critiqued the privileging of biologically essentialist and US- and Euro-centric notions of womanhood and progress in cyberfeminist work, especially the disembodied futures that cyberfeminism envisioned were possible through networked technology (Brophy; Daniels; Gajjala and Mamidipudi). Other scholars of race, gender, and technology, including Lisa Nakamura and Wendy Chun, have taken this work further: in addition to deconstructing and revealing the ways in which technologies have been used to control women, queer populations, and people of color, they have asked how we can develop strategies and tools for survival and subversions, or as Sandoval has called them, "methodologies of the oppressed."

It has been several decades since those early canonical texts by Haraway, Harding, Balsamo, and Wajcman, and cyborgs and cyberfeminists seem to be making a comeback in new iterations. Feminists scholars continue to make important strides in STS, scholars such as Anita Say Chan, Kalindi Vora, Nishant Shah, and Lilly Nguyen expanding the scope of STS to industries of the Global South, and others such as Anne Polack and Alondra Nelson are bringing feminist STS methods to anti-racist scholarship that interrogates the troubling history of medical and pharmaceutical industries in the United States. The contributions of feminists engaged in technology is not restricted to research and scholarship, however, as the early cyberfeminists might have foreshadowed.

In recent years, feminist thinkers and doers have been active in not just critiquing but in remaking the very systems and structures they find problematic; they are engaging in technology both in the modern and classical sense. These important efforts have taken the form of collective organizing and publishing with the intent of rethinking reproductive technologies, platform technologies, surveillance systems, and tools for control and punishment. The distributed collective FemTechNet, for example, has been working to transform higher education and its trajectory toward the corporate university by supporting their situated and localized Distributed Open Collaborative Course (DOCC) that offers structures and resources for teaching college-level courses about gender, sexuality, race and technology. As their manifesto pronounces, "FemTechNet is fueled by our civil rights, anti-racist, queer, decolonizing, trans- feminist pedagogies as we work within the belly of the beast of neoliberal austerity, normalized precarity, neo-colonial techno-missionary evangelism and [Massive Open Online Course (MOOC)] fever towards the radical redistribution, reinvention, and repurposing of techno-logical, material, emotional, academic, and monetary resources." More than an incu-bator for feminist theory or criticism, it is a hub for feminist praxis. Likewise, in the wake of Edward Snowden's seismic revelations, Deep Lab, "a congress of cyberfeminist researchers" was organized at Carnegie Mellon University to "examine how the themes of privacy, security, surveillance, anonymity, and large-scale data aggregation are problematized in the arts, culture and society" (Wagenknecht et al., 4). One of their major projects came out of a five-day hack-a-thon, wherein Deep Lab self-published an Open Access book that chronicled their "visualizations, software, reflections and manifestos" that educated the public about the dangers and potentials of platform tech-nologies as well as of such mysterious spaces as the Dark Web. Then there are the GynePunks, or the TransHackFeminists (THF!), developing open source and Do-it-Yourself (DIY) resources to help cisgender women reclaim control over their bodies by making and owning their gynecological technologies, combining methods and know-ledge that are ancient and new. There are also larger feminist, anti-racist, and trans-futurist groups like Allied Media Projects, which have developed infrastructure and space to help facilitate the work of smaller radical nonprofits and community groups to organize and educate their communities.

Ultimately, these examples represent a small fraction of the abundance of feminist activity that has emerged in and around technology. At their heart, all of these efforts are critical approaches to examining how material and immaterial technologies are informed by the underlying cultures that produce them. Additionally, this work is sensi-tive to the ways these technologies have been used to *other*, *oppress*, and *control* different populations. They recognize that despite our best intentions, we can easily be complicit with traditional patriarchal power structures and industrial complexes. But we can also resist, and these feminist scholars, activists, and artists have given us numerous models for resistance. From DIY GynePunks who have reclaimed the speculum to hashtag campaigns like #sayhername and #metoo, recent digital feminist action by those working at the intersections of gender, race, and technology has not only increased the visibility of gen-dered and racialized violence but also highlighted the novel ways that feminists have appropriated existing designs or commercial tools for educational and liberatory action. Women, trans, and queer people do not need to remain at the mercy of patriarchal tools and ideologies. Instead, we can transform those tools and create new technologies for our own emancipation.

NOTES

1 A prominent example of this occurrence can be seen in the *Oxford Handbook of Feminist Theory*, edited by Lisa Disch and Mary Hawkesworth, published in 2016, which included a chapter on "Cyborgs and Virtual Bodies" by Krista Geneviève Lynes and Katerina Symes among other keyword entries such as "Affect," "Agency," and "Diaspora."

2 Jentery Sayers breaks these down in concisely in the following way: "technological determinism (technology as the sole cause of cultural change), technological instrumentalism (technology as value neutral), technological positivism (technological progress as social progress), and technological essentialism (technology as having some intrinsic nature or essence)."

3 The term "cyberspace" is credited to science fiction author William Gibson, who first used the word to describe an imagined internet in his Sprawl Series, but most notably in his novel *Neuromancer* (1984).

WORKS CITED

Arcy, Jacquelyn. "Emotion Work: Considering Gender in Digital Labor." *Feminist Media Studies* 16.2 (2016): 365–8.

Barber, Elizabeth Wayland. *Women's Work: The First 20,000 Years—Women, Cloth, and Society in Early Times*. New York: W. W. Norton, 1996.

Barrie, Joshua. "Sex Robot Display Model Molested So Much It Breaks before Anyone Can Actually Use It." *Mirror*, September 28, 2017, https://www.mirror.co.uk/news/weird-news/expensive-sex-doll-molested-much-11251239. Accessed January 27, 2018.

Birke, Lynda, and Henry, Marsha. "The Black Hole: Women's Studies, Science and Technology." *Introducing Women's Studies: Feminist Theory and Practice*, 2nd edn. Ed. Victoria Robinson and Diane Richardson. New York: New York UP, 1997.

Boris, Eileen. *Home to Work: Motherhood and The Politics of Industrial Homework in the United States*. Cambridge: Cambridge UP, 1994.

Brophy, Jessica E. "Developing a Corporeal Cyberfeminism: Beyond Cyberutopia." New Media & Society 12.6 (2010): 929–45, https://doi-org.proxy.lib.umich.edu/10.1177/1461444809350901.

Clynes, Manfred E., and Kline, Nathan S. "Cyborgs and Space." *Astronautics*, September 1960, pp. 26–7, 74–6.

Dačić, Anika. "Arts and Crafts Movement—When Women United in Creativity." *Widewalls*. October 18, 2016, https://www.widewalls.ch/arts-and-crafts-movement-women-artists. Accessed January 27, 2018.

Daniels, Jessie. "Rethinking Cyberfeminism(s): Race, Gender and Embodiment." Women's Studies Quarterly 37.1 & 2 (Spring–Summer 2009) 101–24, doi.org/10.1353/wsq.0.0158.

De Kosnik, Abigail. "Fandom as Free Labor." *Digital Labor: The Internet as Playground and Factory*. Ed. R. Trebor Scholz. New York: Routledge, 2013.

Dunlavy, Colleen A. "Technology." *The Oxford Companion to United States History*. Oxford: Oxford University Press, 2001. *Oxford Reference*, 2004, http://www.oxfordreference.com.proxy.lib.umich.edu/view/10.1093/acref/9780195082098.001.0001/acref-9780195082098-e-1511. Accessed January 27, 2018.

Faulkner, Wendy. "The Technology Question in Feminism: A View from Feminist Technology Studies." *Women's Studies International Forum* 24.1 (January–February 2001): 79–95, doi.org/10.1016/S0277-5395(00)00166-7.

"Feminism, Technology, and Race." Facilitated by Anne Balsamo, featuring Lisa Nakamura and Maria Fernandez, FemTechNet. *Vimeo*, September 2, 2013, https://vimeo.com/73647791.

Fernandez, Maria. "Cyberfeminism, Racism, Embodiment." Ed. Maria Fernandez, Faith Wilding and Michelle Wright. *Domain Errors: Cyberfeminist Practices*. New York: Autonomedia, 2002, pp. 29–44.

Gajjala, Radhika, and Mamidipudi, Annapurna. "Cyberfeminism, Technology, and International 'Development.'" Gender and Development 7.2 (July 1999) 8–16, https://www.jstor.org/stable/4030445.

Haraway, Donna. "A Cyborg Manifesto: Science, Technology, and Socialist-Feminism in the Late Twentieth Century." *Manifestly Haraway*. Ed. Cary Wolfe. Minneapolis: U of Minnesota P, 2016, pp. 3–90. Project Muse. https://muse.jhu.edu/book/45083.

Haraway, Donna. "Situated Knowledges: The Science Question in Feminism and the Privilege of Partial Perspective." *Feminist Studies* 14.3 (1988): pp. 575–99. *JSTOR*, www.jstor.org/stable/3178066. Accessed January 27, 2018.

Harding, Sandra. *The Science Question in Feminism*. Ithaca: Cornell UP, 1986.

Hochschild, Arlie, and Anne Machung. *The Second Shift: Working Parents and the Revolution at Home*. New York: Viking P, 1989.

Hossfield, Karen J. "'Their Logic against Them': Contradictions in Sex, Race, and Class in Silicon Valley." *Technicolor: Race, Technology, and Everyday Life*. Ed. Alondra Nelson, Thuy Linh N. Tu, and Alicia Headlam Hines. New York: New York UP, 2001, pp. 34–63.

Lisa Disch and Mary Hawkesworth, eds. *The Oxford Handbook of Feminist Theory*. Oxford: Oxford UP, February 1, 2016; Oxford Handbooks Online, January 6, 2015. http://www.oxfordhandbooks.com/view/10.1093/oxfordhb/9780199328581.001.0001/oxfordhb-9780199328581. Accessed January 28, 2018

Norris, Sian. "The Damage to Samantha the Sex Robot Shows Male Aggression Being Normalized." *NewStatesman*, September 28, 2017. https://www.newstatesman.com/politics/feminism/2017/09/damage-samantha-sex-robot-shows-male-aggression-being-normalised. Accessed January 27, 2018.

Oldenziel, Ruth. *Making Technology Masculine: Men, Women and Modern Machines in America, 1870–1945*. Amsterdam: Amsterdam UP, 1999.

Parker, Rozsika. *The Subversive Stitch: Embroidery and the Making of the Feminine*. New York: Women's P, 1984.

Phillips, Edward. *The New World of Words: Or, Universal English Dictionary* by J. K. Philobibl. London, MDCCVI. [1706]. Eighteenth Century Collections Online. Farmington Hills, MI: Gale, University of Michigan. January 28, 2018 http://find.galegroup.com/ecco/infomark.do?&source=gale&prodId=ECCO&userGroupName=umuser&tabID=T001&docId=CW3313544879&type=multipage&contentSet=ECCOArticles&version=1.0&docLevel=FASCIMILE.

Plant, Sadie. *Zeroes + Ones: Digital Women and the New Technoculture*. New York: Doubleday, 1997.

Sayers, Jentery. "Technology." *Keywords for American Cultural Studies*, 2nd Edn. Ed. Bruce Burgett and Glenn Hendler. New York: New York UP, 2014. http://hdl.handle.net/2333.1/rr4xh08x. Accessed March 13, 2017.

"technology, n." *OED Online*. Oxford: Oxford University Press, January 2018, www.oed.com/view/Entry/198469. Accessed January 27, 2018.

"Technology." *Merriam-Webster.com*. Merriam-Webster, n.d.; Online, January 28, 2018.

Terranova, Tiziana. "Free Labor." *Digital Labor: The Internet as Playground and Factory*. Ed. Trebor Scholz. New York: Routledge, 2013.

"TransHackFeminists (THF!) Convergence Report." Calafou: Colonia Ecoindustrial Postcapitalista. https://calafou.org/en/content/transhackfeminist-thf-convergence-report.

Wagenknecht, Addie, et al. *Deep Lab.* Deep Lab, 2014, CC-BY-NC-SA 4.0, http://deeplab.net

Wajcman, Judy. *Feminism Confronts Technology.* Cambridge: Polity P, 1991.

Wajcman, Judy. *Technofeminism.* Cambridge: Polity P, 2004.

"We Are FemTechNet." Multiple authors, FemTechNet Manifesto, 2014. http://femtechnet.org/publications/manifesto/. Accessed January 22, 2018.

Williams, Raymond. *Keywords: A Vocabulary of Culture and Society.* Oxord: Oxford UP, 2015.

Wilson, George. *What Is Technology? An Inaugural Lecture Delivered in the University of Edinburgh, on November 7, 1855.* Edinburgh: Sutherland and Knox, 1855. Archive.org https://archive.org/details/b21996131.

VNS Matrix (Josephine Starrs, Julianne Pierce, Francesca Rimini, and Virginia Barratt). "Cyber Feminist Manifesto for the 21st Century." *Net Art Anthology*, Rhizome 2016. http://archive.rhizome.org/.

Vora, Kalindi. "Limits of 'Labor': Accounting for Affect and the Biological in Transnational Surrogacy and Service Work." *South Atlantic Quarterly* 111.4: (October 1, 2012): 681–700. doi: https://doi.org/10.1215/00382876-1724138.

Zipf, Catherine W. *Professional Pursuits: Women and the American Arts and Crafts Movement.* Knoxville: U of Tennessee P, 2007.

CHAPTER TWENTY-NINE

Home

SARAH AFZAL

This essay examines the concepts of home and belonging by tracing different threads of the notion of "home" as it has been understood, theorized, and used in feminist scholarship. As a physical space as well as a more abstract concept, the idea of home has been examined in the contexts of domestic spaces, nationality and citizenship, diasporic spaces and their relationship to homeland, and borders that are not only territorial but also separate the domestic from the political and social, the private realm from the public sphere. With a view toward reimagining borders and boundaries as more fluid than in the conventions of the philosophical tradition and liberalism, feminist scholarship has advocated for women pushing back against the borders defined by patriarchal power structures and has also constructed alternative feminist spaces for women, both real and virtual, spaces that women can identify as "home." While home is no longer restricted to a private domestic heteropatriarchal sphere due to changes in the division of labor as demanded by global capital, the expansion of marriage, emergence of multiple gender and sexual identities and expressions, and opening up of digital spaces, women's reproductive rights are still under assault and continue to be a site of conflict, one through which women's bodies continue to be controlled. In this context, the home can be an important site for feminists to politicize anew.

While the old categories assume the home to be stable in ways that restrict the home to the reproduction of life within a heterosexual patriarchal marriage system, now the reproduction of life is often connected to other sites, including newly created technological, virtual, and digital spaces that are being used by women for new and alternative ways of constructing identity and reclaiming subjectivity. As Sara Ahmed points out, "we can think of feminism as happening in the very places that have historically been bracketed as not political: in domestic arrangements, at home, every room of the house can become a feminist room, in who does what where, as well as on the street, in parliament, at the university" (Ahmed 3–4). This essay is an attempt at reclamation as well as reimagination, to examine the potential that new iterations of home can hold for feminist scholarship and feminism across cultures, borders, and languages.

The conventional relationship between women and home has been a contentious one. Since home is traditionally associated with the private, domestic sphere, women's roles have conventionally been associated with activities restricted to domestic life—homemaking, housework, housekeeping, home-economics, childrearing, and other forms of unpaid labor—which conflated home with domesticity and created a binary between the private and public sphere. The roles performed by women, the unpaid labor, at home were not considered "work" since the private, domestic sphere was separated from the public paid labor that constituted "work." Women's work in the household and the roles they performed within the domestic sphere embedded essentialist ideas regarding women's "nature"—their natural roles, attributes, and shared experiences—and reinforced gender roles by creating the category of woman based on biological sex and using this binary model to ensure the continuation and success of a cisheteropatriarchal hegemony and the maintenance of status quo in a heteronormative society.

Subsequent feminist scholarship worked on multiple levels to reform different areas of women's lives. While early feminist scholarship, with Virginia Woolf as the best known but certainly not the only example, dealt with issues of access and worked to ensure a greater participation of women in the field of education, sometimes to prepare them for the workforce but also to give them more grounding in citizenship, subsequent feminist scholarship delved into the categories of difference associated with gender and sought to understand the roots of a binary gender division. Oppression needed to be examined through an intersection between race, class, gender, as well as in relation to histories of colonial and capitalist expansions. Feminist scholarship has not only aimed to open up spaces previously dominated by men; it is also trying to reconfigure the very definition of home from being associated solely with domestic roles such as mothering, care and nurturing, reproduction, domestic labor, and heteronormative sexual and marital relations.

The category of "woman" was already destabilized through earlier feminist scholarship, including French feminist scholars' engagement with fields of Philosophy and Psychoanalysis—such as that presented in the works of Simone de Beauvoir, Luce Irigaray, Julia Kristeva, Monique Wittig, and Hélène Cixous. Other feminist scholarship, such as that of Jacqueline Rose, Gayle Rubin, Judith Butler, and Juliet Mitchell, continued to analyze these categories and discredit the notion of gender binary as "natural" by examining power structures, through the positioning of women who did not participate in many of the roles associated with domesticity, heterosexuality, marriage, reproduction, and motherhood. The notion of domesticity could no longer be considered a point of common or shared experience for women.

At the same time, the intersection between Marxist theory and Feminist Studies played another integral role in destabilizing the notion of home by including a critique of capitalism and blurring the distinction between private and public realms. The specialization of work to paid employment only, as Raymond Williams explains in *Keywords*, was a consequence of the development of capitalist productive relations, as a result of which "to be in work or out of work was to be in a definite relationship with some other who had control of the means of productive effort. Work then partly shifted from the productive effort itself to the predominant social relationship" (Williams 267). Using the Marxist theory of labor, Feminist Studies focused on women's labor at home: women's work in the home was a kind of labor that formed an essential part of profit in a capitalist society but remained unpaid and largely unrecognized as real work. Some, such as Selma James, organized around the demand of wages for housework.

Further destabilization of the category "home" occurred as a result of scholarship that revealed the vastly different experiences women associated with the site of home across cultures and political boundaries. Newer scholarship in the fields of Postcolonial and Transnational studies, intersecting with Feminist Theory, revealed the instability and arbitrariness of borders that made citizenship and nationality unstable categories of identity in relation to home and belonging. Transnational Feminism addresses the globalized experiences of immigrants, migrants, diasporic communities, and refugees who have family links across borders and cultures. Chandra Talpade Mohanty's 1986 essay "Under

Western Eyes" provided the grounds for analyzing, deconstructing, and dismantling the "Third World woman" as a unified monolithic subject as it had been represented in some Western Feminist texts. By critiquing what she termed as the creation of "Third World difference"—the assumption that this singular ahistorical "Third World woman" is oppressed—Mohanty paved the way for discerning and critiquing colonizing tendencies in Western Feminist texts, texts that need to be examined in the context of the global hegemony of Western scholarship, texts that can be considered imperialist.

This was an important step in redefining the home since such an assumption of oppression produces the image of a "Third World woman" as someone who not only is sexually constrained but also, because of being "Third World," must be poor, uneducated, domestic, family-oriented, and so on, thereby creating a binary opposition between this image of the "Third World" woman and that of the self-represented, autonomous Western woman as being educated, liberated, modern, and free. Privileging the figure of the Western woman as the norm, point of reference, or yardstick, and the "Third World" woman as the oppressed figure, repeatedly characterizes Third World women as victims—of their socioeconomic systems, of male violence and control, of religion, and so on. The association of the figure of the "Third World woman" as "domestic" and family-oriented not only assumes that this "Third World" woman is always already oppressed (regardless of the historical specificity, politics of location, and without contextualization within particular social, economic, and power networks) but also implies that sexual liberation in the West lies elsewhere, outside the home, outside the domestic sphere. This takes the focus away from reforming different areas of women's lives across the globe.

In revisiting her 1986 essay "Under Western Eyes" in her 2003 work *Feminism without Borders*, Mohanty builds on the idea of "home" in her previous work as the basis of "homeland," or the construction of national belonging as it is challenged by globalization. Mohanty describes globalization as "the production of an epoch of 'borderlessness'" (Mohanty 172). This borderlessness of globalization creates a global division of labor, where categories of home and work depend on a global capitalist economy, as they change in response to global flows of capital: goods, services, and labor. At the same time, while globalization affects all women, it disproportionately impacts some more than others because of location, socioeconomic class, race, culture, and other identity markers. Such borderlessness underlies Feminist Theory's anticapitalist, decolonial, postnational, and transnational critique. Feminist Theory has expanded the concept of "home" to take on the difficult challenge of connecting the local and the universal, of recognizing local differences alongside global structures, and using what Mohanty calls "common differences" to form the basis of solidarity, a "non-colonizing feminist solidarity across borders" (Mohanty 224–5). Since borders are arbitrary and not entirely rigid, Mohanty argues that by knowing differences and peculiarities, we can see commonalities and connections across borders (236).

The fluidity and arbitrariness of borders destabilized existing notions of home and at the same time allowed feminism to rethink its own borders and boundaries. As a space that promised inclusion and equality, feminist discourse needed to reimagine the home. A space, in its real (architectural), imagined, and virtual form, can be flexible and open to possibilities since, as Elizabeth Grosz articulates, "it moves and changes, depending on how it is used, what is done with and to it, and how open it is to even further changes" (Grosz 7). For Feminist Theory, this meant reimagining home as a space that would be inclusive to diverse sexual and gender identities, multiple forms of marriage and domestic partnership, and non-patriarchal forms of mothering. The conventional cisheteropatriarchal home and family structure falls apart in the face of transsexual and transgender identities because it assumes a fixed gender and sexual identity along a binary division that defines, assigns, and neatly separates the roles of men and women within and outside the home. Queering the home space not only meant being inclusive to non-heteronormative and nonheterosexual forms of domestic arrangements and family structures, but also, through the discourse on transgender and transsexual identities, bodies and desires, destabilizing the notion of having a fixed "gender home." Judith Halberstam, for instance, critiques a type of transsexual paradigm "driven by the subject's sense of not being home in his/her body" (Prosser 490) and argues instead for a "place from which one theorizes 'home'" to alter "the models of gender and sexuality one produces" (Halberstam 148). This calls attention to the way that gender home, like the home space, is also no longer a fixed point of reference for analysis since gender and sexuality are fluid, nonbinary categories.

Halberstam similarly critiques Transsexual theory that articulates a tension between the transsexual's quest for "'home,' a place of belonging to one sex or the other," and the transgender quest for "a world without gender" (Rubin 7). She argues, instead, for a queer hybridity that recognizes what she refers to as the "dangers of investing in comforting but tendentious notions of home." For Halberstam, "some bodies are never at home, some bodies cannot simply cross from A to B, some bodies recognize and live with the inherent instability of identity" (164). Displacing "gender home" also displaces the conventional home, borders, border crossing, and belonging.

While Halberstam recognizes the tendency to use metaphors of travel and border crossing within the discourse on transsexuality as inevitable, she also brings to light the dangers of "transposing an already loaded conceptual frame—place, travel, location, home, borders—onto another contested site [of gender identity]" (175) by pointing out that border crossings are also "laden with the histories of other identity negotiations, and … carry the burden of national and colonial discursive histories" (165). For some migrant or exiled subjects, home can represent "the belated construction of a safe haven in the absence of such a place in the present or the past … a mythic site, a place to anchor some racial and ethnic identities even as those identities are wrenched out of context or pressured into assimilation" or "a fantasy space, a remembered place of stable origin and a nostalgic dream of community" (171). For others, especially queer subjects, home can be at the margins; this is a subject that Gloria Anzaldúa identifies as the border dweller, "a refugee [who] leaves the familiar and safe homeground to venture into unknown and possibly dangerous terrain. This is her home / this thin edge of / barbwire." (*Borderlands/La Frontera* 12–13). For a border dweller, home can be "a space of exclusion whose very comforts depend on the invisible labor of migrant border dwellers" (Halberstam 171). For yet others, a space that can neither be identified in terms of home or borders, but one that is constructed by a community, assumes the identity of a home, a safe space for support, growth, and also resistance; for example, bell hooks's idea of a "homeplace" was a community of resistance as well as a safe space for black women, which was shared globally (hooks 384).

In addition to queering the home space in terms of gender identity and gender roles, queer spaces can also be constructed in a more tangible, architectural way, from converting existing buildings or architectural spaces into new forms or to perform new functions. What is significant here, as Grosz points out, is "the idea that space, or spaces, is the product of a community, as much as it is the product of a designer … leaves the building itself much more open to future use (and transformation)" (Grosz 7). This implies that spaces, both architectural as well as conceptual, can be transformed into sites of resistance; home can be a conceptually constructed space for a community that can act as site of resistance, and it can also be a domestic and familial space where feminism can thrive and resist the cisheteropatriarchal norms of mothering, sexuality, and gender roles and expressions.

For Feminist Studies, redefining home as a space where women can still occupy existing roles, like those associated with mothering and reproduction, but in empowering ways, is significant. However, as Andrea O'Reilly points out in her introduction to *Feminist Mothering*, little discourse exists in feminist scholarship on the subject of feminist mothering, even though patriarchal motherhood has been a concern in feminist scholarship since Adrienne Rich's 1976 book *Of Women Born*. O'Reilly thus aims to develop a theory of feminist mothering by identifying common themes, challenges, and concerns in feminist maternal practice, by exploring various practices of feminist mothering across a broad range of maternal experience (O'Reilly 3). O'Reilly reminds us of an important distinction, first made by Adrienne Rich, between the two meanings of motherhood superimposed on one another: "the term *motherhood* refers to the patriarchal institution of motherhood that is male-defined and controlled and is deeply oppressive to women, while the word *mothering* refers to women's experiences of mothering that are female defined and centered and potentially empowering to women" (3). Mothering is not naturally or necessarily oppressive and can be a site of empowerment when it is freed from the patriarchal institution of motherhood.

In redefining the home as a space that goes beyond the conventional domestic roles that women have previously occupied, feminist scholarship has also paid attention to how the use of the technology and new media is widening the scope of women's workspace. With access to digital spaces, work often entered and sometimes invaded domestic space. With numerous ways of conducting business through online spaces, as well as the ability to work part-time and full-time from home, it is becoming possible to identify domestic space as work space and work space as intersecting with private life. For Feminist Studies, this changes the definition of home from being largely associated with the domestic sphere to a technological site in the paid labor market. Within the larger context of capitalist globalization, work technologization introduces new problems for labor exploitation.

Telework can be seen as part of the feminist struggle against capital in claiming more leisure time, but this ignores the exploitative nature of women's domestic labor. While giving the illusion of freedom, telework increases the length of the working day and increases worker productivity by having women perform both waged and unpaid domestic labor throughout the day. Home here can be seen as a site where capitalism reproduces the "social factory" (Weeks 120). The new social media technologies expand not just productive activities into the home but also turn consumption into production: in engaging in reviews and web commentary, consumers are donating their free labor and leisure time to producing public relations and advertising for commercial companies. The role of the producer has been made over through engaging in activities of consumption, as the border between the home and the shopping mall has broken down.

Other forms of technological use also need to be considered here. Donna Haraway positions the figure of the cyborg as a "cybernetic organism, a hybrid of machine and organism, a creature of social reality as well as a creature of fiction" (Haraway 149). While Haraway is aware of its limitations, she prompts us to imagine the cyborg in terms of its potential of removing hierarchies, blurring boundaries, and eliminating binary, essentialist, or totalizing ways of understanding concepts. This is particularly significant for Feminist Theory as the cyborg removes the polarity between the public and private sphere, defines a "technological polis based partly on a revolution of social relations in the *oikos*, the household," reworks nature and culture, eliminates hierarchical domination, and lets us imagine a world without gender (151). Haraway's cyborg helps us envision a multiplicity of feminist spaces as sites of resistance, reformation, and reproduction, both including and beyond the home. Subsequent feminist scholarship has used Haraway's cyborg figure to link the use of new technologies in locations that are particularly constraining for women due to an interplay between religious and cultural norms, rigid gender roles, and patriarchal domination. The image of the cyborg serves as a common point of analysis for Feminist Theory to speak across borders, bridging homes and communities.

For instance, building on the concept of Adrienne Rich's "politics of location," Kochurani Abraham examines prospects of cyberspace with regard to politics of women's location. She focuses in particular on experiences of women residing in India who are marked by class and caste inscriptions of gender, but the potential that cyberspace holds for them in allowing them to have what Abraham refers to as " 'a space of one's own' in the Woolfian sense" (Abraham 62) is significant for a larger conversation about feminism's relationship to home. Using specific case studies, Abraham shows how the virtual space becomes a "liminal space inviting women to cross the threshold of restricted spaces" (70). In a similar vein, Virginia Saldanha uses case studies and examples of women in rural India who are using information and communication technology (ICT) to acquire a virtual mobility beyond the home due to cultural, religious, or class-based norms and regulations, when their physical mobility is restricted. This is restructuring the home in different ways: opportunities for economic empowerment are increasing through microfinance programs enabled by information technology in some of the poorest segments of society, enabling women to have earnings and savings of their own. This means greater economic independence, potentially leading to more decision-making and agency within a patriarchal household as well as less dependence on the male counterparts of the family. Cases of domestic abuse are being reported due to the ability to collect evidence through mobile phones, and phones are also being used to call for help and help women stay safe in cases of violence. Women have gained and shared knowledge through collaboration, with online tools such as Yahoo! Groups and Google Groups, providing a space, as well, for women to get involved in activism—an example of this is "Feminist India," an online network of women activists who organize protests, provide support in cases of abuse, as well as lobby with the government on laws that affect women (Saldanha 50–2).

Mobility beyond the home is also significant for specific cultural contexts where public spaces are predominantly occupied by men, not because women are prohibited from these spaces, but because they have been deemed "unsafe" for women historically and culturally. "Girls at *Dhabas*"[1] is one such example of a movement that started with a single hashtag on an Instagram account and developed across the country, aiming to reimagine the way public spaces are used in Pakistan. Challenging the fact that women do not get to experience public spaces in Pakistan the same way that men do, this small group of friends started frequenting *dhabas* and posting pictures on Instagram, eliciting widespread response from women all over the country. This led the group to use online spaces such as Tumblr, Facebook, and Twitter to make a larger feminist movement in order to reclaim spaces for women outside of the domestic sphere. The founders of this movement align themselves with "everyday feminism" and focus on the sharing of stories and experiences through these online platforms as a way of empowering women. For the founder, "public space is contentious and political; it becomes feminist because I am a woman who needs to go through a certain mental and physical effort to be in that space" (Khatri). Even the act of taking a selfie is significant because it implies "ownership of position and place. Women are frequently told to stay out of, or remain invisible in, public spaces, and the action of putting all those prescriptions aside to take your own photo in a space you are not traditionally supposed to be in" is an act of reclamation (Khatri). This aligns with Grosz's idea of transforming existing spaces for different purposes, and also signifies the increasing scope of feminism, a kind of borderless cyborg feminism that uses technology-facilitated networking to blur the private/public divide, push the boundaries of home, and reclaim spaces as sites of gathering and resistance.

The figure of the cyborg is also significant in the way it redefines home by changing the way family relationships are maintained across borders that define homelands. ICTs play a major role in the lives of Asian migrant women workers, not only in terms of facilitating job search and recruitment and sending back remittances to contribute to the home and the home economy but also in the maintenance of family relationships. Gemma Tulud Cruz builds on the concept of "transnational mothering," previously defined in the context of Latina immigrant women as a way "to explore how the meanings of motherhood are rearranged to accommodate ... spatial and temporal separations" (Hondagneu-Sotelo and Avila 562). Cruz applies this to the maintenance of transnational family life by Asian migrant mothers who engage with the home through communication with the family, through mothering over the phone or other technological gadgets, and through supporting the family's financial needs, all of which are facilitated by technology (Cruz 99). Distant and transnational maintenance of family ties restructures the home and family as no longer a nuclear activity.

For such new transnational kinship arrangements, bridges are "passageways, conduits, and connectors that connote transitioning, crossing borders, and changing perspectives," and transformation occurs within this "in-between space, an unstable, unpredictable, precarious, always-in-transition space lacking clear boundaries" (1), as Anzaldúa points out in the preface to *This Bridge We Call Home*. For many, the bridge or "in-between" space becomes a kind of "home." The "yearning to belong," as M. Jacqui Alexander points out, "cannot be confined only to membership or citizenship in community, political movement, nation, group, or belonging to a family" but can also include "a desire to reproduce home in 'coalitions'" (Alexander 99). In the twenty-first century, the figure of the cyborg allows for this multidirectional conversation where online spaces can be where women feel at home, find safety and support in the community, and where migrant women can find a connection back to home. Home is virtual, a space without borders, a web of connectivity. The links between women across borders are web links, backlinks, hyperlinks; home is the virtual homepage.

Changing ideas about mothering can give us different ideas of the home. For example, adding a consideration of infertility and unsuccessful fertility treatments to ideas about mothering not only highlights the existence of nonreproductive women but also no longer limits the home to being a site of reproduction—the home is instead also a site of conflict because it essentializes women by forcing them into reproductive roles or valuing them according to their reproductive capacities. Digital culture and virtual networking diversify the way motherhood, maternity, and reproduction are narrativized, as Kumarini Silva elaborates. Silva is primarily concerned with how reproductive labor becomes a way to "(re)domesticate women within contemporary backlash culture" (170). Silva cites a range of examples that highlight this phenomenon: instruction books for mothers emphasizing the need to learn "the womanly art of breast feeding"; articles and stories, such as the cover story for the May 2012 issue of *Time* magazine titled "Are You Mom Enough?" and contradictory attitudes toward breastfeeding mothers ranging from glamorous magazine cover photographs of breastfeeding mothers that eroticize maternal relations, to real life attitudes and social media critiques leveled at women breastfeeding in public[2]. The presence of blogs on mothering, however, provides an alternative to these mainstream or popular culture representations of "good mothering" because of the multiplicity of narratives on motherhood that digital spaces can provide. Personal blogs on mothering can give a range of experiences, including a conversation on difficult personal experiences with breastfeeding, infertility, miscarriages, and postpartum depression.

This is not to assume that all blogs on mothering provide a more diverse representation of motherhood and home or that all challenges associated with motherhood and mothering get the same kind of exposure; it is precisely because there are so many blogs on mothering in the ever-expanding virtual and digital world that there is an increased likelihood of coming across alternative stories of motherhood. In terms of visibility, as Rosemary Hepworth points out, infertile (medically termed as subfertile) women "upon whose bodies new reproductive technologies are developed and measured" still lack visibility (Hepworth 199). With regard to infertility and its treatment through use of reproductive technologies such as in vitro fertilization (IVF), Hepworth points out how previously dominant forms of media, such as newspapers and press releases, privileged success stories from IVF treatments over unsuccessful ones, originating first with scientists and fertility clinics releasing "heart-warming success stories to the press in order to promote the hope narrative, thus serving their pro-research agenda" (202). This points to an interplay of power-relations but also reveals how heteronormative, patriarchal norms are reinforced with happiness measured through a successful treatment that results in reproduction. Home, no longer only a site of biological reproduction but also that of turmoil caused by failed reproduction, allows for different ways of imagining the family: it could be expanded to include nonbiological relationships through adoption and alternative means of reproduction through surrogacy, and it could also be formed without children. This implies that "home" is constructed and there is no single ideal image of home. At the same time, New Reproductive Technologies (NRT) and IVF also provide a greater number of reproductive choices for single women and lesbian couples, which leads to an expansion of types of homes.

Recognizing the blog as a space where public and private are juxtaposed, and where the "blogged-self is an iteration of the blogging self and is therefore simultaneously real and virtual" (Hepworth 208), Hepworth invokes the conceptual figure of the "avatar" who lives online. Many infertility bloggers who feel alienated from their bodies because of the invasiveness of reproductive technologies often express this bodily alienation through the familiar space of the online fertility community, and Hepworth cites examples from bloggers who describe these online spaces—bulletin boards, blogs, online communities—as "home." This "home-for-home, where one can be oneself, is accessed via the internet from the private, domestic space which has often, along with the body, become a place of estrangement" (209). "Home" is neither the domestic space that it used to be idealized as, nor the space of reproduction it was associated with once.

Only recently has a move toward documenting and archiving these stories in a central location begun. *Maternal Narrative Archives*, an emerging digital space for preserving maternal writing, including narratives of pregnancy, birth, and postpartum, is exploring how mommyblogs not only help create identity but also use online writing to challenge the conventional patriarchal idea of motherhood. An archive such as this creates a bridge between academic feminist discourse and the everyday experience of mothering that gets left out of mainstream feminist discourse on motherhood, a practice that Sara Ahmed would identify as "bringing feminist theory home" and "mak[ing] feminism work in the places we live, the places we work" (Ahmed 10). The founder of this archive also invokes the figure of the cyborg when talking about digital spaces where the image of the mother is constantly being remediated and explains how "this remediation of the maternal provides ... a kind of collective cyborg that acts as an oppositional force to totalizing images of motherhood specifically patriarchal motherhood" (Wallace). Wallace examines how "digital life writing has allowed for women to create heterogeneous networked ecologies in digital spaces." This can be seen as a representation of the kind of borderless coalition and affinity that both Haraway and Mohanty have talked about and envisioned for the future of Feminist Studies, which represents home as a networked, mediated, online space.

Feminist scholarship has changed the home in multiple ways: it has helped blur the distinction between the private and public, recognized women's labor within the home, pushed the boundaries of the domestic sphere, changed views on motherhood and familial relationships, transformed and reclaimed the space of home as well as public spaces as a site of feminist resistance and feminist practices, and helped create new spaces, including online and digital spaces, as "homes" for women transnationally. Part of imagining a future feminist home would involve building on existing critiques of capitalism, colonialism, globalization, and power relations that are formed by both local as well as global structures and play out differently across the spaces women occupy worldwide. Brooke Ackerly and Jacqui True acknowledge the way feminist understanding of oppression is not only political but rooted in global power relations and how this helps feminism work across natural, cultural, disciplinary, and conceptual boundaries. Taking this further, they argue for an application of a global lens to feminist research work and point out that investigating the "global dimensions of seemingly domestic research questions is a new frontier of feminist research, one that rivals intersectionality in the scope of its implications for empirical work" (Ackerly and True 470). For them, this challenges us to see the ways "domestic power relations are always already globalized" (470). Some examples they provide of "already globalized" power relation include "Internal and external migration is affected by conditions outside of state boundaries. Militarization is a process that socializes all citizens. States' economic contexts—and therefore women and men's differential access to productive resources—are significantly influenced by policies determined outside their borders and by relationships of trade and aid with other states or multinational corporations. The politics of war and conflict spill over borders and into bedrooms, kitchens, and so on" (470). This reveals, within a feminist analysis of conflicted spaces that women occupy, like that of the home, the "concealed, intersectional exercises of power, much of which are now global" (470). For Ackerly and True, feminist research and activism at the beginning of the twenty-first century should include not just a recognition of the global dimensions of social problems but also the global dimension of their solutions; an awareness of global connectedness can help us reframe and rethink our research methodologies and questions, and produce greater collaboration across disciplinary, cultural, and national borders. This should be paired with a critique of capitalism that is centered around ways in which capitalist structures affect women worldwide, but also around how they affect different women in different proportions.

Feminism ought to be transnational and borderless in order for it to critique the ways in which globalized power structures are borderless and the way in which they affect different spaces and roles women occupy, including those within the home. A feminist analysis of spaces including the home would have to take into account the process of nation-building and construction of identities postindependence, and how these new identities create new internal power dynamics that exist along hierarchies of gender, class, caste, and skin color. At the same time, it would have to analyze global power relations, from a colonial history to a neo-colonialist structure of debt economies, exploitation of labor through sweatshops and call centers, and migrant domestic labor. Both the local and the global would affect women's positioning in the spaces they occupy—including the home—agency and mobility, and the ways those spaces could be transformed into sites of feminist practices, collaborations, and resistance.

NOTES

1 *Dhaba* translates to a roadside food and tea stall.
2 Women are now, however, increasingly breastfeeding in public spaces, at least in the United States, and there have been recent movements that aim to destigmatize the practice of breastfeeding in public. This further redefines the home by bringing reproductive labor, an activity that had historically been restricted to the private domestic sphere for women, into public spaces, making women's unpaid reproductive labor more visible.

WORKS CITED

Abraham, Kochurani. "Women in Cyberspace: A New Key to Emancipatory Politics of Location." *Feminist Cyberethics in Asia: Religious Discourses on Human Connectivity.* Ed. Agnes M. Brazal and Kochurani Abraham. Basingstoke: Palgrave Macmillan, 2014, pp. 61–76.

Ackerly, Brooke, and Jacqui True. "Back to the Future: Feminist Theory, Activism, and Doing Feminist Research in an Age of Globalization." *Women's Studies International Forum* 33.5 (2010): 464–72, doi:10.1016/j.wsif.2010.06.004.

Ahmed, Sara. *Living a Feminist Life.* Durham, NC: Duke UP, 2017.

Alexander, M. Jacqui. "Remembering *This Bridge*, Remembering Ourselves: Yearning, Memory, and Desire." *This Bridge We Call Home: Radical Visions for Transformation.* Ed. Anzaldúa, Gloria and AnaLouise Keating. New York: Routledge, 2002, pp. 81–103.

Anzaldúa, Gloria. *Borderlands/La Frontera: The New Mestiza.* San Francisco, CA: Aunt Lute Books, 1987.

Anzaldúa, Gloria. "Preface: (Un)Natural Bridges, (Un)Safe Spaces." *This Bridge We Call Home: Radical Visions for Transformation.* Ed. Anzaldúa, Gloria and AnaLouise Keating. New York: Routledge, 2002, pp. 1–5.

Cruz, Gemma Tulud. "For Better or For Worse? Migrant Women Workers and ICTs." *Feminist Cyberethics in Asia: Religious Discourses on Human Connectivity.* Ed. Agnes M. Brazal and Abraham Kochurani. Basingstoke: Palgrave Macmillan, 2014, pp. 95–116.

Grosz, Elizabeth. *Architecture from the Outside: Essays on Virtual and Real Space.* Cambridge, MA: MIT Press, 2001.

Halberstam, Judith. *Female Masculinity.* Durham, NC: Duke UP, 1998.

Haraway, Donna. "A Cyborg Manifesto: Science, Technology, and Socialist-Feminism in the Late Twentieth Century." *Simians, Cyborgs, and Women: the Reinvention of Nature*. New York: Routledge, 1991, pp. 149–81.

Hepworth, Rosemary. "Infertility Blogging, Body, and the Avatar." *Feminist Erasures: Challenging Backlash Culture*. Ed. Kumarini Silva and Kaitlynn Mendes. Basingstoke: Palgrave Macmillian, 2015, pp. 198–215.

Hondagneu-Sotelo, Pierrette, and Ernestine Avila. "'I'm Here, but I'm There': The Meanings of Latina Transnational Motherhood." *Gender and Society* 11.5 (1997): 548–71. www.jstor.org/stable/190339.

hooks, bell. "Homeplace (a Site of Resistance)." *Available Means: An Anthology of Women's Rhetoric(s)*. Ed. Joy Ritchie and Kate Ronald. Pittsburgh: U of Pittsburgh P, 2001, pp. 383–90.

Khatri, Sadia. Interview by Afshan Shafi. "Spotlight: Girls at Dhabas." *The Missing Slate*, March 24, 2016. themissingslate.com/2016/03/24/girls-at-dhabas/.

Mohanty, Chandra Talpade. *Feminism without Borders: Decolonizing Theory, Practicing Solidarity*. Durham, NC: Duke UP, 2003.

O'Reilly, Andrea. Introduction. *Feminist Mothering*. Ed. Andrea O'Reilly. Albany: State U of New York P, 2008, pp. 1–22.

Prosser, Jay. "No Place Like Home: The Transgendered Narrative of Leslie Feinberg's Stone Butch Blues." *MFS Modern Fiction Studies* 41.3 (1995): 483–514, doi:10.1353/mfs.1995.0120.

Rich, Adrienne. *Of Woman Born: Motherhood as Experience and Institution*. New York: W. W. Norton, [1976] 1986.

Rubin, Henry. "Do You Believe in Gender?" *Sojourner* 21.6 (February 1996): 7–8.

Saldanha, Virginia. "Digital Revolution—Creating a Flat World for Indian Women?" *Feminist Cyberethics in Asia: Religious Discourses on Human Connectivity*. Ed. Agnes M. Brazal and Kochurani Abraham. Basingstoke: Palgrave Macmillan, 2014, pp. 47–60.

Silva, Kumarini. "Got Milk?: Motherhood, Breastfeeding, and (Re)Domesticating Feminism." *Feminist Erasures: Challenging Backlash Culture*. Ed. Kumarini Silva and Kaitlynn Mendes. Basingstoke: Palgrave Macmillian, 2015, pp. 167–82.

Wallace, Paige. "The Archive: How and Why It Began." *Maternal Narratives Archive*, February 3, 2018, www.maternalnarrativearchives.com/single-post/2018/02/03/The-Archive-How-and-why-it-began.

Williams, Raymond. *Keywords: A Vocabulary of Culture and Society*. 2nd edn., Oxford: Oxford UP, 2015.

Weeks, Kathi. *The Problem with Work: Feminism, Marxism, Antiwork Politics, and Postwork Imaginaries*. Durham, NC: Duke UP, 2011.

CHAPTER THIRTY

Migration

EFFIE YIANNOPOULOU

Feminism and migration are terms referring to sets of embodied thought and lived experience whose histories have crosscut and impacted each other. For years, the migratory flows of women and feminist theories across regional and transnational borders have served to forge links between women in different sites within an increasingly globalized economy. At the same time, contact between women's varied experiences of being in the world, which resulted from this migratory activity, has also contributed to Western feminism's "legitimation crisis" (Kaplan 6) and helped diversify its predominantly white, middle-class and heterosexual political agenda. Postcolonial, black, and transnational feminisms in particular have consistently critiqued Western feminism's racialized gender underpinnings and its privileged collusion with imperialist, neoliberal and heteronormative positions. These newer trends in feminism have thus prompted feminist theorizing and activism to face up to their exclusionary practices and reinvent themselves as heterogeneous and internally differentiated political formations, "multiple, contradictory, wedged ambivalently and precariously between diverse sets of subject positions and subjectivities" (Brah 13).

Today, most contemporary feminisms have issues of multiplicity and diversity high on their agendas and are hard at work seeking to articulate a contingent politics of difference that will allow them to encounter and decode multiple and mobile differences (of class, race, sexual orientation, age, ability, or species) in non-appropriative and inclusive ways. It is perhaps no accident that, being so informed by the tensions inscribing women's multiply located, migratory experience, feminist theory and research have emerged as promising sites especially suited to addressing the complex and multidimensional problematic of migrancy. As I suggest in this chapter, with its attentiveness to the gendered dynamics of migration, feminist thought has worked toward defetishizing the figure of the migrant—unpacking and diversifying the unitary character of a conceptual category that has allowed "different forms of displacement to be gathered together in the singularity of a given name" (Ahmed, *Strange Encounters* 5). It achieves this by bringing into sharper focus the embodied, historically and culturally embedded, and power-bound character of migrant mobilities (Blunt 691), by reconfiguring home in terms of movement (Fortier, "Coming Home"; Brah; Ahmed et al) and foregrounding representation and its contingencies as crucial to how borders, movement, and spaces of belonging and unbelonging are made intelligible and inhabited.

Migration can be understood as referring to material acts of individual or communal relocation, involving leaving what is perceived as home and moving to a different place, and at once as a metaphor that is used to theorize the mobility of identity in a world whose ways of knowing have grown more fluid—identity as migrancy. In that sense, migration is a term that provides a framework for thinking about embodied, cultural, and economic movement across material, subjective, and affective locations in a world of global flows. Whether lived, imaginary, forced, or voluntary, it engages issues such as home and settlement, national belonging, sovereignty and citizenship, travel and mobility, transnationalism, creolization, and diaspora. Though a hallmark of human activity since ancient times, migration in the context of globalization is a multifaceted social process (Hondagneu-Sotelo 112), marked by the diversification in the identity of migrants (Blunt 688; Papastergiadis 39), the widening variation in their resources, a change in the patterns of settlement and return (Piper 136), the proliferation in the direction of migratory movements that are increasingly directed toward and within non-Western locations (Papastergiadis 39, 45) and, crucially, the feminization of the migrant labor force (Piper 151; Silvey 138). The complexity of global cross-border connectivity is further registered in the contradictory languages of migration that produce identities and cultural sensibilities. These languages and sensibilities are played out and acutely felt in the field of public discourses through which both migrants and locals are accorded or dispossessed of meaning and life.

As evidenced by popular media discourses and heated political debates during several recent electoral campaigns in the immigrant-receiving countries of the Global North, migrants—be it documented or undocumented immigrants, political refugees or asylum seekers, educated professionals, "accidental" immigrants of the heart (Kelley), or seasonal migrant laborers—are routinely constructed as alien even within the legal and cultural frameworks that organize apparently difference-loving contemporary multicultures. Post-Brexit Britain might best exemplify the tensions inhering in balancing out the demands of a national imaginary that constructs itself as a defender of civilized, transcultural symbiosis and a new kind of virulent, nationalist backlash that narrates European-Union citizens as strangers. Though clearly a more familiar "other" to the British public than Syrian refugees seeking political asylum in the United Kingdom, both Eastern and Western Europeans residing in Britain are still fetishized as a group of foreign bodies that is being used as a potent bargaining chip in the British government's negotiating strategy with Europe. These Europeans are for the most part constructed as enjoying a closer relationship of proximity to the (white) native Briton. Even so, they are still coded in ways that are as homogenizing as those reserved for the Asian and African migrants currently arriving at Europe's doorstep via the Mediterranean and are represented as a "threat" to British territorial sovereignty and national interests.

Being classed as bodies "out of place," European residents in the UK as much as asylum seekers have been made to move, to borrow from Hanif Kureishi's chilling description of the migrant condition, from "reality" to a nation's "collective imagination." Stripped of "colour, gender and character," they are made into "something resembling an alien," an "example of the undead, who will invade, colonise and contaminate," figures that "we can never quite digest or vomit" (27). Ontologized and cut off from the social and material relations which determine their existence, an effect of what Sara Ahmed terms "stranger fetishism" (*Strange Encounters* 5), migrant subjects are assigned a pre-given meaning through a system of binary distinctions that delegitimates them (legally, culturally, morally, sexually) in discourse and real life, and installs them as signifiers of illegality and subjects in need of surveillance and visa, passport, or residence control. What motivates the staging of migratory subjectivities in terms of a philosophy of "distinction" (Mountz 262) is partly the desire of national communities to preserve subjects and places (of migrant settlement and origin) sealed and firmly bounded, untouched by the fluidity affecting human living and mixing. Clearly, the ideologies of racial and cultural purity that were vital to Western colonial practices continue to fuel contemporary attitudes to migratory mobility and settlement and to determine restrictive, and deeply uneven, strategies of discursive and physical exclusion and inclusion.[1]

Feminist-informed work on migration coming out of different disciplines suggests that these shifting processes of migrant incorporation and expulsion must be addressed within a more complex and nuanced framework of differentiation. Working against earlier elaborations of migration as a monolithic, either-or/us-them binary construct, feminist researchers' engagement with the gendered dynamics of migration has contributed to a perceptual shift in understandings of migrant politics as diverse and contradictory. Feminists call attention, for instance, to the embodied materialities of women's migrant mobilities, the asymmetrical power relations determining their movement across spaces (how some move and some fail to move), and the uneven effects of that movement on their subjective states of being, social positionings, and sense of belonging. They address the political constructedness of borders and boundaries along lines of gender, race, class, nation, caste, or religion (Silvey 139). They also ask to know how different women on the move inhabit, narrate, imagine, and affectively relate to homes—households, families, homelands, or communities that they lost, forcibly abandoned, rejected, or built anew—making us, thus, alive to the fact that homes are not given but "enacted" in relation to the differential dynamics of migratory movement that might have been willingly undertaken, forced, or forbidden (Ahmed et al. 2).

Such gender-inflected approaches to the problematic of migrancy and home are especially indebted to brands of postcolonial and transnational feminism that are concerned with the intersectionality of gender, race, class, and sexuality in the production of transnational spaces and subjects, forms of national and supranational belonging or citizenship and statelessness (Ahmed, *Strange Encounters*; Mohanty; Butler and Spivak; Butler and Athanasiou). They have also been made possible by broader cross-disciplinary feminist inquiries into the work of difference and the limits of diversity (Weedon), the embodied and spatialized basis of subjectivity (Massey), and the importance of power relations, structures of inequality, and historical and cultural determination in shaping patterns of living mediated by representation and discourse.

To begin to understand how feminists have started to debunk the assumptions built into migrant ontology and complicate popular encodings of migration, it is important that we consider their interventions into the politics of mobility and home. In what follows, I will, first, discuss how feminist concern with gendered mobilities has served to highlight the extent to which movement is connected to conditions of privilege and marginality and constitutes, therefore, an embodied practice that is bound to concrete networks of power relations and meaning. This gender-specific critique, as I argue, taps into the concerns of the influential "mobility turn," as it has been emerging across the social sciences, and its expressed desire to rethink contemporary geographies of mobility as historically determined and differential practices that materialize within specific embodied, representational, and material contexts.

Given that migration and home are as intimately connected to each other as mobilities are to immobilities, the final part of this chapter will focus on feminist challenges to dominant ideas of home or the homeland as a unitary and static site of comfort. The presumption of home as static is foundational to analytic discourses that perceive migration in mechanistic terms as a structure of displacement that operates between two fixed points of origin and destination and defines migrant mobility as "rootless" in opposition to the "rooted" sense of belonging afforded to the citizen subject, underwriting the invocation of the migrant as alien. Feminists suggest, instead, that there are no single or final points of departure or arrival and attempt to reconfigure home as a space internally ruptured by the work of intersectional differences, antagonisms, and desires, hence, as a site of nonending negotiation and often uncomfortable incompleteness. Rethinking the limits of attachment to a place and the borders of the communal as being continually adjusted to different relationships of proximity and estrangement allows ethical strategies of inclusion to develop that resist producing the migrant as a given and knowable other with a fixed ontological essence, a figure to be rejected or appropriated at will. Rather, migrants as multiply-situated subjects can alter the language of the host community (the nation) and its public spaces and forge a contingent sense of belonging for both those who cross boundaries and those who stay put. To address these issues, theoretical reflections will be interwoven with readings of artistic and literary responses to migration, the work specifically of Austrian artist Tanja Boukal and British writer and activist Rahila Gupta's short story "Leaving Home."

(MIGRANT) MOBILITIES

Migration cannot be theorized outside spatialized relations of power, outside, that is, its connection with place, home, and enclaves of belonging. Understanding migration begins with the migrants' embodied stories of how they inhabit and move across physical and social spaces, the histories and the conditions of their departures and arrivals. In that sense, recent approaches to mobility that involve research on "the combined movements of people, objects and information in all of their complex relational dynamics" (Sheller, "Mobility" 1) are both informed by and extend the study of migration. As Alison Blunt observes, while research on mobilities and migrations cannot be collapsed onto each other, there are many productive connections between them, particularly in their shared concern with materiality and politics (685). Feminist researchers in these two fields are especially keen on calling attention to the material, situated, and historically distinct conditions framing women's movement and constructions of home as part of their continuing struggle against the abstraction of thought that underwrites masculinist ideas of a universal, common humanity whose rules systematically override, obscure, undervalue, and marginalize women's specificities, experiences, and positions in the world. As I will argue in the next section, feminist concern with materiality, which is at once a concern with locating and reevaluating (sexual) difference, runs parallel to—and at once informs— the production of social theories that are situated within the "new mobilities paradigm" which has proved instrumental in redressing the "unspecified" nature of mobility in an increasingly mobile world (Cresswell, *On the Move* 2).

Whereas absolute space, what is commonly understood as "real" space in Western societies (Smith and Katz 75–6), has been repeatedly critiqued for its assumed transparency and abstract neutrality by Marxist and feminist critics,[2] the notion of mobility has received much less rigorous attention. In spite of its centrality to life experience and the production of knowledge, movement has been routinely coded as a "kind of blank space," contentless, apparently natural, devoid of meaning, history, and ideology (Cresswell, *On the Move* 2, 3). To challenge the ideological transparency of such an encoding, a politics of mobility that seeks to historicize the production of mobile practices has begun to be articulated. For Tim Cresswell, that means reconfiguring forms of mobility as involving "a fragile entanglement of physical movement, representations and practices" ("Towards a Politics of Mobility" 18) that have a history and bear the imprint of specific cultural and social determinations. The dominant conceptualization of mobility as abstract and universalizable must give way, it is suggested, to a more political understanding of mobile practices as at once discursively constituted and embodied acts of relocation that are productive of the social relations, the spaces, and the subjects that traverse them, as much as they are produced by them. Mobility then needs to be reimagined as a resource that is differentially accessed, narrated, experienced, valued, and affectively invested depending on the concrete power contexts within which it materializes. In line with this theoretical take, the focus is currently on "mobilities," which, as a category, comprises a host of terms such as travel, tourism, exile, cosmopolitanism, nomadism, or deteritorrialization, names for relocation which, in alluding to migrant states that share continuities and discontinuities, tend to be seen less as synonyms and more as signs of different critical registers and historical instances (Kaplan 3). Such a differential mobile imaginary is in a position to trouble and complicate simplified notions of migration as a transparent line linking already constituted places of departure and arrival, which, according to Cresswell, is what classic migration theory often assumes. In his argument, a "man and a woman, or a businessman and a domestic servant, or a tourist and a refugee may experience a line of a map linking A and B completely differently" ("Towards a Politics of Mobility" 18, 21).

Through her photographic collage *Memories of Travels and Dreams* (Figure 30.1), Tanja Boukal clearly suggests that such an experience of moving along a line on the map is not simply different for different mobile subjects but, crucially, deeply uneven, conditioned as it is by the asymmetries of power that regulate human spatial crossings. First presented to the public in the summer of 2016 in the context of an art exhibition

FIGURE 30.1 Tanja Boukal's *Memories of Travels and Dreams* (2016)

entitled *A World Not Ours* and organized by the Schwarz Foundation on the Greek island of Samos,[3] Boukal's artwork accords visibility to the power-inflected character of migrant mobility. It reflects on the reality of a tourist island–turned refugee detention camp as a result of uncontrolled migratory activity by visually juxtaposing tourist and migrant mobilities as interlocking and yet fundamentally distinct ways of crossing the narrow sea strip between Samos and Turkey. Advertising a day cruise to the Turkish town of Kusadasi on the shore opposite, the tourist poster at the collage's center promises cheap entertainment to those in possession of leisure time, money, and passports. Surrounding it are scattered photographs of torn life vests, discarded milk bottles, baby shoes, and pink ribbons, witnesses to the perilous migrant passage from Asia to Europe that costs over 3,000 Euros and does not guarantee an arrival.

Mae Henderson's observation that "Border crossings move in different directions and from different locations, some from positions of centrality and dominance, others from positions of marginality and powerlessness" (26) clearly has a special resonance here. If, as Henderson aptly notes, "power relations and positionality shape the consequences and possible inequities" resulting from such events, Boukal's collage openly puts forth the claim that tourists and refugees sail across the Aegean border having set off from diverse positions on the map of power hierarchies. As subjects, they are interpellated through their mobilities by being accorded distinctive subject positions in discourses, which are normatively associated with particular means and styles of moving (Cresswell and Merriman 7). In a global economy of capitalist social relations and policed territorial sovereignty, tourists travel freely, consume commodities, energize economies, and figure as vital components in the construction of transnational culture while refugees move in clandestine and enforced ways that demand to be policed and contained.

Boukal, however, does more than expose the power dynamics—and indirectly engage the histories of cultural and social determination—that control who can move and how. She brings into focus the relational character of mobilities in all their material manifestations. Countering dominant public discourses that stage migration as a threat inherently from the "outside," Boukal's work proposes a framework that identifies a relationship of interdependence connecting privileged and marginal mobilities. Encoded here through their representation as ruins, the synecdochic signs of migration encircle what is represented as a "fenced in" system of Western cultural and economic hegemony, rupturing its borders partly by means of resignifying its spaces. The same beaches that act as holiday resorts for the affluent Westerners are identified as sites of dispossession, death, and burial when their postcard-type photographs are strategically placed among the visual traces of missing migrant bodies. Migrant ruination is shown thus to haunt Europe with a vision of its own finitude and constructedness, suggesting that, as an idea and an institution, "it hasn't always been there" and "it will not always be there, it is finite" (Derrida 44). At once, it also confronts the West with the very precariousness that is lodged, even if foreclosed, at the heart of its self-perception and which migration itself embodies—migrancy posited here, in all its unpredictability, as a constituent element in Western ontological structures and histories.

FEMINIST MIGRATIONS

Feminists have been instrumental in uncovering the extent to which migration is imbricated in the production of power and relations of domination. In that sense, they have contributed to exposing migration as not only producing ruins but also being itself structured by the logic of the ruin, never being completely one as a concept but rather multifaceted and multidimensional. Indeed, the growing body of feminist research into the gendered politics animating migration has called attention to gendered mobilities as being deeply political (Massey) and unevenly enacted in processes that reflect and reinforce social organization along the lines of race, class, nation, sexuality, caste, and religion (Silvey 138; Sheller, "Gendered Mobilities" 257).

Accordingly, it is constructions of gender as iterable performance and an engagement with intersectional materialist politics that inform those contemporary feminist responses to migration which seek to understand gendered mobilities as performed in specific contexts, allowing for differences among women to be analytically focused upon and generating differential (and contingent) understandings of displacement and relocation. Reworking "unmarked masculinist assumptions about the migrant" (Silvey 142), such theoretical approaches draw their energy from the need to situate and historicize the meanings invested in migratory patterns by highlighting their construction as embodied, socially embedded, and materially grounded processes. Their concern with the embodied materialities of women's migrant mobilities has proved vital in unmasking the vested interests served by the abstraction normatively surrounding the concept of movement. Additionally, it has also helped reassess the histories of its connection with women's lives and the frequent celebratory deployment of the idea of migration as a metaphor for liberation in women's worldly relations and writings as well as first-world feminist epistemologies.

To appreciate the political import of admitting to the material conditions (historical, geographical, cultural) that produce varied experiences of migratory mobility for feminist politics, it is important to remember that, in Western modernity, discourses of mobility (physical and discursive) have been actively enlisted to challenge structures of gender inequality often in universalizing ways that mystify and erase the histories of social relations. As it is by now well documented, gender categories have been historically articulated in terms of the spatial division of public and private that maps on to masculine and feminine (Cresswell and Uteng 2). According to this essentializing oppositional structure, the masculine is firmly placed on the side of progress and unimpeded movement forward while the feminine is associated with a sedentary, home-bound existence, often identified with domesticity, tradition, and the past (Parkins 3).[4]

Moving out of, across or between firmly bounded social, racial, cultural, or sexual spaces has been unsurprisingly construed by Western feminists as a sign of women's struggle against patriarchal control and has been accorded the status of an emancipatory gesture crucial to reimagining women's subjective and social positions, self-representations, and futures. When Antiguan-American writer Jamaica Kincaid admits, for example, that "[o]ne of the reasons why I left home was that I was a victim of tradition. I was on the verge of being a dead person because of tradition, and I think women especially have to be very careful of these traditions" (82), she speaks for many, fictional or real-life, women who identify in leaving home a means of survival and a strategy of resistance to hegemonic gender conventions by refusing to inhabit a particular space. "Travel," to quote Trinh T. Minh-ha, "allows one to see things differently," the "itinerary displaces the foundation" (23) and so offers women the promise of self-reinvention. In some feminist epistemologies, migration becomes, for this reason, embraced as a theoretical mechanism which, next to engaging physical movement, is employed as a metaphor that reconceptualizes women's gender identities as open to previously denied possibilities because predicated on movement. Migration, along with its cognate mobile metaphors of the "nomad" and the "rhizome,"[5] becomes celebrated for its anti-foundational thrust as a border-crossing notion that destabilizes and transgresses fixed forms of home and identity, a metaphor for dislocation and the lack of (stable) being that can generate alternative modes of agency, resistance, and subjectivities for women.

However, the narrative that posits migrancy as necessarily subversive has been challenged by materialist, anti-racist feminists who charge it with constructing, as Sara Ahmed puts it, "an essence of migration in order to theorise that migration as a refusal of essence" (*Strange Encounters* 82). What Ahmed finds troubling is the slippage between "literal migration and metaphoric migration" which erases the real and substantive differences between the conditions in which particular movements across spatial borders take place (*Strange Encounters* 80, 82). Caren Kaplan contends, in the same spirit, that "All displacements are not the same" (2), pointing to the "ahistorical universalisation" (3) and the lack of concern for material social relations that underwrite the conflation of different kinds of journeys under the sign of migrancy. The aim of such critiques is not to reduce the importance of migration as a critical term for thinking about movement, culture, and identity but to complicate the feminist narratives that produce the meanings of migration by introducing "questions of context (post-coloniality/globality), historicity, temporality and space" (Ahmed, *Strange Encounters* 81) into the debate. In a similar vein, what Chandra T. Mohanty suggests as a way of repoliticizing hegemonic feminism and the neoliberal politics of mobility thought to frame it is a "return to the radical feminist politics of the contextual" (987) and the need to uncover the complex and contingent relationships of antagonism that allow some subjects to move freely at the expense of others (Ahmed, *Strange Encounters* 86). Such a return involves a renewed concern with the embodiment of migration and how this is practiced in and through the sexed and racialized bodies of women whose meanings and movements intersect, in the context of global interconnectivity, with multiple and scattered structures of domination.

Indeed, as many materialist feminist analyses of women's real-life transnational journeys demonstrate, the migrant mobilities made available to women materialize and are accorded meaning within intersecting and often competing configurations of power and are, therefore, never to be understood, as Rachel Silvey notes, exclusively in terms of "trangressive, agency-driven, potentially empowering moves" (142). Rather, the structural inequalities of gender, class, and race that operate in the state policies of sending and receiving countries, the household as much as the global and local labor markets (Raghuram 194), reveal women's itineraries being often embedded in exploitative and coercive migration flows that are subject to increasing political and social controls.[6] Women fleeing war zones, domestic violence, or the religious curtailment of their freedoms figure perhaps as the most obvious instances of enforced displacement.

Additionally, the increasingly feminized global labor and family migrations (for the purposes of family formation or reunification) have been also read as legitimating and reinscribing gender inequalities through forms of displacement that may not be desirable or evenly experienced by female migrants. The caring professions and domestic work sectors especially are singled out as labor spaces that reinforce the "caring ideologies" so central to restrictive and much challenged constructions of femininity within local and international networks of social reproduction. Filipina women, in Parvati Raghuram's account, for example, are cast by government policies as global caregivers (187) while the Indonesian state is seen by Rachel Silvey as aggressively promoting the out-migration of women to work as domestic laborers in Saudi Arabia where a woman's job "garners low wages, grants little security and few benefits, involves high rates of multiple forms of abuse, and provides only slim chances of occupational mobility" (141). In both these examples, women's migration patterns reproduce patriarchal gender spaces, install transnational women workers as "emblematic figures of contemporary regimes of accumulation" (Brah 179) and reveal their cooption into nationalist projects.[7]

In other words, what is suggested is that there is nothing essentially transgressive about migratory mobilities that can both resist and lend support to hegemonic gender norms. Their meanings and concrete effects are impossible to grasp in the present (Ahmed, *Strange Encounters* 9), hence to stabilize, but must be decided upon in terms of the histories of determination that form the social, cultural, and bodily spaces within which they materialize and the futures they potentially gesture toward. Reconfiguring migration politics as historically grounded, hence differential, contradictory, and incomplete, has an immediate effect, as I argue next, on how the place of home within the context of transnational networks of connection is rearticulated by intersectional, materialist feminists who reconceptualize spaces of inhabitance as embodied, diasporized, and internally ruptured.

(MIGRANT) HOMES

Home, migration and belonging relate to each other in multiple ways. An object of strong affective investments, home has become in today's globally connected world a political question enmeshed with struggles around the formation of familial, communal, national, and transnational identities and boundaries. Whether referencing a familial environment, a national homeland, or just the lived experience of a locality, home oscillates between different modes of articulation that are dependent for their meanings and effects on distinct configurations of migration.

In sedentarist thought, for example, home is valued as a place of roots and spatial and social order while migration is regarded as morally and ideologically suspect (Cresswell, *On the Move* 26). Such a construction of home as a seamless site of belonging, origin, familiarity, and comfort is fundamentally gendered, racialized, and "intrinsically linked with the way in which processes of inclusion and exclusion operate" (Brah 192) within communities. It is at work in masculinist geographies of home as the space of feminine domesticity and in exclusionary nationalist discourses that imagine the national body as a sealed cultural system that casts migrants as alien bodies.

In the context of migration, the desire to defend a bounded conception of home, culture, and identity is perhaps best exemplified by the "refugee camp," this politically contentious "zone of exception" (Agamben 174), which stabilizes the borders of the nation-state by incorporating what lies "outside" the homeland into the sovereign order in the form of a perfectly containable and fixed space of exclusion. Nomadic epistemologies, by contrast, have historically privileged migratory mobility at the expense of notions of attachment to a place and a dwelling which are duly represented as confining, static, and often politically reactionary. In this narrative about movement, home is posited as what needs to be "overcome" (Ahmed *Strange Encounters* 87) and repudiated in order for progressive, forward-moving thinking and action to materialize in the world. It is no accident that feminist nomadic politics and theorizing have made moving away from a symbolically feminized and devalued concept of home into a pivotal ideological gesture in the struggle against essentialist gender discourses. In suggesting, however, that homeless migrancy is the key to destabilizing identities, much of this research continues to construct home as a stable, unitary conceptual category—even if delegitimized by being construed as what is best avoided—and has been critiqued for mystifying the histories of women's differential claims on the experience of being at home (Ahmed, *Strange Encounters*; Kaplan).

Attentive to the embodied materialities and variable forms and conditions of movement, transnational feminist works on migration and inhabitance propose, instead, an equally variable configuration of placement. Informed by the context-specific politics of intersectionality, they call into question the naturalization of home as origin and stasis and bring into focus the multiple senses of belonging that women negotiate and forge through their lived experience of being-at-home. Feminists, for example, have on many occasions critiqued the heterosexualized model of home as comfort by exposing it as a site of gender violence, inequalities, and trauma especially for queer subjects (Hondagneu-Sotelo 115; Fortier, "Coming Home" 409). In the case of the Filipina domestic worker whose story Geraldine Pratt gives, however, her cozily arranged room constitutes a personal refuge and comfort provider. As a contract worker admitted into Canada on a special visa (Cresswell, "Introduction" 18–19), her attachment to this private space strengthens her fragile claim on a new homeland, her pride in her financial independence (she pays for the room and can decorate it in the way she likes), and her hopeful self-representation as a migrant body "in" and not, as popularly assumed, "out of place."

Rather than having an essential meaning in advance of its making (Ahmed et al. 8), home in these cases is produced through the movement of desire, enacted and, hence, constituted as an open-to-possibilities "event rather than a secure ontological thing rooted in notions of the authentic" (Cresswell, "Introduction" 25). Such diverse accounts of migrant women's relationships to rooms, houses, households, families, or homelands in a context of transnational dispersal compel us to rethink the problematic of home as familiarity and sameness. They provide a framework for reconfiguring spaces of inhabitance as contingently structured around multiple forms of estrangement and attachment, as changeable and mobile because differentially embodied, narrativized, remembered, or emotionally registered following changes in the grounds and conditions that make placement and displacement possible.

In the short story "Leaving Home" by the British Asian writer Rahila Gupta, staying put is certainly not without movement for its protagonist Zara, a 21-year-old, second-generation South Asian woman. Split between filial duty toward her immigrant Pakistani parents' expectations to see her married off to a Pakistani man of respectable ancestry and her own desire to go to art school, Zara negotiates multiple belongings. The home that she tries so hard to leave—by arranging a marriage of convenience to a Muslim man whose political asylum applications have been rejected twice and exposing herself to the risk of rape in his hands—signifies on more than one level, complexly weaving together invocations of her parents' house, their immigrant reconstruction of Pakistani culture, and the diasporic space of late-twentieth-century Britain that she is born into. Zara's access to any of these home spaces is highly mediated by her gender, cultural creolization, and generational difference all of which direct her movement between competing codes of gender conduct and cultural belonging.

What impresses in the story is the poignant way in which Zara's struggle to negotiate a multiply ruptured experience of home materializes at the level of lived embodiment. She dresses differently in and outside the home. Her public Punk image—spiked hair with hard pink tips, "skin-tight shiny, black trousers" boots and heavy makeup (32)—becomes transformed, with the help of a public-lavatory "Cinderella act," into one of conformity to household gender rules as her long T-shirt is made to look like a traditional churidar kameez. Zara's gendered and racialized body, in its lived everydayness but also when made into the target of politically and culturally induced sexual violence, functions as the fleshy articulation of incomplete belonging. Zara is never quite fully at home in any of the homely spaces that she moves through. This failure to inhabit home fully is not regrettable but, as Sara Ahmed writes, it is the precondition for an "act of *making*" (*Strange Encounters* 94), making home into a more inclusive communal space by not allowing it to take one form only. Rather than a fixed sense of belonging, it is "motions of attachment," the idea that home "combines forces of movement and attachment at once" (Fortier, "Making Home"), that give shape to what the story suggests at its end (when Zara's mother embraces her daughter's hybridized state of being) might be a more supportive mode of living together.

In this chapter, I have suggested that the questions of migration and home are formulated and made intelligible in relation to each other. How one moves away from or between homes is formative of how one inhabits home and the way in which "processes of inclusion and exclusion operate" at individual and collective levels to regulate "belonging" (Brah 192). Feminist thinkers, especially transnational and postcolonial feminists whose work draws on the materialist politics of intersectionality, have proved instrumental in complicating and reconfiguring notions of migration and inhabitance by insisting on the need to understand them as context-specific, historicized, socially embedded, and embodied processes and states of being. Bringing into focus women's differential relationships to movement and placement within global networks of connection has allowed gender-inflected theorizing on transnational gendered identities, diasporic cultural spaces, mobilities and homes to work toward defetishizing the idea and practice of migration and de-ontologizing migrant subjectivities. It has thus contributed to thinking that has begun to articulate a more radical, ethical and just politics of living together that resists the originary distinction between home and away, preferring to conceptualize them, instead, as spaces that leak into each other—a leakage that under specific circumstances can yield support and acceptance.

NOTES

1 Western imperialist policies and colonial legacies are closely allied to mass migration in immigrant-receiving countries such as Britain and the United States. Ideologies and practices of imperialism continue to encourage legal and cultural suspicion toward new arrivals in both these countries while being at once one of the main causes that have led to migration to the West in the first place. It is by now well known that the waves of mass migration to Britain following the collapse of the British empire in the mid-twentieth century are the result of its colonial history. Millions of ex-colonial subjects move (from former colonies in the Caribbean, Asia, and Africa) to the metropolitan center as a way out of their poverty-stricken, exploited economies and a colonially instilled sense of duty toward the "motherland." In a different, yet equally historically determined context, the US imperialist interventions into Latin-American countries (in the form of direct rule in Puerto Rico or the overthrow of a democratically elected government in Guatemala) have contributed to the political unrest, corruption, and deprivation that have fueled the migratory flows toward the north and the dream of a prosperous, democratic United States. Tellingly, in both Brexit Britain and Donald Trump's United States, the historical connection between Western imperialism and migration are systematically disavowed and erased from political discourse.

2 Since the publication of Henri Lefebvre's seminal study *The Production of Space* (1974), the widely held conception of space as emptiness has come under rigorous scrutiny by Marxist geographers who have shown it to be an ideologically loaded representation that coincides with the "emerging space-economy of capitalism" (Smith and Katz 75–6). Beginning from the premise that space is a thoroughly gendered—and hence political—construction (Massey), feminists like Donna Haraway and Gillian Rose call attention, in their turn, to the masculinism associated with the illusion of transparent space and an all-seeing vision, often described as the "view from nowhere" (Staeheli and Kofman 4) while postcolonial feminists remind us of the invented character of absolute space when probing into the conceptual and cartographic mappings of cultural and racial differences (see, for instance, Sara Ahmed's inquiry into the spatial formations of Orientalism in *Queer Phenomenology* 13, 112–14).

3 Separated from Turkey by less than two kilometers of sea, Samos, like other Greek islands in the north Aegean Sea, has been since 2015 an entry point into Europe for thousands of illegal migrants and asylum seekers who survived a perilous journey at sea (Perlson). The art project was especially designed to complicate populist representations of migrants dominant in the European press and public debates in the middle of the immigration crisis by creating a space for alternative aesthetic and political responses to an issue as socially and politically divisive as that of contemporary migrancy.

4 "The limitation of women's mobility," writes Doreen Massey, "in terms both of identity and space, has been in some cultural contexts a crucial means of subordination. Moreover the two things—the limitation on mobility in space, the attempted consignment/confinement to particular places on the one hand, and the limitation on identity on the other—have been crucially related" (179).

5 "Rhizome" and "nomad" are terms originating in the influential philosophy of Gilles Deleuze and Félix Guattari that has helped us think about our connection to land, culture, and politics in distinctly mobile terms. See, especially, *A Thousand Prateaus* (1987).

6 Aihwa Ong's analysis of "the disjunctures between nations and moral economies [which] create conditions that foster neo-slavery for some foreign maids" in Southeast Asia is pertinent here and revealing (161).

7 According to Parvati Raghuram, Filipina transnational migrant women are inscribed into the nationalist project both as care workers whose remittances help alleviate the state's foreign debt and as household members assigned the primary role of preserving ties across nation-states by maintaining social relations and caring across borders (193).

WORKS CITED

Agamben, Giorgio. *Homo Sacer: Sovereign Power and Bare Life*. Trans. Daniel Heller-Roazen. Stanford, CA: Stanford UP, 1998.

Ahmed, Sara. *Queer Phenomenology: Orientations, Objects, Others*. Durham, NC: Duke UP, 2006.

Ahmed, Sara. *Strange Encounters: Embodied Others in Postcoloniality*. London: Routledge, 2000.

Ahmed, Sara, Claudia Castañeda, Anne-Marie Fortier, and Mimi Sheller. "Introduction: Uprootings/ Regroundings: Questions of Home and Migration." *Uprootings/Regroundings: Questions of Home and Migration*. Ed. Sara Ahmed, Claudia Castañeda, Anne-Marie Fortier, and Mimi Sheller. Oxford: Berg, 2003, pp. 1–19.

Blunt, Alison. "Cultural Geographies of Migration: Mobility, Transnationality and Diaspora." *Progress in Human Geography* 31.5 (2007): 684–94.

Boukal, Tanja. "Memories of Travels and Dreams." *A World Not Ours*. Curated by Katerina Gregos. Schwarz Foundation. Art Space Pythagorion: Samos, August 5–November 5, 2016.

Brah, Avtar. *Cartographies of Diaspora: Contesting Identities*. London: Routledge, 1996.

Butler, Judith, and Athena Athanasiou. *Dispossession: The Performative in the Political*. Cambridge: Polity P, 2013.

Butler, Judith, and Gayatri C. Spivak. *Who Sings the Nation-State? Language, Politics, Belonging*. London: Seagull Books, 2007.

Cresswell, Tim. "Introduction: Theorizing Place." *Mobilizing Place, Placing Mobility: The Politics of Representation in a Globalized World*. Ed. Ginette Verstraete and Tim Cresswell. Amsterdam: Rodopi Editions, 2002, pp. 11–31.

Cresswell, Tim. *On the Move: Mobility in the Western World*. New York: Routledge, 2006.

Cresswell, Tim. "Towards a Politics of Mobility." *Environment and Planning D: Society and Space* 28 (2010): 17–31.

Cresswell, Tim, and Peter Merriman. "Introduction: Geographies of Mobilities—Practices, Spaces, Subjects." *Geographies of Mobilities—Practices, Spaces, Subjects*. Ed. Tim Cresswell and Peter Merriman. London: Ashgate, 2011, pp. 1–15.

Cresswell, Tim, and Tanu Priya Uteng. "Gendered Mobilities: Towards a Holistic Understanding." *Gendered Mobilities*. Ed. Tanu Priya Uteng and Tim Cresswell. London: Ashgate, 2008, pp. 1–12.

Deleuze, Gilles, and Félix Guattari. *A Thousand Plateaus: Capitalism and Schizophrenia*. Trans. and foreword by Brian Massumi. Minneapolis: U of Minnesota P, 1987.

Derrida, Jacques. "Force of Law. The Mystical Foundation of Authority." *Deconstruction and the Possibility of Justice*. Ed. Drucilla Cornell, Michael Rosenfeld, and David Gray Carlson. London: Routledge, 1992, pp. 3–67.

Fortier, Anne Marie. "Coming Home: Queer Migrations and Multiple Evocations of Home." *European Journal of Cultural Studies* 4.4 (2001): 405–24.

Fortier, Anne-Marie. "Making Home: Queer Migrations and Motions of Attachment." Department of Sociology: Lancaster U, 2003. http://www.lancs.ac.uk/sociology/papers/fortier-making-home.pdf.

Gupta, Rahila. "Leaving Home." *Right of Way: Prose and Poetry by the Asian Women Writers' Workshop*. London: Women's P, 1988, pp. 32–45.

Henderson, Mae. *Borders, Boundaries, and Frames: Cultural Criticism and Cultural Studies*. New York: Routledge, 1995.

Hondagneu-Sotelo, Pierrette. "Feminism and Migration." *The Annals of the American Academy of Political and Social Science* 571 (2000): 107–20.

Kaplan, Caren. *Questions of Travel: Postmodern Discourses of Displacement*. Durham and London: Duke UP, 1996.

Kelley, Carol E. *Accidental Immigrants and the Search for Home: Women, Cultural Identity and, Community*. Philadelphia, PA: Temple UP, 2013.

Kincaid, Jamaica. "Jamaica Kincaid with Gerhard Dilger." *Writing across Worlds: Contemporary Writers Talk*. Ed. Susheila Nasta. London: Routledge, 2004, pp. 80–92.

Kureishi, Hanif. "These Mysterious Strangers: The New Story of the Immigrant." *A Country of Refuge: An Anthology of Writing on Asylum Seekers*. Ed. Lucy Popescu. London: Unbound, 2016, pp. 27–30.

Lefebvre, Henri. *The Production of Space*. Trans. Donald Nicholson-Smith. Oxford: Blackwell, 1991.

Massey, Doreen. *Space, Place and Gender*. Minneapolis: U of Minnesota P, 1994.

Minh-ha, Trinh T. "Other Than Myself/My Other Self." *Travellers' Tales: Narratives of Home and Displacement*. Ed. George Robertson, Melinda Mash, Lisa Tickner, Jon Bird, Barry Curtis, and Tim Putnam. London: Routledge, 1994, pp. 9–26.

Mohanty, Chandra Talpade. "Transnational Feminist Crossings: On Neoliberalism and Radical Critique." *Signs* 38.4 (Summer 2013): 967–91.

Mountz, Alison. "Refugees—Performing Distinction: Paradoxical Positionings of the Displaced." *Geographies of Mobilities: Practices, Spaces, Subjects*. Ed. Tim Cresswell and Peter Merriman. pp. 255–69.

Ong, Aihwa. "A Bio-Cartography: Maids, Neo-Slavery, and NGOs." *Migrations and Mobilities: Citizenship, Borders, and Gender*. Ed. Seyla Benhabib and Judith Resnick. New York: New York UP, 2009, pp. 157–84.

Papastergiadis, Nikos. *The Turbulence of Migration: Globalization, Deterritorialization and Hybridity*. Cambridge: Polity P, 2000.

Parkins, Wendy. *Mobility and Modernity in Women's Novels, 1850s-1930s: Women Moving Dangerously*. Basingstoke: Palgrave Macmillan, 2009.

Perlson, Hili. "On Samos, Greece, a Show Takes an Intimate Look at the Refugee Crisis." *Review, ArtNet News*, August 12, 2016. http://www.boukal.at/site/assets/files/1022/2016_08_15_artnet_news.pdf. December 21, 2017.

Piper, Nicola. "Gendering the Politics of Migration." *International Migration Review* 40.1 (2006): 133–64.

Raghuram, Parvati. "Crossing Borders: Gender and Migration." *Mapping Women, Making Politics*. Ed. Lynn A. Staeheli, Eleonore Kofman, and Linda J. Peake. New York: Routledge, 2004, pp. 185–97.

Sheller, Mimi. "Gendered Mobilities: Epilogue." *Gendered Mobilities*. Ed. Tanu Priya Uteng and Tim Cresswell. London: Ashgate, 2008, pp. 257–65.

Sheller, Mimi. "Mobility." *Sociopedia.isa*, 2011, doi: 10.1177/205684601163.

Silvey, Rachel. "Borders, Embodiment, and Mobility: Feminist Migration Studies in Geography." *A Companion to Feminist Geography*. Ed. Lise Nelson and Joni Seager. Wiley-Blackwell, 2004, pp. 138–49.

Staeheli, Lynn A., and Eleonore Kofman. "Mapping Gender, Making Politics: Toward Feminist Political Geographies." *Mapping Women, Making Politics: Feminist Perspectives on Political Geography*. Ed. Lynn A. Staeheli, Eleonore Kofman, and Linda J. Peake. New York: Routledge, 2004, pp. 1–13.

Smith, Neil, and Cindi Katz. "Grounding Metaphor: Towards a Spatialized Politics." *Place and the Politics of Identity*. Ed. Michael Keith and Steve Pile. London: Routledge, 1993, pp. 67–83.

Weedon, Chris. *Feminism, Theory and the Politics of Difference*. Oxford: Blackwell, 1999.

CHAPTER THIRTY-ONE

Diaspora

AVTAR BRAH

According to UN Sustainable Development Homepage, the number of international migrants living abroad worldwide reached 244 million in 2015, a 41 percent increase compared to 2000. The figure includes almost 20 million refugees. Women comprise slightly less than half of all international migrants. Indeed, female migrants outnumber male migrants in Europe and North America, though in Africa and Asia, particularly western Asia, migrants are predominantly men. These global migrations are creating new displacements. These migrants either join existing diasporas or, in the fullness of time, create new diasporas.

EARLIER STUDIES ON POST-SECOND WORLD WAR DIASPORAS

The studies discussed in this section do not always specifically address the questions of gender, yet they are important in laying the terrain of diaspora studies as a field of enquiry. They have been influential in setting the agenda for theoretical and political debate on the subject. They are likely to feature as the formative texts on most courses in diaspora studies. Hence the need to discuss them in constructing feminist narratives in relation to diaspora.

Over the last four decades, the term "diaspora" has gained growing currency to describe communities that have emerged from the migration and resettlement of peoples all over the world. However, the term itself is a very old one, a Greek word derived from the verb "diaspeiro," which was used as early as the fifth century bc by Sophocles, Herodotus, and Thucydides (Dufoix). There has been a long association of the word diaspora with the dispersal of the Jewish people after the Babylonian exile. The Jewish diaspora evokes a history of persecution and genocide, and occupies a particular iconography within European cartography of displacement. It has a specific resonance in European narratives of trauma, especially in relation to the Jewish Holocaust during the Second World War. Yet, to analyze diasporas in the twenty-first century is to take such ancient diasporas as a point of departure rather than as models or ideal types. Safran suggests that diaspora is now deployed as a "metaphorical designation" to describe different categories of people—"expatriates, expellees, political refugees, alien residents, immigrants and ethnic and racial minorities *tout court*" (83)—and it covers a wide variety of different peoples. The current usages of diaspora are likely to emphasize creativity and positive dimensions of diaspora as much as their history of discrimination, disadvantage, and suffering. As Robin Cohen argues, creativity was a feature of ancient diasporas as well, though it has tended to have been overlooked by commentators. Emphasizing the specificity of the current usage of the term "diaspora," James Clifford suggests,

> We should be able to recognize the strong entailment of Jewish history on the language of diaspora without making that history a definitive model. Jewish (and Greek and Armenian) diaspora can be taken as non-normative staring points for a discourse that is travelling in new global conditions. (303)

Robin Cohen in his discussion of different diasporas provides us with "typologies" of different kinds of diasporas. Typologies can be problematic if treated as hermetically sealed categories, but he recognizes that the histories they describe are much more complex and ambiguous than the typology suggests. This point is especially critical because typologies can be misread as standing for permanent and fixed mutual exclusions. Instead, he emphasizes that there are no fixed boundaries between different types of diasporas, and the typology is a heuristic device to conduct an inquiry. His typology includes victim, labor, trade, imperial, and cultural diasporas. It is important to recognize that a given diaspora can take more than one form and others change their positioning over time in that a "victim" diaspora, for instance, may in time become successful economically and politically and may no longer warrant designation as "victim" as is the case of many Jewish communities and the Ugandan Asian refugees who settled during the 1970s in Britain and elsewhere.

There has been some considerable discussion of the criteria by which a group might be considered to constitute a diaspora. There is no final agreement on this except that a diaspora is not casual travel or short-term settlement of a few years but rather decades or more. Drawing upon some criteria identified by Safran (83), Robert Cohen lists nine common features of a diaspora as follows:

- Dispersal from an original homeland, often traumatically, to two or more foreign regions;
- alternatively, the expansion from a homeland in search of work, in pursuit of trade or to further colonial ambitions;
- a collective memory and myth about the homeland, including its location, history and its achievements;
- an idealization of the putative ancestral home and a collective commitment to its maintenance, restoration, safety and prosperity, even to its creation;
- the development of a return movement that gains collective approbation;
- a strong ethnic group consciousness sustained over a long time and based on a sense of distinctiveness, a common history, and the belief in a common fate;
- a troubled relationship with host societies, suggesting a lack of acceptance at the least or the possibility that another calamity might fall the group;
- a sense of empathy and solidarity with co-ethnic members in other countries of settlement; and
- the possibility of a distinctive creative, enriching life in host countries with a tolerance for pluralism. (26)

Although these criteria are offered as common features, they do not, of course, apply to all diasporas and not in the same fashion. For instance, not all diasporas sustain a desire to "return" to the country of origin, other than perhaps for a short visit. Nor do they necessarily start return movements. Similarly, I have reservations about using the term "host," not least because populations in the country of settlement may be antagonistic rather than host-like to the diasporic groups. I also do not endorse an over-emphasis on attachment to the "homeland" because diasporics do not always consider the country of origin as its homeland but instead regard the country of settlement as "homeland." This is not to suggest, however, that the question of home does not have a critical resonance in the diasporic lifeworld. In fact, home is a central trope in diasporic imaginary. I suggest that we need to think of a "homing desire" that is not the same as a desire for the "homeland" (Brah, *Cartographies of Diaspora*). Homing desire is in large part about a sense of belonging, a "returning" that is also "going forward." And as desire it engages our deepest emotionality. It is marked by the unruly imbrications of the conscious within the workings of the unconscious. Rather than the myth of return, it poses a critique of fixed origins. Here the question of homeland is indefinitely suspended. Home is a place of desire but, equally, it refers to the lived experience of a locality. The two articulate and mark cultural creativity, hybridity, and innovation as well as all manner of contradiction.

The theories that emerged from British cultural studies such as those of Stuart Hall and Paul Gilroy dislodged the concept from its emphasis on homeland, return, and exile. Here the emphasis is on diasporic experience and the narratives of displacement of the postcolonial subject. Hall foregrounded a new theorization of identity as "'production,' which is never complete, always in process" (Hall, qtd. in Woodward 51). He distinguished between two conceptions of identity. One regards shared history as something to be recovered that might mask a "one true self" to be mined, excavated and valorized. He argued that the colonial struggles, for instance, foregrounded such a conception of identity. It was a powerful notion of identity that reshaped the world even though it might be seen by some as an essentialist concept. The second view of identity is "as much about 'becoming' as 'being'. It belongs to the future as much as to the past. It is not something that already exists, transcending place, time, history, and culture ... Far from being eternally fixed in some essentialized past, they are subject to the continuous 'play' of history ... identities are the names we give to the different ways we are positioned by and position ourselves within, the narratives of the past" (Hall, qtd. in Woodward 52).

Hall points out that diasporic identities are constituted not just across similarities but equally within and through difference. Here he borrows Jacques Derrida's concept of *différance*—a simultaneous play of differ and deferral—so that meaning is always deferred. This continuous deferral might be a problem only if we see this "cut of identity as natural and permanent rather than an arbitrary and contingent 'ending'" (Hall, qtd. in Woodward 55).

Working along similar lines, Paul Gilroy shows how diaspora poses a challenge to the "'family as building block' basis of the nation state, offering instead anti-national and anti-essentialist accounts of identity formation based on contingency, indeterminacy and conflict, and offering possibilities of different forms of political action" (Gilroy, in Woodward 339). Gilroy critiques essentialist authenticity and purity, challenges formations of ethnic absoluteness at the heart of nationalist projects and valorizes identities that are seen as hybrid, creolized, and syncretic. Yet, these identities are not entirely arbitrary, embedded as they are in the social histories of the groups who live it. In the book *The Black Atlantic*, Gilroy charts diaspora cultural configurations and politics and argues that the Black Atlantic culture is not simply African, American, Caribbean, or British but all of these at once. It is a creolized formation. Inter alia, Gilroy foregrounds the centrality and prominence of music within the various black communities of the Atlantic diaspora as a means of essential connectedness. "But," he argues, "the histories of borrowing, displacement, transformation, and continual reinscription that the musical culture encloses are a living legacy that should not be reified in the primary symbol of the diaspora and then employed as an alternative to the recurrent appeal of fixity and rootedness" (Gilroy, *The Black Atlantic* 102).

My own analysis of diaspora (Brah, *Cartographies of Diaspora*), is refracted through an intersectional feminist optic. However, while it foregrounds intersectionality of axis of power and differentiation, I was not familiar at the time that I developed this idea with the concept of intersectionality as deployed by Kimberle Williams Crenshaw. I came to know and appreciate the power of her theorization at a later stage. I shall return to a discussion of intersectionality. My point of departure was to think through the distinction made by James Clifford between diaspora understood as a "concept"; as "diasporic discourses" and particular historical "experiences." I tried to specify features that may be seen to distinguish diaspora as a theoretical concept from the historical "experiences" of diaspora. I suggested that diaspora may be understood along the lines of historically contingent "genealogies" in the Foucauldian sense. In other words, diaspora serves as "an ensemble of investigative technologies that historicize trajectories of different diasporas and analyze their relationality across fields of social relations, subjectivity and identity" (Brah, *Cartographies of Diaspora* 180).

I wish to stress that diasporas are historically specific rather than transhistorical formations. Historical specificity is crucial in order to understand the relationality between distinct diasporas. Diasporas do not only signify the movement of people but are also associated with that of capital, commodities, cultural processes, artefacts, and information. While the history of a specific diasporic trajectory will make for distinctiveness of social and cultural experience, diasporas may not be theorized as inscribing some transcendental diasporic consciousness. Nor are diasporic cultural life and politics invariably progressive, though this might be a feature of the new social, cultural, and political transformations in the lifeworld of diasporics in a new location. It is worth bearing in mind that diasporas are heterogeneous, contested spaces as are the societies in which they are embedded. Diasporic lives are lived through multiple modalities produced through the intersection of race, class, gender, sexuality, disability, religion, generation, and so on. Construction of a common "we," then, is not a straightforward process but involves complex cultural and political negotiation involving conflict and contestation as much as solidarity. In my approach to studying diaspora I have proposed a multiaxial performative conception of power that operates across multiple intersectional fields. The concept of diaspora in my frame emerges as

> *an ensemble of investigative technologies* that historicise trajectories of different diasporas, map their relationality, and interrogate, for example, what the search for origins signifies in the history of a particular diaspora, and *why* originary absolutes are imagined; how the materiality of economic, political and signifying practices is experienced; what new subject positions are created and assumed; how particular fields of power articulate in the construction of domination and subordination in a given context; why certain *conceptions of identity* come into play in a given situation, and whether or not these conceptions reinforced or challenged and contested by the *play of identities*. (Brah, *Cartographies of Diaspora* 197)

BORDER AND DIASPORA

The concept of diaspora points to the importance of the notion of the border. Gloria Anzaldua's theorization of borders is particularly instructive. There are two insights that hold particular resonance. First, she uses the concept of border to reflect upon social conditions of life at the Texas–US Southwest/Mexican border where—using the terminology of the period in dividing the world into First, Second, and Third World, the last being what is today referred to as the Global South—she says, "the third world grates against the first and bleeds" (Anzaldua 3). She also uses the concept of the border as a metaphor for psychological, sexual, spiritual, cultural, class, gender, and racialized boundaries. Metaphors are not mere abstractions of concrete reality, but rather they undergird the discursive materiality of power relations. A key question relates to how borders are policed and regulated. Who is allowed to cross a border with ease, and who is kept out? Who is considered outsider, alien and as Other? How, for instance, will queer identities be policed in a context saturated with homophobia and heterosexism? How is the position of racialized groups, or economic migrants, regulated in and through immigration control?

Borders are arbitrary constructions, but they are associated with particular meanings depending upon the history within which a particular border is inscribed. Each border speaks its own story distinct from that of other borders. Old borders may disappear under new socioeconomic and political conditions, and new ones created. Thus power relations are crucial to the operations of all borders. Borders signify the sovereignty of the state whereby they come to symbolize the ability of the state to exercise control over the movement of people, goods, capital, trade, information, and so on. It is common to think of territorial borders to be on the edges of the nation state. Yet, they do not stop at the territorial borders, but rather they permeate the national, even global space. Étienne Balibar argues that what is important about borders is what they do at a given historical juncture. Borders are also understood as enacted practices and in this regard may be viewed as located on the body (Whitley). This is the case, for instance, when immigration legislation permits "fishing raids" at places of work and suspected undocumented workers are rounded up. Some immigrants may live under the constant threat of deportation, carrying borders on their bodies. Racism operates in and through constructions of bodies.

This is nowhere more true than in Europe today. Global inequality and poverty run rife in our war riven world. These social and cultural conditions are at the heart of intolerable journeys undertaken by migrants and refugees from the Global South to the Global North. According to media reports, 500,000 refugees arrived at the shores of Southern Europe in 2015, fleeing war-ravaged countries such as Syria and Iraq. Intolerable conditions also attend the plight of people reaching Europe via Libya. They too are trying to escape dire economic and/or political conditions or natural disasters such as famine and floods. Wars, religious insurgencies, authoritarian and repressive political regimes, climate change–related draught and famine, lack of jobs and, as we have already noted, endemic poverty, are all contributory factors in this tragedy. These journeys often begin in the impoverished, sometimes politically unstable and conflict-ridden parts of the world such as Syria, Chad, Eriteria, Somalia, Sierra Leone, Iraq, and other parts of the Middle East, and North and West Africa. Thousands have drowned in the Mediterranean. In July 2017, the death rate reached the dreadful figure of one in forty. Western intervention in Libya destroyed the infrastructure, creating a social vacuum in which infighting factions collide and the broken state cannot prevent these places the center of people smuggling.

The difficulties of border crossing do not always end when one reaches the end of the first stage of the journey. In Europe, the refugees and migrants are faced with racism and xenophobia. Any hopes of a coordinated European response to settle those arriving have failed to materialize with Italy and Greece because of their geographical location, disproportionately bearing the responsibility for the intake of the newcomers. According to the editorial of the British newspaper the *Guardian* of July 9, 2017 ("Refugee Policy Is Wrong and Short Sighted"), "All hopes of a united European response to the refugee crisis seem to have evaporated. There is still no network of commonly funded reception centers. National leaders have shunned the idea of equitable resettlement quotas for EU states. The cornerstone of the European approach remains the hopelessly outdated Dublin Regulation, which insists refugees must be processed by the first EU country they set foot in and can be sent back there if they journey beyond it. And so the injustice of two of Europe's poorer nations—Italy and Greece—continuing to struggle with large number of refugees remains" (*Guardian* 34). When some refugees try to move up to north European countries, they may be faced with incredible obstacles including razor sharp wired boundaries. Even countries such as Germany which welcomed refugees for six months has been giving into internal anti-immigrant political pressure. Yet, it is ironic that 80 percent of the world's refugees are hosted by developing countries. Moreover, migrants make important economic and social contribution to the receiving countries, and their labor is often needed, although perhaps to do low-paid jobs that the local people do not wish to undertake.

The cases cited above highlight the historical specificity of these particular journeys. They also place into relief why it is important to discuss them in relation to diasporas. These migrants arrive under difficult and specific material and psychological conditions. This makes their needs different and distinctive from long-term diasporics but in time they may create new diasporas or become part of existing ones. This, for example, was the case with Asian refugees to Britain from Uganda in the early 1970s. Over the last decades, they have successfully made new lives in Britain and created a new diaspora.

BORDER, POLITICS OF LOCATION, DIASPORA, AND DIASPORA SPACE

A discussion of borders and boundaries, and of home and belonging, brings into focus issues of "politics of location." One early example of the use of the term "politics of location" is that by the feminist scholar Adrienne Rich. Her text is a reflection upon how Rich came to realize the centrality of embodiment to feminist politics, and how embodiment locates you across multiple axes of differentiation and power. She emphasizes the importance of not transcending the personal but claiming it. She discusses how there was a time when she could quote without hesitation Virginia Woolfe's statement, "As a woman I have no country. As a woman I want no country. As a woman my country is the whole world." But she could not do so anymore because, as she says, "As a woman I have a country; as a woman I cannot divest myself of that country merely by condemning its government or by saying three times, 'As a woman my country is the whole world.' Tribal loyalties aside, and even if nation-states are now just pretexts used by multinational conglomerates to serve their interests, I need to understand how a place on the map is also a place in history within which as a woman, a Jew, a lesbian, a feminist I am created and trying to create" (Rich 212). She speaks of how as a white middle-class woman, she was simultaneously "located" by her gender, color, and class. Indeed, she refers to "whiteness" as a politics of location which places her in a position of power vis a vis people of color.

Another contemporary autobiographical account that interrogates the shifting positionalities of whiteness and the simultaneous articulation of position of power with that of subordination is that of Minnie Bruce Pratt entitled "Identity: Skin, Blood, Heart" (1984). She is committed to unpicking power geometries entailed when she, as a white, middle-class, Christian raised in Southern United States, decides to come out as a lesbian, and her family and friends "back home" react negatively. She explores how her sense of belonging and safety had been dependent on her taken-for-granted acceptance of the normative cultural and social codes of her social milieu. These were shaken when she sought to gain custody of her children and had to face the hostility and rejection of people she had understood were her "community." She examines the politics of racism in the United States, both in terms of its structural dimensions as well as its personal manifestations. In contrast, Angela Davis's autobiography of growing up black in southern United States invokes life in the segregated south and charts experiential terrain from the opposite side of the racial divide. Such accounts foreground the ways in which same geographical space may come to articulate different histories so that politics of location emerge as politics of contradiction. Politics of location is the site of the intersectionality of the structural, the personal/subjective, psychic, and experiential.

In my analysis of the concepts of diaspora, borders, and politics of location, these concepts together provide a conceptual grid for analyzing historicized accounts of the movements of people, information, cultures, commodities, and capital. I have called the articulation of these three concepts as "diaspora space." I have described the concept of diaspora space as follows:

> Diaspora space is the intersectionality of diaspora, border, and dis/location as a point of confluence of economic, political, cultural and psychic processes. It is where multiple subject positions are juxtaposed, contested, proclaimed or disavowed; where the permitted and the prohibited perpetually interrogate; and where the accepted and the transgressive imperceptibly mingle even while these syncretic forms may be disclaimed in the name of purity and tradition. Here tradition itself is itself continually invented even as it may be hailed as originating from the mists of time. What is at stake is the infinite experientiality, the myriad processes of cultural fissure and fusion that underwrite contemporary forms of transcultural identities. (Brah, *Cartographies of Diaspora* 208)

Diaspora space references conditions of contemporary transmigrancies, crossing borders, territorial and otherwise, and the multiple power geometries where the play of power is both coercive and productive, and where identities and a sense of belonging are produced and contested. In other words, diaspora space, as distinct from diaspora, highlights the *"entanglement of the genealogies of dispersal* with those of staying *put"* (Brah, *Cartographies of Diaspora* 242).

DIASPORA AND INTERSECTIONALITY

Why is it important to discuss intersectionality in a chapter devoted to analysis of diaspora? It is essentially because diasporas are not homogeneous categories but rather are deeply marked and differentiated by such axis as that of race, class, gender, and sexuality.

In other words, diasporas are inherently intersectional formations. The theorization of intersectionality is a very significant development within feminist analytics. Black women and women of color have played a central role in its emergence and elaboration in the 1960s, 1970s, and since. At its base, intersectionality is about the fact that our experience is marked by a variety of vectors such as race, gender, class, sexuality, and so on. One of the early statements of intersectionality was that by the Combahee River Collective, a group of black lesbian activists in Boston. Written in 1977, this statement is a key document of women-of-color feminism. Its incisive insights are as relevant to scholarship and activism today as they were forty years ago. Although it does not use the term "intersectionality," there is no doubt that the statement is one of the major forerunners to our current debates. Its argument that "we are actively committed to struggling against racial, sexual, heterosexual and class oppression, and see as our particular task the development of integrated analysis and practice based upon the fact that the major systems of oppression are interlocking" (Guy-Sheftall 232) is singularly predictive of subsequent developments in the study of intersectionality. Its emphasis on "simultaneous experience" of different axis of differentiation such as racism, gender, class, and sexuality provides a critical lens on the kaleidoscopic effects of articulating modalities of power. It prefigures later debates on analyzing the concepts of "embodiment" and "experience." As socialist feminists, the member of the Collective foregrounded their politics in a critique of capitalism, imperialism, and patriarchal social relations. This contextualizes US black feminism in the global context of transnational feminism.

In the following decades, the concept of social divisions and that of different axis of power was used by scholars in the same way as intersectionality has been deployed since. For instance, Floya Anthias and Nira Yuval Davis analyze the interconnections of race, ethnicity, gender, and class, and Floya Anthias introduces the concept of "translocational positionality," which resonates with the meanings associated with intersectionality. Braidotti provides interesting insights into the development of the term intersectionality and its transpositionality with other vectors of difference in the constitution of subjectivity, identity, and structural domains. But the term intersectionality itself is said to have been coined by Kimberle Williams Crenshaw. Collins and Bilge note that today the term is widely used by scholars, policy advocates, practitioners, and activists in many different contexts in the world. A definition of the term to which all may subscribe is not an easy task. In 2004, Ann Phoenix and I described the term as "signifying the complex, irreducible, varied and variable effects which ensue when multiple axes of differentiation—economic, political, cultural, psychic, subjective and experiential—intersect in historically specific contexts" (Brah and Phoenix 76). Collins and Bilge offer the following definition:

Intersectionality is a way of understanding and analyzing the complexity in the world, in people and in human experience. The events and conditions of social and political life and the self can seldom be understood as shaped by one factor. They are generally shaped by many factors in diverse and mutually influencing ways. When it comes to social inequality, people's lives and the organization of power in a given society are better understood as being shaped not by a single axis of social division, be it race or gender or class, but by many axes that work together and influence each other. Intersectionality as an analytic tool gives people better access to the complexity of the world and of themselves. (Collins and Bilge 2)

Importantly, Collins and Bilge suggest that intersectional analysis are underpinned by six core ideas that appear and reappear when the concept is used. They are inequality;

relationality; power; social context, and social justice. For a sympathetic, though critical, engagement with intersectionality, see Brah ("Multiple Axis of Power"), and Nash.

Scholars working in the field of diaspora studies do not always address questions of intersectionality. Yet, as I have argued (Brah, *Cartographies of Diaspora*, "Multiple Axis of Power"), diaspora studies and intersectional studies are intimately interconnected. Diasporas are intersectionally heterogeneous and share a common focus on "difference." It is here that the two intersect and overlap. There are many ways in which difference may be analyzed. In my case, I have argued that difference may be theorized across four axes: difference understood as social relation; analyzed as subjectivity; difference theorized as identity; and difference conceptualized as experience (Brah, *Cartographies of Diaspora*, "Multiple Axis of Power"). Although they are presented separately for analytic purposes, they crosscut in practice.

QUEERING DIASPORAS

Studies of sexuality have been limited in the field of diaspora studies, but see, for instance, Fataheh Farahani's examination of the narratives of first-generation Iranian women living in Sweden. Much early work on diasporas has been refracted through the heteronormative lens. More recently, however, this focus is increasingly being challenged. This scholarship interrogates the demands placed by heteronormativity on bodies, desires, subjectivities, and identities. This mapping of queerness onto diaspora decenters these regimes. This queer scholarship challenges nationalist ideologies by foregrounding the impure, inauthentic, and nonessentialist promise of the concept of diaspora. As Gayatri Gopinath argues, "The concept of a queer diaspora enables a simultaneous critique of heterosexuality and the nation while exploding the binary oppositions between nation and diaspora, heterosexuality and homosexuality, original and copy" (11). In other words, "suturing 'queer' to 'diaspora' thus recuperates those desires, practices, and subjectivities that are rendered impossible and unimaginable within conventional diasporic and nationalist imaginaries" (Gopinath 11). The term "queer" is preferred by Gopinath to "gay" and "lesbian" as a critique of the globalization of "gay" identity that judges all "other" sexual cultures and practices as premodern against a model of Western sexual identity. Queer diasporic scholarship also reframes questions of home, a preoccupation in studies of diaspora: "The resignification of 'home' within a queer diasporic imaginary makes three crucial interventions: first, it forcefully repudiates the elision of queer subjects from national and diasporic memory; second, it denies their function as threat to family/community/nation; and third, it refuses to position queer subjects as alien, inauthentic, and perennially outside the confines of these entities" (Gopinath 15). Her text challenges discourses that "forget, excise and criminalise queer bodies, pleasures, desires, histories, and lives" (Gopinath 187).

In a similar vein to Gopinath, El-Tayeb uses queer theory to analyze diaspora and ethnicity. She interrogates the "national" through which exclusion takes place, exploring the means by which minorities are constructed as being outside the national politics, culture, and history and represented as not being British, German, Spanish, and so on. Her book focuses on Europe and delineates the ways in which racialized groups are externalized from Europe and their histories of long-standing connections with Europe are concealed. For her, the alternative community building by a variety of groups she analyses such as the Black Women's Summer School in Germany, might be best conceptualized as "queering ethnicity." The term would seem to refer to the mixing and matching of genres and styles in the cultural processes of performativity which resists notions of purity, authenticity, and "uncomplicated belonging." The term diaspora is important here as it, contrary to that of migration, transcends such binaries as citizen and foreigner and defies linear models of movement from origin to destination. Her notion of diaspora is defined as follows:

> In this study I extend the notion of diaspora to describe a population that does not share a common origin—however imaginary it might be—but a contemporary condition. Within this broadened understanding of diaspora, the concept is transformed from a temporal and spatial displacement focused on the past towards one of productive dislocation directed as the future—mirroring the potential of queering ethnicity as a nonessentialist, and often nonlinear, political strategy. (El-Tayeb xxxv)

Diaspora studies is thus a continually developing field.

WORKS CITED

Anthias, Floya. "Beyond Feminism and Multiculturalism: Locating Difference and the Politics of Location." *Women's Studies International Forum* 25.3 (2002): 275–86.

Anthias, Floya, and Yuval-Davis, Nira. *Racialized Boundaries: Race, Nation, Gender, Colour and Class and the Anti-racist Struggle.* New York: Routledge, 1992.

Anzaldua, Gloria. *Borderlands/La Frontera.* San Francisco, CA: Spinsters/Aunt Lute Books, 1987.

Balibar, Étienne. *Politics and the Other Scene.* London: Verso Books, 2002.

Brah, Avtar. *Cartographies of Diaspora, Contesting Identities.* London: Routledge, 1996.

Brah, Avtar. "Multiple Axis of Power: Articulations of Diaspora and Intersectionality." *The Routledge Diaspora Studies Reader.* Ed. Wilson, Janet and Stierstorfer, Klaus. London: Routledge, 2018.

Brah, Avtar, and Phoenix, Ann. "Ain't I a Woman: Revisiting Intersectionality." *Journal of International Women's Studies* 5.3 (2004): 75–86.

Braidotti, Rosi. *Transpositions: On Nomadic Ethics.* Cambridge: Polity P, 2006.

Clifford, James. "Diaspora." *Cultural Anthropology* 9.3 (1994): 302–38.

Cohen, Robin. *Global Diasporas: An Introduction.* London: U College London P, 1997.

Collins, Patricia Hill, and Bilge, Sirma. *Intersectionality.* Cambridge: Polity P, 2016.

Crenshaw, Kimberle Williams. "Demarginalizing the Intersection of Race and Sex: A Black Feminist Critique of Antidiscrimination Doctrine, Feminist Theory, and Antiracist Politics." *University of Chicago Legal Forum* 140 (1989): 139–67.

Dufoix, Stephane. *Diasporas.* Berkeley: U of California P, 2008.

El-Tayeb, Fatima. *European Others: Queering Ethnicity in Postnational Europe.* Minneapolis: U of Minnesota P, 2011.

Farahani, Fataneh. *Gender, Sexuality, and Diaspora.* London: Routledge, 2017.

Gilroy, Paul. *The Black Atlantic: Modernity and Double Consciousness.* London: Verso Books, 1992.

Gilroy, Paul. *"Diaspora and the Detours of Identity"* in Woodward Kathryn, *Identity and Difference.* London: Sage, 1997.

Gopinath, Gayatri. *Impossible Desires: Queer Diasporas and South Asian Public Cultures.* Durham, NC: Duke UP, 2005.

Guy-Sheftall, Beverly, ed. "A Black Feminist Statement." *Words of Fire: An Anthology of African American Feminist Thought.* New York: New P, 1995, pp. 232–40.

Hall, Stuart. *"Cultural Identity and Diaspora"* in Woodward Kathryn, *Identity and Difference*. London: Sage, 1990.

Nash, Jennifer C. "Re-thinking Intersectionality." *Feminist Review* 89.1 (2008).

"Number of International Migrants Reached 244 Million in 2015." *United Nations*, January 12, 2016, www.un.org/sustainabledevelopment/blog/2016/01/244-million-international-migrants-living-abroad-worldwide-new-un-statistics-reveal/. Accessed September 27, 2017.

Pratt, Minnie Bruce. "Identity, Skin, Blood, Heart." *Yours in Struggle: Feminist Perspectives on Racism and Anti-Semitism*. Ed. E. Bulkin, M. B. Pratt, and B. Smith. New York: Long Hall, 1984.

"Refugee Policy Is Wrong and Short Sighted." *Guardian Editorial*, July 9, 2017.

Rich, Adrienne. "Notes towards a Politics of Location." *Blood, Bread, and Poetry, Selected Prose 1979–1985*. W. W. Norton, [1984] 1994.

Safran, William. "Diasporas in Modern Societies: Myths of Homeland and Return." *Diaspora*. 1.1 (1991): 83–99.

Whitley, Leila M. "More than a Line: Borders as Embodied Site." PhD Thesis, Goldsmiths College: U of London, 2015.

CHAPTER THIRTY-TWO

Community

MINA KARAVANTA

And the migrants kept coming.

—Jacob Lawrence, *The Great Migration*

[I]t is salutary, indeed urgent, to be reminded that our age and our country symbolize not just what has been settled and permanently resides here, but always and constantly the undocumented turbulence of unsettled and unhoused exiles, immigrants, itinerant or captive populations for whom no document, no adequate expression yet exists sufficient to take account of what they go through.

—Edward Said, *Humanism and Democratic Criticism*

The overweening, defining event of the modern world is the mass movement of raced populations, beginning with the largest forced transfer of people in the history of the world: slavery. The consequences of which transfer have determined all the wars following it as well as the current ones being waged on every continent. Nationhood— the very definition of citizenship—is constantly being demarcated and redemarcated in response to exiles, refugees, *Gastarbeiter*, immigrants, migrations, the displaced, the fleeing and the besieged. The anxiety of belonging is entombed within the central metaphors in the discourse on globalization, transnationalism, nationalism, the break-up of federations, the rescheduling of alliances, and the fictions of sovereignty. Yet these figurations of nationhood and identity are frequently raced themselves as the originating racial house that defined them. When they are not raced, they are ... imaginary landscape, never inscape; Utopia, never home.

—Toni Morrison, "Home"

In colonial modernity, community is often aligned with the history of the nation-state and linked with the fixity but also fluidity of the demarcators of ethnicity, race, religion, class, language, sexuality, and gender. It is the effect of the right of the individual to belong to a social and political order either in the sense of "being bound or indebted together" or in the sense of belonging to "what is together as one" (Van Den Abbeele xi).[1] However, community is also related to the deprivation of this right and often signifies the delimitation or even negation of a communal life as the histories of colonialism and neocolonialism, racism, and partition have aptly demonstrated. The histories of the disaster of the human that haunt the rise and development of the modern nation-states, whose bleak histories are summoned by the spaces of the slave plantation and the concentration camp,[2] have associated community with the histories of dispossession and "survivance" (Vizenor 1)[3] or, in Jacques Derrida's terms, expropriation and exappropriation.[4] Dispossession and expropriation refer to destruction and loss while survivance is immanent in the emergence of constituencies and their communities that persevere and develop in the wake of dispossession. Their common cause appears to be negative, lacking a shared property, and untimely as they emerge from within the ruins of disaster. In view of the global migrations and forced dispossessions of human beings and the colonization of indigenous and native lands, the contemporary concept of community has undergone transformations and cannot be restricted to signifying the exceptionalist structure of primordial origins, blood ties, and the myth of the nation as "a homogeneous, empty time" (Benjamin 261). In the present,[5] the nation-state cannot account for the spread of diasporic communities within and across its borders. Its mainstream discourses fail to affirm the potentiality of the sprawling communities of multicultural, interethnic, hybrid, and multilingual characteristics within the metropolises and the global cities that are characterized by new orders of displacement, containment and a "class and spatial polarization" (Sassen 245). This failure contributes to the rise of new forms of xenophobia, racism, and ethnocentrism as various thinkers have recently argued.[6] It has also provoked a messianic desire for communities to come,[7] at least within Eurocentric discourses aspiring to articulate the negative potentiality of community within a socialist or communist horizon or utopia.

As the world becomes discontinuously and unevenly connected, community signifies the rise of diasporic and intercultural communities and the perseverance of the peripheral and nondominant collectivities that seek recognition within the nation or as nations, struggling against their marginalization. It also refers to the perseverance or emergence of collectivities such as the subaltern and indigenous communities that, despite their existence, remain unacknowledged by or at the limits of the national discourses and policies. The twenty-first century attests to the growing tensions between communities that, despite the growing multiculturalism and hybridity of cultures, are still identified by primarily their ethnic, religious, and racial attributes. The current refugee crisis in the Mediterranean gives rise to the new subaltern communities of paperless humans who, having escaped from war, ecological, political, and economic disasters, seek asylum in Europe. This event symptomatically reveals how the history of the stateless as the disavowed human[8] and the figure of the foreigner, a racialized body, as a rhetorical and social device of the national community, are intertwined. It also symptomatically reveals how community is not a given but rather a performative act; it becomes materialized not through the repetition of a common cause, an objective that is instantly shared by a group but rather through a series of minor acts of various constituencies that come from different origins or communities and become affiliated with the ones who offer hospitality in the joint effort of survival and care.

This essay borrows its conceptual vocabulary from Sylvia Wynter's deconstruction of the coloniality of being that permeates cultures and their community poetics in modernity. In her effort to decolonize thinking and articulate an analysis of culture against the discourses of colonialism and race thinking, Wynter offers an important conceptual framework through which community as a myth narrative that consolidates the exceptionalist or fantasy structures of the nation can be systematically deconstructed.[9] By drawing on Wynter's conceptual framework, this essay engages Sara Ahmed, Leela Gandhi, Elizabeth Povinelli, Judith Butler, Chantal Mouffe, Wendy Brown, and Gayatri Spivak's work on community and the other, the foreigner, the subaltern, the refugee, and, in Jacques Rancière's sense, "the part that has no part" (Povinelli 73).[10] It proposes to examine community as the performative act of constituencies who form a hybrid polity of conviviality and survivance against race thinking and in the name of a radical democratic polity-in-the-making.

Rather than "blood and soil," community as a polity-in-the-making is "demarcated and redemarcated" by "exiles, refugees, *Gastarbeiter*, immigrants, migrations, the displaced, the fleeing and the besieged" (Morrison 11) and signifies the "autopoetic mechanisms" (Wynter, "Human Being as Noun?"), "sociogenic codes" (Wynter, "Towards the Sociogenic Principle" 32), and revised "origin narratives" (Wynter, "1492" 30) of the collectivities that seek to rebuild their home in the world. Wynter uses these terms to describe the ways by which humans construct their commonness through mythopoetic processes they engender in their effort to respond to the question of who they are as humans and what genre of "we," the *"propter nos"* ("1492" 47), human collectivities form in the process of their cultural and political development, especially when they are subjected to sovereign structures that delimit their ontological, social, and political potentiality such as colonialism, imperialism, and their epistemological discourses that proliferated a certain idea of the human by destroying or colonizing other ontological, cultural, and political ways of being human. Delinking the "propter nos" (47) from the "Western bourgeois liberal monohumanist *homo oeconomicus*" ("Unparalleled Catastrophe for Our Species?" 47) to rethink it "from the perspective of our 'whole human community'" (63) requires a "gaze from below" (50) that calls into question "the very *being* of being human, as incarnated in its globally hegemonic Western bourgeois definition" and deconstructs the sociogenic codes, discourses, and symbolic practices that constitute what is represented as the universal condition of being *"normally human"* (59).

Although Wynter never writes about community per se, her deconstruction of the coloniality of being unearths the epistemological and philosophical strategies of constructing the human as a narrative of the self as always the same, which underlies the poetics of community in modernity and stresses the link between ontology and polity that runs through community. In colonial modernity, community is haunted by its association with the social and political evolution of the nation-state and its origin narratives and truth statements (Wynter) and is thus related to colonialism, imperialism, and capitalism that exploited and destroyed or, at least, tried to destroy the cultures of the indigenous, the natives, or what colonial discourses identified as the Others. In her work, Wynter remarks how this destruction meant both the systemic dispossession of the natives from their lands in the process of the slave trade and the slave plantation but also the expropriation of the natives and indigenous populations in their own lands as they were invaded, colonized, and christianized by Western Christendom, its military and cultural weapons. In view of this history that continues well into the present, this essay analyzes community as a concept that is transnational and hybrid, the product of affective politics rooted in a common cause that is not a given but the deferred effect of the performative acts not only of those who belong but also of those who wish to belong. These thinkers represented here as a community of method emphasize community as the effect of the minor acts of survival, perseverance, and resistance of constituencies against and beyond the limitations of the political and economic forces of expropriation and dispossession throughout colonial modernity. The refugee crisis, the continuing transformations of what Étienne Balibar identifies as "neo-racism,"[11] the growing numbers of white supremacists in the United States and Europe, and the disavowal of the indigenous and subaltern communities with their systemic exclusion from the state and human rights represent some of the challenges that transnational feminist and anticolonial criticism engages in its variegated and pluralizing effort to articulate a community poetics that does not reproduce the idea of Man as an "overrepresented modality of being human" (Wynter, "Unsettling the Coloniality of Being" 317). These particular thinkers thought together attend to the poetics of community as a polity-in-the-making by gleaning their conceptual analysis from the histories of collectivities that resisted and continue to resist racism, nationalism, and exceptionalism.

In *Encounters: Embodied Others*, Sara Ahmed argues that community is often formed as a collective "we" that is consolidated on the figure of the stranger who does not enter sovereignty as the unknown other but is already known as the outside, the periphery, the margin. A community, a collective and knowable "we" is dependent upon this stranger who is all too paradoxically familiar; his or her presence is unconditional for the condition of a community as a collectivity of the similar and the intimate to exist. In Ahmed's words,

> the stranger is somebody we know as not knowing, rather than somebody we simply do not know. The stranger is produced as a category within knowledge, rather than coming into being in an absence of knowledge. The implications of such a rethinking of the relationship between knowledge and strangers are far reaching: it suggests that knowledge is bound up with the formation of a community, that is, with the formation of a "we" that knows through (rather than against) "the stranger." (55)

The stranger is a "constitutive outside, an exterior to the community that makes its existence possible" (Mouffe 235) through which the community can reproduce the self as same. Tolerant to the presence of others, contemporary multicultural societies that are predominantly exceptionalist in their national discourses are defined by a community poetics that maps its outside space inhabited by those that the dominant historical and political narratives regard as the others. However, these others are the source of a knowledge of sameness, that is, of self as always same to itself. This politics of sameness that produces the stranger as "a category within knowledge" (Ahmed 55) is what Derrida calls "*ipseity*" (*Beast and the Sovereign* 103), which founds the political discourses of sovereignty on a collective and individual level in modern states.

What the stranger offers to a certain collectivity that establishes its sovereign self as a "we" that remains always the same to a certain idea of the human is the possibility of constructing a sense of belonging and identity unburdened by the task of encountering "embodied others" (Ahmed 148). Opposing the generalized and abstract term of the other, Ahmed uses the term "embodied others" to conjure the re-presentation of human beings as others who are coerced into embodying a state of otherness because of race, religion, gender, and ethnicity; their being is mediated by discourses and institutions that mark their bodies as an aberration, that is, a deviation from the norm often likened to the animal as a beastly being. The term also signifies the negative potentiality of these differentially racialized individuals, whose genres of the human and their ontological, political, and social *bios* remain unaccountable and unanswerable to the sovereign politics of a certain community. Ahmed calls for a transnational feminist criticism that deconstructs community as the collectivity of the same; her text critiques the construction of otherness or foreignness within a community poetics that perpetuates the imaginary structure of the nation as an organic community rooted in blood ties. She attends to the history of the foreigner or the stranger not as the other within the same but as the singularity who represents knowledges, has mastered sociogenic codes and can perform autopoetic mechanisms that proliferate the genres of the human that are in danger of being made obsolete by the community narratives that banish them or deem them to be inferior others and unwanted strangers. She thus deconstructs the narrative of community as a structure of the self as same to attend to a polity poetics that does not foreclose but rather remains open to the ones who have been racialized and represented as the others or the ones who are expected to occupy this position from outside the community.

The history of the scarf affair in Europe has been a case in point.[12] In the early and late 1990s, the scarf became the symbol of a battle between state and individual, secular politics and the ethnic symbols of the non-Christian and nonwhite communities in the former imperial metropolises. The history of the scarf affair both in France and in Germany summons the woman's body as the constitutive space of this battlefield. The representation of the scarf affair to primarily Western readers often misreads or disavows the Muslim woman's secular right to affiliate her different subject positions as both a Muslim and European woman, citizen of the state, and member of an ethnic or hybrid community.[13] The various readings and misreadings of the case also revealed how any knowledge relating to the scarf cannot avoid the mediation of a prior knowledge of the other; the scarf can only symptomatically reveal an oppositional practice to secular politics, a remainder of women's oppression in the Arab world, and a sign of the continued interpellation of the Muslim woman's body by an oppressive religious patriarchy that can be contravened by the postimperial and secular politics of the Western state. By demonstrating how the Muslim woman's body can be forced into a secular politics through the removal of the scarf in the public spaces of the knowledge institutions, the state can exert its power as the legal entity to represent the communities of others within its territory and discursive domains. By regulating the women's bodies and misrepresenting religious or cultural differences as a threat to secularism, the state falls into the paradox of a semi-secular politics that justifies its force through the control of the body. The scarf becomes a biopolitical instrument by which the unruly and undisciplined body can be more properly secularized.

The more communitarian approach to the matter suggests that the state and its secular politics outweigh the individual right to an ethnic or religious difference that assumedly threatens this politics whose mission is to protect the individual from cultural and ethnic practices that violate her rights. Instead of protecting the individual, this approach reinforces "liberal exceptionalism" (Povinelli 31). Povinelli explains how liberal exceptionalism

> pivots on the commonsense truth of two competing, or at least incommensurate, political and social discourses and their affective entailments—that in cases of cultural conflict the problem of difference is solved through public reason and in these same cases moral reason must draw red lines across which difference cannot proceed, or a bracket must be put around the difference so that it can be removed from public debate until that time its challenge can be managed. (31)

The recent chapter of the history of the scarf in France is a case in point. Following the terrorist attacks in Paris and then Nice in 2016, the French police in Nice made a woman remove some of her clothing and gave her a ticket for wearing a burkini that several French towns decided to ban on its beaches. She was fined for "not wearing an outfit respecting good morals and secularism" (Quinn, *The Guardian*).[14] The burkini ban was aligned with the fight against religious fundamentalism and the right of a community to defend its secular politics. The irony is that the scarf is also related to the efforts of Muslim women in the West and other places to affiliate secular politics and religious symbols and thus enable themselves to be present in sports, on the beaches, and in the public arena as constituencies that perform their ethnic and religious attachments as constitutive of the public and secular world.

In transgressing religious and secular codes by refusing to be stereotyped as either liberated or victimized, the women who choose to straddle their different subject positions and wear the scarf or the burkini "intertwine gender performativity with precarity" (Butler, *Notes* 32–3). Explaining the connections between gender performativity and precarity in her work, Butler argues how the lives of sexual minorities and certain economically and politically vulnerable populations can challenge the political and social norms by their mere existence: "Gender performativity ... opposed the unlivable conditions in which gender and sexual minorities live" and "precarity designates that politically induced condition in which certain populations suffer from failing social and economic networks of support more than others, and become differentially exposed to injury, violence and death" (33). In the wake of the terrorist attacks often represented as attacks against Western political and social life, the Muslim woman's body is thrown into the midst of two forms of precarity and is rendered politically vulnerable through her gender performance. Hers is a body that performs its difference and marks its otherness by way of remaining elusive or unaccountable to the dominant images that reproduce the woman's body as a sign of women's emancipation and freedom in the public space but also as a spectacle for entertainment and consumption. Looking from below at the faces of the police officers who stand above her and force her to remove the clothing that shields her body from being immediately visible and thus accountable to their power, she is not speechless. She rather holds her right to perform the sociogenic codes and autopoetic mechanisms of her cultural difference as a difference that she displaces and transposes into another setting she cohabits with her others. Her performative hold on these codes and mechanisms in this particular public space endues them with a different meaning and subjects them to deferral and variation. She refuses to ascribe to a community of the same that sees her attire as an element of a terrorist politics that threatens liberty and equality as much as she affirms her presence in the public space by connecting her religious and ethnic codes and mechanisms with a particular secular politics.

This kind of performativity is "always subject to creative deviation, deferral and variation," and retains a " 'possibility of agency' which need not conform to spatial and temporal specificities, and which, we might add, may also remain unrealized" (Gandhi, *The Common Cause* 164). Its realization is immanent in the politics of alliance that her presence as well as the presence of other vulnerable others conjure. Deviating from the rules and defying the norms, she is the other who insists on her "individual self-expression" and refuses to be "denuded of her accents, cries and lamentations" (Willett in Ahmed 144) that make up her "specificity" in a concrete place and temporality. Embodying her otherness by way of performing parallel attachments and inhabiting subject positions in different communities in which she partakes as a woman, Muslim, of European, Arab, and other origins, this other reveals how there is an urgent need for a politics

> that is premised on closer encounters, on encounters with those who are other than "the other" or "the stranger" ("ourselves undressed").... . Thinking about how we might work with, and speak to others, or how we may inhabit the world with others, involves imagining a different form of political community, one that moves beyond the opposition between common and uncommon, between friends and strangers, or between sameness and difference. (Ahmed 180)

The performance of her specificity reveals the other's need to engage in "a process of cultural translation" (Butler, *Parting Ways* 8) that enables a certain traditional or religious element to be transposed through time and space and become a "historical resource" that "comes to bear upon the present" (8). In *Parting Ways: Jewishness and the Critique of Zionism*, Butler examines Jewishness as such a "historical resource," constituted by "the exilic—or more emphatically, *the diasporic*" (15) that can pave the path to a politics of cohabitation against Zionist exceptionalism and Israel's ongoing colonization of the Palestinian lands. This politics of cohabitation that is "unchosen," as in the case of the Palestinian and the Jew, is not just a political problem for the State to resolve, often resorting to forcing the *differend* or the "part that has no part" into disappearance, but primarily "a condition of social existence" (176) that arises from a plural, albeit, uneven coexistence and relies on various material and immaterial interdependences. In a different but relevant to the politics of cohabitation that Butler analyzes in her powerful critique of Zionism, the veil is also an element of the exilic and the diasporic that challenges European exceptionalisms by revealing the multicultural alibis of national exceptionalisms and highlighting the urgency to rethink the politics of cohabitation from the perspective of an in-common that is neither evenly shared nor always anticipated. It thus raises the question of what is shared and transposed through the sharing, desired or unchosen as it might be, and how practices of cultural translation transform and raise new questions about what Butler, following Hannah Arendt, calls "the inclusive and plural cohabitation" (125) that is an unconditional human condition: "To cohabit the earth is prior to any possible community or nation or neighborhood. We might sometimes choose where to live, and who to live by or with, but we cannot choose with whom to cohabit the earth" (125). The politics of "cohabitation … follows from the account of ethical obligation" that is neither restricted to the suffering of those nearby—for this would mean that one's "ethics are invariably parochial, communitarian, and exclusionary" (Butler, *Notes* 104)— nor bound by the abstract idea of the human that refutes any possibility of translation or mediation by the concrete and the specific reality of those in suffering. Nor is this politics of cohabitation related to those at a "distance," which would mean that "I evacuate my situation in an effort to secure the distance that allows me to entertain ethical feeling and even feel myself to be ethical" (104). Butler insists that "ethical relations are mediated" and "questions of location are confounded" (104); community as a polity-in-the-making remains a "never-ending process" (Mouffe 238) that questions the idea of the people by "underscoring the temporal and open-ended character of the people" (Butler, *Notes* 166).

In the context of the current debates on democracy circumvented and circumscribed by race thinking, liberal exceptionalism, and "neoliberal rationality" (Brown 36),[15] transnational feminist thinkers delink community both from a national or ethnic narrative and from a communist utopia that has not yet arrived or that is never to arrive. They engage the place and temporality of the constituencies that are either peripheral to dominant cultures or completely removed and remote from their structures, thus speaking or trying to speak to the inhabitants of the uninhabitable zones of culture. From the favelas to the slums and the refugee hotspots in the Mediterranean to the ghettoed communities sprawled in the global cities, these places are the new terra nullius of postimperial thought. Transnational, anticolonial, and feminist thought wrenches the concept of community from the product of a politics grounded in the narratives of nation and locality and redefines community as a polity-in-the-making. The material and ideological framework of the diasporas, the growth of hybrid and transnational communities across the world as a result of imperialism and transnational capitalism, the perseverance of subaltern and indigenous communities, and the existence of stateless or partitioned communities question the "we" of community and thus question the universalizing rhetoric that appropriates the stranger as a figure within the same.

The figure of the clandestine immigrant, the paperless human washed on the Mediterranean shores with a taciturn, albeit persistent claim, that she be recognized as the human with a right to rights, the human with a right to a polity, is the challenge to community politics and poetics in Europe and other places in the world in the present. Gayatri Spivak calls this figure "the new subaltern" (225).[16] Her arrival at the gates and borders of the various nations that are acting as temporary or permanent hosts challenges the politics and ethics of the common that reproduce collectivity and belonging as the natural consequence of an organic homogeneity. This recent event is a chapter in the long history of "exiles, refugees, *Gastarbeiter*, immigrants, migrations, the displaced, the feeling and the besieged" (Morrison 11) whose bodies are often racialized and turned into an ontological and political exception, thus contributing to what Wynter calls the long history of the "coloniality of being." Spivak calls them "the new subaltern" (225), affiliating them with the histories of subaltern communities in India and other places in the world. An unconstituted alterity that is forced outside hegemonic structures, the subaltern speaks to local histories of global dimensions as it refers to a large number of people and communities that are outside hegemony and thus outside the "available frames of recognizability" (Butler, *Frames of War* 3) and human rights.

The perseverance of what Povinelli calls "the part that has no part" (73) raises the issue of a shared responsibility and accountability to describe these worlds and re-present them so that their histories and persevering presence cannot be forgotten and their alternative polities and "origin narratives" (Wynter) can be thought a time when ecological and economic disasters threaten human collectivities. The existence of these communities has been described by terms such as "'counterrepublics' (Michael Warner), 'new social imaginaries' (Charles Taylor), and 'subaltern counterrepublics' (Nancy Frazer)" (in Povinelli 7). In *Economies of Abandonment*, Povinelli offers her term, "alternative projects of embodied sociality" (7), to think about "how new forms of life, let alone the political thought they might foster, persevere" in spaces defined by "the wavering of death" and where "instances of survival" can be described as "moments of miracularization" (10). Crafting an "anthropology of the otherwise" (10) by working with the Karrabing Indigenous community, Povinelli examines "the modes of the life" of the constituencies and their communities that "exist in the precarious zones of being and not being" and "the modes of their life: social belonging, abandonment and endurance" (31). Although "In Australia, for instance, indigenous rural and urban communities are open broom closets of poverty, disease and despair," they are not "determined by the decomposition that composes them" (135). Their existence that remains unaccountable to the "normative direction around which a practical politics could be built" (189) instantiates a polity-in-the-making. Forced to confront and struggle against state policies that consolidate a "governance of the prior" (36), they formulate polities that insinuate the "governance of freedom" (59).

"The new subaltern" intertwines the history of such subaltern and indigenous communities left outside hegemony in precolonial and postcolonial times with the communities of racialized constituencies across different nation-states in Europe, the United States and other places in the world, and with the recent refugee crisis on the Mediterranean shores that are strewn with the cadavers of those who have not made it and who often remain unnamed. This event is often discussed without any reference to the migration and movement of millions into the countries that are among the poorest ones. Michael Dummett reminds us that "there has been gross inequity in refugee flows to different countries" but some of the poorest countries like Pakistan, Ethiopia, and Sudan "have accepted refugees by the million" when "developed countries complain when a thousand or so arrive" (36). This complaint has taken such gigantic proportions in Europe lately that thousands of people remain stranded in the places of entry which are not the places of their desired arrival. Their protracted status as asylum seekers who remain paperless and stateless condition them to a state of subalternity to which "persons and groups are cut off from upward—and in a sense 'outward' social mobility" (Spivak, "The New Subaltern" 325).

This condition of subalternity that determines the lives of thousands of people stranded in Greece nowadays, especially on the islands of Hios and Lesvos where they are forced to live under bleak conditions, is often described as "bare life" (Agamben, *Homo Sacer* 100), a life that can be sacrificed without being killed, as Agamben argues. In contemporary terms, this means that the life of those forced into this permanent condition of subalternity or statelessness are emptied of the basic human right to rights and can thus be made an exception to the laws that reinforce their right to have a political life, a *bios politikos*. This is especially the case with the immigrants whose applications for asylum are denied and they are either pushed back or stranded in the places of their first entry. However, contemporary thinkers contest the validity of the term "bare life" in view of the perseverance of the subaltern and immigrant communities[17] that do not stop pushing hard on for their entry into hegemony with the help of activists, artists, intellectuals, NGO workers, other immigrants who reside in the host country, and simple civilians who organize themselves individually or through different forms of collective action. They represent "communities of belonging" that "refuse alignment along the secure axes of filiation to seek expression outside if not against possessive communities of belonging" (Gandhi, *Affective Communities* 10) being formed "on behalf of vulnerable strangers" (189). They are "affective communities," as Leela Gandhi calls them in her study of a politics of friendship that underlies western anti-imperialist communities of socialist and homosexual politics in late-nineteenth-century Britain and Europe. Gandhi reconstructs the history of affective communities in her archival analysis of anti-normative collectivities whose affective relations challenge the imperial politics from below and beyond the divisions between the colonizer and the colonized. She thus demonstrates how the "part that has no part" is not systemic noise but the agents of communities of intercultural polities-in-the-making. In *The Common Cause*, Gandhi further develops her work on the histories of "anticolonial counterrepublics" (151) and their community poetics and politics that speak to the "transnational ethical history of democracy in the first half of the twentieth century" (159) and represent historical accounts of polities-in-the making that were formed by dissident groups not represented in the mainstream. Their histories counteract the "business of inclusivity/democracy/the commons" (156) and the current formation of the autonomous subject of neoliberal politics with "an antipositivist art of the possible—namely the 'what if' 'would that' 'if only' 'let us suppose that'" (156). Their common cause is extricated from the minor histories and the subcultures of the dispossessed, the colonized, the subalterns, the refugees who now form new affiliations and engender their new origin narratives against and beyond the state structures that separate the citizen from the subaltern, the autonomous subject from the stateless.

These communities are worth "staying with the trouble" (Haraway 3) of a theoretical and political analysis that refuses to subscribe to the horizon of the "normative" (Povinelli 189) and instead attends to representing and thinking communities in the present as the projects of alternative social and political modalities of being rooted in the human in all of its genres, modes of life, origin narratives and autopoetic mechanisms that cannot be reduced to a certain governance of being. The struggle of subaltern peoples, asylum seekers that do not arrive alone but often in large numbers that suggest that the individual claims are community claims, and immigrants running away from ecological, political, and economic disasters, are examples of "political self-determination ... struggling for sovereignty ... to lay claim to space to move freely, to express one's views, and to seek reparation and justice" (Butler, *Notes* 161). The struggle for sovereignty is a struggle against a certain neoliberal ontology and politics that determines the autonomous subject by way of preconditioning and regulating the genres of the human, that is, the poetics, politics, and aesthetics of human constituencies and their collectivities across the world and throughout time. Such communities of survivance are related to *kairos*, that is, a propitious moment or event that interrupts time, rather than *Khronos*, time as a linear, apparently uninterrupted sequence of events. They challenge and can destabilize the "governance of the prior" (Povinelli 26), undermining the politics and discourses that consolidate the "coloniality of being" (Wynter, "Unsettling the Coloniality of Being" 266).

In view of the histories of perseverance that the subaltern, the foreigner, and the immigrant summon, revealing the allusive ties between the histories of collectivities of the "part that has no part," community presently refers not only to the prior existence of a common cause that preconditions a certain belonging but also to the performative outcome of a coming together of constituencies whose politics of survival and perseverance engenders a poetics of the common formed on affective relations, subaltern politics of resistance, the encounter with the foreigner, and strategic affiliations for the political development of democracy that fight against the reduction of human belonging to the neoliberal mandates. These transnational communities of affective relations rooted in the figure of the migrant who keeps coming represent community as an intercultural and hybrid polity-in-the making, whose common cause "is not merely the condition of passively inhabiting or even participating in/with culture of a given mass or collectivity. It is, rather, an acutely individuated dedication to becoming common—the effect of an idiosyncratic disregard for the self by the self for the cause of inclusive sociality" (Gandhi, *Common Cause* 152). The common cause of these communities of *kairos* is crafted by the antinomian, minor but also persistent performative acts of those who inherit the future and demand their right to live well. Those who keep coming.

NOTES

1 As Georges Van Den Abbeele explains in his timely introduction to the Miami Theory Collective's *Community at Loose Ends*, the *Oxford English Dictionary* offers two etymologies, namely, "com+*munis*" and "com+*unus*" (xi) that respectively signify debt and oneness. I would be remiss not to mention the significant contribution of the Miami Theory Collective to the debates on community in the 1990s and the inheritance of this community of method from the philosophical works of Jean-Luc Nancy and Jean Lyotard, whose essays feature in this collection. The analysis of community as "debt-gift" (Esposito 6) is further developed by Roberto Esposito in *Communitas: The Origin and Destiny of Community*.

2 See Anthony Bogues's analysis of the "historically catastrophic events" (Bogues 40) that mark the massive destruction and extermination of human beings and their collectivities. For a transnational analysis of the concentration camp, see Giorgio Agamben's *What Is a Camp?* Paul Gilroy was one of the first scholars who stressed the urgent need to perform a contrapuntal analysis of the slave plantation and the concentration camp in *The Black Atlantic*

(205–23). See also *Between Camps*, his most recent analysis of the long durée of the ideologies of racial purity and nationalism that examines the interlocking aspects of race thinking immanent in the histories of the slave plantation and the concentration camp that flank colonial modernity.

3 Gerald Vizenor's "aesthetics of survivance" draws its force from "native survivance as an active sense of presence over absence, deracination and oblivion" (1). Native stories suggest not only the survival of communities reacting against state policies and discourses that effect their containment within mainstream discourses and politics; for Vizenor, survivance also signifies the perseverance and development of the native communities' aesthetic and discursive ways of giving an account of themselves and of proliferating their ontological and political ways of perceiving the relations between the individual and her community as a polity in-the-making that is constitutive of and constituted by the world.

4 See Jacques Derrida's *Specters of Marx* and Étienne Balibar's analysis of the concept of exappropriation in *Equaliberty*, 87–94.

5 According to Fredric Jameson, modernity as a narrative persistently renews the sense of the present manifested in the anxiety to periodize transformations, ruptures, and breaks that carry the double-bind promise of continuity and newness. As a "narrative of elucidation" (33) and trope of self-reflexivity that "dramatizes its own claims" (39), it looks to the future as a break from the past, a future that is already present and, yet, unnamed in the available frames of recognizability. See Jameson's *A Singular Modernity: An Essay on the Ontology of the Present*.

6 See Balibar's *Equaliberty*; Judith Butler and Gayatri Spivak's *Who Sings the Nation-State*; and Judith Butler and Athena Athanasiou's *Dispossession: The Performative in the Political*.

7 Giorgio Agamben's *Coming Community* is in dialogue with Jean Luc-Nancy's *Inoperative Community* and Maurice Blanchot's *The Unavowable Community*.

8 See Hannah Arendt's analysis of the stateless in *The Origins of Totalitarianism*.

9 Donald Pease analyzes American exceptionalism by drawing on Jacqueline Rose's "state of fantasy" in *The New American Exceptionalism*.

10 See Jacques Rancière's *Disagreement: Politics and Philosophy*. Below I draw on Elizabeth Povinelli's analysis of the political and social potentiality of the lives of those she calls "the part that has no part"; following Rancière, Povinelli argues that, despite the marginalization of the indigenous communities, their members represent and embody the difference between political acts that transform politics, minor and structurally peripheral to the state as they might be, and policing acts of the State that tries to accommodate and assimilate the political acts of the "part that has no part" to ensure the continuation of its hegemonic order. Jean-François Lyotard's concept of the *differend* is also relevant here. See Lyotard's *The Differend: Phrases in Dispute;* and "A l'insu (Unbeknownst)" in *Community at Loose Ends*.

11 Balibar's analyses "neo-racism" as a " 'racism without races' " (21) that develops in the era of " 'decolonization' " (21) well beyond the pseudoscience of race and is symptomatic of a certain hegemony of race thinking. Balibar coins this term to refer to the substitutional power of race thinking that invents its new targets, that is, the human beings and their collectivities that supposedly represent a threat to the sovereign subjects of the State, by replacing biological with cultural or religious differences. In the early 1990s in Europe that witnesses the "reversal of population movements between the old colonies and the old metropolises, and the division of humanity within a single political space" (21), Balibar remarks how the "category of *immigration*" operates as a "substitute for the notion of race" (20) giving rise to new forms of racism "whose dominant theme is not biological heredity but the insurmountability of cultural differences, a racism which, at first sight, does not postulate the superiority of certain

groups of peoples in relation to others but 'only' the harmfulness of abolishing frontiers, the incompatibility of life-styles and traditions" (21). Balibar's term is prevalent, especially in view of the recent refugee crisis in Europe in the second decade of the twenty-first century. See "Is There a 'Neo-Racism'?" See also Balibar's "For a Democracy without Exclusion" in *Equaliberty*.

12 The headscarf affair ("l'affaire du foulard") began in 1989, the year of the bicentennial anniversary of the French Revolution, when the principal of the Collège de Creil (Oise) expelled three Muslim students who refused to remove their headscarves. This triggered a series of reactions by defenders of the French republican version of secularism (*laïcité*), a concept "whose meaning would be furiously debated in the months and years that followed" (Scott 22), feminists, local and religious community representatives, and the government. In Balibar's words, some of the French intellectuals "tried to point out the flagrant contradiction inherent in expulsions"; the so-called defense of the "young girls against religious fundamentalism, of which sexism is an intrinsic part" paradoxically went hand in hand with their expulsion from school, which meant that they were being sent back "to the communitarian space dominated by precisely this religious sexism" (*Equaliberty* 211). This was the first incident of a series of cases that followed in 1994, 2003 and most recently in 2016 in France. On the headscarf affair, see also Joan Wallach Scott, *The Politics of Veil*; and Seyla Benhabib, *The Rights of Others*.

13 Both Seyla Benhabib and Étienne Balibar thoroughly analyze the scarf affair as symptomatic of the claims (Benhabib) and limitations and failures (Balibar) of secular democracies. See Balibar, *Equaliberty* 209–23; and Benhabib's analysis of the "scarf affair" in France and Germany in *The Rights of Others*, 183–209.

14 See http://www.independent.co.uk/news/world/europe/burkini-ban-why-is-france-arresting-muslim-women-for-wearing-full-body-swimwear-and-why-are-people-a7207971.html.

15 See Wendy Brown's *Undoing the Demos*. Brown explains how "the norms and principles of neo-liberal rationality do not dictate precise economic policy, but rather set out novel ways of conceiving and relating state, society, economy and subject and also inaugurate a new 'economization' of heretofore noneconomic spheres and endeavors" (51). These practices, in other words, strive to capture political and social modalities of being that are outside the referential power of the *homo oeconomicus* defined by Michel Foucault in *The Birth of Biopolitics* as the subject of "irreducible, non-transferable atomistic individual choices" (272).

16 Her work on the subaltern cannot be reduced to this single reference. In this essay, I am interested in how her work addresses the current refugee crisis and the question of human rights it raises. See "Can the Subaltern Speak?" and *A Critique of Postcolonial Reason. Toward a History of the Vanishing Present*. For analysis of the subaltern and human rights, see "Righting Wrongs."

17 See Butler and Spivak's critique of "bare life" in *Who Sings the Nation-State*; also see Derrida's deconstruction of Agamben's analysis of bare life in *The Beast and the Sovereign* (vol. I).

WORKS CITED

Abbeele, Van Den. "Introduction." *Community at Loose Ends*. Ed. Miami Theory Collective. Minneapolis: U of Minnesota P, 1991, pp. ix–xxvi.

Agamben, Giorgio. *The Coming Community*. Trans. Michael Hardt. Minneapolis: Minnesota UP, 1993.

Agamben, Giorgio. *Homo Sacer: Sovereign Power and Bare Life*. Trans. Daniel Heller-Roazen. Stanford, CA: Stanford UP, 1998.

Ahmed, Sara. *Strange Encounters: Embodied Others in Post-coloniality*. New York: Routledge, 2000.

Anderson, Benedict. *Imagined Communities*. New York: Verso Books, 1992.

Arendt, Hannah. "The Decline of the Nation State, and the End of the Rights of Man." *The Origins of Totalitarianism*. New York: Harcourt, Brace & World, 1968, 147–82.

Balibar, Étienne. *Equaliberty*. Trans. James Ingram. Durham, NC: Duke UP, 2014, pp. 67–99.

Balibar, Étienne. "Is There a 'Neo-Racism'?" *Race, Nation, Class: Ambiguous Identities*. Trans. Chris Turner. New York: Verso, 1991, pp. 17–29.

Balibar, Étienne, and Immanuel Wallerstein. *Race, Nation, Class: Ambiguous Identities*. New York: Verso Books, 1991.

Benhabib, Seyla. *The Rights of Others: Aliens, Residents, and Citizens*. Cambridge: Cambridge UP, 2004.

Benjamin, Walter. *Illuminations*. Trans. Harry Zohn. New York: Schocken Books, 1969.

Blanchot, Maurice. *The Unavowable Community*. Trans. Pierre Jorris. Barrytown, NY: Station Hill P, 1988.

Bogues, Anthony. *Empire of Liberty*. Lebanon: Dartmouth UP, 2010.

Brown, Wendy. *Undoing the Demos: Neoliberalism's Stealth Revolution*. New York: Zone Books, 2015.

Butler, Judith. *Frames of War: When is Life Grievable?* New York: Verso Books, 2009.

Butler, Judith. *Notes toward a Performative Theory of Assembly*. Cambridge, MA: Harvard UP, 2015.

Butler, Judith. *Parting Ways: Jewishness and the Critique of Zionism*. New York: Columbia UP, 2012.

Butler, Judith, and Athena Athanasiou. *Dispossession: The Performative in the Political*. Cambridge: Polity P, 2013.

Butler, Judith, and Gayatri Chakravorty Spivak. *Who Sings the Nation-State?* London: Seagull Books, 2007.

Derrida, Jacques. *The Beast and the Sovereign*. Trans. Geoffrey Bennington. Chicago, IL: U of Chicago P, 2009.

Derrida, Jacques. *Specters of Marx*. Trans. Peggy Kamuf. New York: Routledge, 1994.

Dummett, Michael. *On Immigration and Refugees*. London and New York: Routledge, 2001.

Esposito, Roberto. *Communitas: The Origin and Destiny of Community*. Trans. Timothy Campbell. Stanford, CA: Stanford UP, 2010.

Foucault, Michel. *The Birth of Biopolitics: Lectures at the Collège de France 1978–9*. Trans. Graham Burchell. Basingstoke: Palgrave Macmillan, 2008.

Gandhi, Leela. *Affective Communities: Anticolonial Thought, Fin-de-Siècle Radicalism, and the Politics of Friendship*. Durham, NC: Duke UP, 2006.

Gandhi, Leela. *The Common Cause: Postcolonial Ethics and the Practice of Democracy, 1900–1955*. Chicago, IL: U of Chicago Press, 2014.

Gilroy, Paul. *Between Camps: Nations, Cultures and the Allure of Race*. London: Penguin Books, 2010.

Gilroy, Paul. *The Black Atlantic: Modernity and Double Consciousness*. Cambridge, MA: Harvard UP, 1993.

Haraway, Donna. *Staying with the Trouble*. Durham, NC: Duke UP, 2016.

Jameson, Fredric. *A Singular Modernity: An Essay on the Ontology of the Present*. New York: Verso Books, 2012.

Lawrence, Jacob. *The Great Migration: An American Story*. New York: The Museum of Modern Art, 1993.

Leotard, Jean-François. *The Differend: Phrases in Dispute*. Trans. George Van Den Abbeele. Minneapolis: Minnesota UP, 1988.

Miami Theory Collective, ed. *Community at Loose Ends*. Minneapolis: Minnesota UP, 1991.

Morrison, Toni. "Home." *The House that Race Built*. Ed. Wahneema Lubiano. New York: Vintage Books, 1988, pp. 3–12.

Mouffe, Chantal. "Democratic Citizenship and the Political Community." *Dimensions of Radical Democracy: Pluralism, Citizenship, Community*. Ed. Chantal Mouffe. New York: Verso Books, 1992, pp. 225–40.

Nancy, Jean-Luc. *The Inoperative Community*. Ed. Peter Connor and trans. Peter Connor, Lisa Garbus, Michael Holland, and Simona Sawhney. Minneapolis: U of Minnesota P, 1991.

Pease, Donald. *The New American Exceptionalism*. Minneapolis: U of Minnesota Press, 2009.

Povinelli, Elizabeth A. *Economies of Abandonment: Social Belonging and Endurance in Late Liberalism*. Durham, NC: Duke UP, 2011.

Quinn, Ben, "French Police Make Woman Remove Clothing on Nice beach Following Burkini Ban." *Guardian*, August 24, 2016. https://www.theguardian.com/world/2016/aug/24/french-police-make-woman-remove-burkini-on-nice-beach. Accessed on November 29, 2017.

Said, Edward. *Humanism and Democratic Criticism*. New York: Columbia UP, 2004.

Sassen, Saskia. *The Global City*. Princeton, NJ: Princeton UP, 1991.

Scott, Joan Wallach. *The Politics of the Veil*. Princeton, NJ: Princeton UP, 2007.

Spivak, Gayatri Chakravorty. "Can the Subaltern Speak?" *Marxism and the Interpretation of Culture*. Ed. C. Nelson and L. Grossberg. Champaign, IL: U of Illinois P, 1988, pp. 272–313.

Spivak, Gayatri Chakravorty. *A Critique of Postcolonial Reason. Toward a History of the Vanishing Present*. Cambridge: Cambridge UP, 1999.

Spivak, Gayatri Chakravorty. "The New Subaltern: A Silent Interview." *Mapping Subaltern Studies and the Postcolonial*. Ed. Vinayak Chaturvedi. New York: Verso Books, 2000, 324–40.

Spivak, Gayatri Chakravorty. "Righting Wrongs." *The South Atlantic Quarterly* 103.2/3 (2004): 523–58.

Vizenor, Gerald, ed. *Survivance: Narratives of Native Presence*. Lincoln: U of Nebraska P, 2008, pp. 1–25.

Wynter, Sylvia. "1492: A New World View."*Race, Discourse and the Origin of the Americas. A New World View*. Ed. Vera Lawrence Hyatt & Rex Nettleford. Washington: Smithsonian Institution P, 1995, pp. 5–57.

Wynter, Sylvia. "Human Being as Noun? Or *Being Human* as Praxis? Towards the Autopoetic Turn/Overturn: A Manifesto," 2007. http://www.scribd.com/doc/237809437/Sylvia-Wynter-The-Autopoetic-Turn#scribd.

Wynter, Sylvia. "Towards the Sociogenic Principle: Fanon, Identity, the Puzzle of Conscious Experience, and What it is Like to Be Black," *National Identities and Sociopolitical Changes in Latin America*. Ed. Antonio Gómez-Moriana, and Mercedes F. Durán-Cogan. New York: Routledge, 2001, pp. 30–66.

Wynter, Sylvia. "Unsettling the Coloniality of Being/Power/Truth/Freedom: Towards the Human, After Man, Its Overrepresentation—An Argument." *CR: The New Centennial Review* 3.3 (2003): 257–337.

Wynter Sylvia, and Katherine McKittrick. "Unparalleled Catastrophe for Our Species? Or, to Give Humanness a Different Future: Conversations." *Sylvia Wynter: On Being Human as Praxis*. Ed. Katherine McKittrick. Durham, NC: Duke UP, 2015, pp. 9–90.

CHAPTER THIRTY-THREE

Anti-Imperialism

RASHMI VARMA

DISSENTING HISTORIES

This essay elaborates upon the idea of what I call the "dissenting histories" of feminism and anti-imperialism. It aims to situate their historical trajectories within the contemporary political crises faced by both feminism and anti-imperialism. The most recent crisis (in a series of moments of disruption and rupture) seems to have been precipitated by the 9/11 attacks by Al Qaida on the World Trade Center buildings in New York City and the subsequent unleashing of the "war on terror," as well as the ongoing war in Syria and a more generalized global turn toward populist authoritarianism. The global financial crisis of 2008 that for a while seemed to threaten the very foundations of the neoliberal order in the world has further challenged the projects of feminism and anti-imperialism as austerity and the evisceration of welfare have become common sense in country after country.

Although both feminism and anti-imperialism have historically constituted themselves as projects of liberation, questions concerning liberation from what and toward what ends have been key to what has sometimes been a convergence, but also often involved separation and dissension. Specifically in this essay I identify four critical moments of simultaneous convergence and dissension where the concept of anti-imperialism came to constitute an important analytical resource for feminism and feminism challenged the limits of anti-imperialism: (1) what I call "the feminist international" of the first half of the twentieth century leading up to (2) decolonization and the establishment of postcolonial states. I then consider (3) the articulation of anti-imperialism by diasporic black feminists as part of the civil rights and second-wave women's movements in the West, and conclude with (4) the more recent formulations of anti-imperialism that have emerged among sections of the feminist Left, post-9/11, and the subsequent US-UK-led illegal invasion of Iraq. These more contemporary articulations of anti-imperialism, I will argue, do not do justice to the revolutionary aims of earlier anti-imperialist and Third World solidarity projects articulated through such fora as the Non-Aligned Movement (NAM) launched in Bandung in 1955, and the more revolutionary formations such as the Tricontinental, the 1966 Solidarity Conference of the Peoples of Africa, Asia, and Latin America held in Havana, Cuba.[1] In fact, I argue in conclusion that this last moment rolls back the many significant gains that were made in those earlier decades by anti-imperialist feminists, a decline that meshes with the more general diminishing of the Third World project today and is aligned with a dilution of genuine internationalism as borders close in on refugees and migrants.

The essay will demonstrate this concluding point via a critical assessment of the intervention of the group Women Against Fundamentalism (WAF), a feminist anti-racist and anti-fundamentalist group that was established in London in 1989. Through such a reading, or what could be called a critical historical recuperation, I hope to point to some of the most glaring blindspots of anti-imperialism today, as construed by a broadly constituted cultural (academic and activist) Left, and particularly within an intellectual formation that names itself as anti-imperialist feminism.

FEMINIST INTERNATIONAL

My essay thus must proceed by way of a detour through the earlier history of the convergence and subsequent divergence of feminism and anti-imperialism. When in 1924, at the International Conference of Women, an unveiled Huda Sha'rawi, the delegate from Egypt, reported that the Europeans at the conference wanted the Egyptians to be "romantic, ignorant heroines of the European novelists" and that the veil worn by Muslim women was a source of obsession, keeping European feminists ignorant of the real condition of the lives of women in Asia and Africa, she was pointing to an enduring divide within feminism between women from the colonial countries and those from countries under colonial rule (Prashad, *Darker Nations* 55). But where European women were seen as having condescendingly patronized their Eastern counterparts, Huda went on to identify grounds for commonality, springing from the inspiring suffrage campaigns of European women.[2] Even a cursory study of women's movements in the early decades of the twentieth century, in countries such as Turkey, Iran, Egypt, and India, reveals the influence that Western feminism exerted on bourgeois women's movements in the East. Organizations such as the All India Women's Conference (founded in 1927 by Margaret Cousins "for the upliftment and betterment of women and children") and the Egyptian Feminist Union (founded in 1923 by Huda Sharaawi) came out of the belief that women's rights had to be universal, and that even in colonized countries women ought to obtain equal rights.

But it was in the Communist internationals and meetings inspired by a global socialist vision that women found spaces of convergence with a historically specific understanding of anti-imperialism (Young 141–57).[3] The end of the Second World War, in particular, opened up crucial space for anti-fascist, anti-imperial feminists to issue a call for a unified struggle, thus forging a feminist internationalism whose roots lay in opposition to fascism in Europe and colonialism abroad.[4] This was the moment in which "fostered by the shared analysis of imperialism" women from Asia and Africa were able to forge "a solidarity of commonalty for women's shared human rights, and a solidarity of complicity that took imbalances of power between women of the world into account" (Armstrong 305). The "shared analysis" was of course predicated on the common struggles against colonialism in Asia and Africa, mobilizing peasant and working-class women against both foreign rule and domestic social hierarchies.[5]

It was such a transformational milieu that produced an organization such as the Women's International Democratic Federation (WIDF), founded in 1945.[6] At its first international meeting, about forty delegates participated from various strands of Left women's movements. Armstrong notes that this was the only transnational feminist organization at that time that openly opposed colonialism and provided a "systemic critique of imperialism" (320). Such a critical view was the outcome of engaged discussions and interactions between Western feminists focused on anti-fascist struggles in Europe, and their Eastern counterparts who argued vociferously that anti-imperialism was not reducible to anti-fascism. Perhaps the single greatest contribution of WIDF was to acknowledge and then activate the analysis that imperialism was a women's issue. Often in conjunction with WIDF, conferences such as the 1949 Conference of the Women of Asia in Beijing, the 1958 Asian-African Conference of Women in Colombo, and the 1961 Afro-Asian Women's Conference in Cairo were expressive of a consolidating feminist international occurring alongside and critically intervening in the articulation of global anti-imperialist solidarity leading up to decolonization.

While the role of Bandung in articulating a Third World project in 1955 has been widely written about, it was in 1947 that India's first prime minister Jawaharlal Nehru, speaking at the Asian Relations Conference (that included Status of Women and Women's Movement groups), called for Asian solidarity among anti-colonial movements. Post-Bandung, it was the 1957 Afro-Asian People's Solidarity Organization (AAPSO) Conference in Cairo that was to further cement the groundswell of Third World solidarity. These attempts to forge south-south solidarity gained further strength from the establishment of the NAM in the context of an increasingly virulent Cold War contest between the United States and the USSR, even as the UN Declaration of Human Rights revealed the hypocrisy of colonial countries that continued to deny political rights to its subject citizens.

Although concepts of universalism and human rights, and particularly feminist universalism, have come under attack within poststructuralist postcolonial and postmodernist feminist discourse from the 1990s onward (see Dhawan), it is important to remember that the UN Declaration of Human Rights provided decolonizing nations and social movements within them with a crucial rights framework within which to agitate for liberation. In fact, many of the drafters of the resolution came from newly decolonized countries and they worked to ensure that women's rights and the right to national self-determination were important parts of the Declaration. India's delegate Hansa Mehta, a member of the Constituent Assembly in India, is considered to be the author of the opening words "All human beings are equal in dignity and rights," arguing against the standard use of the word "men" (Sahgal, "Who Wrote the Universal Declaration").

From the particular perspective of women's movements, it was the post-Bandung 1957 AAPSO Conference in Cairo that saw "the presence of women not only in the hall but also at the podium" (Prashad, *The Darker Nations* 53). At a plenary speech at the conference, Aisha Abdul-Rahman, journalist, poet, and a well-known critic of monarchy as well as of Nasser's authoritarianism, underlined the convergence of nationalism and feminism. She spoke of how "the renaissance of the Eastern woman has always coincided with liberation movements" and that "the success of these revolutions depends on the liberation of the enslaved half, on rescuing women from paralysis, unemployment and inaction and eliminating the differences between the two halves of the nation—its men and women."[7]

NATIONAL LIBERATION

For the most part, for anti-imperialists, the nation-state has been a crucial if contested site for envisaging freedom from colonialism—whether the nation was conceived as a socialist entity, or, even as for Right-wing anti-imperialism, as a container for the recuperation of traditional political forms within society.[8] Kumari Jayawardene, in her pioneering account of women and nationalism, argues that in fact "nationalist struggles were the first arena of women's involvement in political action" (258). Although women's participation in nationalist anti-colonial movements is often understood to have largely attracted bourgeois women (since social reform, education, voting and property rights were key areas of focus for nationalist women activists), their involvement nevertheless threatened the feudal elites who viewed women's activism as an outgrowth of Westernization. In this, tradition, typically constructed in defense of national culture, was seen as under assault by colonial rule (Chatterjee). Women nationalists thus faced a double bind: on the one hand, they attempted to use modern ideas of emancipation to challenge both native and colonial patriarchies (often also forming autonomous women's organizations) and on the other hand their struggle against patriarchy was seen as strengthening the hand of the colonialists.

Women's participation in the 1919 Egyptian revolution and their active involvement in the Indian national movement from the 1920s onward are key instances of the ways in which women's concerns coalesced with concerns regarding national liberation. This simply underscored the fact that national liberation movements had to prioritize social reform and embark on a project of modernization. This entailed in many cases (from Japan and China to Turkey and Iran) radical transformations of deeply embedded social structures that served to reproduce feudal and dynastic relations.[9] Thus across the board, anti-colonial nationalism put women's issues on the national agenda. In this vein, Jayawardene notes that in most countries "the new body of ideas was seized on by the bourgeoisie and used as an instrument in their attempt to forge a new national consciousness and modern secular political structures" (6).

Although historians and critics are divided about the role of Western education and capitalism in bringing about either nominal or revolutionary changes as part of the anti-imperialist project, the profound influence exerted by capitalism's interruption and intrusion, via colonialism, of the material and social lives of the colonized provided one of the central paradoxes of anti-imperial nationalism. Notions of rights, democracy, secularism, and rationalism emerged as integral parts of nationalist movements. As Jayawardene has noted, the paradox involved a "situation ... where Western secular thought" became "a crucial factor in fashioning a consciousness and in devising structures that would make possible an escape from the domination of Western political power."

It is important to note here that although capitalist development not only produced new social classes from among the bureaucracy, merchants, and traders within colonial society and emancipated women of the bourgeoisie from many suffocating traditions, it offered a severely constrained set of opportunities in education, literacy, and employment, except when those opportunities could bolster the economic bases of colonialism. The introduction of Western modes of clothing and self-styling (that frequently precipitated movements to reject the veil as an example of unfreedom), opened up pathways of social mobility and against physical seclusion, and reshaped the family as nuclear and based on heterosexual monogamous marriage. Social reform (against Sati or widow burning, child marriage, concubinage, polygamy), and technological advancement further altered the material conditions of women's lives. Thus was conjured the birth of the new woman of nationalist discourse—both modern and traditional, educated to uphold the nuclear modern family while retaining attachment to rituals and values.

Most conventional analyses of women's contributions to anti-colonial national liberation movements have largely ascribed feminist activism to bourgeois women, but elided from view in such accounts, however, are the struggles of working-class and peasant women. As colonial capitalism established primacy in colonized territories, women came to be increasingly treated as sources of cheap labor in plantations, industry (especially the textile trade), and agriculture. Thus, from the 1940s onward, many of the nationalist movements did indeed become mass-based and were involved in organizing women on issues of land reforms, debt, nutrition, and so on. These issues had become key particularly for the incorporation of women within Left anti-imperialist parties.

One can therefore discern different but overlapping strains of feminist positions at work within national liberation movements—the strand of social reform, typically articulated in the vocabulary of social welfare and uplift operating within the frame of already existing social arrangements; the strand of feminism more closely allied to nationalist movements, demanding equal rights in the nation, its institutions, and in public life; and the strand of Left-wing mass movements anchored in peasant and working-class mobilization that called for more far-reaching changes within relations of production and reproduction. The latter involved key questions concerning land reform and the nationalization of industries against the stranglehold of national capitalists who were obstacles to the project of socialism in the new nations. Democratic women's movements emerged out of this paradoxical context of imperialism and its interface with nationalist resistance, and women's status became the touchstone of progress in countries throughout the colonized world.

STATE FEMINISM

A crucial fallout of national independence in many previously colonized countries was the consolidation of what came to be known as "state feminism," exemplified by a shift away from the anti-imperialist vision of the 1949 Conference to the more nation-centered 1958 Asian-African Conference of Women in Colombo, where the emphasis shifted to social reform rather than liberation. Similarly, the Afro-Asian Women's Conference in Cairo in 1961 occurred under the ideological auspices of the putative socialist, secular, modernist progressive Egyptian state (Magdy).

The underlying assumption was that the colonial masters had been defeated, and the newly sovereign nation had to be embraced as a container of freedom. In general, women's movements would appear to have been co-opted by newly decolonized states for whom social transformation was not to be subdivided by gender divisions. In situations where they weren't co-opted, they retreated under the ruse that notional equality was the key achievement of newly independent states.

But the betrayal of women in the aftermath of the 1919 Egyptian Revolution had been only the most glaring instance of the limits of women's rights within the framework of anti-colonial nationalism. Although male nationalists such as Ataturk and Fukuzawa fashioned themselves as modernizers of women, they nevertheless were prescriptive in their vision of the role women were to play in the new nations (Jayawardene 257). Kandiyoti refers to Ataturk's project of women's liberation as an exemplar of "paternalistic benevolence" or "state-sponsored feminism" (279, 280), while Magdy points out that under Nasser, whose administration gave Egyptian women the right to vote four years after coming to power in 1956, all civil society organizations were brought under state control. In India, Armstrong has pointed out that the All Asian Women's Conference, sponsored by the anti-fascist and anti-imperialist WIDF, was not supported either by the newly independent government or by Indian feminist nationalists such as Sarojini Naidu and others, forcing the Conference to be moved to Beijing in 1949 (314–15).

Thus, while the period of state feminism witnessed the formation of autonomous women's groups linked to nationalist political groups, these tended to operate away from active engagement with politics into arenas of social welfare and cultural regeneration, such as the arts, handicrafts, education, and the health sectors. Where working-class women were mobilized within trade unions as factory workers, they did so as part of Left-wing organizations. They also formed women's wings of Communist parties, since women's issues continued to be considered a subordinate problem within the party hierarchy in many national contexts.[10]

Ultimately, state projects could only accommodate a significantly limited horizon for the emancipation of women. While many postcolonial states instituted legal equality and anti-discriminatory legal frameworks concerning education, property, and work, there was an accompanying silencing of larger questions concerning structures of family and society that remained embedded in patriarchal tradition. For feminists, the big political lesson to be learnt from this period of co-option was the historical realization that the nation itself was never an adequate ground for liberation, for it could not guarantee liberation from patriarchy, whether traditional, modern, or revolutionary.

IMPERIAL FEMINISM

One key moment in the development of tricontinental diasporic feminism was the emergence in the late 1970s and early 1980s of what came to be known as black British feminism in the UK and emerged under the sign of multicultural or Third World feminism in the United States. Central to what was a post-war postcolonial rearticulation of the concept of "imperialism" was the charge that black American and British feminists leveled at white Euro-American feminists—that of replicating the imperialist relationship within feminism itself. This was a movement and a growing theoretical field that purported to be global and in solidarity with the oppressed populations of the world. After all, the second wave of global feminism had emerged in the wake of civil rights and anti-war movements in the West. Thus, in their famous article, "Challenging Imperial Feminism," published in the journal *Feminist Review*, Valerie Amos and Pratibha Parmar sought to redefine imperialism in terms of the racism they perceived within the dominant feminist movement that was largely shaped by the concerns of bourgeois white women. In the UK, black British feminism emerged in the noxious years of Thatcherism that ironically provided it with a meaningful theoretical urgency, even as on the ground black feminists began to feel the political limits of the politics of difference.

Across the Atlantic, already, the Combahee River Collective, in the context of racism within the American women's movement, made this point very forcefully in their manifesto:

> A Black feminist presence has evolved most obviously in connection with the second wave of the American women's movement beginning in the late 1960s. Black, other Third World, and working women have been involved in the feminist movement from its start, but both outside reactionary forces and racism and elitism within the movement itself have served to obscure our participation.

What black feminists of the Combahee River Collective were expressing was outrage, as condensed in Hazel Carby's stinging call "White Woman, Listen!" not only against elitism and racism within the mainstream women's movement but also within feminist academic production. Formations such as the Combahee River Collective and various Latina/Chicana and Asian American women's activist and artistic collectives launched powerful criticisms of mainstream feminism. At the time, these had a significant impact within feminist theory and in feminist studies departments and organizations and supported the emergence of "different" feminisms under the sign of postcolonialism.[11] It is important to note that the term "Third World women" was deployed strategically in these writings to signal a transnational feminist solidarity before it was called that. Third World feminism in the United States called attention to imperialism abroad as well as within the United States, against women of color.

Chandra Talpade Mohanty noted in her influential essay "Under Western Eyes: Feminist Scholarship and Colonial Discourses" that the resurgence of "colonization" as an analytic category in "the age of Reagan" was being "used to characterize everything from the most evident economic and political hierarchies to the production of a particular cultural discourse about what is called the 'Third World'" (333). What she was calling out was the ways in which feminist scholarship in the West was precisely enabling a slippage from a structural critique of economic and political hierarchies to an almost exclusive focus on the cultural construction of the ideal "Third-World woman" as the exemplary object of study (see also Spivak). Writing about the pathbreaking volume *This Bridge Called My Back* (1981), a collection of poetry and essays by women of color, Chela Sandoval wrote that although "*This Bridge Called My Back* in 1981 made the presence of U.S. third world feminism impossible to ignore on the same terms as it had been throughout the 1970s," it wasn't long before "the writings and theoretical challenges of U.S. third world feminists were marginalized into the category of what Alison Jaggar characterized in 1983 as mere 'description'" (309).

This focus on the "Third-World woman" as exemplary subject of feminist theory chimed in well with the emerging field of postcolonial feminism that sought to puncture the myth of sisterhood as a global movement. As Mohanty ("Under Western Eyes") reflects back on the political moment in which her earlier critique of Western feminist discourse appeared, she acknowledges that her interest had been in theorizing difference, in response to what third world and feminists of color perceived to be the appropriation of their experiences by an increasingly hegemonic Women's Studies establishment. Since then, she has revised this body of work to focus on the materiality of women's lives in different geographic and social locations in the context of neo-imperial global capitalism.[12]

WOMEN AGAINST FUNDAMENTALISM

One such organization that helped to bring to surface the contradictions inherent within feminisms of difference as articulated by postcolonial and diasporic feminists was Women Against Fundamentalism (WAF) in 1989. WAF was formed in the wake of what has come to be known as "the Rushdie affair," in which the publication of Salman Rushdie's novel *The Satanic Verses* saw the emergence of a transnational consolidation of religious fundamentalist forces—from India to Bangladesh, from Britain to Iran, and elsewhere. The *fatwa* issued by Iran's Ayatollah Khomeini against Rushdie, seeking the author's death for the crime of blasphemy, had been preceded by a ban of the book in India as it was perceived to be offending the faith of its Muslim minorities, and by demonstrations in Bradford, London, and elsewhere in the UK by Muslim communities that felt beleaguered by the racist Thatcherite state.[13] The book was publicly burnt and demands of death for

Rushdie were made vociferously in retaliation for what was perceived as an insult to Muslims everywhere.

For many black feminist activists, most prominently those who had earlier established the Southall Black Sisters to advocate against domestic violence faced by black and ethnic minority women in Britain, the Rushdie affair brought to the fore an array of so-called community leaders, almost all male and many with dubious pasts in the Indian subcontinent (later many were identified as war criminals from Bangladesh), who used the moment to carve out a radical presence within an increasingly fractured public sphere in Britain. As these fundamentalist community leaders came to accrue legitimacy as "representatives" of their communities, feminist activists saw a different power situation emerging, caught as they were between British racism and their own communities' social conservatism and growing fundamentalism.[14]

What was notable in the fallout of the Rushdie affair was that many of the male voices to emerge in the wake of the Rushdie affair also included second-generation Asian men who had participated in anti-racist movements, but who along with the more conservative men in the community left no space to dissent from the sexual norms and mores that governed these Right-wing religious political mobilizations. These mobilizations curiously coalesced with seemingly progressive anti-racist positions, united in their understanding of women as objects of protection from the imperialists.

In defending Rushdie's right to write, members of WAF asserted their own right to speak for themselves, to gender equality within communities, to diversity in religious practice and interpretation, to syncretism over purity, and to the right to question religious authority. For the founding of WAF was premised on the understanding that the form of gender politics that was laid bare during the Rushdie affair was not unique to Muslim communities, and that WAF's work had to focus on fundamentalism as a rising powerful force within all religions. Indeed, many WAF activists were engaged in challenging and fighting to abolish blasphemy laws and state-funded faith schools both of which have had the backing of Christian groups in the UK. Most of the activists were politically formed in struggles against religious fundamentalism in places such as Ireland, Pakistan, Israel, and India (Dhaliwal and Yuval-Davis).

WAF's political positions were based in the reality that at the same time that Muslim fundamentalists were carving out a political space for their conservative agendas in the UK, a similar consolidation of fundamentalist tendencies was gaining ground globally. In the United States, a resurgent Christian fundamentalism consolidated its assault on gay and lesbian movements, women's right to abortion, and other issues that were becoming central to the "culture wars" of the 1980s and 1990s. The Christian right was also perpetrating attacks on reproductive rights in Ireland and in Africa and Latin America through funding innocuous sounding charities, while Hindu fundamentalism's rise led to its social and political consolidation in India from the late 1980s via the propagation of a vision of retrograde womanhood in the service of Hindu nationalism. In the face of such movements, WAF defined religious fundamentalism as a modern political movement and ideology seeking to consolidate power either within or in opposition to the state. In this, WAF made a crucial distinction between religious fundamentalism and religious observance, which it saw as a matter of personal choice, but also between religious conservatism and religious fundamentalism.

On this view, it is secularism that offered the strongest guarantee of equality, of justice, and of equal access to the public, while leaving space for individual religious belief and unbelief (Sahgal and Yuval-Davis). One could thus see that WAF was undoubtedly drawing upon an earlier tricontinental vision committed to principles of secularism and socialism as principles best suited for ensuring equality, particularly gender equality, in newly decolonizing nation states.

It is important to note here that national modernity, to whose imagination women were central, was defined in the aftermath of the internationalist convergence of anti-imperialism and nationalism as socialist and secular in country after country. In Turkey, Ataturk styled himself as a modernizer of women's conditions as part of his project of forging a modern, secular Turkish state; in Egypt, the ideology of Arab Socialism was crafted by Nasser when he came to power after the coup of 1952; in India, the Nehruvian state committed itself to socialist planned development and a secular polity; and the revolutionary secular FLN took power in Algeria after defeating the French colonialists. The fact that those projects of secularism and anti-colonial nationalism have suffered decisive setbacks in the twenty-first-century demands that as feminists we need to re-evaluate the dissenting histories of feminism and anti-imperialism not as projects of nostalgia, but as critical aspects of the future.

By 2010, WAF folded as an activist organization, but the circumstances that led up to that moment (Dhaliwal and Yuval-Davis) allow for a critical examination of the fourth moment in the history of feminism and anti-imperialism that this essay seeks to narrativize.

THE NEW ANTI-IMPERIALISM

Two and a half decades after WAF was first formed, religious fundamentalism has spread its tentacles even deeper into our social and political lives and spaces. The impact of fundamentalism is now being felt at a scale and in areas not previously known and has been marked in recent decades by the coming together and networking of cross-border and transnational fundamentalist forces (see Dhaliwal, Nagarajan, and Varma). These developments provide credence to Jayawardene's reflection that the early fervor with which ideals such as secularism and socialism were pursued has now diminished and that "the old pre-capitalist dogmas and religions have proved to be surprisingly enduring" (6). However, one needs to emphasize that resurgent fundamentalism is not just a revival of old dogmas but a new phenomenon that pre-dates 9/11 but was given the status of a global movement as a distinctive modern political force in the age of the "war on terror" as declared by the then US president George W. Bush on the eve of the attack on Afghanistan in December 2001.

Many states in fact have used the cover of the war on terror to discipline, control, and eliminate the fundamentalist terrorist networks that emerged in the wake of the earlier Soviet invasion of Afghanistan from 1979 to 1989 and can be traced back to that period. In most instances, the responses of states where these terrorist networks operate, have been disproportionately militarized and have clearly violated human rights while unleashing prejudice against specific communities. The discourse in European states around refugees and migrants within or at their borders is imbued with fears of what the imperialist historian Niall Ferguson called "Eurabia," conjuring up an image of a civilized Christian Europe swamped by Muslims.

At the same time, the war on terror has enabled states to deploy the rhetoric of human rights and liberation to justify wars that were often mere fig leaves for the neo-imperial ambitions of the West in oil-rich regions. After all, the 2001 invasion of Afghanistan was carried out in the name of saving Afghan women from the Taliban. So, for example, Jasbir

Puar has pointed to the ways in which a concern for the rights of gay and lesbian people provided justification for neo-imperial intervention and occupation.

Certainly, the war on Iraq and Afghanistan was a form of what David Harvey referred to as the "new imperialism," a new stage of the expropriation of the world's resources via military might. But for the vast majority of the international Left the dramatic rise of violent extremism was a potent form of "blowback" (Prashad, "Blowback Time"). The rhetoric of human rights and the fight against terrorism, for the Left, was nothing but a fig leaf for the West's neocolonial greed. The Left liberal defense of culture, religion, and tradition, seen especially in the Left's ambivalent response to attacks on freedom of expression in favor of a politics of hurt sentiments of religious minorities, has of course an unexpected ally from within religious majorities as well, as in Christian fundamentalists in the UK and elsewhere, who, like many academics on the Left, also use the term "secular fundamentalism" to discredit the work of those fighting for the rights of those who are victims of religious extremism (Farris, "Secularism"). Indeed, for many on the Left, the religious fundamentalists seem to be carrying out a heroic anti-imperial struggle (see Tax, *Double Bind*; Cowden).

Indeed, the voices of activists fighting against fundamentalist forces and states with imperial designs, often at the same time, are pointedly marginalized from public discussion, to the detriment of the very principles of gender and race equality that previous iterations of anti-imperialism were allied with. As Rohini Hensman puts it in her account of what she calls "pseudo anti-imperialism," "genuine anti-imperialists do, of course, oppose Western states when they invade and occupy countries, impose authoritarian regimes on Third World peoples, or kill civilians in airstrikes. But pseudo-anti-imperialists, by opposing 'the West' as such, are also rejecting the democratic revolutions carried out by labor activists, feminists, LGBT activists and anti-racists in the West" (51).

The consolidation of fundamentalism globally at the same time as there is increasing control of borders and migration, often along race and class lines, and of a worldwide financial crisis that spurred a wave of austerity measures across the globe, has thus exposed a deep chasm in progressives' thinking about gender, race, and empire, together, as deeply articulated and intersectional. Here I want to suggest that the more recent articulations of anti-imperialism thus blur the lines between anti-imperialism and a defense of minority authoritarianism.

To say then that as anti-imperial feminists some may reject both Western imperialism in all its avatars as well as the consolidation of fundamentalism globally as projects antithetical to women's rights is to enter a minefield. What should have been a fairly logical position for the international Left to take—oppose imperialism and religious fundamentalism—has been rendered into a controversial stand, as feminists struggling for secular public spaces are accused of fueling racism and imperialism, and of being "Western," deracinated secularists (Kumar; Toor; for a critical view see Zia, "The Ethics of Feminist Engagement"; Cowden).

This leads us to a discussion of the circumstances in which WAF found itself divided and adrift and ultimately unable to function as an organization. In 2010, Gita Sahgal, who was one of the founders of WAF and was then heading the Gender Unit of Amnesty International, publicly challenged the organization and protested the stage it was providing to former Guantanamo Bay prisoner Moazzam Begg and his organization the Cageprisoners (now known as CAGE). In Sahgal's view, Begg (who had left home in Birmingham and moved to Peshawar in Pakistan in the late 1990s and had been involved in wars in Bosnia and Chechnya) and Cageprisoners were engaged in promoting jihadi and extremist politics. After Begg's release from Guantanamo in 2005, Cage had projected itself as a defender of human rights, but for Sahgal, who was supportive of the human rights of those who had been illegally captured and kept in detention in Guantanamo, Begg and Cageprisoners were at the same time propagating a very retrograde view of women's position within Islam (see Cowden).[15] As head of the Gender Unit of Amnesty International, for Sahgal, giving a platform to Begg by Amnesty was akin to supporting Cage's extremist ideology.

In simultaneously supporting Begg's rights as a victim of extraordinary rendition and criticizing Cage's support for religious fundamentalist projects, Sahgal was going beyond the binary of the formulation "you are either for us or against us." In fact, WAF itself had worked consistently in breaking the mold within which anti-imperial feminists have often found themselves imprisoned. But this time around, the fear that they may be seen as Islamophobic had gripped many anti-racist, anti-imperialist activists, including some of those who had been long-term members of WAF. The fear of Islamophobia was the air we all breathed. As a consequence, WAF was unable to come up with a united defense of Sahgal's position and soon ceased to exist as an organization. Of course, many of its members continue to be active on the same issues, and a group of former members has recently founded a journal called *Feminist Dissent* based at the University of Warwick. As Dhaliwal and Yuval-Davis put it, WAF continues to be "a source of inspiration, a resource for political analysis and a method for political engagement" (13). But it is impossible to not recognize the inability of WAF to function as an organization in the current climate as symptomatic of this latest moment of divergence of feminism and anti-imperialism, such that secular feminists are now tainted with the charge of "imperialist feminism" (Kumar; Toor). In many ways, the circle is now complete, and the task is to disentangle the many contested histories of feminism and anti-imperialism.

Of course, for the anti-racist self-styled anti-imperialists, the Amnesty case had exposed Sahgal as a "cause celebre for neo-conservatives, the pro-war left and similar Islamophobic groupings" (Miller, Mills, and Massoumi). A series of attacks on secular feminists as "liberal Islamophobes" (Toor; see also Oza), and indeed on the very idea of secularism (Birchall; Farris, "Secularism"; Scott), underscores a profoundly disturbing emergence of contradictory alliances of politics and principles among these critics. For many on the Left, primarily in the imperial states, religious fundamentalists seem to be prosecuting a heroic anti-imperial struggle. Further faced with unprecedented cuts in the social budget and a brutally enforced austerity regime on the domestic front, many in the Left have come to see religious fundamentalism as the lone force in the world that seems to be able to challenge the unilateral power of the imperial countries. Groups like Stop the War Coalition and the Respect Party in the UK have openly allied with fundamentalists to forge what they see as an anti-racist and anti-imperialist agenda (Cowden). For their part, fundamentalists have tended to exploit anti-imperialist traditions to present themselves as radical anti-Western anti-imperialists.

Academic responses to these issues have, on the whole, tended to highlight the instrumentalization of rights-based frameworks, the hypocrisy of Western nation states, and a critique of the civilizational, imperialist, and racist presumptions at the heart of the Enlightenment whose legacies the world is still bearing (Dhawan). Postcolonial theory's critique of the Enlightenment as a Eurocentric, coercive, and authoritarian project has become the common sense of the field (Spivak). While recent attempts to "decolonise Enlightenment" have focused attention on its contradictory and contested legacies, there is nevertheless a sense of discomfort with "the historical triumph of reason and science" that brought with it "terror, genocide, slavery, exploitation, and domination" (Dhawan 11). That is some historical blame to lay on reason and science!

Prominent feminist theorists seem to have been significantly moved by the "war on terror," and seem fascinated by women's participation in religious political mobilizations and immersion in religious identity politics (Mahmood). They have been less interested in the impact of fundamentalism on women and sexual minorities. Much academic work as part of "faiths" literature projects religious groups as important carriers of social capital and providers of welfare support, and also projects religion as "cohesive," and "faith communities" as central players in tackling "radicalization." More recently, Sara Farris (*In the Name of Women's Rights*) elides the entire question of women's rights and religious fundamentalism in her study of what she sees as an unlikely alliance between Right-wing nationalist political parties, neoliberals, and some feminists. She reprises Puar's notion of "homonationalism" as "femonationalism," an ideology that discredits minority Muslim communities and leaders in the West for their retrograde views on gender. The fact that these communities, along with the French state (one of her key examples), practice ideologies detrimental to women's rights finds no airing in her argument.

In part, this retreat from criticism of religious fundamentalism is the consequence of what Chetan Bhatt ("Ethnic Absolutism") has referred to as the "cultural episteme" and is a reproduction of an earlier tendency to treat the ethnic minority subject as particularly fragile and as exemplary victim. This can be seen in the proliferation of academic and journalistic work on "Islamophobia" as the leading issue of our times, typically unmoored from an analysis of racial discrimination and structural causes (Kumar; Kundnani). Arun Kundnani, in his provocatively titled expose of Islamophobia in the West, *The Muslims Are Coming*, writes, "One of the key arguments of this book is that to comprehend the causes of *so-called jihadist terrorism*, we need to pay as much attention to Western state violence and the identity politics that sustains it, as we do to Islamicist ideology. What governments call extremism is to a large degree a product of their own wars" (25, emphasis mine). Among other things, what gets elided in such work is the way in which Islamic states such as Saudi Arabia have openly allied with Western imperial powers while peddling ultraconservative ideologies of gender.

Such work that reprises the figure of the Muslim as the ideal victim of neo-imperialism enjoys a fair degree of prestige in the Western academic establishment, securing for its proponents endowed chairs and ensuring publication by leading Left-wing and theoretically cutting-edge presses and blogs. On the other hand, Muslim men and women challenging fundamentalism are placed in the double bind of being burdened by Right-wing assimilationist pressures to challenge fundamentalism within their communities and a simultaneous criticism by Left-wing forces for pandering to state agendas and imperialism when they do so (Bennoune; Zia, *Faith and Feminism in Pakistan*). Karima Bennoune, law professor and daughter of an Algerian exile, writes about this silenced aspect of Muslim resistance with tremendous poignancy in her riveting account of Muslims fighting against fundamentalism all across the globe: "My father's country (Algeria) showed me in those grim years of the 1990s that the struggle waged in Muslim majority societies against extremism is one of the most important—and overlooked—human rights struggles in the world. This remains true twenty years later" (3).

In the UK context, the problems and paradoxes that were identified by WAF within the context of an assimilationist Thatcherite government at home and resurgent religious political mobilizations across the globe were exacerbated by a New Labor government for whom religious organizations were a critical part of governance. These have been more or less followed by successive British governments, all invested in "multifaithism," a new religious settlement between former colonial states and their minority ethnic populations. A multiculturalist practice based on undemocratic negotiations of the state with an unelected layer of "community leaders" (often religious men) has bolstered the power of ethnic minority religious leaderships in the UK over a number of decades. These tendencies are also reflected in the trajectories and contemporary contexts of other countries, especially those with colonial histories. In the United States, Trump's racist and reprehensible ban on immigrants from seven Muslim nations is poised to further shut down secular spaces for women in particular, as Trump's blatant Islamophobia drives the left into positions that defend Muslim and other minority "cultures" at any cost.

The trends that I have identified here signal a sea change from the earlier period of decolonization in Latin America, Africa, and Asia when a vision committed to a secular, socialist, and internationalist global society was articulated. In Western academia, postcolonial and postmodernist strands of critical inquiry have fed on the allure of cultural relativism as a way to manage difference. Their critique of the Enlightenment as a racist and imperialist project, and a concomitant valorization of the popular and the subaltern, has led, ironically, to a retreat from a critique of religious fundamentalism and patriarchy and a willed amnesia toward anti-colonial struggles. Those anti-colonial and anti-imperial struggles were fought by peoples throughout the colonized world, often by wresting concepts of freedom, liberty, rule of law, rights, secularism, and so on from the "West."

Hope today lies in the fact that in contrast to dominant academic and international NGO-driven work, progressive movements on the ground globally often have stronger analyses of fundamentalism, and seek to combat its influence and impact, as well as seek to highlight progressive interpretations of religion and engender changes in religious, state, and cultural institutions (Bennoune). After all, feminist activists, whether in India or Nigeria or Turkey, or in Latin American countries, in their activism have historically embraced ideas of freedom, secularism, and rights and have a much more nuanced understanding and navigation of the terrain of colonialism, racism, and rights than often seen in the West. They ask the question, Are we to cede all of these ideas to Western imperialism? After all, the history of anti-colonial struggles in fact has involved the attempt to wrench these concepts from their European moorings and to re-signify them for anti-colonialist and progressive aims. That may well be one of the legacies of anti-imperialist feminism that is in urgent need of recuperation.

Implicit in this theoretical foray is the question of what it means to recall this moment from the perspective of the current conjuncture characterized by an exponential expansion of neoliberal austerity, neo-imperial greed, religious fundamentalism, and the consequent rollback of the rights of women and minorities. I argue that this conjuncture necessitates a different kind of analysis than the one that has become standard fare of anti-imperialist feminism, and that we need a new way of looking at the intersection of feminism and anti-imperialism so that a renewed vision and practice of anti-imperialist feminism can be forged. As Hensman puts it bluntly: "To support authoritarian states by word or by deed in the name of opposing capitalism or imperialism is a betrayal of struggles against both" (50). She goes on to argue that

> it is undeniable that capitalism is responsible for unspeakable atrocities and must be fought, but this should not detract from the fight against other forms of oppression. If anything, the struggle against racism and religious bigotry, patriarchy, misogyny and homophobia, xenophobia, nationalism and all forms of authoritarianism should be a

priority, because a working class dominated and divided by these ideologies and politics can never defeat neoliberalism, much less capitalism. Nor can the struggle against capitalism be won without the freedom to express oneself freely, to debate, discuss and organize. (50)

CODA

As a coda, I would like to conjure up the figure of the young guerrilla freedom fighting women of Rojava, members of an autonomous women's army, who have not only successfully pushed back Daesh but are involved in a unique social and political experiment of radical democracy that is feminist, inclusive, secular, and Left-wing (Tax, *A Road Unforeseen*). In them, the truly progressive legacies of anti-imperial feminism live on, and with whom we must stand in solidarity. Sadly, the women of Rojava have received little attention from the international Left.

For a true solidarity to emerge, feminist anti-imperialism will need to go beyond what I would like to call an imperialist anti-imperialism. For behind the figure of the women soldiers of Rojava is also that of Najiya Hanum from Turkey who spoke so eloquently at the Baku Conference about less than a century ago about the dual oppression of "women of the east," oppressed both by class power and the "despotism of their menfolk." Prepared to wage war on both, for Hanum theirs was "a life and death struggle to win our rights by force." It is a struggle that is very much alive today and toward which we must stand in solidarity if anti-imperialism is also going to be a feminist project.

NOTES

I would like to thank Robin Goodman for giving me the opportunity to write this essay, to Subir Sinha for a careful and critical reading, and to members of the editorial collective of *Feminist Dissent* from whom I have learnt so much. In particular, I owe a debt to my coauthors Sukhwant Dhaliwal and Chitra Nagarajan for our essay "Why Feminist Dissent?" that appeared in the inaugural issue of the journal and on which I build my arguments here. I presented a version of this paper as a plenary talk at the conference on "Legacies of the Tricontinental, 1966–2016," Centre for Social Studies, University of Coimbra, Portugal, September 22–4, 2016. I thank Tor Krever for his invitation and the audience for a combative and challenging response. Thanks also to Brenna Bhandar who invited me to speak on this topic as part of Women's Strike! Strike to Win! International Women's Day celebration at the SOAS-Birkbeck UCU Teachout on March 8, 2018.

1 The 1966 Conference is considered to be the largest gathering of anti-imperialists with over 500 participants who represented various national liberation and other guerilla revolutionary movements fighting against their own newly formed postcolonial regimes.

2 Many travelers from the colonized countries reported being impressed by the freedom of European women within the secular, liberal context of European societies. Many of them were already or became subsequently involved in social reform activities back in their own countries. See Grewal.

3 Left-wing women from Europe such as Agnes Smedley and Evelyn Roy participated in the revolutionary struggles of women in the colonized world. Revolutionary groups in London and Paris also sprang up to further the cause of revolutionary anti-imperialism. See Jayawardene (*Feminism and Nationalism in the Third World*) for more on the role of Western women who were socialists and dissidents within their own national contexts (20–1).

4 In the theses Lenin prepared for the Third International (the Second Congress of the Comintern in 1920), from which he was to break away on the question of nationalism, Lenin made a case for making "a clear distinction between the interests of the oppressed classes, of working and exploited people, and the general concept of national interests as a whole, which implies the interests of the ruling class," as well as "an equally clear distinction between the oppressed, dependent and subject nations and the oppressing, exploiting and sovereign nations." (Hensman 30).

5 Lenin clearly wanted to forge "a joint revolutionary struggle of 'the proletarians and the working masses of all nations and countries'" (Hensman 31).

6 Japan's defeat of Tsarist Russia in 1905, the formation of the Chinese Republic of Sun Yat Sen in 1912 after the overthrow of the Qing dynasty, the 1917 Russian Revolution and the subsequent rise of Communist parties in colonized countries, the nationalist Irish Uprising of 1916 culminating in independence in 1949, the launch of the nationalist movement in India from the early decades of the twentieth century, as well as the founding of the Turkish republic under Ataturk in 1922 all contributed to a global sense of political transformation, social revolution, and postcolonial possibilities during the early decades of the twentieth century.

7 Quoted in Afro-Asian People's Solidarity Conference, Cairo, December 26, 1957–January 1, 1958 (Moscow: Foreign Languages Publishing House, 1958, 204–5; in Prashad 54).

8 Jayawardene argues that we cannot overlook the role of Orientalism in constructing and shaping the idea of a pristine tradition for native societies. She goes on to suggest that the idea of a coherent and unified national identity itself was one of the products of colonialism (4–5).

9 In her important book, Kumari Jayawardene provides an overview of the range of countries that were either directly and indirectly subject to imperialism. While India, Sri Lanka, Indonesia, Vietnam, and Philippines were all part of colonial empires, Egypt and Iran possessed a semicolonial status. The Turkish empire was dismembered by colonialism while Japan was subjected to economic pressure and control (1).

10 For the Indian case, see Marik.

11 The collection of essays and creative work coedited by Cherrie Moraga and Gloria Anzaldua, *This Bridge Called My Back: Writings by Radical Women of Colour*, was a landmark contribution to the emergent critique of the imperialism within the mainstream American women's movement.

12 See Mohanty, as well as the work of Marie Mies on gender, colonialism, and the international division of labor for more materialist analyses of feminism and new forms of imperialism.

13 The move to ban the book can be seen as an attempt by the Indian government to make up as it were for a progressive judgment in the Shah Bano case where a divorced Muslim woman's right to maintenance had been upheld by the courts. The right given to Shah Bano was controversial, as it was seen to hurt the sentiments of the mullahs and other conservative elements among Muslims!

14 Dhaliwal and Yuval-Davis write that WAF's members were "primarily united by their position as feminists and as dissenters within their own communities" (8).

15 See also https://www.theguardian.com/world/2010/apr/25/gita-sahgal-amnesty-international. Accessed July 3, 2018.

WORKS CITED

Abu-Lughod, Leila. *Do Muslim Women Need Saving?* Cambridge, MA: Harvard UP, 2015.

Amos, Valerie, and Pratibha Parmar. "Challenging Imperial Feminism." *Feminist Review* No. 17, Many Voices, One Chant: Black Feminist Perspectives. (Autumn 1984), pp. 3–19.

Armstrong, Elisabeth. "Before Bandung: The Anti-Imperialist Women's Movement in Asia and the Women's International Democratic Federation." *Signs: Journal of Women in Culture and Society* 41.2 (2016): 305–31.

Bennoune, Karima. *Your Fatwa Does Not Apply Here: Untold Stories from the Fight against Muslim Fundamentalism*. New York: W. W. Norton, 2013.

Bhatt, Chetan. "Ethnic Absolutism and the Authoritarian Spirit." *Theory, Culture & Society* 16.2 (April 1999): 65–85.

Birchall, Ian. "The Wrong Kind of Secularism." *Jacobin*, November 19, 2015. https://www.jacobinmag.com/2015/11/charlie-hebdo-france-secular-paris-attacks-lacite/. Accessed September 23, 2018.

Carby, Hazel. "White Woman Listen! Black Feminism and the Boundaries of Sisterhood." *The Empire Strikes Back: Race and Racism in 70s Britain*. Ed. Centre for Contemporary Cultural Studies, U of Birmingham. London: Hutchinson, 1982, pp. 212–35.

Chakraborty, Dipesh. *Provincialising Europe: Postcolonial Thought and Historical Difference*. Princeton, NJ: Princeton UP, 2000.

Chatterjee, Partha. *The Nation and its Fragments*. Princeton, NJ: Princeton UP, 1993.

Comahee River Collective, The Combahee River Collective Statement: Black Feminist Organizing in the Seventies and Eighties. Kitchen Table: Women of Color Press, 1986.

Cowden, Stephen. "The Poverty of Apologism: The British Left, Feminism and the Islamic Right." *Feminist Dissent* 1 (2016): 67–80.

Dhaliwal, Sukhwant, and Nira Yuval-Davis, eds. *Women against Fundamentalism: Stories of Dissent and Solidarity*. London: Lawrence and Wishart, 2012.

Dhaliwal, Sukhwant, Chitra Nagarajan, and Rashmi Varma, "Why Feminist Dissent?" *Feminist Dissent* 1 (2016): 1–32.

Dhaliwal, Sukhwant, and Stephen Cowden. "Nationalism, Fundamentalism and the Monopoly on Violence: A Reply to Sara R. Farris." *Verso Blog*, September 20, 2016. https://www.versobooks.com/blogs/2843-nationalism-fundamentalism-and-the-monopoly-on-violence-a-reply-to-sara-r-farris. Accessed July 4, 2018.

Dhawan, Nikita, ed. *Decolonizing Enlightenment: Transnational Justice, Human Rights and Democracy in a Postcolonial World*. Opladen: Barbara Budrich, 2014.

Farris, Sara R. "Secularism is the Fundamentalist Religion of France." *Verso Blog*, August 26, 2016. https://www.versobooks.com/blogs/2817-secularism-is-the-fundamentalist-religion-of-france. Accessed July 4, 2018.

Farris, Sara R. *In the Name of Women's Rights: The Rise of Femonationalism*. Durham, NC: Duke UP, 2017.

Ferguson, Niall. "The Way We Live Now: 4-4-04; Eurabia?" *New York Times*, April 4, 2004. https://www.nytimes.com/2004/04/04/magazine/the-way-we-live-now-4-4-04-eurabia.html. Accessed July 4, 2018.

Grewal, Inderpal. *Home and Harem: Nation, Gender, Empire and the Cultures of Travel*. Durham, NC: Duke UP, 1996.

Harvey, David. The New Imperialism. Oxford: Oxford University Press, 2003.

Hensman, Rohini. *Indefensible: Democracy, Counter-Revolution, and the Rhetoric of Imperialism*. Chicago, IL: Haymarket Books, 2018.

Jayawardene, Kumari. *Feminism and Nationalism in the Third World*. London: Verso Books, [1982] 2017.

Kandiyoti, Deniz. "End of Empire: Islam, Nationalism and Women in Turkey." *Feminist Postcolonial Theory: A Reader*. Ed. Reina Lewis and Sara Mills. New York: Routledge, 2003, 263–84.

Kumar, Deepa. *Islamophobia and the Politics of Empire*. Chicago, IL: Haymarket Books, 2012.

Kundnani, Arun. *The Muslims Are Coming!: Islamophobia, Extremism, and the Domestic War of Terror*. London: Verso Books, 2015.

Magdy, Rana. "Egyptian Feminist Movement: A Brief History." *openDemocracy*, March 8, 2017. https://www.opendemocracy.net/north-africa-west-asia/rana-magdy/egyptian-feminist-movement-brief-history. Accessed March 16, 2018.

Mahmood, Saba. *Politics of Piety: The Islamic Revival and the Feminist Subject*. Princeton, NJ: Princeton UP, 2011.

Marik, Soma. "Breaking Through a Double Invisibility: The Communist Women of Bengal, 1939–1948." *Critical Asian Studies* 45.1 (2013): 79–118.

Mies, Maria. *Patriarchy and Accumulation on a World Scale: Women in the International Division of Labour*. London: Zed Books, 1999.

Mohanty, Chandra Talpade. "Under Western Eyes: Feminist Scholarship and Colonial Discourses." *Feminist Review* 30 (Autumn, 1988): 61–88.

Mohanty, Chandra Talpade. "Women Workers and Capitalist Scripts: Ideologies of Domination, Common Interests, and the Politics of Solidarity." *Feminist Genealogies, Colonial Legacies, Democratic Futures*. Ed. Jacqui M. Alexander and Chandra Talpade Mohanty. Thinking Gender. New York: Routledge, 1997.

Mohanty, Chandra Talpade. "'Under Western Eyes' Revisited: Feminist Solidarity through Anticapitalist Struggles." *Signs* 28.2 (Winter 2003): pp. 499–535.

MillerDavid, Mills, T., Massoumi, N. "Apologists for Terror or Defenders of Human Rights? The Cage Controversy in Context." *openDemocracy*, July 31, 2015. https://www.opendemocracy.net/ourkingdom/tom-mills-narzanin-massoumi-david-miller/apologists-for-terror-or-defenders-of-human-righ. Accessed July 4, 2018.

Moraga, Cherrie, and Gloria Anzaldua. *This Bridge Called My Back: Writings By Radical Women of Color*. San Francisco, CA: Aunt Lute Books, 1981.

Oza, Rupal. "With Us or Against Us." *Counterpunch*, January 21, 2011. https://www.counterpunch.org/2011/01/21/with-us-or-against-us/. Accessed July 4, 2018.

Prashad, Vijay. *The Darker Nations: A People's History of the Third World*. New York: New P, 2008.

Prashad, Vijay. "Blowback Time." *Frontline*, July 25, 2014.

Puar, Jasbir. *Terrorist Assemblages: Homonationalism in Queer Times*. Durham, NC: Duke UP, 2007.

Sahgal, Gita. "Who Wrote the Universal Declaration of Human Rights?" *openDemocracy*, December 10, 2014 (originally published in 2012). https://www.opendemocracy.net/5050/gita-sahgal/who-wrote-universal-declaration-of-human-rights. Accessed March 16, 2018.

Sahgal, Gita. "A Statement by Gita Sahgal on Leaving Amnesty International." *New York Review of Books*, May 13, 2010. http://www.nybooks.com/articles/2010/05/13/statement-gita-sahgal-leaving-amnesty-internationa/. Accessed July 4, 2018.

Sahgal, Gita, and Nira Yuval-Davis, eds. *Refusing Holy Orders: Women and Fundamentalism and Britain*. London: Virago P, 1992.

Sandoval, Chela. "U.S. Third World Feminism: The Theory and Method of Oppositional Consciousness in the Postmodern World." *Geographic Thought*. Ed. George Henderson and Marvin Waterstone. New York: Routledge, 2009.

Scott, Joan. *Sex and Secularism*. Princeton, NJ: Princeton UP, 2017.

Spivak, Gayatri Chakravorty. "*Can the Subaltern Speak?*" *Marxism and the Interpretation of Culture*. Ed. Cary Nelson and Lawrence Grossberg. Urbana: U of Illinois P, 1988, 271–313.

Tax, Meredith. *Double Bind: The Muslim Right, the Anglo-American Left, and Universal Human Rights*. New York: Centre for Secular Space, 2013.

Tax, Meredith. *A Road Unforeseen: Women Fight the Islamic State*. New York: Bellevue Literary P, 2016.

Toor, Sadia. "Imperialist Feminism Redux." *Dialectical Anthropology* 36 (2012): 147–60.

Young, Robert J. C. *Postcolonialism: An Historical Introduction*. Oxford: Wiley-Blackwell, 2001.

Zia, Afiya Shehrbano. "The Ethics of Feminist Engagement: Discussing Feminism-as-Imperialism." *openDemocracy*, January 19, 2015. https://www.opendemocracy.net/5050/afiya-shehrbano-zia/ethics-of-feminist-engagement-discussing-feminismasimperialism. Accessed July 4, 2018.

Zia, Afiya Shehrbano. *Faith and Feminism in Pakistan: Religious Agency of Secular Autonomy?* Eastbourne: Sussex Academic P, 2018.

CHAPTER THIRTY-FOUR

Future

BRIDGET CRONE AND HENRIETTE GUNKEL

INTRODUCTION

In May 2015, Laboria Cuboniks[1] (a collective currently consisting of Amy Ireland, Diann Bauer, Helen Hester, Katrina Burch, Lucca Fraser, and Patricia Reed) published the manifesto "Xenofeminism: A Politics for Alienation" (referred to as XF Manifesto) in which they examine the possibilities for an interplanetary twenty-first-century feminism that projects and remakes a future—a new *future* future—through a proposed large-scale speculative practice embedded in technology, rationality, reason, and universality.[2] The invocation of embeddedness with and through technology is visualized in Diann Bauer's video introduction in which Laboria Cuboniks introduce themselves through avatars and which begins from the space of the desktop. The emphasis on science and rationality at the core of the Manifesto differentiates it from previous forms, in particular cyberfeminism of the 1990s.[3] As such, the XF Manifesto highlights the role of technology in projecting a future, but it does this through attention to a specific kind of alienation that is queer, feminist, and possibly Afrofuturist. Here a constant tension between future and "no future" produces an impossible-possible space, and, as we will propose, an Alien Feminism emerges from this tension. Alien Feminism, we will suggest, is committed to building a futurity from the creative impossibility of the future. Following Luciana Parisi, this is a hyperstitional practice that has "future consequences" and that is based in a collective thinking beyond the bounds of what is or can be thought (216).

Here, the scope of the XF Manifesto and Parisi's (and our own) "Alien Feminism" goes beyond the techno activism of the previous generation of cyberfeminists, initially working in response to and inspired by Donna Haraway's 1984 text "The Cyborg Manifesto" published in her book *Simian, Cyborgs and Women: The Reinvention of Nature* (1991), and it is here that we find the development of the idea of "worlding" and the future orientation that is of such importance to both manifestos. In her multiform worlding practice, Haraway also reminds us of the need for denormalization by arguing that "it matters to destabilize worlds of thinking with other worlds of thinking," or "which ideas we think other ideas with" (Haraway, "Anthropocene, Capitalocene, Chthulucene" n.p.). There are two points of difference to be highlighted between the two moments from which each manifesto emerged. One is the possibilities or impossibilities of thinking the future for now as the future and science fiction itself has become capital (becoming a form of what Mark Fisher has termed SF Capital). The other is the increased urgency of the recognition (and inclusion) of trans, machinic, and hybrid bodies. The XF Manifesto ends with the demand "If nature is unjust, change nature" (0x01A), which must be contrasted to that of VNS Matrix's cyberfeminist manifesto "the clitoris is the direct line to the matrix" (VNS

Matrix). Xenofeminism and our own Alien Feminism builds upon Haraway's call for a politics based on affinity rather than identity and does so through a call to a possible-impossible future.

This constant tension between forward movement and stasis that is set out in the understanding of no future in the present while, simultaneously unleashing a possibility of creating something new has its theoretical precedent in the different, sometimes contradictory conceptualizations of time from a queer perspective—a perspective that puts forward an understanding that for certain groups of people the future is already foreclosed. Lee Edelman's positioning of queer temporality, for example, within an anti-relational, antisocial politics of "no future" breaks with teleological conceptions of reproduction and hope in the context of straight time. His anti-reproductive futurism, which is a queer-theoretical response to the HIV/Aids epidemic in Europe and the United States, foregrounds the fact that certain groups of people are not envisioned in the future project or, respectively, that for certain groups the future is already foreclosed. In *Cruising Utopia. The Then and There of Queer Futurity* (2009), José Esteban Muñoz refers to Edelman's notion of queer time but proposes a conceptualization of the future as queerness's domain while understanding queerness as a potential *future perfect*, as an ideality yet to be reached. He invites us to imagine alternatives to what seems available to us and to dream and enact more radical forms of being together. He insists on the principle of hope and radically reappropriates the concept of the future from a queer of color perspective, demanding a political imagination that is inherently collective in nature and hence works against neoliberalism's push for competitive individualism.[4] As he writes, "we are not yet queer. We may never touch queerness, but we can feel it as a warm illumination of a horizon imbued with potentiality" (1).

Muñoz's queer-theoretical approach to the impossible-possible time helps us think about the notion of future itself. Here we might want to draw on Hugh Charles O'Connell's distinction between the "future" as the "quantitative aspect" (292) of the quotidian passing of time, which O'Connell develops particularly in relation to Mark Fisher's understanding of capitalist realism where although time passes there is no radical sense of the future outside of the conditions of global late capitalism or in relation to what Kodwo Eshun coined the futures industry, and "futurity" as the "qualitative notion of the future as difference" (292). The latter provides an emphasis on the "not yet" of the becoming that can be found not only articulated in queer temporality and the XF Manifesto but also in recent pop-cultural articulations of imagining the world otherwise; Marvel's recent film *Black Panther* (2018) is just one of many examples of this imagining otherwise that is embraced worldwide. We will discuss this sense of futurity—or as Franco "Bifo" Berardi calls it "futurability"—in relation to vertigo and alienation in particular, the key concepts in the XF Manifesto, which alter our conceptions of time. We will use these themes to propose a particular form of feminist futurity—one that projects, fixes, and undoes the future—forming a project that is at once respectful of difference but at the same time universally collectivist in vision (intention).

FREE FALL: "OURS IS A WORLD IN VERTIGO"

Laboria Cuboniks's XF Manifesto begins with an explicit appeal to a tension between world-building and dissolution, between movement and stasis, growth and structure. "Ours is a world in vertigo. It is a world that swarms with technological mediation, interlacing our daily lives with abstraction, virtuality, and complexity" (0x00), they write. This torque between mass, libidinalized movement, and an action that works in the opposite direction to frame or to construct a logic or rationality out of this flow is evidenced through the structural form of the XF Manifesto itself, which is divided into sections that variously suggest movement, flow, and containment: Zero, Interrupt, Trap, Parity, Adjust, Carry, Overflow. These could also be understood as instructions, inspiration, or terms of encouragement—like that found in a self-help guide— equipping the reader with a set of actions to perform within and against the vertiginous flow of life in the twenty-first century. These section headers also circumscribe a circularity that is itself without end—the productive nature of the zero with which we begin emphasizes the importance of mathematics (and computation) to the XF Manifesto but also proposes and, indeed, presents us with a limit from which a world ensues and that ultimately (with the final section, "Overflow") exceeds its bounds. Zero also represents the unthinkable, the impossibility of nothingness within Christian belief and large swathes of Western thought. Therefore, to make a claim for "zero" from the outset is to make a radical demand for creation—the zero and the one from which all ensues. Here the zero undermines the givenness of the world as it is, suggesting instead that it can be produced anew (e.g., in a process of worlding).

Beginning their manifesto with "zero" points to a collective process and calls for a collectivity to come. As Helen Hester writes in another context, "Our name is zero for we are many" (n.p.). Here zero, its relation to mathematics and to collectivity (the more than one) can also be seen to refer to the work of pioneering cyberfeminist and philosopher Sadie Plant whose book, *Zero and Ones: Digital Women and the New Technoculture* is an antithesis of computation, beginning from the neglected foundational history centered on the work of Ada Lovelace. Lovelace was an early nineteenth-century-mathematical genius whose work is often written out of the history of computing, in favor of that of her collaborator William Babbage. Yet, it was Lovelace who "produced the first example of what was later called computer programming" (Plant 7). The "Zeroes and Ones" of Plant's title refers to computational process, zero and one being the components of a digital system, but it can also be seen in the context of the way in which Plant structures the writing of her book—opening its narrative to a plurality of voices and interjections. In this way, the mathematical refers to collectivity and plurality in the work of Plant and other cyberfeminists of the 1990s, as well as the retrieval of lost histories. Yet this has become further complicated as a result of the dehumanizing effects of neoliberalism, as Laboria Cuboniks have noted.[5] As a result, we must now recognize the reference to zero as suggesting the quantification of the human subject such that it is no longer recognized as an individual but a *dividual*—the breakdown of the singular *individual* into something more resembling a mathematical unit. As Gilles Deleuze writes in his essay, "Postscript on Societies of Control," "Individuals have become '*dividuals*,' and masses, samples, data, markets, or '*banks*'" (5).[6]

In responding to this situation, the shape of the XF Manifesto is explicitly left accelerationist for the way it seeks to intervene and to shape a strategy for intervention and to harness the technologization of daily life for feminist ends. That is to say in the words of the manifesto, to construct "a feminism of unprecedented cunning, scale and vision" in which "(T)echnoscientific innovation must be linked to a collective theoretical and political thinking in which women, queers, and the gender non-conforming play an unparalleled role" (0x02). If accelerationism is understood as a politics that is formed around the suggestion that emancipation from capitalism might be found through an acceleration of capital itself—that is, as Benjamin Noys suggested, through a speeding up of capital's movement toward its own destruction—then left accelerationism suggests that this acceleration must be harnessed for the construction of a future. Specifically, it is the means for acceleration that must be seized, and it is for this reason that we see an emphasis on harnessing technology and remaking the possibility of our technological futures. As Patricia Reed has noted elsewhere, neoliberalism presents us with two options concerning technology—one is to embrace it, and this means embracing its relation to capital such that technological innovation is centered upon and mandated by the financial imperatives set by Silicon Valley; the second option is to attempt to withdraw completely. Yet, she suggests there must be a third way that harnesses technology for an explicitly progressive agenda. The XF Manifesto emerges into this context, and it is within context that it must be read; that is, as producing a double movement, on the one hand recognizing the necessity of the acceleration of technological futures and, on the other hand, harnessing, mediating, and world-building.

The notion of vertigo appears here in the context of the speed of movement, technological change, and decentering of the subject that is inherent to neoliberalism. In the essay "In Free Fall: A Thought Experiment on Vertical Perspective," the artist and writer Hito Steyerl has noted that "the present moment is distinguished by a prevailing condition of groundlessness" (1). This groundlessness is addressed very viscerally in Steyerl's film, *Free Fall*, in which free fall—a state that is parleyed through repeated imagery of airplane crashes—represents economic collapse, the 2008 financial crash, as well as the resulting more generalized conditions of vertigo and free fall. Here financial and human bodies alike are in free fall, and the opening scenes of the film present footage of airplane crashes and associated human terror. Significantly, this footage is presented to us through the frame of a computer screen so that we see the image mediated, framed, and presented for us. There are then two things pertinent to us here. First, the intertwinement of financial and human body. Second, through the event of the crash, Steyerl presents us not with images of human horror but with images of images of human horror. We are therefore subsumed and not subsumed into this state of free fall that Steyerl's film presents to us, but we are positioned relative to it—we are outside the frame.

Most usually, the act of falling describes a loss of perspective and a surrender to movement, and free fall is the extreme horizonless manifestation of this. As one of the protagonists in Steyerl's film notes, "Once the process of descent began there wasn't really anything we could do to stop it." This state of loss can be seen in the manner in which free fall or vertigo (its disquieting cousin) are used to describe the breakdown or liquidation of the structures inherent to Fordism—that is, the separation of work and leisure, public and private spaces—into a continuous space of control in which the subject becomes lost to the velocity and disorientations of a continuous space of capital (emphasizing more empathically an inherent loss of perspective).[7] At this point, it is worth noting the difference between falling and free fall where to fall suggests a downward trajectory and a movement from one position to another, whereas free fall might technically not suggest such a movement but could suggest a falling upward or even sideways. Here free fall might be equated with vertigo in its suggestion of an extended state of disquiet, of estrangement and unbalancing. It is a situation in which the world seems to be suspended in motion. Unlike falling (as distinct from free fall or falling in pure gravity), vertigo does not signify an end but rather an elongated present in which the future is curtailed.

Disorientation and the precarity that it produces is thus normalized. It is from this state of vertigo that two important and interlinked points for building a future feminism—or what Lucianca Parisi has termed an "Alien Feminism"—ensue. The first of these is the productive potential of alienation as constituting the tools for the construction of new worlds, and the second is the role of inhumanism in the building of a feminism from the ashes of the capitalist, technoscientific ruination of the human. Both these strands of possibility emerge from the "politics of alienation" that we find in the XF Manifesto, but also importantly from Black Studies and black radical thought, particularly the work of Kodwo Eshun, Zakiyyah Iman Jackson, and Frank B. Wilderson III in addressing the question of inhumanism and the understanding of black subjectivity as marked by the violent disorientations of a state of ongoing vertigo, that "sense of unhinged reality, a communion with death and that realm which exceeds life," as Jackson (23) puts it.

In his article, "The vengeance of vertigo: Aphasia and abjection in the political trials of black insurgents," Wilderson III, importantly, draws the distinction between *subjective vertigo* as vertigo of the event which he describes as "a dizzying sense that one is moving or spinning in an otherwise stationary world, a vertigo brought on by a clash of grossly asymmetrical forces," and *objective vertigo*, "the sensation that one is not simply spinning in an otherwise stable environment, that one's environment is perpetually unhinged stems from a relationship to violence that cannot be analogized" (3). For him, black life takes place at the crossroads where vertigoes meet, at the intersection of performative and structural violence which, in effect, provides us with an understanding of blackness as a "life constituted by disorientation rather than a life interrupted by disorientation" (3). Being in vertigo, then, in this sense, reinvigorates black social and ontological isolation which Jared Sexton understands as the social life of social death in the wake of chattel slavery and places black subjectivity in the position of the inhuman that facilitates the definition of what constitutes the human nevertheless.[8]

What Wilderson III then provides us with is not an additional thought on vertigo proposed in the context of blackness but a reminder that planetary antiblackness and its state of ongoing vertigo has its origin in the Middle Passage, in "the Atlantic cycle of capital accumulation" as Ian Baucom calls it in his book *Specters of the Atlantic. Finance Capital, Slavery, and the Philosophy of History*. This gives an important grounding to the vertigo that the XF Manifesto describes. As Baucom suggests, the free fall of capital inherits "both a geography of history and a form of time, a type of contemporaneity, a complex, enigmatic, Atlantic 'now'" (Baucom 324). Inhabiting this ongoing state of dizziness, that, as Frantz Fanon argues, "haunts the whole of existence" (253) while rupturing it at the same time would call for imagining "otherwise from what we know *now* in the wake of slavery," as Christina Sharpe (18) puts it, toward the need for the unthought, also in relation to so far inaccessible alienations.

ALIENATION AS AN IMPETUS TO GENERATE NEW WORLDS

If vertigo suggests a state of continuous movement, it also marks an immersion within the present moment of this movement with the future suspended and foreclosed. It is this very eradication of the possibility of thinking *forward* that produces the world-building or worlding practice within Xenofeminism. In a place of "no future" (as the Thatcherite ghosts persists in whispering in ears), we have instead the seizing of this alienation from the future as the very possibility of a future. As Laboria Cuboniks write early on in their manifesto, "XF seizes alienation as an impetus to generate new worlds" (0x01). Here it must be said that alienation is corrupted from its Marxist usage and is used in a sense that will be more familiar to queers and Afrofuturists where alienation becomes the vehicle for a world that is *more-than* (more beautiful, more flamboyant, more fantastic as Jack Smith's 1962 film *Flaming Creatures* exemplifies) and that is *new*. Unlike Marxist alienation, freedom is not sought through a negation of alienation or its overcoming but through an acceleration of it. "The construction of freedom involves not less but more alienation; alienation is the labour of freedom's construction … Anyone who's been deemed 'unnatural' in the face of reigning biological norms, anyone who's experienced injustices wrought in the name of natural order" (0x01).[9]

In his essay "Further Considerations on Afrofuturism," Kodwo Eshun defines Afrofuturism (and his growing disquiet with it) as "concerned with the possibilities for intervention within the dimension of the predictive, the projected, the proleptic, the envisioned, the virtual, the anticipatory and the future conditional." This is, he suggests, the temporal dimension of the "not-yet" (289)—a time of becoming, and thus a focus not on being but on what is "not yet." It is this "not yet" that the XF Manifesto seizes upon to assemble its feminist project of "unprecedented cunning and scale" where the terrestrial dimensions of the feminist project are exploded for a project of planetary-scale complexity. This project of thinking beyond existing scales of imagination and ambition and moving toward the unthought can be seen to find their precedence in the work of Afrofuturist Sun Ra, where the focus is on the reinvention of an absolutely new world rather than a future that loops back and forth with a relation to the present. Sun Ra, African American musician, performance artist, and scientist, has, together with his Arkestra, perhaps most profoundly reclaimed, celebrated, and performed an extraterrestrial mode of being. Born as Herman Poole Blount in Birmingham, Alabama, in 1914, Sun Ra effectively undid himself as an earthly nonhuman being, claiming that this was the name of "an imaginary person" that "never existed" and that he had been transported to Earth from the planet Saturn (Szwed): "I think of myself as a complete mystery. To myself" (Sun Ra).

Myth and reality are set face to face in John Coney's film *Space Is the Place* (1974); the relationship between resistance to white supremacy/antiblackness and the performance of disidentification[10] as myth-science is described in a crucial scene in which Sun Ra visits a community recreation center in Oakland, California, where a group of inner-city black teenagers question him about his performance of alien drag[11] at the height of Black Power, Black Nationalism, and Black Panther Party politics. They ask him, how do we *know you are for real?* And he answers,

> How do you know I'm real? I'm not real. I'm just like you. You don't exist in this society. If you did your people wouldn't be seeking equal rights. You're not real. If you were, you'd have some status among the nations of the world. So we're both myths. I do not come to you as reality; I come to you as a myth. Because that's what black people are: myths.

The encounter speaks to the reach of antiblackness into the nonhuman, the irreconcilable chasm between blackness and the human, which Afropessimist[12] writings such as those by Saidiya Hartman and Frank B. Wilderson III point to, but also to Greg Tate's Afrofuturist formulation that Afrodiasporic subjects live the estrangement that science fiction writers envision.[13] The latter reiterates what Donna Haraway argued in her Cyborg Manifesto that "the boundary between science fiction and social reality is an optical illusion" (149). Or in the words of Jared Sexton: "Black life is not lived in the world that the world lives in, but it is lived underground, in outer space" (28)—a quote that points to the varied and various ways that black life lived in, as, under, and despite black (social) death, as

Christina Sharpe puts it, in her temporal analysis of thinking through the afterlife of slavery, which she understands as being in the wake:

> How might we stay in the wake with and as those whom the state positions to die ungrievable deaths and live lives meant to be unlivable? These are questions of temporality, the longue durée, the residence and hold time of the wake. At stake, then is to stay in this wake time toward inhabiting a blackened consciousness that would rupture the structural silences produced and facilitated by, and that produce and facilitate, Black social and physical death. (22)

In this context, then, a move beyond the human as articulated in current discussions around the anthropocene, in scholarship of posthumanism, and also in the XF Manifesto, needs to be understood as necessarily a reach toward blackness, as Z. I. Jackson points out, as "blackness conditions and constitutes the very nonhuman disruption and/or displacement they invite" (215, 216). Similarly, in her discussion of a productive inhumanism, Nina Power (2017) refers to the writings of Frantz Fanon and Wilderson III in which Blackness is excluded from humanism because of the impossibility of redress and redemption. In particular, Wilderson's work points to the limits of an intersectional analysis that is implicit in the XF manifesto, arguing that the structural relation to violence is different in the case of antiblackness than it is in the context of sexism and homophobia, for example.

CONCLUSION

We propose a *future* future feminism, that is an alienating interplanetary twenty-first-century-feminism that takes as its starting point the XF Manifesto and engages it with queer theory, theories of inhumanisms, and Afrofuturism. Because of the temporal scale and ungrounded potentiality of the project both in terms of thinking its inhabitants as well as its site, we must consider this as an Alien Feminism based upon an alien futurity, an alien future-as-difference. As Parisi argues, an Alien Feminism is to propose a practice that has "future consequences" (216). This is therefore a hyperstitional praxis—a historically situated collective thinking and imagining beyond the bounds of what is or can be thought (moving toward the unthought). While this is a far-future practice, it has immediate tractions in its projection of a future body that recognizes "the multiplicity of sexes for which new genders have to be invented" (Parisi 221). Parisi continues, "This involved not simply a rejection of nature, but the invention of a new philosophy of nature: a re-potentiation of what nature is and can be. If sex does not coincide with biological imperatives, so that the body is not limited to the boundaries of the organism but becomes a plane of vectors stretching and curving together to generate assemblages of another kind" (221).

Alien Feminism is driven by trans, machinic, and other bodies, and at the same time by the very question of what it is to have a body. This question arises from the very basis of humanist thought and its relation to colonialism and the Middle Passage, and the various degrees of vertigo that have been experienced either as subjective, objective, or at the crossroads of both. This is a project that demands tactical thinking and practice: we need to prepare ourselves to confront the position of the unthought and to confront the limits of humanist inclusion and to respond to the provocation of this exclusion by dismantling the very basis of inclusion itself. Taking our cue from Wilderson III, who writes, "The human need to be liberated in the world, is not the same as the Black need to be liberated from the world" (33),[14] we recognize the impossible limits of inclusion and wish to rebuild the world from its ruins accordingly. This is to become a vertiginous being, abandoned to a flow but at the same time constructing a future being and system of thought from that place. This is the impossible-possible future that Alien Feminism proposes.

NOTES

1 Laboria Cuboniks is an anagram of "Nicolas Bourbaki," a pseudonym under which a group of largely French mathematicians worked toward an affirmation of abstraction, generality, and rigor in mathematics in the early twentieth century.

2 The XF Manifesto emerges from the conversations and debates surrounding the Accelerationism conference held at Goldsmiths, the University of London, September 2010, which involved such figures as Mark Fisher, Kodwo Eshun, and Benjamin Noys. Also speaking were Alex Williams and Nick Srnicek who subsequently authored "The Accelerationist Manifesto" first published on the *Critical Legal Thinking* blog in 2013 and later in *Accelerate: The Accelerationist Reader* (edited by Robin Mackay and Armen Arvanessian). The XF Manifesto therefore emerges from a frustration at the predominantly male lineup for the accelerationist project as well as frustration at the continuing sense that science, mathematics, and rationality would be a "male" terrain. Accelerationism is a political, philosophical, and artistic project based on the work of Gilles Deleuze and Felix Guattari, Jean-Francois Lyotard as well as Nick Land, Sadie Plant, and other members of the CCRU (Cybernetics Cultural Research Unit based at Warwick University, UK, in the 1990s). It is based upon the theory that in order to be resisted capital must be accelerated. Laboria Cuboniks (established in 2014) is a xenofeminist collective of artists, writers, activists, and academics based across five countries and three continents. Members are active in conferences and exhibitions that address questions of time, technologies, and futurity across Europe, the United States, and Australia.

3 These include artists and activists such as Sandy Stone, Faith Wilding, Shulea Cheang, and the Australia group VNS Matrix (founded in 1991 in Adelaide) who were initially working in response to and inspired by Donna Haraway's 1984 text "The Cyborg Manifesto" published in her book *Simian, Cyborgs and Women: The Reinvention of Nature* (1991). Subsequent scholarship such as Sadie Plant's *Zeroes and Ones* (discussed further in this text) and Katherine N Hayles *How We Became Posthuman* (1999) also form important contributions to this field.

4 See, for example, Fisher.

5 There is a diverse range of literature on the effects of neoliberalism on the conception of the individual which might include Michael Hardt and Antonio Negri's *Empire* (2000), Christian Boltanski and Eve Chiapello's *The New Spirit of Capitalism* (2006), and Wendy Brown's *Undoing the Demos* (2015).

6 In this respect, we must recognize the difference in focus of the XF project in comparison with that of the preceding cyberfeminism such that where cyberfeminism's project lies in the inclusion and participation of women with technology, the XF project addresses the bounds of the human within the dehumanizing effects of "a world in vertigo" (while still advancing a gender-positive position). They write, "Xenofeminism endeavours to face up to these obligations as collective agents capable of transitioning between multiple levels of political, material and conceptual organisation." (0x06) Here the role of reason as well as "(S)ystematic thinking and structural analysis" (0x05) are important to the XF Manifesto.

7 Deleuze describes this in his essay, "Postscript on Societies of Control," as producing a situation in which "the man [sic] of control is undulatory, in orbit, in a continuous network."

(6) Here then there is a loss of the self to the free fall of capital such that the human body and capital are intertwined. This might most pertinently be understood as the shift from "the idea of multiplicity (as manifested in the distributed touch of the typist) to be theorised as a signifier of a radical gender political potential, rather than as, say, a quality of an expendable and exploitable employee operator" as Hester points out.

8 Or in the words of Wilderson, "My status as a sentient being who is not a Human being, someone who cannot be recognized by and incorporated into the world, someone who exists to facilitate the renewal of others, has *shaped* the rhetorical strategies of my analysis just as it shaped the rhetorical strategies of [Black Liberation Army] testimonies" (28).

9 Laboria Cuboniks harness the alienation prevalent in Reza Negarestani's work as an inherent facet of human cognition—to think it to be estranged from the world, and as such alienation is "an enabling condition of rational agency" for Negarestani—but they enhance this through the specific lens of the experience of gendered, homophobic, or racial violence; "anyone who's experienced injustices wrought in the name of the natural order."

10 Disidentification is a term coined by José Esteban Muñoz in his analysis of minority drag performances in downtown New York.

11 A concept proposed by Tim Stüttgen: "When it came to performing masculinity, his despotic alien drag could not be farther away from the performance of the black macho that was shaped in American racism but also appropriated in Blaxploitation cinema. One could also argue that performing the alien or the cyborg would reflect on the radical disruption blacks experienced from whites in the time of slavery. Many levels beyond the classic gender drag performance by drag queens and drag kings, the notion of alien drag would remind us of the radical dehumanization slaves went through in slavery the moment they were put onto a ship" (Stüttgen).

12 Afropessimism developed from an understanding that slavery continues to exist in the social and political life of black people in the United States, with Saidiya Hartman, for example, stating, "I, too, am the afterlife of slavery" (in *Scenes of Subjection* 1997, 6). David Marriott's *On Black Men* (2000), as well as Jared Sexton and Wilderson III, both mentioned in this text, are key thinkers in the field.

13 "[T]he condition of alienation that comes from being a black subject in American society parallels the kind of alienation that science fiction writers try to explore through various genre devices—transporting someone from the past into the future, thrusting someone into an alien culture, on another planet, where he has to confront alien ways of being. All of these devices reiterate the condition of being black in American culture. Black people live the estrangement that science fiction writers imagine." (Greg Tate in Dery 211–12)

14 Similarly, in "The Labor of the Inhuman, Part I: Human," Reza Negarestani suggests that inhumanism is a commitment to the human, where the human is a "constructible hypotheses, a space for navigation and intervention." (1) This demands a careful unpacking or unpicking and examination of what it is to be human.

WORKS CITED

Baucom, Ian. *Specters of the Atlantic: Finance Capital, Slavery, and the Philosophy of History*. Durham, NC: Duke UP, 2005.

Cuboniks, Laboria. *Xenofeminism. A Politics of Alienation*. 2015. http://www.laboriacuboniks. net. Accessed March 11, 2018.

Deleuze, Gilles. "Postscript on the Societies of Control." *October 59* (1992): 3–7.

Dery, Mark. *Flame Wars: The Discourse of Cyberculture*. Durham, NC: Duke UP, 1994.

Edelman, Lee. *No Future: Queer Theory and the Death Drive*. Durham, NC: Duke UP, 2004.

Eshun, Kodwo. "Further Considerations of Afrofuturism." *The New Centennial Review* 3.2 (2013): S.287–302.

Fanon, Frantz. The Wretched of the Earth. Trans. C. Farrington. New York: Grove Press, 1968.

Fisher, Mark. *Capitalist Realism: Is There No Alternative?* London: Zero Books, 2009.

Haraway, Donna. "Anthropocene, Capitalocene, Chthulucene: Staying with the Trouble." 2014. http://opentranscripts.org/transcript/anthropocene-capitalocene-chthulucene/. Accessed March 12, 2018.

Haraway, Donna. *Simian, Cyborgs and Women: The Reinvention of Nature*. New York: Routledge, 1991.

Hartman, Saidiya. Lose Your Mother: A Journey along the Atlantic Slave Route. New York: Farrar, Straus and Giroux, 2007.

Hester, Helen. "After the Future: *n* Hypotheses of Post-Cyber Feminism." 2017. http://beingres. org/2017/06/30/afterthefuture-helenhester/. Accessed March 11, 2018.

Jackson, Zakiyyah Iman. "Sense of Things." *Catalyst: Feminism, Theory, Technoscience* 2.2 (2016): 1–48.

Mackay, Robin, and Avanassian, Armen. *Accelerate: The Accelerationist Reader*. Falmouth, UK: Urbanomic, 2014.

Marriott, David. On Black Men. New York: Columbia University Press, 2000.

Muñoz, José Esteban. *Cruising Utopia. The Then and There of Queer Futurity*. New York: New York UP, 2009.

Negarestani, Reza. "The Labor of the Inhuman, Part I: Human." *e-flux journal* 52 (2014): February 2014.

Noys, Benjamin. *Malign Velocities: Accelerationism and Capitalism*. London: Zero Books, 2014.

O'Connell, Hugh Charles. "'We Are Change': The Novum as Event in Nnedi Okorafor's *Lagoon*." *Cambridge Journal of Postcolonial Literary Inquiry* 3.3 (2016): 291–312.

Parisi, Luciana. "Automate Sex: Xenofeminism, Hyperstition and Alienation." *Futures & Fictions*. Ed. H. Gunkel, A. Hameed, and S. O'Sullivan. London: Repeater, 2017, pp. 213–30.

Plant, Sadie. *Zero and Ones: Digital Women and the New Technoculture*. London: Fourth Estate, 1997.

Reed, Patricia. "The Cold War and the Collective Subject." Talk for the WHAP! Lecture series at Calarts. Los Angeles, CA: West Hollywood Public Library, November 17, 2017.

Sexton, Jared. "The Social Life of Social Death: On Afro-Pessimism and Black Optimism." *InTensions* 5 (2011): 1–47.

Sharpe, Christina. In the Wake. On Blackness and Being. Durham: Duke University Press, 2016.

Steyerl, Hito. "In Free Fall: A Thought Experiment on Vertical Perspective." *e-flux*, 24 (2016). http://www.e-flux.com/journal/24/67860/in-free-fall-a-thought-experiment-on-vertical-perspective/. Accessed March 11, 2018.

Stüttgen, Tim. *In a Qu*A*re Time and Place. Post-Slavery Temporalities, Blaxploitation, and Sun Ra's Afrofuturism between Intersectionality and Heterogeneity*. Berlin: b_books, 2014.

Sun Ra. Interview with Jennifer Rycenga. 1988). Retrieved from http://joelasqo.com/blog/2014/11/05/msppiano-w-ubu-ra-big-band-set-3-845pm-◉-reconnaissance-fly-set-1-7pm-◉-electropoetic-coffee-set-2-8pm-◉-wed-12-nov-center-for-new-musics-friendly-galaxies-sun/. Accessed September 23, 2018.

Szwed, John. *Space Is the Place: The Lives and Times of Sun Ra*. London: Canongate Books, 1998.

VNS Matrix. *A Cyberfeminist Manifesto for the 21st Century*. Billboard. Sydney: Tin Sheds Gallery, 1992.

Wilderson III, F. B. "The Vengeance of Vertigo: Aphasia and Abjection in the Political Trials of Black Insurgents." *InTensions* 5 (2011): 1–14.

INDEX